MARKETING

5E

James L. Burrow, PhD

Australia • Brazil • Mexico • Singapore • United Kingdom • United States

Acknowledgments

Grateful acknowledgment is given to the authors, artists, photographers, museums, publishers, and agents for permission to reprint copyrighted material. Every effort has been made to secure the appropriate permission. If any omissions have been made or if corrections are required, please contact the Publisher.

Cover Image Credits

Lightbulb: ImageFlow/Shutterstock.com; Background images: Bloomicon/ Shutterstock.com; DECA logo: © DECA Inc.

For product information and technology assistance, contact us at
Customer & Sales Support, 888-915-3276

For permission to use material from this text or product, submit all requests online at **www.cengage.com/permissions**
Further permissions questions can be emailed to
permissionrequest@cengage.com

National Geographic Learning | Cengage
1 N. State Street, Suite 900
Chicago, IL 60602

National Geographic Learning, a Cengage company, is a provider of quality core and supplemental educational materials for the PreK-12, adult education, and ELT markets. Cengage is a leading provider of customized learning solutions with employees residing in nearly 40 different countries and sales in more than 125 countries around the world. Find your local representative at **NGL.Cengage.com/RepFinder.**

Visit National Geographic Learning online at
NGL.Cengage.com/school

ISBN: 978-0-357-13574-7

Library of Congress PCN Number: 2020901512

Printed in the United States of America
Print Number: 02   Print Year: 2021

CONTENTS

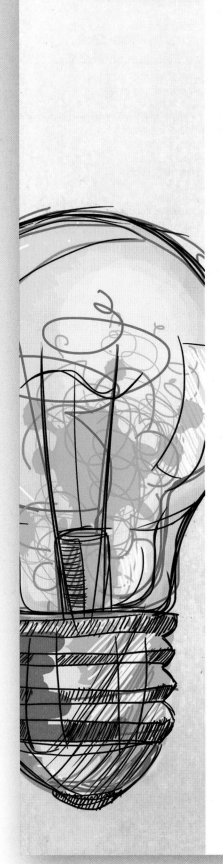

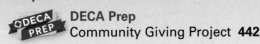

PREFACE

Marketing, 5e

Keep your marketing course current with innovative industry technology, research, and strategies with the first-ever digital solution to provide continuous access to the latest trends in marketing.

In *Marketing, 5e*, students learn how current marketing technologies and practices relate to their personal goals and future careers. Students will be able to recognize effective marketing applications to create strategic plans for a variety of business endeavors. This edition maintains the hallmark integrated marketing approach seen in previous editions as students learn the foundations and functions needed to successfully market goods, services, and ideas to consumers. Professional development, customer service, and digital marketing strategies including social media, are presented as key marketing skills for success. Emphasis on the Career Clusters, DECA Performance Indicators, and real-world applications highlight how these skills can be used in everyday life and future careers. While students study business, economics, selling, human relations, communications, logistics, promotion, product planning, and pricing, they also understand why marketing is crucial across all business operations.

WHAT'S NEW?

MindTap for *Marketing, 5e*, includes additional timely features such as examples of advertisements, stats and facts, digital marketing strategies, Internet research activities, and case studies that will be updated between editions to keep your course current in this evolving area of business.

Enhanced design in the print textbook makes the text easier to read and offers a more engaging, magazine style to highlight current issues in marketing that are incorporated into this edition.

Course Competencies defined by NBEA's National Standards for Business Education, National Marketing Education Core Competencies, TEKS, current DECA Prep Performance Standards, and Career Cluster Standards for Marketing.

Build Your Marketing Plan feature is now highlighted throughout both the print textbook and Mind-Tap online solution. Marketing Plan Worksheets are now available on both the Student Companion Site as well as in MindTap for each chapter. The majority of marketing plan instruction is found in Chapters 4 and 9, but this feature offers hands-on practice applying new skills to a marketing plan at the end of every chapter.

New pedagogical features such as ***Let's Start a Band!***, ***Case Studies***, and ***Build Your Portfolio*** increase student engagement with marketing concepts as well as their personal goals and career plan.

Transform Your Course with

Measurable Outcomes

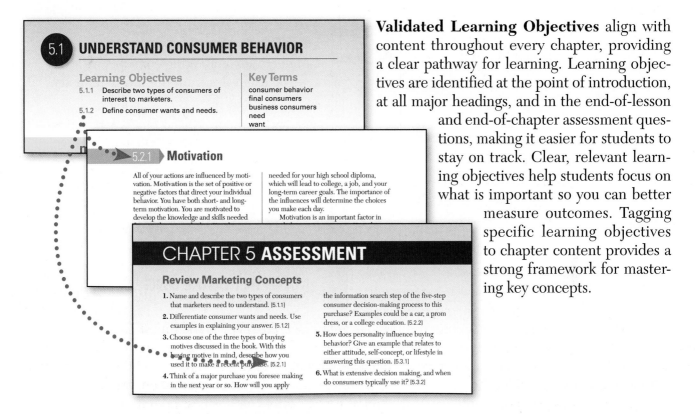

Validated Learning Objectives align with content throughout every chapter, providing a clear pathway for learning. Learning objectives are identified at the point of introduction, at all major headings, and in the end-of-lesson and end-of-chapter assessment questions, making it easier for students to stay on track. Clear, relevant learning objectives help students focus on what is important so you can better measure outcomes. Tagging specific learning objectives to chapter content provides a strong framework for mastering key concepts.

Marketing, 5e, is aligned to current DECA Performance Indicators and was reviewed by Chris Young, DECA's Chief Program Officer to ensure all DECA Prep Events and Assessments are up-to-date. National Geographic Learning, a part of Cengage, is a proud member of DECA's National Advisory Board.

This edition of ***Marketing*** prepares students for careers under the national Marketing, Sales & Service Career Cluster and fully aligns to the **Precision Exams' Marketing Fundamentals (400)** and **Marketing I (401)** industry certifications. Precision Exams' certifications are backed by national industries and offer knowledge standards that are updated every 2–3 years. Working together, Precision Exams and National Geographic Learning, a part of Cengage, focus on preparing students for the workforce with exams and content that are kept up to date and relevant to today's jobs. To access a corresponding correlation guide, visit the accompanying Instructor Companion Website for this title at nglsync.cengage.com. For more information on how to administer the Marketing Fundamentals and Marketing I exams, or any of the 180+ exams available to your students, contact your local Sales Consultant. Find your Sales Consultant at cengage.com/repfinder.

Transform Your Course with

Engaging and Relevant Content

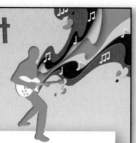

Let's Start a Band!

> "I think musicians and artists are the most philanthropic people I know. The charity record of the music business would hold up to the work of anybody."
>
> – Glenn Frey, Eagles

It's only been a couple of weeks and things are coming together a lot faster than I thought they would. The band members get along, at least most of the time. And the music's getting better.

Today was one long, tough session. It took us a while, but we finally got it right. I just hope we can repeat it tomorrow.

Anyway, Layla came up to me after the rehearsal and asked if I thought the band should stand for something. I know she volunteers at an animal shelter, but I wasn't sure what she meant. She said she thinks we should use our music to help increase awareness of an important issue, like animal welfare. I told her that while I didn't disagree, not every band member may share her commitment.

I told her I'd think about it and I have. I'm concerned that becoming involved in something controversial might cause the band to lose audience members. People want to be entertained, not preached to. How do we walk that fine line, and should we even want to?

Let's Start a Band!
Connects key marketing concepts with specific examples from the music industry.

"I really like how the story comes full circle in a way that emphasizes that business and marketing activities are just as important in the entertainment industry as the talent is."

- Dan Harper, Truman High School, Independence, MO

MATH IN MARKETING

Breakeven Point
The breakeven point is the number of unit sales a company must make to cover the expenses of a venture. Below the breakeven point, expenses exceed revenues, and a company will lose money. At the breakeven point, sales will exactly cover all expenses. Once the breakeven point is exceeded, a company will begin to make a profit.

To calculate the breakeven point, you need to know the total fixed cost of a venture, the selling price per unit, and the variable cost per unit of a good or service. The breakeven point is the total fixed cost divided by the difference between the selling price and the variable cost per unit.

$$\text{Breakeven point} = \frac{\text{Total fixed cost}}{\text{Per unit price} - \text{per unit cost}}$$

For example, a clothing store at the mall wants to print and distribute flyers advertising its new line of sweaters. The fixed cost of the flyers is $2,400. The selling price of each sweater is $50, and the variable cost of each sweater is $10. The breakeven point for the flyer is 60 sweaters.

$$\frac{\$2,400}{\$50 - \$10} = \frac{\$2,400}{\$40} = 60$$

If the store sells fewer than 60 sweaters, the store will lose money on the flyer. If it sells exactly 60 sweaters, the cost of the flyer will be covered exactly. If it sells more than 60 sweaters, the store will make a profit.

Do the Math

1. At the same clothing store, a display unit for jeans costs $1,800. If the jeans sell for $45 with a variable cost of $9, what is the breakeven point for the display?
2. What would be the breakeven point if the store installs a second $1,800 display unit for a different brand of jeans that sell for $54 with a variable cost of $18 each?

Math in Marketing
Addresses math concepts that are essential to marketers.

MARKETING COMMUNICATION

Manage Online Reputation
Nearly every company or organization has an online presence. For many, it is their initial point-of-contact with the public, and it results in customers forming a first impression, often everlasting. In managing its online reputation, a company must go beyond creating content and monitoring social media. It must pay attention to what customers are saying, whether they are tweeting about the company's latest product or posting about a consumer experience on Yelp. Although user-generated content can be beneficial, opening the company or organization up to feedback does have some risks.

Negative product reviews or other critical comments about the company's brand can affect sales and, in some cases, go viral reaching a vast audience. Because everyone has the right to express their opinion about any company, addressing criticism publicly without hiding negative online comments is optimal. Yet most companies' initial response to a negative review or comment is either to do nothing or take it down from the company website.

Think Critically

Imagine you are in charge of a company's website. Write guidelines for the public forum part of the company's site. Be sure to make the guidelines clear. The guidelines should also address the balance between the customers' desire to be heard and the company's desire to show itself in a positive light. *Build your portfolio*

Marketing Communication
Describes challenges, techniques, devices, and media used to convey marketing information.

Transform Your Course by
Building Career Skills

Planning a Career In...
COMMUNITY RELATIONS

Did you ever experience a positive change in your life because you knew how to prepare for an event? For example, maybe you avoided a serious house fire because you regularly changed the batteries in your smoke detector.

Public awareness campaigns reach out to communities to improve the quality of life within the community. Whether informing people about Lyme disease or reminding them

spend the next hour reviewing the print and radio "Ride the Bus" ad campaigns that will run for the rest of the summer. Reminding commuters how they can help reduce smog by riding the bus is an effective way to both increase ridership and minimize smog.

After lunch, Jada gives a presentation on the city's new "fare assistance" program to representatives from various social service agencies. Jada needs to inform the elderly,

Planning a Career in …
Provides information related to one of the career clusters and encourages students to begin thinking about a career choice.

21ST CENTURY SUCCESS SKILLS
Your Personal and Professional Image

Businesses are aware of the importance of the first impression—the image a product and its package conveys, the cleanliness and appearance of a store and its merchandise, and the impression its employees make. If you walk into a law office, you expect a different image from one you might encounter in an auto repair shop. If that image does not meet your expectation, you may not feel comfortable or confident becoming a client or customer.

Everyone makes decisions based on first impressions. As you walk down the halls of your school each day, you notice what other students are wearing. At the beginning of a new semester, the appearance and attitude of your teachers influence your initial feelings about them and the class.

Personal Care and Appearance

There are many elements to personal appearance, starting with cleanliness, skin and hair care, and personal hygiene. Regular bathing keeps you fresh. Brushing your teeth freshens your breath and maintains a healthy and beautiful smile. An easy-to-maintain and attractive hair style, clean and trimmed nails, and healthy skin increase personal attractiveness and self-confidence.

Language and Voice Tone

Your language and tone of voice are the final pieces of your successful image. No matter what the setting or with whom you are speaking, use positive,

21st Century Success Skills
Introduces basic skills needed in the business world and teaches students how to market themselves.

WORKING IN TEAMS

Working with a team, select a product and list all the marketing activities that must occur in the exchange between the business and the customer. Outline how the exchange would work without marketing. As a team, discuss why marketing is needed.

Working in Teams
Allows students to experience group dynamics that enhance the learning process and discover the benefits and concerns of shared decision making.

Build Your Portfolio
Icons highlight activities and projects that students can use to create a porfolio showcasing their work.

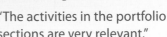

"The activities in the portfolio sections are very relevant."

- Mark Drummond, West Deptford High School, West Deptford, NJ

Apparel and Accessories Marketing Series Event

DECA PREP

Build your Portfolio

In the fashion industry, what goes around comes around. Today's popular styles often are styles that were popular 20 to 30 years ago.

The manufacturer of a popular pique cotton tennis shirt with a reptile emblem has made an incredible comeback from its popularity 30 years ago. Then, the well-constructed cotton tennis shirt sold for $35 to $42. Retro clothing has made an incredible comeback, and now the reptile tennis shirt commands a retail price ranging from $79.50 to $165.

Your marketing strategy must describe the target market, the advertising campaign, and the pricing strategy for the shirt manufacturer. You will have 10 minutes to plan your marketing strategy and 10 minutes to present the strategy to the shirt company CEO and answer questions about your plan. You will meet in the CEO's office to present your plan.

Performance Indicators Evaluated

• Explain the concept of marketing strategies.

DECA Event-Prep Projects
A **full page event-prep project** at the end of every chapter assists student with competitive-event preparation and includes critical-thinking questions.

Transform Your Course with

Comprehensive Assessment Options

Marketing Matters & Essential Question

Provides instructors with "bell-ringer" discussion topics to help assess student knowledge prior to beginning the lesson.

marketing matters

The activities associated with marketing may be misunderstood. Marketing has been accused of creating a false need for unnecessary products. Some people feel that marketing is a waste of money and only serves to increase the price customers pay. Others claim that high-quality products do not need marketing because the products will sell themselves.

essential question

What are the common criticisms consumers have of marketing? Which do you think are correct and which are incorrect?

Lesson Assessments

Include review questions and activities that relate back to the learning objectives, as well as DECA activities which focus on DECA prep and require students to apply critical thinking and decision-making skills.

2.1 ASSESSMENT

What Have You Learned?

1. Why is customer satisfaction important to a business? [2.1.1]
2. How does marketing result in lower prices for consumers? [2.1.2]
3. Name four ways in which marketing benefits society. [2.1.3]

Make Academic Connections

1. **Visual Art** Using magazines or online sources, find images that illustrate ways in which marketing benefits society. Make a collage with the illustrations. [2.1.3]
2. **Consumer Economics** Marketing is said to improve exchanges between businesses and consumers. Make a list of at least five products or services that you buy or use. Describe how marketing has improved the exchange process for each of these products or services. Organize this information in a spreadsheet. [2.1.2]

Connect to ◇DECA

You work for a food processing company that is considering selling its product globally. The owner has no experience marketing products internationally and has asked for your advice. Using presentation software, prepare a two-minute presentation on how international trade can benefit the business. Include two specific ways that marketing can support the company's efforts. Give your speech to your teacher (judge). [2.1.3]

CHAPTER 5 ASSESSMENT

Review Marketing Concepts

1. Name and describe the two types of consumers that marketers need to understand. [5.1.1]
2. Differentiate consumer wants and needs. Use examples in explaining your answer. [5.1.2]
3. Choose one of the three types of buying motives discussed in the book. With this buying motive in mind, describe how you used it to make a recent purchase. [5.2.1]
4. Think of a major purchase you foresee making in the next year or so. How will you apply

Marketing Research and Planning

1. Some products are sold to both business consumers and final consumers. Name at least one business consumer use and one final consumer use for each of the following items: pencil, balloon, rubber band, radio, sofa, all-terrain vehicle, bagel, pesticide, suitcase, blanket. Here is an example: [5.1.1]

Item	Business Use	Final Consumer Use
banana	restaurant	family lunches

2. Marketers strive to capture your attention with advertisements that address meaningful buying motives. Choose an advertisement from each of the following media: magazine,

the information search step of the five-step consumer decision-making process to this purchase? Examples could be a car, a prom dress, or a college

5. How does personal behavior? Give an either attitude, self answering this que
6. What is extensive do consumers typic

Write an email to t elements of the ma important, and wh action with each cu following words or behavior, consumer needs, wants, buyin extensive decision- 5.2.2, 5.3.2]
4. Using Internet new announcement of a Analyze the announ personal, cultural, influences to which

Marketing Management and Decision Making

1. In order to learn more about customers, many organizations use customer feedback cards like the one shown below for a restaurant. The organizations use the information to improve their products and services and increase customer satisfaction.

In an effort to help your school provide better service, work with other students to develop a customer feedback card to give to students at your school. The customer feedback card should be designed to find out from students what they like and dislike about your school. You may wish to ask questions about the curriculum, classes, teachers, atmosphere, spirit, extracurricular activities, grades, homework, facilities, and any other

items relevant to your school. Survey at least 15 students.

After the surveys have been completed and collected, use a computer spreadsheet program to record and tabulate the responses. Then determine the mean, median, and mode for each question. (The mean is the average of all the responses to a question. The median is the middle value when all answers are arranged in order. The mode is the response that was given most frequently.) Prepare tables, charts, and graphs to display the survey results. Based on the results, draw several conclusions about student attitudes. Make recommendations for improvements to your school. [5.3.1]

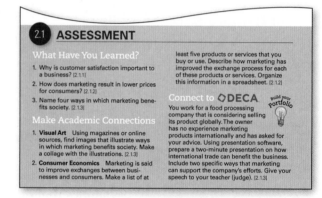

Fine Foods and More Restaurant
We value your opinions and strive to meet your expectations. Tell us how you like us by circling the rating that best represents your view of our restaurant.

WHAT DID YOU THINK OF OUR SERVICE?				
	Poor			Excellent
Menu		2	3	4	5

Chapter Assessments

Provide review questions and numerous scenario-based activities that enable students to work through real-world situations.

Cengage Learning Testing by Cognero

Cognero is a flexible, online system that allows instructors to author, edit, and manage test bank content from multiple Cengage Learning solutions, create multiple test versions in an instant, and deliver tests from your learning management system or classroom.

Transform Your Course with
Digital Solutions that Enhance Teaching and Learning

Connect to **MindTap**

NEW! MindTap for *Marketing, 5e*

- A highly personalized, cloud-based solution
- Unique digital platform with readings, application activities, multimedia, and assessments all in a single Learning Path
- Automatic grading allows students to receive immediate feedback
- Teachers can monitor student engagement and progress in real time
- Connect to MindTap icons in the print text make it clear when to integrate additional digital activities into your course

Digital Features

Stay Current with RSS Feeds in MindTap with curated, up-to-date articles from professional journals teachers can choose to incorporate in their class for discussion or additional projects.

Careers Videos in MindTap offer video interviews of real professionals discussing a typical day, some challenges, and exciting aspects of different careers in marketing.

Build Your Portfolio icons highlight activities and projects where students will create a document or artifact that they can share with their future employers to validate career-ready skills.

Other Digital Features

- Flashcards
- Glossary
- Internet Activities
- Lesson Reviews
- Chapter Quizzes
- Chapter Tests
- Study Tools

Instructor's Companion Site

Also available! The Companion Site for *Marketing, 5e*, includes teaching materials and NEW supporting activities. Login at nglsync.cengage.com to access these resources and more:

- Teacher's Resource Guide
- PowerPoint Presentations
- Internet Activities
- Correlations

Getting Ready to Start Your Class?
Need Help Getting Started?

NGL SYNC

National Geographic Learning, a part of Cengage, offers **NGLSync** access with every course. NGLSync is your portal to online courses, instructor and student resources, test banks, rostering, and more!

Find NGLSync User Guides and Video Trainings at www.cengage.com/coursepages/NGL_DigitalFulfillmentSupport.

Unsure whether you have access? Contact your Sales Consultant at www.ngl.cengage.com/RepFinder.

EVENTS

Reviewers

James T. Conklin II
Business Education and Math Teacher
Sheboygan Falls High School
Sheboygan Falls, Wisconsin

Mark Drummond
Marketing Education Coordinator
West Deptford High School
West Deptford, New Jersey

S. Michele Duncan, M.S. Ed. & C.A.S. Ed.
Marketing Education Educator
Nansemond River High School
Suffolk, Virginia

Dan Harper
Business/Marketing Instructor, DECA Chapter Advisor
Truman High School
Independence, Missouri

Jason Hendrickson
Business Teacher
North Central High School
Indianapolis, Indiana

Don R. Ide
Marketing Instructor / DECA Advisor
Lynnwood High School
Bothell, Washington

Mark Murphy
Business Teacher and Instructional
  Technology Coordinator
Mars Area High School
Mars, Pennsylvania

Michael Murphy
Business Teacher
Walpole High School
Walpole, Massachusetts

Christopher Young, CAE
Chief Program Officer, DECA Inc.

About the Authors

James L. Burrow, PhD, has a background in marketing and human resource development. During his career, he was a university faculty member in Iowa, Wisconsin, Nebraska, and North Carolina, teaching marketing, marketing education, and human resource development. In addition, he worked with businesses and other organizations as a consultant on marketing and performance improvement strategies. He is retired from the faculty of North Carolina State University. Dr. Burrow holds a BA and MA from the University of Northern Iowa and a PhD from the University of Nebraska.

Contributing Author

Hyde Park Publishing Services, owned by Jeanne R. Busemeyer, was the contributing author on this edition of *Marketing*. Jeanne has a BA in English from Miami University and an MBA with emphasis in Marketing from Xavier University. She has worked as a consulting editor on several earlier editions of this book as well as many other business education titles including *Principles of Business, Contemporary Economics,* and *Law for Business and Personal Use.* Hyde Park Publishing Services associate Michael O'Bryant, a retired Mason High School teacher, assisted Jeanne with this project.

CHAPTER 1

MARKETING TODAY AND TOMORROW

Connect to MindTap

See how effective advertising leads to successful marketing strategies.
Click on Chapter 1, Visual Focus, **in your MindTap.**

Let's Start a Band!

> ## "The hardest thing to do in this business is start a band nobody's ever heard of."
>
> – *Michael Penn, Singer–Songwriter, Composer*

When I got to the garage it looked like most of the players were already there. After a few quick intros I started getting ready. Gael, who I already knew, was setting up his drums. We had started out together when neither of us were very good. He got better. I just hoped I had.

Edwardo, whom I just met, held a trumpet to his side and was talking to Layla. I'd heard Layla perform and thought that with her presence and pipes she was a great pick to front this band. Malik with his guitar and Jake with his bass were warming up. Both could play, and I thought to myself, this just might work.

I had some doubts and a lot of questions when Naomi approached me with the idea of putting a band together. What kind of music would we play? Where would we play? Would we get paid? Naomi's passion and enthusiasm were infectious, but it was her honesty that got me in the door. She admitted she didn't have all the answers. But if I could share her dream and help her realize it, we would figure it out together. It wasn't an easy decision, but there I was, in a garage, ready to step off.

Naomi entered the garage. She hesitated and surveyed the room, her eyes lingering on each one of us. Then she strode to her keyboard and said with a smile, "Come on you hacks. Let's put this band together."

When we finished, I sat down on a folding chair convinced. Although it sometimes sounded like musical chaos, the last two hours showed me that with practice this group was good enough to make it. But I knew from experience that a good sound wasn't always enough. There are a lot of great bands out there. To really get noticed, to really be successful, I thought we would have to do more. But what? I'm not sure. So, I want to ask you. What should we do next?

1.1 WHAT IS MARKETING?

Learning Objectives

1.1.1 Explain the importance of studying marketing.

1.1.2 Describe the nine marketing functions.

1.1.3 Define marketing.

Key Term

marketing

marketing matters

Marketing is one of the most important business functions in U.S. and international companies. It involves a wide range of activities necessary to success in all organizations, both for-profit and not-for-profit, and provides the basis for many exciting jobs and careers. Knowing about marketing concepts and developing marketing skills can help you achieve success throughout your career.

 essential question

Why is marketing such an important part of most businesses? What jobs and careers do you think are related to completing marketing activities?

1.1.1 ▶ Why Study Marketing?

Businesses, individual consumers, and the economy all benefit from effective marketing. This chapter introduces marketing in a way you may not recognize. Even though *marketing* is a well-known word, it is often misused or misunderstood. Marketing activities and jobs have changed a great deal over the years and will continue to change. Even though marketing in one form or another has been around for centuries, some businesses still do not understand marketing well or use it effectively.

Marketing influences all business operations and includes a number of different activities. Marketing is now seen as essential to the success not only of manufacturers, retailers, and other

businesses but also of government agencies, hospitals, law offices, schools, and churches. Successful businesses and other organizations recognize the difference between effective and ineffective marketing. They develop an approach to marketing that responds to the needs of their customers. They know that effective marketing leads to satisfied customers and a successful, profitable business.

Where Does Marketing Take Place?

Marketing is one of the most visible aspects of business. You typically do not see products being manufactured, accountants maintaining the financial records of a business, or human resource employees hiring and training personnel. But you do see evidence of marketing every day. Marketing includes advertisements in all types of media, products being transported, and marketing researchers conducting surveys in shopping malls.

As a consumer, you are not involved in most business operations, but you make marketing decisions and participate in marketing activities every day. You are involved in marketing when you decide to make a purchase in a store or on the Internet, when you decide whether to pay for an item with cash or credit, and when you have a bulky item delivered to your home.

As you study marketing, you will learn how businesses use marketing effectively and profitably. You will see how you can use marketing skills in your personal life. Those skills can help you make better purchasing decisions as a consumer. They can help you as you complete an application for college or an interview with a potential employer. Marketing skills also are needed for many exciting and well-paying business careers and can help you achieve leadership positions in any organization.

How do Businesses Use Marketing?

Every business today is involved in marketing (**Figure 1-1**). Companies devote a large part of their resources to marketing activities. Large businesses have marketing departments that employ many types of marketing specialists. Small companies employ people who complete marketing activities as a part of their jobs. While some businesses may not view themselves as involved in marketing, they still need to understand and use many marketing concepts as they work with their clients and customers.

What are Marketing Job Opportunities?

There are many types of marketing jobs, ranging from selling to inventory management. Careers in advertising, sales promotion, customer service, credit, insurance, transportation, and research require preparation in marketing. Marketers work for manufacturers, law offices, hospitals, museums, professional sports teams, and symphonies.

Many entry-level jobs relate to marketing. These jobs include retail clerk,

ALL TYPES OF BUSINESSES USE MARKETING		
Businesses Devoted to Marketing Activities	**Businesses with Major Marketing Activities**	**Businesses with Limited Marketing Activities**
advertising agencies	retailers	law offices
marketing research firms	manufacturers	medical centers
import/export offices	banks	accounting firms
freight companies	real estate agencies	government agencies
finance and credit firms	insurance companies	universities
telemarketing companies	automobile dealers	construction businesses
travel agencies	farmers and ranchers	public utilities

FIGURE 1-1 Some businesses are more actively involved in marketing than others, but all businesses complete marketing activities.

bank teller, stock person, telemarketer, and delivery person. From these jobs, you can advance to marketing management jobs, some requiring further education and experience. Marketing positions are among the highest-paid jobs in most companies. Because of the change and growth in marketing, many people view marketing as the most diverse and exciting career area of the 21st century.

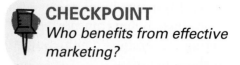

CHECKPOINT
Who benefits from effective marketing?

1.1.2 ▶ Marketing Functions

Many marketing activities need to be completed before a product or service is ready to be advertised and sold. Those many activities can be grouped within major marketing *functions* or related activities designed to accomplish an important marketing goal.

© iStockphoto/PhilAugustavo.

Which marketing function ensures that prospective customers are able to locate, obtain, and use a company's products and services?

Many marketers recognize nine marketing functions: Market Planning, Product and Service Management, Distribution, Pricing, Promotion, Selling, Marketing-Information Management, Financing, and Risk Management. You will learn more about the functions and how each one is used as a part of effective marketing in later chapters. Here is a description of each.

1. **Market Planning**   Identifying and understanding the markets a company wants to serve and developing effective marketing strategies for each market.

2. **Product and Service Management** Assisting in the design and development of products and services to meet the needs of customers.

3. **Distribution**   Determining the best methods and procedures to use so prospective customers are able to locate, obtain, and use the products and services of an organization. Some marketers today refer to distribution as *channel management*.

4. **Pricing**   Establishing and communicating the value of products and services to prospective customers.

5. **Promotion**   Communicating information to prospective customers through advertising and other promotional methods to encourage them to purchase the organization's products and services.

6. **Selling** Direct, personal communications with prospective customers in order to assess needs and satisfy those needs with appropriate products and services.

7. **Marketing-Information Management** Obtaining, managing, and using market information to improve decision making and the performance of marketing activities.

8. **Financing** Budgeting for necessary financing, and providing financial assistance to customers to assist them with purchasing products and services.

9. **Risk Management** Providing security for products, workers, and customers, and reducing the risks associated with marketing decisions and activities.

Each marketing function occurs every time a product or service is developed and sold. The performance of the activities described in the functions is the responsibility of marketers. Marketing is a complex part of business and is very important to the success of businesses and to the satisfaction of customers.

How Companies Use the Marketing Functions

When you understand the marketing functions, you will be able to recognize the activities being performed by companies as they develop new products, improve marketing procedures, and respond to customer needs. You can find examples of these functions in hundreds of different forms.

Apple used *product/service management* by combining the technologies used in the iPod, iPhone, and MacBook to produce the iPad.

Redbox and Netflix redefined the movie rental business through their innovative *distribution* strategy. Today Redbox's bright red kiosks are disappearing, and Netflix no longer rents DVDs, as both have become online streaming companies.

Many professional firms recognize the importance of the selling function. Selected executives in law offices, accounting firms, and banks complete professional sales training in order to effectively obtain new clients and handle their needs.

An example of *marketing-information management* is the use of electronic scanners at supermarket checkouts. The scanned data provide information about inventory levels and purchases so that managers can ensure the best and freshest assortment of products available.

To reduce its inventory of existing homes during a slump in housing sales, a major construction company offers customized decorating and new furnishings

How might store owners use the information collected by electronic scanners to help market directly to customers?

to customers who sign a purchase contract within 30 days. Rather than cutting the price of the home, this *pricing* incentive allows the company to maintain sales levels while competitors continue to struggle.

Businesses selling expensive products, such as oceanfront condominiums, personal aircrafts, or yachts prepare high-quality *promotional* brochures that provide detailed product information for events like trade shows. They also digitally deliver product-individualized information for each buyer. Well-trained salespeople follow up with each customer to provide personalized presentations of the customized product and help customers make the best purchase decision.

Major automobile manufacturers demonstrate the *financing* function when they maintain their own financing organizations. For example, GM Financing, a subsidiary of General Motors, makes loans or provides leases to consumers who purchase their products from local dealers.

Marketing Core Standards for Employment

Marketing jobs exist in every industry and within most companies. Marketing jobs are found at the lowest and highest levels of a company and are available for people with varied amounts of education and experience. Job opportunities in marketing are available to match many interests.

Career programs in Marketing Education provide the most comprehensive preparation opportunities for high school students considering full-time employment in marketing after graduation or for those considering additional education after high school. A Marketing Education program incorporates complementary learning experiences—introductory and advanced courses in marketing, and when appropriate, structured work experiences through internships and cooperative education. The program may be aided by affiliation with a CTSO (Career and Technical Educational Student Organization), which provides students with educational support to enhance their learning. CTSOs include such groups as DECA or FBLA (Future Business Leaders of America), an organization that helps students transition to the business world.

To prepare for careers in marketing, you need a broad understanding of marketing functions and activities. You will also need to develop skills in one or more of the functions. Careers in marketing require strong academic preparation including basic and advanced mathematics. You will want to develop effective interpersonal and communication skills, and excel in creativity as well as critical thinking. Organizational, analytical, and decision-making skills also need to be developed. Be prepared to demonstrate your abilities as a leader no matter what your job or role in an organization. Most students preparing for marketing careers will want to plan for education beyond high school.

Want to know more about what is trending with this topic? Click on **Lesson 1.1, Marketing Decisions,** *in your MindTap.*

Connect to
MindTap

CHECKPOINT
Which of the marketing functions occurs when a product is developed and sold?

Marketing Defined

Because marketing involves so many functions and activities, developing a definition that effectively describes it is difficult. The American Marketing Association (AMA) presented a simple definition in 1960. The AMA described marketing as "the performance of business activities that direct the flow of goods and services from producer to consumer or user." As marketing developed and was applied to a broad set of organizations, its definition became more complex. Marketing today also includes customer research and product development activities. It applies to nonprofit businesses and to organizations not considered businesses (churches, schools, libraries). Marketing is used not only for products and services but also for individuals (political candidates, artists, sports stars) and ideas (stop smoking, recycle, stay in school).

The AMA's most recent definition of marketing communicates how marketing has changed over the years. It defines marketing as "the activity, set of institutions, and processes for creating, communicating, delivering, and exchanging offerings that have value for customers, clients, partners, and society at large."

Because marketing can be applied in different ways in various organizations, and because marketing needs to be easily understood, the following definition describes the value marketing offers to those who use it: **Marketing** is the creation and maintenance of satisfying exchange relationships.

Carefully consider all parts of this definition in order to understand marketing. *Creation* suggests that marketing is involved from the beginning as products and services are being developed. *Maintenance* means that marketing must continue to be used as long as a business or organization is operating. *Satisfaction* of both the business and the customer is an important goal of marketing. When products and services are exchanged, the needs of everyone involved must be met as well as possible. *Exchange relationship* refers to any exchange that involves people giving and receiving something of value (**Figure 1-2**).

 CHECKPOINT
What kinds of relationships exist when marketing is successful?

Business/Organization	Customer	Exchange
movie theater	moviegoers	convenient and enjoyable access to entertainment
grain farmer	cereal manufacturer	high-quality wheat delivered for processing
physician	patients	treatment for illnesses and injuries; health care
college	students	courses, degrees, professional development
commercial airline	business travelers, individuals, families	safe, on-time, and comfortable transportation between cities
city government	citizens	clean and well-maintained streets, police and fire protection, enjoyable living

FIGURE 1-2 Marketing involves many types of exchanges.

Why is it important for both the company and the customer to be satisfied when doing business?

1.1 ASSESSMENT

What Have You Learned?

1. Successful businesses and other organizations recognize the difference between effective and ineffective marketing. What approach to marketing do these organizations typically develop? [1.1.1]

2. Which marketing function involves determining the best methods and procedures to use so prospective customers are able to locate, obtain, and use the products and services of an organization? [1.1.2]

3. In the definition of marketing, what is the exchange relationship? [1.1.3]

Make Academic Connections

1. **Visual Art**   Draw or use technology to create a picture, graphic, or other visual representation of the definition of marketing and common activities that are a part of marketing. [1.1.3]

2. **Careers**   Use the career center in your school or the Internet to identify a marketing job that would have major responsibilities for each of the nine marketing functions. Prepare a chart that lists the function, the job title, and a brief description of the job responsibilities. [1.1.2]

Connect to ◇DECA.

Build your Portfolio

Develop a two-minute presentation on the importance of marketing for businesses, other organizations, and consumers. Make sure to include an explanation of the definition of marketing. Prepare an outline of your presentation and one visual aid. Submit your presentation to your teacher (judge). [1.1.1]

1.2 BUSINESS NEEDS MARKETING

Learning Objectives

1.2.1 Explain why businesses need marketing.

1.2.2 Explain how marketing developed as a part of business.

1.2.3 Describe the functions of business.

Key Terms

self-sufficient
bartering
specialization of labor
money system
central market
production
merchandising
operations
accounting and finance
management

marketing matters

Over time, marketing developed into a sophisticated and complex business function. Several simple business activities that were taken for granted in the past have become important marketing tools today. For example, 100 years ago, providing credit to regular customers was common and was managed with a pen and paper to record customers' purchases. Today, providing financing options, including credit, is a complex process that requires computerized records and entire divisions of a business.

essential question

Why are many of the same marketing activities that were used more than 100 years ago still needed today even if the methods to complete the activities have changed?

1.2.1 ▶ The Need for Marketing

Ever since people began exchanging things with each other, there has been a need for marketing. In the past, marketing was viewed as a simple set of activities that helped a business sell its products to more customers. The first businesses developed ideas and activities designed to attract interest and sell their products.

Business executives know that marketing must be carefully planned and coordinated with other business activities. The approach to managing marketing activities changes as organizations understand what makes marketing effective.

Marketing is necessary in every business. Some people believe that if a business offers a good product, marketing is not necessary. However, if customers do not know about the product or where to purchase it, are unable to get to the place where it is sold, cannot afford the price being charged, or do not think it is a good value, they will not purchase it. A variety of marketing activities are required so that customers will be able to purchase the product and will be satisfied with their decision.

Marketing cannot be successful if the product is not what the customer wants or if the quality is low. Although customers may be encouraged to buy a product through advertising, selling, or a very low price, if they do not view the product as satisfying a need, they will not purchase it. If a customer decides to buy the product but it is defective or does not work the way the customer was led to believe, the customer will likely return it for a refund. Even if the product is not returned, the customer is unlikely to buy the same product again. He or she also may develop a negative attitude about the business that sold the product.

Businesses and other organizations use effective marketing to provide satisfying exchanges of products and services with customers. The ways marketing is used have changed over the years, but the need for marketing has not changed.

CHECKPOINT
Why does a business need marketing if it has a good product or service?

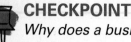

WORKING IN TEAMS

Form a team and discuss products you have purchased that you later found were not what you expected. Why did you make the purchase, and what did you do when you became dissatisfied? As a team, suggest how businesses that understand marketing can do a better job of satisfying customers. Also suggest what responsibilities individual consumers have to make better purchase decisions.

1.2.2 ▶ The Development of Marketing in Business

There have been times in history when people were self-sufficient. Being **self-sufficient** means you do not rely on others for the things you need to survive. People were able to find or produce the food and materials needed for themselves and their families. That type of lifestyle required hard work and was very risky. Self-sufficient people had to have good hunting, fishing, or farming skills as well as the ability to produce shelter, clothing, and other necessities. They often could not obtain everything needed to survive because of poor weather, competition with other people, sickness, or lack of skills.

Bartering

Some people who found they were not successful at being self-sufficient tried to find other ways to survive. They discovered that when they did not have certain things they needed, other people often did. If each person had something that the other person valued, they were able to make an exchange, so each would be better off than before. Exchanging products or services with others by agreeing on their values is known as **bartering**. A system of bartering was developed so that people could exchange with others to obtain the things they needed.

In an early bartering system, someone who was a good hunter but was not able to grow grain might exchange products with a person who had extra grain but needed meat. People who had developed skills in weaving cloth might barter with people who raised animals. Exchanging products through bartering was one of the first examples of marketing. Bartering still takes place today among individuals and businesses. Can you identify examples of bartering in your neighborhood or community or on the Internet?

Specialization of Labor

People discovered they had interests or skills in certain kinds of work while they were not as good at or were uninterested in other types of work. When people concentrated on the work they did well, they were able to accomplish much more than when they tried to do a variety of things. Concentrating on one thing or a few related activities is known as **specialization of labor**. Specialization of labor made it possible for people to produce larger quantities of a product rather than trying to produce many different products. Therefore, more of that product would be available to exchange with other people.

Money Systems

As specialization of labor became more common and a greater variety and quantity of products were available, bartering was not always possible. Not all people needed the products of others, and it was not always possible to reach agreement on what products were worth so that they could be exchanged directly. To assist with the exchange, a money system was developed. **A money system** established the use of currency as a recognized medium of exchange. With money, people could obtain products even if they did not always have something to exchange. Those with products to sell could do so for money, which could then be used for future purchases. The development of a money system is another example of marketing.

Central Markets

With many people producing more types of products and with people having money to purchase the items they needed, the demand for products increased. Locating and gathering all the products people wanted and needed was a difficult process. Much time was spent traveling to sell and purchase products. To solve that problem, central markets were developed. A **central market** is a location where people bring products to be conveniently exchanged. Central markets

© iStockphoto/buzzbuzzer.

Shopping centers and malls are more modern versions of the central market. How do you think developers decide where to locate a new shopping center?

were often located at places where many people traveled, such as where rivers or roads met.

Towns and cities developed at those locations and became centers of trade. People brought the products they wanted to sell to the markets. When people needed things they could not produce, they would travel to the market to make purchases. Developing locations where products could be bought and sold was another step in the development of marketing.

Other Marketing Activities

As central markets expanded, other types of business services were created to make exchanges easier. It was not always possible for sellers and buyers to travel to the markets at the same time. Therefore, individuals often formed businesses to purchase products from producers and hold them for sale to purchasers as needed. Other businesses were started to loan money to buyers or sellers, to help with transportation of products, or to locate products that were not available in the market but that customers wanted. Each of those activities resulted in the development of another marketing activity and made the exchange process more effective for those who produced products and those who purchased and consumed the products. Soon marketing became a complex set of activities with some businesses specializing in marketing while others used the services of marketing businesses. Exchanges became easier as businesses added marketing services and improved the services they already provided.

CHECKPOINT
How did the development of central markets aid in the growth of business?

1.2.3 ▶ The Functions of Business

From the previous discussion of the development and improvement of marketing activities, you can see that marketing is an important part of business and that businesses cannot be effective without marketing. But marketing alone cannot ensure success. Other important business functions are production, operations, accounting and finance, and management. These business functions are shown in **Figure 1-3** and are discussed below.

Production

The primary reason for a business to exist is to provide products or services to consumers and to earn a profit. The **production** function creates or obtains products or services for sale. Think of the variety of products and services available, and you can see that production can take various forms.

RAW MATERIALS Production includes obtaining raw materials for sale to customers. Mining, logging, oil drilling, and similar activities are examples of this type of production.

PROCESSING Other businesses take raw materials and change their form

FIGURE 1-3 Marketing is one of several important business functions.

through processing so that they can be used in the production of other products or in the operation of businesses or equipment. Examples include oil refining and the production of steel, paper, plastics, and food products.

AGRICULTURE Another example of production is agriculture. Food and other materials are grown for consumption or for processing into a variety of products.

MANUFACTURING Manufacturers use raw materials and other resources to produce products for sale to consumers or to other businesses. Manufacturers have produced most of the products you, your friends, your family, and businesses consume.

SERVICES Creating and providing services is also an example of production. Although a physical product is not provided to the customer, offering a service such as preparing tax returns, styling hair, providing lawn care, or performing a concert meets customer needs just as making consumable products does.

MERCHANDISING Finally, some businesses do not produce or manufacture products. Instead, they accumulate products for resale to customers. Offering products produced or manufactured by others for sale to customers is known as **merchandising**. Retailers and wholesalers are examples of merchandising businesses. Although merchandising is not production, it makes the products of other businesses available for sale.

Operations

The ongoing activities designed to support the primary function of a business and keep it operating efficiently are known as **operations**. A business must perform many activities to successfully produce and market products and services. It must maintain buildings and operate equipment. It must obtain, transport, and store products. It must prepare and maintain records. The business must perform these ongoing activities well to be successful.

Accounting and Finance

Business operations are complex with a variety of activities occurring at once. Because businesses need money to finance those activities, they must carefully monitor and manage it. Many types of money, including cash, checks, and credit, are used in a business. The **accounting and finance** function plans and manages financial resources and maintains records and information related to a business's finances.

Financial managers begin by determining the amount of capital needed for the business and where that capital will be obtained. They must develop a budget and then monitor and update it. Most businesses borrow money for major purchases as well as for some day-to-day operations. Determining sources for borrowing, interest rates, and loan payback schedules are important responsibilities of accounting and finance personnel. Managers rely on accounting and finance personnel to provide the financial information they need to plan the activities of the business.

Management

Even in the smallest businesses, time must be spent developing plans and organizing work. Someone must determine what the business will do, how it can best meet the needs of customers, and how to respond to competitors' actions. Problem-solving, managing employees, and evaluating the activities of the business are ongoing responsibilities of managers. The **management** function involves developing, implementing, and evaluating a business's plans and activities.

Managers are responsible for everything that occurs in the business including the work of the employees. They must develop objectives and plans, make sure the appropriate resources are available, be responsible for buildings and equipment, and assign responsibilities to others. Managers are responsible for the performance of the company, including whether it is profitable.

Marketing

Marketing is also an important function of business. All businesses need to complete a variety of activities in order to make their products and services available to consumers and to ensure that satisfying exchanges occur.

Want to know more about marketing in the information age? Click on **Lesson 1.2, Digital Marketing,** *in your MindTap.*

Connect to MindTap

Coordination of Business Functions

Each of the functions of an effective business depends on the other functions. Products can be produced, but if the company is not operated or managed well, adequate records are not maintained, or marketing is ineffective, the products will not be sold at a profit. In the same way, operations maintains buildings and equipment and management plans and coordinates the work occurring in all parts of the business. Finance and accounting provide information to the other parts of the business to make sure that adequate funds are available and are used efficiently.

Some organizations have not been successful in coordinating business functions. Functions operate independently and often compete. Products are produced that cannot be sold. Marketing activities are planned without considering costs. Managers concentrate on specific activities without considering whether their decisions have negative effects on other functions. As a result, product quality and customer service decline while prices increase. Customers become unhappy about the declining product quality and service and rising prices. Competitors who are better organized can take advantage of those situations.

Companies develop *business plans* that help managers coordinate the various functions. This is a written description of the business idea and how it will be carried out. A company's business plan includes several components, including a *marketing plan*. This is a written description of the marketing strategies a business pursues and the way the business will operate to accomplish each strategy. You will learn more about marketing planning in Chapters 4 and 9.

CHECKPOINT
How can the lack of coordination among the business functions affect a company?

1.2 ASSESSMENT

What Have You Learned?

1. Why does a business's approach to marketing change over time? [1.2.1]
2. What is a central market? [1.2.2]
3. Which business function takes raw materials and other resources to produce products for sale to consumers or to other businesses? [1.2.3]

Make Academic Connections

1. **Geography and History**   Use the Internet to locate and print a map of your state. Mark the locations of five towns and cities that were central markets early in your state's development. Identify why each town or city provided a good location for a central market. [1.2.2]

2. **Economics**   International trade requires that currencies from different countries be readily exchanged. Develop a table identifying 10 countries other than the United States, the name of the currency of each country, and the current exchange rate of that currency with the U.S. dollar. [1.2.2]

Connect to ◇DECA

Build your Portfolio

Your team members are the managers of a company whose expenses are increasing while sales and profits are declining. Each team member will assume the role of manager of one of the main business functions. Discuss how the function each manager represents can work with the other functions to identify the main problems facing the business and to develop a plan for improvement. Using presentation software, make a three-minute team presentation of your recommendations to your teacher (judge). [1.2.3]

THE MARKETING CONCEPT

Learning Objectives

1.3.1 Define the marketing concept.

1.3.2 Explain how businesses implement the marketing concept.

Key Terms

marketing concept
market
marketing mix
product

promotion
distribution (place)
price

marketing matters

An important principle of effective marketing is to identify products and services that customers want and then provide them at an appropriate price. Companies spend many hours and hundreds of millions of dollars every year trying to identify new products that customers will buy. Often the new products are just improvements or changes to existing products. Other times, entirely new product categories are created that have not existed in the past.

essential question

How can marketers effectively identify and introduce new products for customers in a way that results in success for the business?

1.3.1 ▶ Define the Marketing Concept

Marketing was not always viewed as an important part of business. Indeed, the term *marketing* was not even used in business until the last half of the 20th century. In the early 1900s, businesses were mostly concerned about producing products that the business believed customers could afford and would purchase. One of the biggest challenges facing businesses back then was getting the products from the places where they were produced to the places where customers could purchase and use them. There were not many choices of transportation methods, and roads and highways were not well developed. A business's primary challenge to increasing sales was to be able to deliver the products to a larger number of customers.

As consumers increased their standard of living and had more money to spend, their demand for newer and better products increased. Demand was usually greater than the available supply of products. Businesses concentrated on production and seldom had to worry about marketing. Customers were often eager to buy new products and would seek out the manufacturer when they heard of a product they wanted.

Over time, production processes improved, there was more competition among producers and manufacturers, and consumers had more choices of products and services. Businesses had to compete to get customers to buy their products. They began to engage in basic marketing activities, such as advertising and selling, to persuade customers that their products were superior to those of competitors.

Satisfy Customer Needs

As it became more and more difficult and expensive for businesses to sell their products, some businesspeople began to realize an important fact. Businesses could no longer be successful by just producing more products or increasing their advertising and selling efforts. They had to produce products that customers wanted. The most successful businesses considered customers' needs and worked to satisfy those needs as they produced and marketed their products and services. That philosophy of business is now known as the marketing concept. The **marketing concept** is using the needs of customers as the primary focus during the planning, production, pricing, distribution, and promotion of a product or service.

Applying the marketing concept is not as easy as it might sound. Businesses must accomplish three activities if they want to use the marketing concept successfully (**Figure 1-4**):

1. To identify what will satisfy customers' needs.

2. To develop and market products or services that customers believe are better than other choices.

3. To operate profitably.

Many businesses successfully identify and respond to needs of customers. Fast-food restaurants provide breakfast menus and late-night hours in order to make their products available when customers want them. Many banks provide secure online services so that customers can pay bills, transfer money, check account balances and even deposit checks using their home computer or a mobile application on their cellphone or mobile tablet. Hospitals offer wellness programs, weight loss clinics, and fitness centers to attract clients and broaden their image. Colleges offer courses for area high school students to earn college credits prior to graduation and to interest students in enrolling full-time at the college.

ELEMENTS OF THE MARKETING CONCEPT

FIGURE 1-4 The marketing concept focuses on identifying and satisfying customer needs.

For basic customer service and marketing situations that involve simple interactions and a limited number of responses, businesses are turning to *chatbots*. These are computer programs that simulate voice or text to communicate with people. They appeal to younger consumers who are accustomed to engaging with technology and desire immediate responses. The use of chatbots appeals to businesses because they are relatively inexpensive, compared to human customer service providers, and can be used any time of the day. Chatbots also function as virtual assistants in many operating systems, such as Apple's Siri and Cortana for Windows. Dedicated chatbot appliances, such as Amazon's Alexa and Google Assistant, are becoming increasingly common as are messaging apps like WeChat and Facebook messenger.

Why do you think a business would choose to use virtual assistants and chatbots to provide customer service?

When Customer Needs Are Not Satisfied

Businesses that do not use the marketing concept are more concerned about producing products than understanding customer needs. Once products are developed, they rely on traditional marketing activities to sell those products. Often when automobile manufacturers or home builders have difficulty selling their products it is because they are not producing the type, style, or quality of cars or houses customers want. They then turn to advertising, price reductions, rebates, and pressure selling to persuade customers to buy a product the customers do not prefer.

Retail stores sometimes buy products that they believe will sell but then find that customers are not willing to buy them. The stores then have to cut prices, increase advertising, use special displays, or find other strategies to persuade customers to buy the products. The extra expenses of marketing products that customers may not have a strong interest in buying can lead to reductions in profit or even losses for the business.

Sometimes, after purchasing the product, customers may decide it is not what they wanted. They may return the product or become unhappy with the product and the company. They may be reluctant to buy from that company in the future and may express dissatisfaction to prospective customers, resulting in reduced sales for the company.

CHECKPOINT

What should a business have as its primary focus during planning, production, pricing, distribution, and promotion of a product?

1.3.2 # Implement the Marketing Concept

Companies that believe in the marketing concept operate differently from those that do not. These companies follow a two-step process. First, they identify the market, and then they develop a marketing mix.

Identify the Market

The first step is to identify the market or markets the company wants to serve. A **market** is a description of a unique group of prospective customers a business wants to serve and their location. An example of a market for a bicycle manufacturer may be people who ride bicycles in the mountains for health and fitness. A potential market for a sports arena may be teens within 80 miles of the arena who attend concerts more than twice a year.

Develop a Marketing Mix

The second step is to develop a marketing mix that will meet the needs of the market and that the business can provide profitably. A **marketing mix** is the blending of four marketing elements—product,

© iStockphoto/vadimguzhva.

distribution, price, and promotion—by the business. The marketing mix is sometimes referred to as the *4 Ps of marketing* with *place* used as an alternate term for distribution.

Let's illustrate a possible marketing mix for the two markets described earlier. The bicycle manufacturer may decide to offer three types of mountain bikes. It can sell through a selected group of bicycle shops. The price can range from $480 to $1050. It can be promoted by advertising in two fitness magazines, on a cable sports channel, on selected travel and cycling Internet sites, and by salespeople in the bicycle shops.

The sports arena manager could choose a marketing mix for concerts that includes groups whose recent titles are among those most frequently downloaded from Internet music sites. Performances could be scheduled on Saturday or Sunday evenings and priced at $90 for reserved seating and $45 for open seating. The arena could promote the concerts on the three area radio stations with the highest audience ratings for listeners age 15 to 25. It also could develop specific social media websites for each concert and encourage word-of-mouth "buzz" marketing.

Each of the elements of the marketing mix provides many alternatives to better satisfy the market. The development and implementation of the marketing mix will be discussed in detail in other chapters. Basic definitions of each marketing mix element follow.

- **Product** is anything offered to a market by the business to satisfy needs, including physical products, services, and ideas.

MARKETING COMMUNICATION

Get the Word Out

Word-of-mouth promotion has been around since the beginning of business, and it is still an important promotional tool. Stories of positive experiences spread orally or by electronic means by satisfied customers can have a powerful influence on family members, neighbors, and friends. On the other hand, there can often be no stronger negative influence than people talking about their negative experiences with a product or a business. Businesses have developed methods to try to influence word-of-mouth promotion. Some of those methods are:

After-sale follow-up. Making contact with purchasers in person, on the telephone, and with letters and emails to make sure they are satisfied with their purchase.

Recognition and special services. Publicly recognizing purchasers in promotions and newsletters or at events.

Incentives. Offering purchasers small financial incentives, discounts, or special purchases for recommending the business and its products to prospective customers.

The Word of Mouth Marketing Association (WOMMA) describes several new methods to encourage positive messages from satisfied customers. They include:

Buzz marketing. Using high-profile entertainment or news to get people to talk about your brand.

Product seeding. Placing the right product in the right hands at the right time and providing information or samples to influential individuals.

Conversation creation. Creating interesting or fun advertising, tweets, emails, catch phrases, entertainment, or promotions designed to start word-of-mouth activity.

Think Critically

1. If you are the marketing manager for a new brand of sunglasses, what would you do to increase the positive word-of-mouth promotion by customers?

2. During this course, keep a "Marketing Ideas" file. Write ideas, phrases, concepts, and plans you think would be effective in marketing. The file you create will help you develop useful ideas in the future. Start your Marketing Ideas file by writing down new ways to encourage positive word-of-mouth promotion.

Build your **Portfolio**

- **Promotion** includes the methods used and information communicated to encourage customers to purchase and to increase their satisfaction.

- **Distribution** or **place** includes the locations and methods used to make the product available to customers.

- **Price** is the amount that customers pay and the methods of increasing the value of the product to the customers.

Although each definition is written to describe marketing of products by a business, non-business organizations and individuals also can develop marketing mixes.

CHECKPOINT
What four marketing elements make up the marketing mix?

1.3 ASSESSMENT

What Have You Learned?

1. Successful marketers consider customers' needs and work to satisfy those needs as they produce and market their products and services. What is the term for this approach? [1.3.1]

2. Why does the use of chatbots for customer service and simple marketing interactions appeal to businesses? [1.3.1]

3. What is the first step in implementing the marketing concept? [1.3.2]

4. Name the 4 Ps of the marketing mix. [1.3.2]

Make Academic Connections

1. **Math** A company is considering two marketing mixes. With the first, it projects it can sell 8,500 units at a price of $23.50 per unit with total costs of $176,000. Unit sales for the second mix are projected at 9,875 at a price of $19.90 with total business costs of $158,500. What is the projected profit (total income minus total costs) for each one? [1.3.2]

2. **Management** Choose one of the businesses described in the lesson—the bicycle manufacturer or the sports arena. Identify a specific new market for the business. Then plan the marketing mix elements the business should offer to meet the needs of the identified market. Prepare a three-paragraph report explaining your decisions. [1.3.2]

Connect to ◇DECA

Build your Portfolio

You are a consultant working with the owner of a new restaurant. You have been asked to provide advice on how to make effective marketing decisions. Write a report to the restaurant owner (judge) describing the meaning and importance of the marketing concept in guiding marketing planning. Be prepared to answer questions about your ideas. [1.3.1]

Businesses are aware of the importance of the first impression—the image a product and its package conveys, the cleanliness and appearance of a store and its merchandise, and the impression its employees make. If you walk into a law office, you expect a different image from one you might encounter in an auto repair shop. If that image does not meet your expectation, you may not feel comfortable or confident becoming a client or customer.

Everyone makes decisions based on first impressions. As you walk down the halls of your school each day, you notice what other students are wearing. At the beginning of a new semester, the appearance and attitude of your teachers influence your initial feelings about them and the class.

You have your own personality and preferences, and that affects your dress and grooming choices. The world would be boring if everyone looked, dressed, and acted alike. On the other hand, dress and grooming decisions affect your success. Personal image, whether in business, school, or social situations, is formed by clothing, personal care and appearance, and language and voice tone. A warm smile, direct eye contact, and a firm handshake go a long way in establishing successful relationships.

© iStockphoto/ozgurdonmaz

Clothing

Don't overdress or underdress. Choose styles that reflect your personality and fit the setting. Clothing does not have to be expensive, but it should be pleasing, not startling, to others. You do not have to be conservative, but you also should not dress so differently from others that the only thing people remember about you is how you dress.

Personal Care and Appearance

There are many elements to personal appearance, starting with cleanliness, skin and hair care, and personal hygiene. Regular bathing keeps you fresh. Brushing your teeth freshens your breath and maintains a healthy and beautiful smile. An easy-to-maintain and attractive hair style, clean and trimmed nails, and healthy skin increase personal attractiveness and self-confidence.

Language and Voice Tone

Your language and tone of voice are the final pieces of your successful image. No matter what the setting or with whom you are speaking, use positive, personalized, and appropriate language. Demonstrate your interest by carrying on your side of a conversation but not dominating it. Show knowledge without being overbearing. How you speak and what you say convey a great deal about you, especially to those who are just getting to know you.

Develop Your Skill

Use a digital camera to take a picture of yourself dressed for three situations: going to school, going to work at a job you would like to have, and going to a social activity.

Show the photos to three people—a close friend, a businessperson, and a teacher or other adult who knows you well. Ask for honest feedback on whether the image you convey in each photo fits the situation. Ask each person to provide two positive comments and two recommendations that will help strengthen your image in the way you dress and your personal care and appearance. Use their feedback to set goals for personal improvement. Keep the pictures as a reminder of your goals and progress.

1.4 THE CHANGING ROLE OF MARKETING

Learning Objectives

1.4.1 Compare and contrast the four different emphases companies have placed on marketing over the years.

1.4.2 Summarize how marketing is changing in businesses and other organizations.

Key Terms

relationship marketing
employee empowerment

marketing matters

Marketing is an important tool for businesses. In addition, many organizations that are not businesses also find benefits in performing marketing activities. For example, colleges routinely send recruiters all over the United States and even to other countries to attempt to persuade students to attend their school.

 essential question

How can non-business organizations use marketing generally and marketing functions specifically to help the organization achieve its goals?

1.4.1 ▶ The Changing Approach to Marketing

Although marketing is necessary in all exchanges, businesses have not always believed marketing was important to their success. They expected customers to take most of the responsibility for completing marketing activities. It took many years before businesses began to realize the value of effective marketing. There are several changes in the role that marketing has played in U.S. businesses during the past century. The historical development of marketing is summarized in **Figure 1-5**.

Production Emphasis

From the Civil War into the 1920s production processes were very simple and few product choices were available.

People had limited money to spend on products and mostly purchased just basic necessities. Transportation systems were not well developed, so it was difficult to get products from where they were manufactured to customers throughout the United States.

Businesses were driven by innovations such as Henry Ford's assembly line and the efficient work principles developed by Fredrick W. Taylor. They focused on developing new products and improving production. They believed that if they could reduce manufacturing costs, they could pass the savings on to consumers and increase sales. Their only marketing effort was devoted to distribution—moving products from the producer

PRODUCTION ERA	SALES ERA	MARKETING DEPARTMENT ERA	MARKETING CONCEPT ERA
Civil War–1920s	1930s–1940s	1950s–1960s	1970s–Today
Emphasis on producing and distributing new products	Emphasis on using advertising and salespeople to convince customers to buy a company's products	Emphasis on developing many new marketing activities to sell products	Emphasis on satisfying customers' needs with a carefully developed marketing mix

FIGURE 1-5 Businesses have approached marketing differently over the years.

to locations where customers could buy them.

Sales Emphasis

Effective production methods were not enough to overcome the economic conditions of the Great Depression and World War II during the 1930s and 1940s, causing many businesses to fail. They could no longer rely on customers buying their products just because they were able to get the products to them. Companies began to rely on sales and promotional techniques to convince customers that their products were better than the products of competitors. Good salespeople could introduce products that customers had not purchased before and demonstrate the advantages of ownership. Some historians note that these companies were more interested in selling the product than they were in satisfying the customer.

Marketing Department Emphasis

After World War II, the U.S. economy expanded rapidly, and wage levels increased for consumers as their hours of work declined. Consumers had more money to spend and more time to enjoy the use of many products. Companies increasingly found that consumers were not easily convinced to make purchases when they had many choices available to them. With that, companies began manufacturing products to satisfy customers, moving their emphasis from selling, which focuses on the needs of the seller, to marketing, which focuses on the needs of the buyer. This was an evolutionary change as companies sought to find different ways to convince consumers to purchase their products. They began to develop marketing departments that were responsible for developing those new methods.

One of the first efforts of the new marketing department was to expand the use of advertising. Advertising had an important role of informing consumers about a company's products, the reasons to buy the products, and where they could locate the products. The use of newspapers and magazines, the expanded use of radio, and the growth of television provided outlets to reach consumers with many forms of advertising.

New methods of getting products to customers were developed including catalog sales with mail delivery to rural areas, expanded and improved truck and rail distribution, and the use of airplanes to move perishable products rapidly. The expanding number of retail stores and the growth of city shopping centers gave customers easier access to product choices. Competition brought product prices down, and customers were offered credit to make purchases more affordable. As companies worked to find more ways to encourage customers to buy, they increasingly relied on marketing to find ways to expand markets and sell more products.

Marketing Concept Emphasis

The marketing department emphasis showed that marketing could be a very important tool for businesses. A number of activities were now available that had not been used in the past. However, marketing was becoming quite expensive, and it did not always guarantee a company's success. Marketers also began to misuse marketing activities. These unethical activities might have increased sales, but they also led to customer complaints. Examples included high-pressure sales, misleading advertising, and customer services that were not provided as promised. Even today some people have a negative attitude toward marketers and some marketing activities.

Marketers also discovered that no matter how hard they tried, there were some products that customers did not want to buy. If customers did not believe that a product would satisfy their needs, marketing was not effective. Yet marketers were not involved in developing the company's products.

MATH IN MARKETING

The Consumer Price Index (CPI)

Marketers are responsible for developing strategies to sell a company's products and services to consumers. Those consumers must decide how to spend the money they have available to get the greatest value and satisfaction from the purchases they make. Competition among businesses, improvements in technology and business procedures, and greater productivity from employees cause product prices to decrease over time. However, inflation results in increases in the prices customers pay. To measure the effect of inflation on consumer prices, the federal government calculates the Consumer Price Index (CPI). The CPI compares the cost of a group of products and services commonly purchased by consumers from year to year.

The base year, or a CPI of 100, was established as 1983. Years prior to the base year have a CPI less than 100, and years after the base year have a CPI greater than 100. For example, the CPI for 1915 was 10.1, for 1950, 24.1, and for 2010, 218.1. If a consumer purchased $350 of goods and services in 1983, those same purchases would have cost $35.35 in 1915 ($350 × 0.101), $84.35 in 1950 ($350 × 0.241), and $763.35 in 2010 ($350 × 2.181).

Do the Math

1. If the cost of the average new home in 1983 was $73,500 how much could we expect the price to increase due to inflation by 2021 if the CPI for that year is 270?
2. If the actual cost of the average home was much more or less than what would be expected based on the CPI, what could account for the difference?

In the 1970s, some companies began to realize they could be more successful if they listened to consumers and considered customer needs as they developed products and services. The marketing concept uses the needs of customers as the primary focus during the planning, production, pricing, distribution, and promotion of a product or service.

When the marketing concept was adopted, marketing became more than the work of one department. Marketing personnel worked closely with people in other parts of the company. Activities were completed with customer satisfaction in mind. By coordinating the efforts of the departments in the company and by focusing on satisfying customers' needs, companies were able to develop and market products that customers wanted and that could be sold at a profit. Since its first use in the 1970s, the marketing concept has proven to be effective.

Improving the Marketing Concept

The marketing concept has directed the efforts of many businesses for nearly 40 years, and it still achieves the desired goals—satisfied customers and profitable sales. You will learn in later chapters that even when a company's competitors use the marketing concept, each business can be successful because it focuses on satisfying the needs of customers. However, the marketing concept continues to change as businesses find ways to improve the way they complete marketing activities. In the 21st century, important improvements are strengthening the marketing concept. Two of them are an emphasis on relationship marketing and employee empowerment.

Want to know more about what is trending with this topic? Click on **Lesson 1.4, Global Marketing,** *in your MindTap.*

Connect to MindTap

A third improvement is attention to social responsibility, as discussed in the next chapter.

RELATIONSHIP MARKETING

Businesses have learned that selling to a customer once is not enough. It costs a company a great deal of money to identify new customers, inform them of products, and convince them to purchase. Retaining customers so they continue to purchase from the company again and again can greatly increase profits. The extra efforts required to replace a lost customer can greatly reduce profits.

Businesses are now implementing relationship marketing. **Relationship marketing** focuses on developing customer loyalty by which customers continue to purchase from the business for a long period of time. Customers prefer to shop and buy from businesses they trust and that they believe provide good products and great service. Companies that use relationship marketing stay in contact with customers, determine ways to provide better products and services to meet customer needs, and immediately try to solve any problems the customers may

WORKING IN TEAMS

Work with your team members to identify several businesses that you believe do a good job of relationship marketing. Discuss what the business does that demonstrates interest in customers and how those things encourage customers to return again and again.

have. Keeping current customers satisfied is important because the cost to obtain a new customer is estimated to be at least five times more than the cost of retaining an existing one.

EMPLOYEE EMPOWERMENT   To most customers, a business is represented by the employees with whom they deal on a regular basis. If an employee has an uncaring or indifferent attitude, cannot answer customers' questions, appears unconcerned about a problem, or is unable to solve a problem, a customer will become dissatisfied and shop elsewhere.

Employee empowerment is an approach to customer service that gives employees the authority to solve many customer problems. When a company empowers its employees, it trusts them to make good decisions in the best interest of both the company and the customer. Empowered employees are given training to understand the resources that are available to them when they work on a problem. They are also given guidelines to determine appropriate solutions. Businesses have learned that empowered employees who understand the marketing concept make good decisions that satisfy customers.

CHECKPOINT
Name the four major emphases in the development of marketing's role in business since 1900.

1.4.2 ▶ The Changing View of Marketing

Marketing today is different from marketing 15 or 20 years ago. If you look at the history of business, you can see that marketing played a role in even the simplest early businesses. But businesspeople did not recognize the full value of marketing as a business tool until recently.

As the role of marketing in business changed, so did the way businesspeople viewed its importance. Previously, marketing was considered to be a tool to help a business sell its products and services. It was thought to be unnecessary if sales were high. Today, businesspeople see that marketing contributes in several important ways. Marketing provides information about customers and their needs through market research. It provides many ways to serve customers better, including distribution, pricing, credit, and customer services. Marketing can increase customer satisfaction by solving customer problems. It can help businesses become more profitable by coordinating activities and controlling costs.

Marketing in Other Organizations

Because marketing has been used so successfully by businesses, other types of organizations now depend on marketing as a tool. Libraries, churches, government agencies, and community organizations are using marketing activities. Some non-business organizations use marketing well, whereas others do not.

You can evaluate the marketing efforts of non-business organizations to decide if they understand their value. If the organization relies on promotion with brochures, advertisements, and public service announcements, they likely view marketing as a way to convince consumers of their organization's value. If they use marketing to determine what products and services to offer, where to make them available, how to help consumers determine the value of their services, and how to communicate effectively with consumers, they have adopted the marketing concept. The marketing concept works well for businesses and other organizations.

Analyze a case study that focuses on chapter concepts. Click on Chapter 1, Case Study, in your MindTap.

Connect to MindTap

make decisions that will result in sales and profits for the business. Marketers have varied amounts of experience and education.

Marketing is an exciting and challenging career area. If you are interested in marketing as a career, you can begin now to develop and demonstrate the needed knowledge and skills. Marketing offers many opportunities for you no matter your educational and career path both now and in the future.

Marketers' Roles Today

Marketing managers are responsible for a large number and variety of activities. They work with many people inside and outside a company. Marketing managers are ultimately responsible for a large chunk of the company's budget. People involved in marketing need information about customers, competitors, and market conditions. This information helps marketers

CHECKPOINT
What types of organizations other than businesses use marketing?

1.4 ASSESSMENT

What Have You Learned?

1. Name the four approaches to marketing from the Civil War to present day. [1.4.1]

2. What is the focus of relationship marketing? [1.4.1]

3. How can marketing increase customer satisfaction? [1.4.2]

Make Academic Connections

1. **History** Choose an item you use now and that has been used since 1900. Explain how that item would have been marketed in each of these eras: 1900–1930, 1931–1950, 1951–1980, 1981–present. [1.4.1]

2. **Communication** Compose a letter to the owner or manager of a business that you believe has a low level of customer service. Describe the reasons for your beliefs and explain how relationship marketing and employee empowerment might help the business. [1.4.2]

Connect to ◇DECA

Build your Portfolio

You have decided to run for the office of president of a student organization in your school. Prepare a two-minute speech you would deliver to the members of the organization in which you describe the importance of using marketing as a way to increase the number of new members in the organization. Deliver the speech to your teacher (judge). [1.4.2]

CHAPTER 1 ASSESSMENT

Review Marketing Concepts

1. When are consumers involved in marketing activities? [1.1.1]

2. Choose three of the marketing functions. Describe each function and give an example of how it is used in a specific business. [1.1.2]

3. Using the example of a business that provides tutoring for SAT and Advanced Placement exams, define the customer and exchange that takes place. [1.1.3]

4. Assess a company's marketing effort if a customer purchases a product but the product is not what was expected? What is the likely result? [1.2.1]

5. Identify the factors that led to the development of the central market. [1.2.2]

6. Compare and contrast manufacturing and merchandising businesses. [1.2.3]

7. What are the three activities businesses must accomplish in order to use the marketing concept successfully? [1.3.1]

8. Choose something you have purchased and used recently. Describe that product in terms of the 4Ps of marketing. [1.3.2]

9. Explain how relationship marketing can benefit a business. [1.4.1]

10. Compare the way businesspeople view marketing today with how they viewed it 20 years ago. [1.4.2]

Marketing Research and Planning

1. Find an article from a current magazine or newspaper that describes how a company developed a new product or service, improved a marketing procedure, or responded to customer needs. Prepare a brief oral report describing the activity and how it does or does not illustrate the marketing concept. [1.3.1]

2. Identify and record examples from your own experience for each of the following:

   a. Five marketing activities you have seen in the last week.

   b. Five businesses in your community that have marketing as an important activity.

   c. Five careers in marketing.

   d. Five examples of businesses devoted to performing marketing functions.

   e. Five descriptions of markets. [1.1.1]

3. Identify 10 people who vary in age, gender, occupation, and other personal characteristics. Ask each person the following three questions. Record their answers:

Build your Portfolio

   a. What do you believe "marketing" means?

   b. When you hear the word "marketing," are your feelings positive, negative, or neutral?

   c. Do you believe most people involved in marketing are attempting to meet your needs as a customer? Yes or no? [1.1.1]

When you have completed the interview, write a summary of your findings for question (a) using a word-processing program. Then using a spreadsheet program, enter the gender, age, and occupation of each person you interview in the first three columns. In the fourth column, enter each interviewee's answer to question (b), and in the fifth column, enter the answers to question (c).

Using the graphing function of the spreadsheet program, create several graphs or charts that illustrate the data you recorded.

4. Businesses may have problems when the business functions are not coordinated. An important way to increase customer satisfaction and make a profit is to organize the functions so that they cooperate rather than compete. For each of the following pairs of business functions, identify a problem that might result if the two functions compete. Then identify a way that customer satisfaction or company profits could improve if the functions are coordinated. [1.2.3]

Business Functions

production and marketing

finance and marketing

operations and production

management and finance

5. The two statements below express opinions often held by people who do not understand marketing. Using a word-processing program, develop a paragraph of at least five sentences for each of the statements that demonstrates why the opinion is not correct. [1.1.1]

"My business offers high-quality products, so it does not need marketing."

"Customers have been complaining that my products are not as good as they would like. I need to use marketing to be sure those poor products are sold."

Marketing Management and Decision Making

1. Managers regularly make decisions about the price of products to provide a good value for customers, make a profit for the business, and ensure that products are sold. Often the original product price is not the selling price. Collect information on price reductions for at least 10 products. Gather the information from products you, your family, or friends have purchased by checking prices in stores in your community or in advertisements. Identify the original price and the reduced price for each product. Then complete the following activities:

   a. Calculate the amount and percentage of decrease in price for each product. For example, if a gaming console originally sold for $150 and is on sale for $125, the price reduction is $25 ($150 − $125). The percentage of decrease is the price reduction divided by the original price. For the gaming console, the percentage of decrease in price is 16.7% ($25 ÷ $150).

   b. Assuming the business makes 4% net profit on each sale, determine how much reduction in profit the store will have for each product. For the gaming console, at the original price, the profit would have been $6 ($150 × 0.04). At the reduced price, the profit is $5 ($125 × 0.04). The reduction in profit is $1.

   c. Using the marketing concept, determine reasons why the manager of the business may have decided to reduce the price for each product you identified. Suggest other things the manager might have been able to do to avoid reducing each product's price. [1.3.1]

2. Each of the marketing functions provides exciting career opportunities. There are marketing jobs available for people with varied levels of education, experience, interests, and talents. Use the classified section of a newspaper or a website that lists jobs. For each of the nine marketing functions, find two jobs that have duties related to it. One job should be open to people with a high school diploma and little or no experience. The other should require a college degree and several years of experience. Use the information to prepare a

career poster or work with a team to develop a bulletin board to inform others about jobs available in marketing. [1.1.2]

3. From 1793 to 1861 the United States government did not issue paper money. Instead paper money was issued by state-chartered private banks. Eventually 7,000 varieties of these easily counterfeited forms of currency were in circulation. With no federal regulation, the need to keep track of the value of the notes caused confusion and circulation problems. Some entrepreneurs published "bank note reporters" listing the value of different bank currencies, identifying counterfeits, and reporting insolvent banks. Eventually the financial pressure of the Civil War forced the U.S. government to issue its own paper money called "Greenbacks" and imposed a tax on state bank notes driving them out of circulation. What marketing problems would arise today if there were 7,000 forms of currency in circulation? Do you believe the rise in crypto-currencies such as bitcoin could potentially create the same kinds of problems? Explain your answer. [1.2.2]

Let's Start a Band Follow-Up Discussion

Work in small teams to discuss the question posed at the end of the opening vignette. What should the band do next? Discuss how applying the marketing concept can help the band become successful.

Build Your Marketing Plan

Build your Portfolio

The ability to build a solid marketing plan based on a company's marketing strategy is an essential skill in business. At the end of each chapter you will have the opportunity to develop this skill by focusing on each of the elements of a marketing plan. As part of the first step in this process, you will choose a specific product or service for which you will build your marketing plan. You might want to select a school-related product or service. Your teacher will work with you on developing your idea. By the end of the course, you will submit a final marketing plan to your instructor. Your plan will reflect the information you have gathered and analyzed as part of these chapter-end activities and should clearly outline and articulate your marketing strategy.

In this chapter you learned about the different functions of marketing. You will now apply this learning to the development of your marketing plan. To access the chapter-specific tools that you will need to complete this activity, please navigate to Chapter 1 ➜ Build Your Marketing Plan in MindTap. Alternatively, you can access these tools online at NGLSync. Please visit www.nglsync.cengage.com, and search for the companion website that accompanies this book by entering the ISBN, author, or title. Once you locate this companion website, navigate to Build Your Marketing Plan ➜ Chapter 1.

Marketing Communications Series Event

DECA PREP

Build your Portfolio

The Marketing Communications Series Event consists of a 100-question multiple-choice Career Cluster® exam and role-plays. The role-play portion of the event requires participants to accomplish a task by translating what they have learned into effective, efficient, and spontaneous action. Students have 10 minutes to prepare their strategy for the role-play and another 10 minutes to explain it to the judge and answer questions related to the presentation.

You are the marketing manager for Solid Trust Homes, a large national home builder that builds homes around the country. Your company has earned numerous awards for building high-quality homes. However, the company's success is in jeopardy because of consumer complaints about faulty construction. Expediting the building process to meet deadlines has resulted in building errors, unhappy customers, and lost profits due to the need for reconstruction.

Solid Trust Homes retains some of the best attorneys to represent the company in lawsuits brought against it by unhappy customers. Most states have laws that require new homeowners to take cases not involving warranties to arbitration. Arbitration is an expensive process in which an agreed-upon third party hands down a decision to which the disputing parties must adhere. This strategy is unpopular with home buyers because they have less money to spend on the legal process than large home builders.

There has been an alarming increase in the number of complaints filed by Solid Trust Home customers. Your company has a successful track record of defending itself in these cases because it has great attorneys and insurance to cover court costs. However, unhappy customers are now legally picketing at your large home design centers, using billboards to publicize complaints about the quality of work, and reporting problems with your new homes to the media. Solid Trust Homes has called upon you to help stop the unfavorable publicity. You must outline a strategy that includes steps to overcome all the negative publicity that Solid Trust Homes has received due to poor construction and unhappy customers. The goal is to create satisfied customers who, through word-of-mouth, will share positive comments with prospective customers.

Performance Indicators Evaluated

- Explain the nature of positive customer relations. (Customer Relations)
- Demonstrate a customer-service mindset. (Customer Relations)
- Handle customer/client complaints. (Customer Relations)
- Explain warranties and guarantees. (Product/Service Management)

Go to the DECA website for more detailed information. **www.deca.org**

Think Critically

1. Why must a home builder follow up with customers?
2. What is the problem that a company faces with one unhappy customer?
3. What may be the public's opinion about a company that has the finest lawyers to defend it?
4. Why should Solid Trust Homes consider developing a Consumer's Bill of Rights or Customer Satisfaction Pledge?

CHAPTER 2

SOCIALLY RESPONSIBLE MARKETING

See how effective advertising leads to successful marketing strategies.
Click on Chapter 2, Visual Focus, **in your MindTap.**

Let's Start a Band!

"I think musicians and artists are the most philanthropic people I know. The charity record of the music business would hold up to the work of anybody."

– *Glenn Frey, Eagles*

It's only been a couple of weeks and things are coming together a lot faster than I thought they would. The band members get along, at least most of the time. And the music's getting better.

Today was one long, tough session. It took us a while, but we finally got it right. I just hope we can repeat it tomorrow.

Anyway, Layla came up to me after the rehearsal and asked if I thought the band should stand for something. I know she volunteers at an animal shelter, but I wasn't sure what she meant. She said she thinks we should use our music to help increase awareness of an important issue, like animal welfare. I told her that while I didn't disagree, not every band member may share her commitment.

I told her I'd think about it and I have. I'm concerned that becoming involved in something controversial might cause the band to lose audience members. People want to be entertained, not preached to. How do we walk that fine line, and should we even want to?

2.1 THE IMPACT OF MARKETING

Learning Objectives

2.1.1 Explain how marketing affects businesses.

2.1.2 Describe how marketing affects individuals.

2.1.3 Discuss ways marketing benefits society.

Key Term

international trade

marketing matters

Consumers have a lot to consider when deciding what to buy. "Is the price right?" "Is the product what I need?" "Will the product perform as expected?" "Does this shirt match those shoes?" "Is there a guarantee or warranty in case it is defective?" People ask themselves these and many other questions when making most purchasing decisions.

 essential question

How can consumers improve the way they make decisions about the products and services they purchase? How can businesses help consumers make better decisions?

2.1.1 ▶ Marketing Affects Businesses

Marketing helps businesses find customers and sell their products and services profitably. Many people question the value of marketing. Some people believe it adds too much to the cost of products. Others believe it encourages people to buy things they really do not want or need or that it promotes unhealthy lifestyles. Still others suggest that if businesses produce quality products and services, there is no need for marketing.

It is important to examine the role of marketing in the economy and to society. What does marketing contribute to businesses, individuals, and society? If there are problems with marketing, what can

be done to eliminate them? What can be done to avoid the problems in the first place?

Critical Business Function

Marketing is an important business function. Businesses may have the best accountants, managers, and economists working for them, but without customers, the business will not survive. Marketing is how the business gets customers.

Even though businesses have not always understood marketing or used it effectively, they could not have existed without it. Marketing is responsible for the activities leading to the exchange of a business's products and services for the customer's money. Distribution, financing, promotion, and the other marketing functions are needed to make the exchange possible.

Businesses that use the marketing concept benefit even more from marketing. In those businesses, marketing is used to identify and understand customers. Using market research and marketing information systems, the business can determine customer needs, attitudes, likes, and dislikes. Then the business can carefully develop products and services that meet the needs of the customers and earn a profit. The business also can determine the best way to promote the product to customers and ensure that the product is readily available to them.

Customer Satisfaction

Marketing helps a business satisfy customer wants and needs. Manufacturers developing a new brand of laundry detergent will make better decisions if they are aware of what consumers like and dislike about the current choices. Marketing also helps the business make better decisions about what to sell and how to sell it. The manager of a clothing store will want to know what consumers are expecting in terms of styles and prices before purchasing new items to sell. When customers find that their wants and needs are met by the business, they are more likely to be loyal and continue to purchase from that

How does customer satisfaction relate to the marketing concept?

business. It is more cost-effective for a business to hold on to existing customers. So, effective marketing is important to the success of businesses.

 CHECKPOINT
How do businesses that use the marketing concept benefit more from marketing?

2.1.2 ▶ Marketing Helps People

Individuals benefit from marketing because it improves the exchanges that occur between businesses and consumers. By doing so, it also can make their lives easier. While many people do not easily recognize the benefits of marketing, there are numerous examples of its value.

Consider going to a supermarket to purchase party supplies. You want the store to be conveniently located. You also want the store to stock an adequate supply of your favorite brands of decorations, drinks, and snacks. When you enter the store, you should be able to locate the products easily. The prices should be clearly marked and affordable. Store employees should be able to answer your questions and help you check out and bag your purchases. The store should offer convenient methods of payment, including cash, check, and credit or debit card. You might even expect the store to offer discounts or special savings on their products.

Each of the activities described for the purchase of your party supplies is an example of marketing. Those activities make it easier for you to shop. The business benefits because you purchase the products. You benefit because the business is able to satisfy your needs.

Better Products at a Lower Price

Marketing provides other benefits to individuals that may not be as obvious. Marketing continually evaluates consumers' likes and dislikes and unmet needs. Based on this information, improvements are made to products and services, and new products are developed. As a result of marketing activities, more products are available to satisfy the needs of more customers. This results in more sales. The increase in sales allows businesses to produce products more efficiently, which leads to lower prices for consumers.

For example, the first personal computers were very basic and not very powerful, but they cost several thousand dollars. When

Want to know more about marketing in the information age? Click on **Lesson 2.1, Digital Marketing,** *in your MindTap.*

Connect to MindTap

WORKING IN TEAMS

Working with a team, select a product and list all the marketing activities that must occur in the exchange between the business and the customer. Outline how the exchange would work without marketing. As a team, discuss why marketing is needed.

introduced to the marketplace, most consumers did not know how computers would benefit them. Today's personal computers cost as little as a few hundred dollars, so they are accessible to almost everyone, and they are thousands of times more powerful. They have many features to make them easy to use and are helpful for a variety of work and personal activities. Computers allow users to modify photographs, prepare personal budgets, perform online banking, listen to music, play complex online games, talk to friends, and even get an education. All of this was made possible through improved technology and the work of marketers who let consumers know what they could accomplish with computers.

Enhanced Social Interaction

Marketing also helps consumers build lifestyles and friendships and pursue other social activities. All consumers want to present an image to their friends and family that says something about who they are. You might wear a certain T-shirt or brand of jeans to let people know something about yourself. You also might participate in lifestyle activities such as skateboarding, gaming, or dancing. Marketing helps consumers find their place in the world by providing the raw materials they use to develop a sense of who they are.

Marketing also provides venues for consumers to share time with others. You might go to the movies with friends. You might keep in touch with people through Facebook, Twitter, Pinterest, or other social media sites supported through marketing. You might even be part of a brand community that allows consumers who share a love or respect for a particular brand to come together in celebration of that brand. In such ways, marketers help consumers develop relationships with others throughout their community and the world.

Expanded Job Opportunities

Because many jobs in the United States have some marketing responsibility, acquiring an understanding of marketing will enhance your employment opportunities. Entry-level jobs in sales often lead to higher-level marketing positions. Jobs in customer service, warehouse and inventory management, and marketing research are financially rewarding career areas that require marketing skills. A knowledge of marketing can benefit all career areas because all businesses need to plan, promote, price, and distribute their products and services. You can combine your interest in a particular industry with your marketing knowledge for a rewarding career.

Marketing skills also are valuable because they can help you accomplish your goals. For example, marketing skills can help you get elected to an office in a club, prepare for college or for a job, plan a fundraising activity for an organization, or start your own business.

 CHECKPOINT
How do individuals benefit from marketing?

What goals do you have that marketing skills might help you achieve?

© leolintang/Shutterstock.com.

Does society benefit from marketing? This question often is debated, but the evidence seems to indicate there are many positive effects of marketing for society (**Figure 2-1**).

New and Better Products

Marketing helps to identify and develop new and better products and services for consumers. Many of those products and services are beneficial to society in general. For example, more efficient automobiles use less gasoline and cause less pollution. Biodegradable products reduce the growing need for landfill space. Improvements made to safety products such as airbags and motorcycle helmets continue to reduce the number and severity of injuries from accidents. All of these products were developed to meet the needs of consumers and society.

Marketing encourages businesses to provide products and services that consumers want. It also helps educate consumers to make better purchasing decisions. As a result, natural resources and raw materials can be used more efficiently rather than being wasted on products consumers will not buy.

Improved Standards of Living

Marketing improves the standard of living in a country. The standard of living is based on the products and services available to consumers, the amount of resources consumers have

BENEFITS OF MARKETING
New and better products meet consumer needs
Consumers make better decisions
Natural resources are used more effectively
Standard of living improves
Awareness of important issues increases
International trade increases

FIGURE 2-1 Marketing benefits consumers, businesses, and society.

to obtain the products and services, and the quality of life for consumers. Countries that have well-developed marketing systems are able to make more and better products available to consumers. Those countries also have more jobs for their citizens and higher wage scales as a result of marketing.

More Awareness of Important Social Issues

Marketing also helps to inform consumers of issues that have an impact on them as individuals and on society. Marketing can help inform you to stay away from certain products that may be harmful to your health, such as cigarettes and alcohol. Additionally, it can help raise awareness of societal issues such as the need to stop texting while driving or how to prevent the spread of disease throughout your community.

Want to know more about what is trending with this topic? Click on **Lesson 2.1, Global Marketing,** in your MindTap.

Connect to MindTap

Improved International Trade

Marketing has been particularly effective in improving international trade. **International trade** is the exchange of products and services with people in other countries. International trade has many benefits for the participating countries and for the consumers in those countries. Think of the number of products you buy that are produced in another country. Just as the United States is a large consumer of foreign products, many U.S. businesses sell products internationally. Without marketing, international trade would be difficult.

Marketers help determine where products can be sold and how to sell them in countries that may have very different business procedures, money systems, and buying practices. Methods of shipping and product handling must be identified or developed. Decisions about customer service must be made. Promotional methods that are appropriate for the people in each country or region must be developed to ensure that customers understand the products and their benefits.

> **CHECKPOINT**
> *Name four ways in which marketing benefits society.*

2.1 ASSESSMENT

What Have You Learned?

1. Why is customer satisfaction important to a business? [2.1.1]
2. How does marketing result in lower prices for consumers? [2.1.2]
3. Name four ways in which marketing benefits society. [2.1.3]

Make Academic Connections

1. **Visual Art** Using magazines or online sources, find images that illustrate ways in which marketing benefits society. Make a collage with the illustrations. [2.1.3]
2. **Consumer Economics** Marketing is said to improve exchanges between businesses and consumers. Make a list of at least five products or services that you buy or use. Describe how marketing has improved the exchange process for each of these products or services. Organize this information in a spreadsheet. [2.1.2]

Connect to ◇DECA
Build your Portfolio

You work for a food processing company that is considering selling its product globally. The owner has no experience marketing products internationally and has asked for your advice. Using presentation software, prepare a two-minute presentation on how international trade can benefit the business. Include two specific ways that marketing can support the company's efforts. Give your speech to your teacher (judge). [2.1.3]

2.2 CRITICISMS OF MARKETING

Learning Objectives

2.2.1 Discuss three common criticisms of marketing.

2.2.2 Explain how marketing can be used to solve social problems.

Key Term

green marketing

marketing matters

The activities associated with marketing may be misunderstood. Marketing has been accused of creating a false need for unnecessary products. Some people feel that marketing is a waste of money and only serves to increase the price customers pay. Others claim that high-quality products do not need marketing because the products will sell themselves.

essential question

What are the common criticisms consumers have of marketing? Which do you think are correct and which are incorrect?

2.2.1 ▶ Common Complaints

If used inappropriately, marketing can have negative effects. The misuse of marketing has led to some criticisms and has created a negative image for some marketing activities. Businesspeople must take criticisms of marketing seriously. If consumers have a negative opinion about an important part of a company, it can affect whether they will do business with it.

Marketing Causes Unneeded Purchases

Because of marketing, consumers have many choices of products to purchase. Those products are readily available in many stores. They are displayed in ways that make them easy to purchase, and they are packaged to attract attention. Advertising is used extensively to encourage people to consider specific brands of products. Credit and special financing arrangements are often available for expensive products to make them seem more affordable. Marketing activities and the power of promotion can increase the sales of products and services.

Businesses using the marketing concept should carefully consider the potential impact of marketing activities on consumers. Although it might seem appropriate to use any tool that will result in more sales of a product, the long-term results of the sale should also be considered. If a customer buys a product because of marketing rather than because the product is really needed, there is a good chance the customer will be dissatisfied. How many times have you purchased something and then quickly decided you really did not want or need the item? What actions did you take?

In your opinion, is the use of credit a positive or negative outcome of marketing? Explain your answer.

© robertindiana/Shutterstock.com.

product does not meet customer needs, businesspeople should avoid using marketing strategies such as promotion and price reductions to try to sell it. This often will lead to dissatisfaction with both the product and the business.

Finally, the business must nurture long-term relationships with customers. One sale is not enough. The business will be successful only when customers return repeatedly because they are satisfied with the business and believe the business cares about their needs.

Marketing Causes Social Problems

For as long as marketing has been around, it has been associated with various social issues. For instance, during the Great Depression of the 1930s, marketers were blamed for creating a culture that focused on excess and hedonism. During the more recent Great Recession of 2008 to 2009, marketers were criticized for selling consumers houses they could not afford, which led to overextension of credit and increases in defaults and foreclosures.

Additionally, marketing and advertising have been blamed for a variety of current health and psychological problems such as obesity, anorexia, low self-esteem, depression, anxiety, smoking, alcoholism, high-blood pressure, and a host of others. In other words, in addition to being blamed for selling individuals products they don't need, marketing is also criticized for selling products that may be harmful.

To address this criticism, businesses should be mindful of the impact their products have on people and society. They also should be aware of how advertising influences individuals and the culture as a whole. Finally, marketers need to be mindful of history in order to prevent repeating mistakes made in earlier decades and even centuries.

Many consumers simply return the item for a refund. The business has now lost the sale, and it also has a product that is worth much less and perhaps cannot be resold. The business is left with returned merchandise, an unhappy customer, and possibly a bad reputation among the customer's friends.

To respond to this criticism, businesspeople must carefully match products to the needs and wants of customers. They also must evaluate products that do not sell to determine why customers do not want them. In doing so, the business can make better planning decisions in the future to offer products and services that customers want.

Marketing should start with ensuring that the company's products are high quality and meet consumer needs. If a

Marketing Wastes Money

Some people believe marketing activities serve only to raise the cost of their purchases. However, economists who study the impact of marketing activities on product prices have demonstrated that marketing results in lower prices in the long run. Because of marketing, products can be sold to more customers. This, in turn, creates more competition among businesses. When consumers have more choices of products, they will usually buy those that are reasonably priced. That encourages businesses to keep prices as low as possible to be competitive. According to the economists, increased sales volume and competition result in lower prices for consumers.

Marketing May Be Misused

There are many examples of businesses that rely on marketing to sell poor-quality products. Think of the used automobile with many mechanical problems that is sold because the salesperson convinced the customer that the car is in good condition. There are numerous tales of people buying land based on information in a brochure or from a high-pressure salesperson only to discover that the land is in a swamp or on the side of a steep mountain. Marketing is misused in those situations to misrepresent poor products.

CHECKPOINT
Name four common complaints about marketing.

MARKETING COMMUNICATION

Manage Online Reputation

Nearly every company or organization has an online presence. For many, it is their initial point-of-contact with the public, and it results in customers forming a first impression, often everlasting. In managing its online reputation, a company must go beyond creating content and monitoring social media. It must pay attention to what customers are saying, whether they are tweeting about the company's latest product or posting about a consumer experience on Yelp. Although user-generated content can be beneficial, opening the company or organization up to feedback does have some risks.

Negative product reviews or other critical comments about the company's brand can affect sales and, in some cases, go viral reaching a vast audience. Because everyone has the right to express their opinion about any company, addressing criticism publicly without hiding negative online comments is optimal. Yet most companies' initial response to a negative review or comment is either to do nothing or take it down from the company website.

Think Critically

Imagine you are in charge of a company's website. Write guidelines for the public forum part of the company's site. Be sure to make the guidelines clear. The guidelines should also address the balance between the customers' desire to be heard and the company's desire to show itself in a positive light.

Build your Portfolio

Marketing Solves Problems

When used effectively, marketing can help to solve important problems and contribute to social improvement.

Marketing Increases Public Awareness

Our society faces many serious problems. Concerns about health care, crime levels, poverty, diseases, racism, education, unemployment, drug use, teenage pregnancy, and the environment all require the attention of many people if solutions are to be found. Marketing contributes to the solutions in several ways. Through communication, people are more aware of social problems and how they affect individuals and the country. Consider the number of times you have received information on using seat belts, recycling, the dangers of drugs and alcohol, and reasons to stay in school. Marketers have been responsible for developing the advertisements and public service announcements you have seen. Marketers also have been responsible for creating new products to help minimize some of these problems.

Marketing has encouraged people to eat healthier food, quit smoking, contribute money to charity and relief organizations, and support research into cures for diseases such as AIDS and cancer. Marketing has encouraged people to vote and to avoid drinking and driving. Many important social issues are now receiving much attention because of effective marketing.

Many businesses now promote the use of green marketing. **Green marketing** consists of marketing activities designed to satisfy customer needs without negatively impacting the environment. Businesses promote the importance of environmentally friendly products and encourage consumers to purchase

© BP North America

"Electric cars won't happen overnight. There's got to be a way of making fuels cleaner."

▲ Scott Takeda/Writer

Reducing sulfur is one way. We voluntarily introduced cleaner burning low-sulfur gasoline, six years before E.P.A. mandates. Today it's available in over 40 U.S. cities. This year, we're introducing low-sulfur diesel fuel for bus fleets in major U.S. cities. When used with new filter technology, this fuel helps reduce air pollution and can cut emissions by up to 90 percent.

It's a start.

bp

beyond petroleum   bp.com

How does this BP ad relate to green marketing?

such products. BP promotes the use of more environmentally friendly fuel in the advertisement shown here.

Marketing Helps Match Supply with Demand

Providing products and services through distribution is a function of marketing. However, products and services are not always available when and where consumers most need them. For example, if there is a drought in one part of the country, the supply of hay and grain may not meet the demand of farmers and ranchers in that area. At the same time, there might be an excess supply in other areas. An effective distribution system can move the hay and grain quickly from one part of the country to another, helping to match supply and demand.

Oil products and gasoline can be distributed throughout the country using an extensive network of pipelines. If a greater supply of natural gas or heating oil is needed in northern states during an especially cold winter, it can be routed away from areas that have less demand. Marketing helps to prevent or reduce the impact of problems that could otherwise result in serious outcomes for society.

> **CHECKPOINT**
> *Define green marketing.*

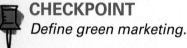

2.2 ASSESSMENT

What Have You Learned?

1. How can marketers respond to the criticism that marketing causes unneeded purchases? [2.2.1]

2. Why should marketers be mindful of history in approaching how to market their products? [2.2.1]

3. Which marketing function helps match supply with demand for products? [2.2.2]

Make Academic Connections

1. **Social Studies**   Marketing is responsible for many successful public awareness campaigns, such as *Don't Drink and Drive, Buckle Up,* and *Just Say No.* Think of a problem that is prevalent in society today. Write a blog post that would contribute to a public awareness campaign for the problem. Include a visual in your post. [2.2.2]

2. **Economics**   Explain the effects marketing has on the following issues:
   a. Competition
   b. Pricing
   c. Supply and demand [2.2.2]

Connect to ◇DECA

Build your Portfolio

You are a marketer in the farming industry. Apple growers in your state have an oversupply. This is forcing them to slash prices and is threatening to put them out of business. Develop a two-page plan that outlines three specific ways marketing can help balance the supply and demand of apples. Present your plan to your teacher (judge). [2.2.2]

Planning a Career In...
COMMUNITY RELATIONS

Did you ever experience a positive change in your life because you knew how to prepare for an event? For example, maybe you avoided a serious house fire because you regularly changed the batteries in your smoke detector.

Public awareness campaigns reach out to communities to improve the quality of life within the community. Whether informing people about Lyme disease or reminding them to have cancer screening check-ups or change the batteries in their smoke detectors, these campaigns increase awareness on many vital issues.

Job Titles

- Community Outreach Coordinator
- Public Relations Officer
- Community Relations Liaison
- Director of Media
- Social Service and Outreach Manager
- Programs Specialist
- Cancer Society Community Relations

Needed Skills

- A bachelor's degree is usually required.
- Excellent written and oral communication skills are helpful.
- Ability to stay abreast of current trends in your industry is required.

What it's like to work in... Community Relations

Jada arrives at her office at 9:00 A.M. As the Customer Communications Manager for her city's publicly funded city bus system, she will spend the next hour reviewing the print and radio "Ride the Bus" ad campaigns that will run for the rest of the summer. Reminding commuters how they can help reduce smog by riding the bus is an effective way to both increase ridership and minimize smog.

After lunch, Jada gives a presentation on the city's new "fare assistance" program to representatives from various social service agencies. Jada needs to inform the elderly, low-income residents, and students about this assistance. The presentation feedback the agency representatives provide will help her accomplish that goal. The bus system strives to provide transportation to as many citizens as possible.

At 4:00 P.M., representatives from a local advertising agency meet with Jada and her team to review the new posters designed to increase ridership. Featuring endorsements of riders from all walks of life, the posters are intended to increase ridership throughout the community.

What About You?

What issues do you believe are important to a community's well-being, and how would you like to promote those ideas?

Discover more about the outlook for this career and watch a video about a related career. Click on **Chapter 2, Planning a Career In...** *in your MindTap.*

2.3 MARKETING AND SOCIAL RESPONSIBILITY

Learning Objective

2.3.1 Explain the three factors involved in increased social responsibility for businesses.

2.3.2 Explain ways by which businesses improve their own practices.

2.3.3 Discuss how ethical issues affect marketers' professional responsibilities.

Key Terms

social responsibility
consumerism
boycott
ethics
code of ethics
self-regulation

marketing matters

One of the stakeholders of any business is the society in which the company operates. As marketing continues to influence consumers and products, it should also look at the influence the company has on the society, culture, and environment in which it does business.

 essential question

What can both businesses and consumers do to make sure that products and services meet consumer expectations?

2.3.1 ▶ Consumer Protection

Marketers must be aware of the effects of their activities. They must be willing to pay attention to society's needs to determine how businesses can address those needs. In a global world, they also must pay attention to the differences in needs across cultures.

Businesses today are expected to aid in solving the problems facing society. Concern about the consequences of actions on others is called **social responsibility**. When making decisions, businesspeople realize that they must consider factors beyond what their customers want and what is most profitable for the business. Most businesspeople recognize that their businesses cannot be successful

in the long run if society is facing major problems.

Increased social responsibility of businesses involves three factors. The growth of consumerism, government regulation, and improving business practices are each playing a role (**Figure 2-2**).

The Growth of Consumerism

Consumerism is the organized actions of groups of consumers seeking to increase their influence on business practices. Individual consumers can have only a small influence on the activities of a business.

Social Responsibility Must Be Shared

CONSUMER GROUPS

BUSINESS

GOVERNMENT

FIGURE 2-2 Consumer groups, government, and business organizations all play a role in improving society.

However, when organized as a group, consumers have a much greater impact. They can speak out and meet with businesspeople to recommend changes. They also can use the money they spend on purchases to influence decisions.

Although consumers have always attempted to influence business practices, consumerism became an important influence on businesses in the 1960s when President John F. Kennedy presented the Consumer Bill of Rights. The Consumer Bill of Rights identified four rights that all consumers should expect:

1. The right to adequate and accurate information
2. The right to safe products
3. The right to product choices
4. The right to communicate their ideas and opinions to business and government

As a result of the attention focused on those rights, consumers have become very active in ensuring that their rights are protected. Some ways used to protect consumer rights are consumer education, consumer information, lobbying, and product boycotts. Consumer groups develop materials and educational programs to be used in schools and other places to help people become better-informed consumers.

There are a number of consumer organizations that test products to determine whether they are safe and whether they provide a good value for the price. The organizations often publish the results in books, magazines, and on the Internet or have a telephone service so people can call for product information before making a purchase. Consumer lobbyists work with national and state legislators to develop laws to protect consumer rights.

Finally, consumers have found they can influence business practices by the way they spend their money, their consumer *votes*. If a group of consumers is dissatisfied with the actions or products of a business, they can organize a boycott. A **boycott** is an organized effort to influence a company by refusing to purchase its products. For example, many consumers stopped using BP gas stations after the oil spill in the Gulf of Mexico. Consumer groups also reinforce positive business practices by encouraging their members to purchase products from businesses that respond to consumer needs.

Government Regulation

The U.S. government significantly influences business practices. The welfare of consumers is at the core of many of the laws and regulations enacted by government. These laws are designed to improve the social impact of business practices. Businesses must comply with consumer protection laws or risk fines and a loss of business. Some important consumer laws are described in **Figure 2-3**.

CHECKPOINT
What are the four rights all consumers should expect, according to the Consumer Bill of Rights?

CONSUMER LAWS	
Legislation	**Purpose**
Sherman Antitrust Act, 1890	To increase competition among businesses by regulating monopolies
Food and Drug Act, 1906	To control the content and labeling of food and drug products by forming the Food and Drug Administration (FDA)
Federal Trade Commission Act, 1914	To protect consumer rights by forming the Federal Trade Commission (FTC)
Robinson–Patman Act, 1936	To protect small businesses from unfair pricing practices between manufacturers and large businesses
Fair Packaging and Labeling Act, 1966	To require packages to be accurately labeled and fairly represent the contents
Consumer Credit Protection Act, 1968	To require disclosure of credit requirements and rates to loan applicants
Consumer Product Safety Act, 1972	To set safety standards and to form the Consumer Product Safety Commission (CPSC)
Americans with Disabilities Act, 1990	To prohibit discrimination and ensure equal opportunity for persons with disabilities
Telemarketing and Consumer Fraud and Abuse Prevention Act, 1994	To prohibit deceptive telemarketing practices and regulate calls made to consumers' homes
Millennium Digital Commerce Act, 1999	To regulate the use of electronic contracts and signatures for Internet business transactions
Gramm–Leach–Bliley Financial Modernization Act, 1999	To limit the sharing of consumer information by requiring financial services companies to inform consumers about how private information is handled
Dodd–Frank Wall Street Reform and Consumer Protection Act, 2010	To regulate financial markets in order to protect consumers from unfair lending practices and set up the Consumer Financial Protection Bureau

FIGURE 2-3 Federal legislation is one method of increasing the social responsibility of businesses.

Most businesses recognize their responsibility to consumers and to society. If consumers are dissatisfied with the business's practices, they will soon stop buying the company's products. If social problems exist, the government may increase regulation of business or increase taxes to pay for programs designed to solve the problems. Businesses do not want increased regulation or taxes.

Individual businesses and business organizations are working to improve business practices in several ways. They have established codes of ethics and engaged in self-regulation and social action.

Codes of Ethics

Ethics are moral principles or values based on honesty and fairness. **A code of ethics** is a set of standards or rules that guide ethical business behavior. An organization's code of ethics encourages honest and proper conduct and practices. Businesspeople recognize that the inappropriate or illegal behavior of one company can have a negative effect on the whole industry. They attempt to influence that behavior by agreeing on standards of conduct. By agreeing to a code of ethics, businesspeople encourage responsible behavior. In some industries, the codes of ethics are enforced by penalties and are applied to businesses that violate the standards. The American Marketing Association (AMA) Statement of Ethics prescribes ethics norms and values for marketers (**Figure 2-4**).

Self-Regulation

Individual businesses and groups of businesses in the same industry have developed procedures to respond to consumer problems and to encourage customers to work directly with the businesses to solve problems. Taking personal responsibility for actions is known as **self-regulation**. The Better Business Bureau is a consumer protection organization sponsored by businesses. The purpose of the Better Business Bureau is to gather information from consumers about problems, provide information about improper business practices, and attempt to solve problems between businesses and their customers.

Many businesses have customer service departments that work to solve consumer problems and to provide consumers with information about the company and its products. The Butterball Turkey Talk-Line has been in operation for more than 30 years. It is open every year during the months of November and December, with experts answering consumers' questions about how to prepare a Butterball turkey for their holiday meals. In addition

Ethical norms:
- Do no harm.
- Foster trust in the marketing system.
- Embrace ethical values

Ethical values:
- Honesty
- Responsibility
- Fairness
- Respect
- Transparency
- Citizenship

FIGURE 2-4 The American Marketing Association Statement of Ethics prescribes ethical norms and ethical values for marketers.

Source: https://www.ama.org/AboutAMA/Pages/Statement-of-Ethics.aspx

to the telephone talk-line, the turkey experts now answer questions via email, social media, live chat, and text.

Some industries, such as homebuilding, developed procedures consumers can use to resolve problems. Problems that cannot be resolved between the customer and the business are referred to an independent panel that can help determine a fair solution.

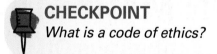
© Bochkarev Photography/Shutterstock.com.

Social Action

Businesspeople are concerned about the world in which they live. Many are active in helping to solve some of society's serious problems by investing time and money to help their communities. For example, Microsoft has a long history of giving back to society. Through its Microsoft Philanthropies program, the company aims to "make the benefits and opportunities of technology accessible to everyone." Other initiatives include Microsoft's Technology Education and Literacy in Schools (TEALS) program and the Microsoft Giving Program, through which Microsoft employees donate technological services in their communities. McDonald's sponsors Ronald McDonald Houses for families with children who are hospitalized with serious illnesses. Operating worldwide, Ronald McDonald Houses help ease the burden for families while their children receive medical treatments.

> **CHECKPOINT**
> *What is a code of ethics?*

2.3.3 ▶ Ethics in Marketing

Each day you can see many examples of businesses that feel a social responsibility to help their community and its people. Business ethics has received a great deal of attention recently. Most businesspeople behave ethically. However, the actions of a few people can cause customers to wonder if ethical behavior is really valued in business.

Responsibility to Customers

Marketers deal directly with customers. They ask customers to spend money for products intended to satisfy needs and wants. Because of this relationship, marketers have a special responsibility to behave ethically. People place a high value on ethical business behavior. Businesspeople are expected to be honest and fair in dealings with customers, employees, and other businesses.

Each marketer must behave ethically. Decisions and actions should be evaluated to determine if they are honest and fair. Sometimes there will appear to be conflicts in what is best for the business, its employees, customers, competitors, and society in general. Some people suggest that the decision should be based on what is best for most people. Others believe an action is right or wrong based on how it will affect the people directly involved.

Want to know more about what is trending with this topic? Click on **Lesson 2.3, Marketing Decisions,** *in your MindTap.*

Connect to
MindTap

ConAgra Foods once recalled all varieties of its Peter Pan Peanut Butter product because of a possible link to salmonella poisoning. Although initial product tests did not indicate the presence of salmonella, ConAgra voluntarily recalled the peanut butter and offered consumers a refund. ConAgra acted responsibly and ethically by making consumer health and safety a priority. Upon further investigation, ConAgra discovered that there was salmonella contamination caused by water damage experienced during a flood at one of its plants. ConAgra closed the plant to make renovations that would result in safe production processes.

Harm and Accountability

In some cases, unethical behavior of marketers may not appear to cause any real harm. If dishonesty results in a customer buying your product rather than your competitor's, or if you can conceal a mistake you made, you may believe that it does not matter. But marketers must remember that their emphasis must be on

MATH IN MARKETING

Ethical Marketing Pays Off

Not only is honest marketing the ethical thing to do, but it makes business sense as well. Ideally, a company wants to build brand loyalty and enter into long-term relationships with its customers. Loyal customers purchase repeatedly from the same company. Over a lifetime, these purchases can really add up. And when customers are happy with a product or service, they will recommend it to others.

It may be tempting for a company to try to increase sales through deceptive marketing that overstates the benefit of its product. This practice is not only unethical, but it also can result in fewer profits for the company in the long run.

Do the Math

1. Two car dealerships, Dealership A and Dealership B, both make an average of $1,000 profit for every car they sell. Using deceptive sales and pricing, Dealership A sells 100 cars in May. However, none of those 100 customers ever buy from Dealership A again. Dealership B is honest with its customers but sells only 70 cars in May. However, 30 of those customers buy an average of three more cars from Dealership B throughout their lifetime. What is the difference in the monthly and long-term profit between Dealership A and Dealership B from those customers?

2. Dealership B's repeat customers also each recommend Dealership B to six friends. Fifty percent of those friends end up buying a car from Dealership B. How much profit does Dealership B make from this word-of-mouth promotion?

what is best for everyone in an exchange. Marketers' actions affect many others, both inside and outside the business.

In other cases, unethical behavior does have obvious negative consequences for individuals and businesses. Improper marketing can harm customers. Society is hurt by businesses that have no concern for the products and services they sell or how or to whom they are marketed. Senior citizens often fall prey to the unethical business practices of salespeople who sell them poor-quality or unneeded products or services. Finally, many unethical business practices are illegal. People have been fined and imprisoned as a result of unethical actions.

Some businesses are developing education programs and operating procedures to help employees understand how to make ethical decisions. They want to improve the ethical image of all businesses and ensure that customers believe they will be treated fairly.

CHECKPOINT
Why do marketers have a special responsibility to behave ethically?

2.3 ASSESSMENT

What Have You Learned?

1. What is the term for businesses' concern about the consequences of their actions on others? [2.3.1]

2. How can the government regulate business? [2.3.1]

3. What does a code of ethics encourage businesspeople to do? [2.3.2]

4. How can businesses help employees understand how to make ethical decisions? [2.3.3]

Make Academic Connections

1. **Government** Many consumer laws exist to protect consumer rights. Research one of these laws. Write one paragraph describing the purpose of the law and the history surrounding it. [2.3.1]

2. **Ethics** Although most businesses act ethically, some do not. Search newspapers or the Internet for recent stories about *Build your Portfolio* businesses that used unethical marketing tactics resulting in harm to consumers. Report about the unethical activities in a one-page paper. [2.3.3]

Connect to ◇DECA *Build your Portfolio*

Your investor relations team works for a large public corporation that regularly makes sizable contributions to charity and relief efforts. The annual shareholder meeting is coming up. Some vocal shareholders have expressed a concern that the contributions are cutting into the corporation's profits. Your team has been asked to prepare a three-minute presentation for the meeting to address the following question: If a corporation is supposed to maximize its shareholders' return on investment, how can it justify giving millions of dollars to social causes? Use presentation software in preparing the presentation. Make your team presentation to your teacher (judge). [2.3.2]

Connect to MindTap

Analyze a case study that focuses on chapter concepts. Click on **Chapter 2, Case Study,** *in your MindTap.*

Review Marketing Concepts

1. Why is marketing an important business function? [2.1.1]

2. How does an understanding of marketing help you expand your job opportunities? [2.1.2]

3. According to the textbook, what are the four positive effects of marketing on society? [2.1.3]

4. Why should businesses nurture long-term relationships with customers? [2.2.1]

5. Explain how marketing results in lower prices for products in the long run. [2.2.1]

6. What is "green marketing" and why do you think it is important? [2.2.2]

7. What are the effects of a consumer boycott? [2.3.1]

8. Describe three examples of businesses using self-regulation to help customers solve problems. [2.3.2]

9. What are the two approaches to ethical decision making involving consumers? Which approach makes the most sense? Explain your answer. [2.3.3]

Marketing Research and Planning

1. The four consumer products in the table below have undergone major price decreases since they were introduced. Those price decreases occurred because of improved technology and effective marketing and resulted in higher sales. The prices listed for each product are typical of the prices charged when the products were first introduced and more recent prices. [2.1.2]

Product	Introductory Price	Recent Price
Hand-held calculator	$ 138	$ 14
Quartz watch	$ 320	$ 16
Microwave oven	$ 860	$ 60
Personal computer	$2,800	$349

a. For each product, find the price reduction and percentage decrease from the introductory price to the recent price.

b. Assume that you planned to buy all four of the items. Calculate the total cost of the purchases if all were purchased at the introductory price. Now calculate the total cost if all were purchased at the recent price. Calculate the percentage savings to you if

you were able to make all purchases at the recent price. What would the price saving be if you adjusted the introductory prices for inflation? (See the CPI inflation calculator at http://data.bls.gov/cgi-bin/cpicalc.pl)

c. List four other products with large price decreases from the time they were first introduced until now.

d. Why has there been such a drastic change between the introductory prices and the current prices of this item? [2.1.2]

2. Review the business section in five issues of a print or online newspaper or business magazine (*BusinessWeek, Fortune,* or *Money,* for example). Identify all articles that relate to the social responsibility of businesses. For each article, determine

a. The primary issue involved;

b. Whether the problem is being addressed by consumer groups, government, businesses, or a combination;

c. The type of action being proposed to solve the problem.

After you have collected the information, summarize your findings in a one-page written report. Before submission, check the document for correct grammar, spelling, punctuation, and format. [2.3.1]

3. The following statements describe marketing activities that may result in a problem for society. For each statement, describe a problem that may result from the practice and one way that consumers, government, and businesses could respond.

    a. Fast-food restaurants use a large amount of packaging.

    b. Credit card companies use advertising to encourage people to use credit for more of their purchases.

    c. A hospital cannot afford to admit patients who do not have health insurance.

    d. A market research organization asks a large number of personal questions during interviews. [2.2.1]

4. For each of the following positive results of marketing, provide specific examples demonstrating that those contributions do exist. Cite examples other than those listed in the section "Marketing Solves Problems."

    a. Marketing increases public awareness of problems and solutions.

    b. Marketing helps match supply and demand to solve serious problems. [2.2.2]

Marketing Management and Decision Making

1. Work in small teams to prepare a code of ethics for students and teachers. When you are finished, share your group's code of ethics with the other groups. Identify the areas of agreement and disagreement in the various codes of ethics. Discuss how the students in the class could enforce the code of ethics through self-regulation. [2.3.2]

2. Advertising fast-food and producing bottled water are situations in which businesspeople must decide how their decisions can be socially responsible. Choose one and then answer the questions that follow. Use the Internet to conduct a brief investigation into the social responsibility issue you choose.

    a. Who is affected by the business's decisions? How is each group affected?

    b. What is a possible action that can be taken by a concerned consumer group, government, or group of businesses? By the business involved?

    c. What do you believe is the most socially responsible action? Why? [2.3.1]

3. Work with a partner to plan a campaign to increase awareness of a social problem in your school or community. The purpose of the campaign may be to raise money for a school function, to fulfill a community need (such as cleaning up a local park), or to meet another need. Consider how marketing can be used throughout the campaign process.

    • What is the social problem the campaign addresses and who is the audience?

    • How can market research help you develop a successful campaign?

    • What kind of promotions will you use?

    • Do you need sponsors or investors to help finance the campaign?

Prepare an oral presentation using visual aids describing the purpose of the awareness campaign. Communicate your marketing plans and the goals you want to accomplish. [2.2.2]

Let's Start a Band Follow-Up Discussion

Work in small teams to discuss the question posed at the end of the opening vignette. Should the band use music to help increase awareness for an important social issue, or should it focus solely on the goal of entertaining its audience? Is it possible to accomplish both goals?

Build Your Marketing Plan

In this chapter you learned about the social responsibility of business and how it relates to marketing. You will now apply this learning to the development of your marketing plan. To access the chapter-specific tools that you will need to complete this activity, please navigate to Chapter 2 ➔ Build Your Marketing Plan in MindTap. Alternatively, you can access these tools online at NGLSync. Please visit www.nglsync.cengage.com, and search for the companion website that accompanies this book by entering the ISBN, author, or title. Once you locate this companion website, navigate to Build Your Marketing Plan ➔ Chapter 2.

Apparel and Accessories Marketing Series Event

DECA PREP

Build your Portfolio

In the fashion industry, what goes around comes around. Today's popular styles often are styles that were popular 20 to 30 years ago.

The manufacturer of a popular pique cotton tennis shirt with a reptile emblem has made an incredible comeback from its popularity 30 years ago. Then, the well-constructed cotton tennis shirt sold for $35 to $42. Retro clothing has made an incredible comeback, and now the reptile tennis shirt commands a retail price ranging from $79.50 to $165.

The popular reptile-emblem shirt can once again be seen on college campuses, on tennis courts, at social gatherings, and in schools throughout the country. The shirt has not really changed from 30 years ago, but innovative marketing, selective merchandising, and high demand from other countries have caused the price of the shirt to soar. Only the top-end department stores and high-priced specialty stores currently are allowed to sell the retro tennis shirt brand. However, outlet stores for the brand have been selling the popular reptile tennis shirt at greatly reduced prices.

You have been asked by the CEO of the tennis shirt manufacturer to determine additional means to sell the very popular shirt without lowering the price. You must describe how the advertisements in the United States will vary from the advertisements in Mexico, where high-income individuals are purchasing many of the shirts from outlet malls.

Your marketing strategy must describe the target market, the advertising campaign, and the pricing strategy for the shirt manufacturer. You will have 10 minutes to plan your marketing strategy and 10 minutes to present the strategy to the shirt company CEO and answer questions about your plan. You will meet in the CEO's office to present your plan.

Performance Indicators Evaluated

- Explain the concept of marketing strategies. (Market Planning)
- Describe the functions of prices in markets. (Economics)
- Explain the concept of competition. (Economics)
- Discuss the global environment in which businesses operate. (Economics)
- Explain marketing and its importance in a global economy. (Marketing)

Go to the DECA website for more detailed information. **www.deca.org**

Think Critically

1. Why is it important to determine the target market(s) for the shirt?
2. What types of stores are the best outlets for the popular retro shirts?
3. What can the shirt company do to show responsibility to society?
4. Why should the company consider selling the shirts in other countries?

CHAPTER 3

THE ECONOMIC BASIS FOR MARKETING

Connect to MindTap

See how effective advertising leads to successful marketing strategies.
Click on Chapter 3, Visual Focus, **in your MindTap.**

Let's Start a Band!

"People don't buy plastic and paper,
they buy emotions."

– Scott Young, CEO, Wherehouse Entertainment

We've been preparing for weeks. We're ready, but for what? The few feelers we put out to different venues received a lukewarm response. In our excitement and single-minded focus, I fear we may have lost sight of reality. Does this area really need another band?

Gael put out the idea of playing for free or at least really cheap. He thought that might get some people to come out and hear us play. Then, if enough people liked what they saw and heard, we could begin charging.

Malik suggested that Naomi contact someone he knows in a popular band in the area. "Ask him if we could open for them," he said. "They already have a following, and it would put us in front of an audience I think would like our music."

Edwardo reminded us that we need to make sure that when we do get a chance to play before an audience, we're well prepared. First impressions are important, and if the audience does not leave satisfied, we might not see them again.

I'm not sure how, but I know we've got to get out there. You got any ideas?

3.1 SCARCITY AND PRIVATE ENTERPRISE

Learning Objectives

3.1.1 Identify the basic economic problem and how it influences marketing strategies.

3.1.2 Describe the characteristics of the U.S. private enterprise economy and how it operates.

Key Terms

scarcity
command economy
free economy
mixed economy
private enterprise

profit motive
value
consumers
demand
producers
supply

marketing matters

Knowledge of economics and how people make economic decisions improves marketers' ability to make marketing decisions. Unlimited needs and wants, combined with limited resources, produce scarcity. Scarcity is the basic economic problem. People always want more than they can buy, so they must make choices. The way those choices are made determines the type of economic system a society has. The United States has a private enterprise economy, which has many of the characteristics of a free economy. Consumers' independent decisions about what they want to purchase and producers' decisions about what they will produce drives America's economy. The government's role in making economic choices is limited.

essential question

How does the availability of product choices and the amount of money each consumer has to spend affect their purchasing decisions?

3.1.1 The Importance of Economic Understanding

Effective marketing relies on the principles and concepts of economics. Knowledge of economics and how economic decisions are made improves marketing decision making. It also results in increased customer satisfaction and higher profits for the company.

An understanding of the types of competition that businesses face also

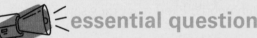

Want to know more about what is trending with this topic? Click on **Lesson 3.1, Marketing Decisions,** in your MindTap.

Connect to MindTap

contributes to better marketing decisions. Marketers also must learn how to interpret economic information to improve marketing decisions. Marketers and other businesspeople should recognize that the increased competition most businesses face places a new importance on understanding and using economic information.

The Basic Economic Problem

People's wants and needs are unlimited. They seldom feel their wants and needs are completely satisfied. Conversely, resources are limited. There are never enough available to meet everyone's wants and needs. For example, producing a car requires a variety of resources, including glass, rubber, steel, and plastic. Yet each of those resources is in limited supply. They also are used to produce items in addition to cars. So, there may not be enough resources to make as many cars as people might want.

Unlimited wants and needs, combined with limited resources, result in **scarcity**. Scarcity is the basic economic problem. Because of scarcity, choices must be made. How will limited resources be used to satisfy people's unlimited wants and needs? Because wants and needs will always be greater than the available resources, choices and tradeoffs must be made. The available resources will have to be allocated to satisfy some wants and needs but not others.

Scarcity creates difficult problems for a society. Resources are used to produce certain products and services. Other products and services are not produced. What is produced and for whom it is produced must be determined. The way those decisions are made indicates the type of economic system a society has.

Economic Questions

An economy organizes the use of limited resources in a way that will satisfy the individual and group needs of people in the economy. All economies must answer three questions:

1. What goods and services will be produced?
2. How will they be produced?
3. For whom will they be produced?

Economies are organized into different economic systems based on how these three economic questions are answered. The type of economic system determines who owns the resources. It also determines how decisions are made regarding the use of resources. Which needs are satisfied and how resources are distributed also depends on the type of economic system. Even the cost of resources depends on the economic system.

In a **command economy**, the government answers the three economic questions. It attempts to own and control important resources and to make the decisions about what will be produced and consumed. In a **free economy**, also known as a *market economy* or *capitalism*, resources are owned by individuals rather than the government. The market

Think of all the resources used to make a car. What other products require the use of these same resources?

© bibiphoto/Shutterstock.com

provides answers to the three economic questions. Decisions are made independently with no attempt at government regulation or control. In a **mixed economy**, some goods and services are provided by the government and some by private enterprise. The U.S. economy and the economies of most other nations in the world are mixed economies.

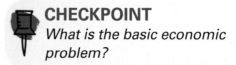

CHECKPOINT

What is the basic economic problem?

3.1.2 ▶ America's Private Enterprise Economy

The United States has many of the characteristics of a free economy. The U.S. economic system is often called a private enterprise or free enterprise economy. **Private enterprise** is based on independent decisions by businesses and consumers with only a limited government role regulating those relationships.

Characteristics of Private Enterprise

Several important characteristics define a private enterprise economy.

- Resources of production are owned and controlled by individual producers.

- Producers use the profit motive to decide what to produce. The **profit motive** refers to the use of resources to obtain the greatest profit.

- Individual consumers make decisions about what will be purchased to satisfy needs.

- Consumers use value in deciding what to consume. **Value** is an individual view of the worth of a product or service. Consumers make decisions of worth by comparing the cost of something they are considering purchasing with available alternatives.

- The government stays out of exchange activities between producers and consumers unless it is clear that individuals or society are harmed by the decisions.

Because businesses have a great deal of independence in a private enterprise economy, the decisions they make can determine whether they succeed or fail.

CONSUMERS AND PRIVATE ENTERPRISE Individuals who purchase products and services to satisfy needs are **consumers**. They have limited resources, or money, to satisfy their needs. Consumers determine what products and services will be successful in an economy. Consumers create demand for products and services when they select those they believe will provide the greatest satisfaction for the price. **Demand** is a relationship between the quantity of a product consumers are willing and able to purchase and the price.

Consumers gather information about available products and services so they can select those that appear to best satisfy their needs. For example, clothing is a basic consumer need. Some consumers sew their own clothes. Some purchase basic and inexpensive clothing. Others spend a great deal of money on a large and expensive wardrobe.

*Want to know more about marketing in the information age? Click on **Lesson 3.1, Digital Marketing,** in your MindTap.*

Connect to **MindTap**

PRODUCERS Businesses that use their resources to develop products and services are **producers**. They hope to sell those products and services to consumers to earn a profit. Producers create a supply of products and services when they offer them for sale to consumers. **Supply** is a relationship between the quantity of a product that producers are willing and able to provide and the price.

Producers gather information about the types of products and services consumers want so they can provide those that are most likely to be purchased. For example, an athletic shoe manufacturer conducts research to determine which athletic and exercise activities are increasing and decreasing in popularity. Based on the research, the company may decide to produce more cross-training shoes than running or walking shoes. The economic concepts of supply and demand will be discussed in detail in Lesson 3.2.

GOVERNMENT Under ideal circumstances, government allows consumers and producers to make decisions without any interference. However, in some cases, consumers or producers may be placed at an unfair disadvantage or society may be harmed by the decisions of producers or consumers. For example, a producer may make misleading claims about a product or sell products that can be hazardous when used. A small manufacturer may be unable to introduce new products due to pressures applied to distributers by a much larger competitor. In those situations, the government can enact laws and regulations to help maintain an effective economy.

Economic Forces

An example of decision making in a private enterprise economy illustrates how the system operates. Suppose a city has a variety of entertainment options but has no social club for teenagers. Many teenagers indicate a need for some type of club and suggest they would visit it and spend money there if one was developed. Even though it appears that the need for the new type of business exists, no one is required to open a teen social club. It will be developed only when someone recognizes the need, determines that a club could be

Why do retailers offer so many different kinds of clothing?

opened and operated profitably, wants to operate that type of business, and has the resources to do so.

Members of city government might recognize the need for a teen club. They may see teenage crime rates increasing, have concerns expressed to them by teenagers and parents, or just want to meet important needs of city residents. Based on that concern, city leaders may encourage the development of a teen club through tax incentives or other economic assistance. They may even decide to develop and operate a teen center as a city service.

In a private enterprise economy, government would not typically get involved with developing and operating a teen center. It would rely on the profit motive to encourage the development of a new business and on consumers to express their needs for products and services to businesses.

 CHECKPOINT
In a private enterprise economy, when does government get involved in exchange relationships?

3.1 ASSESSMENT

What Have You Learned?

1. Explain the difference between a command economy and a free economy. [3.1.1]

2. What is the profit motive? [3.1.2]

Make Academic Connections

1. **Social Studies** Prepare a one-page paper describing the basic economic problem and include an example of it. Explain how different economic systems (command, free, mixed, and private enterprise) handle this problem. [3.1.1]

2. **Consumer Economics** Consumers gather information about available products and services so they can select those that appear to satisfy their needs. Compile a list of resources—either print or online—that consumers can use to do this, briefly describing each one. [3.1.2]

Connect to ◇DECA

Build your Portfolio

You work for a clothing manufacturer that would like to sell its products in China. You have been asked to explore the marketing opportunities in China. Conduct research to determine the key differences between the Chinese and U.S. economic systems. Using presentation software, develop a two- to three-minute presentation on the key economic factors that would have an impact on marketing your clothing line in China and present it to your teacher (judge). [3.1.1]

THE LAW OF SUPPLY AND DEMAND

Learning Objectives

3.2.1   Explain microeconomics and the concept of consumer demand.

3.2.2   Identify factors that affect supply and its relationship to demand.

Key Terms

macroeconomics
microeconomics
opportunity cost
demand curve
law of demand
economic market

economic resources
supply curve
law of supply
market price

marketing matters

Microeconomics analyzes the interaction of consumer demand with producer supply to predict how changes in one affect the other. Major considerations are consumers' needs and wants and the availability of alternatives. When the independent decisions of consumers and producers are combined, they can be illustrated as curved lines on a two-dimensional graph that intersect at the market price.

essential question

What factors do consumers consider when determining if a product's price is a fair value?

3.2.1 ▶ Microeconomics and Consumer Demand

Economics attempts to understand and explain how consumers and producers make decisions concerning the allocation of their resources. That understanding helps consumers and producers use their resources more effectively. It also helps government decision makers determine if and when they should become involved in the economy as they work to maintain balance between producers and consumers and to maintain a strong economy.

Economics operates on two levels. The first level, **macroeconomics**, studies the economic behavior in the economy.

Macroeconomics looks at the big picture. It helps to determine if society's resources are being used as effectively and efficiently as possible. Macroeconomics studies the decisions of all consumers and producers and the effects of those decisions on the economy.

The second level, **microeconomics**, examines relationships between individual consumers and producers. Microeconomics looks at small parts of the total economy. Microeconomics studies how individual producers and consumers make decisions about what to produce and what to consume.

While a broad understanding of economics is important to marketers, they are most concerned about microeconomics. Information about how consumers make purchasing decisions and how much they are willing to pay can be very important in selecting target markets and developing effective marketing mixes. Marketers must also understand how a business's competitors make decisions about what they will produce and the prices they are likely to charge. Microeconomics looks at supply, demand, and the level of individual product prices. Marketers need to pay special attention to the relationship between supply and consumer demand for their products.

Factors Affecting Demand

A number of factors influence consumers' decisions regarding what to purchase and how much to pay. First, if a need or want is important or strong, a consumer might be willing to spend more money to satisfy it. For example, if you are at a baseball game and your favorite player hits three home runs, obtaining a shirt with the player's name on it may seem very important to you. You may be willing to pay much more to buy the shirt right away at the ballpark rather than waiting to make the purchase later at a sporting goods store.

Another factor that affects consumers' decisions is the amount of the product or service available. If a large amount of product is available, consumers will usually place a lower value on it. Imagine walking through a farmers' market where a large number of producers are selling fresh fruits and vegetables. As a consumer, you see there are many choices of sellers and a large quantity of each product available. Therefore, you will probably be careful not to overpay for the fruits or vegetables you want. However, if there are a large number of customers but only a few farmers at the market, the customers may pay much higher prices to be sure they get the items they need.

A third factor is the availability of alternative products that consumers believe will satisfy their needs. If consumers believe there is only one product or brand that meets their needs, they are willing to pay a higher price. If several options seem to be equally satisfying, consumers are more careful about how much they pay. The choice you make also reflects the **opportunity cost** of the decision. This is the value of the alternative items or activities you must pass up. Opportunity cost may be measured in dollars spent, but it also may be the opportunities lost when the choice is made.

How does the amount of produce for sale and the number of vendors at a farmers' market affect consumer demand for the produce?

An example of opportunity cost is your choice of entertainment for an evening. If there are very few activities you and your friends can choose, you will likely be willing to pay quite a bit for a specific activity you would really enjoy. However, if you identify many options (going to a movie, a new restaurant, an amusement park, or renting a video game) and each seems enjoyable, you may consider the cost more carefully. You might decide to rent the video game because it is the least expensive option and you and your friends will still enjoy it. The opportunity cost of renting the video game is the opportunity that you lost from doing the other activities.

law of demand: When the price of a product is increased, less will be demanded. When the price is decreased, more will be demanded.

All of the consumers who will purchase a particular product or service comprise an **economic market**. Economists believe that the consumers in an economic market view the relationship of products and prices in the same way.

CHECKPOINT
How do microeconomics and macroeconomics differ?

Analyze Demand Curves

Economists try to determine how much consumers are willing and able to pay for various quantities of products or services. The relationship between price and the quantity demanded is often illustrated in a graph known as a **demand curve**. A demand curve for movies is shown in **Figure 3-1**. As the price of movies increases, fewer people buy tickets. As the price decreases, more tickets are sold. This relationship is known as the

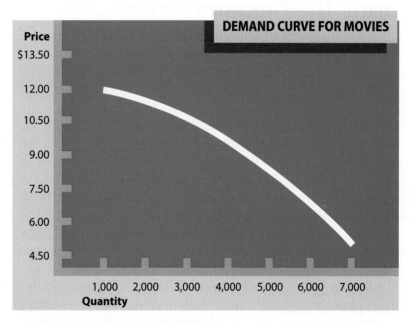

FIGURE 3-1 As the movie price increases, the number of consumers willing and able to pay that price decreases.

3.2.2 ▶ Product Supply

Several factors influence what and how many products or services a business will produce. These include the possibility of

profit, the amount of competition, and the capability of developing and marketing the products or services.

One of the most important reasons for businesses to operate in a private enterprise economy is to make a profit. Businesses will try to offer products and services that have a good chance of making a large profit, rather than products and services likely to yield either a small profit or the likelihood of a loss. Business managers carefully consider both the costs of producing and marketing products and the prices they will be able to charge for those products. That analysis helps in determining the most profitable choices to produce.

Dealing with Competition

When looking for opportunities, businesses consider the amount and type of competition. When competition is intense—with many businesses offering the same types of products or services—there are fewer opportunities for success than when there

MATH IN MARKETING

Measuring the Demand Curve

Economists have a way of quantifying demand curves so that businesses can use them to develop better marketing strategies. This method of quantifying is referred to as *elasticity of demand*. In economics, elasticity means responsiveness to change. Elasticity of demand measures how much consumer demand for a product changes when the price is raised or lowered.

If demand is highly elastic, the demand curve is more horizontal, and a small change in price will have a big effect on consumer demand. If it is inelastic, the curve is more vertical, and demand remains relatively constant.

Elasticity is quantified by calculating the ratio of the percentage change in the quantity demanded over the percentage change in price. To illustrate, let's say a movie theater's research indicates that if it raises its ticket price from $8 to $10, the average number of tickets it sells will decrease from 300 to 250 per day. To calculate the elasticity of demand, first calculate the percentage of change in number of tickets sold: 50/300 = 17%. Then calculate the percentage change in price: $2/$8 = 25%. Now calculate the ratio of the change in demand (17%) over the change in price (25%): 17/25 = 0.68.

When the ratio is greater than 1, the demand is said to be elastic, and raising prices decreases overall revenue. When it is less than 1, demand is inelastic, and raising prices increases revenue. The theater's revenue should increase even if fewer tickets are sold.

Do the Math

1. Research for a bicycle shop indicates that if it lowers the price it charges for a tune-up from $60 to $40, it will sell twice as many tune-ups. Calculate its elasticity of demand.

2. Is its demand elastic or inelastic?

3. If the shop's costs per tune-up remain the same regardless of how many tune-ups it does, what should it do to maximize profits?

is little competition. When possible, suppliers may choose to offer products and services that have few competitors. Another option when there is a lot of competition is to change the product to make it different from those offered by other businesses. For example, an owner of an apartment complex in a community where there are many vacant apartments may provide free cable TV for residents. The owner may extend short-term leases or may offer furnished apartments if those types of services are not available in other apartment complexes.

Finally, businesses use the resources available to develop products and services. **Economic resources** are classified as natural resources, capital, equipment, and labor. The specific types of resources a business has available will determine the types of products and services it can develop and sell. Some resources are very flexible, enabling a business to change and offer new products quickly. For example, if the owners of an electronics store found that equipment such as fax machines and scanners were no longer profitable, they could change the products sold in that part of the store to some that are more profitable such as multifunction printers. Other businesses have more difficulty changing products. Companies that own oil wells or coal mines, for instance, have few options because the natural resources they own are their products. They will continue to sell the oil and coal even at times when those products are not as profitable

until they can obtain or develop other resources.

Analyze a Supply Curve

Some economists predict how the quantity of products and services changes at various prices. The graph of the relationship between price and quantity supplied is known as a **supply curve**. An example supply curve for sunglasses is shown in **Figure 3-2**. The graph shows that as the price increases, producers will manufacture more sunglasses. As the price goes down, fewer will be manufactured. This relationship is known as the **law of supply**: When the price of a product is increased, more will be produced. When the price is decreased, less will be produced.

Whenever possible, producers use their resources to provide products and services that receive the highest prices. Just as with demand, economists believe that all producers in the same economic market respond in similar ways when determining what to produce. Like

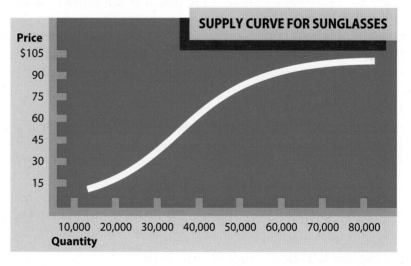

FIGURE 3-2 As the price consumers want to pay for sunglasses decreases, so does the quantity that manufacturers will be willing to supply.

consumers, producers see a relationship between products and prices.

Intersecting Supply and Demand

We learned that suppliers and consumers make independent decisions. When the decisions of many consumers of the same product are combined, they form a demand curve. A demand curve illustrates the quantity of a product or service that will be demanded at various prices. When the decisions of all the suppliers of the same product or service are combined, they form a supply curve. That curve illustrates the quantity of the product that will be supplied at various prices.

Figure 3-3 shows a demand curve and a supply curve for a particular type of notebook computer. The demand curve shows that fewer will be purchased as the price increases. As expected, computer manufacturers are willing to supply a larger number of computers if prices are high and fewer if prices are low.

To determine the number of notebook computers that will actually be produced and sold, the two curves must be combined. The combined curves are shown in **Figure 3-4**. Notice that the two lines cross or intersect at a price of $1,300 and a quantity of 450,000 computers. The point where supply and demand for a product are equal is known as the **market price**. At that price, 450,000 computers will be manufactured and sold.

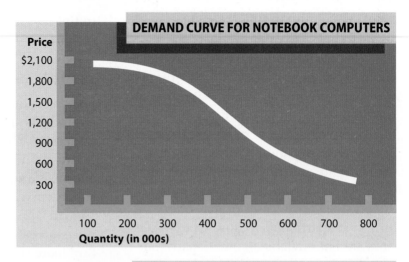

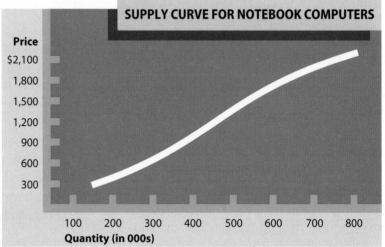

FIGURE 3-3 Consumers and suppliers respond very differently to price changes. The demand curve illustrates consumers' responses, and the supply curve illustrates suppliers' responses.

Each product in a specific market has its own supply and demand curves. And each market has price and quantity relationships that are unique and result in different curves on the graphs.

CHECKPOINT

What are the main factors that businesses consider when deciding what and how much to produce?

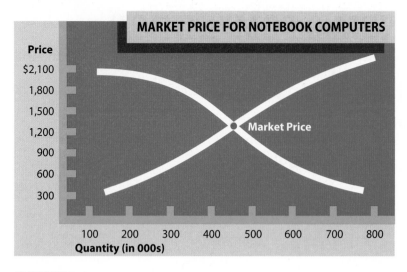

MARKET PRICE FOR NOTEBOOK COMPUTERS

Price

$2,100
1,800
1,500
1,200 • Market Price
900
600
300

100 200 300 400 500 600 700 800
Quantity (in 000s)

FIGURE 3-4 The point at which the demand curve and the supply curve for notebook computers intersect is the market price.

© wavebreakmedia/Shutterstock.com.

In the market for notebook computers—or any other product—at what point do the demand curve and the supply curve intersect?

3.2 ASSESSMENT

What Have You Learned?

1. Which level of economics studies how individuals make decisions about what to produce and what to consume? [3.2.1]

2. What are the three factors that affect demand? [3.2.1]

3. What are the three factors that affect supply? [3.2.2]

4. Where would you find market price on a combined supply and demand curve? [3.2.2]

Make Academic Connections

1. **Visual Art**   Create a picture, poster, or other visual representation of macroeconomics and microeconomics. [3.2.1]

2. **Economics**   Use the following data to create supply and demand curves for cameras. [3.2.2]

Quantity Demanded	Price	Quantity Supplied
100	$70	750
200	60	550
400	50	300
700	40	150

Connect to ◇DECA

Build your **Portfolio**

You work for a party planning company that has declining sales and profits. Consider the factors that affect the demand for your services. Based on these factors, develop a plan to improve your business. Write a two-page report for your teacher (judge) describing possible reasons for the decline in business and your recommendations to increase demand for your services. [3.2.1]

Learning Objectives

3.3.1 Define pure competition and monopoly.

3.3.2 Explain the characteristics of oligopolies and monopolistic competition.

Key Terms

pure competition
monopoly
oligopoly
monopolistic competition

marketing matters

A company's response to consumer demand is strongly influenced by the competitive structure of the industry it is in and the market it serves. The type of competition—or in some extreme cases, the lack of competition—determines how much control a business has over pricing and what strategies it should follow to obtain the greatest long-term profits. Each type of competition produces a unique demand curve. Identifying the type of demand a business faces is important in developing marketing strategies.

essential question

What are the factors in a market that give a business the least and greatest amount of control over prices it can charge?

3.3.1 ▶ **All-Out Competition or No Competition at All**

The type of competition found in a market affects consumer and supplier decisions alike. If consumers see a variety of products that seem to be very similar, they will be less willing to pay higher prices. If suppliers are in a market with many other businesses offering similar products, they will have difficulty raising their prices. Businesses must determine the type of competition they face and the amount of control they have over the prices they can charge to make effective marketing decisions.

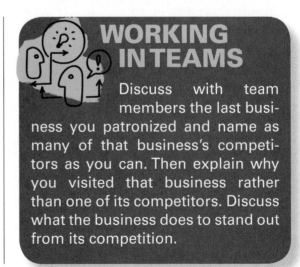

WORKING IN TEAMS

Discuss with team members the last business you patronized and name as many of that business's competitors as you can. Then explain why you visited that business rather than one of its competitors. Discuss what the business does to stand out from its competition.

Two characteristics are important to determine the type of economic competition in a specific market:

1. The number of firms competing in the market.
2. The amount of similarity or difference between the products of competing businesses.

Economists use these characteristics to define four forms of economic competition—pure competition, monopoly, oligopoly, and monopolistic competition.

Pure Competition

A few markets contain a large number of suppliers with very similar products. In these markets, consumers have a great deal of control over choices and prices. Because the suppliers are unable to offer products that consumers view as unique, they must accept the prices that consumers are willing to pay, or the consumers will buy from another business. This market condition is known as **pure competition**. In pure competition, many suppliers offer very similar products.

The traditional examples of industries in pure competition are producers of agricultural products such as corn, rice, wheat, and livestock. Each producer's products are just like every other producer's products. There are many producers, so customers have no difficulty finding a business that will sell the products. Because customers have so many choices of suppliers and the products of all suppliers are similar, prices will be very competitive. No single supplier will be able to raise the price. Other examples of markets in which businesses face something close to pure competition are those for many of the low-priced consumer products you purchase—milk, bread, paper clips, bottled water, school supplies, and the like.

An example of the demand curve for a business in a purely competitive market is shown in **Figure 3-5**. In theory, it is a straight line at one price. That suggests that the supplier will receive the same price no matter how much of the product the supplier is willing to sell. Therefore, businesses have no control over price if they want to sell their products.

Monopoly

The opposite of pure competition is a monopoly. A **monopoly** is a market in which one supplier offers a unique product. In this market, the supplier has almost total control, and the consumers will have to accept what the supplier offers at the price charged. This occurs because of the lack of competition.

Because of the obvious advantage a business has in monopoly markets, governments attempt to control them. Therefore, there are few examples of monopolies that actually dictate prices.

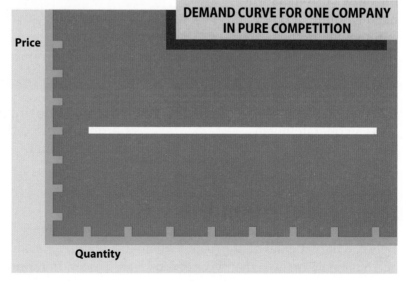

FIGURE 3-5 In pure competition, the seller must accept the market price no matter how much of the product is sold.

Utility companies that supply communities with electricity, gas, or water are typically organized as monopolies. There is only one supplier of each product because it would be very inefficient to have several companies extending gas and water lines or electrical service to every home. Once a home is supplied with the utilities, it would be easy for the company to raise the price. The consumer would have no choice but to pay the higher price or go without the gas, water, or electricity. Therefore, government agencies regulate the prices that the utility companies can charge.

Other examples of markets that can operate much like a monopoly are some local telephone and cable television services and businesses that are the only ones of their type in a geographic area. For example, if you are driving down an interstate highway in a rural area and there is only one gasoline station at the only exit within many miles, that business can operate much like a monopoly for those customers who need gasoline or other automotive products and services. A pharmacy or grocery store in a neighborhood where there is no other similar business also can operate much like a monopoly for those

customers who are unable to travel to a competing business.

In theory, the demand curve facing a business that has a monopoly would look like the one in **Figure 3-6**. There is a fixed demand for the product because there are no other businesses offering a similar product that the consumer needs. Therefore, if unregulated, the business can charge any price it chooses. The consumer either pays the price set by the business or goes without the product.

CHECKPOINT
Distinguish pure competition from monopoly based on the two characteristics that economists use to define types of competition.

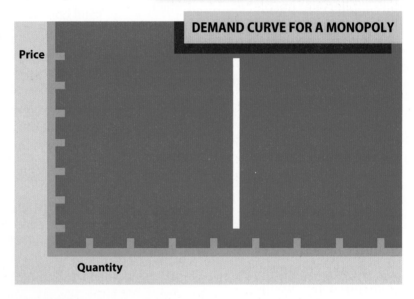

FIGURE 3-6 In theory, a business in a monopoly can charge any price because it is selling a unique product.

3.3.2 ▶ Between the Extremes

Between the extremes of pure competition and monopoly are two other types of economic competition—oligopoly and monopolistic competition. In an **oligopoly**, a few

businesses offer very similar products or services. In **monopolistic competition**, there are many firms competing with products that are somewhat different.

Oligopolies

Consider the problems and advantages facing businesses in oligopolies. If the businesses work together, they will be like a monopoly and have a great deal of control in the market. On the other hand, if they are very competitive, the similarity of their products or services will give consumers choices, much like in pure competition. In that case, the consumers will have more control, and prices will be lower.

The airline industry is an example of an oligopoly. Only a very few large airlines compete for national travel in the United States. It is difficult to see important differences between airlines that serve the same cities. Therefore, if one airline wants to increase its number of passengers, it will often do it by reducing prices. To counter that effort and to keep passengers from flying with the competitor, other airlines will reduce their prices as well.

To increase profits, an airline may want to increase ticket prices. However, one airline will not usually succeed in increasing prices alone. If the airline industry wants higher prices to cover operating expenses and contribute to profit, competing companies will need to cooperate in raising their prices as well. Depending on the industry, government agencies may attempt to regulate that type of activity, making it illegal for businesses to work together to set prices. Notice, however, that if one airline announces a price increase or decrease, competitors are usually very quick to match the change.

Other examples of industries with characteristics of an oligopoly are automobile manufacturers, insurance companies, interstate delivery services, computer manufacturers, Internet

What are the advantages and disadvantages of an oligopoly, such as the airline industry, to consumers?

© photobac/Shutterstock.com.

service providers, and companies offering long-distance or wireless telephone services. On the local level, some businesses operate as oligopolies because there are only a few businesses offering almost identical products and services to the consumers in that market. Some examples in medium- to large-size communities are movie theaters, banks, and hospitals.

The demand curve facing businesses in an oligopoly is difficult to describe. For an individual business, the demand curve will look like the demand in pure competition because one business cannot influence the price it can charge to any great extent. **Figure 3-7** shows an example of a demand curve for one company in an oligopoly.

The demand curve for all of the businesses combined in an oligopoly will look much closer to that of a monopoly. Cooperatively, the businesses have a great deal of control over prices. Consumers who want the product or service will have to purchase from one of the few companies in the market or go without. A demand curve for the entire industry in an oligopoly is shown in **Figure 3-8**.

Monopolistic Competition

By far the most common type of economic competition most businesses face is monopolistic competition, where many firms compete with products that are somewhat different. The fewer the number of competitors and the greater the differences among the competitors' products or services, the greater the control each firm will have in the market. With more competitors and only minor differences, businesses will have very limited control.

Most of the products and services you buy are in markets with monopolistic competition. As a consumer, you typically have choices of businesses or products.

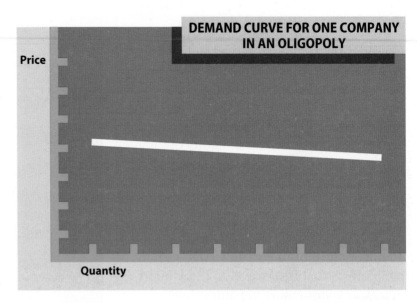

FIGURE 3-7 One business in an oligopoly will have little influence over the price it can charge.

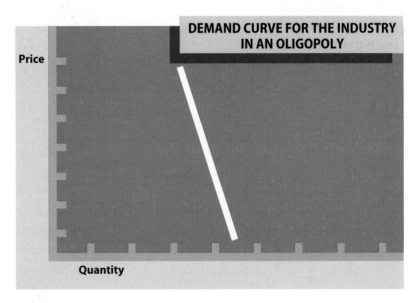

FIGURE 3-8 Because there are few firms in an oligopoly, the total industry has much more control over prices.

When you have choices, you usually select the one providing the most satisfaction at the best value. Examples of businesses and products in monopolistic competition include restaurants, automobile

How does the athletic shoe industry represent monopolistic competition?

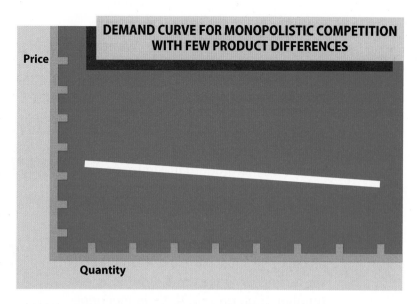

FIGURE 3-9 When there are few differences among products, businesses will have little price control.

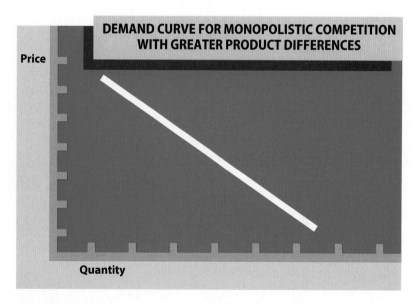

FIGURE 3-10 With greater product differences, businesses have more control over prices.

dealerships, athletic shoes, consumer electronics, and cosmetics.

The demand curve for businesses in monopolistic competition falls somewhere between that of pure competition and monopoly. The fewer the differences, the less control business has, so the demand curve is more horizontal. An example of this type of demand curve is shown in **Figure 3-9**. The greater the differences among products and services, the more control the business has, so the demand curve is more vertical. An example is shown in **Figure 3-10**.

Understand the Competition

It is important for businesspeople and especially marketers to know the type of economic competition they face and to act accordingly in order to maximize profits. A business in pure competition will not be able to exercise much control in the market, while one in a monopoly will have almost total control. Businesses in an oligopoly must pay careful attention to the actions of competitors. For the largest number of businesses, those in monopolistic competition, the differences between competing products will be very important. Wherever possible, marketers will want to do things that result in products that are different from and better than those of competitors. In that way they will have more control in the marketplace.

*Want to know more about what is trending with this topic? Click on **Lesson 3.3, Global Marketing,** in your MindTap.*

Connect to MindTap

CHECKPOINT
Compare and contrast oligopolies and monopolistic competition.

What Have You Learned?

1. What are the two characteristics important to determining the type of economic competition in a market? [3.3.1]
2. In what type of economic competition do many suppliers offer very similar products? [3.3.1]
3. If a business's demand curve is a straight vertical line at one quantity, in what type of market does it compete? [3.3.1]
4. What type of control do businesses in a monopolistic competition have when there are few differences among products? [3.3.2]

Make Academic Connections

1. **Technology** Use the library or Internet to find a change in technology that you believe increased economic competition in the United States. Find another change that you believe reduced economic competition. Use visuals or a written report to communicate your findings. Make sure to describe how the technology affected competition. [3.3.1]

2. **Management** Most restaurants face monopolistic competition. What changes could a restaurant manager make to increase profits? [3.3.2]

Connect to ◇DECA

Build your Portfolio

You have been hired by the owner of a new ice cream shop in your community to analyze the competition. Create a list of questions you think need to be answered to help you complete an effective analysis of the competitive environment. Submit these questions to the owner (judge), and explain the importance of each question. You should also present a list of sources and/or techniques you will use to gather information for your analysis. [3.3.1, 3.3.2]

3.4 ECONOMIC UTILITY

Learning Objectives

3.4.1 Define four types of economic utility.

3.4.2 Explain how marketers use utility to increase customer satisfaction.

Key Term

economic utility

marketing matters

Although consumers rarely analyze precisely how they decide to buy products or services, they unconsciously make buying decisions based on the satisfaction they expect to receive from them. Businesses therefore try to increase consumers' satisfaction by making improvements to products and services. Economists have developed a concept called economic utility and identified various types of utility to explain why consumers get more or less satisfaction from different products. For businesses, economic utility is important to help them develop better products.

 essential question

What must businesses do with their products and services in order to increase the satisfaction they provide to consumers?

3.4.1 ▶ Utility Means Satisfaction

Most people would like to purchase more things than they can afford. Because of limited resources and unlimited needs, they have to choose among products and services. People select those that provide the greatest satisfaction for the money they are able or willing to spend. You may have to choose between attending a concert and purchasing a new video game, for example. Saving for college may be more important than buying a car.

To analyze how people make choices among competing products, economists use a concept called economic utility. **Economic utility** is the amount of satisfaction a consumer receives from the consumption of a particular product or service. Products that provide great satisfaction have a higher economic utility, while those providing less satisfaction have a lower utility.

Businesses use economic utility to increase the chances that consumers will buy their products or services. If a consumer believes that a particular product will provide higher utility than other choices, that product is more likely to be purchased. The four primary ways businesses can increase the economic utility of a product or service are changes in form, time, place, and possession.

Form Utility

The physical product provided or the service offered is the primary way that consumer needs are satisfied. Form utility results from changes in the tangible parts of a product or service.

Some products and services are in a more usable form than others. One product may be constructed better or have features that consumers want. One service provider—a hair stylist, for example—may be more skilled than another.

Time Utility

Even though a product is in the form a customer wants, it may not be available when the customer wants it. Time utility results from making the product or service available when the customer wants it. Examples include a bank that stays open in the evening and a cable television service that provides movies on demand.

Place Utility

Just as some consumers are concerned about when a product is available, others may want to purchase or consume the product at a particular place. Making products and services available where the consumer wants them is place utility.

Check-cashing outlets and businesses that provide mailing, photocopying, and printing services are successful if they are

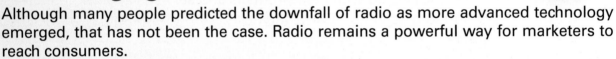

MARKETING COMMUNICATION

The Changing Face of Radio

Although many people predicted the downfall of radio as more advanced technology emerged, that has not been the case. Radio remains a powerful way for marketers to reach consumers.

In 1996, the government passed the Telecommunications Act, which deregulated the radio industry and allowed large companies to buy many radio stations across the country. Today a few companies dominate the radio market. Although some listeners complain that this decreases the diversity of radio programming, it also helps radio stations keep expenses down and makes it easier for advertisers to reach their audience.

With the advent of satellite and online radio, the format has changed once again. Satellite radio companies such as SiriusXM beam a digital signal to receivers via satellite. This allows listeners access to hundreds of stations anywhere in the country. Currently, satellite radio is a subscription service and boasts of being "commercial free" on many of its music stations. However, it does allow "promos," or short product messages. Internet radio, delivered through a home computer, often broadcasts traditional radio stations, but many independent Internet-only stations have emerged as well. All this ensures that radio will remain a valuable tool for marketers.

Think Critically

1. What type of economic utility does broadcasting a local radio station online have for listeners?
2. What are the advantages for a local radio station to be on the Internet?
3. How do national radio broadcasts, such as those via satellite or Internet, differ from local radio stations in terms of the types of advertisers they will attract?

located where consumers and businesses who need those services reside. A convenient location for products and services is an important utility for people with busy lives.

Possession Utility

A product may be in the form a consumer wants and be available at the right time in the right place, yet the consumer still may not be able to purchase the product because of a lack of resources. Possession utility results from the affordability of the product or service. It is usually not possible for a business to decrease the price just so a product can be sold. Yet there are other ways besides cutting the price to make a product more affordable.

Credit allows people to purchase things for which they do not have enough cash at the time. They can then pay for the product when the credit bill is received or pay gradually with monthly payments. For example, automobile dealerships lease new automobiles. Leases make it possible for customers to drive new cars without having to make a huge down payment. Saving money until you have enough to pay cash for a major purchase such as a car also provides possession utility and prevents you from going into debt.

Finding ways to finance, rent, or lease products has become an important business activity today. It is a valuable way to offer possession utility to customers.

CHECKPOINT
What are the four types of economic utility?

What is the benefit of renting rather than buying a tuxedo for a formal dance? Why do you think renting a prom dress is not a popular practice for women?

© Monkey Business Images/Shutterstock.com.

3.4.2   Utility as a Marketing Tool

Businesspeople who use the marketing concept try to identify customer needs and develop marketing mixes to satisfy those needs. Economic utility supports the marketing concept. It identifies ways to add value to products and services through changes in form, time, place, and possession. Economic utility can be a particularly effective marketing tool when a business focuses on the unique needs and characteristics of each target market. When economic utility is improved, so is customer satisfaction. Marketers need to determine what changes customers would like to have in products and services in order to develop an effective marketing mix. There are many possible ways to improve products and, in turn, improve product demand.

WORKING IN TEAMS

Make a list of your last 10 purchases. For each, tell which form of economic utility was the most important to your buying decision. After all team members have shared their lists, determine which type of utility drove the majority of your team's purchasing decisions. Discuss why you think that particular factor was so important.

 CHECKPOINT

How does the marketing concept relate to the concept of economic utility?

3.4   ASSESSMENT

What Have You Learned?

1. Define economic utility. [3.4.1]
2. Which type of economic utility results from changes in the tangible parts of a product or service? [3.4.1]
3. When can economic utility be an effective marketing tool? [3.4.2]

Make Academic Connections

1. **Creative Writing**   Compose either a jingle or script for an advertisement for a local business, focusing on one type of economic utility—form, time, place, or possession. [3.4.1]
2. **Geography**   Use the Internet to locate and print a map of your neighborhood or community. On the map, mark as many locations of grocery stores/supermarkets as you can find. Then write an explanation of which store you would most likely patronize if place utility were the most important consideration. What about form utility? Possession utility? Time utility? [3.4.1]

Connect to ◇DECA

Build your Portfolio

You are the manager of a medium-size appliance store, and you want to increase sales in your store. Consider the different types of economic utility. Using presentation software, prepare a two-minute presentation you would deliver to the store owner (judge) in which you describe at least three ways you can improve economic utility to accomplish your goal. Submit your presentation to your teacher. [3.4.2]

Connect to MindTap

Analyze a case study that focuses on chapter concepts. Click on **Chapter 3, Case Study,** *in your MindTap.*

The old adage "a picture is worth a thousand words" still holds true. With a highly scheduled, multitasking society, people want to get the information they need, quickly understand it, and move on.

Data analysis often begins with spreadsheets that help automate the analysis of raw data. The results of the data analysis can be presented in charts, graphs, and tables. Charts and graphs facilitate swift decision making by presenting understandable relationships among variables in a visual form. Tables provide a concise method to summarize data. Effective data summaries do not overwhelm the target audience with an excessive amount of data.

Choosing a Data Summary Tool

When deciding which type of data summary tools to use, keep your audience in mind. Certain types of graphs are far more common, and therefore easier to understand. Line graphs, bar charts, and pie charts are among the most frequently used.

A line graph is helpful for conveying changes over a period of time. The slope of the line indicates whether the variable has an increasing or decreasing trend. If the line goes up and down frequently, it may represent cyclical changes. A bar graph often conveys variations in quantity at specific points in time or among different elements or groups. Those quantity changes are usually displayed on the vertical axis.

Pie charts are effective for illustrating percentages of a whole. To ensure the pie chart is easy to interpret, limit pie slices to five or six.

Each chart or graph should be concise, presenting an important relationship. Start with a simple meaningful title. The graph axes and variables should be labeled. The unit of measurement as well as the item being studied should be easily distinguished. Using consistent units of measurement throughout a graph is important to avoid distortions when presenting information.

Presenting the Results

The analysis process may build a strong visual case to understand a relationship between two or more items. Likewise, data analysis may provide a startling "aha" moment that contradicts previous beliefs. Although it may be tempting to omit data or vary the way the information is presented, you must always maintain the integrity of your data and share important analyses. Your audience is relying on your objectivity to help guide their decision making.

Photodisc/Getty Images

Interpreting Data

Learning how to interpret the charts and graphs of others is also an important skill. Pay close attention to the units of measurement, the source of the data, and any possible bias in the presentation. Ask yourself whether the conclusions made from the analysis are reasonable. When you have doubts, ask to see the original data on which the analysis was based.

Develop Your Skill

Build your Portfolio

Review local or national newspapers (*USA Today*, for example) for articles that present data in tables, charts, and graphs. Determine which present information in an understandable way and which seem to present a biased view or confuse the reader. Use a spreadsheet program to record numerical information about your class or school. Summarize important relationships in a chart and a graph. Review the results with fellow students or a teacher.

CHAPTER 3 ASSESSMENT

Review Marketing Concepts

1. What types of services does government in a country that has a mixed economy provide, and why do you think the government is best suited to provide these services? [3.1.1]

2. Define value and explain its role in consumer decision making. [3.1.2]

3. Why do you think government regulates food production? [3.1.2]

4. What is the difference between macro-economics and microeconomics in terms of the decisions consumers and producers make? [3.2.1]

5. What is the relationship between demand for a product and its price? [3.2.1]

6. What does the supply curve for tacos illustrate about the number of tacos a Mexican restaurant is willing to supply? [3.2.2]

7. You are evaluating two businesses to purchase. One of them operates in a pure competition system and the other in a monopoly. Based on this, which business would you choose? Would the consumer benefit from your decision? Why or why not? [3.3.1]

8. A car dealership, which operates in an oligopoly, raises prices to increase profits. Will this strategy be successful? Why or why not? [3.3.2]

9. Explain why car dealerships stress monthly payments in their advertising instead of the total price for the automobile? Which utility are they trying to address? [3.4.1]

10. Explain how a company that markets computers adds value to its product by addressing the utilities of form, time, place, and possession? [3.4.2]

Marketing Research and Planning

1. Businesses can be classified into the four types of competition—pure, monopoly, oligopoly, and monopolistic competition—based on the number of competitors and the amount of similarity between the products. Use the advertising section of your local telephone directory, a business directory, or online sources to identify two businesses that fit into each of those four categories. Explain each decision based on the two factors listed. [3.3.1, 3.3.2]

2. Select a popular food item that is sold through your school's cafeteria or in a vending machine in your school. Determine the current price for the item. Then use spreadsheet or presentation software to construct a chart showing the following price increases and decreases for the product:

+10%, +25%, +50%, +100%, −10%, −25%, −50%, −90%

Survey five people from your school. Ask each person how many of the food items they typically purchase in one week at the current price. Then ask each person how many of the items they would purchase at each of the price increases and decreases. Based on the results, construct a demand curve to illustrate the effect of price changes on demand for the product. [3.2.1]

Build your **Portfolio**

3. You have been an economist for the United Nations for the past 15 years. Now, in the year 2034, a large industrial colony is being developed on the moon. It will be populated with 2,000 people initially, and there are plans to expand it until nearly one million people are living in the colony by 2055. The United Nations is studying the best form of economic system to develop on the colony.

   Prepare a two-page report in which you compare three types of economies—command, free, and mixed. Discuss the advantages and disadvantages of each for consumers, businesses, and the government. Make a recommendation on the most appropriate system for the colony. Consider factors such as resources available, supply and demand, the amount of competition, and so forth. [3.1.1]

4. When a marketer analyzes a demand curve, it is important to determine what effect changes in price and quantity demanded would have on the amount of money the business will receive from selling the product. The amount received is known as the total revenue and is determined by multiplying the price by the quantity demanded.

   For example, if the price of a product is $8.50 and the quantity demanded at that price is 1,550 items, the total revenue would be $13,175 ($8.50 × 1,550). The information in the table was taken from the demand curves for two different products. Calculate the total revenue for each price listed. Then construct a demand curve for each product. [3.2.1]

PRODUCT 1		PRODUCT 2	
Price	Quantity Demanded	Price	Quantity Demanded
$1.00	350,000	$250	1,125
$2.50	280,000	$325	950
$3.25	225,000	$400	600
$4.00	175,000	$500	425
$4.75	75,000	$850	250
$5.50	25,000	$1,000	200

Marketing Management and Decision Making

1. Marketing managers must be creative in determining ways to improve products and services to increase customer satisfaction. For each of the following three items, determine changes that could be made in form, time, place, and possession utility. Then recommend the one change for each product you believe would be the most effective in improving customer satisfaction and explain why.

   a. Vending machine selling snacks

   b. A handheld electronic game player

   c. A college recruiting high school seniors
   [3.1.1]

2. Tasha Formby is a recent college graduate with a degree in Business Administration and coursework in computer information systems and marketing. She completed a summer internship with a computer manufacturer. She worked full time another summer at a company that provides commercial printing services to small businesses. She was in charge of design work using computer software.

   Tasha decides to open her own printing business. There are already three large printing companies in the city. Those businesses compete for the printing services of the large and small companies in the area. There are eight other small printing businesses, each of which serves individual consumers rather than businesses.

   Tasha decides to compete with the larger companies rather than with the small printers. She believes there is more opportunity for larger printing jobs and that her computer background could help her with the businesses' needs.

After operating the business for six months, Tasha is becoming concerned. Prospective customers are more concerned about her prices than the personalized service she provides. The larger printers are usually able to offer lower prices. It also seems that the larger printing businesses have more control over the prices they charge, raising prices for some customers and lowering them for others.

a. What type of competitive environment do you believe Tasha's business is facing? Explain your answer.

b. Would she face the same type of competition if she sold to individual consumers? Why or why not?

c. What can Tasha do to improve the chances of success for her new printing business? [3.3.1, 3.3.2]

Let's Start a Band Follow-Up Discussion

Work in small teams to discuss the question posed at the end of the opening vignette. What are your ideas for getting the band in front of the right audience? Think in terms of supply and demand and economic utility.

Build Your Marketing Plan

Build your Portfolio

In this chapter you learned about why marketers need to understand the economic/competitive environment for the product/service. You will now apply this learning to the development of your marketing plan. To access the chapter-specific tools that you will need to complete this activity, please navigate to Chapter 3 ➔ Build Your Marketing Plan in MindTap. Alternatively, you can access these tools online at NGLSync. Please visit www.nglsync.cengage.com, and search for the companion website that accompanies this book by entering the ISBN, author, or title. Once you locate this companion website, navigate to Build Your Marketing Plan ➔ Chapter 3.

Food Marketing Series Event

Build your Portfolio

You are to assume the role of merchandise manager for Vandalay T's, a popular brand of high-quality tomatoes. The marketing manager (judge) has asked you to decide how the company should respond to rising oil prices.

Vandalay T's was introduced 15 years ago when the economy was soaring and consumers had a lot of disposable income. The company sells tomatoes to higher-end grocery stores in urban metropolitan cities. Vandalay T's are known for their quality and appearance, for being a healthy snack, and for their moderate price.

The prices of food and fuel oil have risen in tandem in recent years. This past year, the oil industry was hit hard due to many events. Modern agricultural companies such as Vandalay T's use oil products to fuel farm machinery, to transport other inputs to the farm, and to transport their products.

Vandalay T's cannot afford to pay the higher price for oil and continue to sell the tomatoes at moderate prices. The marketing manager (judge) has come up with two possible solutions to the rise in oil prices and wants you to determine which is the best option for Vandalay T's.

Solution #1: Raise the price of Vandalay T's all at once. With oil prices more than doubling, Vandalay T's would have to increase the price of the tomatoes significantly to offset the higher fuel costs.

Solution #2: Raise the price of Vandalay T's gradually over a period of time. This would not affect the consumers as much as increasing the price at once, but it would affect Vandalay T's profits.

You will explain which solution you have chosen and the reasoning behind your choice to the marketing manager (judge) in a meeting to take place in the marketing manager's (judge's) office.

Performance Indicators Evaluated

- Explain the concept of economic resources. (Economics)
- Explain the principles of supply and demand. (Economics)
- Discuss the global environment in which businesses operate. (Economics)
- Identify factors affecting a business's profit. (Economics)
- Demonstrate connections between company actions and results. (Marketing)

Go to the DECA website for more detailed information. **www.deca.org**

Think Critically

1. Should Vandalay T's announce the price increase to customers or keep it to themselves? Explain your answer.

2. How will the price change affect Vandalay T's marketing plan?

3. What would be the biggest benefit of going with the solution you did not choose?

CHAPTER 4

MARKETING BASICS

Connect to MindTap

See how effective advertising leads to successful marketing strategies.
Click on Chapter 4, Visual Focus, **in your MindTap.**

Let's Start a Band!

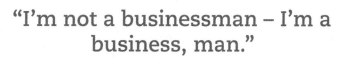

> "I'm not a businessman – I'm a business, man."
>
> *– Jay-Z, Rapper, Songwriter, Record producer*

Things are working out. We've got regular gigs at a couple venues and seem to be building a following. But we were talking the other day, and I said I was worried maybe we've reached our peak in this town. Maybe we need to take our show on the road.

Naomi wondered if we were getting complacent. Maybe we need to change the sets, add new songs, and dump some of the old ones before we start sounding stale.

Jake believed our sound was key. "If we play well, the audience will show."

Layla agreed but wondered how well we knew our audience. She said, "If we know why they're coming, we would have a better idea of what to do and how to do it."

"That's easy, Layla," Gael responded. "They're coming to see you."

"It's fine if they come to see me the first time. But after that I want them to come to *hear* me," she responded.

We ended up agreeing that, while we know what we're playing, we didn't know much about who we were playing for. If we didn't figure it out soon, we might just be playing for ourselves. So what do you think? Do you think we're right?

4.1 CHANGES IN TODAY'S MARKETING

Learning Objectives

4.1.1 Explain how marketing practices today differ from those in the past.

4.1.2 Explain why marketers need to understand their customers when applying the marketing concept.

Key Terms

integrated
market opportunities

marketing matters

Marketing today is much different from marketing just a few decades ago. It is more complex and more interconnected with other business functions. For those reasons, it is even more important that businesses focus on making the best marketing decisions possible. Today's businesses know they must plan marketing activities carefully. Satisfying customer needs has to be their primary objective. Even the best products and services will fail if they do not fit the needs of customers.

 essential question

In what ways do you think marketing has changed since the days of your childhood? Since your parents' childhood?

4.1.1 ▶ Marketing Has Changed

Marketing has changed dramatically in recent years. Understanding how marketing practices differ from those of the past will help you use marketing more effectively.

From Few to Many

Marketing has expanded in scope from a few activities to a variety of activities. The earliest use of marketing was to move products from the producer to the consumer. Then promotion and sales were added to help persuade customers to buy a business's product. Today, businesses complete a wide range of marketing activities, from research to offering customer credit. Effective marketers understand all of the marketing tools and know when and how to use them.

From Independence to Integration

Marketing has changed from an activity that was an independent part of most businesses to one that is well integrated with other business functions. In the past, marketing was not well understood by businesspeople who did not have marketing backgrounds. Marketers often worked by themselves and had little contact with others in the business. Planning for marketing was done after other business planning was complete. Now, marketing is **integrated**, meaning it is involved in all important business decisions and considered an essential part of the business. Companies develop marketing strategies as a part of their business plans.

From Problems to Opportunities

Once thought of as a problem-solving tool, marketing now is regarded as an opportunity-creation tool. In the past, businesses often called on marketing when they faced a problem. If inventory was too high, marketers were asked to increase sales and promotion efforts. If competitors were attracting customers away from a business, they were asked to find weaknesses in the competitor's programs.

Today's businesses do not wait until problems occur. They continuously look for market opportunities. **Market opportunities** include new markets as well as ways to improve a company's offerings in current markets. Marketing is responsible for identifying and planning for opportunities.

From Expense to Investment

Marketing used to be thought of as an expense, but now it is viewed as a critical investment. Marketing can be very expensive. In the past, when businesses faced financial problems, marketing was seen as a place to cut costs. Most businesspeople today recognize that companies will not be able to make a profit if products remain unsold. Effective marketing is an investment because it is responsible for matching a company's offerings with market needs. Spending money to improve marketing usually results in increased profits.

An understanding of how to use marketing is an important business skill.

Marketing is a valuable business asset in today's competitive world. People who understand the basics of marketing are in high demand in the business world. Those basics include understanding the marketing concept as well as how to plan a marketing strategy, respond to competition, and integrate marketing into the business.

From Product to Market Orientation

There was a time when people would invent a product and then figure out how to sell it to customers. The idea was to create a market for the product, and whether the customers needed or wanted the product was not important. Today, most businesses will investigate the marketplace for what will help customers in satisfying their needs. As you read in Chapter 1, this is known as the *marketing concept*. Rather than creating a market for a product, it focuses on creating a product to fulfill a market need.

CHECKPOINT
How do today's marketing practices differ from those used in the past?

© bikeriderlondon/Shutterstock.com

Why do you think it is important to learn about marketing regardless of your career choice?

MARKETING COMMUNICATION

Pinpointing Promotion

Imagine you are walking down the street and pass a music store. Suddenly, your cell phone rings, and you receive an advertisement for the new release of your favorite musical artist. Wireless telephone and Internet services offer a new method of providing specific advertising messages to consumers. The message is targeted to those people who have an interest in the product. It can also be sent at a specific time when the consumer may be most interested in making a purchase.

This targeted advertising uses global positioning system (GPS) technology that is integrated into many cell phones. The GPS can identify where the user is at any time. If you are walking through a mall, a store could send you a digital coupon for 20 percent off of a purchase if you visit the business within the next 15 minutes. If you are driving down the interstate, ads from gas stations and restaurants may encourage you to stop.

Think Critically

1. Why is the targeted marketing used with GPS technology more likely to boost sales than traditional media advertising such as TV ads?

2. There are concerns that businesses and others will misuse the new technology to pinpoint your location at any time. Do you think there should be restrictions on the use of GPS technology for marketing purposes? Why or why not?

3. Would you be willing to complete a survey from your cellular service provider that helps identify your interests? Why or why not?

4.1.2 ▶ What Does Marketing Mean to a Business?

The marketing concept has changed the way businesses operate. It is more than just a new way to complete marketing activities. It requires a totally new approach to thinking and planning. The marketing concept keeps the main focus on customers' needs during the planning, production, distribution, and promotion of a product or service. That may seem simple, but these two examples show how complex it can be.

Reliable Auto Service

Maria Santoz has always enjoyed repairing cars. As a teenager, she bought older cars,

fixed them, and resold them at a profit. She studied auto mechanics in high school and took classes at a local community college to become a certified mechanic. She got a job at a franchised auto repair center, but she soon became dissatisfied with it. She had to complete repairs as quickly as possible and use inexpensive repair parts rather than those specified by the manufacturer. Maria wanted to be able to spend more time with each car to make sure that all problems were identified and repaired with the best available parts.

After a few years, Maria decided to open her own auto repair business. She rented a small building on the edge of a large shopping center two miles from her home. Maria opened Reliable Auto Service and was pleased with the early response. She didn't spend a great deal on advertising because the store's location and signs seemed to attract customers. Many people liked the convenience of being able to leave their car while they were shopping. They also said they had more confidence in an auto repair business whose owner worked on their car. Now that she owned the business, Maria knew she would be able to give each car special attention and the best possible service.

It didn't take long, however, for Maria's customers to start complaining. Many were upset when they had to leave cars overnight while Maria completed repairs. They also were concerned that repair costs were higher than they were used to paying. Maria told them that the price reflected the high-quality parts and a guarantee for all repairs. Customers responded that other businesses also offered guarantees at much lower prices. Maria's business began declining. She was disappointed that customers did not value the quality of her work.

Derek's Designs

Derek Sloan combined his talents in art and sewing to work with the community theater. He designed and made the costumes for the theater's productions. Several of the actors and actresses were impressed with his unique designs. They asked him to create some items for their personal wardrobes.

Derek enjoyed the work, and word-of-mouth referrals from his customers soon resulted in more orders than he could fill. Because of his success, he hired several people so that he could expand into a full-time business. He believed that he could sell his products through small businesses that would use the unique designs to compete with larger stores. He contacted several small retail chains hoping to find one that would agree to buy and distribute his fashions.

After three contacts, Derek was discouraged. Retailers agreed that the clothing was unique and well-constructed. However, the first retailer felt the fashions did not fit the image of her store. The second retailer was willing to buy one or two of the designs if Derek could produce a large volume of each in various sizes. Derek preferred to produce a variety of designs and styles. The last contact was willing to display Derek's fashions but required a full display for each store in the chain and was unwilling to pay until 60 percent of the original order was sold. Derek could not afford that investment. He could not understand how his current customers could be so excited about his work, yet he could not interest any retailers to cooperate in building his business.

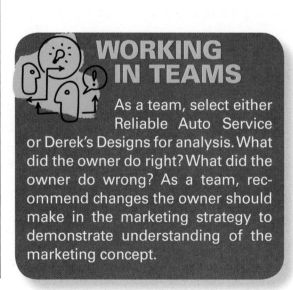

WORKING IN TEAMS

As a team, select either Reliable Auto Service or Derek's Designs for analysis. What did the owner do right? What did the owner do wrong? As a team, recommend changes the owner should make in the marketing strategy to demonstrate understanding of the marketing concept.

Focus on Customer Needs

The experiences of Maria and Derek illustrate the difficulty of applying the marketing concept. Their businesses both offered a quality product or service. Initial reactions from customers were positive, yet they were unable to develop a successful business strategy. They were unsuccessful for several reasons.

1. They were concerned only about the product or service.
2. They believed that they knew what customers wanted.
3. They did not study the market.
4. They failed to use a variety of marketing tools available to them.

It is not just new businesses that do not use marketing effectively. Car manufacturers, large retailers, and service businesses fail, often after many years of successful operations. A business that is unwilling to study the needs of its customers when planning and marketing products and services is taking a big risk. Competitors who understand and use the marketing concept will turn that understanding into an advantage.

CHECKPOINT
What different approach to marketing planning is required of businesses that use the marketing concept?

4.1 ASSESSMENT

What Have You Learned?

1. What was the earliest use of marketing? [4.1.1]
2. Define market opportunities. [4.1.1]
3. What is the main focus of companies that believe in the marketing concept during planning, production, distribution, and promotion of their product or service? [4.1.2]

Make Academic Connections

1. **Math**   Maria Santoz can purchase economy car batteries for $28 each and sell them for $42. She can buy heavy-duty batteries for $68 and sell them for $86. Research tells her that if she stocks both economy and heavy-duty batteries, she can sell 22 economy batteries and 13 heavy duty batteries per month. What would be her total sales and total profit if she sells all of the batteries? [4.1.2]

2. **Communication**   Market opportunities can be either totally new markets or ways to improve a company's current offerings in existing markets. Choose a business in your community. Write a three-paragraph memo to the owner or manager identifying a possible market opportunity and the reasons you think the company should consider the opportunity. [4.1.1]

Connect to ◇DECA

Build your Portfolio

Derek Sloan of Derek's Designs has asked you to help him use the marketing concept to improve his business. Using presentation software, develop a two-minute presentation explaining the changes you recommend in his approach to marketing. Give your presentation to your teacher (judge). Be prepared to answer questions about your recommendations. [4.1.2]

PLAN A MARKETING STRATEGY

Learning Objectives

4.2.1 Describe how the marketing concept transforms business planning.

4.2.2 Explain the importance of understanding the customer.

4.2.3 Discuss how businesses develop the right marketing mix.

Key Terms

strategy
market segment
market opportunity
   analysis
target market

marketing matters

When a business uses the marketing concept, it starts by researching potential customers and their needs. Only then does it move on to planning the product. The product is planned as part of a comprehensive marketing mix. All elements of the marketing mix focus on satisfying the needs of the target market customers that the company's research has identified.

essential question

How do companies benefit when identifying a unique group of customers and considering the group's specific needs when planning each element of the marketing mix?

4.2.1 ▶ Put Marketing Up Front

Every business decides how it will attempt to achieve its goals. Most businesses use carefully prepared plans to guide their operations. A plan that identifies how a company expects to achieve its goals is known as a **strategy**. A company's marketing strategy provides the clearest indication of whether it understands the marketing concept.

With the marketing concept, the company believes it will be most successful if it can respond to the needs of customers. It recognizes that those needs may differ among various consumer groups. It also realizes that customer needs can change over time.

As shown in **Figure 4-1**, before doing anything else, the company will begin its planning by identifying potential customers and studying the needs of those customers. Marketers as well as others will be involved in the research and in using the results to plan the products and services to be developed. The company will attempt to develop products and services that respond to customer needs rather than what the company thinks should be offered. Marketing planning and product planning will occur at the same time, involving many people in all parts of the

HOW DOES THE MARKETING CONCEPT AFFECT PLANNING?	
Without the Marketing Concept	**With the Marketing Concept**
1. Develop a product. 2. Decide on marketing activities. 3. Identify potential customers.	1. Conduct research to identify potential customers and their needs. 2. Develop a marketing mix (product, distribution, price, promotion) that meets specific customer needs. 3. Develop a plan for adapting to changes in customer needs.

FIGURE 4-1 With the marketing concept, planning begins with customer needs.

company. Marketing will be directed at meeting the identified needs of the customers rather than developing ways to persuade people to buy something they may not need.

CHECKPOINT

What is the name for a plan that identifies how a company expects to achieve its goals?

4.2.2 ▶ Understand the Customer

Consumers have many choices of products and services they can purchase to meet their needs. Today, consumers are well informed and experienced in gathering information. With the Internet, they have more avenues available for collecting that information. Consumers often spend time comparing products and services before they make decisions. If buyers are dissatisfied with the purchase or find a better choice later, they will likely return the original product for a refund.

Bringing a new product to the marketplace is expensive. It takes time and money to develop, produce, distribute, and promote products. When a new product enters the market, it must compete with many products offered by other companies. These companies also have invested a great deal and do not want their products to fail. The competition

among products is very intense. Think about how much time, money, and effort Coke and Pepsi put into making sure that their product remains top-of-mind when it comes to consumers' soft drink choices.

Identify Customer Needs

Successful companies are usually those that meet customer needs. Think of your favorite businesses or the products you purchase regularly. They usually are not the only choices you have, but they meet your needs in specific ways better than the other choices. The reasons may be higher quality, convenience, better prices, or a unique image. Satisfying exchanges occur when you spend your money for products and services that meet your needs, and the business is able to make a profit on the sale of its products.

Meeting customer needs is not easy. First, many customers are not sure of their needs or may have conflicting needs. Second, while consumers have many needs, they typically have limited amounts of money available to satisfy those needs. They may not have enough money to buy the product that best meets their needs. Finally, the needs of individuals can vary widely. Their perceptions of the products or services that will meet their needs also may vary. Compare your feelings about specific products or services with those of your friends or family. You will find that there often are differences of opinion.

Businesses tend to deal with customer needs in one of two ways. Some businesses don't view the specific needs of consumers as important. They think either that consumers don't understand their own needs or that businesses can influence consumer needs with well-designed products and effective prices and promotion. In other words, if they can effectively produce and market products, consumers will buy their products. These businesses feel that most consumers are similar in terms of their needs and purchase behavior.

Other businesses think that an understanding of consumer needs is an important part of their business activities. They study needs and try to understand how consumers evaluate products and services to make decisions about what to purchase. The businesses recognize that consumer needs can be quite different, so they try to identify groups of consumers who have similar characteristics and needs. They feel that they can do a better job of satisfying consumers if they can develop products and services that respond to what the consumer wants and expects.

Satisfy Customer Needs

The business that is concerned about consumer needs follows the marketing concept. It begins with a focus on the customer and strives to satisfy customer needs better than its competitors. The business studies markets to identify and focus its efforts on groups of consumers with unsatisfied needs. Through marketing research, the business gathers and analyzes consumer information. It categorizes customers according to characteristics, needs, and purchasing behavior. A group of similar consumers within a larger market is known as a **market segment**.

After identifying distinct market segments, the business analyzes each one. It tries to determine which market segments can be served most effectively and which have the strongest needs, the most resources, and the least competition. It tries to identify other characteristics that can provide the business with opportunities for success. Studying and prioritizing market segments to locate the segment with the best potential based on demand and competition is known as **market opportunity analysis**.

Once segments have been identified and prioritized, the business selects those segments on which it will focus its efforts. The segments selected become the business's target market. A **target market** is a clearly defined segment of the market to which a business wants to appeal. The business can then use the information it has collected from the research to make production and marketing decisions specifically focused on that target market.

CHECKPOINT
What is a market segment?

Much of a company's planning efforts are used to determine what to sell and how to present it to the customer. Marketing strategies need to be planned in order to make the products and services available to the targeted customers.

A business that follows the marketing concept bases the planning process on customer needs. It knows that product planning and marketing must work hand in hand. Therefore, it will carefully coordinate the development of the marketing mix.

The Marketing Mix

The *marketing mix* is a blend of the four marketing elements—product, distribution, price, and promotion. The company makes many decisions to ensure that a satisfying product is available to the selected markets at the time, in the location, at the price, and with the information that best meets customers' needs. An effective strategy will bring together many complex activities. A business will be able to control a large number of the activities, but it will usually have to involve other businesses to help with its plans.

Create the Right Mix

Some of the decisions in the marketing mix are obvious while others are not. The results of one decision affect others. For example, if an improvement is made to a product, then the company might need to increase the price. Developing the best marketing mix requires the cooperation of many people as well as careful planning and creativity.

A business uses the marketing concept because it believes that the best decisions can be made when the needs of consumers are an important focus of the planning. By combining the planning of product, distribution, pricing, and promotion, as shown in **Figure 4-2**, the company has the best opportunity to develop a satisfying, competitive, and profitable mix. Businesspeople need to understand each of the mix elements and all of the choices available in order to develop a good marketing mix.

FIGURE 4-2 Effective marketing strategies combine the parts of the marketing mix to satisfy customers.

DEVELOP PRODUCTS When the term *product* is used, many people think of the basic offering of a company, such as an automobile, a tablet computer, or a meal at a restaurant. But there is much more to the product. Each competitor must make decisions that will make the product it offers under its brand different from and better than the products competitors offer.

Parts of the product decision that can improve customer satisfaction include special features such as a unique design, construction, size, color, or operation. Accessories may be available that make the product easier to operate and more useable.

A company can improve its products by offering services to customers before or after the sale. Services can be related to the purchase, delivery, installation, or maintenance of the product. Guarantees and warranties should be considered as a part of some products because they make customers more confident in the purchase of the product.

Another part of the product decision is the use of the product. Often products have more than one use. Customers may be dissatisfied if they are not able to use the product in the way they want. Packaging is needed not only to protect the product but also to provide customers with information about how to use the product.

Finally, the product may have additional benefits associated with it that go beyond the straightforward use of the product. For instance, a push mower not only provides the consumer with the ability to keep a neatly manicured lawn, but it also provides the consumer with exercise. As another example, a lip gloss may provide the consumer with colorful lips as intended, but it can also protect the lips from becoming chapped on a cold, windy day.

MAKE DISTRIBUTION DECISIONS

Distribution is a critical part of a business's marketing decisions. It has an important impact on customer satisfaction by making the product available where and when the customer wants it. Examples of distribution problems include products that are damaged during shipment, poorly packaged, or assembled incorrectly. Poor distribution often leads to customer dissatisfaction.

While some products and services are exchanged directly between the producer and the customer, other businesses are usually involved in the distribution process. Manufacturers must rely on wholesalers and retailers to get products to the consumer. Similarly, a retailer must locate sources of the products its customers want and obtain them.

Try to trace the distribution path for the products you purchase. Sometimes it is almost impossible to identify the companies involved in each part of the distribution process or even the company that manufactured the product. Activities such as order processing, product handling, transportation, and inventory control must be completed efficiently in order for companies to get the product to the customer. If one company fails, the entire marketing effort may fail.

PRICE PRODUCTS AND SERVICES

Price is probably the most difficult marketing decision to understand and plan. Theoretically, price is determined from the interaction of supply and demand. That relationship is important in setting the best price, but it is almost impossible to set the price of a specific product in a specific business using only supply and demand. Businesses must develop specific procedures to set prices that are competitive yet allow the business to make a profit.

First the business needs to set its objectives in pricing its products and services. Is the goal to increase the sales volume of a particular product or to make the most profit possible on each sale? Each goal will result in a different price. Many businesses set their prices the same or slightly lower than their major competitors. That pricing strategy may be necessary in some situations, but it also can create problems.

Calculating the price involves several elements. The price must be acceptable to customers, but it must cover all costs and allow for a reasonable profit. Production, marketing, and operating costs make up a large percentage of the final price of most products, so the net profit available often is very small. Prices must be calculated carefully, so that businesses make a profit after expenses are paid.

Another part of the pricing decision is how price is presented to customers. Normally, retailers use a price tag or sticker, and customers pay the price that is marked. Manufacturers may communicate price through catalogs or price lists or by sales representatives as a part of their sales presentation.

Businesses commonly offer discounts from their list prices to some or all of their customers. Prices also can be changed by markdowns, allowances, trade-ins, and coupons. Finally, credit is commonly used to allow customers to purchase a product without paying the full price at the time of purchase.

PLAN PROMOTION Promotion communicates the value and benefits of a product or service to help consumers make decisions. Advertising and other promotional methods are powerful tools if used to support effective marketing programs. However, they can easily be misused and can have no impact or even a negative effect on consumers.

Think of promotions you think are particularly good. Now try to determine the impact of a specific promotion on your purchase behavior. It is difficult to determine the influence of just one promotion on a decision, even if it is memorable. You can never notice or respond to all the promotional messages you encounter each day.

When planning promotion, businesspeople select from a variety of methods. The most common methods are advertising, personal selling, sales promotion, visual display, and publicity. The choices will be based primarily on the objectives the company wants to accomplish and the audience it wants to reach. A company needs to plan carefully to reach the target markets with an understandable message that helps the consumer make appropriate decisions.

Promotion is a unique type of marketing tool. It does not create economic utility by itself. It is used to communicate the value and benefits of other product and marketing decisions to the consumer. Promotion cannot do a great deal to help a company that has a poor product, excessively high prices, or ineffective distribution.

CHECKPOINT
Why should marketing mix elements be planned together rather than separately?

MATH IN MARKETING

Pricing, Promotion, Profits

Part of any company's marketing strategy involves pricing products and services while planning promotions to advance objectives. The way these strategies are implemented has a direct impact on sales and profits. For example, a boutique clothing store sells a high-quality brand of designer jeans. The cost and expense for the jeans amount to $60 per pair.

Do the Math

1. How much profit will the company make under each of the following scenarios? (1) sell 10 pairs of jeans at full price for $100; (2) sell 15 pairs of jeans at a discount for $80; or (3) sell 25 pairs of jeans at full price for $100 by spending $500 on promoting the brand. Which scenario would be most profitable?

2. The store buys 25 pairs of jeans and sells 10 pairs for full price. How much profit would it make on the remaining 15 pairs if it sells them for $80 each and spends $150 to promote the sale? What is the total profit on the 25 pairs?

4.2 ASSESSMENT

What Have You Learned?

1. For a company implementing the marketing concept, which should occur first: marketing planning or product planning? [4.2.1]

2. What do marketers conduct when they study and prioritize market segments to locate the best potential based on demand and competition? [4.2.2]

3. Which marketing mix element does not create economic utility by itself? [4.2.3]

Make Academic Connections

1. **Visual Art** Draw or use a computer to create a picture, graphic, or other visual representation of the marketing mix a company uses for one of its products. Make sure your visual includes each of the four elements of the marketing mix. [4.2.3]

2. **Language Arts** Some companies have a specific target market for their products and services while others appear to be marketed to everyone. Locate an advertisement for a company that demonstrates a clear target marketing strategy and another that does not. Determine how the language used in the two advertisements helps communicate the marketing strategy. Use the two ads to verbally describe your conclusions. [4.2.2]

Connect to ◇DECA

Build your Portfolio

You are part of a team responsible for planning a marketing mix for a new fast-food breakfast item targeting health-conscious families. Develop a description of each mix element. Using presentation software, make a three-minute team presentation of your decisions and explain to your teacher (judge) how you applied the marketing concept. [4.2.3]

Planning a Career In...
MARKETING RESEARCH

What makes top companies so successful? How does a business know when to launch a new product or run a big sale? How do competing companies that sell similar products differentiate them?

Marketing research enables companies to determine consumers' needs and wants. Products can then be developed or refined to meet consumers' needs. For example, marketing research enables cell phone manufacturers to know the screen size customers prefer as well as the types of apps they like to have preloaded on their phones.

Job Titles

- Focus Group Facilitator
- Marketing Research Analyst
- Survey Sales Representative
- Marketing Research Account Executive
- Media Research Analyst
- Research and Development Manager

Needed Skills

- Depending on the type of research, educational requirements vary from a BA to an MA or PhD degree.
- A blend of coursework in business, quantitative analysis, and information science is beneficial.
- Strong analytical skills and attention to detail are important.

What it's like to work in... Marketing Research

It's 7:15 A.M. and Dimetri, a marketing research associate at a consumer products company, is reviewing what consumers need most from a laundry detergent. The results, obtained from a recent focus group, indicate that effectiveness at stain removal, colorfastness, and value were the most important factors to consumers. Dimetri will incorporate questions on these attributes into the online survey he is developing for current and prospective customers.

Dimetri's afternoon team meeting focuses on the most effective way to deliver coupons to consumers. Six weeks ago, in three separate test markets, coupons for the laundry detergent were distributed via newspaper ads, by having retailers' cash registers print out coupons when a competing brand was purchased, and by making coupons available through the Internet. By comparing coupon distribution methods to recent sales in test markets, the group hopes to determine which method of coupon distribution was the most effective.

What About You?

Would you like to contribute to product enhancements through conducting marketing research projects?

Discover more about the outlook for this career and watch a video about a related career. Click on **Chapter 4, Planning a Career In...** *in your MindTap.*

Learning Objectives

4.3.1 Detail the stages of consumer decision making.

4.3.2 Explain how businesses can use the marketing concept in various types of competition.

Key Terms

decision
want

marketing matters

People follow a fairly predictable series of steps in making purchase decisions. They follow those steps to identify and evaluate various products and services that might satisfy their needs. By providing the right information at the right time when consumers are making a decision, businesses try to demonstrate to consumers that their products will deliver the best value. If that does not happen, consumers will likely choose another product. Much of a business's marketing strategy depends on the type of competition it faces from other businesses. The number and types of competing businesses affect the choices consumers have and how businesses will compete with one another.

 essential question

What steps do consumers follow when making a decision? What types of factors influence how consumers make purchase decisions?

4.3.1 ▶ Consumer Decision Making

Consumers make decisions every day. A **decision** is a choice among alternatives. Decisions are made to satisfy a need or solve a problem. Once a need is identified, it then leads to a **want,** which is a culturally defined way the consumer can fill the need. Consumers want to choose the alternative that provides the most satisfaction or the greatest value. Without choices, there would be no need for a decision.

If marketers want to satisfy customer needs and wants, they must understand how consumers choose what they will buy. Researchers agree that people follow a series of decision-making steps when making a commitment to purchase. The

consumer decision-making process is used most often with infrequent, important buying decisions.

The Stages of a Decision

Understanding the decision-making process is an important marketing skill. Knowing where consumers are in that process helps marketers offer the right information at the right time. The result should be a more effective exchange.

Figure 4-3 illustrates the five stages in consumer decision making. Consider an important decision you have made as you study each stage to help you understand it.

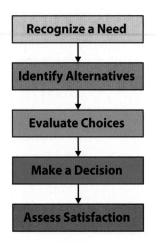

FIGURE 4-3 Consumers make a series of decisions before making a purchase.

STAGE 1—RECOGNIZE   The typical purchasing process begins when the consumer recognizes that a need exists. Prior to that time, the consumer may have been aware of many products and services but took no action. Once a specific need is identified, the consumer moves through the stages of decision making. If the need is urgent, the process may occur quickly. If not, the consumer may take time before making a decision.

STAGE 2—IDENTIFY   Once a need is recognized, the consumer becomes interested in finding a solution. That solution arises in the form of a want. That interest leads to identifying products or services that relate to the want and sources of information that can help the consumer make an effective decision.

STAGE 3—EVALUATE   When several choices have been identified, the consumer then gathers information and uses it to evaluate the choices. An evaluation is done to determine if any one choice seems to be better, more available, or more affordable than other choices. Consumers must determine if one product or service meets their needs better than the other products and services they are evaluating. Some consumers spend very little time and use a small amount of information to evaluate choices. Some consumers are careful and objective in making decisions while others are much less rational.

STAGE 4—DECIDE   When the consumer is comfortable with the evaluation, a decision is made. The decision will be to select one of the available choices, to gather more information, or to do nothing.

STAGE 5—ASSESS   The final step in the process is to determine whether or not the choice was correct. If the consumer tried a specific product, it will be evaluated to see if it satisfied the need. If it did, the decision will likely be repeated the next time the same need occurs. If it did not satisfy the need, the purchase decision will probably not be repeated.

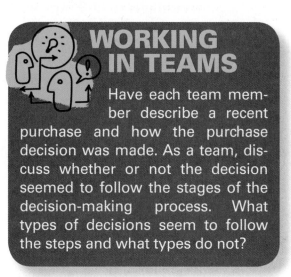

WORKING IN TEAMS

Have each team member describe a recent purchase and how the purchase decision was made. As a team, discuss whether or not the decision seemed to follow the stages of the decision-making process. What types of decisions seem to follow the steps and what types do not?

Marketers Rely on Information

Marketers are often described as creative people. Indeed, a great deal of creativity is needed to plan a marketing mix. Developing new product features and uses, preparing promotional materials and activities, and demonstrating value to customers depends on the creativity of the people involved. However, marketing is increasingly becoming a scientific process. Information is gathered to improve decisions, and alternative methods are studied to determine which are most effective. Information is also a key component of the creative process itself.

Conducting research is an important marketing activity. It is the way in which marketers learn about their customers. Marketers need to be skilled in organizing research, analyzing the data collected during research, and using research results. The most important type of research for most businesses is the study of potential and current customers. Companies need to clearly identify their customers, characteristics that make groups of customers differ, important customer needs, and how customers make purchase decisions.

Want to know more about what is trending with this topic? Click on **Lesson 4.3, Digital Marketing,** *in your MindTap.*

Connect to MindTap

Additionally, research about competitors will identify the type of competition and the strengths and weaknesses of competing companies. Finally, businesses study alternative marketing strategies to determine which ones are most effective and most profitable.

Marketers are using more and more information to make decisions. Most companies are developing marketing information systems that collect and store a variety of information. That information is readily available, often through the use of computer databases, when decisions need to be made.

CHECKPOINT
What are the five stages in the consumer decision-making process?

4.3.2 ▶ Respond to Competition

The private enterprise economy offers many opportunities for businesses. A person who wants to start a business and has the necessary resources can probably do so. The private enterprise economy is also good for consumers. Because of the opportunities for people to operate businesses, consumers typically have many available products and services from which to choose.

Even though private enterprise offers many opportunities, it also presents challenges to businesspeople. When there are many businesses in a market, competition is usually intense. Consumers can select

from among a number of products and services. They expect real value from businesses. Otherwise, they will purchase from a competitor. Value is not always the same for every consumer. It may mean higher quality, more service, or lower prices. Businesses that are unable to meet customer expectations better than their competitors may not be able to survive.

Marketers need to identify the type of competition a company faces and develop an appropriate marketing strategy. Using the marketing concept provides direction for developing effective strategies.

Intense Competition

The most difficult type of competition businesses face is a market in which they compete with others offering very similar products. One example is *pure competition*, where there are many businesses offering the same product. Another example is an *oligopoly*, where only a few companies compete in the same market but offer products in which consumers see few, if any, differences. Businesspeople can study the customers in the market to determine if there are some groups who are not currently satisfied with the choices available.

Companies that face intense competition need to examine their marketing mix. With careful study of consumer needs and their experience with available products, businesses may be able to identify ways to change or improve products, features, or the services offered with the products. New product uses might be identified. The goal of any product change is to make the product different from that of competitors so that it is more satisfying to the target market.

Examining other parts of the marketing mix may also help a business compete. Distribution can focus on making the product available at better locations and times, with more careful handling or better customer service. Pricing can offer alternative methods of payments or greater ease of obtaining credit. It can provide extended time for payment, or it could provide the opportunity to lease rather than own.

© Africa Studio/Shutterstock.com.

Promotion can provide more personalized or detailed information. It can use nontraditional methods or media. It can also communicate with the customer after the sale to aid in the use of the product.

Limited Competition

Some businesses have the advantage of offering a product or service with little or no direct competition. In economic terms, this situation is known as a *monopoly*. Businesses facing limited competition often operate in very different ways than those facing intense competition. They do not have to worry as much about price or even promotion because consumers are restricted in their choice of products. Therefore, a business usually will concentrate on maintaining its advantage in the market. It will try to keep competing businesses from entering the market. It will protect its location and concentrate on keeping its product or service as unique as possible.

Customers using the products and services of a monopoly business often become dissatisfied with their lack of choice. They believe that without competition they pay higher prices and receive poorer service. They also must deal with a company that may be more concerned about protecting its market and making a profit than meeting the needs of consumers.

Consider the only hospital in a community where the next closest hospital is 60 miles away. That hospital would be in a market much like a monopoly with no direct competition. It would be difficult for patients and their families to drive 60 miles to the alternative hospital. The hospital administrators would not have to be concerned about the people who need hospital services. They could offer the services that provided the highest level of profit. Customers might not be happy, but they would have little choice in the matter.

While it may not be as profitable in the short run, the hospital administrators could adopt the marketing concept to make operating decisions. As a result, consumers will be more likely to use the local hospital for a variety of services and to encourage others to use it. They will be less likely to look for other places and other methods to meet their health care needs.

The same analysis could apply to the only convenience store, supermarket, or other retail business in a neighborhood. It could also apply to the only distributor of fuel or agricultural supplies in an area or to a government agency or school system. Each of these businesses has the characteristics of a monopoly and can decide whether or not to adopt the marketing concept.

Monopolistic Competition

Most businesses face competition somewhere between monopoly and intense competition. They have many competitors, but customers see some differences among the choices. The customers will attempt to determine which of the available products and services best meet their needs. It is important for the companies to have clearly identified differences that result in customers selecting their brands from among all of the available choices.

Companies in monopolistic competition find the marketing concept to be of most value. Because customers already recognize the unique choices available to them, they attempt to select the brands

© Monkey Business Images/Shutterstock.com.

What product differences could a restaurant specializing in hamburgers offer customers in an effort to differentiate its product from competitors' products?

that are most satisfying. Companies that use the marketing concept focus on specific groups of customers and attempt to identify their needs. Then they will use the full range of decisions within the marketing mix to develop products and services for those customers. Changes and improvements in the product, distribution, price, and promotion can make the brand not only different from its competitors but also more attractive to potential customers.

Here are some examples of the use of the marketing concept. A manufacturer of portable digital music players makes its product smaller and more durable and offers the product in a variety of colors and styles. A child-care center keeps children overnight to meet the needs of parents who have evening jobs. A supermarket accepts orders and payments on its website or by telephone and has the order ready at curbside for the customer at a convenient drive-up location. In each case, a change is made in the marketing mix that is designed to improve the mix, make it stand out from the competition, and respond to an important need of the target market.

CHECKPOINT
Why is the marketing concept useful for businesses facing monopolistic competition?

4.3 ASSESSMENT

What Have You Learned?

1. Why are the consumer decision-making steps important in marketing planning? [4.3.1]

2. What is the most important type of research for most businesses? [4.3.1]

3. If a company decides to change a product to better compete in a market, what should be the goal of that change? [4.3.2]

4. For which type of competition do companies find the marketing concept to be of most value? [4.3.2]

Make Academic Connections

1. **Technology** Using the drawing tools of a word-processing program, create a flowchart that illustrates each stage of the decision-making process. Fill in the flowchart with information about an important purchasing decision you made. [4.3.1]

2. **Management** For each of the three types of competition discussed in the lesson, identify a business in your community that you believe faces that type of competition. For each business, decide whether or not you believe the business is using the marketing concept in its response to competition. Act as the marketing manager for one of the businesses and write a paragraph explaining how the business could use the marketing concept more effectively. [4.3.2]

Connect to ◇DECA

Build your Portfolio

Your marketing research team must prepare a short survey to determine the most important reasons consumers are loyal to a specific business or brand. Survey 15 people and analyze the results. Prepare a short report with two supporting charts or graphs. Submit the report to your teacher (judge) and be prepared to answer questions about the research. [4.3.1]

THE VARIED ROLE OF MARKETING

Learning Objectives

4.4.1 Explain how the role of marketing differs in various types of businesses.

4.4.2 Identify ways marketing is used by non-business organizations.

Key Terms

pull strategy
push strategy
channel of distribution
channel members
non-business organization

marketing matters

Marketing activities must be performed every time an exchange of products and services occurs. That exchange may occur between businesses, a business and a consumer, or even between consumers. The same basic marketing functions and activities are used in all exchanges. Each exchange involves a supplier, a consumer, and a complete marketing mix. Marketing tools are used by non-business organizations and even individuals. However, there are differences in the ways that various types of businesses use marketing tools. Marketing principles can apply to a variety of types of exchanges even when profit is not the ultimate motive.

essential question

How do various types of businesses and non-businesses make marketing decisions?

Marketing in the Business World

The entire marketing mix and all marketing functions are important to all types of businesses. However, each type of business places a different emphasis on marketing mix elements and marketing functions.

Producers and Manufacturers

Producers and manufacturers develop the products and services that businesses and consumers need. Because of that role, the product element of the marketing mix usually receives the most attention. Distribution is also important as the companies must make sure the products get to their customers. Unless manufacturers and producers distribute products directly to users, they must rely on other businesses to make good decisions about product distribution, pricing, and promotion. Even if manufacturers and producers do not sell their products directly to the final consumers, they must still understand and respond to the needs of consumers. In addition to the design of products, other marketing activities must meet consumer needs as well. Manufacturers and producers also must be able to satisfy the needs of the businesses involved in the marketing channels for the products.

Producers and manufacturers also play a role in the promotion of products to the customer. They may promote their product directly to the customer so that the customer will request the product from retailers who will then request the product from manufacturers. This is known as a **pull strategy**. Or, they may promote the product to wholesalers and retailers who will then, in turn, promote the product to customers. This is a **push strategy**.

Channel Members

A **channel of distribution** is made up of all of the businesses involved in completing marketing activities as products move from the producer to the consumer. **Channel members** are the businesses used to provide many of the marketing functions during the distribution process. The producer places emphasis on the product element of the marketing mix. Other channel members place less emphasis on the product, although they must have the products that customers want.

After deciding what products and services to offer, channel members then focus their attention on the other mix elements. Wholesalers emphasize distribution planning. Many wholesalers also help their customers with financing and provide marketing information.

Retailers are responsible for most final pricing decisions. They use a variety of promotional activities to encourage consumers to purchase their products. Channel members must work closely with both producers and customers to make sure the marketing mix is satisfactory to everyone involved.

Want to know more about what is trending with this topic? Click on **Lesson 4.4, Marketing Decisions,** *in your MindTap.*

Connect to
MindTap

Service Businesses

Service businesses face unique marketing challenges. Most service businesses work directly with their customers rather than through a channel of distribution. Therefore, they are responsible for the entire marketing mix. Also, services are usually developed and delivered by people, making it more difficult to control the quality of the service each time it is provided.

Because of the characteristics of services and the expectations of customers, the product mix element is very important for service businesses. The business must develop procedures to provide consistent customer service.

Distribution planning also is important because the service must be available where and when the customer wants it. If the business is not conveniently located, sales may be lost. If the business offers more services than the customers want, expenses will be high.

Service businesses usually have more control over pricing than businesses that sell products. It is more difficult for customers to determine the appropriate price for a service or to compare the prices of several companies because one business may offer the service differently from its competitors. Services are more difficult to promote because the customer may not be able to see or examine them before making a decision to buy. Services that customers are not familiar with may require a great deal of promotion.

CHECKPOINT
What unique marketing challenges do service businesses face?

Does a service business need to develop a marketing mix? Why or why not?

4.4.2 ▶ Marketing by Non-Business Organizations

The successful use of marketing has moved from the business world to other non-business organizations. A **non-business organization** focuses on something other than providing products and services for a profit. Examples are government agencies, churches, schools, museums, and even professional organizations. Like for-profit businesses, a non-business organization must satisfy its customers' needs in order to achieve the organization's goals and maximize its effectiveness.

Just as businesses have not always understood marketing and have mis-used it, many non-business organizations have made mistakes with their marketing efforts. They often emphasize promotion and treat people as if they all have the same needs and interests. The unique characteristics of several types of non-business organizations suggest how they might approach marketing.

Government Agencies

Most government agencies have many of the characteristics of a monopoly. They seldom have competition for the services they provide. Citizens usually pay for fire and police protection, garbage collection, street repairs, and other city, state, and federal services through taxes. As a result, they have no choice but to pay the cost established by the government for those services. It becomes easy for those providing the services to feel they know what citizens want and how best to provide it. They may not be concerned about a high level of customer service. They may be more concerned about controlling costs to meet their budget.

Today, however, many government officials and employees recognize the importance of providing quality services and responding to customer questions and concerns in positive ways. They are making information and services available in more convenient and accessible ways. Many government agencies are now using e-government where information and services are readily available through well-designed and secure websites. Citizens can transact their business with government in a convenient, secure way using the Internet.

Government agencies also have worked with the pricing element of the marketing mix. While they may not be able to reduce the prices of services, they have made it possible to use credit or debit cards for payments or to spread payments over a period of time rather than requiring full payment all at one time. Promotion also has become a popular marketing tool for government agencies to inform customers of services and to build a positive image.

Nonprofit Organizations

Nonprofit organizations have a unique situation. They do not operate with a profit motive. However, they still need adequate resources to provide services to people in need. Often, they must rely on fundraising from people who will not directly benefit from the organization's services. They must be able to convince people of the value of those services and the need to support the organization financially. Promotion is a very important marketing mix element for many nonprofit organizations.

Nonprofit organizations provide products and services for their clients. The product mix element is important to make sure the products and services provided meet the clients' needs. Because many organizations serve clients across the country and even worldwide, distribution decisions also are important. Distribution may involve shipping food, clothing, and other products to impoverished areas or transporting people to help with relief efforts.

Want to know more about what is trending with this topic? Click on Lesson 4.4, Global Marketing, in your MindTap.

Connect to
MindTap

All American Red Cross
Disaster Assistance Is Free

© FashionStock.com/Shutterstock.com.

Which element of the marketing mix does this photo of the Red Cross, a global nonprofit charity, illustrate?

Support for Non-Business Organizations

Many organizations seek help from people who understand marketing and know how to use the marketing concept to identify target markets and develop marketing mixes. These organizations are moving beyond using marketers simply for promotional help and are enlisting them to help develop their "product" as well as the message associated with that product. With the help of marketers and increased understanding of and use of marketing tools, those organizations have seen positive results. They now view marketing as an important part of their efforts.

CHECKPOINT

Why is marketing important to non-business organizations?

4.4 ASSESSMENT

What Have You Learned?

1. Which marketing mix element usually receives the most attention from producers and manufacturers? [4.4.1]

2. What is a channel of distribution? [4.4.1]

3. How does the focus of a non-business organization differ from the focus of a typical business organization? [4.4.2]

Make Academic Connections

1. **Visual Art** Think of a product you have purchased recently. Draw or use a computer to create a picture, graphic, or other visual representation of a channel of distribution involving three or more businesses that are responsible for producing and distributing that product. The visual should show each business and the marketing activities that each business performs as a part of the channel of distribution. [4.4.1]

2. **Government** Locate the website of a local, state, or federal government agency. Analyze the website for evidence of the use of marketing. Decide whether or not you believe the agency understands the marketing concept. Prepare a two-paragraph report describing your findings and conclusion. [4.4.2]

Connect to ◇DECA

Build your Portfolio

As the membership chairperson for your local DECA chapter, you are responsible for developing a marketing plan for increasing membership. Prepare three computer slides that summarize your decisions about a target market and marketing mix. Use the slides to present your ideas to your teacher (judge). [4.4.2]

Connect to MindTap

*Analyze a case study that focuses on chapter concepts. Click on **Chapter 4, Case Study,** in your MindTap.*

CHAPTER 4 ASSESSMENT

Review Marketing Concepts

1. Explain how marketing that is integrated with other business functions helps a company to apply the marketing concept. [4.1.1]

2. What is the likely result when a company believes it knows what customers want without researching the market? [4.1.2]

3. How does the marketing concept affect planning? [4.2.1]

4. Why it is difficult to understand customer needs? [4.2.2]

5. What services might a car dealership offer a customer who purchases a new car? Why would providing these services benefit the dealership? [4.2.3]

6. Which of the five steps of consumer decision making do you think is most important? Explain your answer. [4.3.1]

7. You are a marketing manager who works in a market with intense competition for your company's products. What would be your strategy for increasing sales? [4.3.2]

8. What unique marketing challenges does a service business face? [4.4.1]

9. Why might a church use marketing to achieve its goals? [4.4.2]

Marketing Research and Planning

1. Marketing involves understanding customers and their wants and needs. To demonstrate two views of customers, create two documents in a word processing or page design program. For each document, find online images to create a collage of pictures. One document should illustrate customers that are all alike and would respond to a mass-marketing approach. The other should illustrate customers who represent different market segments and would respond to target marketing. [4.2.2]

2. The type of competition a company faces affects the type of marketing strategy it will use. Locate an advertisement for a local business that faces intense competition (auto dealership, supermarket, cell phone service, etc.) and another advertisement for a company that faces limited competition (utility company such as electricity, natural gas, telephone, cable, etc.). Create an electronic presentation that compares the marketing strategies of each company by highlighting differences in the advertisements. [4.3.2]

3. Brand names often have a significant impact on a consumer's perception of quality. Survey 10 people to find their perception of the quality of the products represented by the following brands: Alphabet (Google), Amazon, Apple, Rolex, Walt Disney. Ask them to use a rating scale where 1 is the worst quality and 10 is the highest quality. Use a computer spreadsheet program to create a chart. Record each person's responses in your chart and find an average quality rating for each product. Prepare three written conclusions from the data. [4.2.2]

4. Develop a marketing strategy including a description of a target market and a complete marketing mix for a house-painting service. Make sure that you consult the textbook to include all of the variables of each mix element. Describe the decision-making

process you think the target market will follow to choose a painting service. Identify and justify the type of competition such a service would face in your community. [4.2.2, 4.2.3, 4.3.2]

5. Use an Internet search engine or an online library research service to find a recent article on the use of marketing by non-business organizations. Then compose a 150- to 200-word summary of the article's main points. [4.4.2]

Marketing Management and Decision Making

1. One service that is gaining in popularity is a shuttle service for children whose parents work. These shuttle services provide rides to and from after-school activities such as dancing, gymnastics, music lessons, and sports practices. The service is gaining in popularity as more parents are unable to transport their children because they are still at work.

   You are responsible for completing a market opportunity analysis, determining the type of competition a children's shuttle service would face, reviewing the stages of decision making for a parent considering the service, and describing each of the marketing mix elements you would recommend.

   To analyze the potential for a children's shuttle service in your community, prepare written answers to the following questions:

   a. What individuals, groups, or organizations are potential customers for the service?

   b. What type of information is needed to determine if there are enough potential customers for the business? What are some possible sources to determine the number of potential customers?

   c. What are two possible market segments for the service, and what are the important needs of each segment?

   d. What type of competition would exist for this service in your community—intense, limited, or monopolistic competition? Who are the major competitors?

   e. What information would a customer need about the service at each stage of the decision-making process?

   f. Based on your market analysis, what are the most important factors to focus on to ensure you provide a satisfying product, effective distribution (place), a reasonable price, and effective promotion of the new business? [4.2.2]

2. A successful business needs to study its customers and their wants and needs. As these needs and wants change, marketers must be able to identify new markets or customer groups for old products or services. Pick-up trucks, fast-food, and photo-processing services are products that have been on the market for a long time. Traditional markets are changing, so marketers are looking for new markets for each of those products. For each product, prepare a table that describes and compares (a) a traditional market, (b) the marketing mix for the traditional market, (c) a new market, and (d) the marketing mix for the new market. [4.2.3]

3. Two years ago, Nick began to sell his own pasta sauce to local independent retailers and at farmers markets. Nick's grandfather owned and operated an Italian restaurant for 40 years, and Nick uses his grandfather's recipe for the sauce. Up to now Nick has done little marketing, and the sauce has succeeded by word-of-mouth marketing. Recently Nick has begun selling online, and the success has put a strain on his ability to keep up with production.

   Nick needs to decide if he wants to continue to grow the business. If so, he will need to make a sizable investment in improving his production capabilities. However, he understands that a commitment to increasing production will have an effect on other aspects of the business, including distribution and marketing. He also understands that much of his success so far is due to familiarity with the product's legacy. He wonders if the product can be successful in the crowded pasta sauce market outside the region where people do not know its history. Should Nick's Pasta Sauce remain a local product and maintain current production levels and channels of distribution? Or should Nick try to broaden its market? Explain the effect either decision would have on distribution and marketing.

Let's Start a Band Follow-Up Discussion

Work in small teams to discuss the question posed at the end of the opening vignette. Discuss why the band needs to understand its audience (target market) and how it might use the consumer decision-making process to inform some of its decisions.

Build Your Marketing Plan

Build your Portfolio

In this chapter you learned the importance of developing a marketing strategy. You will now apply this learning to the development of your marketing plan. To access the chapter-specific tools that you will need to complete this activity, please navigate to Chapter 4 ➔ Build Your Marketing Plan in MindTap. Alternatively, you can access these tools online at NGLSync. Please visit www.nglsync.cengage.com, and search for the companion website that accompanies this book by entering the ISBN, author, or title. Once you locate this companion website, navigate to Build Your Marketing Plan ➔ Chapter 4.

Business Solutions Project Event

DECA PREP

Build your Portfolio

The Business Solutions Project uses the project management process to work with a local business or organization to identify a specific problem with the current business operations and implement a solution. Examples include talent acquisition, employee on-boarding, policies and procedures, technology integration, customer service improvement, safety operations, marketing and promotion activities, and productivity and output enhancement.

This project is limited to 20 numbered pages, including the appendix and excluding the title page and table of contents. Major parts of the written project include the Executive Summary, Initiating, Planning and Organizing, Execution, Monitoring and Controlling, Closing the Project, Bibliography, and Appendix.

You have been hired by your city to conduct research for attracting an appropriate company and additional business activity to your community. You must consider the population of your city, the available workforce, economic incentives, and the marketing and distribution of the products/services produced by the company you are trying to attract to your community. You will prepare a written entry for this project and an oral presentation to sell your research findings. The oral presentation must cover all performance indicators. You must present a compelling reason for a company to locate in your city.

Performance Indicators Evaluated

- Describe the project in an organized, clear, and effective presentation. (Communication)
- Identify the marketing information needs of the research project. (Marketing-Information Management)
- Interpret descriptive statistics for marketing decision-making. (Marketing-Information Management)
- Explain the findings and recommendations. (Communication)
- Demonstrate professional appearance, poise, and confidence. (Communication)

Go to the DECA website for more detailed information. **www.deca.org**

Think Critically

1. What are the greatest assets that your city has to offer a potential business?

2. Why must you describe the workforce in detail when trying to attract a business to a community?

3. How can tax incentives be used to attract businesses to a community?

4. Why is it important to describe the demographics of your community when presenting to a potential business?

CHAPTER 5

MARKETING BEGINS WITH CONSUMERS

5.1 Understand Consumer Behavior

5.2 What Motivates Buyers?

5.3 Influence Consumer Decisions

See how effective advertising leads to successful marketing strategies.
Click on Chapter 5, Visual Focus, **in your MindTap.**

Let's Start a Band!

"We're the McDonald's of rock. We're always there to satisfy and a billion served."

– Paul Stanley, Kiss

We're still struggling to understand what gets people to come to our performances.

Layla says she often sees the same faces at our shows. "A lot has to do with the performance," she told us. She also thinks some people come because we've taken a stand on an important issue." We sing about it. We promote it. They respond to it.

Naomi thought for a moment before replying. "I don't disagree. But I think most people come because they like what we do. Just look at the response we get from our encore. I think we could play all night and they would never leave."

"That's right," chimed in Gael. "Let's not forget the old saying, 'Keep the Customer Satisfied.' I think Simon and Garfunkel even wrote a song about that."

"Simon and who?" Malik asked. "Never heard of them."

Jake answered enthusiastically. "They were a great folk-rock duo who had their biggest hits in the 1960s. I know them because my grandparents had an old turntable and a collection of 45s, which were small records with one song on each side. "Keep the Customer Satisfied" was on the flip side of their biggest hit, "Bridge Over Troubled Waters." My grandfather told me that Simon wrote "Keep the Customer Satisfied" when he was tired from touring. Hey, maybe we should adopt it as our theme song."

With that we all rolled our eyes and groaned, "We'll think about it." But don't you think he had a point?

UNDERSTAND CONSUMER BEHAVIOR

Learning Objectives

5.1.1 Describe two types of consumers of interest to marketers.

5.1.2 Define consumer wants and needs.

Key Terms

consumer behavior
final consumers
business consumers
need
want

marketing matters

In order to apply the marketing concept effectively, marketers study consumer behavior. There are two basic types of consumers—final consumers who make purchases for their own consumption and business consumers who make purchases for their business or to resell to customers. Both final consumers and business consumers make purchases to satisfy wants and needs. By understanding the reasons consumers buy and the needs and wants they are attempting to satisfy, business marketers can make sure their products and services match what consumers are looking for.

essential question

Why do marketers need to understand the behavior consumers use to satisfy wants and needs?

5.1.1 ▶ Consumer Behavior

Marketing begins with customers. This is key to understanding the discipline, because without customers, there is no business. Marketers must understand their customers' buying behavior. They must continually consider consumers' wants and needs as they plan and implement their marketing strategies. The study of consumers and how they make their consumption decisions is called **consumer behavior**. This field of study explores factors that influence how people purchase and use products and services.

Why do marketers need to understand the behavior of their customers?

© michaeljung/Shutterstock.com.

Marketers analyze customer needs in several ways and use the information to make wise marketing decisions. To do this they need to understand the two types of consumers: final consumers and business consumers.

Final Consumers

Final consumers buy products or services for personal use. The traditional view of a consumer is someone who enters a retail environment, locates and purchases a product, takes it home, and then uses the product. Final consumers gather information about products and services and make purchases in many different ways. These include going to a retail store or using the Internet or mobile apps or other purchasing methods. When you go to a local store to purchase a notebook for your marketing class, you are a final consumer. Family members taking a trip to a regional shopping center are final consumers. A homeowner contracting with a landscaping service to provide monthly lawn maintenance, and a photography buff searching the Internet for a new camera lens are both final consumers.

*Want to know more about what is trending with this topic? Click on **Lesson 5.1, Global Marketing,** in your MindTap.*

Connect to
Mind Tap

Business Consumers

Business consumers, on the other hand, do not make purchases for personal use. **Business consumers** buy goods and services to resell or use in producing and marketing other goods and services. An example of a business consumer is the manufacturer of the notebook you purchased. The manufacturer buys paper, glue, ink, wire, and other materials to produce the notebook. It will purchase other supplies it needs to package, store, ship, and promote its products. It will also purchase the office supplies needed to run the business. When a manufacturer purchases material to produce products it will sell to its customers, it is a business consumer.

> **CHECKPOINT**
> *What types of consumers buy products or services for personal use?*

WORKING IN TEAMS

Form a team and identify 10 products and services that final consumers typically use. Now review each product and service on the list and discuss whether it could be used by a business consumer. As a team, identify similarities and differences in how the products and services would be marketed to each of the groups.

© Iakov Filimonov/Shutterstock.com.

What types of materials and supplies does a business that makes and sells artisan bread need to purchase?

All consumers have wants and needs. A **need** is anything that you require to live. Needs are considered the root of all human behavior and rise from a lack of something in the consumer. When you are hungry, you need food. When you are thirsty, you need something to drink. When you are lonely, you need companionship.

A **want** is a culturally defined way to fulfill that need. When you are hungry, you need food, but you want a pizza. When you are thirsty, you need something to drink, but you want orange juice. When you are lonely, you need companionship, but you want to play video games with your friends. Often, the products and services you purchase to satisfy wants are not essential for living but are important for maintaining your lifestyle.

Hierarchy of Needs

Marketers rely on Abraham Maslow's classic work on motivation when studying human needs. Maslow, a psychologist, identified five areas of needs that people have (**Figure 5-1**). They are physiological, security, social, esteem, and self-actualization needs.

Maslow believed that these groups of needs are satisfied in a hierarchy and that other needs become important as a person satisfies the needs at each level. Everyone must satisfy physiological needs. You must eat, sleep, and breathe to exist. After these needs are generally satisfied, you can start to satisfy security needs. Although it is important to be secure, it is only important to be secure after you have satisfied your physiological needs. At the next level, social needs are certainly important, but only after you meet physiological and security needs.

Gaining respect and recognition from others satisfies esteem needs. Running for student council might be an attempt to satisfy esteem needs. The need for self-actualization usually involves intellectual growth, creativity, and accomplishment. Attending college or taking music lessons also might satisfy self-actualization needs.

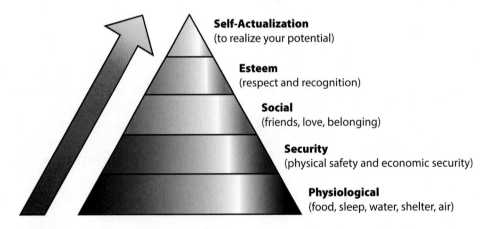

Self-Actualization
(to realize your potential)

Esteem
(respect and recognition)

Social
(friends, love, belonging)

Security
(physical safety and economic security)

Physiological
(food, sleep, water, shelter, air)

FIGURE 5-1 Maslow's hierarchy of needs illustrates the progression people follow in satisfying needs.

Different People, Different Levels

Marketers must recognize that people are at different levels on the needs hierarchy. Some people focus on security needs while others, on esteem needs.

Housing provides a good example of how consumers' needs differ. The physiological need for housing is served by a home that provides protection from the weather. A house that is in a fairly safe neighborhood and has a security system would satisfy the need for security. For a family with young children, a house that is in a neighborhood with lots of young families might satisfy social needs. A house might satisfy esteem needs if it is well maintained and the yard is landscaped. Self-actualization needs might be satisfied when the owner designs or builds the home.

CHECKPOINT
What are the five levels of Maslow's hierarchy of needs?

5.1 ASSESSMENT

What Have You Learned?

1. What is consumer behavior? [5.1.1]
2. Which type of consumer buys goods and services to resell or use in producing and marketing other goods and services? [5.1.1]
3. Explain the difference between needs and wants. [5.1.2]
4. Which category of need in Maslow's hierarchy must be fulfilled first? [5.1.2]

Make Academic Connections

1. **Visual Art**   Use old magazines and newspapers to locate and clip pictures that represent each level of Maslow's hierarchy of needs. Use them to create a poster or other visual that illustrates the hierarchy in the correct order of needs. [5.1.2]
2. **Math**   A building supply store sells to business and final consumers. Last month the average sale to businesses was $856.08, and the average sale to final consumers was $43.95. There were 128 business customers averaging 5 purchases during the month, and 2,593 final customers that averaged 2.3 purchases per month. Calculate the total monthly sales for each customer type, the overall total monthly sales, and the percentage of total sales for each customer category. [5.1.2]

Connect to ◇DECA

Build your Portfolio

Your advertising team must develop two 30-second radio advertisements for a new hybrid SUV on the market. The first should appeal to consumers' need for an economical vehicle. The second should appeal to their self-esteem needs. Record the advertisements and present them to your teacher (judge). [5.1.1]

WHAT MOTIVATES BUYERS?

Learning Objectives

5.2.1   Identify the three categories of buying motives.

5.2.2   Describe the five steps of the consumer decision-making process.

Key Terms

motivation
buying motives
emotional motives
rational motives

patronage motives
buying behavior
consumer decision-making process

marketing matters

People have motives for the purchases they make. Motives can be emotional or quite rationale. Often consumers don't think consciously about what motivates their decisions, but every decision they make is influenced by many factors. Whatever the motivation, the consumer decision-making process generally follows a series of steps. Sometimes those steps are completed quickly with little consideration. At other times a long, thoughtful process is needed. Marketers must understand what motivates consumers and their decision making in order to be an effective influence in the final decision.

essential question

How do the buying motives influence the way consumers make purchase decisions and the types of purchases they make?

5.2.1 ▶ Motivation

All of your actions are influenced by motivation. **Motivation** is the set of positive or negative factors that direct your individual behavior. You have both short- and long-term motivation. You are motivated to develop the knowledge and skills needed for a good career and salary. You also are motivated by happiness and enjoyment.

When you wake up in the morning, you may be motivated to stay in bed for another hour of sleep. But you also recognize that you should get out of bed and prepare for school. The motivation for that choice may be the chance to socialize with friends. You also have the longer-term motivation to complete the courses needed for your high school diploma, which will lead to college, a job, and your long-term career goals. The importance of the influences will determine the choices you make each day.

Motivation is an important factor in your behavior as a consumer. Your decisions to spend money on products and services are influenced by what marketers call buying motives. **Buying motives** are the reasons that you buy. There are three categories of buying motives that drive consumers to purchase products or services or respond to ideas: emotional motives, rational motives, and patronage motives.

Emotional Motives

Emotional motives are reasons to purchase based on feelings and emotions. Emotional motivation is based upon the principle that consumers wish to seek pleasure and avoid pain. Forces of love, affection, passion, and happiness are emotions that consumers like to have because they bring them pleasure. Guilt, fear, or anxiety are emotions that consumers want to avoid. Such emotions often compel consumers to acquire products that will help them attain or avoid those emotions.

What would motivate you to continue your education and obtain a college degree?

Marketers realize that a person's emotional motives are frequently very strong and can have an important influence on decisions and behavior. For example, Hallmark advertisements encourage you to buy greeting cards based on the emotions of love and affection. Because of your feelings for others close to you or because of a special event such as Mother's Day, a birthday, or a friend's illness, you want to express your feelings with a card and a short note.

Fear also is an emotional motivator that marketers may use to encourage consumers to buy products. People who buy security systems for their home or automobile are motivated by the fear of having their home burglarized or their vehicle stolen. Organic food marketers appeal to the fear of pesticides and other dangers in our food supply. Due to illnesses and deaths caused by tainted meats and vegetables in recent history, consumer motivation to make sure food purchases are safe to eat has increased. Marketers understand emotional motivation and use it to plan marketing mixes that appeal to those motives.

Rational Motives

Emotional motivation is not always appropriate or effective. Consumer behavior also can be influenced by rational motivation. **Rational motives** are reasons to buy based on facts or logic.

Rational motives include factors such as saving time or money or obtaining the highest quality or greatest value. Rational buying motives may influence many purchases, but they are especially important for many expensive purchases. Even if emotions play a role in your purchase of a house or car or your selection of a college, you will still want to consider the quality and value of your choice.

How do you decide to buy a new computer system? Although your current computer may still work, you may want a more powerful and faster operating system, upgraded sound or graphics cards, a larger monitor with touchscreen capability, or the latest software and Internet security. These attributes all affect the functioning of the computer and your satisfaction with its use.

Automobile purchases can be emotional but usually include a number of rational motives. As a prospective owner, you may consider the quality history of the car, the service and repair record of the dealership, and the maintenance costs. Fuel economy versus engine size may be an important factor. Do you want to purchase the additional safety options or the extended warranty? All of these are a part of the rational decision making that goes into most automobile purchases. But vehicle purchases also can be influenced by your emotions when you catch sight of that new convertible!

Business consumers also have both emotional and rational motives. However, they try to avoid basing purchases on emotions because it does not make good business sense. The emotions of fear, friendship, and enjoyment may result in poor purchase decisions for a business if those emotions are allowed to influence the process.

Instead, the business will evaluate choices, looking for the best price, fastest delivery, most favorable credit terms, and highest-quality products. Those are all rational motives.

Patronage Motives

The third type of buying motivation, **patronage motives**, are based on loyalty. Patronage motives encourage consumers to purchase from a particular business or to buy a particular brand.

Loyalty is influenced by positive previous experiences or a close identification with the product or business. Consumers

> *Want to know more about what is trending with this topic? Click on Lesson 5.2, Marketing Decisions, in your MindTap.*

Connect to
MindTap

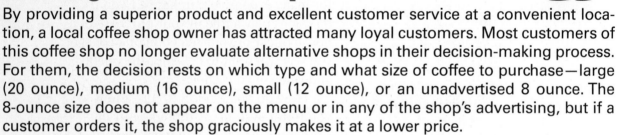

MARKETING COMMUNICATION

Deciding on Your Next Cup

By providing a superior product and excellent customer service at a convenient location, a local coffee shop owner has attracted many loyal customers. Most customers of this coffee shop no longer evaluate alternative shops in their decision-making process. For them, the decision rests on which type and what size of coffee to purchase—large (20 ounce), medium (16 ounce), small (12 ounce), or an unadvertised 8 ounce. The 8-ounce size does not appear on the menu or in any of the shop's advertising, but if a customer orders it, the shop graciously makes it at a lower price.

The shop recently announced it will be raising prices an average of 1 percent on all beverages. This increase is expected to boost profits by 11 percent. However, the increase will not affect all sizes across the menu. It affects only about a third of the beverages, mostly the lower-priced ones that have a lower profit margin. The owner justifies the price increase by citing an increase in commodity prices. Although prices are already relatively high, the shop owner believes that demand will remain high as customers regard "premium" coffee as an affordable luxury.

Think Critically

1. Why might the shop choose not to advertise or promote its smallest and least-expensive beverages?
2. Why would the shop increase its prices only on lower-priced drinks?
3. Why would the shop cite an increase in commodity prices as a reason for price increases?

develop loyalty for various reasons. They might like the low prices, high quality, friendly staff, great customer service, or convenient location. They may be loyal because it is a business or brand name their family has used for years and years. People are often loyal to a local or neighborhood business. Some identify with the people who work in the business, who are featured in advertising for the product, or who appear to share their beliefs and values.

Business consumers also may be influenced by patronage motives. They may return to the same business time after time to purchase raw materials and supplies because they have been satisfied with the quality and service in the past. They may prefer a local supplier rather than risk working with a company located in another state or country. The important point to remember is that people who are motivated by patronage are very loyal to the product, service, or brand. Businesses encourage and cultivate patronage motives so that customers are less likely to consider products of their competitors.

 CHECKPOINT
Describe the three different categories of buying motives.

5.2.2 ▶ The Consumer Decision-Making Process

To help customers make good decisions, marketers need to understand buying behavior. **Buying behavior** refers to the processes consumers use and the actions they take when they purchase services and products. When marketers understand the process customers go through when selecting goods or services, they help them make better decisions.

A consumer often goes through five steps when making a purchase decision, as shown in **Figure 5-2**. The **consumer decision-making process** is the process by which consumers collect and analyze information to make choices among alternatives. Decision making, as it applies to a specific purchase, moves through the following steps: problem recognition, information search, alternative evaluation, purchase, and postpurchase evaluation.

You may not address every step in the process for every buying decision you make, however. Sometimes, you might recognize a problem and automatically know what you will purchase. Other times,

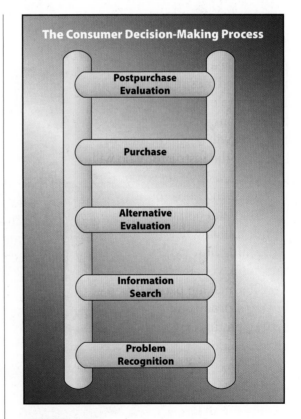

FIGURE 5-2 Consumers follow a series of steps when making purchase decisions.

you may decide not to purchase anything as your information search reveals the cost is too high. Or, instead of purchasing yourself, you might drop a hint to a parent or friend to get the item for you as a birthday gift.

The strength of the need and the urgency to satisfy the need are also important. You have many needs at any given time, but some become strong and even urgent at particular times. If you haven't eaten for most of the day, you will likely be quite hungry and look for food choices. If you have been working very hard for some time, you may try to identify ways you can relax and enjoy yourself. When a need is strong or urgent, it may result in a much faster decision with fewer choices considered. When a need is not as strong or urgent, you may delay the decision-making process or take more time to complete the steps.

1. Problem Recognition

The first step in the decision-making process occurs when you recognize a need, desire, or problem. For example, if playing guitar becomes an important goal, then you will begin the task of choosing the instructor who will give you lessons. Once you recognize the need for artistic outlet and define the way of fulfilling that need as learning how to play the guitar, you are on the decision-making path to buying a product or service, in this case, guitar lessons.

2. Information Search

After identifying a need or problem, you gather information

© 4contrast_dot_com/Shutterstock.com

about alternative solutions. The process you use to identify alternatives depends on your past experience. If the need is one you have satisfied before, then you may be ready to identify choices. With a problem you have not yet encountered, identifying a solution may be more difficult.

Satisfying a hunger need may be relatively easy because you can identify your favorite foods and restaurants, and you know how much money and time you have available. Although the choice will not be the same each time, you usually will be able to identify a few businesses or products that seem appropriate based on your specific needs at the time. If you are in an unfamiliar location or want to try something different, you will need to identify alternatives.

Choosing a guitar teacher is an example of a problem you have not yet encountered. It is not likely you have gone through that decision-making process. After you recognize the need to learn to play the guitar, you must find a way to accomplish that goal, including locating a good teacher or finding aids to help you teach yourself. You may ask your friends for recommendations. You might surf the Internet, ask for recommendations from a local music store, check with a music teacher at school, or phone the music department of a local college. Your goal is to identify choices of instructors, so you can choose the one that best fits your level of experience, schedule, and resources.

When identifying alternatives, you also need to gather information about each alternative. The type and amount of information to gather will depend on what information is readily available, the amount of time you have to gather information, and the importance of the need.

You may not know what information is important at the time you are identifying alternatives. You may gather some initial information only to learn later that you do not have the type or amount you need. You may rely on others to help you determine the information you need if you are not well informed about the problem or have no experience with it. Over time, you will become more effective in your information search.

3. Evaluate Alternatives

After gathering information, you evaluate the various alternatives to determine which is best. Sometimes this involves summarizing the information, comparing the pros and cons of each choice, making tradeoffs between price and various options, and ranking the alternatives. Evaluating guitar instructors might involve determining whom you can afford, what hours and locations the instructor is available, how you will get to the lesson, and the reputation of each instructor. Based on these evaluations, you will make a decision.

You may decide you do not have adequate information to make a decision, that you do not have the needed resources to make a purchase, or that your need is not strong enough to justify the cost compared to other important needs. Depending on that information, you may decide to forgo satisfying the need or to continue gathering and evaluating information. You may even decide to consider additional alternatives. For instance, you may decide to forego a teacher altogether in favor of a computer game like Rocksmith that teaches guitar using a video game system or PC.

4. Purchase

You will make the purchase if a suitable choice is available that appears to satisfy the need or solve the problem and that you can afford. The purchase step involves agreeing with the business selling the product on what you will buy, the price, payment method, and how you will obtain the product or service. The purchase decision involves agreement on the entire marketing mix.

In the case of your decision to take guitar lessons, you may choose to take lessons from a retired professor from the local university who comes highly recommended by several of your friends. She will give you a half-hour lesson each Saturday morning at your home at a price of $50 per lesson. You can pay cash each time, or you can pay for a full month of lessons in advance for a savings of $5 per lesson. You may also supplement what the teacher provides you with the purchase of software that will help you with your lessons.

5. Postpurchase Evaluation

Each time you make a purchase and use the product or service, you will begin to realize whether it met the need or solved the problem. You will either be satisfied or dissatisfied with the purchase. After you have had several guitar lessons, can play some simple songs, have worked with the instructor, and know how the lessons fit into your schedule, you will have a better idea of whether you are committed to the time and effort required to learn to play the guitar well. If you are satisfied with your lessons and your decision, you will probably continue and may even recommend your instructor to your family and friends. If you are not satisfied, you will probably find a new instructor or quit taking lessons altogether.

In making your postpurchase evaluation, you will determine whether the need or want was as important as you originally believed. You may decide the need was not important enough to warrant the effort and expense, so you will not give it as much attention the next time it arises. You may decide the need was important to you, but the choice you made is not providing the satisfaction you believed it would. In that case, you will usually not make the same decision again. Instead, you will learn from your experience. The next time you recognize the same need or encounter a similar problem, you will choose a different alternative and evaluate the information more carefully.

Marketers pay attention to post-purchase satisfaction to make sure that customers are satisfied with their purchase and will become regular customers. Toll-free telephone numbers, email, or live chat alternatives with customer service departments let consumers easily obtain help, ask questions, or express concerns. The goal is to reassure customers that they made the right choice, resolve any customer problems and concerns immediately, and increase customer satisfaction.

> **CHECKPOINT**
> *What are the five steps of consumer decision making?*

5.2 ASSESSMENT

What Have You Learned?

1. What are the three categories of buying motives that drive consumers to purchase products or services or respond to ideas? [5.2.1]

2. What type of buying motives are based on feelings? [5.2.1]

3. What is the consumer decision-making process? [5.2.2]

4. Why are marketers concerned with consumers' postpurchase evaluation of the products they purchase? [5.2.2]

Make Academic Connections

1. **Psychology** Work with a team to prepare a bulletin board display that demonstrates the use of the three types of buying motives by businesses. Provide examples of products and services that are effectively marketed using emotional, rational, and patronage motives. [5.2.1]

2. **Language Arts** Compose a fictional story (humorous, mystery, or romance) about a person who encounters a major problem and solves that problem through the purchase and use of a product. Build the story around each of the steps of the consumer decision-making process. [5.2.2]

Connect to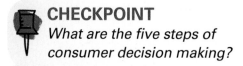

> Build your Portfolio

Your marketing research team has been identifying sources of information that students use most often when making purchase decisions. Prepare a two- to four-question survey and distribute it to 15 students in your school. Analyze the results and develop a three-minute oral presentation of your results with two supporting charts or graphs. Present the report to your teacher (judge) and be prepared to answer questions. [5.2.2]

5.3 INFLUENCE CONSUMER DECISIONS

Learning Objectives

5.3.1 Describe important influences on the consumer decision-making process.

5.3.2 Explain how consumers and businesses use each of the three types of decision making.

Key Terms

personal identity
personality
attitude
self-concept

lifestyle
culture
reference group

marketing matters

Making purchase decisions is a complicated process. It is not as simple as seeing a product and deciding to buy it. Many factors influence consumers' buying decisions, including individual personality characteristics and personal image, the social and cultural environment of the consumer, and the influence of others. How and which of those influences affect decisions depends on the consumer's experience with the product or service and whether the consumer views the purchase decision as routine or complex. If marketers are able to analyze and understand the factors influencing purchase decisions for their products, they can make decisions that influence and support their prospective customers.

essential question

What factors influence a consumer's decision to buy? How do those factors affect the marketing mix a business uses?

5.3.1 ▶ Influences on Buying Decisions

To remain profitable, businesses must provide customers with products and services that meet their wants and needs. Knowing what influences a customer's buying decision is a key part of implementing the marketing concept. By understanding what motivates and influences customer purchases, businesses are able to provide products and services at the right place and time. Many internal and external factors influence purchase decisions. Two important factors are individual characteristics and the cultural and social environment.

Individual Characteristics

Each consumer is different. Even though a person is a member of a family, community, and other personal, social, and career groups and organizations, a person's identity is a major influence on decisions and actions. **Personal identity** consists of the characteristics that make a person unique. Important factors that make up personal identity include personality, gender, ethnicity, and age.

PERSONALITY   The first individual characteristic that influences buying behavior is personality. **Personality** is a pattern of emotions and behaviors that define an individual. How would you describe your personality? Are you outgoing, serious, or shy? People often express their personality in the products and services they choose, including their clothing, hobbies, and social activities. Personality also often is factor in decisions about whether to save money for the future or spend it on immediate needs.

Personalities influence buying decisions because everyone has individual preferences based on attitude, self-concept, and lifestyle choices. **Attitude** is a frame of mind developed from a person's values, beliefs, and feelings. You may already have formed attitudes about the value of education, the use of credit, or the need for conservation that shape your purchasing decisions. **Self-concept** is an individual's belief about his or her identity, image, and capabilities. **Lifestyle** is the way a person lives as reflected by material goods, activities, and relationships. Decisions about type and location of jobs, housing, family size, leisure activities, and community involvement are all a part of a person's lifestyle.

GENDER   An individual's gender influences many decisions and actions. Dress, grooming, social relationships and activities, family roles, and career choices tend to differ for men and women. Although gender roles and influences are changing, marketers identify differences in the product and service choices of each gender.

ETHNICITY   A set of characteristics uniting a group based on ancestry, country of origin, language, and traditions is known as *ethnicity*. The impact of ethnicity on a person's attitudes and actions varies based on individual identity and the views and values of others. Some individuals have a strong ethnic identification and demonstrate it in many lifestyle choices including dress, social activities, and food choices, among other factors.

AGE   A person's age has a major influence on consumer behavior. The age of a person generally indicates the types of products and services he or she will be interested in and the brands and features that are important. The entertainment industry often develops television shows, movies, and music to a specific age group. Not only are the shows, movies, and music different for every generation, but the accompanying advertising messages and media differ as well.

© ilyasadovski/Shutterstock.com.

How do you express your personality in the products and services you choose?

Cultural and Social Environment

The second important influence on a person's buying decisions is their cultural and social environment. **Culture** is the history, beliefs, customs, and traditions of a group. A group's culture has a strong influence on individual values and behaviors. Traditionally, culture has been defined by the activities, relationships, and institutions shared by a group of people over many generations. If the culture places a high value on families, its members spend a great deal of time on family activities, and family members exert a strong influence on individual choices and decisions. In other cultures, individual independence is valued, and young people are prepared and encouraged to take personal responsibility for important decisions at an early age.

Today, in the United States and some other parts of the world, culture is less important than social environment to many people due to the mobility of people and increasing diversity. A *social environment* is made up of the groups and organizations that people live and interact with on a regular basis. It has an influence on the values and behaviors of the people who are members of the group or organization.

Social environment may be defined by a community, a neighborhood, or even a social or business organization. Your school is a part of your social environment. In many parts of the United States, high school students have a car at their disposal. In other areas, high school students do not even expect to get a driver's license, much less own a car.

Some of the strongest influences on individual choices and behaviors are drawn from a person's reference groups. A **reference group** is a group of people or an organization that an individual admires, identifies with, and wants to be a part of. Reference groups might be clubs, social or civic organizations, business groups, or even informal groups of peers and others who have characteristics or lifestyles to which individuals aspire. If you are currently a member of a reference group or if you want to identify with a group in which you are not a member, you will shape your behavior and your image around what you believe the group expects. Marketing that connects consumers with the images and actions of their reference group and encourages them to "join the group" by purchasing and using the products and services preferred by group members is often very effective.

Want to know more about marketing in the information age? Click on **Lesson 5.3, Digital Marketing,** *in your MindTap.*

Connect to MindTap

CHECKPOINT
What are the four factors that make up personal identity?

© dotshock/Shutterstock.com.

Consumers spend varying amounts of time and consider different factors when making decisions. It takes different decision-making skills to buy toothpaste than it does to borrow money to buy a house. The three types of decision making are routine, limited, and extensive decision making (**Figure 5-3**).

Routine Decision Making

Routine decision making is used for purchases that are made frequently and do not require much thought. For routine purchases, the consumer is familiar with the products available, often chooses the same brand, or can make an easy substitution if the usual choice is not available.

Food and snacks, personal supplies, and basic necessities are most often purchased using routine decision making. You buy them regularly when you know you will need them or when you run out. You either choose your favorite brand if you have a preference or choose among two or three brands if you view them as similar. In that case you will buy the one that is most convenient or has the lowest price at the time. You basically give very little thought to the purchase because it has become a part of your routine.

Businesses use routine decision making when making regular purchases such as operating supplies or standardized raw materials needed for the production process. The business will often use one supplier and will reorder from that company whenever necessary. The business may have a backup supplier to ensure a reliable supply.

Limited Decision Making

Limited decision making takes more time than routine decision making. Often, limited decision making is associated with a product that is more expensive or is purchased less frequently. When you go to the mall to buy a pair of jeans, you might try on several styles, compare prices, and consider the color and feel of the fabrics of a few selections before you make a decision. This is an example of limited decision making. You will usually identify and complete a reasonable comparison and evaluate a few alternatives before making a decision. You are not absolutely certain of the best choice, but you generally know what you are looking for and the important factors that will influence your decision.

However, limited decision making does not apply to more expensive items. Something as simple as buying a soft drink can involve limited decision making. If you are a Coke drinker and the store is out of Coke, what do you do? You may consider some other flavor choices that are Coke products, or you may decide that Pepsi is a reasonable alternative. Or you might decide to go to a different store. Choosing a movie for an evening's entertainment with friends is another example of limited decision making. You may already have a preferred movie and theater, so the decision is routine. However, often you will spend time on the Internet reviewing the new releases and checking theatre times and locations before making the final decision.

Businesses use limited decision making for many purchases, such as office equipment, furniture,

© pikselstock/Shutterstock.com.

and even selecting a parcel delivery service. The business knows generally what it needs, but it sees value in comparing several alternatives to determine if there are price or quality differences. Even for routine purchases, such as office supplies, limited decision making might be used if a new supplier offers substantially lower prices that the purchasing agent needs to evaluate or if a change in equipment or procedures requires the purchase of a new product that the current supplier does not carry.

Extensive Decision Making

The third type of decision making is extensive decision making. Extensive decision making occurs when the consumer methodically goes through all five steps of the decision-making process. Normally, customers use extensive decision making for expensive purchases such as an automobile, home, or family vacation. Consumers do not make the decision lightly. They spend time and effort evaluating alternatives and arriving at a decision. They carefully review their needs and match them with the best choice possible. Differences among choices may not be evident or may involve a number of factors that consumers need to carefully analyze in order for them to be comfortable with the decision.

Extensive decision making is used in business for first-time purchases or those that involve a large investment. Perhaps a business needs a new computer system or several new delivery vehicles. The purchasing agent will conduct an extensive search for the best deal before reaching a purchase decision. The company may require suppliers to prepare a written proposal with complete descriptions of the product. Those in

TYPES OF DECISION MAKING		
Type	**Used for**	**Example Products**
Routine	Purchases made frequently that do not require much thought.	Food and snacks Toothpaste
Limited	Products that are more expensive or not purchased frequently.	Clothing Entertainment options
Extensive	Expensive, significant, or complicated purchases. Consumer goes through all five steps of the decision-making process.	Electronic devices Automobile Vacation

FIGURE 5-3 Consumers use three types of decision making when faced with a purchase decision.

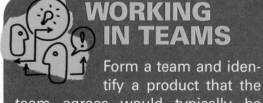

WORKING IN TEAMS

Form a team and identify a product that the team agrees would typically be purchased using each of the three types of decision making. Now compare where each product is usually purchased, what factors are most important in deciding what to purchase, and what information consumers need in order to decide what product or brand to purchase.

the business who have special expertise with the particular product will review the proposals. Extensive negotiations may occur with the vendors before a final decision is made.

Marketers' Role in Decision Making

Why do marketers need to understand the decision-making process prospective customers use? Marketers want to match their products and services to the needs and expectations of customers. They want to be able to provide the information customers want in order to make the best choice. If consumers choose a product using routine decision making, they do not want to be overwhelmed with information. On the other hand, if they are making a difficult choice using extensive decision making, they will want more information related to the factors they view as most important.

Marketers want the opportunity to explain the benefits of their products and services and to demonstrate how they can satisfy consumer needs. By studying consumers, businesses should be able to develop products and services that match the needs and expectations of their

MATH IN MARKETING

Breakeven Point

The breakeven point is the number of unit sales a company must make to cover the expenses of a venture. Below the breakeven point, expenses exceed revenues, and a company will lose money. At the breakeven point, sales will exactly cover all expenses. Once the breakeven point is exceeded, a company will begin to make a profit.

To calculate the breakeven point, you need to know the total fixed cost of a venture, the selling price per unit, and the variable cost per unit of a good or service. The breakeven point is the total fixed cost divided by the difference between the selling price and the variable cost per unit.

$$\text{Breakeven point} = \frac{\text{Total fixed cost}}{\text{Per unit price} - \text{per unit cost}}$$

For example, a clothing store at the mall wants to print and distribute flyers advertising its new line of sweaters. The fixed cost of the flyers is $2,400. The selling price of each sweater is $50, and the variable cost of each sweater is $10. The breakeven point for the flyer is 60 sweaters.

$$\frac{\$2,400}{\$50 - \$10} = \frac{\$2,400}{\$40} = 60$$

If the store sells fewer than 60 sweaters, the store will lose money on the flyer. If it sells exactly 60 sweaters, the cost of the flyer will be covered exactly. If it sells more than 60 sweaters, the store will make a profit.

Do the Math

1. At the same clothing store, a display unit for jeans costs $1,800. If the jeans sell for $45 with a variable cost of $9, what is the breakeven point for the display?

2. What would be the breakeven point if the store installs a second $1,800 display unit for a different brand of jeans that sell for $54 with a variable cost of $18 each?

customers. When those customers are taking the time to consider alternatives, marketers have the opportunity to explain their products through appropriate communication channels. The customer may want only a limited amount of information or may expect extensive communication with the business. Without the needed information, the customer will likely move on to another choice. On the other hand, if customers routinely buy the same thing because they are brand loyal, the business will focus on making the product available and reminding customers of the value of the brand.

 CHECKPOINT
Rank the types of decision making according to the time and research consumers typically devote to each type.

5.3 ASSESSMENT

What Have You Learned?

1. Name the four factors that make up your personal identity. [5.3.1]

2. What is a frame of mind developed from a person's values, beliefs, and feelings? [5.3.1]

3. Define reference group. [5.3.1]

4. What kind of decision making do consumers use when they are familiar with the products available, often choose the same brand, or can make an easy substitution if the usual choice is not available? [5.3.2]

5. With what kind of decision making do marketers have the best opportunity to explain the benefits of their products and services and how they can satisfy consumer needs? [5.3.2]

Make Academic Connections

1. **Sociology**   Interview a parent, older relative, or leader of a community cultural organization about the influence culture or ethnicity has had on his or her life. Write a summary of the interview. Compare the person's views and attitudes with your own and describe the differences and similarities. [5.3.1]

2. **Technology**   Use the Internet to locate detailed information on three different brands of a digital camera. Prepare a table that compares the three brands based on at least five features, noting differences and similarities among the brands. Also identify the price of each brand. Based on the analysis, which brand would you choose? Why? [5.3.2]

Connect to ◇DECA.

Build your Portfolio

A shoe manufacturer is introducing a new moderately priced athletic shoe targeted at females between the ages of 12 and 15. The company wants to use a strong reference group appeal to promote the shoe. Develop a unique brand name and sketch a simple print advertisement to introduce the shoe. Make sure the reference group appeal is evident in the ad. Present your ideas to your teacher (judge) and explain why you think the advertisement will be effective. [5.3.1]

Connect to MindTap

Analyze a case study that focuses on chapter concepts. Click on **Chapter 5, Case Study,** *in your MindTap.*

Planning a Career In...
CUSTOMER SERVICE

Did you ever have a question about a product that required a call for help to a company's toll-free number? Do you use the "live chat" feature for help when ordering products online? Has your family ever tried to get an inaccurate charge on a credit card bill adjusted?

Most corporations employ customer service representatives to answer product questions, resolve customer issues, and follow up with purchasers to make sure they are satisfied with the company's products. Customer service personnel may meet customers in person or may respond by telephone, email, or even live chat sessions on a computer.

Job Titles

- Customer Care Representative
- Bilingual Financial Care Representative
- Account Coordinator
- Online Operations Associate
- Customer Support Administrator
- Order Expeditor

Needed Skills

- Most positions require a high-school diploma or equivalent.
- Complex or regulated products may require representatives to have a college degree.
- The ability to remain positive and composed is important when faced with concerned customers and supervisors who monitor some contacts.
- Bilingual skills will increase marketability.

What it's like to work in... Customer Service

As a Customer Service Representative for a hospital billing department, Vanessa often encounters emotionally draining situations. Vanessa just completed a conference call with two insurance companies and the parent of a young cancer patient. Midway through chemotherapy, the parent's insurance carrier changed. New authorizations were required, and a few bills were not paid on time because of the transition. In addition to caring for a very ill child, the exhausted parent had to spend time resolving the insurance issues. Vanessa was able to resolve the insurance issue and devise an affordable payment plan for the overdue bills.

During the afternoon, Vanessa had a conversation with the son of a new elderly patient. The son was trying to determine if his father had coverage for medical care. The changes in government insurance programs for the elderly often lead to confusion about benefits.

What About You?

Do you have the patience and compassion required to assist customers with a variety of questions and problems?

Connect to MindTap

Discover more about the outlook for this career and watch a video about a related career. Click on **Chapter 5, Planning a Career in...** *in your MindTap.*

CHAPTER 5 ASSESSMENT

Review Marketing Concepts

1. Name and describe the two types of consumers that marketers need to understand. [5.1.1]

2. Differentiate consumer wants and needs. Use examples in explaining your answer. [5.1.2]

3. Choose one of the three types of buying motives discussed in the book. With this buying motive in mind, describe how you used it to make a recent purchase. [5.2.1]

4. Think of a major purchase you foresee making in the next year or so. How will you apply the information search step of the five-step consumer decision-making process to this purchase? Examples could be a car, a prom dress, or a college education. [5.2.2]

5. How does personality influence buying behavior? Give an example that relates to either attitude, self-concept, or lifestyle in answering this question. [5.3.1]

6. What is extensive decision making, and when do consumers typically use it? [5.3.2]

Marketing Research and Planning

1. Some products are sold to both business consumers and final consumers. Name at least one business consumer use and one final consumer use for each of the following items: pencil, balloon, rubber band, radio, sofa, all-terrain vehicle, bagel, pesticide, suitcase, blanket. Here is an example: [5.1.1]

Item	Business Use	Final Consumer Use
banana	restaurant	family lunches

2. Marketers strive to capture your attention with advertisements that address meaningful buying motives. Choose an advertisement from each of the following media: magazine, Internet, television, and radio. Select ads that demonstrate each of the three types of buying motives—emotional, rational, and patronage. Use copies of the magazine and Internet ads. Prepare a written description of the television and radio ads. Classify the type of buying motive used in each advertisement. [5.2.1]

3. You are the manager of a new furniture store that is opening in three days. You believe strongly in the marketing concept and want your salespeople to pay attention to customers' needs as they help perform their sales duties. Write an email to them to remind them of the elements of the marketing concept, why it is important, and what they can do to put it into action with each customer. Be sure to use the following words or phrases: customers, buying behavior, consumer decision-making process, needs, wants, buying motives, lifestyle, and extensive decision-making process. [5.1.2, 5.2.1, 5.2.2, 5.3.2]

4. Using Internet news services, find a corporate announcement of a new product or service. Analyze the announcement to identify the personal, cultural, social, and reference group influences to which the product or service appeals. Cite specific language that provides evidence of the appeal being used. [5.3.1]

5. Some consumer advocates believe that marketers use research on consumer motivation and buying behavior to exploit them with emotional appeals and social pressures. What do you think? Is identifying buying motives and using them in a marketing campaign an ethical or unethical practice? Write an essay that takes a position on the ethical question and defend your viewpoint. [5.2.1]

Marketing Management and Decision Making

1. In order to learn more about customers, many organizations use customer feedback cards like the one shown below for a restaurant. The organizations use the information to improve their products and services and increase customer satisfaction.

In an effort to help your school provide better service, work with other students to develop a customer feedback card to give to students at your school. The customer feedback card should be designed to find out from students what they like and dislike about your school. You may wish to ask questions about the curriculum, classes, teachers, atmosphere, spirit, extracurricular activities, grades, homework, facilities, and any other items relevant to your school. Survey at least 15 students.

After the surveys have been completed and collected, use a computer spreadsheet program to record and tabulate the responses. Then determine the mean, median, and mode for each question. (The mean is the average of all the responses to a question. The median is the middle value when all answers are arranged in order. The mode is the response that was given most frequently.) Prepare tables, charts, and graphs to display the survey results. Based on the results, draw several conclusions about student attitudes. Make recommendations for improvements to your school. [5.3.1]

Fine Foods and More Restaurant
We value your opinions and strive to meet your expectations. Tell us how you like us by circling the rating that best represents your view of our restaurant.

WHAT DID YOU THINK OF OUR SERVICE?				
Poor				**Excellent**
Menu	1	2	3	4	5
Portion size	1	2	3	4	5
Atmosphere	1	2	3	4	5
Service	1	2	3	4	5
Cleanliness	1	2	3	4	5
Prices	1	2	3	4	5

Thank you for sharing your views with us!

---

2. Electricity generated through solar energy is fast becoming a reliable alternative for homeowners. Assume you are a marketing specialist for a cellular telephone company that sells solar panels for homes. Identify a target market for the solar panels. Identify important needs, personal identity characteristics, and the personal and social influences for the prospective customers. Then describe the consumer decision-making process customers would follow and the buying motives to which you would appeal. Use a computer to design a one-page brochure you would use to introduce the solar panels to the target market. [5.1.2, 5.2.1, 5.3.1]

Let's Start a Band! Follow-Up Discussion

Work in small teams to discuss the question posed at the end of the opening vignette. Discuss what motivates the band's audience to attend its performances. How important is customer satisfaction to retaining the audience?

Build Your Marketing Plan

In this chapter you learned about the importance of understanding the behavior of current and potential customers. You will now apply this learning to the development of your marketing plan. To access the chapter-specific tools that you will need to complete this activity, please navigate to Chapter 5 ➔ Build Your Marketing Plan in MindTap. Alternatively, you can access these tools online at NGLSync. Please visit www.nglsync.cengage.com, and search for the companion website that accompanies this book by entering the ISBN, author, or title. Once you locate this companion website, navigate to Build Your Marketing Plan ➔ Chapter 5.

Automotive Services Marketing Series Event

Build your Portfolio

Quick Stop is a busy gas station/convenience store. You are the assistant manager for this popular store. The pumps that allow customers to pay with credit cards are very popular. Unfortunately, many of those pumps need repair because they do not read the credit cards correctly, and/or they do not give the customer a receipt.

Recently, you have listened to many angry customers complain about high gas prices. Customers become increasingly frustrated when they have to go inside the store/station to pay for or obtain a receipt for their gas purchase or when pumps are covered with plastic bags, indicating that they are not operational. Some customers have even indicated that they will take their business to a competitor.

Your task is two-fold: (1) You must convince the owner of the station to repair the gas pumps immediately, and (2) you must create a special promotion to bring back loyal customers to your service station. You will present your proposal to the owner of the service station.

Description of the Proposal Write down the main points that you want to emphasize to the owner of the service station.

Description of Promotion Plan Outline your plan for a promotion to keep loyal customers coming to your service station. Remember, they are upset about high gas prices, problems with the "pay at the pump" service, and inoperable gas pumps.

Role Play Translate what you have learned into effective, efficient, and spontaneous action, demonstrated in a role play.

Performance Indicators Evaluated

- Explain the nature and scope of the product/service management function. (Product/Service Management)
- Explain the nature of positive customer relations. (Emotional Intelligence)
- Evaluate the customer experience. (Product/Service Management)
- Coordinate activities in the promotional mix (Marketing Communications)

Go to the DECA website for more detailed information. **www.deca.org**

Think Critically

1. Why must self-service stations carefully maintain their pumps?

2. What type of incentive would be good for loyal customers of the service station?

3. How will improved customer service affect the number of employees needed to work each shift at the service station?

4. How do rising gas prices lead to customer dissatisfaction at a service station?

CHAPTER 6

MARKETING INFORMATION AND RESEARCH

6.1 Understand the Need for Marketing Information

6.2 Find and Manage Marketing Information

6.3 Use Marketing Research

6.4 Collect Primary Data

See how effective advertising leads to successful marketing strategies.
Click on Chapter 6, Visual Focus, in your MindTap.

Let's Start a Band!

> "Technology is going to play a huge part in tomorrow's music business. And the companies that will win are going to be the most equipped to understand how to use data to further an artist's career."
>
> – *Troy Carter, CEO, Atom Factory (entertainment and arts management company)*

We all agreed we need a better understanding of our audience.

Jake suggested that the band keep a record of all its performances, tracking information like venue, time, day of the week, audience estimates, and admission price.

Layla added, "I'm not sure just how to do it, but after each performance we should take note of the audience's response to both our overall performance and to specific sets and songs."

Naomi chimed in, "I agree. It should help us decide how to organize the sets and what songs to set aside."

"It would also help us judge how successful our experiments with the performance are," commented Edwardo.

Not everyone was entirely convinced. Gael seemed disinterested while Malik was a bit hesitant saying, "I'll go along with this, but it sounds too scientific to me." He continued, "When I'm playing, I can feel what the audience responds to. I think this might be a big waste of time. Music is about emotion. This isn't."

I'm not sure where I stand. I realize that we can't always go by our gut, but it's music. It's feelings and emotions. How would you handle this?

6.1 UNDERSTAND THE NEED FOR MARKETING INFORMATION

Learning Objectives

6.1.1 Explain the importance of information in making marketing decisions.

6.1.2 Describe the categories of information needed by marketers.

Key Term

discretionary purchases

marketing matters

The marketing concept is based on satisfying customer needs, so it is essential for a business to know and understand prospective customers. When implementing the marketing concept, businesses start with information about customers, their needs, attitudes, and expectations. Marketers can use the information to confidently select the markets they will serve and plan effective marketing mixes tailored to those customers.

 essential question

How can marketers benefit by gathering and understanding information about the similarities and differences in needs and purchase behavior of individual customers?

6.1.1 ▶ Start with Information

When a business follows the marketing concept, it needs information about the market before it can start the marketing planning process. Competitive and economic factors facing businesses today increase the need to gather and study information. Marketers recognize that an understanding of consumers, expanding choices, competition, and the global marketplace will help them make better decisions.

Consumer Differences

Most businesses recognize that consumers have very different needs and wants and likely view product and service choices quite differently. Businesses know that if they are to meet the specific needs and expectations of consumers, they will need detailed and specific information about them. They must be able to determine the similarities and differences among market segments and decide how they can best meet the unique needs and wants of those segments.

Expanding Choices

Customer needs are changing, and so are the choices customers make to satisfy those needs. Consumers are able to satisfy their basic needs much more easily than they could in the past. They have moved beyond satisfying their basic needs and are devoting more resources to satisfying their wants by making discretionary purchases. **Discretionary purchases** are not essential, so consumers can decide whether or not to purchase them.

Consumers have many choices of most products and services as well as ready access to information about those choices. In order to develop a marketing mix that will satisfy consumer wants, businesses must have a clear understanding of expanding consumer choices and consumer purchasing decisions.

Competition

Competition is becoming much more intense for most businesses. It is more difficult to make marketing decisions that will ensure customers will prefer one company's products over those of competitors. Gathering information about competitors' products and marketing activities in order to determine their strengths and weaknesses will help businesses to be more competitive.

The information gathered will help determine the product's *points-of-parity* (similarities) as well as its *points-of difference* (differences). Finding the proper balance between the two and identifying and communicating the unique benefits of a product as compared to its competitors is important in determining the most effective marketing strategy.

When a company's products are very similar to competitors' products, it will try to compete for sales by emphasizing such things as brand name, availability, or price. It may also try to compete by developing unique designs, product improvements, or special features.

Decision makers need information that enables them to make the best and most profitable product and service choices that improve on competitors' offerings. The correct product design and marketing decisions can be very profitable, but the wrong choices can result in losses for the company.

The Global Marketplace

As businesses develop an international focus, the differences among customer groups and the number of distinct market segments can become even greater. Even if businesses believe that they understand the consumers in their own country quite well, they will not have as much confidence about consumer groups in other countries that they have never served. Gathering information about the country and its people, as well as about the laws and regulations that apply to conducting business there, can help the company to enter the global marketplace.

*Want to know more about what is trending with this topic? Click on **Lesson 6.1, Global Marketing**, in your MindTap.*

Connect to MindTap

> ### CHECKPOINT
> *When a business follows the marketing concept, what is the first thing it needs to begin marketing planning?*

Many companies make marketing decisions with too little information or the wrong types of information. Others may become overwhelmed with too much information. Consider the approaches of two apparel companies as they decide on their apparel lines for the upcoming year.

Approaches to Planning

J'Borg Apparel is deciding on next year's designs for its lines of shirts and shorts. The members of the design team meet and share their ideas about possible changes. Several of the designers suggest that J'Borg should keep its basic designs from this year because they have been so successful. They think the company should simply develop new colors and some additional accessories. Another group thinks that customers may be tiring of the company's current casual offerings and will want more tailored styles. They argue that entirely new designs for its lines of apparel should be developed.

Dominique Designs is J'Borg's primary competitor. Dominique's designers are also meeting to consider changes in product lines. Before the meeting, the design team requests information from the company's marketing manager. The marketing manager provides records on each of the company's products. Those records identify the quantity sold by size and color for each week of the year. They also show the region of the country and the retail store in which sales were made. Original prices of products sold, markdowns, and the number of items returned or unsold are also recorded.

The marketing manager also distributes copies of a report that was purchased from a national apparel manufacturing association. It presents information on total consumer apparel purchases in the United States for each of the past five years for ten major categories of apparel. Sales are broken out for four geographic regions of the country and are categorized by age and gender and by type of retail store where products are sold. The report also identifies the top six brands of apparel and shows the percentage of total sales contributed by each brand over the five-year period. The final section of the report discusses the anticipated changes in the economy and in customer expenditures for apparel for the next year.

Finally, the marketing manager shares the results of a marketing research study completed during the past month. Four groups of consumers from across the country were invited to a meeting to discuss their attitudes about apparel

What type of information would a clothing design business need to gather from customers in order to decide on design changes?

© Diego Cervo/Shutterstock.com.

and their ideas about purchases they expected to make. The consumer groups discussed ten questions about designs, brands, and value. The results of the discussions are summarized in the research report. All Dominique designers have studied the market information, and they discuss it before deciding on next year's designs.

How will each of the companies decide whether to make design changes and the types of designs to use for the next year? Which company's decisions do you think are most likely to be successful? What is the biggest difference in the way Dominique Designs makes decisions compared to J'Borg Apparel?

Categories of Information

Put yourself in the position of the marketing manager for a national chain of yogurt stores. It is your responsibility to collect information to help store managers decide what they can do to increase sales and profits. What information do you think is needed?

Each type of business needs specific information, but there are general categories that all businesses should consider. Those categories are consumer information, marketing mix information, and information about the business environment. **Figure 6-1** provides examples of the types of information needed for each of the three categories.

As the marketing manager of the yogurt stores, you will need information from each of the categories. You will want to help store managers determine who their customers are, where they live, how much they spend on desserts, how they make decisions on what and when to purchase, and how they feel about your store and its brand of yogurt.

You will want to know what new flavors to add, if other food products should be sold, whether specific locations or certain store layouts are more effective, the prices to charge, and the most effective promotional messages and methods. A study of internal operations such as

TYPES OF INFORMATION NEEDED FOR EFFECTIVE MARKETING DECISIONS		
Consumers	**Marketing Mix Elements**	**Business Environment**
• Age • Gender • Income • Education • Family size • Occupation • Attitudes • Primary needs • Purchase frequency • Brand preferences • Information needs • Media preferences • Shopping behavior	• Product: basic products, product features, services, product packaging, guarantees, after-sale customer service • Price: credit choices, discounts • Place (distribution): location and method of sale; type of distribution used • Promotion: promotion and sales methods; promotional message; promotional media	• Type of competition • Competitors' strengths • Competitors' strategies • Economic conditions • Government regulations • Consumer protection • Ethical issues • Tax policies • Proposed laws • International markets

FIGURE 6-1 Marketers need information to make effective decisions.

costs of operations, training requirements for employees, and management methods may help determine the best ways to operate the stores.

Your store managers will want to know if the economy will change in the next year, if there will be new competitors or if current competitors are making important changes, if taxes or government regulations will increase, and even specific information such as whether the city is planning to make street improvements in front of a store.

There are many reasons to collect information. However, all the reasons can be summarized in two statements.

1. Effective marketing information improves the decisions of businesses.
2. Effective marketing information reduces the risk of decision making.

If a business can make better decisions that increase the likelihood of making a profit, the time and money spent gathering information is a good investment.

CHECKPOINT
What are the three general categories of information needed by businesses for making effective marketing decisions?

6.1 ASSESSMENT

What Have You Learned?

1. What are discretionary purchases, and why are they important to marketers? [6.1.1]

2. How does a company compete for sales when its products are very similar to its competitors' products? [6.1.1]

3. What are the two major reasons a business should collect information about its market? [6.1.2]

Make Academic Connections

1. **Psychology** Businesses respond to differences in consumer needs by offering choices of the same product. Select a company that offers at least three choices of the same product. Examine the product and product information to determine the differences and the customer characteristics or needs to which each appeals.

Prepare a one-page report or a summary chart of your analysis. [6.1.1]

2. **Economics** Review several recent issues of a local or statewide newspaper. From the news reports, identify five factors that could affect the economic environment for consumers and businesses in the next six months. Suggest how each factor might affect businesses in your community. [6.1.1]

Connect to ◇DECA

Build your Portfolio

Your marketing research team works for a local movie theater. Your goal is to increase the number of moviegoers and the average amount each customer spends on concessions. As a team, determine three specific types of information you will need for each category: consumers, marketing mix, and business environment. Decide why each type of information is needed. Make a team presentation of your ideas to your teacher (judge). [6.1.2]

FIND AND MANAGE MARKETING INFORMATION

Learning Objectives

6.2.1 Describe common sources of internal and external market information.

6.2.2 Explain the five critical elements of an effective marketing information system.

Key Terms

internal information
external information
marketing
    information
    system (MkIS)

input
storage
analysis
output

marketing matters

In order to use information effectively, businesses first need to know where to find it. They also need to develop marketing information systems to get the most out of the information they have. As one of the functions of marketing, marketing information management is used to improve decision making and the performance of marketing activities.

essential question

Why is it important for a business to have a systematic way to gather, analyze, and use market information rather than just reviewing all information that is available when a decision needs to be made?

6.2.1 ▶ **Sources of Market Information**

Where do you go to find the most recent movies available for viewing on your computer, tablet, or smart TV? What is a good source of information to help you learn about careers or college choices? If you want to know the best price to pay for a specific model of automobile, where do you turn for help? Each of these decisions requires information. For most decisions, there is usually more than one information source. Factors that influence your choice of an information source may include its availability, how quickly it can be accessed, how complete or

accurate you believe it to be, and your past experience with the source.

Businesspeople need information to make marketing decisions. As they determine what information they need and where to obtain it, they go through a similar process. The process can be summarized in the following steps:

1. Identify the types of information needed.

2. Determine the available sources of each type of information.

3. Evaluate each source to determine if it meets the organization's needs in terms of accuracy, time, detail, and cost.

4. Select the sources that best meet the identified needs.

5. Enter the information into a marketing information system.

Marketing information can come from one of three sources: internal sources, external sources, and marketing research. Internal and external information sources are discussed next while marketing research will be discussed in Lesson 6-3.

Internal Information Sources

Internal information is information developed from activities that occur within the organization. A great deal of information flows through a business. Much of it is useful for marketing decision making. Three categories of information a company generates internally are customer records and sales information, production and operations reports, and performance information.

CUSTOMER RECORDS AND SALES INFORMATION Customer information is essential in order to plan marketing directed at those customers. Therefore, customer records are an important information source. Many companies keep a complete record of all transactions they have with a customer. They record what is purchased, the dates of purchase, and the quantities purchased. If the customer purchases accessories or related products, then or at a later time, that information also is recorded and matched with the original purchase. Detailed information on payments and credit is also recorded. If the customer requires service, a service record is prepared. Customer problems and complaints also should be a part of their record. When a customer stops buying the product

Why should a salesperson take notes while talking with a customer?

or service, the record should not be discarded. It should be analyzed to determine why the customer was lost.

To target products and marketing activities to specific customers, information more detailed than sales records is needed. That information includes demographics such as age, family size, income, and mailing and email addresses. Businesses also need to understand customer needs, interests, and attitudes. They need to know how consumers make buying decisions, such as where they gather information, what choices are considered, where they decide to purchase, and when.

Customer information can be gathered through marketing research, but some businesses have discovered other ways to get it. Detailed profiles might be completed on a customer by the salesperson as a part of the selling process. For example, many realtors ask prospective buyers to supply a great deal of information in order to locate the best possible home for them. Salespeople who work in clothing and apparel stores record information about their regular customers' needs and preferences. Customers may be asked to provide profile information in response to an advertisement, special offer, or when registering a new product purchase.

One of the most common ways to collect customer information is through store loyalty cards. Prospective and current customers are provided with special incentives for signing up for the loyalty program. In order to join, the consumer completes a detailed profile form. Based on that profile, each consumer is sent regular mailings or email messages providing new product information, special purchase opportunities and discounts, and promotional information for products and services the company believes the customer will want to buy. The cards often are linked to the customer's cell phone number and email address, enabling the promotions to be sent by text or email.

The Internet helps companies build and use a consumer database. Nearly everything someone does online can be collected. Big Data, as it is often called, is data collected using software that searches the Internet for public information about consumers. This often is done by third parties, who then sell the information to retailers. The retailers use the information for direct marketing.

Analyzing Big Data to look for specific information or patterns is called *data mining*. Various analytic software tools

are available to perform these searches. Grocery stores use data mining to analyze information about consumers. Based on the information they gather, they create RFM (recency, frequency, monetary) customer groups and develop a marketing strategy for each group. For example, customers who spend a lot of money but shop infrequently receive different promotions than customers who spend less but shop frequently.

Tracking customer website visits is another way to collect consumer information. Website tracking software often is used to identify the customer, the products they purchase, and whether they are browsing or buying. The information collected can then be used to send ads or offer discounts. The search terms used by customers also provide information for retailers. The more specific the term used, the more likely the customer is to make a purchase.

Actively collecting and retaining customer information may result in a consumer database of thousands of people for a business. This gives rise to privacy concerns for customers. The company must inform each individual that the information is being collected and maintained and provide information about the company's privacy policies. Effective data management and security procedures must be put in place to protect the information from misuse, loss, or theft.

PRODUCTION AND OPERATIONS REPORTS Production and operations activities are important to marketing. Products and services must be available when customers want them. Quality standards need to be met. Expenses need to be controlled in order to price products and services competitively. Information

*Want to know more about marketing in the information age? Click on **Lesson 6.2, Digital Marketing,** in your MindTap.*

Connect to MindTap

about production and operations activities also needs to be collected and shared regularly with the people planning marketing activities.

When companies that make up a channel of distribution work closely together and share operating information, they can meet customers' needs much better and operate more efficiently. In that way all members of the channel benefit. Those companies can develop information systems that can quickly share information about sales, costs, inventory levels, and production and delivery schedules.

PERFORMANCE INFORMATION

The success of a business is judged by its performance. Some people believe the only important performance measure is profit, and managers certainly must pay attention to the bottom line. However, managers need to consider other performance measures as well, including sales, costs, quality, and customer satisfaction.

Performance is typically measured in three ways. For companies that have operated for a number of years, there are records of past performance. Current sales or costs can be compared to those of a previous month or year to determine if performance is improving

or declining. A second method is to compare performance with that of similar businesses. Information on other businesses is available from external information sources.

The most important performance measure is the comparison of actual performance with expected or planned performance. When managers plan marketing activities, they develop goals, performance standards, and budgets. Those plans need to be compared frequently with actual performance to determine if the company is meeting expectations.

External Information Sources

External information provides an understanding of factors outside of the organization. Marketers cannot plan effectively without understanding consumers, competitors, the economy, and other changes going on around them. Marketing research is an important method of collecting and analyzing external information. In addition, there are many valuable sources of external information that businesses should be aware of and review regularly.

GOVERNMENT REPORTS People often think that regulation and taxation are the roles of government in business. However, another important activity of federal, state, and local governments is to supply information that businesses and consumers can use. There are a number of agencies that regularly collect helpful marketing information.

Probably the best-known data collection agency is the U.S. Bureau of the Census. Every 10 years, the Census Bureau conducts a complete census of the country's population. The report of that census is very detailed and specific. It is an excellent resource for learning about the number of people and important characteristics of individuals and households in specific areas of the country. Census data is available in digital form for easy analysis. Some companies analyze census data and sell reports to businesses.

The population of the United States is not the only census the federal government completes. Others include the Census of Manufacturers, Retail Trade, Wholesale Trade, Transportation, and County Business Patterns. The Census Bureau conducts many of the studies either every five years or every ten years. It also issues yearly updates of some data.

There are literally thousands of other databases, reports, and information sources available from government offices. One of the most difficult parts of using government information is determining just what is available. Information is developed on agriculture, education, housing, health, and international trade as well as many other areas of interest to businesses. Much of the current and historic federal government data can now be accessed online.

TRADE AND PROFESSIONAL ASSOCIATIONS

Trade and professional associations are organized to serve people and businesses with common interests. Members of the association may be a part of the same industry, such as travel, retail, export, or corn growers. Other associations, such as the American Management Association and the National Association of Professional and Executive Women, provide services for people in particular job categories.

Most associations provide information specific to the needs of their members. That information may be published through websites, journals, newsletters, or in detailed research reports. Some associations have research services, libraries, or data services that members can use.

BUSINESS PUBLICATIONS

Business publications, websites, and blogs are useful sources for current information on the economy, legislation, new technology, and business ideas. However, there are thousands of publications, websites, and blogs, and it is impossible to keep up with all of them. Still, it may be important to find relevant ones to subscribe to or follow and to develop effective research skills. Publications worth following may include general business newspapers and magazines such as *The Wall Street Journal*, *Forbes*, and *Bloomberg Businessweek*, as well as more specialized publications such as *Black Enterprise*, *Wired*, *Fast Company*, *Adweek*, or *E-Commerce Times*. Each publication also has websites and blogs which contain additional business information and insights. Additionally, there are important sites and blogs that do not have a print component such as Venture-Beat or TechCrunch.

COMMERCIAL DATA AND INFORMATION SERVICES

There are a number of businesses that collect, analyze, and sell data. Experian, Equifax, and TransUnion are the three major credit reporting agencies for consumer credit. Dun & Bradstreet maintains the largest worldwide business database and offers tailored reports to its customers. Nielsen is one of the best known of many companies that conduct marketing research on a number of topics and sell the information to business customers.

CHECKPOINT
What is the key difference between internal and external market information?

Marketing Information Systems

Businesses need a great deal of information to operate successfully. With all of the information needed, businesspeople could spend most of their time gathering and studying information.

A **marketing information system (MkIS,** pronounced M-K-I-S) is an organized method of collecting, storing, analyzing, and retrieving information to improve the effectiveness and efficiency of marketing decisions.

Manage Information

Each business develops its own marketing information system. In a very small new business, an MkIS may be as simple as a filing cabinet in which the owner collects, organizes, and stores customer information, business records, and other information important to the business. Today, however, even small businesses maintain computerized records. Large businesses may have an information management unit with a dedicated computer system and a staff of people who collect and analyze information and prepare reports. The information management staff is charged with collecting information in a cost-effective manner that is complete, accurate, easy to use, timely, and affordable.

Design a Marketing Information System

All effective marketing information systems contain five elements. Those elements are input, storage, analysis, output, and decision making. In planning an MkIS, questions relating to each system element need to be answered. The questions and related elements are shown in **Figure 6-2**.

INPUT How do you make decisions? If you want to be as objective as possible and make good decisions, you must gather information. **Input** is the information needed for decision making that goes into the system.

Routine information about customers, competitors, and business operations is used for marketing decisions. Marketers need to know what customers purchase, in what quantities, and at what prices. They must know where customers buy their products and what factors influence them.

DESIGNING AN MkIS	
Question	**MkIS Element**
What information is needed to develop and implement the marketing strategy?	Input
How should the information be maintained so it is in a usable form and easy to access when needed?	Storage
What methods should be used to organize and study the information in order to make effective marketing decisions?	Analysis
How and when should the information be made available for most effective use?	Output
In what ways should the information be used to improve marketing?	Decision Making

FIGURE 6-2 A marketing information system (MkIS) is designed to help marketers obtain, store, organize, and use information to improve decisions.

Marketing is influenced by the activities of competitors. Information is needed on which businesses are competing in specific markets, the marketing mixes they use, their strengths and weaknesses, their market share, and their profitability. Marketers can use information about competitors' business operations to determine what activities are effective or ineffective.

Occasionally, additional information that the business does not routinely collect is needed for a decision. In that situation, a marketing research procedure is used to collect the information. You will learn about collecting marketing research information in Lesson 6.3.

STORAGE   Have you ever rushed to a class only to discover that your assignment was not in your notebook? Many of us are very good at collecting information. We may not be as good at storing it so that we can locate it when needed. **Storage** involves the resources used to maintain information, including equipment and procedures, so that it can be accessed when needed.

A storage system in an MkIS has several characteristics. Most important, it must protect the information. If information is lost or damaged, it is not available when a decision must be made. Some business information is very confidential. The storage system should be designed so that only authorized people can access the information. Finally, the storage system should be organized so that information is easy to locate when it is needed.

Most of the information storage in business is done using computer technology. After data is entered into the computer, it is stored and maintained on a hard drive or using third-party cloud storage such as Good Drive for Work, Microsoft OneDrive for Business, or Dropbox Business. Careful planning is done to

Why is it important for MkIS output to be well organized and easy to understand?

make sure that backup copies of all data are maintained and that information is secure. When using third-party cloud storage, which is relatively inexpensive, easy access to the data also is important. Information and records maintained on paper must be organized and stored in filing cabinets.

ANALYSIS   Information in an MkIS is collected and maintained in order to improve decision making. **Analysis** is the process of summarizing, combining, or comparing information so that decisions can be made. In order to plan a promotional budget, a manager may examine the budgets for other products or for past years. The effectiveness of one business in a channel of distribution may not be apparent until that company's sales are compared with those of similar companies. The costs for national and international customers can be compared to determine differences in serving each type of market.

The type of analysis needed is usually determined when planning the marketing information system. Procedures are developed to obtain needed information from storage, to organize it, and to complete the needed analysis. Specific computer programs are available that assist with those procedures. For example, database and spreadsheet programs have procedures for common types of business data analysis using existing formulas and graphing tools. Companies that complete a large amount of data analysis usually employ people skilled in organizing and analyzing data.

OUTPUT   For managers and other decision makers, the most important part of an MkIS is the output. Many people never see information being collected, stored, or analyzed. They are given only summaries or reports to use in decision making. **Output** is the result of analysis provided to decision makers. Output is usually written information or graphics. It is provided in print form or accessed by decision makers using a computer. If it is not well organized or if it uses language or data that is difficult to understand, it may be misused or not used at all.

People who need output to make decisions should have access to it. However, business output is often confidential, and access is restricted and secure. The use of the Internet to store and access information makes data security a bigger issue than it was in the past.

DECISION MAKING   The purpose of a marketing information system is to improve decision making. Decisions should be better and should be made more quickly if an MkIS is well designed. The decision-making process includes who is involved in the decision, when decisions need to be made, any policies or procedures that should be considered, and the information needed by the decision makers.

Some decisions are routine, and the result of the analysis will determine the decision that should be made. For example, information in the MkIS of an office supply store shows when computer paper needs to be reordered, based on inventory levels. The analysis program in the computer determines that 200 cases of paper are needed.

*Want to know more about what is trending with this topic? Click on **Lesson 6.2, Marketing Decisions,** in your MindTap.*

Connect to MindTap

It searches the vendor list to determine which approved vendor has the lowest current price. The vendor is selected, the reorder quantity is identified, and a purchase order is sent to the vendor. This type of routine decision requires no management attention.

Other decisions are unique. A major credit card company considers whether to offer a money-back guarantee on all products consumers purchase using the card. The guarantee is viewed as an important service that will encourage people to use the credit card and could attract many more customers. The results will affect the company, the businesses that accept the credit card, and competing credit card companies. The decision to add the guarantee means important changes in the entire marketing mix. Once the company announces the new service, it will be difficult to end the service even if it proves to be too expensive to maintain. That decision requires a great deal of time and information, and many of the company's managers will be involved in making it.

 CHECKPOINT
What are the five elements of an effective marketing information system (MkIS)?

6.2 ASSESSMENT

What Have You Learned?

1. What are the three sources of internal information that can be useful for marketing decision making? [6.2.1]

2. What type of information provides an understanding of factors outside of an organization? [6.2.1]

3. Name the five elements in a marketing information system. [6.2.2]

Make Academic Connections

1. **Technology** Use the Internet to locate three sources of information you would recommend to a small business owner as an aid in planning. Using computer presentation software, develop three slides that describe the information sources and why you are recommending each one. [6.2.1]

2. **Success Skills** Choose one of the following personal decisions—choosing a college or applying for a full-time job after graduation. Describe five types of information you will need for the decision and five information sources you will use. Write a two-sentence description of each of the components of an MkIS that will help you make the decision. [6.2.1]

Connect to ◇DECA

Build your Portfolio

Some businesspeople are concerned about the time and expense required to gather and analyze all of the information needed to make marketing decisions. Develop a two-minute persuasive speech to convince a business owner of the value of marketing information. Make sure to address both concerns of time and cost. Give your speech to your teacher (judge). [6.2.2]

USE MARKETING RESEARCH

Learning Objectives

6.3.1 Describe the four steps involved in implementing a marketing research study.

6.3.2 Identify the steps needed to gather and study data relevant to a problem.

6.3.3 Explain how to prepare reports and present proposed solutions.

Key Terms

marketing research
primary data
secondary data
population
sample
random sampling

marketing matters

A well-organized and efficient marketing information system should provide the information needed for making regular and routine decisions. However, marketers also are required to make decisions that relate to one-time problems or new situations. This often presents the need for information that has not been anticipated or previously collected. Marketing research uses tried and tested problem-solving procedures to gather the information needed.

essential question

How does marketing research provide information not currently available in a business's MkIS to aid decision makers?

See the Problem Clearly

Suppose a business is considering entering a new market in which it has no experience. Maybe a company's engineers have developed a prototype product that has never been sold before. In situations like that, the company's MkIS will likely not have adequate information to support the required marketing decisions. **Marketing research** is a procedure designed to identify solutions to a specific marketing problem through the use of scientific problem solving.

You probably have studied and used scientific problem solving in other classes. If you have, you already know the steps involved in that process. Those steps are shown in **Figure 6-3**. This so-called *scientific method* is used to ensure that a careful and objective procedure is followed in order to develop the best possible solution.

FIGURE 6-3 Effective marketing research uses the scientific problem-solving procedure.

Define the Problem

Marketing research is used when a business needs to solve a specific and unique problem. The first step is to be certain that the problem is clearly and carefully defined. That is not always an easy step. Sometimes the problem is very clear—to identify the characteristics of a market or select a new advertising medium. In other cases, you may not know the real problem. If sales are declining, the problem might be that customers' needs are changing, they are dissatisfied with some part of the marketing mix, or a competitor may have introduced a new product choice. Consumers may believe the economy is not strong and may be less willing to spend money. Usually decision makers and researchers gather and study specific information before they fully understand the problem.

Defining the problem involves preparing a written statement of the problem. The statement should be reviewed by several people to make sure it is understandable. The problem should be specific enough that researchers know what to study, whom to involve in the study, and the types of solutions or results that might be appropriate.

Analyze the Situation

An important part of scientific problem solving is to understand the circumstances surrounding the problem well enough to determine how to solve it. Analyzing the situation allows the researcher to identify what is already known about the problem, the information currently available, and even possible solutions that have already been attempted.

During the analysis step, the researcher reviews available information and gathers information from people who might have ideas or additional information. Reviewing similar problems or other studies that have previously been completed can help the researcher decide how to study the current problem.

It is possible that a careful situation analysis by itself may result in the identification of a solution. If the decision maker is confident in the proposed solution and has limited time or money to study the problem further, the marketing research process will come to an end. A good marketing information system frequently provides the necessary information, and further study is not needed.

Develop a Data-Collection Procedure

After thoroughly reviewing the situation and the available information, the researcher decides what additional information is needed and how to collect it. In this step, the actual marketing research study is planned. The researcher needs to know where to obtain information and the best and most efficient ways to obtain the information. There are two types of data that can be collected—primary data and secondary data.

PRIMARY DATA   Information collected for the first time to solve the problem being studied is **primary data**. This type of data is obtained through data collection designed specifically in response to current needs of the company.

SECONDARY DATA   Information already collected for another purpose that can be used to solve the current problem is **secondary data**. Examples of secondary data include company records, government reports, studies completed by colleges and universities, information from industry trade associations and other business groups, and research reported in magazines.

CHECKPOINT
Once a problem has been clearly defined, what three things should a marketer identify?

6.3.2 ▶ Gather Information

Have you ever participated in a marketing research study? A common research method is to question study participants. A great deal of specific information can be obtained using questionnaires presented online or sent through the mail, with telephone interviews, or by stopping people in shopping malls to ask questions. No matter what method is used to gather the information, procedures must be carefully developed and followed to be sure the results are accurate.

Select the Participants

The selection of participants in marketing research is one of the most important decisions to be made. In most situations, there are many more potential consumers than a company can afford to involve in the research. Researchers usually collect information from a small percentage of possible consumers. In order for the results to be accurate and the research to be useful, that smaller group must be representative so that its members will give responses similar to those of the larger group. Research results will be misleading if they do not reflect the views or behavior of the prospective customers.

Researchers use several terms to describe the people who are the focus of study. All of the people in the group the company is interested in studying are known as the **population**. A smaller group selected from the population is a **sample**. To make sure a sample is representative of the larger group, the researcher will use random sampling. With **random sampling**, everyone in the population has an equal chance of being selected in the sample.

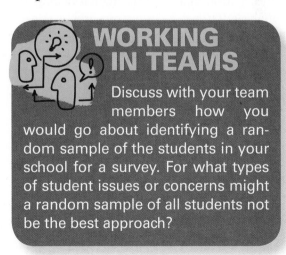

WORKING IN TEAMS

Discuss with your team members how you would go about identifying a random sample of the students in your school for a survey. For what types of student issues or concerns might a random sample of all students not be the best approach?

Collect the Data

Research procedures should be carefully planned in advance to ensure that needed information is obtained and that the collection and review of information is done objectively. Procedures for primary data collection are particularly important. When gathering information directly from other people, researchers must be careful to maintain the privacy of the individual and treat the person ethically. A great deal of consumer research is conducted by telephone calls to people's homes. The number of calls they receive and the time of day they received the call may upset many people. Some businesses unethically tell consumers that they are conducting a research study when they are really collecting personal information or attempting to sell a product or service.

Analyze the Data

Once information is collected, it needs to be reviewed to determine whether it can aid in developing a solution to the problem. For small amounts of information or simple studies, the information may not be difficult to review. However, most marketing research studies collect a large amount of information that requires a great deal of analysis. Therefore, most research is analyzed using computers and statistical programs in order to increase the speed and accuracy of obtaining the results.

After the study is complete, researchers examine the information collected. That information may be in the form of answers to surveys, observations that have been recorded, or data collected from an experiment. The information needs to be organized so that it is meaningful and easy to study.

NUMERICAL DATA   Numerical data is the easiest to organize. Researchers total the number of responses to each question or for each factor being observed. When more than one group is involved in the research, it is typical to compare the responses of the groups. The simplest form of comparison is done by calculating the percentage of responses or average response (mean, median) of each group. Advanced levels of comparison can be made to determine the relationships between two or more variables. For example, the researcher may want to study the relationship between the number of times an advertisement runs on a television station and the number of customers who call a business seeking information about a product. Another comparison could be to determine if there is a relationship between the price of a product and the level of customer satisfaction identified through a survey of recent purchasers.

NON-NUMERICAL DATA   Some research information is not numerical, so it is much more difficult to analyze. When customers respond to open-ended questions or observers describe how a consumer acted in a specific situation, there is not a common set of specific answers recorded. There are special methods for people trained to analyze this type of information. Results can be classified into broad categories that are identified before the information is collected or categories that are determined by looking for similar ideas from the responses. This type of classification allows for summaries of the non-numerical information.

Prepare Results

The results of the study are usually organized into tables, charts, and graphs. Pie charts and bar graphs are common ways of summarizing information. This makes it easier for decision makers to analyze a great deal of information in a brief time and to make comparisons of information from different groups and sources.

The research results are often summarized and analyzed in more than one way. This allows marketers to consider several possible solutions. Studying and analyzing marketing research is an important marketing skill. Marketing research departments and companies employ research analysts to complete those tasks.

CHECKPOINT
Why is it important to select the right people to participate in a marketing research study?

6.3.3 ▶ Propose a Solution

The purpose of marketing research is to identify strategies for a company to follow when implementing and improving marketing activities. Scientific problem solving often begins with the development of a *hypothesis* (or possible solution) to the problem. After the research results have been organized, they need to be studied to determine if the findings support the proposed solution or suggest an alternative solution.

In most cases, the marketing researchers completing the study do not make the final decisions about solutions. Instead, they prepare a report of the research results for decision makers who then carefully study the report. The report needs to be accurate, objective, understandable, and meaningful.

Research Reports

Marketing research reports are usually presented in writing and orally. Effective communication is an important skill for all marketers, especially market researchers. Researchers must keep these two considerations in mind when preparing a marketing

How do marketing research reports help in the decision-making process?

© Gorodenkoff/Shutterstock.com.

research report. First, they must know who will be receiving and studying the report. Just as a marketing mix should respond to the needs of customers, the research report must be prepared to meet the needs of its users. Second, they must include in the report a clear description of the purpose of the study and the research procedures they followed to collect the information. Without an understanding of the problem being studied and the methods used, those receiving the report may misunderstand or misinterpret the results.

A research report, whether written or oral, is usually organized like the study. A research report begins with a statement of the problem or the purpose of the research. This introduction also provides a brief discussion of why the study was needed. The report then summarizes the data that was collected.

The next part is a description of the procedures used in the study. This includes the population studied and the way a sample was obtained. It also describes the method used to collect information including surveys, observations, or experiments. The report continues by presenting the results of the research and concludes with a summary and recommendations.

Present Research Results

The most important part of the research report is the presentation of results. In a written report, the results are presented in the form of tables, charts, and graphs with brief written explanations. In an oral presentation, the results are presented using visuals. Those visuals usually are prepared and presented using presentation software. They often are supported with printed information with the presenter providing explanations and answering questions.

The research report concludes with a summary that emphasizes the most important information from the study. It also may contain recommendations for solutions if requested. Sometimes the research will not completely demonstrate that a solution will be successful. Marketers will need to decide if they have enough information or if they need to continue to study the problem.

When to Use Marketing Research

Although marketing research can be expensive and time consuming, it can be a valuable tool. Deciding whether to use research is based on two factors. How much risk is the business facing from the problem being studied, and how much time and money will be required to gather the information?

If there is little risk or if the possible solutions are not too expensive to implement, there is little need for research. However, if a business faces a complex issue that may substantially affect sales, costs, and profits, research will be very important.

Because many decisions must be made almost instantaneously, most businesses maintain research budgets and conduct ongoing studies to reduce the time needed to gather information. Businesses try to reduce the need for special research studies by building extensive information databases as a part of their MkIS. Today's marketers recognize the value of using information to support marketing planning.

CHECKPOINT
What two things are important when preparing a research report?

6.3 ASSESSMENT

What Have You Learned?

1. What are the two types of data market researchers can collect, and what is the difference between them. [6.3.1]

2. Why would a market researcher use the random sampling method to select participants for a study? [6.3.2]

3. What two factors do managers consider in deciding whether to use research to study a problem? [6.3.3]

Make Academic Connections

1. **Ethics** Use the Internet to locate information on the rights of research participants. Based on that information, prepare a short ethics statement that researchers could use to respect and protect the rights of research participants. [6.3.2]

2. **Math** There are 8,536 dog owners in a town and a pet supply store wants to survey those owners to determine what types of dog-grooming services and supplies they prefer. The researchers want to have completed surveys from 4 percent of the owners and experience has shown that 60 percent of all people asked will complete a survey. How many people should be selected to participate in order to have the correct number of completed surveys? [6.3.2]

Connect to ◇DECA

Build your Portfolio

Your local DECA chapter has a large membership, but attendance at monthly after-school meetings is frequently low. Only about 30 percent of members participate in the competitive events programs. You have been asked to recommend marketing research that will help the chapter develop a solution to the problem. Develop a written outline of the study, making sure to follow the steps of scientific problem solving. Using presentation software, prepare a two-minute presentation of your marketing research plan and present it to your teacher (judge). Be prepared to answer questions about your plan. [6.3.1]

Businesspeople are presented with a variety of numerical data and must be able to understand the information and use it to make decisions. Are sales, profits, and expenses increasing or declining? Are products profitable or not? Do we have a greater share of a market than our competitors?

Consumers also must be able to understand numbers they encounter such as "50% off" or "6.5% financing available." How do those numbers influence your decisions?

Statistics is a type of mathematics that analyzes and presents numerical data in understandable forms including tables, charts, and graphs. Statistics are used to describe the characteristics of a group of numbers so they can be interpreted, compared, and used for decision making.

As a student, you also need to understand statistics. Your teacher hands back a test, and you received a B for a grade. While you may feel good (unless you expected an A), you really don't know a lot about your performance. If you find out you answered 86 of 100 items correctly, you know a bit more about your performance. If your teacher tells you the average score of the 40 students in the class was 83, you know even more and can compare your performance to others.

How would the additional information provided below affect your understanding of your performance and that of the other students?

- Student test scores ranged from 97 to 63.

- More students scored 85 than any other score.

- The distribution of grades was 4 As, 13 Bs, 20 Cs, 2 Ds, and 1 F.

The statistics help you better understand your performance because you recognize how your grade and score compare with other students like you who took the same test. To understand and use statistics you need the following information:

Do you have enough information to make a decision? One or two test scores tell you little about your possible semester grade. Knowing how three or four students performed does not give a true indication of how you performed in a class of 40.

Is the information representative of all of the information available? If student scores on this test are very much higher or lower than typical tests, you won't know much about your overall performance.

Is the information presented in a way to aid understanding or does it confuse or mislead? Tables, graphs, and charts may leave out important information or present it in such a way that it misrepresents the real meaning.

Develop Your Skill

Over a period of several weeks, collect 20 examples of statistics used by businesses in news stories and advertisements. Classify each example in a 3-row × 2-column table according to the following categories:

- *Row 1*—The statistics DO or DO NOT present an adequate amount of information to be understandable and useful.

- *Row 2*—The statistics DO or DO NOT appear to be representative of all the related information available.

- *Row 3*—The statistics DO or DO NOT appear to be presented to confuse or mislead the reader.

Develop charts or graphs that communicate the results of your research in an understandable and meaningful way.

Learning Objectives

6.4.1 Describe how to conduct marketing research surveys.

6.4.2 Explain the reasons for and limitations of using observation.

6.4.3 Identify various types of marketing research experiments.

Key Terms

survey
closed-ended questions
open-ended questions

focus group
observation
experiments
test markets
simulations

marketing matters

When completing marketing research, the data collection method you choose will depend on the type of information you need. To find out how people shop for a product, you would use a different method than you would if you wanted to know how they use the product. You would use a different method to determine consumers' attitudes toward advertising than you would to identify the quantity of a product they consumed during the year. The data collection method should be as efficient as possible to collect accurate data.

essential question

Why do marketing researchers need to be skilled in completing several types of primary research?

6.4.1 ▶ Conduct Surveys

A **survey** is a planned set of questions to which individuals or groups of people respond. The survey can be completed orally or by recorded responses. People can be surveyed in person, through the mail, by telephone, by email, online, or even by using interactive technologies. With some methods, consumers are presented with questions on a computer or television screen. They may key their responses on the computer keyboard, push buttons on a

special keypad provided by the researcher, or enter information on a telephone using voice responses or a keypad.

Most surveys use **closed-ended questions** that offer two or more choices as answers, such as:

- Yes or no
- Agree or disagree
- Select a, b, c, or d
- Rate this item on a scale of 1–10

Occasionally, researchers use **open-ended questions** to allow respondents to develop their own answers without information about possible choices. Examples of open-ended questions include:

- What are the most important features of this product?

- How does the durability of brand A compare to brand B?

- How did you feel about your shopping experience at Z-Mart?

MATH IN MARKETING

Allocate Advertising Dollars Based on Survey Results

As part of a marketing team for a local book festival, your team's goal is to increase event attendance by 10 percent. At the latest event a survey was taken of attendees while they were waiting in line to make their purchases. One of the questions was "Where did you hear about the book festival?" The respondents could choose all answers that applied. The results were as follows:

A coalition of local public and academic libraries, 45%; event website, 35%; newspaper, 33%; bookstore, 25%; social media and other online, 25%; public radio station, 20%; commercial television station, 8%; public television station, 6%; local magazine, 5%; local private library, 4%; local university, 3%; bus banners, 3%.

The advertising budget for the event was $20,000 and was distributed as follows:

Coalition of public libraries for print materials (flyers, bookmarks, etc.), $6,000; event website, $0; newspaper, $0; bookstore, $0; social media, $0; online ads, $2,500; public radio station, $2,000; commercial radio station, $0; public television station, $3,500; local magazine, $0; local private library for print materials (flyers, bookmarks, etc.), $500; local university for print materials (flyers, bookmarks, etc.), $2,500; bus banners, $3,000.

Do the Math

1. As a member of the marketing team for the event, write a report suggesting how the $20,000 marketing budget should be spent, based on the survey information. Justify the expenditures. (Keep in mind that in reality, a marketing plan and budget would not be based on a single question from one survey.)

2. Reevaluate the marketing budget with the following considerations. Along with the library coalition and the local bookstore, various local media partners are supporting the event. The total value of the coverage provided by the media partners is worth more than $100,000. Some partners are compensated monetarily for expenses, while others are compensated through the exposure received for being connected to the event. Though the newspaper values its ad support at $58,000, and the commercial TV at $15,000, no funds are allocated to them. The bookstore, which ran ads in its newsletter and website, received compensation by taking a percentage of the total sales. Armed with this new information, would the team change the allocation of the funds? Adjust the report to reflect any of these changes.

Focus on the Issues

Open-ended questions often are used when researchers are attempting to identify the problem or are completing a situational analysis. They may not be certain of which alternatives to include in closed-ended survey questions. In that case, researchers may discuss the problems with consumers using open-ended questions to get more specific information.

A popular research method used to gather information using open-ended questions is a focus group. A **focus group** is a small number of people brought together to discuss identified elements of an issue or problem. Focus group participants are carefully selected to ensure that the group is representative of a larger group of people or because participants are experts about the topic being studied. A skilled facilitator uses a planned set of open-ended questions to guide the discussion and gather ideas. The discussion is videotaped or recorded, and a summary is prepared for analysis.

What do you see as the benefit of using a focus group to gather information about a product?

© StockLite/Shutterstock.com.

Question with Clarity

Survey questions must elicit information that will help to solve the problem. They must be written in such a way that each respondent understands what is being asked, is encouraged to respond honestly, and is not directed toward one answer so that the results are biased. Questions should be short, clear, and simple. Each question should deal with only one concept and use language that the respondent will understand.

The survey should be organized in a way that makes it as easy as possible to complete. Directions should be clear enough so that the respondent knows how to record answers and what to do with the survey when finished. The respondent should be assured that the answers will be treated confidentially.

Surveys should only ask questions necessary to accomplish the objectives of the research. Many people will not answer surveys that appear to be too long or complex. Gathering unnecessary information can be both misleading and, in some cases, unethical. It may also provide confusion in solving the marketing problem by introducing information that is not relevant.

CHECKPOINT

Why do market researchers sometimes use open-ended survey questions?

A second method of gathering information is by observation. **Observation** collects information by recording actions without interacting or communicating with the participant. The purpose of observation research is to see the actions of the participants rather than to have them recall or predict their actions. This usually results in greater accuracy and objectivity, and less chance of bias. However, using observations to gather data requires more time and expense than using surveys. It also is difficult to gather information from a large number of participants using observation.

Observations must be carefully planned in order to keep from changing the participants' actions as a result of the observation. If people know they are being watched, their actions may be very different. Trained observers typically know what to observe and how to record information quickly and accurately. In some situations, observations can be made using technology with video cameras, audio recordings, or with other types of equipment designed to gather information about the actions of people.

One equipment-based observation method is the use of eye-tracking technology. A retail store may be interested in how customers examine displays. Using close-up video recordings, researchers can determine where the eyes look first, how long customers focus on certain products, how they search the entire display, and what they look at when making a product choice. This information can be very helpful in

organizing and placing specific brands in displays. The same type of equipment is used to study how consumers read magazine and newspaper advertisements or view web pages on the Internet.

In some cases, researchers are interested in learning how participants behave in normal situations. In other cases, researchers may ask people to participate in a planned situation in order to learn how people respond to specific, controlled activities. For example, a business might want to know how customers would react if a certain type of sales presentation is used. Another might want to study consumer responses to a new piece of equipment, such as the screen layout on a smartphone.

Barcode scanners used at the checkout counters of many retail stores are another form of observation using technology. The scanner can record the types and quantities of products purchased, the timing of purchases, how payment was made, whether coupons or other promotions were used, and what items were purchased at the same time. You can learn about purchasing behavior in this way without asking the consumer any questions.

CHECKPOINT

Why are the results of observations generally considered more accurate than survey results?

6.4.3 ▶ **Perform Experiments**

The most precise and objective information is obtained through experimentation. **Experiments** are carefully designed and controlled situations in which all important

factors are the same except the one being studied. Scientific research is done by planning and implementing experiments and then recording and analyzing the data.

Marketers use experiments to determine whether changes in a single element of the marketing mix will affect customer behavior.

Experiments are not used as often as surveys or observations in marketing research. That may be because it is difficult to carefully control factors related to a marketing experiment while making them realistic for consumers. It also takes a great deal of time to organize an experiment and operate it long enough to determine if significant differences result. The actions of competitors can affect experiments undertaken in actual markets.

Implementing the marketing concept suggests many opportunities for research to determine the best market segments to serve and the appropriate mix elements to provide. For example, a company may want to determine if a customer's geographic location makes a difference in purchasing behavior. An experiment in which two groups of customers from different areas are provided the same marketing mix may help to answer the question. As another example, a business owner may be uncertain about the effect of a price increase on sales volume. An experiment can be developed in which everything except the price is held the same for two groups of customers. One group is given a discount while the other is not. The experiment can demonstrate changes in the amount of sales resulting from the price difference.

Test Markets

Because of the need for control over important conditions, experiments are difficult to manage. Some companies have developed test markets. **Test markets** are specific cities or geographic areas in which marketing experiments are conducted.

In gathering research information, why are experiments more difficult to conduct than observational research?

© antoniodiaz/Shutterstock.com.

6.4 | Collect Primary Data   173

The test markets are selected because they reflect consumer and competitive characteristics important to the company.

To prepare for a test market, companies gather detailed information about consumers, competitors, and past marketing activities in the area. The companies try new product ideas or make marketing changes in the test markets. They collect data on the product performance for several months and compare it with previously gathered information. In this way, they can attempt to predict the performance in their total market based on the results in the test market.

Simulations

Sometimes experiments are not possible in actual markets. **Simulations** are experiments where researchers create the situation to be studied. For example, a business may want to see how children respond when playing with a new toy. Rather than observing children playing in their homes or schools, the business may organize a play center. Then they bring groups of children

MARKETING COMMUNICATION

Today's Fragmented Media

Fifty years ago, people got their information from a limited number of media outlets. Towns had one or two newspapers. There were only a few network television and radio stations and a limited number of magazines. However, with the introduction of the World Wide Web in 1993, the choices facing market planners has expanded.

Compared to today, planning and executing a marketing campaign was simple. Now cable and satellite television offer hundreds of stations, and bookstores and newsstands carry magazines that cater to every interest, lifestyle, and hobby. There is AM, FM, and satellite radio, and the Internet is growing exponentially. While there are more media sources from which to choose, in general, each one draws a smaller audience because viewers are now spread over more media outlets. This phenomenon is known as *media fragmentation*.

With the increasingly fragmented media, marketers need to work harder to reach a broad audience. For instance, because a TV commercial during a popular network show today does not reach as many people as one during a popular show in 1980, marketers have to run the commercial on many different stations and will often make it available on the Internet as well.

Think Critically

1. Make a list of different media fragments with which marketers may need to contend.
2. What are some advantages to consumers of fragmented media?
3. How does fragmented media make it more difficult for marketers to reach potential buyers?

Sources: Bergstrom, Guy. "Why Audiences are Fragmented, and What You Can Do About It." The Balance Small Business. June 12, 2017. https://www.thebalancesmb.com/why-audiences-are-fragmented-and-what-you-can-do-about-it-2295929; Kuefler, John. "Media Fragmentation: 10 Things You Can Do Right Now." Callahan. June 1, 2019. https://callahan.agency/media-fragmentation-ten-things-you-can-do-right-now-1/

into the center and observe them under more carefully controlled circumstances. An automobile maker trying to improve the driving experience can build a small area that duplicates the front seat and dashboard of a car. By changing the design and positions of the seat, steering wheel, and controls, the company can determine which is most satisfying.

Many simulations are now done on computers. Computer graphics allow research participants to visualize a change and react to it. Architects can use computer software to develop a complete external view of a proposed building from all sides. The software allows the viewer to enter all doors and immediately see the interior of a room. The software could be used to test consumers' attitudes about changes in the architectural plans of the building before final design decisions are made.

*Analyze a case study that focuses on chapter concepts. Click on **Chapter 6, Case Study,** in your MindTap.*

Connect to MindTap

CHECKPOINT
Why do marketers use experiments in collecting primary data?

6.4 ASSESSMENT

What Have You Learned?

1. Why should researchers avoid gathering unnecessary information in market research surveys? [6.4.1]

2. Why is it important that participants in a market research study not know they are being observed? [6.4.2]

3. Based on what criteria do companies select test markets? [6.4.3]

Make Academic Connections

1. **Communication** Join with five to eight students to form a marketing research focus group. Assign one member as the facilitator and one member as a recorder. The topic of the focus group is positive and negative customer service experiences. When you have finished, have the recorder summarize the results of the discussion. [6.4.1]

2. **Science** Prepare a two-paragraph written comparison of the similarities and differences between conducting an experiment in a science laboratory and conducting a marketing experiment in a test market. Based on your understanding of the scientific process, make two recommendations of how to conduct effective marketing experiments. [6.4.3]

Connect to ◇DECA

Build your Portfolio

Your marketing research team is responsible for surveying parents about the factors they consider when choosing a restaurant for dining with their children. Prepare a written survey with three closed-ended and two open-ended questions. Present your survey to your teacher (judge) and explain why each question was included and the value of the results. [6.4.1]

CHAPTER 6 **ASSESSMENT**

Review Marketing Concepts

1. Why do you think a company would want to gather information about its competition? [6.1.1]

2. Explain the statement, "Effective marketing information reduces the risk in decision making." [6.1.2]

3. Which source of marketing information, internal or external, do you think is better? Explain your answer. [6.2.1]

4. Describe how having a marketing information system would benefit a business. [6.2.2]

5. Explain why defining the marketing problem is important to a successful marketing research effort. [6.3.1]

6. Which is easier to analyze: numerical or non-numerical data? Explain your answer. [6.3.2]

7. In your own words, what two considerations should researchers keep in mind when preparing a marketing research report? [6.3.3]

8. In your opinion, are open-ended or closed-ended questions more useful to market researchers? Explain your answer. [6.4.1]

9. How is the use of barcode scanners at the checkout counters of retail stores a form of gathering research by observation? [6.4.2]

10. Why would a company use test markets to help understand its market and clients? [6.4.3]

Marketing Research and Planning

1. Using an Internet search engine and browser, find the FedStats home page, which is a gateway to statistics from more than 100 federal agencies. Select your state from the MapStats drop-down menu, and then locate the most recent population statistics for your state and county. What percentage of your state's total population resides in your county? Describe what other kinds of information is available on this website. Identify several ways that marketers could use the data provided by FedStats. [6.2.1]

2. A marketing information system (MkIS) has five components: input, storage, analysis, output, and decision making. You want to earn a high grade on your next marketing test, so you decide to develop a system to organize and review the information you are learning. Plan an MkIS you could use. Using pictures or brief descriptions, identify your (a) inputs, (b) storage, (c) analysis, (d) outputs, and (e) decision making that will result in a high grade on your test. [6.2.2]

3. Categories of information for marketing researchers include business data, consumer information, economic information, government data, and information about specific industries. Use the library or Internet to identify two information sources for each of these categories. For each information source, prepare a note card that describes the publication name, publisher, copyright date or frequency of publication, and type of information included in the publication. [6.2.2]

4. Identify which of the five steps in scientific problem solving is described by each of the following marketing research activities:

   a. After receiving the surveys from the respondents, the analyst tabulates the results and prepares charts illustrating the survey results.

   b. The manager reviews sales records for the past five years to see if there have been changes in the geographic location of customers during that time.

c. After considering several methods to collect information, researchers decide to organize two test markets using different distribution methods to determine which is most effective.

d. The managers listened to the report of the research results and decided to implement the research team's top three recommendations.

e. In a discussion with salespeople, the marketing manager agrees that there has been an increase in the number of customer complaints about the cost of repair parts for the product. [6.3.1]

Marketing Management and Decision Making

1. The band boosters at your school are planning a fundraising activity. They want to sell two-pocket folders that can hold full-size papers. The folders would be printed and assembled by a local company and sold to students and faculty. The boosters want your help in determining a design for the folder, the price to charge, and the best ways to promote the folder in school to achieve a high sales volume. Prepare a proposal of three to five pages describing a marketing research study that will help the boosters answer their questions. Include the following sections in your proposal: identify the problem, design the research method, select the participants, analyze the data, and report the research results. The proposal should include at least two of the three types of data collection—survey, observation, and experiment. [6.3.1]

2. An important part of the marketing research process is analyzing the data after it has been collected. The chart below shows the data collected from a study of store and brand choices for four age groups of consumers. One thousand people were surveyed, and the respondents indicated their preferred store and brand.

Calculate the following information from the data in the chart and develop tables, charts, or graphs to illustrate the results.

a. Determine the total number of participants who prefer each store and each brand. (To determine the total, add the numbers in each column.)

b. Using the totals from part a, calculate the percentage of the total number of participants who prefer each store and each brand. (To calculate the percentage, divide the total of each column by the total number of participants.)

c. For each of the age categories, calculate the percentage of respondents who prefer each store and each brand. (Divide the number of respondents in each preference category by the total number of participants in that age category.)

d. Illustrate the rank order of stores and the rank order of brands for each age category.

Age	Store Preference			Brand Preference		
	Bardoes	**Kelvins**	**1-2-3**	**Motif**	**Astra**	**France**
16–20	38	82	130	80	106	76
21–25	56	20	174	156	90	18
26–30	110	64	76	104	98	60
31–35	44	120	86	54	30	128

(Rank order shows the store and brand that is most preferred, next most preferred, and so on.) Then illustrate the rank order of stores and brands when the responses of all age categories are combined.

e. Using the information you have summarized for parts a through d, develop two conclusions about store and brand preferences for the sample surveyed. [6.3.2]

Let's Start a Band Follow-Up Discussion

Work in small teams to discuss the question posed at the end of the opening vignette. Should the band use marketing research to help it understand its audience? Why or why not?

Build Your Marketing Plan

In this chapter you learned about the importance of conducting marketing research to marketing planning. You will now apply this learning to the development of your marketing plan. To access the chapter-specific tools that you will need to complete this activity, please navigate to Chapter 6 ➜ Build Your Marketing Plan in MindTap. Alternatively, you can access these tools online at NGLSync. Please visit www.nglsync.cengage.com, and search for the companion website that accompanies this book by entering the ISBN, author, or title. Once you locate this companion website, navigate to Build Your Marketing Plan ➜ Chapter 6.

Buying and Merchandising Operations Research Event

Build your Portfolio You have been hired by a national home improvement chain store to conduct customer research. The company's current advertising campaign emphasizes personalized customer service, using actual testimonials from satisfied customers. Now the company wants to survey a cross section of customers to determine if the store is delivering on its promises. The purpose of your research is to determine customer perception of the company, expectations for customer service, and level of customer satisfaction. You will analyze current media and its effectiveness and propose a strategic plan to include institutional promotion campaign activities for the home improvement store chain.

Executive Summary Write a one-page description of the project.

Introduction Describe the business or organization and the target market. This part of the written entry should include geographic, demographic, and socioeconomic factors about the community.

Research Methods Used in the Advertising Media Analysis Describe the design for the advertising media and methods used to conduct the advertising media analysis.

Findings and Conclusions Describe the advertising media available and provide a cost analysis of it. Describe the advertising media's potential impact on the target market. Provide a rationale for the selection of the most cost-effective media.

Proposed Strategic Plan Highlight the goals, objectives, and rationale of the strategic plan. Outline the proposed institutional promotion campaign activities, timelines, and the budget.

Bibliography and Appendix These are the last two sections of the report. The appendix is optional.

Performance Indicators Evaluated

- Describe the nature of target marketing in marketing communications. (Market Planning)
- Identify product's/service's competitive advantage. (Product/Service Management)
- Conduct advertising tracking studies. (Marketing-Information Management)

Go to the DECA website for more detailed information. **www.deca.org**

Think Critically

1. Why should a popular national home improvement store conduct customer research?

2. What incentive could be offered to customers to make sure they respond to a survey?

3. Why is it important for a store to validate its level of customer service before highlighting the service in advertisements?

4. Why should a popular company pay attention to the customer service of its competitors?

CHAPTER 7

COMPETITION IS EVERYWHERE

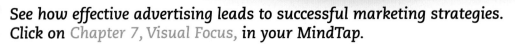

See how effective advertising leads to successful marketing strategies.
Click on Chapter 7, Visual Focus, in your MindTap.

Let's Start a Band!

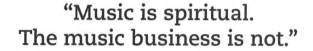

> ## "Music is spiritual.
> ## The music business is not."
>
> – *Van Morrison, Singer–Songwriter, Record Producer*

After a show one night I asked the group, "Why does our audience come to see us? What is it about us that they really like?" I wanted to know what we can do to set ourselves apart.

"You know, it's called show *business*," Layla emphasized. "Image is everything. The image we create will set us apart," she said.

Gael worried that if we focused on creating an image, we might look like fakes or sellouts.

"No, it doesn't mean we change who we are," Naomi answered. "It just means we commit to a specific tone, look, and feel. Something fans can relate to."

Malik turned to Layla and said, "I want them to leave saying they've never heard—or seen—anything like us before."

Eddie pointed out that no matter what direction we take, we have to remain true to ourselves. Our music must be authentic.

Me? I didn't respond. That's why I came to you. Do you think we can both create a unique image to set us apart *and* be authentic?

Learning Objectives

7.1.1 Describe the benefits and categories of market segmentation.

7.1.2 Explain how to identify market segments and determine their potential.

Key Terms

market segmentation
mass marketing
geographic segmentation
demographics
psychographics

product usage
benefit segmentation
market opportunity
market potential
market share

marketing matters

Businesses focus their marketing efforts on potential customers who are most likely to buy their products and services. They identify market segments or groups of consumers that share certain characteristics. Those characteristics may be personal factors such as age, education, income, or gender, or they may identify where consumers live, their lifestyles, needs, interests, or other factors that influence what they might want to purchase.

essential question

How do consumers' personal characteristics affect their purchase decisions?

7.1.1 ▶ Market Segmentation

In order to compete in a free enterprise economy, businesses direct their efforts and resources toward achieving specific goals. As an important part of their efforts, they devise marketing strategies to compete for sales dollars, customers, market share, or any goal they have set.

The Benefits of Segmentation

A *market segment* is a group of individuals or organizations within a larger market that share one or more important

Is it possible for this group of teenagers to represent more than one market segment? Explain why or why not.

© Riccardo Piccinini/Shutterstock.com

characteristics. These shared characteristics result in similar product or service needs. Everyone belongs to many market segments. For example, you may belong to one segment of the population that enjoys salsa dancing and another segment that drinks flavored water.

Businesses use marketing information and market research to complete market segmentation. **Market segmentation** is the process of dividing a large group of consumers into subgroups based on specific characteristics and common needs. Recognizing the needs of a specific segment of prospective customers enables a business to develop marketing strategies that match those needs.

Some businesses may be unwilling to spend the extra time and money required to gather and analyze information in order to segment a market. Instead they use **mass marketing**, which directs the company's marketing mix to serve a large and heterogeneous group of consumers. With market segmentation, the company views its competition as businesses that offer products and services that appeal to the selected market segment. Mass marketing considers all of the consumers in a market as potential customers and therefore every other business competing in that market as a competitor. By appealing to a more diverse group of customers with different needs and competing with many more businesses, success may be more difficult. However, advantages of mass marketing include higher potential sales volumes and efficiencies of scale in a much larger market.

Large companies with high-volume production and vast distribution networks reaching many national and international markets can use mass marketing quite effectively. However, smaller or more specialized businesses have found a mass marketing strategy difficult to maintain. Companies that believe in the marketing concept recognize that the increased time and expense of market segmentation will enable them to identify groups of customers and understand their needs.

Segmentation Categories

Using market segmentation, marketers can classify consumers into groups based on important categories including geographic location, demographic characteristics, psychographics, product usage, and expected benefits.

GEOGRAPHIC SEGMENTATION

Classifying consumers into markets based on where they live is **geographic segmentation**. These markets might be as large as a country or as small as a ZIP code. Just as companies vary in size and scope, the group of customers they want to reach also varies.

Geographic segmentation is based on the concept that people who live in the same geographic area might have the same wants and needs. Consumers who live in Minnesota are more likely to have an interest in cold weather sports than people who live in south Texas. A political party may want to send newsletters on a particular issue to voters in specific congressional districts.

DEMOGRAPHIC CHARACTERISTICS

The descriptive characteristics of a market such as age, gender, race, income, and educational level are referred to as **demographics**. The population of the United States can be described using two demographic characteristics—education

Want to know more about what is trending with this topic? Click on **Lesson 7.1, Global Marketing,** in your MindTap.

Connect to MindTap

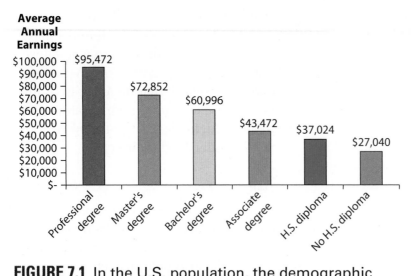

FIGURE 7.1 In the U.S. population, the demographic characteristics of education and income are closely linked.

Source: Bureau of Labor Statistics, 2018, https://www.bls.gov/careeroutlook/2018/data-on-display/education-pays.htm

and income (**Figure 7-1**). Often marketers want to serve a market segment that has similar demographic characteristics. Types of music, cable TV channels, magazines, and restaurant menus may be developed to appeal to different ages, education levels, or ethnic groups. You belong to many demographic market segments. Marketers may segment you according to your age, gender, ethnicity, religious affiliation, and even your body type.

PSYCHOGRAPHICS

People's interests and values are referred to as **psychographics**. Examples of psychographics are the way you spend your time and make your lifestyle choices. Lifestyle research has been particularly valuable in establishing market segments. People's lifestyles and social interests combine to influence the type of housing and transportation they prefer, where they choose to live, how they spend

*Want to know more about what is trending with this topic? Click on **Lesson 7.1, Marketing Decisions,** in your MindTap.*

Connect to
MindTap

their time, and even how often they eat away from home.

Psychographic segmentation allows businesses to find segments with wants and needs unique from the mass market. It is responsible for the creation of many unique products, from automobile models, home décor, and health care products to coffee shops and sports venues.

PRODUCT USAGE

Marketing strategies can differ based on **product usage**, meaning how frequently consumers use products and the quantity of product used. Product usage is based on people's behavior, so this type of segmentation also may be referred to as *behavioral segmentation*. Some people have a preferred beverage and drink it several times a day. Others vary their beverages at meals but may have a particular choice for breaks or when exercising.

The quantity of a beverage consumed at one time varies and accounts for the range of container sizes used for beverages. Some people consume only a few ounces of a drink at one time. They may want to purchase a small container or want a resealable container to maintain the freshness of the beverage. However, with the popularity of the 32-ounce or larger-size soft drinks at convenience stores and fast-food restaurants, it is evident that some people expect to drink a large quantity at one time. By segmenting the market based on usage, businesspeople can make sure each group has the preferred size and type of container to meet their consumption needs.

Other examples of marketing products based on product usage include planning hotel services for frequent business travelers and offering cellphone plans suited to the number of phones in a family and the number of minutes, text messages, and data used in one month.

Customer experience is a part of product usage. Experience ranges from none to extensive. Of experienced users, some have tried the product and don't like it. Others believe it is one of several appropriate alternatives, but they have no preference. Still other customers purchase and use it regularly as their preferred choice. The type of experience will help determine whether a market segment represents a valuable group of potential customers and what type of marketing effort is needed.

BENEFIT EXPECTATIONS As you learned earlier, each product or service on the market has a value or utility to the consumer. Consumers have specific benefits they expect to receive when using a particular product or service. **Benefit segmentation** divides consumers into groups depending on specific values or benefits they expect or require from the use of a product or service. An example of using benefit segmentation can be seen with shampoo. There are many market segments for a product as simple as shampoo based on the expectations and requirements of consumers. There are shampoos for consumers with oily hair, dry hair, or normal hair. There are also shampoos for people with dandruff as well as for those who shampoo daily versus once a week or less. There are even shampoos with conditioners added for people who want

How can market segmentation be used to devise a marketing strategy for a hotel?

one-step hair care. Add the various scents and additives and you can see the infinite number of segments that can be created based on benefits.

Segmenting the Business Market

Just as marketers segment the consumer markets, they also segment business markets. Business markets are segmented by the type of company and the major activities and operations of the business. The size of the business and its geographic location, including whether the company operates in multiple states and even internationally, may be important segmenting criteria. Finally, the types of products and services purchased, the volume and frequency of purchasing, and the type of buying procedures used help to segment business customers.

CHECKPOINT

Why do businesses that believe in the marketing concept use market segmentation rather than mass marketing?

There are two reasons to segment a market. First, by carefully analyzing a market based on segmenting characteristics, a business has a better understanding of the market and the potential customers. Second, with detailed information on market segments, a business can identify the best market opportunities. A **market opportunity** is an identified market with excellent potential based on careful research.

Identify Possible Segments

To successfully segment a market, a business must recognize possible factors that affect consumer purchasing. It also must collect information to determine if market segments are alike or different in their purchasing behaviors and consumption patterns. Identifying market segments involves the following steps:

1. **Select a market or product category to study.** The market will be a large group of consumers who have similar but broad needs, such as entertainment or transportation, or who are likely to purchase a category of products such as computers or sporting goods. The market or product category is often one in which the business has experience, or it may be a new category for the business. The business may be looking for new product ideas, new customers for their products and services, or new opportunities for both customers and products.

2. **Choose a basis for segmenting the market.** Determine what factors seem to lead to the greatest differences among customers and may affect their expectations and choices.

3. **Gather information for analysis.** This step will usually involve a combination of reviewing current customer information, identifying and collecting additional information, and completing marketing research.

4. **Identify the segments that exist in the market.** Based on the information collected, several potential segments are identified and described based on unique characteristics that influence the market potential, such as geographic location or product usage.

5. **Use market information to choose the markets that present the greatest and least amount of potential.** Those with the greatest potential will be analyzed further to select the target markets that will be the focus for the company's marketing efforts.

Determine Market Potential

Once market segments have been identified, they must be analyzed. To be an effective market segment, it must have the potential to be profitable. Each segment should be evaluated on the following criteria:

1. Number of potential consumers

2. Customers' interest in the product or service and other mix elements

3. Money customers have available to make the purchase

4. Business's ability to communicate with and distribute the product to consumers

Businesses operate to make a profit, so it is important to estimate the market potential. The **market potential** is the total revenue that can be obtained from a market segment. Because it is unlikely that one company will attract all customers in a given market, businesses also calculate their market share. **Market share** is the portion of the total market potential that each company expects in relation to its competitors.

For example, the total market potential for plastic storage bins in one city is estimated at $1,850,000 per year. One manufacturer is introducing a new type of plastic storage bin and expects to capture 12 percent of the total market in the city in the first year. To calculate the company's planned market share in dollars, multiply $1,850,000 by 0.12 for a total of $222,000.

The company also can determine the market potential and market share in units instead of dollars. If the average price of a plastic storage bin is $9.25, the market potential in units is $1,850,000 divided by $9.25, or 200,000 units. The company's planned market share is 12 percent of 200,000 units, or 24,000 plastic storage bins (200,000 × 0.12). The company has the potential of selling 24,000 storage bins in this market segment in this city.

CHECKPOINT
What is the relationship between market potential and market share?

ASSESSMENT

What Have You Learned?

1. Which market segmentation strategy classifies consumers on characteristics such as age, gender, race, income, and educational level? [7.1.1]

2. Which market segmentation strategy is also called behavioral segmentation? [7.1.1]

3. Why does a business need to identify the segments of a market it wants to enter? [7.1.2]

Make Academic Connections

1. **Visual Art**   Draw a large circle that represents the mass market of all television viewers. Now draw and label five smaller circles within the large circle that represent a television show or a cable television channel that has a particular focus (example: The Food Network). For each small circle, identify several characteristics of a market segment that enjoys the shows or channels. [7.1.1]

2. **Math**   In one quarter, worldwide sales of smartphones were 355.6 million units. Samsung had a market share of 20.3%, followed by Huawei with 14.6%, Apple with 13.2%, Xiaomi with 9.5%, and OPPO with 8.4%. How many smartphones did each company sell? How many units were sold by all other companies, and what market share did those sales represent? [7.1.2]

Connect to ◇DECA

Build your portfolio

Your team manages a new jewelry store in your community. Identify a specific market segment based on demographic and psychographic characteristics for your products. Prepare two visuals that describe your market segment. Make a three-minute presentation to your teacher (judge) justifying your decisions. [7.1.1]

21ST CENTURY SUCCESS SKILLS
Be an Effective Listener

You encounter many events and activities in your life where listening is required. How well you listen can affect your success in many ways. Academically, it is important to listen during class. Focused listening and careful note taking will help you prepare for homework, projects, and tests.

Listening in social situations also is important. A friend may need you to listen to a problem and provide emotional support. When you are at a meeting or other gathering with people you don't know well, listening to the conversation of those around you may give you clues about their interests and allow you to comfortably interact.

In business, effective listening can mean the difference between success and failure. Businesspeople must listen to customers, coworkers, and even competitors to be successful.

In all situations, it is important to use "active listening." Active listening goes beyond simply hearing what the speaker says. It involves recognizing the emotions behind the words. Suppose your friend, who is trying to qualify for a college scholarship, says, "That calculus test was hard. I only got a C+." Using the active listening technique, you might reply by saying "Does that make you worried about how that grade will impact your chance to get the scholarship? Do you want to talk about it?"

Being a good listener requires patience and generosity. You should give the speaker your full attention, staying focused on the topic and their concerns.

Components of Effective Listening

There are several specific components to effective listening. They are decoding, comprehension, drawing a conclusion, and feedback.

Decoding a message involves translating what the speaker said into the real meaning of the message. Comprehension involves determining how the message relates to the overall topic. When the listener decides how to respond to the message, the listener is drawing a conclusion. Feedback is given to the speaker by both verbal and nonverbal responses.

Improve Your Listening Skills

Several barriers may interfere with your listening ability. Preconceived attitudes about the speaker or the topic can interfere with understanding the message. Background activity or noises that distract the listener's attention can interfere with listening. A speaker's biases can also impact the information being conveyed. You should always try to assess the logic and accuracy of the speaker's message.

You can convey your interest in what is being said through body language. Maintaining eye contact, smiling, and leaning toward the speaker all signal that you are listening attentively.

Techniques to improve listening skills include being prepared to listen, reducing distractions, asking questions to clarify main points, refraining from judgment, and paraphrasing what was said to confirm your understanding. In complicated or prolonged listening situations, taking notes will help you remember what you heard.

Develop Your Skill

Let your parents know that for one week you are going to try to improve your listening skills. Whenever your parents talk to you, give them your full attention. Eliminate any background noise, including TVs, computers, or music players. If they are outlining family plans for the week or giving instructions, take notes on what they say to capture the main points. See how smoothly the next day flows. Continue this practice through Friday. On Saturday, ask your parents for feedback on whether they have noticed an improvement in your listening skills.

Learning Objectives

7.2.1 Explain the various bases for positioning a product to distinguish it from the competition.

7.2.2 Describe the three common positioning strategies.

Key Terms

market position
positioning strategy
consumer perceptions

marketing matters

Businesses know that people usually consider a number of products or services as alternatives when they try to satisfy specific needs. Marketers carefully plan marketing mix elements to influence how a product or service is perceived. When planning a marketing mix, they should consider how it affects consumer perceptions, how it compares to the mixes of competitors, and how it will be affected by the business and economic environment.

essential question

Why should a company's product have a unique image that appeals to consumers and differs from competitors' products?

7.2.1 Bases for Positioning

In order to influence consumers' purchases, businesses position their products and services to highlight how they differ from those of competitors. **Market position** refers to the unique image of a product or service in a consumer's mind relative to similar competitive offerings. Products may be positioned using various methods. An example of how the various positioning methods can be used for a product as simple as laundry detergent is shown in **Figure 7-2**.

Product Feature

One way to position a product is to highlight a product feature or attribute. For example, certain toothpastes have ingredients that whiten teeth. The manufacturer says, "Our toothpaste does everything every other toothpaste does, and in addition, it helps make your teeth white." The positioning is accomplished with the specific product feature and related promotion that identifies the feature and its value for the consumer.

Price and Quality

This positioning strategy may stress a higher price as a sign of quality, or it may emphasize a lower price as an indication of value. Mercedes Benz does not apologize for the high price of its automobiles. Instead, it suggests that because they are high-priced they offer a unique,

	Laundry Product A	Laundry Product B
Product Feature	Cleans quickly and easily	Leaves fresh scent
Price and Quality	Low price, good value	Higher price for highest quality
Use or Application	Use as pre-wash on tough stains	Use for hand-washing delicates
Product User	Homemaker's reliable friend	New generation's discovery
Product Classification	Used by Olympic athletes	Used by professional laundries
Competitor	Gets out dirt Product B can't	Gentler on clothing than Product A

FIGURE 7.2 Competitors develop marketing mixes that emphasize the market positions of their products. These laundry products are positioned to appeal to different markets.

high-quality image. With its promotions, Walmart implies that its products are well suited for consumers' needs with the advantage of being priced lower than competitors' products. Walmart's positioning goal is accomplished by creating the desired level of quality in the product and establishing an appropriate price. This serves to convince customers they get a good value when they shop there.

Use or Application

Stressing unique uses or applications can be an effective means of positioning a product. Arm & Hammer baking soda used to be a staple for homemakers who regularly baked bread, biscuits, and rolls for their families. As families began purchasing rather than baking those products, the market for Arm & Hammer's product declined. The company changed its positioning strategy by developing and promoting new uses and applications for baking soda ranging from deodorizing the refrigerator to brushing teeth to keeping the cat's litter box fresh.

Product User

This positioning strategy encourages use of a product or service by associating a personality or type of user with the product.

For a time, PepsiCo suggested that Pepsi products were consumed by a young, active "Pepsi Generation." Athletic apparel manufacturers use images and obtain endorsements of popular professional athletes.

Product Classification

The objective for product class positioning is to associate the product with a particular category of products. For example, Amtrak, which offers rail-passenger service, uses strategies that model the look, service, and scheduling associated with airlines.

Competitor

Sometimes marketers demonstrate how their products are positioned against those of competitors that hold a strong market position. When the Korean automobile manufacturer Hyundai introduced its new, larger, and more luxurious Genesis models, it began to compare itself to the well-known luxury brands sold in the United States. The company did not think consumers would immediately believe Hyundai had the most luxurious products. However, it wanted consumers to think of its Genesis models when considering the purchase of a luxury automobile. It was successful enough that Genesis eventually became its own brand and was often rated highest among luxury brands. As another example, Samsung often compares the features of its smartphones with those of the Apple iPhone when introducing a new model. Anytime you see an ad comparing one product with a well-known competitor's products, a competitor positioning strategy is being used.

WORKING IN TEAMS

As a team, identify a new consumer product that has recently been introduced. Discuss the marketing mix being used to market the product. What would it take to get you to try the new product? Why might you decide to continue with your current product choice rather than switch to the new product?

CHECKPOINT
What are six common bases for positioning?

MATH IN MARKETING

Big Ten Expansion—Which Numbers Count?

When the Big Ten Conference announced two new teams, many of the league's fans were puzzled. The newest teams, Rutgers and Maryland, had not enjoyed much recent athletic success. Other candidates such as the University of Connecticut, the University of Louisville, and the University of Cincinnati in the Midwest had much better athletic records in the major sports.

How did the Big Ten decide which teams to add? They chose the schools with the most television households in their media market. Maryland was in the nation's 8th largest market while Rutgers was in the country's largest, New York City. Big Ten marketers can demand a higher price for the networks to carry their games and get the Big Ten network onto cable and satellite systems in two large media markets.

Do the Math

1. Research the top U.S. television markets and compare the list to cities that have major professional sports teams in a professional football, baseball, basketball, or hockey league. Based on the television market size, list the top five cities which are candidates for expansion for that league.
2. From a marketing perspective, what other considerations would a sports league have in making a decision to expand to a new city?

Select a Positioning Strategy

All businesses need to develop a positioning strategy. A **positioning strategy** outlines how a company will present its product or service to the consumer and how it will compete in the marketplace with other businesses offering similar products and services. Positioning strategies are based on the following factors:

1. Consumer perceptions
2. Competitors in the marketplace
3. Changes in the business environment

Why is consumer perception important for a restaurant?

Consumer Perceptions

Consumer perceptions are the images consumers have of competing goods and services in the marketplace. The objective is for marketers to position their products to appeal to the desires and perceptions of a target market. A group of consumers that has a distinct idea of the image desired for a product or service might represent a target market. A business will do well with a target market when those consumers perceive the attributes of its products as being close to their ideal image. Over the years, Hershey has done an excellent job of responding to consumer perceptions. For years, its product was perceived by many consumers as the ideal chocolate bar. However, in recent years, several competitors have entered the premium chocolate market, forcing Hershey to expand its product line and increase its promotional efforts.

Competition

Businesses are concerned about the perception consumers have of the company and its products in relation to those of competitors. Ideally consumers perceive a business's products to be superior to its competitors' products or services based on the attributes the company emphasizes in its marketing strategy.

A great deal of marketing effort is used in competitive positioning. The pricing, promotion, product development, and distribution strategies are all planned with an eye toward the competition. Certain products, such as soft drinks, must be carefully positioned in relation to competition because image is important to consumers as they choose a brand. Coca-Cola and Pepsi have staged a very fierce and competitive promotional battle for many years to gain a stronger competitive position. This competition has been referred to as the "Cola Wars."

Companies must be careful not to base their positioning decisions solely on the actions of their competitors. Each company has unique strengths and weaknesses as well as specific goals. A competitor's new

*Want to know more about what is trending with this topic? Click on **Lesson 7.2, Digital Marketing,** in your MindTap.*

Connect to MindTap

marketing strategy should be watched carefully, and information should be collected on the effect it has on a company's customers and its market share.

Business Environment

Organizations should continually pay attention to possible changes in the business environment that might affect the position of their products or services. These include new products entering the market, changing consumer needs, new technology, negative publicity, and resource availability. Manufacturers of golf clubs have been significantly affected by the introduction of new materials used in shaft construction as well as new club head designs. Restaurants have had to respond to the banning of plastic straws in some areas due to environmental concerns.

Colleges have discovered they must respond to the needs of nontraditional students, including more part-time and older students. Colleges have responded by offering convenient schedules, adding more parking, and expanding online course offerings. In each case, these business environment changes have affected marketing strategies and even the types of products and services offered.

CHECKPOINT
Why should businesses be cautious when using competitive positioning?

ASSESSMENT

What Have You Learned?

1. What is a company's market position? [7.2.1]
2. What are the three factors on which a positioning strategy is based? [7.2.2]

Make Academic Connections

1. **Communications** Use print, Internet, radio, or television advertisements to prepare an exhibit of the six bases for positioning described in the lesson. The exhibit can be in the form of a poster, audio or video recording, or another medium. [7.2.1]
2. **History** Use Internet or library research to identify and study a company that has operated for more than 50 years and has made a major change in the market position of a key product. Write a one-page report that describes the reasons for the change, including responses to consumer perceptions, competitors' actions, or changes in the business environment. [7.2.2]

Connect to ◇DECA

Build your Portfolio

A new bank in your community has asked your marketing team to propose an idea for a successful market position. Prepare a print advertisement that clearly communicates the image you have selected. Present the advertisement to your teacher (judge). Identify the basis for the market position chosen and explain why your team believes it will be effective. [7.2.1]

COMPETE FOR MARKET SEGMENTS

Learning Objectives

7.3.1 Distinguish between direct and indirect competition.

7.3.2 Distinguish between price and nonprice competition.

7.3.3 Describe the benefits of competition to consumers.

Key Terms

direct competition
indirect competition
price competition
nonprice competition

marketing matters

Market segments are important because they contain the potential customers for marketers' products. Competition is the rivalry between two or more businesses to secure a dominant position in a market. The products of some businesses are almost identical, resulting in fierce competition and pressures to reduce prices in order to attract customers. Other businesses have products that have notable differences, making competition less intense.

essential question

What effect does competition between businesses have on changes and improvements to the products offered for sale?

7.3.1 ▶ Direct and Indirect Competition

Just as there are different types of market segments and positioning strategies, there are different types of competition that businesses face when positioning their products. To be able to compete successfully, businesses must be able to identify and reach a market segment that has a need for their product or service and position itself effectively against its competitors.

The type of competition faced by a business will affect its positioning. There are two major types of competition that businesses must recognize and address—direct versus indirect competition and price versus nonprice competition.

Direct competition is competition in a market with businesses that offer the same type of product or service. This is a common form of competition. For example, Holiday Inn and Ramada compete with each other for travelers' dollars.

Businesses that compete directly must know who their competitors are. For example, McDonald's has obvious competitors such as Burger King and Wendy's. It also competes against other fast-food restaurants such as KFC, Taco Bell, and Chipotle. These are all direct competitors even though they may offer different menu items. In competing with these businesses, McDonald's tells consumers why its menu items taste better and are a better value. McDonald's goal is to convince every customer that it offers the best choice among all competing brands.

Indirect competition occurs when a business competes with other companies offering products that are not in the same product category but that satisfy similar customer needs. A movie theater competes directly with other area theaters, but it competes indirectly with Netflix and the on-demand feature of many cable television services, and even more broadly with other entertainment choices.

If McDonald's promotes its products as easy and convenient to obtain, then it might be competing indirectly with meals offered at the deli counters of many supermarkets and convenience stores. McDonald's also might find itself competing with easy-to-prepare frozen meals that can be popped into the microwave for a quick individual or family meal. Remember that you have limited dollars to spend on a meal, and there are many factors that can affect your choice of the type of meal and the place to purchase it. How does McDonald's compete with all of the indirect competitors available to consumers in the marketplace?

The marketing managers at McDonald's have some important decisions to make. One decision they must make involves the features of their products they will highlight or the benefits they will emphasize. Will it be quality, variety, price, convenience, or a family-friendly atmosphere? Each market segment places value on different things, and each

What is the direct and indirect competition for a small neighborhood grocery store?

business must appeal to the characteristics of its target segments. McDonald's will compete differently for a market segment that wants a fast breakfast before school or work than it does for the young family segment that wants affordable and nutritious menu choices for both adults and children. The recent addition of McCafés in most McDonald's restaurants shows that it views businesses such as Starbucks and Dunkin' Donuts as competitors.

CHECKPOINT
How do direct and indirect competition differ?

7.3.2 ▶ Price and Nonprice Competition

Because most consumers have limited dollars to spend and are looking for the best value, some marketers decide to emphasize price when they compete. Rivalry among businesses on the basis of price and value is called **price competition**. Look at the various weekly advertisements from your local supermarkets for an excellent example of price competition. Restaurants use price competition with their lunch or early evening dinner specials. Another example of price competition is airfares. If an airline decides to enter a new market, it will often offer a very low fare for the first weeks or months. In response, the competing airlines offering flights between the same cities will lower their fares for a time.

The opposite of price competition is nonprice competition. **Nonprice competition** occurs when businesses decide to emphasize factors of their marketing mix other than price. Those factors might include product quality, brand name, location, or special customer service. Nonprice competition occurs for several reasons. First of all, some businesses do not have a great deal of control over their price in relation to competitors. Insurance companies may not have much control over the price they can charge for policies because a state government agency regulates the industry's prices. Therefore, they focus on nonprice issues such as an easy-to-complete application, personalized services from an insurance agency, a mobile app that allows the policyholder to interact with the company, and prompt claims service when the policyholder suffers a loss.

A company also might choose to use nonprice competition when its product is priced higher. A small business may not be able to compete with large companies due to higher costs and lower volume. The small business may want to identify a specific market segment that is looking for factors other than price when making a purchase. The small business could emphasize individualized attention, delivery, set-up, and after-sale service, or even the long history of the business owners in the community as a balance for higher prices.

Nonprice competition is effective when the market segment values something other than price. The consumers must recognize a unique quality in the product that leads to a product preference regardless of the price. These qualities might be service, quality, credit, location, guarantees, or a unique image.

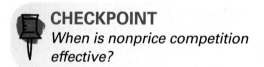

CHECKPOINT
When is nonprice competition effective?

7.3.3 ▶ Benefits of Competition

Consumers benefit in many ways from competition. One benefit is that competition forces businesses to offer reasonable prices for the products and services that consumers use. If businesses want to be successful, they must price their products in line with others in the same classification. As a result, the consumer is given the most value for the least amount of money.

A second benefit of competition is that it encourages improvements in products with the addition of unique features and benefits. Each company is looking for a way to make its product distinctive so that it attracts the attention of the market segment. The benefit to consumers is that they continue to see changes and improvements in product features and quality, often at little additional cost.

Third, to match their competition, businesses must continuously search for new product ideas. Bicycle manufacturers saw a need for a bicycle that was a cross between a traditional road bike and a mountain bike. They created a new cycling product known as a hybrid bike. Rugged, lightweight, and easier to pedal and maneuver, the hybrid bike is popular among weekend bikers and avid members of bicycle clubs.

Finally, competition offers consumers the benefit of a wide variety of products from which to choose. The market segments are so diverse that businesses make sure there are products to meet all consumers' wants and needs. An example of this is the range of television channels available to viewers. Today, with cable or satellite television services, viewers can access more than 200 television channels as well as music channels and premium movies. Each channel competes with the other channels for viewership, and cable and satellite services compete to provide these services. Viewers benefit from that type of competition by gaining more entertainment choices and greater price competition.

CHECKPOINT
How do consumers benefit from competition among businesses?

7.3 ASSESSMENT

What Have You Learned?

1. What type of competition occurs when a business competes with other companies offering products that are not in the same product category but that satisfy similar customer needs? [7.3.1]

2. What type of competition do newspaper ads featuring weekly specials at supermarkets represent? [7.3.2]

3. Why does competition often result in changes and improvements in product features and quality? [7.3.3]

Make Academic Connections

1. **Geography** Use an Internet mapping program such as Google Maps to prepare a map of a large shopping area in your community or a larger city close to you. Use the mapping feature to locate several businesses in direct competition with each other. Then locate several other businesses that compete indirectly. Print a copy of the map and use it to mark the business locations and type of competition each business faces. [7.3.1]

2. **Consumer Economics** Visit a large electronics store or use the Internet to identify three competitive brands of a popular electronic product. Gather the following comparative information: (1) brand name, (2) current list price and current sale price, (3) three features that are similar to those of competitors, (4) two features that are different from competitors. Develop a table to compare the brands using your findings. [7.3.1, 7.3.2]

Connect to ◇DECA

Build your Portfolio

Develop a two-minute informative speech on how principles of the free enterprise economy contribute to the benefits that consumers receive from competition described in the lesson. Prepare PowerPoint slides to accompany your presentation. Deliver your speech to your teacher (judge). [7.3.3]

LEARN ABOUT THE COMPETITION

Learning Objectives

7.4.1 Discuss the types of information businesses need to know about their competitors.

7.4.2 Describe how businesses collect market intelligence.

Key Terms

market intelligence
trade shows

marketing matters

In order to compete with other businesses, a company needs to find out all it can about those competitors. Athletic teams have used scouts for many years. They attend the competitors' games to analyze their strategies, tactics, strengths, and weaknesses. The information is used to prepare their own teams to be more effective competitors. The same is true in business. In order to compete effectively, businesses take a number of steps to learn as much as they can about their competitors. The process in business is called gathering market intelligence.

essential question

What types of information about competitors will help a business develop its marketing strategy? Are there types of information or ways the information is used that would be considered unethical?

7.4.1 ▶ Types of Competitive Information

Marketers want to develop each element of the marketing mix for their products and services to best meet the wants and needs of their consumers. But understanding wants and needs of market segments is not enough. In order to make sure the company's offerings will be the best available, a business must be aware of the strategies its competitors will use. A company needs to gather information on each of the competitors' marketing mix elements.

Pricing Strategies

When businesses are in direct competition, competitors' pricing strategies are very important. Are competitors planning a sale, or are they going to raise the price and add features, options, or services? For example, if Chrysler reduces the price of all of its cars and trucks as part of a year-end promotion, there will be a significant difference between its prices and the prices of its competitors if the competitors do not offer similar price incentives. Even though Toyota may believe it has established a brand preference in the minds of many consumers, will Chrysler's price cuts be enough to influence them? For some people, the answer would be yes, because for that segment price is the most significant factor when making a final choice between competing Toyota and Chrysler models. For others, the answer would be no because they value other factors for which they are willing to pay a higher price.

Distribution Decisions

The second area to study is the distribution systems that competitors use. Are competitors' products conveniently available to customers in a large number of locations or is distribution selective? Do competitors make it more convenient for consumers to purchase by offering Internet or catalog sales?

An important part of satisfying the wants and needs of the consumer is to have the product in the right place at the time the customer wants to purchase it. If the competition is planning on distribution changes, its products might be more convenient to purchase than yours. However, making products available at more locations adds to the cost, which usually must be passed on to the customer, or it will result in lower profits for the company. Making distribution changes usually requires a great deal of time and may involve other businesses, so they need to be planned carefully.

Product/Service Planning

The third type of competitive information involves changes to the products and services offered. One of the greatest challenges to a business is anticipating the introduction of a new product or service by a competitor. A new product usually will result in at least a temporary shift in consumer purchases until customers decide whether or not they like the new product. If customers prefer the new product, it may be difficult for a business to entice them back even when it is able to obtain and offer a similar product choice.

When Pepsi introduced a clear cola, Coke did not put a comparable product on the market to compete. Coke may have decided that the clear cola was not significant competition, or it may have believed that the product would not succeed. However, if it had been successful, Coke would have had to scramble to develop a competing brand, or it would have risked losing market share.

WORKING IN TEAMS

As a team, list three well-known brands of consumer products. Each team member should write a statement describing the image of each brand as he or she perceives it. Compare the statements for each brand and determine the amount of agreement on the image. Discuss the reasons for similarities and differences in perceptions.

Promotional Efforts

More attention may be focused on competitors' promotional efforts than on any of the other mix elements. Promotional strategies can be changed quickly. A unique promotional activity can grab consumers' attention. A well-timed promotion can have a direct effect on the sales of the business running the promotion and on its competitors.

If a furniture store runs a promotion offering discount prices and special financing for an upcoming weekend, how should competitors respond? Will they have time to plan and promote a similar sale? Should they allow the competitor's plans to influence their marketing strategy if it has already been determined? What effect will the promotion likely have on the competitors' sales during that weekend and for several weeks if the promotion results in high sales volume for the business?

Most promotions are designed to support other changes in a business's marketing mix—a new product introduction, opening a new location, or a special sale or price incentive. Competitors need to consider how to respond not only to the promotion but also to the other changes in the marketing mix.

Want to know more about what is trending with this topic? Click on **Lesson 7.4, Marketing Decisions,** *in your MindTap.*

Connect to MindTap

Competitive Market Position

There are other factors that affect each business's competitive edge. Is a new competitor entering the market? If so, what has that competitor's success been in similar markets? Has the business identified a new market segment it wants to serve? If so, is the competition for that segment the same as or different from its current markets? What effect will entering the new market have on existing customers?

How does the financial strength of a company's competitors compare? Do they have the money available to develop new products and improve old ones? Do they have the financial flexibility to respond to pricing changes?

What are the competitive strengths and weaknesses of the other companies? Do they emphasize customer relationships and service, or do they appear to be more focused on mass markets and low prices? Do they have well-known brands with strong customer loyalty? Do they have flexible and efficient distribution strategies? Are they viewed as innovative market leaders, or are they more traditional and conservative in their business practices?

Factors such as these can make the difference between success and failure of a product or service in the marketplace. Studying competitors to understand the strengths and weaknesses and to be able to anticipate and be prepared for competitors' actions is essential for the future success of a business.

> **CHECKPOINT**
> *What are the five types of information that businesses need to know about their competitors?*

7.4.2 ▶ Collect Competitive Information

The process of gaining competitive market information is called **market intelligence.** As a part of their marketing information systems and marketing research procedures, businesses determine the types of competitive information they need, the best sources for each type of information, and the procedures they will use to obtain and analyze the information. They then incorporate the information into their marketing planning.

Information Sources

Businesses engage in the following activities to gain information about the competition:

1. Instruct salespeople and other employees to be alert to information about competitors' products, prices, and anticipated changes.

2. Purchase and analyze competitors' products. The business can use the information to make product changes and recognize the areas where the competitive products have advantages and disadvantages.

3. Collect and study newspaper and magazine articles, government and university research reports, and other public information on competitors, new product research, and marketing trends. Companies may use employees or hire information services to collect and summarize the latest industry news.

4. Attend trade shows. **Trade shows** are exhibitions where companies associated with an industry gather to showcase their products. Vendors attending the

MARKETING COMMUNICATION

Attending Trade Shows

Attending trade shows is a great way for marketers to gather competitive intelligence. These events also give companies the chance to showcase their products and gauge market response to them, meet with current and potential customers, and enhance the morale of the team.

Most shows are sponsored by industry trade associations. This means that the people attending the shows are likely prospects for the company's products, all under one roof. Participation may be costly, however. Expenses include the cost of the booth or table, materials used in displaying products, pamphlets and other handouts for visitors, and possible travel expenses.

A company should set specific goals for attending the show, and then decide whether a given show will meet those goals. In addition to preparing the booth display and marketing materials, pre-attendance activities would include promoting the show to customers, setting up interviews with members of the media, writing a script for the staff, and devising a method to collect contact information for visitors. When the show is over, each lead must be followed-up.

Think Critically

1. You work as an assistant marketing manager for a company that manufactures industrial equipment. Your supervisor asks you to think of ways to collect the names of the people who will visit your booth at a trade show. Write an email to your supervisor that contains at least three ideas.

2. The staff returns to the office with hundreds of names of prospective customers. Draft the introduction to a letter to send to each lead, thanking them for visiting the booth and indicating the next step.

Source: https://www.legalzoom.com/articles/why-trade-shows-are-important-for-your-small-business

What do you think would be the main benefit to marketers attending a trade show?

trade show can gather information on what competitors are displaying and listen to customer opinions on the latest products.

5. Subscribe to professional association and trade group publications and special research reports.

6. Study customers and customer records. Businesses can learn a great deal about the competition by gathering information from customers.

7. Use the Internet. The Internet is becoming one of the best sources of current competitive information. Company websites provide a great deal of information intended for customers and investors, but the information also is useful to competitors.

Businesses do not collect competitive information randomly. Large businesses have staff responsible for working with market intelligence and conducting marketing research, including research on competitors. Their objectives are to identify the strengths and weaknesses of key competitors, assess their current marketing strategies, and predict their future actions.

Ethics in Information Gathering

Some individuals and companies have used unethical methods to obtain information. It is not always easy to determine whether or not a method is ethical. However, the usual standard is that if a competitor has information it considers to be private and does not disclose to people outside the business, obtaining and using that information would be unethical. In the same way, obtaining information through false pretenses or by accessing data from restricted locations is unethical. In some instances, it also may be illegal.

Unethical actions might involve coercing a customer or supplier to provide competitive information. More complex and illegal activities are attempting to access private areas of a company's electronic data system and attempting to bribe an employee for access to private information.

Companies should communicate their expectations about the confidentiality of information to employees, suppliers, and customers. Many companies include guidelines in their codes of ethics about sharing information with others and obtaining and using competitive information.

CHECKPOINT
What are some of the best sources of market intelligence?

7.4 ASSESSMENT

What Have You Learned?

1. What categories of information does a company need to collect on its competitors? [7.4.1]
2. What is the term for the process of gaining competitive market information? [7.4.2]
3. Why is the Internet a good source of finding current competitive information? [7.4.2]

Make Academic Connections

1. **Writing** You are the marketing manager for a local supermarket. Prepare a list of 20 questions that you need to answer in order to understand the business's competitors. Include questions about each of the marketing mix elements and about the supermarket's competitive market position. Compare your list of questions with those developed by other students. [7.4.1]
2. **Language Arts** You and a colleague are gathering information from a competitor's public website when you access a link to a confidential report on a new product under development. It is obvious that the report was intended to be confidential, but the link had not been protected. Role play with another student what you would do with the report, what you would say to your boss, and whether you would inform the competitor about the unprotected report. [7.4.2]

Connect to ◇DECA

Build your Portfolio

You are responsible for market intelligence for the Scion division of Toyota. Locate advertisements or other product information on the Honda Element. Prepare a one-page written competitive analysis describing the strengths and weaknesses of each of the mix elements for the Honda Element. Present your report to your teacher (judge) and be prepared to answer questions. [7.4.2]

Connect to MindTap

*Analyze a case study that focuses on chapter concepts. Click on **Chapter 7, Case Study,** in your MindTap.*

CHAPTER 7 **ASSESSMENT**

Review Marketing Concepts

1. You are a manager at a senior living facility. What segmentation categories would you analyze in pinpointing the facility's market segment? [7.1.1]

2. Why is it important for a company entering a new market to know its market potential as well to estimate the market share it will capture? [7.1.2]

3. You are selling memberships to a golf/tennis club. Which method would you use to position the club in the market? Explain your answer. [7.2.1]

4. Why should businesses be cautious when basing positioning decisions on their competitors' actions? [7.2.2]

5. What is the direct competition and indirect competition for a taxi service? [7.3.1]

6. How does competition based on price relate to the economic concept of scarcity? [7.3.2]

7. From your viewpoint as a consumer, what do you see as the best benefit of market competition? [7.3.3]

8. In gathering competitive information, why do you think a company would focus more attention on competitors' promotional efforts than on the other mix elements? What is the downside of focusing on competitor's promotions? [7.4.1]

9. You just made a new friend who works for a competitor. Your friend does not know where you work and talks about her job and company a lot. She has shared a lot of information that you think would help your company and are considering sharing it with your boss. What would be the ethical thing to do in this situation? [7.4.2]

Marketing Research and Planning

1. Use the Internet to access the U.S. Census Bureau's home page. Type in the name of your state and city or county in the search bar. Below the box of various statistics about the area, click on "View" in the QuickFacts box. Review the information listed and choose three demographic characteristics that could be important to a business operating in your county or city. For each characteristic, identify a segment of the population and a product or service that could be targeted to the segment. For example:

   Characteristic: Age
   Segment: Persons 65 and over
   Product or service: Financial management services for retirement [7.1.1]

2. Businesses decide to compete using price or nonprice competition. Locate two newspaper advertisements that clearly demonstrate a strategy of price competition and two advertisements that stress nonprice competition. Cut and paste each advertisement onto separate sheets of paper. For each ad, highlight and use margin notes to describe how the businesses using price competition characterize or draw attention to the price and how the businesses using nonprice competition emphasize other factors that customers should consider. [7.3.2]

3. It is important to position a product or service in relation to your competitors. The objective of positioning is to cause your product or service to occupy a prominent position in your customer's mind as compared to the competition. Using the list below, decide which of the six positioning methods would

be most important for each product or service. After you have made your selection, explain why you selected that technique. [7.2.1]

a. urgent care medical centers

b. imported perfume or cologne

c. home office furniture

d. personal fitness classes

e. farming tractors

f. environmentally safe laundry detergent

4. A medium-size rural community has three major grocery stores that have 94 percent of the total market. The remaining 6 percent is shared by small, locally owned stores. It is estimated that the total market potential for grocery items for this town is $37.5 million. There are approximately 25,000 potential customers in this town. [7.1.2]

a. What is the total market share in dollars for the three major grocery stores?

b. What is the total market share in dollars for the small, locally owned stores?

c. What is the market share in dollars for each major grocery store if they all have an equal share of the market?

d. One of the major grocery stores has recently remodeled and expanded and has begun to stay open 24 hours. As a result of these changes, this store has increased its market share to 45 percent of the total market. What is its new market share in dollars?

e. Assuming that the locally owned stores still have 6 percent of the market, what market share is left for the other two major stores in dollars?

5. An important part of competitive success is gathering market intelligence on competitors. Select one of the types of businesses below. Make a list of five types of market intelligence the business needs and identify why it is valuable in planning a marketing strategy. For each type of business listed, identify one possible source of that information. [7.4.2]

a. pizza delivery

b. inter-city bus line

c. travel agency

d. furniture rental store

e. radio station in a large city

Marketing Management and Decision Making

1. You are a marketing consultant in your local community. There is an association of downtown businesspeople called the Business Improvement Bureau. It is an organization that is interested in improving the marketing practices of the individual businesses as well as improving the business economy of the entire community. Members have lunch together once a month and usually invite a guest speaker. You have been invited to speak to the organization this month about positioning in the market. Prepare a presentation, including visual aids, for a speech to the Business Improvement Bureau. The talk and discussion are scheduled to last

approximately 10 minutes. Your presentation could include a discussion of positioning, the results the members could expect with effective positioning, and a discussion and examples of the six positioning techniques. Make sure to explain how positioning can work for the entire business community as well as for individual businesses. Your visual aids should emphasize the important aspects of your speech. [7.2.1]

2. Due to a recession, you have become aware of an intense interest in your area in pricing. You think there is a business opportunity in this phenomenon. Specifically, you think that businesses and organizations in

your area would pay to receive up-to-date competitive price information. You have decided to open a business with several classmates called Partners In Pricing. PIP will use various methods to determine the prices of an assortment of products and services sold by area businesses. It will also collect consumer perceptions of competitors' prices.

You will offer the service of finding out what competitors' current prices are for products and services. You will comparison shop in stores; call for prices on the telephone; read advertisements in newspapers, magazines, and circulars; and visit with business and organization owners directly to acquire this information. You will also conduct frequent consumer surveys via telephone and interviews in area shopping malls.

Prepare for marketing your business by describing how you would use each of the positioning techniques for PIP. That is, what attributes would you claim to have, what is unique about your price and quality, and how will your customers be able to use the information you provide them? Also, who are your competitors, how would you classify yourself in the larger arena of business, and who will be your most prominent users? Use your answers to these questions to prepare a threefold brochure or a promotional website that you will use to recruit your first customers. [7.4.1]

Let's Start a Band! Follow-Up Discussion

Work in small teams to discuss the question posed at the end of the opening vignette. Can the band both create a unique image and be authentic? Discuss how the band can identify its competitive advantage and position itself for success.

Build Your Marketing Plan

Build your **Portfolio**

In this chapter you learned how to study the competition in order to identify market opportunities. You will now apply this learning to the development of your marketing plan. To access the chapter-specific tools that you will need to complete this activity, please navigate to Chapter 7 ➔ Build Your Marketing Plan in MindTap. Alternatively, you can access these tools online at NGLSync. Please visit www.nglsync.cengage.com, and search for the companion website that accompanies this book by entering the ISBN, author, or title. Once you locate this companion website, navigate to Build Your Marketing Plan ➔ Chapter 7.

Sports and Entertainment Marketing Team Decision Making Event

Build your Portfolio

The Dynamos are a new professional soccer franchise located in Houston, Texas. The team has been using the local university soccer field for home games. However, after the team recently won a national championship, a new professional stadium is being planned. Sugar Land and Pearland are Houston suburbs that have made serious bids for the soccer field to be built in their communities.

Downtown Houston has Minute Maid Park for professional baseball, Toyota Center for professional basketball, and NRG Stadium for professional football. The light rail system transports fans from satellite parking lots to all three sporting venues. New restaurants and hotels have located near Minute Maid Park. Downtown Houston has become a hub for social activity. The city of Houston has a piece of property near Minute Maid Park that they propose be used to build a professional soccer field for the Dynamos. The city will give the Dynamos a property tax break as an incentive.

Houston is a diverse city with a large Hispanic/Latino population. Sugar Land, located 30 minutes from downtown Houston, is an upscale planned community with a population of 100,000. Pearland is a rapidly growing suburb also located 30 minutes from downtown Houston.

Your team will meet with the President/General Manager for the Dynamos to discuss the pros/cons of all proposed locations for the soccer stadium. You must convince the President/GM to locate the stadium in downtown Houston. Your presentation must describe the target market for soccer, the product/service offered, potential corporate sponsors, proposed publicity for the team, multiple uses for the new soccer stadium,

potential sponsorships, and the economic impact of locating in downtown Houston.

You have 30 minutes to prepare your presentation, 10 minutes to present it to the judge, and 5 minutes to answer the judge's questions about your proposal.

Performance Indicators Evaluated

- Determine the relationship between government and business. (Economics)
- Identify factors affecting a business's profit. (Economics)
- Identify data monitored for marketing decision making. (Marketing-Information Management)
- Describe the need for marketing data. (Marketing-Information Management)
- Describe the nature of target marketing in marketing communications. (Market Planning)
- Develop product positioning concept for a new product idea. (Product/Service Management)

Go to the DECA website for more detailed information. **www.deca.org**

Think Critically

1. Why must a sports venue have the versatility to house other entertainment events?

2. Why do cities compete for professional sports teams?

3. Why should a team pursue government incentives when deciding where to locate?

4. Who are the target markets? What promotions can be used to attract the target markets to the stadium?

CHAPTER 8

SOCIAL MEDIA AND E-COMMERCE

Connect to MindTap

See how effective advertising leads to successful marketing strategies.
Click on Chapter 8, Visual Focus, **in your MindTap.**

Let's Start a Band!

> "For the music business, social networking is brilliant. ... You have this amazing thing now called fan power ... And it's free."
>
> – Simon Cowell, *Television Producer, Critic*

We were about four hours into a five-hour trip back from a gig. Everyone but Naomi seemed asleep. With her ear buds in, she laid her head back and closed her eyes. After a few minutes she slipped the buds from her ears. Speaking just loud enough for me to hear over the din of the road, she said, "We need to do better."

"What do you mean?," I asked.

She responded, "We need to do better with social media. We can have a better presence."

"We use Instagram, Snapchat, and Musical.ly. We're on ReverbNation. We all tweet. What more is there?" I asked.

"Let's be more thoughtful with how we use it," she said. "We need to make sure we engage our fans. Listen to them. Give them a voice. We can tell people about the band, our shows, or anything else the audience may be interested in. But we need to keep it short, sweet, and personal, like the things we talk about in this van. Let's show our fans who we really are and let them tell us who they are."

I got what she was saying, and replied, "I once saw a band that after every show turned around and had a picture taken with the audience in the background. Then they posted it on Instagram."

Naomi smiled and said, "That's what I'm talking about. Now get some sleep."

But I couldn't sleep and kept thinking. We all know how to use social media, but the problem is, how can we make it part of our marketing plan?

TECHNOLOGY, THE INTERNET, AND E-COMMERCE

Learning Objectives

8.1.1   Explain the impact of technology on business and society.

8.1.2   Explain how businesses and consumers use the Internet.

8.1.3   Discuss the advantages and disadvantages of e-commerce.

Key Terms

technology
innovation
e-commerce
click-only businesses
brick-and-mortar businesses
brick-and-click businesses

marketing matters

The use of technology—tools, machines, and computers—is essential for all types and sizes of businesses. Most businesses and consumers are quick to adopt technology when it makes a task easier, less expensive, or more effective. The Internet is one technology that has dramatically changed how products are developed and marketed. However, the need remains for companies to apply basic marketing skills and the marketing concept to achieve success.

essential question

How should businesses determine whether or not to adopt new technology as a part of their marketing strategy?

8.1.1 ▶ The Impact of Technology

Technology is defined as the practical application of scientific knowledge. It is anything people develop to improve the way something is accomplished. Technology applications typically involve machinery and equipment. However, technology also includes the processes, methods, and knowledge used to improve the effectiveness or efficiency of work.

Technology can be divided into two categories: basic technology and high technology (often called hi-tech). *Basic technology* is the tools, equipment, and machines that make physical labor easier or faster. *High technology* is the advanced procedures, techniques, and tools that replace most physical labor and automate procedures. With the development of high technology, less physical effort is required to complete work, but additional mental and intellectual effort is required of the workers who use it.

The simplest examples of basic technology—wheels, levers, hammers, and knives, for example—were tools the earliest humans used to support their survival. Later the development of gears, pumps, drills, and engines led to the Industrial Revolution. Many important technologies followed, from the harnessing of electricity to the development of powered air flight. Basic technologies are still used today to assist workers in construction, agriculture, and manufacturing. They also are used to make household tasks easier and faster.

The term *high technology* was first used in the middle of the twentieth century. High technology usually involves computers, software programs, and quality controls. Its use has increased the speed and quality of work for both businesses and consumers. High technology is used to improve everything from manufacturing, communications, and health care, to work, entertainment, and leisure activities around the home.

High technology has led to major changes in industries such as engineering, medicine, communications, and energy. Manufacturing procedures, agricultural production and food processing, transportation, and military operations all have changed dramatically with advancements in high technology. The work and personal lives of almost everyone have changed through advancements in computer technology, electronics, and the Internet.

A concept similar to technology is innovation. An **innovation** is the introduction of something new that makes a significant change or improvement. An innovation can be a major change in a product, process, or idea. An innovation results in an improvement in how something works or the way something is done, or in a solution to a problem or need. The major advances in technology have been innovations that were then incorporated into the business activities completed in our economy and the products and services we use.

The Internet is a recent innovation that has led to remarkable changes in both business and marketing. In just a few years it has become a major means of marketing goods and services to both businesses and consumers around the world. Electronic commerce, popularly known as **e-commerce**, includes all the activities involved in the exchange of goods, services, and information that relate to buying and selling goods over the Internet.

The Internet and digital communication technologies also have resulted in the rapid growth of social media, another innovation, which is used by both consumers and businesses. Both e-commerce and social media will be examined in this chapter.

CHECKPOINT
How does basic technology differ from high technology?

How does the Internet affect you in your daily life?

In the late 1970s, the introduction of the personal computer gave households and workplaces alike an important tool. Electronic communication among computers became realistic with the introduction of the World Wide Web in 1991. That same year, the National Science Foundation opened the Internet to commercial use. Since then, with improved and lower-cost computer technology and growing access to the Internet, millions of people around the world have been able to instantly access information and communicate with one another.

Today, consumers use the Internet daily to gather product information, locate businesses, compare prices, and make purchases. Most businesses use the Internet to interact with customers and other businesses by purchasing and selling products online, providing and exchanging business information, and offering customer service and support. Although e-commerce is a multibillion-dollar part of our economy, it is still evolving as companies continue to learn how to use the Internet effectively as a business and marketing technology.

Business Activities on the Net

Technology allows businesses to complete many activities using the Internet. For example, an automobile manufacturer uses video conferencing to bring designers from several countries together to work on new car and truck models. A company headquartered in the United States transmits data overnight to Ireland where accounting specialists maintain many of the company's financial records. A chemical company has sensors installed in the chemical tanks of customers which triggers a computer program to automatically order a new supply of that chemical when the level drops to a certain point.

From Bricks to Clicks

Some businesses use the Internet for only a few activities whereas others use it in nearly every aspect of the business. Companies that complete almost all of their business activities through the Internet are known as **click-only businesses**. Companies that still complete most of their business activities by means other than the Internet are called **brick-and-mortar businesses**. The name "brick-and-mortar" suggests that the company relies on actual buildings such as retail stores, offices, or factories to conduct its business. Many traditional businesses have developed ways to use the Internet to support their business activities. Companies that combine traditional business operations with extensive use of the Internet are known as **brick-and-click businesses**.

*Want to know more about what is trending with this topic? Click on **Lesson 8.1, Global Marketing,** in your MindTap.*

Connect to MindTap

CHECKPOINT
How do businesses and consumers use the Internet to buy and sell products?

While there are many benefits of conducting business on the Internet, in order to be successful, businesses also must be aware of the downsides.

Advantages of E-Commerce

Businesses that conduct e-commerce have advantages over those that do not. The Internet allows immediate access 24/7 to prospective customers all over the world. Customers can order products day or night, 365 days a year. They can review operations manuals and other product information that has been placed online.

Doing business on the Internet also allows businesses to gather detailed and specific information about prospective and current customers that can be used to tailor a satisfying marketing mix and maintain regular and personal contact with customers. It also facilitates customer service, allowing customers to send their concerns and questions to a company at any time and receive a response immediately. The Internet also allows businesses to update product information quickly.

Some products can be delivered directly to your computer as a result of e-commerce. For example, e-tickets are replacing paper tickets for air travel, concerts, and movies. You can purchase postage or order package delivery online, print mailing labels from your office or home, and have letters or packages picked up at your door. You can download a movie or the latest musical release from your favorite artist instantly.

The Internet enabled small businesses to compete more easily with larger businesses because an e-business is less expensive to start and operate and affords easier access to customers. Companies can enter international markets by having their website translated into the languages of the countries in which it wants to sell.

Disadvantages of E-Commerce

Not everything about the development of e-commerce has been positive. While the Internet provides an easy way for people to start or expand a business, they still must have specialized knowledge and the drive to succeed. If not properly managed, products may not be described correctly, or errors can occur in order processing. Meeting customer service needs, such as providing answers to questions and supporting customers any time of the day, seven days a week can be a challenge. Businesses engaged in e-commerce also need to develop distribution channels, warranty and repair services, methods for accepting returns, and secure websites for accepting credit card payments to serve customers who order online. Because it is easy for a fraudulent business to develop a web presence, consumers need to be aware of potential frauds and scams and be sure to maintain personal security online.

One of the greatest disadvantages of e-commerce is that it changes the nature of competition. A brick-and-mortar company generally competes with similar

© stockyimages/Shutterstock.com

businesses in the same geographic area. With the Internet, businesses face competition from businesses offering similar products both locally and online. This makes predicting demand for products more difficult. Many consumers use the web to gather information and compare prices. They may go to a local business to examine the product or determine a correct size, but then make the purchase from the online business with the lowest price. This practice is known as *showrooming*. As a result, the local business may find it very difficult to compete on the basis of price.

The Marketing Concept Applied to E-Commerce

Businesses involved with e-commerce need to understand the marketing concept in order to be successful. When people in many locations can view information about a company's products and services, the business must understand who its target market customers are, their needs and wants, and how its marketing mix can satisfy those needs and wants. The business must be able to offer the products and services that customers want. It also must be able to distribute them effectively, make purchases affordable, make ordering and payment of products easy, and provide information in the form of descriptions and pictures. The business must answer questions, provide expected services, and solve problems after the sale. All parts of the marketing mix—including distribution—are important for successful e-commerce.

CHECKPOINT
How does competition change for businesses that become involved in e-commerce?

8.1 ASSESSMENT

What Have You Learned?

1. What is e-commerce? [8.1.1]
2. What is the term for companies that combine traditional business operations with extensive use of the Internet? [8.1.2]
3. Explain the practice known as *showrooming.* [8.1.3]

Make Academic Connections

1. **History**   Choose an industry. Possible examples include engineering, medicine, communications, energy, or agriculture. Research to identify changes in the industry brought about by high technology. Write a paragraph to identify how a task was accomplished before and after the specific technology was introduced. Also explain the benefit of the technology to the industry. [8.1.1]

2. **Foreign Language**   Locate the website of a U.S. business that provides an alternate site in a language other than English. Locate the website of a company in a non-English speaking country that provides an alternate site in English. Identify three to five differences other than language between the alternate websites. [8.1.2]

Connect to ◇DECA

Build your Portfolio

Working in teams, use an online survey tool (Google docs, Survey Monkey, etc.) to develop a four-item questionnaire to determine what customers like and dislike about online shopping. Survey at least 15 people of different ages. Summarize the data and prepare a two-page report of your findings. Present the written report to your teacher (judge) and be prepared to answer questions. [8.1.3]

Planning a Career In...
E-MARKETING

E-marketing is a rapidly evolving means to reach consumers. You engage with e-marketing when you search for information about products online, make purchases through a company's website, and click on ads linked to a web search. A growing number of careers are part of the e-marketing industry.

Job Titles

- Interactive Marketing
- Marketing Web Master
- E-commerce Project Manager
- Search Marketing Specialist
- Online Marketing Manager
- E-commerce Marketing Analyst

Needed Skills

- Varying educational levels from a high school diploma to a PhD are needed in the broad range of e-marketing careers.

- A solid business background, strong analytical abilities, and effective written communications skills are needed.

- A background in computer hardware and software, including database software, open sourcing, web application programming, and search engine design are required for some jobs.

What it's like to work in... E-Marketing

Evelyn, a digital marketing manager for a professional baseball team, was reviewing a report of the number of visits to the team's website. Of particular interest was the amount of traffic resulting from a link from a sports memorabilia website on which the team had purchased advertising space.

A phone call about the electronic team newsletter interrupted the report review. The newsletter, available to fans either by signing up to be added to a distribution list or by clicking a link on the team website, was scheduled for release the next day. Confirmation was needed regarding which product promotions would be included in the newsletter.

In the afternoon, Evelyn ran an Internet sales review meeting. Sales of tickets, clothing, and memorabilia were correlated to variations in website traffic. To determine the most effective advertising methods, the group reviewed the relationship among banners, sponsored sports websites, and keyword advertising links from other sites to increased website traffic and resulting sales.

What About You?

Would you like to help increase online revenue through the creative use of Internet marketing? Are you interested in being part of a new and exciting career area?

Discover more about the outlook for this career and watch a video about a related career. Click on **Chapter 8, Planning a Career In...** *in your MindTap.*

THE EMERGENCE OF SOCIAL MEDIA

Learning Objectives

8.2.1 Trace the milestones in communication technology that led to the introduction of social media.

8.2.2 Define social media.

8.2.3 Describe the ways marketers use social media.

Key Terms

blog
social media
sociability
geo-tagging
outbound marketing
inbound marketing
social network
crowd-sourcing

word-of-mouth (WOM)
word-of-mouth marketing
influencers
real-time marketing
viral marketing

marketing matters

Social media is a relatively new phenomenon, but it has become so popular in recent years that it's hard to imagine a world without it. In a short time, social media revolutionized the way you live your life, the way you connect with others, and the way you do business. Social media can be used as a tool for discovering new products, as entertainment, and as a way to stay in touch with friends. Marketers use social media to connect with customers and to help them make purchasing decisions.

essential question

Why has social media grown so rapidly as both a personal communications tool and a business resource?

8.2.1 ▶ A Brief History of Social Media

Social media has grown faster than any other media type in the history of human communication and interaction. Never before has a type of media spread so rapidly and had such an impact on the human population. The term *media* refers to a tool that is used to store or deliver information. Social media allows two or more users to generate, access, and deliver information almost simultaneously. The telephone was an early form of social media.

Beginnings of Social Media

The start of the modern notion of social media began in the early seventies. In 1971, in a lab in Cambridge, Massachusetts, a computer engineer sent a message from his computer to another computer in the same room, creating what would become known as *email*. The late 1970s saw the rise of *bulletin board systems* (BBS). A BBS was a digital equivalent of a physical bulletin board—a location where users could post messages for others to read and respond to.

The first web browsers also appeared in the late 1970s. These software programs allowed users to navigate the information on this new network of computers. The network of computers was not nearly as widespread or sophisticated as it is today. Much of this network simply connected universities, research laboratories, and government facilities and was known as ARPANET, an early version of the Internet.

Early Applications

Once the personal computer made its way into people's lives during the 1980s and 1990s, people could connect with one another from their homes and offices. Instant messengers allowed people to "chat" online, sending real-time messages back and forth in a format that resembled actual conversation. In 1994, a new website that would become known as GeoCities allowed users to generate their own websites. GeoCities became one of the first true social media sites where users could generate their own content on virtually any topic they desired and present it to other users. This is where some of the earliest weblogs, or blogs, made their first appearance. A **blog** is a website that contains a consumer's own experiences, observations, and opinions in a journal-like format.

In 1997, the website Sixdegrees.com allowed users to create personal profiles

Want to know more about what is trending with this topic? Click on **Lesson 8.2, Marketing Decisions,** in your MindTap.

Connect to MindTap

and list acquaintances. Five years later Friendster was launched as the first networking site that encouraged people to connect with real-world friends online and then meet new friends through those contacts. Myspace and Facebook followed in subsequent years, surpassing Friendster's success.

A pivotal moment in social media came in 1999 with the release of the file-sharing software Napster. Within a year of its initial release, more than 20 million users had downloaded the software, making it one of the fastest-growing brands of all time. Consumers used the software to share music and information about that music as well as about themselves. Napster demonstrated the power of consumer connectivity, and marketers quickly took notice of what social media could do.

CHECKPOINT
Name the significant milestones in communication technology that led to the development of social media.

8.2.2 ▶ Social Media Defined

Social media is any web-based or mobile media technology that connects people. But social media does more than just connect—it enables open communication with groups of people. Social media also allows users of the various media to generate their own content and collaborate with others in the generation of content. Simply put, **social media** includes any technology that allows people to have conversations and share content they have created.

Social Media vs. Traditional Media

Social media differs from the traditional media formats marketers have used in two very specific ways. First, traditional media formats have a one-way flow of information. Content is broadcast to a mass audience through the television, radio, billboards, or print ads. The mass audience receives that information but traditionally has been unable to respond to it directly. The Internet provides the audience with a more direct and immediate method for starting a conversation with the marketer.

With social media, the marketing communication process becomes even more direct. Social media not only allows the receiver of the message to comment on the information provided, but also to share it with friends, add to it, and even redefine it. In other words, the receiver becomes a part of the conversation. If you have ever posted a comment about an online video, written a blog entry, or posted a review on a company's website, then you have taken part in this conversation. Social media allows the audience to provide feedback to a company and allows the audience to share the information with other consumers (**Figure 8-1**).

Second, whereas most content supplied in traditional media is generated by a central source such as a studio, a publisher, or an advertising firm, most social media content is created by the audience itself. For example, the videos that are posted on YouTube are not created by YouTube. They are created by millions of users around the world. That is why content on social media sites often is referred to as *user-generated content*. Sometimes users share videos that were created for traditional media, such as television. This helps marketers reach consumers they otherwise would not have reached.

The Power of Sociability

In recent years, **sociability**, or the inclusion of one or more aspects of social media, has become a standard on websites, even those that exist primarily for other purposes, such as business and government. Consumers have come to expect social media functionality on the websites they visit. As new forms of social media are developed, they are often quickly adopted by existing

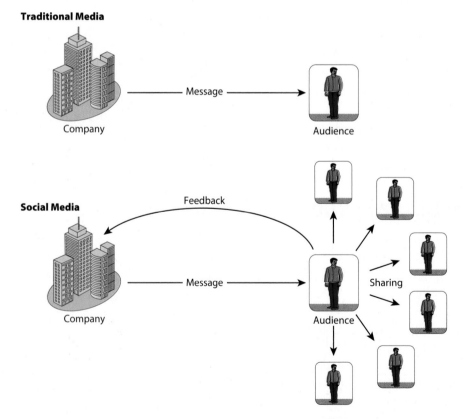

FIGURE 8-1 What are the major differences between traditional and social media? How might this affect how quickly a message is spread?

websites. For example, GPS-enabled mobile technology has introduced **geo-tagging**, or using mobile devices to add a location to posts on social media platforms. Foursquare, Facebook, and photo-sharing sites such as Instagram all allow for geo-tagging. For example, a customer who enters a restaurant might "check in" on Foursquare, which posts the location to a website for others to see and comment on. Stores and restaurants sometimes give incentives, such as discounts, to people who check in from their establishment. These check-ins are essentially a form of free promotion for the business.

© StockLite/Shutterstock.com.

What are the pros and cons of geo-tagging from a consumer's perspective?

CHECKPOINT
What is social media?

8.2.3 ▶ Social Media and Marketing

As social media evolved, marketers needed to figure out ways to insert themselves into the conversations people were having about companies and their products. On social media, marketing is an ongoing discussion, a sharing of ideas about what a company has to offer. A company can craft its own commercial message about its products or services, but it has little control over the conversations that occur in response.

For this reason, marketers must have a well-planned approach to social media. They must be truthful and treat their customers with respect. Marketers are no longer just talking at their audience. They are entering into a relationship with them. Effective social media marketing not only has to get people's attention, it has to engage them. Companies understand the need to give consumers a new and unique experience.

The two-way conversation means that companies engage in **outbound marketing**, where a company initiates contact with potential customers. They must have an **inbound marketing** strategy as well, where potential customers come to them.

Social media marketing allows companies to monitor consumer trends and adapt to them. Marketers also have developed algorithms to track social media. The algorithms enable marketers to better understand their target audience, allowing them to send the appropriate content to the precise target at the proper time.

Perhaps the biggest change social media has brought to marketing is the speed with which it continues to evolve. As new technology and new social media platforms are developed, marketers need to adapt and react quickly to change.

Types of Social Media

There are several common types of social media available to marketers, although not all social media falls neatly into one of the categories. A social media platform typically is a blend of these types. New forms and applications of social media are constantly being developed and evolving. Social media platforms also are becoming more and more integrated.

BLOGS   The term *blog* is a blend of the words "web" and "log." A blog typically is a website where one person regularly posts commentary, descriptions, or other content, and an audience can comment on it. *Micro-blogging*—posting very short updates such as on the popular website Tumblr—is one type of a blog.

SOCIAL NETWORKS   A website that links people or organizations into communities based on common interests, goals, or beliefs is called a **social network**. Social networks typically allow a user to create a profile that identifies him- or herself within that digital community. Facebook is an example of a social network.

COLLABORATION   The Internet makes it easy for large groups of people to collaborate on a single project. When thousands of people each contribute a small amount of work or knowledge, they have the ability to collectively achieve something massive. This large-scale virtual collaboration is sometimes called **crowd-sourcing**. Wikipedia, the online encyclopedia, is one example of this. Collaboration is discussed further in Lesson 8.3.

CONTENT COMMUNITIES   Some social media sites create communities around specific types of media content. YouTube for videos, Flickr and Pinterest for photography, and Pandora and Spotify for music are just a few examples. Many of these sites feature user-generated content.

ENTERTAINMENT   Online games such as Second Life and The Sims Online have evolved to incorporate elements of social media. Participants can create profiles, interact with one another, and share information in digital environments that are sometimes incredibly sophisticated.

REVIEWS AND OPINIONS   Online reviews are part of today's word-of-mouth marketing and give consumers a way to voice their opinions. For example, consumers can review businesses and products with Google, give their opinion on a third-party review site such as Yelp, evaluate them in a Facebook post, or leave reviews about products and vendors on Amazon. Studies show that many consumers trust reviews from total strangers as much as personal recommendations and that reviews influence the purchasing decision of two-thirds of consumers. Thus, it is extremely important for marketers to monitor and respond to online reviews of their business and products.

Google, one of the most important review sites, ranks review sites at the top of their search results. This means that whenever someone searches for a business, its reviews are usually at the top of the search results pages. So the more reviews a company can get on sites such as Yelp, Angie's List, and TripAdvisor, the higher the chances of it showing up on the first page of Google.

Before looking at product reviews, consumers look at star ratings and the total number of reviews for the item. While there will always be negative reviews, having a blend of good reviews and bad reviews makes a business look authentic. Of course, having too many negative responses could prove disastrous. The goal is to have consistent, quality responses that will aid in showing how well the business is doing in providing customer service.

Word-of-Mouth Promotion

Social media allows marketers to harness the power of word-of-mouth promotion. **Word-of-mouth (WOM)** is the passing of information among people through oral communication, and it often takes the form of storytelling. Before the invention of writing, information about history, religion, science, industry, health care, and culture was passed down generation after generation through word-of-mouth communication. This oral tradition took many forms, from folktales to songs to epic ballads.

Today, this oral tradition is supplemented with our ability to write, photograph, and otherwise store information about our world and our place in it. In so doing, we ensure that our stories can be passed from one person to another and even survive into future generations. WOM has become more sophisticated and less reliant on the "mouth" part of the equation. Though we are still concerned about our history, culture, and so on, consumers also use word-of-mouth to discuss the brands and products they use and like.

Marketers have long turned to the power of WOM to help support their own marketing endeavors. For marketers, WOM happens when a consumer of a particular product or brand communicates information about that product or brand to another consumer. When this WOM is positive, it can benefit marketers because consumers tend to find such consumer-generated WOM more credible than marketer-generated materials.

Word-of-mouth marketing—which is different from simple WOM—occurs when a consumer is somehow rewarded for passing along information about products and services. The idea behind word-of-mouth marketing is to get people who like a product or service to tell others about it. When people talk positively about a product, they create "buzz." Marketers increasingly use social media such as Twitter, Facebook, Instagram, and YouTube to generate buzz.

Marketers may compensate endorsers to promote their product or service on social media. These paid endorsers, called **influencers**, are individuals who have established a following and credibility in a specific area that enables them to influence the purchase decisions of others. For example, when Google launched its Gmail email service, it gave free accounts to key influencers. Individuals could not get a Gmail account unless a current member invited them. Limiting the supply created buzz and drove

© Roman Samborskyi/Shutterstock.com.

up demand. Gmail, through word-of-mouth marketing, quickly became a major player among email providers.

Some of the most effective influencers are industry leaders and thought leaders who've gained respect because of their qualifications, position, or experience about a topic. They are bloggers, product reviewers, industry experts or some other trusted source of information, whose opinions are sought because they often have large followings on blogs and social networks, Current popular social media platforms include YouTube, Instagram, Snapchat, Facebook, Twitter, and Twitch. Social media influencers may be celebrities. However, as influencers, celebrities may lack credibility with a product's target audience.

Using influencers on social media enables businesses to target specific demographics, as their audience may be more clearly defined than that of other marketing outlets. With the effective use of social media, marketers have found that influencers can drive customer engagement and word-of-mouth communication.

Real-Time Marketing

Marketers know that consumers seek immediate gratification and information and want to be a part of the latest trends. In response, companies have adjusted how they market to consumers by using real-time marketing. At first real-time marketing simply involved a marketing strategy that focused on current events, trends, and customer feedback. That changed with the rise in popularity of social media and consumers' use of smart phones, tablets, and laptops to keep them entertained, updated, and informed.

Real-time marketing gathers information about consumers' online activities as they are occurring through the use of advanced consumer analytics. The collected data includes customer demographics and other information such as their online search and shopping history. Within minutes, a company can convert the information into a personalized marketing message directly related to the customer's interests and preferences. It sends the message in the form of specific ads, texts, and banners regarding company products and services.

Advantages of Social Media

Social media has some distinct advantages over traditional media as a way for companies to identify, reach, and build relationships with customers (**Figure 8-2**).

COMMUNITY CONCEPT   Social media is based on the concept of community—people interacting and sharing information with one another—and it is designed to make the sharing of ideas fast and easy. If a marketer's message reaches and is meaningful to the right virtual communities, it can spread much faster than it could via traditional media.

This occurs because social media communities are organized around shared ideology, interests, or beliefs. When one person in a social media community is interested in a company's message, there's a good chance that others in that community also will be interested. So, the message is passed along repeatedly, spreading throughout the community. Because it resembles the spread of a disease, marketers often call this "viral marketing" with the message said to be "going viral." **Viral marketing** is

ADVANTAGES OF SOCIAL MEDIA OVER TRADITIONAL MEDIA			
Community Concept	**Trusted Sources**	**Promote Dialogue**	**Promote Sharing**
Interaction Shared ideology, interests, or beliefs	Recommendations from friends	Messages to and from consumers	Links to other social media sites
"Viral marketing"	"Endorsing the message"	"Conversation with audience"	"Buzz worthy content"

FIGURE 8-2 Social media has many important advantages over traditional media for marketers. Can you think of any other advantages social media might have?

a promotional approach utilizing word-of-mouth marketing that encourages satisfied customers to pass along marketing messages through word-of-mouth via the Internet. Viral marketing allows the information to spread rapidly and has allowed marketers to have an almost instantaneous impact on large numbers of people.

TRUSTED SOURCES An important advantage social media has over traditional media concerns the source of the messages. Every day, we receive messages from a wide variety of sources, some we believe and trust more than others. Many of your social media connections are with people you know and interact with frequently. So even if a message originates from a business, if it is passed along to you by a friend, you are likely to trust it. By passing it along to you, your friend is endorsing the message and giving it more importance.

PROMOTES DIALOGUE Another advantage of social media is that it allows for dialogue. With traditional media marketers talk *to* consumers. With social media, however, they have a conversation *with* them. Marketers can use social media not only to send a message about

their product or service, but also to receive messages from their customers, to answer customers' questions, and to collect information that could aid in product development.

How much time per day do you spend on social media?

© Stasique/Shutterstock.com

PROMOTES SHARING With social media, marketers rely on their audience members to share their message with one another. They try to make it as easy as possible for people to pass along their message. For instance, they may add links to Facebook, Twitter, or other social media sites. More importantly, marketers have to create something that people want to share—something that's interesting,

*Want to know more about marketing in the information age? Click on **Lesson 8.2, Digital Marketing,** in your MindTap.*

Connect to
MindTap

entertaining, or useful. Content that people share with one another is sometimes said to have "talk value" or be "buzz worthy" meaning simply that the content is interesting enough to share.

CHECKPOINT
Name six types of social media.

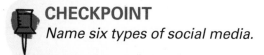

8.2 ASSESSMENT

What Have You Learned?

1. What was ARPANET? [8.2.1]
2. Explain the two differences between traditional media and social media. [8.2.2]
3. What is the term for using mobile devices to add a location to posts on social media platforms? [8.2.2]
4. What is the goal for a company with regard to customer reviews on social media? [8.2.3]

Make Academic Connections

1. **Visual Art** Locate the main website of a social media outlet, and then study the features of that social media format. Create a poster that illustrates how the main features can help a small company to promote its product and how it can encourage customers to become part of the conversation. [8.2.3]

2. **Communication** Identify an influencer on social media for a product or category of products you purchase. Find specific examples in social media of messages the influencer has posted. Write a paragraph explaining why the messages are or are not effective. [8.2.3]

Connect to ◇DECA

Build your
Portfolio

Working with a team, prepare a social media plan for promoting a farm that sells organic fruits and vegetables. Identify three types of social media that should be used and prepare an example message for each type. Present your plan and examples to your teacher (judge). [8.2.3]

8.3 SOCIAL MEDIA AS A MARKETING TOOL

Learning Objectives

8.3.1 Describe the four distinct characteristics of early marketplaces that apply to social media.

8.3.2 Identify three strategies marketers use to develop effective social media messages.

8.3.3 Explain how marketers can use social media platforms in marketing their products and brands.

Key Terms

trending
hashtags
collaboration

marketing matters

Social media can be a powerful marketing tool. Many companies now use social media every day to strengthen relationships with current customers and attract the attention of new ones. To use social media effectively in marketing, a company needs to develop a social media mindset and recognize that strategies that work with traditional marketing methods may not work with social media.

 essential question

Why is social media attractive to marketers who are attempting to connect with customers?

8.3.1 ▶ Social Media Characteristics

The very first marketplaces began to appear along trade routes sometime between 3000 and 1000 BC. Those marketplaces allowed people to gather together to barter for items that could help fulfill their various consumption needs. Those early markets had four distinct characteristics.

1. Marketplaces were personal and interactive. Merchants spoke with customers who provided feedback. Customers could see and touch the product and often see it being made.

2. The interaction had immediacy. Consumers came to the market, interacted with merchants, and left with purchases.

3. The success of any one merchant depended on word-of-mouth. If a merchant failed to satisfy a customer or, worse yet, cheated that customer, word would travel quickly through the marketplace. A business survived solely on the basis of customer recommendations.

4. Because people have a basic need and desire to connect to other people, marketplaces became an important place for people to connect with one another.

How would you compare shopping at a farmer's market today with shopping at one of the early marketplaces?

Many events in the history of modern marketing, however, have distanced the marketplace from the customer. Advertising provided marketers with an opportunity to separate themselves from the customer. It also required them to create a generic message that reached as broad an audience as possible. Throughout much of recent history, there has been a complete divide between the marketer and the consumer, with communication technologies such as television, radio, print, and even the Internet forming a barrier between them.

Social media is helping to break down the barriers that divide marketer from consumer. The four characteristics of the early marketplaces can be seen in social media today. Marketers need to address each of them.

1. **Personal and Interactive** Social media allows marketers to interact with consumers on a personal level. It allows customers to converse directly with the marketers of a product or brand.

2. **Immediacy** Social media allows customers and marketers to communicate in real time. Sometimes it is difficult to anticipate how consumers will react to an ad. If the reaction is negative, social media allows marketers to make changes or address issues immediately.

3. **Word-of-Mouth** Social media is essentially a word-of-mouth technology. Word-of-mouth traditionally referred to oral communication. But word-of-mouth marketing in social media is usually done using other formats such as writing, texting, filming, recording, or photographing. Word-of-mouth has gone digital, and it allows consumers to recommend or criticize a company in a public forum.

4. **Connectivity** One of the basic human needs is to connect to other humans. We not only like to be in the presence of others, we crave it and, in fact, need it in order to survive. As such, customers don't *have* to get on sites such as Facebook and join communities via Twitter and Pinterest, they *want* to. They want to because it allows them to connect with others, just as those early marketplaces did. In short, social media has converted those early marketplaces to a digital format that turns the entire world into one big marketplace. And we all want to be a part of it.

CHECKPOINT
What four major characteristics of the early marketplaces apply to marketing via social media?

Social media shares quite a bit with more traditional forms of marketing. However, dealing with the social media marketplace requires a slightly different approach to strategic thinking. As a marketer, social media requires you to think about your relationship with the customer as a series of small interactions, to develop a social media mindset, and to keep content at the forefront.

Small Interactions

Traditional advertising and promotion opportunities are often one-size-fits-all events. For example, a grocery store might send a generic set of coupons to everyone in its database even though many of those people do not purchase any of the items. The idea is to send everything you have and see what works. Companies may try to do the same thing with their social media, for example, sending a generic tweet containing a coupon to everyone in the database.

With social media, however, marketers have an opportunity to develop smaller, more focused interactions with customers. These interactions are more personal, and they result in greater customer support and loyalty than coupons do. For instance, what if the grocery store in question sees that you purchase milk at the end of the week? The store can tweet you a reminder that you may be low on milk, or it can

MATH IN MARKETING

Web Analytics

When using social media in marketing, it is important for companies to know how many people they are reaching and the types of interactions that make a difference. *Web analytics* is the study of how users interact with websites. It can shed light on the effectiveness of a website by providing a variety of measurements or *metrics* concerning how pages are being shared and how much time visitors spend on a page.

One useful metric indicates the *bounce rate,* which is the percentage of visitors who leave a website rather than viewing another page within the site. The bounce rate is calculated by dividing the total number of visitors to one page only by the total number of visitors to the website.

Another measure that can aid in determining the effectiveness of a page is to track the "conversion" of a desired goal or action. The most common conversion is a sale, but this also refers to other activities such as submitting contact information. A *conversion rate* is calculated by dividing the number of goals or actions by the number of visits.

Do the Math

1. Calculate the following bounce rates:
   a. A website has 175 visitors with 146 viewing only one page.
   b. A website has 220 visitors with 90 viewing only one page.
2. Calculate the following conversion rates:
   a. A website has 225 visitors where 57 of them make purchases.
   b. A website has 225 visitors and 163 of them submit contact information.

send you a message suggesting that fresh-baked chocolate chip cookies go great with a cold glass of milk. The point is that social media allows companies to use their own research to develop smaller, more intimate interactions with customers.

Social Media Mindset

In order to develop these small interactions with consumers, you first need to develop a social media mindset that allows you to explore the opportunities this technology offers. This requires incorporating social media not just into various marketing efforts, but also to build it into your strategic thinking so it becomes part of the planning process.

Social media requires making targeted connections. Unlike most promotional efforts that are broad in their reach and scope, social media provides the opportunity to pinpoint a small group of consumers, even individuals. It also provides you with an opportunity to surround yourself with customers who like you and your product. And it gives your customers the opportunity to participate.

Customers are willing to participate in social marketing when the content you provide is meaningful to them, and when that content seems genuine. In other words, when you send them a reminder about milk or suggest cookies, it has to feel real, not forced.

Content Marketing

In the world of social media, content rules. It can be compared to the product's role in the marketing mix, in that even with the best distribution system, exciting promotion, and reasonable prices, if consumers do not like the product, your marketing effort will fail. Without good, suitable content that consumers find interesting, your social media efforts will fall flat. To be successful, you need to create content you can generate quickly and that consumers find easy to digest. For instance, you might build an infographic that can be sent out on Facebook or Pinterest that provides a lot of information in a simple pictorial. The idea is to manage your content so that you don't bore your audience with information they don't need.

CHECKPOINT
Identify three strategies marketers use to develop effective social media messages.

8.3.3 ▶ Social Media Platforms

Not all social media platforms are created equal. Think about how you use your own social media. For example, during study hall you post a blog entry discussing an assignment for class. Then before heading to lunch, you post on your Facebook page an interesting article you found while researching for the assignment. At lunch, you spend a little time tweeting your opinion about a band you saw last weekend. You use each of these social media formats in a different way and for a different purpose. Here are a few of the more popular formats with an explanation of each.

Facebook and Sharing

Facebook, the largest of the social media platforms, is a site where sharing is the norm. You share tidbits of information about yourself ranging from pictures of friends or family to statements of philosophy to your relationship status. You share this information not only throughout your network of friends, but potentially with third parties, fourth parties, and beyond. The information you submit to Facebook—the conversation you start—goes out into the world to be changed by others through discussion, reposting, and further sharing.

Marketers interested in developing a Facebook presence must be willing to not only share their own experiences but also to give their customers an opportunity to share their experiences with the brand—positive or otherwise. The key to this engagement is developing an openness that develops trust through honest conversation and discussion. If you want your customers to share with you, you have to share with them as well.

In addition to establishing relationships with customers on Facebook, companies can also use it to sell products. The Facebook Marketplace feature makes it convenient for customers to browse for products among all vendors and purchase those they like.

Instagram and Sharing

Instagram is a free photo-sharing platform with which users upload and share photos and videos using their smartphone. Users can configure their accounts to share photos on other platforms including Facebook, Twitter, Tumblr, or Flickr. Companies that have visual products should consider having a presence on Instagram, which is owned by Facebook. All the platforms share a lot of the same features and ad-targeting options. While easy to use, Instagram content is short-lived. Without a visual product or quality photographs, another platform may be a better choice.

Twitter and Trending

Though people can share their thoughts and activities via Twitter, this social media site falls into a slightly different realm of sharing known as trending.

Trending refers to a topic or discussion that is currently popular in social media or other web-based formats. The platform provides an ability to generate a live stream of immediate opinion among a huge group of people.

Twitter allows users to send short, 280-character messages, known as "tweets," to other users who have chosen to follow them. Twitter has been used in a variety of creative ways. Users tweet everything from what they had for lunch to links to interesting articles or websites. People have used Twitter to post "on-the-ground" updates from events ranging from rock concerts and high school graduations to social movements such as the Arab Spring.

For businesses, Twitter is a social messaging platform that allows companies to engage and interact with their target audience, making it ideal for customer service. In addition to allowing marketers to share information and content, it also is a tool for micro-blogging, branding, reputation management, networking, and promotion.

Marketers who wish to understand the cultural trends of the moment should monitor the Twitter accounts of their followers. The content that marketers generate should keep up with those current trends. Growing a following on Twitter takes more than sending out tweets whenever your company has a product being released or an upcoming event. It requires engaging followers to retweet to amplify the message so more people see it.

Hashtags enable users to track topics on Twitter by classifying or categorizing messages using words or phrases preceded by a hash sign (#). At one time Twitter was the only place hashtags were used, but eventually they began to appear online and offline. As marketers developed an understanding of how hashtags were used, they adopted them for marketing and advertising purposes.

YouTube and Consumer Content

YouTube enables the sharing of videos. Users can view, like, share, and comment on the videos posted. They also can create and post their own videos to share with others. Some videos on YouTube are completely original, whereas others build on existing properties.

How has social media enabled people who enjoy sharing their musical talent with others?

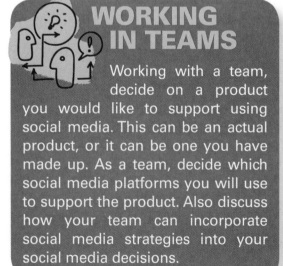

WORKING IN TEAMS

Working with a team, decide on a product you would like to support using social media. This can be an actual product, or it can be one you have made up. As a team, decide which social media platforms you will use to support the product. Also discuss how your team can incorporate social media strategies into your social media decisions.

YouTube (and other sites such as Flickr, WordPress, etc.) promotes this user-generated content and distribution. Some marketers have even allowed consumers to make their own commercials to post on YouTube. They also have encouraged consumers to modify existing commercials or other content without bringing up copyright infringement issues. The idea is to have consumers work with your content. As they do, they take psychological ownership of the brand which, again, can promote both patronage and loyalty.

For a business, YouTube provides an affordable way to publish video content that can be integrated into its website. Because it is owned by Google, any content posted on YouTube is searchable in both platforms and can help with a company's results.

Wikipedia and Collaboration

Wikipedia is a free encyclopedia that was founded on the notion of collaboration. **Collaboration** is similar to sharing in that it involves people coming together to share information and ideas about solving problems. Wikipedia users collaborate in writing the entries, or *wikis*. Wikipedia and other wiki sites involve users collaborating on, generating, and providing information to others on a variety of topics, including companies and brands.

Marketers often stay out of the way when it comes to this type of collaboration. The idea is that your consumers are talking about you, and you can learn a lot from them—especially your mistakes. For instance, marketers may read their company's entry on Wikipedia and see

MARKETING COMMUNICATION

More on Web Analytics

As marketers develop their websites, they also need to develop ways to analyze the sites' effectiveness. The conversion (goal) is often sales generated by the site. Other goals include identifying how a page performs based on how long a visitor stays or tracking where the visitor goes next. Analytics may even give the marketer the visitor's geographic location. The most popular website statistical service is Google Analytics, which is used by more than 27.3 million websites worldwide.

Although Facebook is best known as a means to share comments and updates with friends, family, and coworkers, businesses also may use this platform to build followers. Marketers can use Facebook Audience Insights, which is Facebook's web page analysis tool, to optimize content by accessing sharing metrics and demographic information. It allows users to keep track of page views, unique views, fan statistics, wall posts, video and audio plays, photo views, and other useful information. For example, if a customer links to the company's website in a Facebook status message, that data is included in the analytics for the company's domain. Information can be gathered regularly, allowing content managers to view daily or monthly statistics. Tracking social media platforms such as Facebook and Twitter through analytics helps companies develop content better aimed at their customers' interests.

Think Critically

1. Why is it important for a business to have a goal for its website, Facebook page, or any other social media? When a goal is established, why are analytics important?

2. Choose a school event or activity and write two posts for its Facebook page. Then state the target audience of each post as well as its purpose, such as sales, attendance, or awareness. Be prepared to share your posts with the class.

Sources: "Google Analytics Usage Statistics." *Built With*. 2019. https://trends.builtwith.com/analytics/Google-Analytics; "Learn More About the People that Matter to Your Business with Facebook Audience Insights." *Facebook Business*. May 8, 2014. https://www.facebook.com/business/news/audience-insights

that a statement about customer service is incorrect. The first impulse is to correct the mistake. However, what if the mistake is a misconception about the company's approach to customer service? The company can learn from the mistake, work to change the misconception, and then let customers who have learned to see the company's customer service differently correct the mistake.

As a student, you may use Wikipedia as a starting point in your research, but you should not cite Wikipedia articles in your research papers, as the information may not be correct. You can, however, evaluate the validity of some parts of Wikipedia's articles by checking the footnotes to evaluate their source material.

CHECKPOINT
What does the term trending *mean as applied to social media?*

8.3 ASSESSMENT

What Have You Learned?

1. Which social media characteristic allows customers and marketers to communicate in real time? [8.3.1]
2. What does having a social media mindset require of a marketer? [8.3.2]
3. Define trending. [8.3.3]

Make Academic Connections

1. **Management** Identify a business in your area that uses social media. Based upon the different uses for media formats (sharing, trending, consumer content, and collaboration), discuss how effectively the business uses the formats in question. Act as the social media manager for the business and write a paragraph explaining how the business could use its social media more effectively. [8.3.3]

2. **Ethics** Investigate copyright infringement. Then, pick a social media site and locate its terms of use. Read through those terms to find statements about copyright infringement. Based upon what it states and your additional understanding of infringement, what are some common mistakes people make that violate infringement laws on that site? [8.3.3]

Connect to ◇DECA

Build your Portfolio

You have been asked to give advice to the owner of a small office supply business on how social media can make the business more competitive with larger businesses. Prepare three recommendations for specific ways the business can use social media. Present your ideas to your teacher (judge) and justify each recommendation. [8.3.3]

Connect to MindTap

*Analyze a case study that focuses on chapter concepts. Click on **Chapter 8, Case Study,** in your MindTap.*

CHAPTER 8 ASSESSMENT

Review Marketing Concepts

1. Explain how the Internet qualifies as an innovation with respect to business. [8.1.1]

2. Compare and contrast brick-and-mortar, click-only, and brick-and-click businesses. [8.1.2]

3. Do you think showrooming is an unethical consumer practice? Why or why not? [8.1.3]

4. Why is the telephone considered an early form of social media? [8.2.1]

5. What do you think is the advantage of user-generated content for social media sites? [8.2.2]

6. Explain how marketing on social media differs from radio or television advertising in terms of the flow of information. [8.2.2]

7. With respect to the message delivered, what are the advantages of real-time marketing techniques compared to traditional radio and television marketing? [8.2.3]

8. What does it mean when a marketing message "goes viral" and why does it occur? [8.2.3]

9. Compare and contrast the connectivity aspect of the first marketplaces with that of social media. [8.3.1]

10. Why should marketers think about their relationship with consumers as a series of small interactions? [8.3.2]

11. You would like to use social media to help you sell your collection of action figures. Which platform would be your best choice? Explain your answer. [8.3.3]

Marketing Research and Planning

1. Some companies are well suited to be click-only businesses, and others are better suited to remain brick-and-mortar businesses. Use a business directory for your community and identify five businesses that you believe could be effective click-only businesses and five others that you believe should operate as brick-and-mortar businesses. Explain why you selected each business. Share your lists with other students and compare your answers. [8.1.2]

2. Businesses have many types of social media categories available to them as they develop their social media presence. Think of your favorite brand and then use the Internet to see how all the different categories are utilized by the brand and by consumers of the brand. Discuss how effective the company is in using those different categories. [8.2.3]

3. Companies can creatively utilize social media in many ways to help promote their brand. Identify a company you think has used social media in a creative fashion. Describe the social media used and discuss the strategies you think provide structure to the use of social media. Do you think the company can continue to use this creative approach to their social media messages? Why or why not? [8.3.2]

4. The growth of the Internet has been remarkable as more and more people gain access to it and businesses move into e-commerce. Statistics for Internet use are reported on many websites. Use the Internet

to locate two different websites that report data on the amount of Internet sales in several countries, including the United States, over several years. Using spreadsheet software, prepare a bar chart that presents data from both websites. It is likely that the data will not be the same on each website. Why do you think it is difficult to obtain accurate data on the use of the Internet? [8.1.2]

5. Pick a social media platform such as Facebook, Pinterest, Twitter, or Instagram and research the history and usage of that format. Develop a set of characteristics of the format that marketers need to be aware of as they decide whether to use it. Include a list of advantages and disadvantages associated with that platform. [8.3.3]

Marketing Management and Decision Making

1. You are the social media director for PetSit, a company that provides pet care/boarding services, and have been asked to develop a social media marketing campaign. Choose three different social media formats and write an entry for PetSit's social media campaign for each one. [8.3.3]

2. Understanding marketing will help you to market yourself. Take a look at how you use social media and examine the strategies you have in place to market yourself. Also take a look at what you have posted on your various sites to see how you might be perceived. Then think of yourself as a brand. How do you think potential customers of that brand will perceive you? Now, imagine you will be applying for a job and know your potential employer will be reviewing your social media sites. How would you change them? Prepare a written report on how you would present brand "You" via the each of the social media accounts you have. [8.3.2, 8.3.3]

3. Pick an industry you think will benefit from a more effective usage of social media. Be sure to pick an industry and not a particular brand within that industry (for example, the music industry or the pet-grooming industry). Now, find a trade organization for that industry (e.g., RIAA for the music industry or the National Dog Groomers Association for pet-grooming). Imagine you are the social media director of that trade organization

and you have been charged with two specific tasks. (1) Given the purpose of the trade organization as expressed on its website, develop a plan for the use of social media by that trade organization. (2) For the various companies and brands within your industry, write a list of recommendations about how to use social media. [8.3.2, 8.3.3]

4. Pick a brand you like and familiarize yourself with how that brand uses social media to convey its messages. Now imagine you are the social media director for that brand and you only have the resources to utilize one social media format. Pick the one you would choose and explain why you would choose it. Be sure to prepare tables, charts, and graphs to help you make your argument as to why the social media format you've chosen is the best option given the needs of your brand and how it currently uses social media. [8.3.3]

5. Bruce loves movies and likes to watch as many as he can. He spends a lot of time in his room downloading movies and watching them on his computer. If he likes the movie, he saves it on an external hard drive so he can watch it again and again and even share it with friends. If he doesn't like the movie, he just deletes it and downloads another. Sandy loves music and is an avid collector of rock-and-roll albums. She often downloads entire albums that feature songs she's heard on other people's Pinterest or YouTube accounts. If she likes the album, she will buy

it on vinyl because she thinks it sounds so much better that way. In both cases, social media has allowed these users to share a media product. However, only one of these benefits the marketers of the products. Social media will allow users to share and even modify products and brands in such a way that they can benefit or hurt the companies who created those brands. In either case, copyright infringement has occurred, which is the unlawful duplication of copyrighted property for commercial purposes or material gain. Explain how each example hurts or benefits the marketers who generated the materials the consumers have downloaded. [8.2.1]

6. Name and describe the six types of social media and provide an example of a company that specializes in providing that type of social media. Describe the social media provider and what it does. Then, select a business that uses that type of social media, and describe how it goes about using it. Finally, determine whether you think the company's use is appropriate, and explain why or why not. [8.2.3]

Let's Start a Band! Follow-Up Discussion

Work in small teams to discuss the question posed at the end of the opening vignette. How can the band most effectively integrate social media into its marketing plan?

Build Your Marketing Plan

In this chapter you learned about integrating social media into a company's marketing strategy. You will now apply this learning to the development of your marketing plan. To access the chapter-specific tools that you will need to complete this activity, please navigate to Chapter 8 ➔ Build Your Marketing Plan in MindTap. Alternatively, you can access these tools online at NGLSync. Please visit www.nglsync.cengage.com, and search for the companion website that accompanies this book by entering the ISBN, author, or title. Once you locate this companion website, navigate to Build Your Marketing Plan ➔ Chapter 8.

Buying and Merchandising Team Decision Making Event

DECA PREP

Build your Portfolio

Holiday Joy is an online specialty store offering gifts, ranging from $5 to $50, for nationally recognized holidays. Customers who order gifts online can use all major credit cards to pay for their purchases. Females, aged 55 to 70, make up 70 percent of the customer base for Holiday Joy. Many of the customers prefer shopping at home instead of going to the store or mall. Follow-up customer surveys indicate that high-quality gifts are the main reason for repeat business at Holiday Joy. Customers also like the reliable, speedy delivery of orders.

Holiday Joy would like to expand its target market to attract younger consumers aged 25 to 54. The vice president of Holiday Joy is considering teaming up with school organizations such as DECA to make the company's products available via the Internet as fundraising products. She has asked your team to develop a fundraising strategy to increase sales for the company. Develop a plan for the student organizations to use that describes how to distribute information to the expanded target market (females aged 25 to 54) and assist customers in placing their orders online. You must also develop a system to ensure the sale is credited to the appropriate school organization.

Holiday Joy's vice president has asked for a suggestion for a reasonably priced gift to give customers who purchase more than $50 of merchandise. She would also like suggestions on how to update the website to promote products more effectively.

You will present your recommendations to the vice president. You will have ten minutes for your presentation, and the judge has five minutes to ask questions.

Performance Indicators Evaluated

- Acquire knowledge of client's products/brands (Selling)
- Explain the role of business websites in digital marketing (Promotion)
- Explain the use of social media for digital marketing (Promotion)
- Implement digital marketing campaign (Promotion)
- Explain the relationship between customer service and distribution (Operations)
- Explain the nature of positive customer relations (Customer Relations)
- Pitch marketing communications idea to client (Selling)

Go to the DECA website for more detailed information. **www.deca.org**

Think Critically

1. Why must the website for Holiday Joy be easy to use?

2. What is the benefit of having students assist customers with the online ordering process?

3. How does ordering online make the sales process simpler?

4. What incentives could Holiday Joy use to increase sales within its new target market?

CHAPTER 9

DEVELOP A MARKETING STRATEGY AND MARKETING PLAN

9.1 Elements of a Marketing Strategy

9.2 Marketing Mix Alternatives

9.3 Consumer Purchase Classifications

9.4 Marketing Planning

*See how effective advertising leads to successful marketing strategies.
Click on Chapter 9, Visual Focus, in your MindTap.*

Let's Start a Band!

> ## "I wish there had been a music business 101 course I could have taken."
>
> – *Kurt Cobain, Singer–Songwriter for the rock band Nirvana, †1994*

It was late and I just finished the idiot check after a gig. After climbing into the van, I felt it was a good time to bring up something that had been on my mind.

"I think we need to plan for our future," I said to the group. "We need to write down our marketing plan." I paused a moment and was surprised there were no protests. But I knew they were thinking, "OMG, he sounds like my parents."

I continued, "I read somewhere that this job is half business and half music, and 'If you don't plan, you plan to fail.' Now, we haven't failed. In fact, I think we've done a pretty good job of analyzing the market and finding out where we fit in it. We've defined our music, and we've defined our audience. We're developing a brand and offering something unique and valuable. We just need to write it down."

Maybe they were too tired, but nobody responded. So I went on. "We need to establish some goals. Not expectations. We need to put in writing what we want to achieve. Then we can map out how we're going to get there. We need to be honest with ourselves about what we'll do to achieve those goals."

Still no response. "I'm not saying this will be set in stone. But it will give us a roadmap for the future. Rather than starting over when we add a new goal, we can see what's worked for us in the past and throw out what hasn't."

I knew they were tired and told them to think about it. But can you help me explain to the band why we should write a marketing plan?

9.1 ELEMENTS OF A MARKETING STRATEGY

Learning Objectives

9.1.1 Describe how market segments are defined.

9.1.2 Identify the four criteria that an effective target market must meet.

Key Term

marketing strategy

marketing matters

In order to develop satisfying exchange relationships with customers, businesses need to develop and follow a marketing strategy. The process begins with identifying a target market or markets and then choosing a target that provides the best opportunity for the company to offer a satisfying marketing mix.

essential question

How do the personal characteristics of individuals affect their wants and needs as well as the choices of products and services they make to satisfy those wants and needs?

9.1.1 Differentiate Market Segments

A **marketing strategy** specifies the way an organization plans and coordinates marketing activities to achieve its goals. An organization that believes in the marketing concept develops a marketing strategy with the goals of satisfying customer needs and making a profit. In most instances, those organizations follow a two-step process. First they carefully select a target market. Then they develop a marketing mix for it. You will learn about selecting a target market in this lesson and about developing a marketing mix in Lesson 9.2.

Start with a Market

A *market* includes all of the consumers available for a business to serve by selling a product or service. However, because the people in a market can be so different, it is nearly impossible for a business to serve all customers well. What if a business came into your classroom to sell items for students who will be graduating next spring? It is possible that not everyone in the room is a senior, so some would not be in the market for graduation products this year. Each person has different plans for graduation. Some students have no plans yet and will not make them for several months. Others probably made plans as early as last summer and already may have purchased the things they will need for graduation.

Recognize Differences and Similarities

Your class is a very small market. It is likely that the business visiting your class also will be interested in all seniors in your school and other schools in your city and state. It might want to serve students who will be graduating from colleges and universities as well as from high schools. Some companies also offer products for graduates from adult education programs, junior high schools, and even preschools. It is highly unlikely that those graduates all want the same things. The differences among all of the people who buy graduation products will affect purchasing decisions and the information they need.

Segmenting Factors

Markets are made up of many segments. *Segments* are components of a market in which people have one or more similar characteristics. **Figure 9-1** shows the major categories often used to segment markets along with examples of common characteristics for each. Marketers start with the needs and wants of consumers in segmenting markets. If a product does not appeal to an important consumer need or want, it will remain unsold. People in a market segment share one or more of these needs or wants. They also may share similar demographic, psychographic or lifestyle, behavioral, and geographic characteristics.

Demographic characteristics include age, income, location, and education level. Psychographic or lifestyle characteristics include activities, customs, traditions, and attitudes. The attitudes of potential consumers are especially important in segmenting markets. They indicate how consumers feel about the type of products and specific brands. Geographic characteristics relate to where customers are located, from neighborhood and city, to region, state, and country.

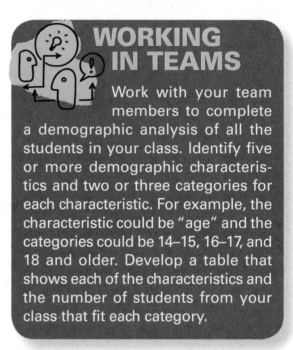

WORKING IN TEAMS

Work with your team members to complete a demographic analysis of all the students in your class. Identify five or more demographic characteristics and two or three categories for each characteristic. For example, the characteristic could be "age" and the categories could be 14–15, 16–17, and 18 and older. Develop a table that shows each of the characteristics and the number of students from your class that fit each category.

FACTORS USED TO SEGMENT A MARKET				
Needs and Wants	Demographics	Psychographics/ Lifestyle	Behavioral	Geographics
Necessities Convenience items Luxuries	Age Gender Education Occupation Income Geographic location	Interests Hobbies Values/beliefs Religion Attitudes Leisure activities	Preferences and habits Decision making styles Buying behavior patterns	Location of customers (neighborhood, city, region, state, or country)

FIGURE 9-1 Businesses study a variety of information to identify unique market segments.

Buying behavior refers to the way consumers make their purchase decisions. These *behavioral segmentation* factors could include their previous experience with products, the sources of information they use, whether decisions are rational or emotional, and how much time they take to gather and evaluate information before making a decision. Marketing information systems and marketing research are used to gather information in order to organize markets into segments.

Niche Marketing

Some market segments include a broad range or large group of consumers. In contrast, to target a more specific market segment, *niche marketing* is used. This concentrated form of marketing is created by identifying extremely specific consumer wants and needs. Consumers who have these specific wants and needs comprise the market *niche*. Once a niche is identified, initially there is often little or no competition for that market segment. An example of niche marketing is Whole Foods, which found its niche by targeting health-conscious consumers concerned with nutrition and willing to pay a premium for organic food.

CHECKPOINT
What does a marketing strategy specify?

9.1.2 ▶ Select Target Markets

Rather than trying to satisfy every person in a market, a business will be more successful in meeting customer needs by concentrating on a specific target market. A *target market* is a clearly identified segment of the market to which the company wants to appeal. In order to be an effective target market, it must meet four criteria:

1. The people in the target market have common, important needs and must respond in a similar way to marketing activities designed to satisfy those needs.

2. The people outside the target market have enough differences from those in the market that they will not find the marketing mix satisfying.

3. The company has adequate information about the people in the target market so they can be identified and located.

4. The important wants and needs of the target market and their buying behavior are understood well enough to develop an effective marketing mix.

The business selling graduation products should study the market of students who will be graduating. The business can then identify segments based on the type of school, its location, and graduation date. Other segments could be based on factors such as the age, gender, or even income.

After identifying several segments, the company would study needs, attitudes, and family customs to see if they are similar or different among the

How many different market segments might this group of students represent?

segments. The company also would collect information to see when and how each segment makes purchase decisions about graduation products. Then it will identify which segment offers the best marketing opportunity. That will become the target market.

It is possible for the company to select more than one segment for a target market. To be successful, the segments must have enough common needs that they respond in the same way to marketing efforts. For example, males and females from the same school may be a part of one target market. Or all graduating seniors from high schools in the Midwest may be similar enough to be considered one target market. Larger companies often work with several target markets at the same time. Each target market requires a unique marketing mix that responds to the differences among the target markets.

CHECKPOINT
What four criteria must be satisfied in order to have an effective target market?

9.1 ASSESSMENT

What Have You Learned?

1. Why are people's wants and needs an important basis for identifying market segments? [9.1.1]

2. Name four demographic factors used to segment a market. [9.1.1]

3. Define target market. [9.1.2]

Academic Connections

1. **Technology**   Locate the website of a company that manufactures computers. Review the website and identify three unique market segments for which the company produces computers. Using information from the website, describe the main factors that differentiate each segment. [9.1.1]

2. **Economics**   Use the library or the Internet to identify government publications or other sources of information about the demographic characteristics of your community. Prepare an alphabetized bibliography of the publications with a brief description of each. [9.1.1]

Connect to ◇DECA

Build your Portfolio

You are a consultant to a company that manufactures athletic uniforms. The company produces a large catalog and sends it to every sports team it can identify. Prepare a three-minute presentation for the company's president on the value of focusing marketing efforts on one or more target markets using a unique marketing mix for each target market. Provide an example target market and marketing mix. Present your ideas to your teacher (judge). [9.1.2]

With 24/7 contact available—whether through email, cell phone, instant messaging (IM), texting, or blogs—you are accustomed to receiving information in a continuous, ongoing stream. But sometimes you are using so many devices at once, you forget that your objective is communication. Keep in mind that the communication devices you use are merely the tools that allow you to communicate—that your goal is the communication itself.

Just as courtesy is necessary for face-to-face communication, it also is required when using electronic communication. These courtesies are particularly important for business interactions. While meeting with others, communication devices that would cause distractions should be turned off.

Developing strong interpersonal relationships with coworkers is extremely important. These relationships are strengthened through face-to-face interactions. Therefore, although it may be tempting to text, email, or call your coworkers, it is often worthwhile to walk down the hall and have a brief chat with them instead.

Patience is important. Although a request for information can be delivered instantly, you may not receive an immediate response. The recipient's schedule and the need to gather information before responding will affect response time.

Texting and instant messaging often alter spelling and style conventions to facilitate fast communication and to minimize keystrokes. Although these conventions, such as the use of all lowercase letters, are considered appropriate for personal electronic communications, they are not appropriate for electronic or written communications in the workplace. Utilize good grammar and standard English when preparing all work-related communications, from texts to formal written documents.

Signatures added to electronic communications such as emails and IMs should include only pertinent contact information. Including political or religious quotations or symbols or links to websites or blogs may violate your employer's policies and detract from the original message.

Many employers monitor employees' use of email and the web. You should know and adhere to your employer's email and Internet usage policies.

Keep in mind that the web and its various components, such as websites or blogs, are internationally accessible. Use restraint when posting information on websites. Confidential or negative information regarding an employer should not be posted on personal blogs.

As part of the background check for job applicants, many employers search the web to find information about job applicants. Publicly recorded instances of bad behavior could hurt your chances of getting hired.

Develop Your Skill

Consider some sensitive information you need to communicate to three people. Outline what your message is and why you need to share it. Define the goal you want to achieve by conveying your message.

Prepare three scripts for communicating the message—one for a phone conversation, one for an email, and one for an IM. Using each type of technology only once, relay the messages to all three people.

Which type of delivery medium was most effective at conveying the message you intended? Which delivery method promoted ongoing, harmonious relationships with the people involved?

Learning Objectives

9.2.1 Describe the eight components of the product mix element.

9.2.2 Discuss important influences on distribution, price, and promotion.

9.2.3 Analyze the four stages of a product life cycle.

Key Terms

brand
image
guarantee
warranty
product life cycle

marketing matters

The most important function of marketers is designing and implementing the marketing mix. The four elements of the marketing mix include all of the activities that marketers will complete to satisfy the target market. Marketers recognize that there are many ways to make a product more appealing to customers. Effective marketing involves careful study of each marketing mix element to determine what can be changed and to identify the effect of the changes on the target market and on company profits.

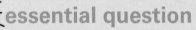

essential question

If a company changes the product element of the marketing mix, will it also have to change one or more of the other mix elements? Why or why not?

9.2.1 ▶ Fine-Tune the Product Mix Element

Have you ever shopped for an item only to find that you really have very few choices? Although there may be two or three brands available, each of the brands is almost identical to the others. This problem often occurs when businesses try to sell products to a large market. They have to offer a product that will appeal to the average consumer. If you are not average, you probably will not be satisfied with the resulting product.

When customers see few differences in competing products, they often look for the lowest price. This reduces the profit margin for businesses. To avoid this situation, businesses can try to differentiate their products from the competition to be more satisfying to customers. However, the trade-off is that they probably will not be able to focus on as large a market.

The product or service as a marketing mix element includes anything the business offers the customer that will be used to satisfy needs. Even for very simple products, businesses can make many choices when developing the product element of the marketing mix.

The product mix element is made up of many components. Not all of the components will be used with every product or service. In some cases, all the target market wants is the basic product. At other times, services and a guarantee are important. Both research and creativity are needed to develop an effective product. Marketers need to be familiar with all of the possible changes that can be made in a product and select the most satisfying combination to serve a target market. Changes could be made in the basic product, product features, product options, associated services, brand or image, guarantee or warranty, packaging, or product use.

Basic Product

The most important part of this mix element is the basic product offered. The basic product is a computer, an automobile, a pair of jeans, or a box of breakfast cereal. It is the first factor considered by the consumer in deciding whether or not to purchase. If the basic product does not meet an important need, the consumer will not consider it. Basic services also can be part of a marketing mix. Movie theaters, child-care, home cleaning, and tax preparation businesses all offer a basic service.

Product Features

Businesses can add features to a basic product or service to make it different from and better than competitors' offerings. Most basic products are sold with many additional features. Consider the product offerings of automobile dealers. Every automobile today has hundreds of features. Some—such as seat belts, outside rearview mirrors, safety bumpers, and emission control equipment—are required by law. Others—such as carpeted floor mats, heated seats, locking gasoline covers, and multi-speaker music systems—are included to satisfy the common needs of automobile purchasers.

Examples of features on other products include a shirt that offers easy-care fabric, double-sewn buttons, and color choices. A shampoo may contain a conditioner and a pleasant scent. A business telephone may have multi-line and intercom capabilities, 50-number memory, a digital display screen, and Bluetooth headset compatibility. Consumers expect many of these features, and they will not buy products that do not include them.

Options

Features are added to improve the basic product. Some businesses make decisions about the features they offer to customers. Customers are not given choices. They must accept the features the company offers. Other companies give customers choices of the features to be included on the product they purchase. Those choices are known as *options*. When you order telephone service, you are given choices such as call waiting, call forwarding, and caller ID. Some customers choose one or more of these options, whereas others choose just the basic service.

Associated Services

If your family has purchased a major appliance such as a washer or refrigerator, the salesperson probably offered a maintenance contract. The maintenance contract is an associated service that will pay for repair work if the appliance fails to operate properly. In many cases, services that come with a product make the product easier to use. For example, if you purchase a computer system, you might want someone to

What types of features might each family member prefer when purchasing a large-screen television for their home?

set it up and make sure it works properly. When purchasing or leasing a car, you may have the option of purchasing a service package that provides basic maintenance for a set number of miles or years.

Brand/Image

A **brand** is a unique name, symbol, or design that identifies a product, service, or company. For some products you purchase, the brand name may be one of the most important factors in your decision. In fact, you may refuse to buy a pair of jeans unless they are American Eagle, athletic shoes unless they are Converse, or even a can of soda unless it is a Coke.

Your parents may not always understand why you want to buy certain brands, but they are probably just as loyal to particular brands of automobiles, foods, or clothing. One of the important reasons for brand loyalty is the image of the brand. The **image** is a unique, memorable quality of a brand. Some brands have an image of quality, others of low price, and still others of innovation. To be effective, the image must match important needs of the consumer.

Guarantee/Warranty

When customers purchase products or services, they want to receive a good value. If they are concerned the product is poorly constructed, will not work properly, or may wear out quickly, they may be unwilling to purchase it. Companies offer guarantees or warranties with products as insurance that the product will be repaired or replaced if there are problems. A product **guarantee** is a general promise or assurance of quality whereas a **warranty** is a specific written statement of the seller's responsibilities related to the guarantee.

Packaging

An often-overlooked part of the marketing mix is the package. Packaging provides protection and security for the product until the consumer can use it. It serves other purposes as well. The package can provide information that helps the customer make a better purchasing decision. It can be useful in promoting the product by attracting attention and illustrating the product in use. Packaging can even make the product more useful for the consumer. For example, producers of orange juice found that sales increased when a plastic spout with a cap that could be screwed on and off was added to their cardboard carton.

Some companies offer eco-friendly packaging for consumers who are trying to minimize their impact on the environment. For example, these consumers purchase soft drinks and yogurt in glass bottles rather than plastic containers and prefer paper bags to plastic because the materials can be recycled. Some packaging companies are producing biodegradable packages that will break down in a landfill. Examples are compostable cellophane bags for dry food and containers made of plant fiber for take-out food.

Uses

The final part of the product element of the marketing mix is the use of the product. It is possible that products and services can be more satisfying to customers or can appeal to new markets if other uses are found. A classic example of expanding markets through new product uses is duct tape. Johnson & Johnson developed a strong waterproof tape that was used to keep the contents of soldiers' ammunition cases dry. Following the war when that demand decreased, they found that the tape could be modified for use as an easy-to-apply, permanent adhesive for the joints of heating and air conditioning ductwork. Because of the high demand for housing at the end of the war, demand for duct tape grew. Today, duct tape is sold in multiple colors and strengths for uses from simple home repairs to apparel trim.

 CHECKPOINT
Name the eight components of the product mix element.

9.2.2 ▶ Distribution, Price, and Promotion

The product or service a company offers is certainly an important element of the marketing mix. However, in order for the company to be successful, the product must be known to consumers in the target market, available when they want it, and offered at a satisfactory price.

Distribution

Distribution is the marketing mix element that facilitates the physical exchange of products and services between businesses and their customers. There are many distribution decisions to make. Important questions that should be answered in planning distribution include:

- Where will the customer obtain the product?
- Where will the customer use it?

- Are there special requirements to transport, store, or display the product?
- When should distribution occur?
- Who should be responsible for each type of distribution activity?

In addition to these general distribution decisions, many products require specific attention to physical distribution factors including the type of transportation, inventory control, product handling, protective packaging, order processing, and customer service.

Price

Price as a marketing mix element is defined as the amount a buyer pays as well as the methods of increasing the value of the product to the customers. There are several questions to answer about how to develop and present the price that can affect the customer's perception of value. They include:

- Does the business want to increase sales, increase profits, or enhance the image of the product?

- Should price be based on costs, what customers are willing to pay, or what competitors are charging?

- Will there be one price for all customers?

- Will customers be allowed to negotiate price? Will discounts or sales be used?

- Will the price be clearly communicated through a price tag or other visible display accompanying the product?

- Are there things that clearly satisfy the customer and make the product a better value than alternatives?

Promotion

Consumers need information about product and service choices and help in making the best purchasing decisions. Businesses use the promotion element of the marketing mix to provide that information and assistance. Promotion includes the methods used and information communicated to customers to encourage purchases and increase their satisfaction.

Maybe more than any of the other mix elements, businesses have many decisions to make that relate to promotion. In doing so, they need to answer these questions:

- Will promotions be directed at a general market or specific segments? Who is involved in the decision-making process and who makes the final decision? Where are the customers in the decision-making process?

MATH IN MARKETING

One Price Doesn't Always Fit All

Pricing strategies can vary widely. Some companies want to make the markup a fixed percentage above cost. Others choose a fixed amount. Still others want to match competitors or to set prices to maintain a certain market share. However, one of the best pricing strategies is to capture value through differential pricing.

Differential pricing is selling the same or similar products to different customers at different prices. This can be done through the use of sales, coupons, rebates, or volume purchases. Other examples include setting different prices for adults, children, and seniors, or offering discounts to students or members of the military or other organizations.

Do the Math

1. A music venue offers all of its customers a 40 percent discount on concert tickets for regional bands. It also offers an additional 10 percent discount to "members" who purchase a $25-dollar membership card that is good for a year. If the original price of all concert tickets purchased is $25, how many does a member have to buy to make back the cost of the membership?

2. A restaurant serves 100 meals a day at an average of $20 a meal. Twenty percent of its customers are seniors (who also average $20 a meal). If the restaurant trying to increase profits offers seniors a 25 percent discount, how many new customers would it have to attract to increase profits?

- Is the specific goal of promotion to increase knowledge, to change attitudes, or to influence behavior?

- What specific information does the audience need to make a decision?

- Will promotion be most effective through advertising, personal selling, sales promotion, publicity, or some other form of communication?

- What is the total amount of money needed for effective promotion? When should the money be spent, on what activities, and for which media?

- When and how can feedback be obtained to determine if customers understand the message?

CHECKPOINT
In addition to the product or service being offered, what other elements must marketers consider in developing a marketing mix?

9.2.3 ▶ Analyze the Product Life Cycle

The competition a company faces affects its marketing decisions. An important tool to identify types of competition is life-cycle analysis. A **product life cycle** identifies the stages a product goes through from the time it enters the market until it is no longer sold.

Products go through four stages in their life cycle (**Figure 9-2**). The stages of the life cycle are determined by changes in the amount and type of competition. By studying the competition, a business can determine the type of marketing mix needed in each stage of the product life cycle.

Introduction

In the first stage of the product life cycle, a new product is introduced into the market. It is quite different from existing products, so customers are not aware of it or don't realize how it can satisfy their needs. Because it is new, there are no direct competitors. It will be competing with older, established products that are currently meeting customer needs.

As with many new things, few people will want to be the first to try the product. The business needs to identify those consumers who are very dissatisfied with current products and those who are most likely to want to experiment with something new. These people are the target market for the new product and will become the *early adopters* of the product.

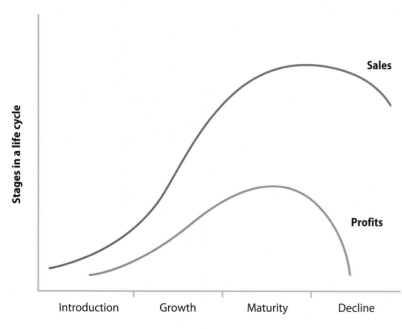

FIGURE 9-2 Competition affects sales and profits in each stage of the product life cycle.

The product itself will be basic because it has just been developed. It will likely not have many features or options. To assure the customers of the quality of the new product, the company may offer a guarantee or warranty. A well-known brand name also may encourage people to buy the new product.

The product will not have to be widely distributed in the market because only a small number of customers will buy it initially. It would be too risky and too expensive for the company to try for widespread distribution immediately. The company will select those locations where the target market will be most likely to buy this type of product.

The price may be high at first so the company can recoup the many expenses it incurs in developing the product. Or the price may be set below cost in order to penetrate and develop a presence in the market. Early adopters often are willing to pay a higher price because they have no other similar products to use in comparing the price.

Promotion needs to inform the target market that a new product is available and show how it will satisfy an important need. Customers need to know where they can purchase the product. Often promotion in the introductory stage of the life cycle will emphasize that the product is new and exciting to encourage people who want to be the first to own something.

Growth

If a new product is successfully introduced, it eventually attracts more customers, and sales begin to grow rapidly. Competitors see that the new product offers opportunities for sales and profits, so they enter the market with their own version of the product as soon as they can. With this growing market and increasing competition, the marketing mix must change.

Competitors need to offer something different from the first brand in order to attract customers. They will add features and options to make their brand better. They also may provide customer services that customers want. Brand name will be very important as each business tries to show consumers that its choice is best.

Because more consumers are now buying the product, it must be distributed more widely. To be as efficient as possible, manufacturers often will use other businesses to distribute and sell their products. Because customers now have choices, each business tries to be sure its brand is available where and when the customer wants it. They concentrate on improving their order processing and handling, transportation, and customer service activities in order to satisfy customer needs better than competitors.

Customers see a range of prices during the growth stage. They have many choices of brands, features, options, and services. Brands with a quality image charge higher prices. Those just entering the market or presenting an economical image have lower prices. Businesses emphasize the value customers receive from the unique qualities of their brand.

Promotion in the growth stage becomes more competitive. It focuses on attracting customers who have not yet tried the product as well as demonstrating the advantages of specific brands. More money is spent on promotion. Unique messages are directed at specific segments of the market. The messages aim to inform prospective customers, persuade those making decisions, and remind those who have purchased about the wisdom of their decision.

Maturity

During the maturity stage of the life cycle, sales peak and profits begin to decline. Consumers are aware of the product and either buy it or not based on their needs. Many businesses now offer their own brand of the product. Therefore, the level of competition is more intense as businesses compete for sales.

The products of competing companies are very similar in the maturity stage. The features and options that were successful have been adopted by all of the companies whereas those that were not successful have been eliminated.

Because customers view the products in this stage as very similar, they pay much more attention to price. Prices will be very competitive, and businesses will regularly offer discounts or sale prices to encourage customers to purchase their brands.

Companies will increase the availability of products to make sure customers can easily obtain them. The products will be sold through many locations. A company

During which stage(s) of the product life cycle are you likely to find products on sale?

also may decide to *reposition* a product in the market by attempting to change how consumers perceive the brand. For example, they can do so by making changes in the design of the product or by offering extended services such as a warranty.

Promotion is very important in the maturity stage. Companies continually remind customers of their brand name and try to persuade them that their company's brand is the best. Because of the large number of customers in the market, a great deal of money is spent on promotion to try to persuade them to buy.

Because sales have peaked, yet costs continue to increase, profits start to go down in the maturity stage. A few companies may still be profitable, but many will struggle, and some will be unable to survive.

Decline

A market declines when most consumers decide that a product no longer satisfies them or when they discover new and better products. Sales drop rapidly, and there is little or no profit available to companies with products still in the market. When a market declines, businesses try to get out as quickly as possible unless they have many loyal customers.

For products in the decline stage of the life cycle, there is little opportunity for product improvement. Examples of products in the decline stage are products that represent old technologies such as typewriters and VCRs (videocassette recorders). Because sales and profits are declining, companies are not willing to invest in product changes. Some companies may use their resources to focus on producing new products that incorporate newer technology. For example, IBM phased out its manufacture of typewriters

© Little Pig Studio/Shutterstock.com.

in the early 1990s as it focused on the manufacture of personal computers. Some companies may try to identify other uses of the product to broaden the market and retain customers.

Distribution will be cut back to only the profitable locations. Companies may save money in distribution by keeping inventory levels low and cutting back on customer service.

Price is a difficult mix element to manage in this stage of the life cycle. Because profits are declining, businesses want to keep prices from dropping further. Only the most loyal customers will pay that high price, however. In most cases, prices have to be reduced to continue to sell the product, and even that may not be enough to keep customers.

Because promotion is expensive, companies cut back on the amount of promotion during this stage to reduce costs. They choose less-expensive media and promote much less frequently. Because there are fewer customers interested in the product, companies can use more direct methods of communication to keep their loyal customers as long as possible.

 CHECKPOINT
What are the four stages of a product life cycle?

9.2 **ASSESSMENT**

What Have You Learned?

1. What are product options? [9.2.1]
2. Which element of the marketing mix makes the product known to consumers in the target market? [9.2.2]
3. In which stage of the product life cycle do sales peak and profits begin to decline? [9.2.3]

Academic Connections

1. **Visual Art**   Illustrate a product using graphic design software. If possible, import a photo of the product into the software file. Label each component of the product discussed in the lesson, including those not visible. Write a brief explanation of each component. [9.2.1]
2. **Economics**   Create a 4 × 3 table using word processing or spreadsheet software. Identify a product that represents each stage of the product life cycle. Write the product name in the first column. In the second column, describe the type of competition businesses selling that product face. In the third column, describe the most important marketing mix element(s) for businesses in that market. [9.2.3]

Connect to ◇DECA

Build your Portfolio

Your team is responsible for proposing a marketing mix for the company that is selling graduation items to seniors in your school. Prepare a one-page brochure that identifies the target market and describes each of the marketing mix elements your team recommends. Use the brochure to make a presentation to your teacher (judge). [9.2.2]

Learning Objectives

9.3.1 Describe the four consumer purchase classifications.

9.3.2 Explain how the purchase classifications affect marketing planning.

Key Terms

staple goods
impulse goods
emergency goods
shopping goods
attribute-based goods

price-based goods
specialty goods
unsought goods

marketing matters

By observing and analyzing the way consumers shop, marketers have identified four basic groups into which products and services fall. The groups are based on consumers' perception of their need for the product. These consumer purchase classifications—convenience goods, shopping goods, specialty goods, and unsought goods—can be used in developing effective marketing mixes. Each classification requires a different mix to respond effectively to consumers' needs and wants.

essential question

What do consumers consider about a product or service before deciding whether to purchase it?

9.3.1 ▶ How Consumers Shop

Consumer purchase classifications describe the ways consumers shop for products based on their needs and perception of them. The four major purchase classifications are convenience goods, shopping goods, specialty goods, and unsought goods.

You do not purchase all products in the same way. For some purchases you are very careful, spending a great deal of time and comparing several brands before making a decision. For others, you know what you want and will buy it as quickly and conveniently as possible. Finally, there are some products you do not know about and so would not consider buying. Through careful study of the ways consumers purchase products, marketers have developed the purchase classification system to help plan marketing strategies. The purchase classifications are based on two important factors:

1. The importance of the purchase to the consumer.

2. The willingness of the consumer to shop and compare products before making the purchase.

Convenience Goods

Consumers want to make many of their purchases as easily as possible. The specific reason for making that convenient purchase decision determines whether the product or service is a staple, impulse, or emergency good. All three are types of convenience goods but for different reasons.

STAPLE GOODS Products that are regular, routine purchases are **staple goods**. You need to buy them frequently, are aware of the needs they satisfy, and probably have a preference of brands. These are products you routinely pick up when you go to a store. Staple goods include bread, milk, toothpaste, snack foods, and many other regularly purchased products.

Because you know you will need them, you make regular purchases. You will typically purchase them at a convenient location or when you make a routine shopping trip. It is not likely you will shop around in order to buy a staple good. If the store you are in does not have your favorite brand, you may buy another brand, or you may wait to buy it until the next time you go shopping.

IMPULSE GOODS How many times have you walked into a store to buy one or two items and left with several more purchases than you planned? Items purchased on the spur of the moment without advance planning are **impulse goods**. Some examples are candy, magazines, low-cost jewelry, unique items of clothing, and inexpensive new products. Impulse goods are often the items you see displayed near checkout counters in retail stores.

Consumers do not actively shop for impulse goods. They purchase them when they see the product displayed or advertised. At that point they identify an important need that they believe can be satisfied by the product. Because of the strong need and a belief that there is no real value to be gained in comparing other products or brands, the consumer makes the purchase immediately.

EMERGENCY GOODS You may have a favorite brand of gasoline or soft drink. When given a choice, you select those brands and may even go out of your way to find them. But when the fuel gauge on your car is on empty, you will probably pull into the nearest gasoline station and buy that brand of gas. If you are very thirsty, you may be willing to buy another brand of soft drink or even a different beverage if your favorite is not available. Products or services purchased as a result of an urgent need are **emergency goods**. Common examples of emergency goods are automobile towing services, umbrellas, ambulance services, and plumbing repair services.

What type of convenience goods would the items at this airport newsstand be considered? Explain your answer.

© Arina P Habich/Shutterstock.com

As with impulse goods, consumers do not actively shop for emergency goods. They decide to purchase only because the situation creates an urgent, important need. Because of the emergency, the consumer is unable or unwilling to shop and compare products before purchasing.

Shopping Goods

Most of the major purchases made by consumers are **shopping goods**. These products and services are typically more expensive than convenience goods. Consumers believe that the need is important, the amount of money to be spent on the purchase is significant, and real differences exist among the choices of products and brands. Therefore, they are willing to spend time shopping and comparing alternatives before making a final purchase decision. Examples of shopping goods include clothing, cars, houses and apartments, stereo equipment, major appliances, colleges, dentists, and vacation locations. Shopping goods are either attribute-based or price-based.

ATTRIBUTE-BASED GOODS For most shopping goods, consumers see a number of different choices. Each brand may have a different set of features or services. Prices may vary or some brands may be purchased on sale or using credit. When a variety of differences exist and the consumer considers a number of factors to determine the best value, the products are **attribute-based goods**.

PRICE-BASED GOODS Some people evaluate major purchases and decide that several products or brands are basically alike. Each will provide the same general level of satisfaction. Yet the consumer believes the price is likely to be quite different among the choices. Because the need is important and the cost is high, it is worth the time needed to shop for the best possible price. Products that consumers believe are similar but have significant price differences are **price-based goods**.

Specialty Goods

There are some products and services that are so satisfying that the consumer will not consider buying anything else as a substitute. Products that have this strong brand loyalty are known as **specialty goods**. People often think of very well-known and expensive products as specialty goods. Automobiles such as Rolls Royce, Porsche, or Jaguar fit this description. Lear jets and Rolex watches also are specialty goods.

Inexpensive and regularly purchased products also are treated as specialty goods by some customers. Do you shop for your clothing at the same store or website every time? Do you believe that one company makes the best cell phones or laptop computers? If you do and you would not typically consider another choice, then they would be specialty products and businesses. Even such things as chewing gum and toothpaste can be specialty goods if the customer will not buy a different brand.

The two factors that determine if a product is a specialty good are its importance in satisfying an individual's need and the willingness of the customer to delay a purchase until the specific product or brand is located. In the case of specialty goods, consumers believe the brand is the only thing that will provide satisfaction. That belief is usually based on very positive past experiences with the brand and less positive experiences with others. Because of the strong belief in the brand, customers

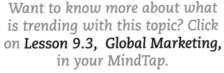

*Want to know more about what is trending with this topic? Click on **Lesson 9.3, Global Marketing,** in your MindTap.*

Connect to
MindTap

Why might some people want to purchase only Nike athletic shoes?

will not compare brands when shopping. They will not make a purchase until they can find their choice. If that means waiting or traveling to another store, the customer is willing to do so. This type of customer loyalty is very valuable to businesses.

Unsought Goods

Whereas consumers go to great lengths to find specialty goods, **unsought goods** are those products that consumers don't know about or don't think of buying. If you were choosing things to purchase in the next year,

would the choices include life insurance or legal services to prepare a will? Those typically are not considered important needs for young people, so they would be unsought goods for you. Nevertheless, when you get older and have a career and a family, either or both of those items may become much more important and could become shopping goods or even specialty goods.

When a product or a specific brand of a product is first introduced into the market, consumers are not aware it exists, so it is unsought. As soon as they become aware of the product, they decide if it is something that might meet a need. If a product or service does not fill a customer need, it remains unsought and unsold. Even if the business makes it easy to buy the product through telephone or Internet sales or a salesperson visiting the person at home, consumers will not purchase an unsought product.

CHECKPOINT
What are the four consumer purchase classifications?

9.3.2 ▶ Use Purchase Classifications in Marketing

Just as life-cycle stages provide important information about competition, consumer purchase classifications help marketers better understand consumer behavior. That understanding is used in planning the best marketing mix. Each purchase classification requires a different mix in order to effectively respond to consumer needs.

Convenience Goods

Consumers want to purchase convenience goods as easily as possible. They do not see important differences among products and brands that make it worth their time to shop and compare. Therefore, businesses need to emphasize product location (convenience) in the marketing mix. The product mix element will focus on brand, packaging, and image.

Price is important for staple goods. Prices cannot be set higher than similar products in the same location, or the consumer will switch brands. For impulse goods, price is less important, and for emergency goods, price is only a minor consideration. Promotion is used to remind people of brand and image for staple goods, the need to be satisfied for impulse goods, and location and availability for emergency goods.

Shopping Goods

Because consumers are willing to shop and compare, the marketing mix for shopping goods is different from the marketing mix for convenience goods. Products and services no longer have to be available in the most convenient locations. Promotion emphasizes the qualities of the product or service that consumers believe are most important. Promotion often helps consumers compare products or brands.

Consumers are interested in the best combination of features, options, services, and uses. For attribute-based shopping goods, the product mix element is very important. For price-based shopping goods, price is the most important. While customers want a quality product, they believe that several products are very similar. They search for the best possible price. Businesses must demonstrate that they have the lowest price or the best possible financial terms. They also need to emphasize price in promotional activities.

Specialty Goods

The marketing mix element emphasized for this category will depend on why consumers believe the product or service is a specialty good. Specialty good status typically results because the product is unique or of high quality. In that case, the business will emphasize the product in marketing planning to ensure that the quality or uniqueness is maintained. Promotion reminds consumers of the reasons they prefer the product.

Consumers also may prefer a product or service because of its location. Some people select a bank, a physician, or even a college because it is close to home or work. Marketing activities for these products would emphasize location over product features. In other cases, price is the reason for specialty status. Consumers may buy only one brand because they believe it has the best price. Again, marketing would maintain that price so that consumers remain satisfied. Promotion that is able to create excitement, a unique image, or a belief that one product is far superior to others may result in the product being treated as a specialty good for at least a short time.

Unsought Goods

The marketing mix developed for unsought goods is particularly important. New products are considered unsought goods at first. If these products are not well marketed, there will be no demand, and they will fail. Consumers must be aware of the product, how it satisfies needs, and where they can purchase it. If a business is successful with the promotion and distribution mix elements, the product will quickly become a convenience, shopping, or specialty good. If a product is new, the marketing mix will emphasize promotion and distribution.

If customers are aware of the product or service and it remains unsought, the mix must be very carefully developed. The product is most important. The business must evaluate the product to determine why consumers do not want it. The

What type of goods does this local deli owner offer, and what would be the best way for him to market his products?

product must be redesigned to make it more appealing to consumers and to relate to their important needs. Promotion can then be used to show consumers how the product will meet their needs.

Businesses must market unsought goods carefully. Consumers may become upset if they believe a business is trying to sell them something they do not need. If consumers develop a negative attitude toward a product or a business, it will be difficult to sell them products in the future. Businesses that successfully sell unsought goods use a target market strategy. They identify the specific segments of the market that have needs related to the product or service. They then develop very personalized marketing mixes to work with those target markets at times and locations where there is a good chance to be successful. Some businesses are so effective with their marketing that a regularly unsought good becomes a specialty good for customers.

CHECKPOINT

For which consumer purchase classification is product location generally most important?

9.3 ASSESSMENT

What Have You Learned?

1. What two factors form the basis of the four purchase classifications? [9.3.1]
2. Name the two types of shopping goods. [9.3.1]
3. What should the promotion for specialty goods remind consumers of? [9.3.2]

Academic Connections

1. **Writing** Tour a retail store or supermarket and identify one product that fits each of the four consumer purchase classifications. Write a paragraph describing how each product is marketed in the store. [9.3.1]

2. **Ethics** Promotion can be a powerful marketing tool to persuade people to purchase something they otherwise might not buy. However, when misused, it might result in dissatisfied customers and a poor image for the company. Write five guidelines for marketers describing the ethical use of promotion when marketing impulse goods and unsought goods. [9.3.2]

Connect to ◇DECA

Build your Portfolio

You are introducing a new unsought good—an insurance policy that provides protection for damages suffered from personal identity theft that occurs when a person is using the Internet. It will cost $5 a month (added to the customer's Internet bill) and will only be promoted via the Internet. Use presentation software to prepare three slides that outline the marketing mix you propose for the unsought good. Present your slides to your teacher (judge). [9.3.2]

9.4 MARKETING PLANNING

Learning Objectives

9.4.1   Define marketing plan.

9.4.2   Describe the market analysis section of a marketing plan.

9.4.3   Explain how a marketing strategy is developed.

9.4.4   Explain the purpose of an action plan.

Key Terms

marketing plan
market analysis
mission statement
SWOT analysis
positioning statement
action plan

marketing matters

The marketing plan serves as a guide for coordinating marketing activities. Developing an effective marketing plan requires the commitment of time and attention by senior marketing managers. It also involves gathering information about the company, competition, changes in the business environment, and current and prospective customers.

essential question

How can a company determine whether its marketing plan is effective?

9.4.1 ▶ What Is a Marketing Plan?

To aid in decision making and coordinating the people, activities, and resources involved in successful marketing, businesses must develop a marketing plan. A **marketing plan** is a clear written description of the marketing strategies of a business and the way the business will operate to accomplish each strategy. The marketing plan is based on marketing strategy.

Marketing strategies must be developed very carefully. They need to be based on a complete study of a market and the possible ways the business can serve the market. If marketers are not careful in developing the strategy, they will likely make decisions based on their own opinions rather than the target market's needs.

In order to develop an effective marketing plan, a business needs an organized, objective method to plan each part of a marketing strategy and determine how the business should operate to make sure the strategy is successful. The process of developing a marketing plan encourages the marketer to gather and analyze information, consider alternatives, determine what competitors are likely to do, and study customers' possible responses. Based on that study, procedures can be planned to achieve the marketing strategy. The marketing strategy describes what the business wants to do, and the marketing plan details how the strategy will be implemented and evaluated.

Executing a marketing plan in most businesses involves many complex activities. To be successful, the activities need to be coordinated with one another and with the activities occurring in other parts of the business. A great many decisions must be made, and often a large amount of money and other resources must be committed by the business from the time of production until the sale of the product. Coordination of decisions and resources will be needed in order for the business to make a profit once the products have been sold. Many people are involved in carrying out marketing activities. To make the best use of the time and efforts of those people, their activities should be coordinated as well.

Marketing plans are developed for a specific time period, often six months to one year. Companies may have an overall marketing plan, but they usually develop a specific plan for each major product. The preparation of the plan is usually coordinated by the top marketing manager with input and assistance from many other people. Usually companies have a number of researchers, analysts, and support staff working continuously on preparing and updating marketing plans.

Companies that successfully prepare and use marketing plans have procedures to gather and analyze information. Much of the information used in developing marketing plans is already available in the company's marketing information system (MkIS). Records of production, operations, and sales are maintained. Detailed information on specific customers and their purchasing history is available. In addition, most businesses regularly gather and study information about competitors, business trends, and the economy. The business also should be aware of other groups and organizations that provide planning information, such as government agencies, trade associations, and private research firms. Finally, businesses must be prepared to complete marketing research when adequate information is not available.

Marketing plans are developed in three stages. The results of each stage are described in the written plan. **Figure 9-3** provides an outline of the three sections of the marketing plan and the stages of development they represent.

CHECKPOINT
What is a marketing plan?

© wavebreakmedia/Shutterstock.com

How does a company benefit by having employees working on marketing plans on a continuous basis?

Develop the Market Analysis

The first stage of development is to analyze the market. A **market analysis** provides information used in developing a marketing strategy that is competitive, meets customer needs, and can be implemented effectively. A market analysis needs to be carefully prepared, clearly written, and effectively communicated to everyone who has a role in implementing the marketing strategy.

The market analysis is discussed in the first section of the marketing plan. It includes information about the purpose and mission of the business, a description of current markets and strategies, information about the business's primary competitors, and an analysis of its strengths, weaknesses, opportunities, and threats (SWOT).

Company Mission Statement

A company's **mission statement** identifies the nature of the business or the reasons the business exists. It is most often developed to describe broad categories of products or services the business provides (transportation, health care, legal services) and the types of customers the company wants to serve (business travelers, resorts in the Sunbelt, single parents with children under age 18).

By identifying the mission or purpose, marketing planners concentrate their efforts in areas where the company is known and works best. An example of a mission statement for an auto dealership is "to offer quality automobiles at fair prices, to provide fast and effective service, and to treat all customers with courtesy and respect."

MARKETING PLAN OUTLINE

I. **Market Analysis**
   A. Purpose and Mission of the Business
   B. Description of Current Markets and Strategies
   C. Primary Competitors
   D. SWOT Analysis
      1. Internal Analysis
         a. Strengths
         b. Weaknesses
      2. External Environment Analysis
         a. Economy
         b. Laws and Regulations
         c. Costs
         d. Competition
         e. Technology
         f. Social Factors

II. **Marketing Strategy**
   A. Marketing Goals/Expected Outcomes
   B. Target Market Description
      1. Identifying Characteristics
      2. Unique Needs, Attitudes, Behaviors
   C. Marketing Mix Description
      1. Product/Service
      2. Distribution
      3. Pricing
      4. Promotion
   D. Positioning Statement

III. **Action Plans**
   A. Activity Schedule
      1. Responsibilities
      2. Schedule
      3. Budget
   B. Evaluation Procedures
      1. Evidence of Success
      2. Method of Collecting Evidence

FIGURE 9-3 A complete marketing plan describes the three stages of development.

MARKETING COMMUNICATION

Vision Statement

A *vision statement* is a statement about what an organization wants to be once it achieves its mission. While the mission statement focuses on what the organization does today, the vision statement focuses on what the organization wants to do in the future. Vision statements are the inspiration for a company's planning, announcing what it is trying to build. It answers the question "where do we want to go?" In some cases it can reflect what an organization dreams of becoming. Here are some examples:

Amazon: "To be Earth's most customer-centric company; to build a place where people can come to find and discover anything they might want to buy online."

Ikea: "To create a better everyday life for the many people."

Facebook: "To give people the power to share and make the world more open and connected."

Microsoft: "Empower every person and every organization on the planet to achieve more."

Human Rights Campaign: "Equality for everyone."

Think Critically

1. Write a vision statement for a school club or organization, such as band, a sports team, or drama club. Limit the vision statement to one sentence.

2. Exchange your vision statement with another member of the class. Discuss the statements and suggest edits, revisions, or even a new approach to improve the statement. After discussing your partner's input, make the necessary changes.

Sources: O'Donovan, Kirstin. "The First Thing All Amazing Startups Work on for a Refreshing Beginning." Lifehack. 2019. https://www.lifehack.org/articles/work/20-sample-vision-statement-for-the-new-startup.html; Ward, Susan. "Vision Statement Definition with Vision Statement Examples." The Balance. September 8, 2018. https://www.thebalancesmb.com/vision-statement-2947999

Current Markets and Strategies

After identifying the mission, the planners briefly review the current marketing efforts of the company. The review identifies the markets in which the company is operating and the marketing strategies it is using. It also provides a summary of current results and effectiveness. This reminds the planners and readers of activities underway in the business.

Determining the activities that are effective as well and those that are not helps planners decide whether to continue with the same strategies or to plan changes. A company might discover that its advertising costs are increasing at a rate much faster than its sales. In that case, it needs to determine if the costs can be controlled, or if the increased advertising might pay off in the long term with faster sales growth. Some products or markets might be outperforming others. Recognizing why those strategies are effective while others are not helps determine where to direct resources in the future.

Primary Competitors

An analysis of the competitors in the same product categories and serving similar customer groups is an important part of the marketing plan. In addition to identifying each competitor, an objective evaluation of the important strengths and weaknesses of each competitor is completed. This evaluation helps decide how to compete with each of those businesses. For example, if a competitor is known for keeping prices very low, it may be difficult for another company to develop a strategy that emphasizes price. On the other hand, if a competitor is having difficulty providing repair services for the products it sells, another company may be able to attract new customers by emphasizing its customer service department.

SWOT Analysis

The **SWOT analysis** portion of the market analysis identifies a business's strengths and weaknesses and the opportunities and threats it faces. (In the acronym SWOT, S stands for *strengths*, W stands for *weaknesses*, O stands for *opportunities*, and T stands for *threats* the company faces in attempting to meet a specific goal.)

An accurate analysis is important because it can inform the marketing team whether the goal is attainable. If not, a new goal must be set, and the SWOT analysis repeated. The company can use the SWOT analysis in developing a marketing strategy by matching opportunities with strengths.

A SWOT analysis reviews the strengths (not only what it does well but how it does well) and weaknesses that come from within the organization. This is called an internal analysis. The opportunities and threats that come from external factors also are explored.

INTERNAL ANALYSIS

The *internal analysis* is a thorough and objective review of the current operating and financial performance of the company. The company's strengths and weaknesses are determined by reviewing and comparing current and past performance with company goals. Analyzing products and production methods, marketing activities, personnel, and financial performance can identify areas where the company is meeting expectations and where it is not. Careful analysis should lead the marketing team to find ways to convert the threats and weaknesses to strengths, to minimize their impact, or to avoid them entirely.

The internal analysis can be compared with competitive data to determine where the company has advantages and disadvantages. If a company has a unique production process that competitors have been unable to duplicate, it should be emphasized. If customers believe the company has a better customer service record, it will be important to use it in the next marketing plan. On the other hand, if the company is having difficulty competing on the basis of price, strategies should be developed to avoid direct price competition. If distribution costs are consistently higher than planned or if inventory levels cannot be maintained to achieve needed sales, those operations can be reviewed and changed.

EXTERNAL ENVIRONMENT

The analysis of the *external environment* identifies any factors outside of the company that may affect its performance. Those factors include the economy, competition, laws affecting the business, technology, changes in costs, and the expectations and needs of society. An example of the effect of technology on business was the introduction

Want to know more about marketing in the information age? Click on **Lesson 9.4, Digital Marketing,** *in your MindTap.*

Connect to MindTap

and acceptance of transmitting legal documents with electronic signatures. That change required the development of new technology to create and transmit secure and identifiable electronic signatures for letters, orders, contracts, and other legal documents. It also required new laws that recognized electronically signed documents as legal business transactions. With those changes, many official business communications could be prepared and transferred almost instantly rather than waiting for delivery through the mail.

CHECKPOINT
What is the purpose of the SWOT analysis portion of the market analysis?

9.4.3 ▶ Develop the Marketing Strategy

In terms of assuring company's success, developing the marketing strategy is the most important activity involved in developing the marketing plan. The *marketing strategy* is the description of the way marketing will be used to accomplish the company's objectives.

Developing a marketing strategy begins with stating the company goals on which the strategy is based. The goals are followed by a full description of the target market, the marketing mix, and a specific positioning statement (**Figure 9-4**).

Determine Goals and Outcomes

The marketing strategy is based on a specific statement of the goals the company plans to achieve or the expected outcomes of the marketing efforts. The company determines whether the marketing strategy is effective based on whether the goals have been met. Marketing goals include such things as increasing sales or profits for certain products, increasing the market share for a product in a particular geographic area or target market, increasing the effectiveness of particular parts of the marketing mix such as distribution or customer service, or other specific results.

Define a Target Market

The marketing strategy will clearly identify the target market to be served. The target market will be defined completely so it can be located, so the company's employees will understand the market's characteristics and the target customers' needs and wants,

DEVELOP A MARKETING STRATEGY	
Determine goals and outcomes	States the goals the company plans to achieve or the expected outcomes of the marketing efforts
Define target market	Allows the target market to be located and the company employees to understand the market characteristics and customer's needs and wants.
Specify the marketing mix	Describes each mix element in marketing the product.
Develop a positioning statement	Describes the unique qualities of the marketing mix that make the product satisfying to the target market and that differentiate it from the competition

FIGURE 9-4 Follow these four steps in developing the marketing strategy for a product.

Specify the Marketing Mix

A complete description of each mix element is included in the marketing plan. Product, distribution (place), price, and promotion are described specifically and completely so that everyone involved in implementing the mix understands the company's plans. A description of the marketing mix is presented in the marketing strategy section of the marketing plan, and the activities and budgets needed to implement each element of the mix are developed in later sections.

Develop a Positioning Statement

A **positioning statement** is a specific description of the unique qualities of the marketing mix that make it different from the competition and satisfying to the target market. For example, a discount store positions itself as the one-stop place to shop for home products for a family on a budget.

and so it is clear that the marketing mix is appropriate for that target market.

Although each target market is unique, it is possible for an organization to serve several target markets at once. When more than one market is identified, marketing planners must remember that each market requires a specific marketing mix. A specific product or target market may have its own marketing plan or a specific section of the overall company marketing plan devoted to it.

CHECKPOINT

What are the four steps in developing a marketing strategy?

How can setting a specific sales goal help a business determine the effectiveness of its marketing strategy?

Photodisc/Getty Images

Develop the Action Plan

The final section of the marketing plan is called an **action plan**. It identifies actions needed to accomplish and evaluate the marketing strategy.

Activity Schedule

Completing each part of the marketing strategy requires a series of activities. The activities must be determined along with a description of how and when they will be completed. Responsibility for completing each activity must be assigned.

Many people both inside and outside the company are involved in marketing. Their activities must be coordinated in order to be successful. For example, if a manufacturer introduces an individual-serving smoothie blender, the production schedule must be coordinated with distribution to retailers and the advertising schedule. If the new blender is advertised to consumers before the retailer has the product, both the consumer and retailer will be unhappy with the manufacturer. If the blender will be sold online, the website must be prepared, and online customer support personnel must have product information to answer questions and provide technical support.

In addition to assigning responsibilities and developing schedules, planners must determine budgets for the various marketing activities. Without a budget, overspending can easily occur or some marketing activities may not have enough funds to be implemented effectively.

Evaluation Procedures

Evaluation procedures must be developed to determine if the action plan is effective. The evaluation procedures measure whether the marketing activities were completed correctly and on time. They will also determine if the marketing objectives identified earlier in the marketing plan were accomplished.

Information can be collected to determine if target markets are responding to the marketing mix and if their needs

> *Want to know more about what is trending with this topic? Click on* **Lesson 9.4, Marketing Decisions,** *in your MindTap.*
>
> Connect to
> **MindTap**

Why is it important that all marketing activities are identified, scheduled, and assigned to someone for completion as a part of the action plan?

© Henryk Sadura/Shutterstock.com

are satisfied. Each mix element should be studied. Specific marketing activities should be evaluated to determine if the quality is acceptable and if they were accomplished within the established budget for the activity.

Information collected in the evaluation is used to make improvements in marketing activities while the plan is being implemented. As soon as problems are identified, actions should be taken to correct those problems. Evaluation information is also essential when developing the next marketing plan.

CHECKPOINT
Why does a marketing plan need an action plan?

9.4 ASSESSMENT

What Have You Learned?

1. What is a marketing plan based on? [9.4.1]
2. What does a mission statement identify and what does it describe? [9.4.2]
3. What is the value of the positioning statement as a part of the marketing strategy? [9.4.3]
4. Why should the action plan include a budget? [9.4.4]

Academic Connections

1. **Research** You are a member of the marketing planning team for a large electronics retailer. Use the Internet to locate current information you think planners should consider on competitors' performance, consumers of electronic products, and changes occurring outside the company. Write a memo to your team summarizing the information. [9.4.2]

2. **Communication** Review advertising or websites of three well-known companies that have unique images. Identify information you believe provides an effective positioning statement. Write each positioning statement on a note card. See if other students can guess the company from the statement. [9.4.4]

Connect to ◇DECA

Build your Portfolio

Your marketing team is advising a new restaurant that caters to the lunch crowd near an industrial park. The people who eat there are a mix of managers, office personnel, and factory workers. Develop a marketing strategy for the business, including a positioning statement. Present your ideas to your teacher (judge). [9.4.4]

Connect to MindTap

*Analyze a case study that focuses on chapter concepts. Click on **Chapter 9, Case Study,** in your MindTap.*

Review Marketing Concepts

1. You are opening a video game sales and rental business. What are some characteristics of the consumers in the market segment you wish to reach? [9.1.1]

2. How does the target market for the floral department of a grocery store chain differ from the target market for a neighborhood flower store? [9.1.2]

3. You are in the market for a new case for your mobile phone. Make a list of possible features and options available for the basic product. Which of these appeals to you, and why? [9.2.1]

4. Mario enjoys baking cookies for his family and friends, and they are always encouraging him to start a baking business. What distribution considerations will he have if he decides to pursue this idea? [9.2.2]

5. Mario decides to open a kiosk in the mall to sell his cookies. His business, now in the growth stage, is doing well and he is making a profit. However, a restaurant in the mall has begun to sell a cookie very similar to his. What can he do to respond to this competition? [9.2.3]

6. What type of goods—convenience, shopping, specialty, or unsought—does the operator of a video game sales and rental business provide? [9.3.1]

7. How has online shopping affected the way consumers shop? Which type of goods are consumers more likely to shop for online? Explain your answer. [9.3.1]

8. Contrast the amount of thought a consumer gives to purchasing a convenience good versus purchasing a shopping good. [9.3.2]

9. Why do you think it is important for a marketing plan to be in written form? [9.4.1]

10. Analyze the external environment of Mario's cookie kiosk at the mall in terms of how each factor will affect his business. Factors include the economy, competition, laws affecting the business, technology, changes in costs, and the expectations and needs of society. [9.4.2]

11. Why do you think it is important for a marketing goal to be specific rather than general? [9.4.3]

12. Explain in simple terms what the evaluation procedures in the action plan section of a marketing plan try to achieve. [9.4.4]

Marketing Research and Planning

1. People have different needs and different ways of shopping for products and services. Therefore, it is likely that the same product or service can fit into several of the product/service purchase classification categories. For the following products, describe the consumer purchase behavior that would be used for each of the categories in the classification system. [9.3.1]

   a. movie
   b. groceries
   c. gasoline
   d. hotel

2. Use the Internet to search for announcements and articles about a large public corporation's plans for a new business venture. Describe the product or service of the new venture and the marketing strategy, including target markets, the marketing mix, and the positioning statement. What types of information did the company gather about the external environment and prospective customers in planning for the venture? [9.4.3]

3. Select one of the following products or services to use for your work on this activity: a professional music group, athletic/running shoes, or a magazine. Identify four people to interview. Determine the information you need to obtain from each person in order to develop a target market description and to classify his/her purchase behavior in the product/service purchase classification system. Conduct the interviews and complete the following activities: [9.1.1]

   a. Develop market segment descriptions of each person.

   b. Determine whether the four people would be part of one target market or more than one.

   c. Identify the appropriate consumer purchase classification for each person interviewed and explain why you selected that classification.

4. Make four columns across a piece a paper. Label each column with these headings: Introduction, Growth, Maturity, Decline. These are the phases of the product life cycle. Below each column heading, list at least three products that you think are in that phase. If you think that, with improvements, the product has repositioned itself from Maturity back to Growth, list it in the Maturity column with an arrow pointing back to the Growth column. [9.2.3]

5. As part of a marketing plan for a school event or activity such as a play or sporting event, do a SWOT analysis with the goal of increasing attendance. Divide your paper into a two-by-two grid. Write 'Strengths" in the upper left box, "Weaknesses" in the upper right box, "Opportunities" in the lower-left box, and "Threats" in the lower right box. Fill in the boxes with the main points of your analysis using a few concise words or phrases. Exchange your completed SWOT analysis with a partner. Discuss the analysis with your partner and suggest edits, revisions, or even a new approach to improve the clarity of the analysis. After receiving your partner's input on your analysis, consider the input and then make the necessary changes. [9.4.2]

Marketing Management and Decision Making

1. The mature stage of the product life cycle is very difficult, especially for smaller businesses. There are many competitors appealing to a large market. They have very similar products and are increasing their distribution and promotion. Many businesses are starting to decrease their prices to encourage consumers to switch to their business. Because most businesses (and especially large businesses) are appealing to the mass market, smaller businesses may have the opportunity to be successful by using the marketing concept when planning a marketing strategy.

   You are a marketing consultant for a small hotel. The business is finding it increasingly difficult to compete with the national chains that have large advertising budgets, can offer a variety of services, and are willing to cut their prices to attract businesspeople and weekend travelers. Prepare a four-page report for the hotel owner that briefly describes the meaning of the marketing concept and why it can help the hotel develop a marketing strategy. Describe a marketing strategy that could be implemented to help the hotel compete with the large chains. Provide a rationale to support the strategy. [9.2.3]

2. An association of homebuilders collected data on the sales of various styles of manufactured windows. One window style presents an interesting example of a product life cycle. It was introduced in 2009 and remained on the market until 2020. The table below

summarizes its market performance during that time. Develop a table that illustrates the following information for each of the years listed:

a. average dollar sales per manufacturer

b. average sale price of each window

c. average cost of each window

d. total profit or loss for the industry

Input the data from the table into a spreadsheet program. Construct a graph of the life cycle for the windows, illustrating total industry dollar sales for each year. [9.2.3]

Year	Number of Manufacturers	Total Units Sold	Total Sales in Dollars	Total Product Cost
2009	1	800	36,000	$ 38,400
2010	3	2,800	123,200	126,000
2011	5	4,500	193,500	189,000
2012	6	5,700	245,100	228,000
2013	9	10,800	464,400	410,400
2014	15	22,500	945,000	787,500
2015	15	23,000	954,500	828,000
2016	13	23,000	943,000	851,000
2017	12	22,500	877,500	855,000
2018	8	18,000	684,000	693,000
2019	4	10,500	393,750	404,250
2020	2	4,800	177,600	182,400

*Note: This data is hypothetical.

Let's Start a Band! Follow-Up Discussion

Work in small teams to discuss the question posed at the end of the opening vignette. Why does the band need a written marketing plan?

Build Your Marketing Plan

Build your Portfolio

In this chapter you learned about making decisions relating to a company's marketing strategy. You will now apply this learning to the development of your marketing plan. To access the chapter-specific tools that you will need to complete this activity, please navigate to Chapter 9 → Build Your Marketing Plan in MindTap. Alternatively, you can access these tools online at NGLSync. Please visit www.nglsync.cengage.com, and search for the companion website that accompanies this book by entering the ISBN, author, or title. Once you locate this companion website, navigate to Build Your Marketing Plan → Chapter 9.

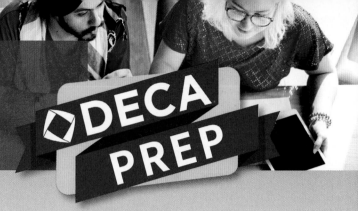

International Business Plan Event

DECA PREP

Build your Portfolio

The International Business Plan Event provides an opportunity to develop a proposal for a new international business venture. You will prepare a written proposal for a new business venture for a foreign country.

This project will be completed by one to three team members. Participants will choose a new business, product, or service to introduce to a foreign country. Each individual or team must conduct thorough research to determine the trade area, economics, culture, and political climate of the chosen country. The demographics for your selected country must be a good match for your idea. After you have determined the best international market for your new business, product, or service, you must persuade an international banker (judge) to grant the needed loan.

This project consists of a written document and an oral presentation. The body of the written entry is limited to 30 numbered pages, including the appendix (if one is attached) but excluding the title page and table of contents. The oral presentation may be a maximum of 15 minutes in length. The first 10 minutes will include an explanation and description of the project followed by 5 minutes for the judge's questions.

The body of your international business plan will consist of the following parts:

Executive Summary Write a one-page description of the project.

Introduction Include a brief description of the proposed business, product, or service.

Analysis of International Business Situation Provide an economic, governmental, and legal analysis of the trading country; provide trade area and cultural analysis.

Planned Operation of the Proposed Business Describe the proposed organization, proposed product/service, and proposed strategies.

Planned Financing Provide projected income and expenses.

Bibliography List all resources used.

Appendix Inclusion is optional.

Your presentation and business plan must thoroughly cover demographics, geography, and psychographics of the country where you intend to conduct business.

Performance Indicators Evaluated

- Write product/service proposal. (Professional Selling)
- Participate as a team member. (Emotional Intelligence)
- Describe small-business opportunities in international trade. (Entrepreneurship)
- Process [research] data to translate marketing information into useful insights/knowledge. (Marketing-Information Management)
- Determine factors affecting business risk. (Economics)

Go to the DECA website for more detailed information. **www.deca.org**

Think Critically

1. Why have more companies expanded operations to include international business?

2. Why is understanding a country's culture important when conducting business there?

3. What risks are involved with conducting international business?

4. What resources can entrepreneurs use when doing business in another country?

CHAPTER 10

DEVELOP SUCCESSFUL PRODUCTS

See how effective advertising leads to successful marketing strategies.
Click on Chapter 10, Visual Focus, in your MindTap.

Let's Start a Band!

> "I think forming a bond with fans in the future will come in the form of constantly providing them with the element of surprise."
>
> – *Taylor Swift, Singer–Songwriter*

The other day I brought up the idea of selling T-shirts. Gael agreed, but said he didn't want us to go overboard. Ignoring his comment, I went on to say that our fans have been asking for T-shirts and we could probably make a little money with them as well.

"Fine," said Gael. "Get some shirts and we'll sell them at our gigs."

Then everyone seemed to talk at once.

"What will they look like?"

"What about color? We need to get the right color."

"I want something cool. Something that stands out, with a little style."

"They have to be high quality. If they're cheap, they'll do us more harm than good. Our fans will think we're ripping them off, and we'll lose the trust we've built up.

"What about sizes, and how many of each size? We don't have a clearance rack to get rid of them if there aren't enough of one size and too many of another."

I finally held up my hands and everyone stopped talking. Why did I think this was going to be easy? Do you think it's worth the hassle?

START WITH A PRODUCT

Learning Objectives

10.1.1 Explain how customers view products.

10.1.2 Describe how marketers keep a consumer focus during product development.

Key Term

product

marketing matters

Businesses tend to view products as the physical items they produce and sell. Consumers see products as ways to satisfy their wants and needs. Marketers play an important role in bridging that gap. They must make sure businesses stay focused on consumers' needs as products are being developed. Marketers need to serve as the customers' representative in the product development process by gathering information, suggesting product improvements, and testing marketing mixes. By doing so, they help the business develop products that satisfy needs better than existing or competing products.

essential question

How do customers' experiences with products that fail to meet their needs affect how they satisfy the same needs in the future?

10.1.1 ▶ Products Meet Customer Needs

A **product** is anything tangible a business offers to a market to satisfy customer needs. It is important for marketers to realize that consumers view a product differently from how the business views it. Businesspeople often see their products as the first part of the definition—anything they offer to a market. Businesses focus on what they offer—the tangible objects. Consumers have a different view of products. They are concerned about their needs, and they view products as ways to satisfy those needs. The differences in those views can result in problems when businesses develop and market products.

What are your motives when you decide you need to make a purchase? For example, you buy shoes for an important basic need—to protect your feet. That is the need. However, few people think only of protection when shopping for shoes. There are additional "wants" they try to satisfy with their shoe purchase, including to convey a certain style and image, to be able to play a sport, or to get a good value. A generic pair of tennis shoes

Want to know more about what is trending with this topic? Click on Lesson 10.1, Global Marketing, in your MindTap.

Connect to MindTap

would fulfill the need to protect the feet. A pair of customized Nikes, however, would also fulfill the wants of conveying style and image as well as the ability to play a sport.

A product is more than a tangible item for consumers. The physical characteristics of the product are important. It must be durable, attractive, and safe. But beyond those qualities, the product must be useful to the consumer and meet the consumer's needs and wants. If not, the consumer will not be interested in buying the product no matter what its physical characteristics.

Focus on the Customer

Businesspeople sometimes misunderstand the wants and needs their products are meeting. For instance, some restaurant owners believe people come to their restaurant mainly to satisfy their hunger—to fulfill their need for food. They fail to realize that few people who eat in restaurants do so just to satisfy physical hunger. Instead, consumers decide on a restaurant for many reasons, including menu variety, taste, speed and quality of service, atmosphere, location, and price. If a restaurant owner is not aware of those reasons—those wants—the business probably will not be successful.

A second misunderstanding some businesspeople have is believing they know better than consumers which needs their products satisfy. U.S. automobile manufacturers made that mistake when they believed consumers were more interested in style and design than in safety and economy. They recognized their error only after foreign automobile manufacturers including Toyota, Honda, and Datsun

Explain the difference between how businesses and consumers view products.

designed models to respond to the safety and economy needs and captured a large part of the U.S. automobile market. U.S. manufacturers struggled to maintain profitability until they began to design and produce automobiles that customers viewed as comparable and even superior to foreign competitors.

Another misunderstanding businesspeople may have is believing their products will satisfy many different market segments. For example, some believe that the same products and same approach to marketing will work with both teenagers and older adults.

Businesses also need to remember that customer needs can change, and different consumer groups have unique needs and experiences. Careful study of markets before making decisions about new products or changes in existing products will pay off for businesses that follow that strategy.

CHECKPOINT
How does a consumer's view of a product tend to differ from that of the business that sells it?

10.1.2 ▶ Product Development as a Marketing Function

A company that believes in the marketing concept uses the needs of customers as the primary focus during the planning, production, distribution, and promotion of a product or service. With that philosophy, marketers should be actively involved with others in the business—as well as with consumers—in the design and development of new products.

Product Development Process

Marketing is the eyes, ears, and mouth of the customer in a business. Marketing is the direct link between a business and its customers. Marketers work with customers every day, whether in selling, promotion, product distribution, marketing research, or the many other marketing activities that occur in a business. Because of that close contact, marketers are in a good position to understand customers—what they like and do not like, how they view competing products, and whether they are satisfied with current products. Marketers must represent the consumer in the business as products are designed and developed.

There are three important roles for marketers in the product development process. Marketers gather information, design marketing strategies, and conduct market tests.

GATHER INFORMATION The obvious role for marketers in product development is market research. Gathering and studying market information and using the results to assist in product planning keeps the focus on consumer needs and competition rather than on the views of those involved in planning.

Marketers can collect information in many ways and from many sources. Feedback from salespeople is very important in understanding both customers and competitors. Analysis of sales data will determine items that have not sold well. It will identify customer complaints and product returns. Marketers might meet regularly with consumer panels to discuss new product ideas and customer experiences. Those discussions provide information for product changes and improvements.

Marketers who are actively involved in product planning usually develop a marketing information system. It allows the information from many sources to be collected, stored, and analyzed to improve new product decisions.

Entrepreneurs who are planning a business also need to conduct research. After relying on your own experiences in developing an idea that solves a need you have, you might then ask your friends if the idea would help them. This anecdotal information may provide valuable insight and can serve as a springboard for beginning a business.

DESIGN STRATEGIES   Companies develop new products to meet specific objectives. If the company's goal is to increase its share of a specific market, it might develop a different product than if the goal is to enter a new market. A new company that cannot risk financial failure with a new product may approach product development differently from an experienced and profitable company.

A marketing strategy combines decisions about a target market and an appropriate marketing mix. Marketers participate in developing an effective strategy by identifying target markets, determining company strengths and weaknesses, and evaluating competitors. They use that information to propose alternative marketing mixes.

New businesses also need to develop sound design strategies. They need to pay attention to competitors who provide a product that suitably meets the customers' needs. They also need to consider competitors who might quickly develop a product to compete with theirs.

CONDUCT MARKET TESTS   After a product and the remaining parts of the marketing mix have been designed, most companies conduct tests to determine if the new product will be successful. Testing

Why do you think product development is so important in the fashion industry?

is a way to reduce failure and to avoid spending money on products and in markets that will not be successful.

Test marketing has become expensive and can tip off competitors to new marketing strategies. Competitors may try to influence the test market results. Companies constantly look for new ways to conduct market tests. Sophisticated computer programs allow companies to simulate the marketing of products and determine expected levels of sales and profits.

New companies have an advantage when it comes to market testing. If a company can test a concept quietly, it can fly under the radar of most of the bigger companies and introduce the product long before those companies notice.

The Product Planning Function

Businesses that are marketing oriented involve marketing personnel in product planning. Therefore, an important marketing function is product/service planning—assisting in the design and development of products and services that will meet the needs of prospective customers. The key parts of the definition are *assisting*, meaning that marketers work cooperatively with others in product development, and *meet the needs*, meaning that the products are designed to satisfy customers.

CHECKPOINT
What are three important roles for marketers in the product development process?

10.1 ASSESSMENT

What Have You Learned?

1. Define *product*. [10.1.1]
2. What is the product/service planning that marketers conduct? [10.1.2]

Make Academic Connections

1. **Writing** Choose a product you have purchased that did not meet your needs. Write a one-page letter to the customer service department of the business from which you purchased the product. In your letter, identify the reasons for your dissatisfaction with the product and describe how you think the product could be improved. [10.1.1]

2. **History** Choose a company or a product that you consider innovative. Use the library or Internet to learn more about the company or product, its history, and the factors that contributed to it being innovative. Prepare an oral report with visuals summarizing what you learned. [10.1.2]

Connect to ◇DECA

Build your Portfolio

Your team has been asked to gather consumer information for a new streaming service introduced six months ago to compete with Netflix and Hulu. Prepare a five-item questionnaire to determine the attitudes of subscribers toward the streaming service and the improvements they would like to see. Give the questionnaire to 10 people and summarize the results using tables and charts. Make a team presentation of the questionnaire and results to your teacher (judge). [10.1.2]

Planning a Career In...
VIRTUAL PRODUCT DEVELOPMENT

Did you ever wonder how someone takes a great idea and turns it into a manufactured product?

Think of how quickly new cell phone models are introduced. Virtual product development (VDP) software allows companies to bring new products to market more quickly than ever before. To stay competitive, the mobile phone manufacturers keep developing phones with improved functions to meet customers' evolving needs.

VPD utilizes state-of-the art software to streamline the development of manufactured items. The sophisticated software integrates multiple planning modules, allowing team members to quickly redesign products to meet changing customer preferences.

Job Titles

- Industrial Design Engineer
- Virtualization Program Manager
- Simulation Engineer
- Manager, Virtual Prototyping
- Product Development Manager

Needed Skills

- At minimum, a bachelor's degree is required. More complex positions may require a graduate degree.
- Strong problem-solving, analytical, and multitasking skills are necessary.

Discover more about the outlook for this career and watch a video about a related career. Click on **Chapter 10, Planning a Career In...** *in your MindTap.*

- Creativity, aesthetic sensibilities, and design principles training is needed.

What it's like to work in...Virtual Product Development

Nadira, an Industrial Designer for a cell phone manufacturing company, is reviewing customer feedback based on VDP software for two distinct cell phone prototypes. This feedback came from two sources.

Nadira's VPD supplier developed an interactive, web-based game to test enhanced cell phone features found on the two prototypes. The game had built-in incentives for accuracy and thorough analysis.

A link on the game's website also provided users the opportunity to design their own prototypes. Users could select the most appealing combination of features when designing their ideal cell phone.

Using the combined results from the game and design modules, Nadira, along with the Product Engineer, designed a final virtual prototype.

To confirm she has properly incorporated the features that are most important to customers, Nadira will have her VPD supplier post the final prototype on the company's website to obtain final customer feedback. By virtually fine-tuning the cell phone model, Nadira has provided her company with significant cost savings. She has spared her company the expense of manufacturing multiple tangible prototypes.

What About You?

Would you like to be involved in using VDP software to obtain customer feedback in developing customer-focused products?

Learning Objectives

10.2.1 Describe the parts of the product mix element.

10.2.2 Discuss the three levels in the product design process.

10.2.3 Explain the importance of product lines, packaging, and brand development.

Key Terms

product line
product assortment
brand
trademark
brand loyalty
licensed brand

marketing matters

When a new product is developed, marketers must make many decisions about its final form and the total product mix. They start with a basic product, be it a toothbrush, an automobile, or a software program. Then they add enhancements to make it more appealing to a target market. Finally, they decide on a brand name, packaging, and accessories that will attract and satisfy potential buyers.

essential question

How do all of the parts of the product mix elements—including features, enhancements, accessories, and even packaging—offer greater satisfaction to consumers than would be possible with just the basic product?

10.2.1 ▶ Parts of the Product Mix Element

Even a product that seems very simple is made up of many parts. Think of the toothbrush you used this morning. Is it like every other toothbrush you could have purchased? What makes it unique? Why did you purchase it rather than one of the many other brands available?

The basic product for a toothbrush is easy to describe—it is a plastic handle and head with bristles. Even with that basic product, there are choices. The handle may be long or short, contoured for an easier grip, bent to allow it to fit comfortably inside your mouth, and manufactured in several colors. The head also comes in various shapes and sizes. The bristles can

be firm, medium, or soft. They can be short, long, or varied with shorter bristles in the middle. Bristles can be manufactured from several different materials.

Even with all of the possible variations, many people believe that all toothbrushes are quite similar. Yet there are still more features to choose from. There are compact toothbrushes that collapse into a small case that you can carry with you. There are disposable toothbrushes that come with toothpaste already applied. And there are battery-powered toothbrushes in many varieties. Some models are part of a complete dental care system. The rechargeable handle can be used with the toothbrush, a tooth polisher, a water pick, and a flossing tool. There is even a sonic toothbrush that offers 10 to 20 times the strokes per minute than the typical battery-powered toothbrush.

Most toothbrushes are sold with a brand name. Some are well-known consumer brands, such as Colgate. Others are brands specifically associated with tooth care, such as Oral-B.

Offering a guarantee or testimonial is another way to differentiate products. A manufacturer may guarantee replacement if the product is defective or may refund the purchase price to consumers who are not satisfied. Or it may offer a testimonial from a professional group, such as the American Dental Association, that attests to the quality of the product.

The toothbrush example shows that even simple products can be complex.

Why is product planning important for all products, even simple ones such as a toaster?

Photodisc/Getty Images

Businesses have many choices in the development of new products to differentiate them and meet consumer needs and wants.

CHECKPOINT
Why does developing even a simple product involve so many decisions?

10.2.2 ▶ The Levels of Product Design

Product design moves through three levels. It begins with the basic product. Then, the basic product is modified and improved by adding features and options. Finally, services and complementary products are planned to make it as useful as possible to consumers.

Basic Product

The basic product is the product in its simplest form. Consumers should be able to easily recognize the important need the basic product addresses. Most products have basic versions, and all competitors offer very similar basic products.

Enhanced Product

The basic product responds to an important customer need. However, we know that consumers usually are trying to satisfy multiple needs and wants with one purchase. They evaluate products to see which one provides the best and most specific satisfaction. Companies add enhancements to their basic products to meet those needs.

Enhancements include features and options. For example, bicycles are manufactured in several frame sizes, in models ranging from mountain bikes to racing bikes, and with a single gear ratio or up to 24 speeds.

Choices of materials used in manufacturing, seat design, and tire construction are available. Some bicycles have shock absorbers built into the frame. If you go to a large bicycle shop or a manufacturer's Internet site, you may be able to select from several hundred different bicycles or even customize a bike. Other types of enhancements to a basic product are levels of quality, styling differences, colors, brand names, and packaging.

Each enhancement changes the basic product. Some customers may view the change as an improvement, increasing the satisfaction they receive. Others may view the change as unneeded or even dissatisfying. Enhanced products make it possible for companies to satisfy several target markets with one basic product. Different combinations of features, options, and brand names are developed with the needs of one target market in mind.

Extended Product

Businesses can improve the satisfaction provided by a product in ways other than product enhancements. They can improve customer satisfaction if the business offers services, guarantees, information on effective use of the product, and even additional products that improve the use of the primary product.

Services are an effective way to meet additional customer needs beyond those directly related to the use of the product. Examples of important customer services that could influence product choice are credit, delivery, installation, repair services, and technical support.

Companies also can improve customer satisfaction by suggesting additional products that should be purchased so that the primary product can be used more effectively. For example, a skilled photography equipment salesperson will ask how you will use a camera and the types of pictures you plan to take. Based on that information, she will recommend additional products such as additional lenses, a tripod, a memory card, or flash attachment to ensure you receive the greatest enjoyment and value from your purchase.

CHECKPOINT
Name the levels of product design.

For a travel agency that sells vacation packages, what is the basic product, and what features, options, or other extensions could it add to improve customer satisfaction?

© Pierre-Yves Babelon/Shutterstock.com.

When consumers evaluate products to determine the one that is most satisfying, they are interested in more than just the physical product. Four important considerations in planning the product mix are the product line, product assortment, packaging, and brand development.

Product Line

New or small companies often offer only one product to a target market. As they grow and gain experience, they can expand into other markets and develop a product line. A **product line** is a group of similar products with slight variations in the marketing mix to satisfy different needs in a market. A company that manufacturers bath towels may offer various colors, sizes, and levels of quality to give customers choices. A soft drink bottler offers not only different sizes and types of containers for a flavor of soda but usually has many flavors in its product line. It may even sell fruit juices and flavored waters in addition to soft drinks.

As companies add items to their product line, they usually increase the number of potential customers and the satisfaction of individual consumers. However, the company is also adding to the costs of manufacturing, distribution, inventory control, and other related marketing activities. An expanded product line also requires additional display space for retailers. The retailer must make a decision whether to stock items from the complete product line of the manufacturer or use the space for the products of competing companies or even entirely different products. In a supermarket display of soft drinks, snacks, or cereal, you can see examples of companies' extensive product lines and the competition they have for display space.

VARIATION IN QUANTITY/SIZE
Product lines can be developed in several ways. One of the easiest ways to expand from one product to several is to vary the product size. The identical food item may be packaged in three sizes—for example, single serving, 4 servings, and 10 servings. Facial tissue may be sold in a pocket-sized cellophane wrapper, a box of 250 tissues, or a multiple-box pack. Another type of quantity variation is to have different sizes for the same basic product. For example, bed sheets are sold in twin, full, queen, or king size. In this case, the product itself is manufactured in varied sizes rather than just changing the quantity in a package.

VARIATION IN QUALITY Differences in quality also can be used to develop a product line. Items such as paintbrushes, carpenter or mechanic tools, lawn mowers, computers, and even clothing often are sold in varying levels of quality. Consumers who use the products infrequently may not need the best possible quality and would prefer to save money in exchange for accepting a slightly lower quality. Adding features to the basic product may produce several levels of product choices that vary in quality. Automobile and appliance manufacturers often have a very basic model at a low price and several other models with selected features and options at higher prices.

Product Assortments

In addition to product line decisions, companies plan product assortments. A **product assortment** is the complete set of all products a business offers to its market. Retail stores provide the best example of product assortments. Some specialty retailers offer customers very complete assortments. For example, lawn and garden

Why would a boot manufacturer want to offer more than one style of boot?

centers have a very complete assortment of products homeowners need. Other general merchandise retailers, such as discount and department stores, also stock products in many different categories. They probably will not have as complete an assortment in one line as the specialty store, but they respond to a broader set of customers' product needs.

Some manufacturers specialize in one product category. For example, mattress producers offer a full assortment of mattresses. Other manufacturers may have a product assortment in many different product categories, such as a full assortment of camping products or many types of home furniture.

Packaging

Most products are sold in a package. The package serves the dual purpose of protection and promotion. In addition, some packaging improves the use of the product. Containers with pour spouts built into the package, resealable liners, and handles for carrying are developed to solve customer problems related to the use of the product.

Want to know more about what is trending with this topic? Click on **Lesson 10.2, Marketing Decisions,** *in your MindTap.*

Connect to
MindTap

EASE OF USE   When designing the package, manufacturers must carefully consider the ways customers use a product. For example, if a cereal box is taller than the shelves in the customer's home, it will not be purchased. A manufacturer of a liquid cleaner found that people would not buy a large economy size because the container could not be lifted and poured with one hand in the way people were used to handling the product.

SAFETY   When planning the packaging of products, safety and protection are important concerns. Products used by children certainly need to have safe packaging. A manufacturer of individual servings of puddings and fruits learned that children would lick the lid of the container when it was removed. As a result, the metal lid was covered with a plastic coating to avoid nicks and cuts. Glass and other fragile products need well-designed packages to ensure that they are not broken during shipment and display.

ATTRACTION   The promotional value of packaging is important for many products. Impulse items often are purchased because of an attractive package that clearly shows the use of the product. Perfumes and colognes usually have very expensive and uniquely designed containers to convey a certain image.

HANDLING   Packaging can be helpful in the display and security of products. In stores where products are displayed for customer self-service, the package may need to be designed to hang from a hook or to lie flat on a shelf. Small or expensive items are often packaged in large containers to reduce the chance of theft.

How can packaging help the attractiveness of a product?

ENVIRONMENT There is growing concern about the type and quantity of materials used for packaging. Manufacturers are increasingly using recycled materials for packaging and developing materials that are biodegradable. Many retailers are reducing the amount of packaging used or are helping consumers reuse or recycle packaging material. For instance, deodorant used to come packaged in a small box in addition to the container that actually held the deodorant itself. Walmart insisted that deodorant marketers do away with the unnecessary boxes. This change not only benefitted the environment, but also resulted in savings for consumers.

Brand Development

Do you know the brand names of the shoes and clothing you are wearing? Do you have a favorite brand of pizza or automobile? In what stores do you prefer to shop? Each of these questions demonstrates that the brand of products can be very important to consumers' purchase decisions. **A brand** is a name, symbol, word, or design that identifies a product, service, or company.

A brand provides a unique identification for the company and its offerings. To ensure that other companies cannot use a brand, a company registers a trademark for it with the federal government. **A trademark** is the legal protection provided to the owner for the words or symbols used to identify a product or service.

Consider how difficult it would be to shop if there were no brand names. Although you purchase some products without considering the brand (think of the paper you use to write in school), in most cases you consider the brand as part of the purchase decision. Positive or negative experience with a brand will influence your future purchases. Businesspeople know that brand recognition resulting from advertising often increases a product's sales.

The goal for a business in using branding is to gain customer recognition of the brand in order to increase the likelihood of a sale. Businesses want brands that convey a particular image and that can be recalled to encourage repeat purchases. There are several levels of consumer brand awareness as shown in **Figure 10-1.**

LEVELS OF BRAND RECOGNITION	
Non-recognition	Consumers are unable to identify the brand.
Recognition	Consumers can recall the brand name, but it has little influence on purchases.
Preference	Consumers view the brand as valuable and will choose it if it is available.
Insistence	Consumers value the brand to the extent that they reject other brands.

FIGURE 10-1 Branding is effective when consumers prefer or insist on a specific brand.

Another goal for branding products is to reduce the likelihood that customers will switch to other brands in the same product category. By providing a brand that customers can trust, companies prevent customers from trying another brand even if the company increases the price by a little bit. Ultimately, companies are seeking to develop brand loyalty with their customers. **Brand loyalty** is a consumer's commitment to repurchasing, using, and even promoting a particular brand over all others.

Both manufacturers and retailers may develop brands. Individual products can have their own brands, or groups of products can carry a *family brand*. Breakfast cereals are often sold under a family brand, such as Kellogg's.

MARKETING COMMUNICATION

Marketing U

By branding their names, logos, and even their team mascots, colleges and universities are reaping profits through the marketing of officially endorsed merchandise. Besides the traditional school supplies and apparel, many universities sell products covering a wide range of uses while appealing to the desire to proudly display school spirit. Consumers can purchase merchandise for their pets branded by UCLA, decorate their tree during the holidays with University of Alabama ornaments, or sleep on crimson pillowcases featuring Harvard's signature H.

Access to buying collegiate merchandise was once limited to buying branded items, usually a cap, sweatshirt, or T-shirt, at stores around the campus. Now, colleges and universities, especially the big-name schools, have opened up the buying channels from coast to coast.

The institutions themselves tend to concentrate their marketing efforts on their core educational services. They farm out their school branding and merchandise development and distribution to outside manufacturers, retailers, and distributors.

Think Critically

Take an inventory of items available that bear your school's name, logo, or mascot. Then examine your school as a brand and determine its level of recognition. Write a paragraph explaining how the items aid in promoting the school's image.

Some companies offer licensed brands to add prestige or a unique image to products. A **licensed brand** is a well-known name or symbol established by one company and sold for use by another company to promote its products. Disney and Sesame Street are examples of companies that license the use of character names and images for products ranging from toys to clothing. Professional and college sports teams license their names and mascot images for use on many products. Some people prefer to purchase products with those brands rather than similar products that do not carry the licensed brand. Professional athletes such as LeBron James and Tony Hawk license their names for use on sporting goods, apparel, and computer games.

CHECKPOINT
Name the four product mix components.

10.2 ASSESSMENT

What Have You Learned?

1. Why do businesses offer consumers so many product choices? [10.2.1]
2. What level of product design do features and options represent? [10.2.2]
3. What is a business's goal in using branding? [10.2.3]

Make Academic Connections

1. **Visual Art**   Use an advertisement or product catalog to locate a picture of a consumer product. Copy or cut the picture and paste it on poster paper. Or, import a digital file of the image into design software. Using different colors, highlight the basic product, enhanced product, and extended product. Identify each of the components. Provide a legend to identify the meaning of each color. [10.2.1]

2. **Research**   Popular movies and movie characters such as Spiderman are often licensed for use by other companies to promote their products. For a current or recent movie, identify as many licensed users of the movie or its characters as you can find. Create a table that lists the company, the product, and a brief description of how the licensed movie or character is used in promotion. [10.2.3]

Connect to ◇DECA

Build your Portfolio

A company has created a new product that combines sunscreen and insect repellant on individually packaged moist tissues for convenient use. It has asked you to create a unique brand name and a supporting image or other visual for the new product. Complete the project and present it to your teacher (judge) with a brief discussion of why you think it will be effective. [10.2.3]

PRODUCTS FOR CONSUMERS AND BUSINESSES

Learning Objectives

10.3.1 Define consumer markets.

10.3.2 Describe the categories of business products.

Key Terms

consumer markets
business markets

marketing matters

The two broad market categories—consumer markets and business markets—have very different reasons for buying products. But product planning for both categories should be based on an understanding of the market in which the product will be sold. Marketers must know who will use the product, its purpose, and the needs customers are attempting to satisfy with it.

essential question

How will marketing be similar or different if a company's target market is made up of businesses rather than individual consumers?

10.3.1 Consumer Markets

Individuals or socially related groups who purchase products for personal consumption comprise **consumer markets**. When you, your family, or your friends buy products for your own use or for others to use, you are part of the consumer market. You make purchase decisions based on the satisfaction you receive from using the product. If you are buying the product for a friend or family member, you are interested in buying something that person will find to be satisfying.

Because final consumers or their family and friends will use the products they purchase, they have a clear idea of the reasons they are making the purchase. They locate and purchase the products that best meet their needs. To satisfy consumer demand, businesspeople must be aware of consumers' needs and how they choose products to satisfy those needs. As discussed in Chapter 9, the consumer purchase classification system is based on two factors:

1. The importance of the purchase to the consumer

2. The willingness of the consumer to shop and compare products before making the purchase

Businesses can use the classifications to decide how to market each category of product in consumer markets.

CHECKPOINT
What are consumer markets?

When are you part of the consumer market?

Business Markets

Companies and organizations that purchase products for the operation of a business or the completion of a business activity comprise **business markets**. These include producers, manufacturers, retailers, nonprofit organizations, government agencies, schools, and other organizations that provide products or services for consumption by others. Business markets make purchase decisions based on what is needed to effectively operate the business, to meet the needs of employees and customers, and to produce the business's products and services.

Business markets make purchase decisions based on customer demand. A movie theater needs to buy enough popcorn, oil, and boxes to meet its customers' needs for popcorn during the movies. If the theater purchases too much, some of the product will not be sold, and money will be lost. If the theater purchases too little, customers will be dissatisfied, and sales will be lost.

Developing products for the business market requires an understanding of how the businesses use the products.

A *business product classification* system aids in understanding the business market. The categories of business products include capital equipment, operating equipment, supplies, raw materials, and component parts.

Capital Equipment

Capital equipment includes a business's land, buildings, and major pieces of equipment. They are usually the most expensive and most important products purchased. They must meet the specific needs of the business so that it operates effectively. Often they are custom designed, so they will have little value to other businesses. Costs for capital equipment range from thousands of dollars to hundreds of millions of dollars. A large office building, delivery vans, and sophisticated computer systems are examples of capital purchases. Most companies purchase the products using long-term loans from finance companies or manufacturers. Some capital equipment is leased rather than purchased.

Operating Equipment

Smaller, less-expensive equipment used in the operation of the business or in the production and sale of products and services is known as *operating equipment*. This type of equipment makes production or operations more efficient and effective. Examples of operating equipment are tools, small machines, and furniture. These items usually have a shorter life than capital equipment and must be replaced from time to time. They also are more standardized, meaning that the same type of operating equipment may be used in many different businesses.

Supplies

The products and materials consumed in the operation of the business are *supplies*. A business needs paper, pencils, and paper clips, as well as cleaning supplies and parts for routine repairs of equipment. Some supplies are purchased and used in small quantities and are quite inexpensive. Others, such as fuel, electricity, or packing materials, may be needed in large quantities and are a major expense for the company. Most supplies are standardized, meaning they are not uniquely developed for one business. They are available from many suppliers and are used in a large number of different businesses.

Raw Materials

Producers and manufacturers buy many products that become part of the products they make. Often they purchase *raw materials*, which are unprocessed products used as basic materials for the products to be produced. Logs are purchased by lumber

In what types of businesses would lumber be considered a supply?

© sirtravelalot/Shutterstock.com

producers, oil by plastics manufacturers, and grain by cereal processors.

Purchasers of raw materials need to have an adequate supply and a standardized quality of raw materials in order to maintain a planned level and quality of production. The price of the raw materials is important because the cost has a big influence on what the company needs to charge for its finished products. The purchasing company will want to sign a long-term contract with the supplier of the raw materials to ensure that it has a continuing supply and to be assured of the cost.

Component Parts

Component parts are also incorporated into the products a business makes. However, *component parts* have been either partially or totally processed by another company. For example, a computer manufacturer will buy computer chips from a chip manufacturer. These chips already have been carefully developed and are simply installed as a part of the computer assembly. The same manufacturer buys parts for a hard drive and power supply from another company. Those parts must be incorporated as part of the final assembly of the computers.

Component parts can be designed for the needs of one company, or they can be standardized for use by many companies. As with raw materials, the purchasing company is concerned that a dependable source of supply is available when needed, that the component parts meet the final product requirements and quality standards of the company, and that costs are reasonable.

> **CHECKPOINT**
> *What are the five categories in the business product classification system?*

10.3 ASSESSMENT

What Have You Learned?

1. What two factors form the basis of the consumer purchase classification system? [10.3.1]
2. What are component parts? [10.3.2]

Make Academic Connections

1. **Technology** Identify five relatively new technology products. Using the Internet, locate a picture of the use of each technology by consumers and another picture of its use in businesses. Using design or presentation software, create a visual that illustrates the consumer markets and business markets for each product. [10.3.1, 10.3.2]

2. **Math** A movie theater has determined that 34 percent of moviegoers will purchase popcorn and 52 percent will purchase a soft drink. The average popcorn sale is $7.50, and the average soft drink sale is $6.00. The theater expects to sell 900 movie tickets on Saturday. Calculate the popcorn and soft drink sales the theater can expect.

Connect to ◇DECA

Build your Portfolio

You are the fundraising manager for your DECA chapter. Each year the club works with a water-bottling company to sell contracts for home-delivery service to consumers in your area. You believe the chapter can make more money by also selling contracts to businesses. Prepare a three-minute persuasive presentation of the benefits of selling to both consumer and business markets. Present your ideas to your teacher (judge). [10.3.1, 10.3.2]

Learning Objectives

10.4.1 Describe the different ways businesses define *new products*.

10.4.2 Describe the six steps in new product development.

Key Terms

new product
prototype
test market

marketing matters

Without new products, companies have a hard time ensuring customer satisfaction and keeping up with their competition. Yet developing successful new products is not easy. The risk of failure is high, and development and testing are expensive.

essential question

What activities does a business need to complete in order to develop and bring a new product to market?

10.4.1 ▶ What Is a New Product?

Few products are really brand new in the sense that no other products like them have been available before. Many "new" products are changes and improvements to existing products. Others are new to a particular market but have been sold previously in other markets.

When the personal computer was first designed in the 1970s, it was completely new. Computers were not available for individual purchase and use before the development of the personal computer. Today, there are hundreds of choices of personal computers

as features are added and technology allows for smaller, faster, and easier-to-use machines.

You are probably familiar with companies that promote products as new and improved. Brands of laundry detergent, toothpaste, diapers, and potato chips often use the words *new* and *improved* to attract attention in a competitive market. In many cases, it is difficult to see what really is new or better about the product. Because some companies have misused the term *new* for products that really were not new, the Federal

*Want to know more about marketing in the information age? Click on **Lesson 10.4, Digital Marketing,** in your MindTap.*

Connect to
MindTap

Trade Commission regulates how and when the term can be used. It allows a company to call a product "new" for only six months after introducing or changing it. A **new product** must be entirely new or changed in an important and noticeable way.

Fashions, music, ethnic foods, and other specialized products may be new in some markets but already well known in others. A product or service may become popular in one part of the country and then spread to other parts. Some companies enter international trade with products that are already successful in their home country.

A new use for a product can be discovered, leading to new markets. Video cameras were first installed on large commercial vehicles to allow drivers to see when backing up. Now cameras

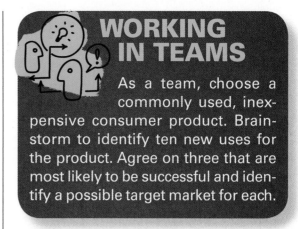

WORKING IN TEAMS

As a team, choose a commonly used, inexpensive consumer product. Brainstorm to identify ten new uses for the product. Agree on three that are most likely to be successful and identify a possible target market for each.

are installed on private automobiles to alert drivers if children or obstacles are behind the car.

CHECKPOINT

When is a product considered to be new?

10.4.2 ▶ Steps in New Product Development

Companies identify and develop new products carefully. They screen out products that are not likely to be successful before investing large sums to produce and market them. The screening process assures that the products meet an important market need, can be produced well and at a reasonable price, and will be competitive with other products in the market. Most companies use the following steps as part of their new product development process.

Idea Development

The most difficult step in new product development usually is finding ideas for new products. You may see a new product on the market and say, "I could have thought of that." But few people have successful new product ideas. Because

products are developed to meet consumer needs, gathering information from consumers may generate ideas for new products. Many companies have consumer panels that meet regularly to discuss ideas for new products.

Important sources of new product ideas are problems customers have that they cannot seem to solve with current products. Often, salespeople who work with customers every day have ideas for new products or product improvements based on what they see and hear.

Developing new product ideas can be a very creative process. Therefore, it is important for people involved in the new product planning process to think creatively. Tools such as brainstorming, creative thinking exercises, and problem solving are used to identify product ideas for testing.

Idea Screening

To encourage a large number of new product ideas, companies do not evaluate ideas in the initial idea development stage. Once numerous ideas have been identified, the second step is to carefully screen them to select those that have the greatest chance for success. Businesses develop criteria for selecting the best ideas, such as:

- Is there an identified market with a strong need for the product?
- Is the amount of competition in the market reasonable?
- Do we have or can we obtain the resources to produce the product?
- Is the product legal and safe?
- Can we produce a quality product at a reasonable cost?
- Is the product environmentally friendly?

Other criteria are not as straightforward and may be tailored to company circumstances. For example, some companies will not want to develop products that compete with their current products.

What are some ways companies can develop ideas for new products?

Others will select products that can be developed with current equipment and personnel to control costs. Some companies seek opportunities to move into new markets, so they want product ideas that meet the new market needs. Coming up with the initial investment required to produce the new product may be more difficult for some companies than others.

Strategy Development

After determining that the product idea seems reasonable, the business will create and test a sample marketing strategy as a first step in developing a business proposal. In this step, it conducts research to identify an appropriate target market with the need and money to pay for the product.

Next, the business plans and analyzes alternative marketing mixes to determine the possible combinations of product, distribution, price, and promotion. Again, it carefully studies each choice to determine if it is appropriate for the target market and if the company can effectively implement that mix. Based on that study, the company selects the best possible mix. If the research in this step shows that an effective mix cannot be developed, the company would drop the idea.

Financial Analysis

If the company determines that a new product idea meets a market need and can be developed, it will complete a financial analysis. It will estimate costs of production and marketing and forecast sales projections and profits. Companies may use computer models that determine best-case and worst-case possibilities. Companies need to understand the type of competition (from pure competition to monopoly) and the level of demand in determining what prices to charge and the amount of sales to expect. They match the results of the analysis against company goals and profit objectives.

Product Development and Testing

After careful research and planning, the company may decide to move forward. Manufacturers will plan the production process, obtain the needed equipment and materials, and train personnel. Retailers will identify a producer or manufacturer to supply the products and negotiate contracts for producing or purchasing the items.

For expensive or risky products, the company may decide to test the idea. It may develop a **prototype**, or model, to test quality and costs before beginning full-scale production. Another testing strategy is a test market. With a **test market**, the company produces a limited quantity of the new product and implements the marketing mix in a small part of the market. If the market test is successful, the company will go forward with the new product. If not, it can end production or change the product before spending a large amount of money.

Product Marketing

The last step in product development is full-scale introduction into the market. A great deal of preparation is needed for this step. The company must plan all of the

MATH IN MARKETING

The Cost of Being Read

The financial analysis book publishers conduct is difficult and complex. Once a publisher decides a new book meets a market need, it completes a financial analysis. One aspect of the analysis is the cost of producing the book. The costs can be broken down into several categories. One is the pre-press phase. This includes most steps before the book goes to press such as the internal layout and the cover design, photography and artwork, formatting, editing and proofreading, and indexing.

Printing cost depends upon a number of factors. The dimensions of the book and the number of pages must be determined in order to make an accurate analysis. Other considerations are the quality of paper used and the number of colors used in printing. Decisions about whether to print a paperback or hardback book and the type of binding used also factor into the cost. Finally, the quantity of books printed will have a major effect on cost of book production.

Do the Math

1. Calculate total production costs and cost per book on a 250-page paperback. The printing and shipping (P&S) costs for the book are $4,000 for 1,000 copies. The book is to be printed in black and white and the pre-press costs (PPC) are $3,000. If 5,000 copies are printed, the printing costs rise to $6,000; for 10,000 copies the cost is $8,000. Calculate total costs for print runs of 1,000, 5,000, and 10,000.

2. If you increase the page count to 500 pages, both the printing costs and the pre-press cost will rise 30 percent. Calculate the production cost and the cost per book for 1,000 copies, 5,000 copies, and 10,000 copies of a 500-page book.

marketing mix elements. It must involve cooperating companies such as wholesalers, retailers, transportation companies, and advertising agencies. Production levels must be high enough to have an adequate supply of the product available to meet sales requirements. Marketing personnel need to be prepared for their responsibilities. All activities and schedules must be coordinated.

If all of the steps in the new product planning process have been carefully completed, the opportunity for success is very high. However, marketers still need to continue to study the market carefully. It is possible that conditions will change, competitors may anticipate the new product, or consumers will not respond as predicted. Adjustments in the marketing strategy may be needed as the market develops.

 CHECKPOINT
Name the six activities in the new product development process.

10.4 ASSESSMENT

What Have You Learned?

1. Why did the Federal Trade Commission step in to regulate the use of the term *new product*? [10.4.1]

2. Name three tools companies use to identify ideas for new products. [10.4.2]

Make Academic Connections

1. **Science**   Companies are introducing many new products and changes to existing products in response to environmental concerns. The effort is referred to as *green marketing*. Select a green product and compare it to existing products that are less environmentally friendly. Describe the differences in ingredients, product design, or packaging and the benefits they provide. [10.4.1]

2. **Entrepreneurship**   Conduct research on a young entrepreneur whose business resulted from a new product or service idea. Find out how the person came up with the idea and then developed it into a successful business. Prepare a short oral report on your research. [10.4.2]

Connect to ◇DECA

You have been hired as the vice president of marketing for a company that has a history of new product failure. They have not involved marketing in product development in the past. Prepare a one-page memo for the CEO on the value of involving marketing and following a careful new product development process. Describe how the company could benefit from your ideas. Present your memo to your teacher (judge). [10.4.2]

Analyze a case study that focuses on chapter concepts. Click on **Chapter 10, Case Study,** *in your MindTap.*

CHAPTER 10 ASSESSMENT

Review Marketing Concepts

1. Businesses often misunderstand the teenage market. Identify a business that tries to sell a product to you but makes mistakes in trying to match it with your needs and interests. What mistakes did they make? What advice would you give to the company about how to change the product? [10.1.1]

2. Marketers can gather market information in many ways. Which of the following two information sources do you think provides more valid information: feedback from salespeople or analysis of sales data? Explain your answer. [10.1.2]

3. Your company is developing a new kitchen floor cleaning tool for home use called Super Mop. What kind of guarantee could it offer to customers who aren't satisfied with the product? [10.2.1]

4. Tool maker ABO manufactures a tool set for homeowners. Describe the ways ABO could provide extended product enhancement to ensure customer satisfaction. [10.2.2]

5. How can registering a trademark protect each of the following product mix components: a product line, the packaging, and a brand? [10.2.3]

6. Super Mop has become the best-selling mop on the market. Your company is considering adding other products and creating an assortment of products. What products would you add to the Super Mop product assortment? [10.2.3]

7. Think of a purchase you made recently and answer these questions about it. (1) How important was the purchase to you? (2) Did you shop around and compare products before making the purchase? Based on your answers, what was the consumer purchase classification? (Recall from Chapter 9 that the four major purchase classifications are convenience goods, shopping goods, specialty goods, and unsought goods.) [10.3.1]

8. What is the difference between capital equipment and operating equipment? From your point of view, which purchase is more important for a business? [10.3.2]

9. Discuss the reasons the Federal Trade Commission allows a company to call a product "new" for only six months after introducing or changing it. [10.4.1]

10. Why do you think companies generate but do not evaluate ideas for new products in step one of the new product development process? [10.4.2]

Marketing Research and Planning

1. Study advertisements, product catalogs, and merchandise available for sale in stores in your community. Identify at least three products that fit into each of the following categories:

   a. Products that are completely new

   b. Products that have significant changes or improvements

   c. Products that have been sold elsewhere but are new to the local market

   Using those products, create a poster or a display that illustrates the concept of new products. [10.4.1]

2. Businesspeople often describe their products in terms of the physical characteristics and features. Consumers evaluate products on the

basis of the needs that can be satisfied. For each of the following product descriptions, identify the consumer needs to satisfy or the benefits consumers will receive as a result of using the product. [10.2.1]

Product Descriptions

a. cell phone with camera and music player

b. online personal banking services

c. takeout restaurant food

d. computerized tax preparation software

e. stationary bicycle with fitness monitor

3. Identify any consumer product that has been on the market for at least five years. On a large sheet of paper or poster board, draw three concentric circles to look like a practice target. Alternatively, you may use design software to create this visual.

Label the innermost circle *Basic Product*.

Label the middle circle *Enhanced Product*.

Label the outer circle *Extended Product*.

Study several brands of the product you selected to identify the components that are basic, enhanced, and extended parts. Based on that analysis, use words or drawings to illustrate each part of the product in the appropriate circle. [10.2.2]

4. Products are planned to respond to consumer needs. Those that best meet those needs are likely to be successful. For each of the common consumer needs listed (a–j), identify a product that has been successful for several years because it meets the need very well. [10.2.2]

a. health

b. beauty

c. education

d. friendship

e. safety

f. economy

g. excitement

h. hunger

i. convenience

j. status

Marketing Management and Decision Making

1. Companies use product lines to be able to serve several target markets with the same basic product. Variations in the product's size, quality, features, etc., are used to meet specific needs of a market. Identify a consumer product that has a product line of at least four specific and different products. Prepare a chart that describes each of the specific products in the product line. For each one, identify the factors that make the specific product stand out from the others in the product line. Then describe the characteristics of the target market to which you think each product is designed to appeal. [10.2.3]

2. If you receive a $1 coin as change, would you keep it or treat it like a dollar bill? Most people opt to keep it, and this explains why the U.S. government has trouble getting $1 coins into circulation. Getting the right mix of coins in the United States has always been the responsibility of the federal government. At various times in its history, the United States has had in circulation the half-cent coin, the two-cent coin, the three-cent coin, the half-dime coin (it would be replaced by the five-cent coin), a twenty-cent coin, and various denominations of gold coins.

With most industrialized countries no longer issuing paper currency in dominations as low as one dollar, many people have been advocating that the United States follow suit. In the long run, the dollar coin is less expensive to make than paper currency. The decision has fallen on the United States

Mint, which has been trying get a $1 coin into widespread circulation. In trying to get the mix correct, it has tried several different designs. It introduced the Eisenhower dollar in 1978. This proved too large, so the mint tried a smaller design with the Susan B. Anthony dollar in 1979. It was thought to be too similar to the quarter in shape, size, and color to be accepted. The Mint attempted to address these issues when it introduced the Sacagawea dollar in 2000. However, despite heavy marketing in print, radio, and television, it did not gain widespread circulation.

Consider future marketing decisions facing use of the $1 coin in the United States. After Canada began minting its dollar coin, the "Looney," it soon began to phase out its paper dollar. In 1996 it introduced the "Toonie," or two-dollar coin. Do you think this approach would work in the United States? Why might the public object to eliminating paper $1-dollar bills and just use coins? Do you think these objections can be overcome by marketing? Explain your answer. [10.2.3]

3. A new company has started to take advantage of people's interest in nature and the environment. The company sells individual flowers that are no more than four inches tall and are planted in two-inch square plastic pots. The flowers are blooming and with proper care should live for several months or longer. They will be sold through supermarkets, gift shops, and even vending machines. You have been asked to help in the design of the package for the flowers. Create a package that will protect the flower, provide an appropriate display, and provide information on the care of the flower. Also develop a brand name for the product that will appear on the package. [10.2.3]

Let's Start a Band! Follow-Up Discussion

Work in small teams to discuss the question posed at the end of the opening vignette. Explain the pros and cons of the band selling T-shirts to its fans. Design a prototype for the band's T-shirt and present it to the class.

Build Your Marketing Plan

Build your Portfolio

In this chapter you studied the product element of the marketing mix. You will now apply this learning to the development of your marketing plan. To access the chapter-specific tools that you will need to complete this activity, please navigate to Chapter 10 ➔ Build Your Marketing Plan in MindTap. Alternatively, you can access these tools online at NGLSync. Please visit www.nglsync.cengage.com, and search for the companion website that accompanies this book by entering the ISBN, author, or title. Once you locate this companion website, navigate to Build Your Marketing Plan ➔ Chapter 10.

Sales Project

Build your Portfolio

The Sales Project uses the project management process to raise funds for the local DECA chapter. Example projects include sports tournaments, t-shirt sales, 5K races, school merchandise sales, catalog sales, sponsorship development initiatives, fashion shows, pageants, restaurant nights, value cards, and yearbook sales.

Your group has earned a large sum of money baking cookies every Tuesday to sell in the school cafeteria. The school administration has given you permission to expand your business operation in school and throughout the community. You may consider opening a school store, taking custom orders from the community, and/or diversifying your product line. You must present a project management plan for your extended operation. The main body of your plan consists of the following parts:

Executive Summary Write a one-page description of the project.

Initiating Explain the type of project proposed, a brief description of the major product/service involved, sources of information (resource materials, presentations, etc.), and a brief description of advisors and their involvement. Describe the trading area, market segment, and customer buying behavior.

Planning and Organizing Define the project goals, human resources required, schedule, quality management plan, risk management plan, and proposed projected budget.

Execution, Monitoring, and Controlling Describe the project implementation, unusual or unforeseen challenges or successes, and methods of handling them.

Closing the Project Define the learning and earning outcomes of the project. Recommend improvements for the project. Describe plans for improving the learning and earning outcomes of the project.

Bibliography List all resources used.

Appendix The appendix is optional. Include in the appendix any exhibits appropriate to the written entry but not important enough to include in the body. Items to include in the appendix may include questionnaires used, letters sent and received, general background data, and minutes taken at meetings.

Performance Indicators Evaluated

- Initiate project. (Project Management)
- Develop project plan. (Operations)
- Determine sales strategies. (Selling)
- Explain the nature of a promotional plan. (Promotion)
- Evaluate project success. (Operations)
- Implement teamwork techniques to accomplish goals. (Emotional Intelligence)

Go to the DECA website for more detailed information. **www.deca.org**

Think Critically

1. Why must a successful business conduct research before expanding its operation?
2. What is the advantage of custom cookie orders?
3. What is the best way to take custom cookie orders?
4. What special distribution considerations must be made for the product being sold?

CHAPTER 11

SERVICES NEED MARKETING

See how effective advertising leads to successful marketing strategies. Click on Chapter 11, Visual Focus, in your MindTap.

Let's Start a Band!

"Nowadays, with the state of the music business, for any artist, whether you're up-and-coming or you've been in it for a while, you have to explore different revenues and different ways of expressing yourself."

– Mary J. Blige, Singer–Songwriter, Actress

So the other night, I'm coming back from a gig. I'm riding in the van with the others and Eddie says he has an idea. He tells us he was watching some documentary on cable the other night, called "Everything's Coming up Profits: The Golden Age of Industrial Musicals." It's about these dudes in the '60s and '70s who companies hired to write musicals about their products. Everything from tractors to toilets. The audience for the shows were the companies' employees.

That got my attention. But I wondered what this had to do with us.

He continued, "What I'm saying is we don't always have to play at a concert or a festival or a club. There are other audiences for our music, like companies looking for bands to play at functions like picnics and parties, even business shows and conventions."

I'm starting to think this may not be a bad idea. But how would we get started?

11.1 WHAT ARE SERVICES?

Learning Objectives

11.1.1 Explain the growing importance of services to the U.S. economy.

11.1.2 Describe four important qualities of services that are not shared by products.

Key Terms

service
intangible
inseparable
perishable
heterogeneous

marketing matters

Services are the biggest and fastest-growing part of the U.S. economy. New services are continually being created in industries that didn't exist a few years ago. Marketing services poses different challenges than marketing products because services possess four key characteristics that products do not. Unlike products, services are intangible, inseparable, perishable, and heterogeneous.

 essential question

Why are service businesses growing more rapidly than goods-producing businesses? What unique characteristics of services need to be considered when completing marketing planning?

11.1.1 ▶ Growth and Importance of Service Industries

Marketing can be applied to both products and services. Products are tangible objects, such as cars, video games, tables, and hamburgers. They are usually easy to see and understand. Services are more difficult to define, in part because the term is used in different ways.

In marketing, the term **service** is defined as an activity that is intangible, exchanged directly from producer to consumer, and consumed at the time of production. Services cover a broad range of activities, such as banking, entertainment, and health care. Some services are support activities that come with the sale of a product, such as delivery, gift wrapping, and installation.

The service sector is the largest and fastest-growing employment area in the U.S. economy. Service jobs are found in industries such as communication, entertainment, information technology, recreation, and of course, marketing. **Figure 11-1** describes projected job growth in several service industries.

One service-providing industry with numerous job opportunities is health care. The gradual aging of the population will place the health-care sector as a dominant source of overall projected employment growth.

There are more services available today than ever before. People pay for childcare, image consulting, carpet

Industry	10-Year Growth Rate	Number of Jobs Added (in thousands)
Solar photovoltaic installers	105%	11.8
Wind turbine technicians	96%	5.6
Home health aids	47%	431.2
Personal care aids	39%	777.6
Physician assistants	37%	39.6
Nurse practitioners	36%	56.1

FIGURE 11-1 These service industries are projected to have the greatest job growth in the United States from 2016 through 2026.

Source: https://www.bls.gov/news.release/pdf/ecopro.pdf

Why do you think people spend more on services during times of prosperity?

cleaning, security services, and party planning. Businesses hire the services of landscapers, interior designers, electricians, and accountants. Services marketing is big business. There are many reasons that the growth of employment in the service sector in our country is faster than job growth in the goods-producing sector.

Prosperity

Although the economy experiences ups and downs over time, continuing economic expansion is an important reason for the growth in the U.S. service sector. Today, many people have more discretionary income to spend on services. Americans are spending a greater percentage of their income on services and less on manufactured goods.

Automation

A second reason why job growth in the service industry is faster than job growth in the goods-producing industry is that the goods-producing industry is becoming more automated and less labor intensive. Companies use fewer people to produce their goods because of the increasing use of technology. Former manufacturing workers often turn to the service industry for continued employment.

Complexity

A third reason for the increase in service industry employment is that many high-technology products require complex installation, repair, and training.

Entire new service areas have opened up around the computer and information technology industries. Firms specialize in training, consulting groups specialize in applications, and other companies specialize in repairing and maintaining equipment. The rapid growth in the renewable energy industry as well as use of the Internet and wireless technology for communication and e-commerce have led to many new service jobs that didn't exist 20 years ago.

CHECKPOINT
What are three reasons for the growth of employment in service businesses in the United States?

11.1.2 ▶ Unique Qualities of Services

Four important characteristics distinguish services from products. Services are intangible, inseparable, perishable, and heterogeneous.

Intangible

The most important difference between goods and services is that services are intangible. **Intangible** means that the service cannot be touched, seen, tasted, heard, or felt. Examples of intangible services include babysitting, vision examinations, and travel planning. Unlike products, they do not have a physical form.

The intangibility of services presents special challenges for marketers. Because people cannot see or handle a service, marketers must focus on the benefits customers will receive. Promotional activities need to be carefully conceived so consumers can visualize the benefits the services provide. Travel planning, for example, relies heavily on photos, posters, videos, and travelogues to encourage customers to select vacation destinations. The objective and challenge of travel planning, or tourism marketing, is to get customers to imagine what it is like to be at a particular tourist location.

Inseparable

A second characteristic of services is that their production and consumption are inseparable. **Inseparable** means that the service is produced and consumed at the same time. Services such as a college class, a spa treatment, or a car repair are produced and consumed simultaneously. In many cases, the customer is actually involved in the production of the service. When you fly to another city on an airline or go to a concert with friends, you are demonstrating the inseparability of production and consumption in a service business.

This simultaneous production and consumption of services requires marketers to pay special attention to the distribution component of the marketing mix. Distribution involves having the service available where and when it is needed or wanted by the consumer. An example of ineffective distribution would be to locate a child day-care center in a retirement community. Because of its location, it probably would not attract many customers. On the other hand, a hotel limousine service located at the airport would be a good distribution strategy.

Perishable

Another characteristic of services is their perishability. **Perishable** means that services unused in one time period cannot be stored for use in the future. Because of perishability, marketers are concerned about lost opportunity. An empty seat in a theater or an airplane cannot be sold later.

After the movie has been shown or the flight has departed, the revenue that could have been earned from another paying customer is lost.

Airlines work very hard to fill seats on every flight. They recognize that money is lost on each empty seat and can never be retrieved. That is why airlines offer discounted fares and special promotions when they know there will be empty seats. This is the airlines' attempt to overcome the perishability of their service.

The pricing component of the marketing mix is crucial in the sale of perishable services. Prices must be set to assure the business the greatest number of sales while covering expenses and allowing for a profit.

© AboutLife/Shutterstock.com.

Why is the pricing component so important for a perishable service provider such as a movie theater?

MATH IN MARKETING

Travel Services Track the Sale of Space

Travel service businesses, including hotels and airlines, sell a highly perishable asset—space. If a hotel room or airline seat goes unsold for one night or one flight, it can never be recovered. Industry-specific measures have been developed to track the effectiveness of sales efforts from one time period to another. The lodging industry, for example, tracks "revPAR" (which stands for "revenue per available room") to gauge how effectively each hotel fill its rooms. It tries to avoid the use of deep discounts just to sell rooms or inflexible rates that lead to more unsold rooms. With revPAR, room rates and occupancy percentages are combined in one easy-to-compare measure of the sale of hotel space.

Airlines use similar performance measures. Available seat miles (ASMs) equal the total number of seats on all scheduled flights multiplied by the total flight miles. Revenue passenger miles (RPMs) include only seats that are occupied by paying passengers. Load factor is RPM divided by ASM, expressed as a percentage. The measure of space sales lead to the most effective balance of prices and rooms or seats sold.

Do the Math

1. If a hotel manager's goal is to increase revPAR by 20% next month, what are the different ways to accomplish this? (Note: Adding rooms is not an option.)

2. If an airline's RPMs increase by 20% while its load factor declines, what is the likely explanation?

Heterogeneous

Another characteristic of services is heterogeneity. **Heterogeneous** means there are differences among services. Services are usually performed by people. Because people differ in their skill level or even their enthusiasm for a job, delivery of a service often is not consistent. People who use a tax-preparation service or an appliance-repair business expect high-quality service. If the quality of the service declines, people will likely look for a new service provider.

Marketers who sell services need to pay particular attention to the marketing concept and satisfying the wants and needs of the consumer through the marketing mix. The heterogeneity of services gives marketers an opportunity to design services to meet the unique needs of a market segment and deliver it in a consistent, satisfying way.

CHECKPOINT

What four characteristics distinguish services from products?

11.1 ASSESSMENT

What Have You Learned?

1. How does a prosperous economy lead to job growth in the U.S. service sector? [11.1.1]

2. Why is the production and consumption of services said to be inseparable? [11.1.2]

Make Academic Connections

1. **Visual Art**   Draw or use technology to create a picture, graphic, or other visual representation of one of the unique qualities of services. [11.1.2]

2. **Economics**   Search the World Bank website to find the percentage of service jobs in the economies of 10 countries of your choosing. Present your findings in a graph format. Include the United States as one of the countries you select. [11.1.1]

Connect to ◇DECA

Build your Portfolio

You work for an amusement park. The owner wants your help in determining the number of guests the park would need each day to fill each ride all day. Make up the details including the number of rides at the park, the average number of seats per ride, the duration of each ride (allowing for time to load and unload) and the number of hours per day the park is open. Assume that all guests ride each ride one time. Include your calculations in presenting the plan to your teacher (judge). [11.1.2]

Learning Objectives

11.2.1 Describe five ways marketers categorize service businesses in order to develop effective marketing mixes.

11.2.2 Identify the three types of service standards used to evaluate service quality.

Key Terms

labor intensiveness
discretionary income
service quality

marketing matters

Marketers classify service organizations in a variety of ways as they develop marketing plans. Businesses and other service organizations may be alike in some ways and quite different in others. Marketers can develop a better marketing mix for services when they consider the various categories of service businesses. Maintaining a high level of customer satisfaction requires a high level of service quality. Marketers can evaluate service quality by comparing it to the services provided by competitors, by establishing objective standards, and by studying customer feedback.

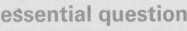

essential question

What types of standards might a business use to determine if customers are satisfied with the services provided? Will the standards differ based on the type of business and type of service? Why or why not?

11.2.1 ▶ Service Organization Classifications

A variety of organizations and businesses provide services to the public. Organizations such as churches, dry cleaners, painters, day-care facilities, basketball teams, health clubs, barbers, law offices, and insurance companies are all service providers. The development and marketing of services can vary widely across types of services.

Marketers classify services in order to develop viable and appropriate marketing plans. Service organizations can be classified by the type of consumers that make up the markets they target, their organizational goals, their degree of labor intensiveness, the amount of contact they have with customers, and the level of skill they require.

Types of Consumers

As with products, there are two types of consumers for services—business consumers and individual consumers.

A business consumer might employ a cleaning service, a security service, a grounds-maintenance service, and an equipment-repair service. Businesses that provide these services to other businesses must offer services tailored to business needs. The services must be available where and when the business wants them.

Individual consumers might employ a cleaning service, a lawn service, an auto-maintenance service, and a computer-repair service. For these consumer-oriented services, the target market and marketing mix will be different from those offered to businesses.

A marketing mix designed to reach business customers might stress personal selling and quantity price discounts. In contrast, a marketing mix designed to reach individual customers might stress personalized attention; advertising through print, television, and Internet; and more standardized pricing. As a marketer, you need to know your market and its specific wants and needs in order to satisfy it.

Goals of the Organization

Some organizations have profit-making as a goal, whereas others operate as not-for-profit organizations. Most businesses that compete with one another in providing services people pay for are profit-making organizations.

Many not-for-profit organizations offer services as well. Examples of not-for-profit organizations that offer services are universities, libraries, museums, government programs, churches, and social agencies. The goals and motives of these organizations differ from those of for-profit organizations. Their goals might be serving the community, making the public aware of a message or idea, increasing knowledge, or changing attitudes. Money normally is not a motivating factor for not-for-profit service organizations. Still, they are equally interested in delivering high-quality services that consumers need and want.

Labor Intensiveness

Labor intensiveness refers to the amount of human effort required to deliver a service. Services range from those that are extremely labor intensive to those that are totally reliant on equipment. Most combine labor and equipment and fall somewhere in between.

Equipment-based services are provided with the use of machinery. These services require few people to deliver the services. Examples include automated car washes, dry cleaning, and vending machines. People-based services generally are more labor-intensive. Guitar lessons, manicures, teeth cleaning, and guided tours are examples of people-based services.

As a marketer, you will emphasize different parts of the marketing mix depending on whether your service is labor or equipment intensive. When marketing equipment-based services, you will pay special attention to the distribution or location of your services. Locating an automatic car wash on a busy avenue is more appropriate than locating it on a quiet residential street. Placing an automatic bank teller machine in a safe, well-lighted place for a drive-through location gives customers a greater sense of security.

MARKETING COMMUNICATION

TV Doctors of America

"I have no idea what I'm doing, I'm just a TV doctor," says a sincere Alan Alda in an ad that was part of health insurer Cigna's "TV Doctors of America" campaign. Alda, who for 12 years played a doctor in the television series M*A*S*H, was one of several actors who appeared in the TV spots. Rather than using a traditional marketing message, the ads used humor and celebrity to highlight preventive care and at the same time position Cigna as a reliable health partner.

According to the Centers for Disease Control (CDC), only half of Americans get annual check-ups. The CDC estimates that if everyone had an annual check-up, 100,000 lives could be saved each year. With that statistic in mind, Cigna launched the TV Doctors campaign across television, digital, and social channels giving an amusing and relatable slant on its message to get a physical check-up.

To produce the ads Cigna looked at television's highest-rated medical dramas and comedies. The research pointed to "M*A*S*H," "ER," "Scrubs," "House," and "Grey's Anatomy" and identified the most-recognizable actors from each. After assessing their trustworthiness and likeability, it chose the ones who ranked the highest to deliver its message.

In conjunction with the campaign, Cigna launched a Health Improvement Tour. The tour traveled to 65 cities nationwide delivering nearly 7,000 free screenings for blood pressure, cholesterol, blood sugar, and body mass index at nearly 100 events. Within two years Cigna saw an 18 percent increase in annual check-ups among Cigna customers.

The TV Doctors of America campaign continued for several years encouraging people to take control of their health and get an annual checkup—from a real doctor.

Think Critically

1. What in the message of the "TV Doctors of America" campaign can be viewed as aligning with the goals of a non-profit organization?

2. How did Cigna promote the quality of its service with the "TV Doctors of America" campaign?

Sources: "America's Favorite TV Doctors Scrub Up to Join Cigna In Campaign Promoting Preventive Care, Helping to Save Lives." Cigna. September 15, 2017. https://www.multivu.com/players/English/8163851-cigna-americas-tv-doctors-go-know-take-control/

"Cigna: 'The TV Doctors of America.'" *Journal of Advertising Research*. 2018. www.journalofadvertisingresearch.com/content/cigna-tv-doctors-america

Mitchell, Stuart. "America's Favorite TV Doctors of America are Now On-Call." Ethical Marketing News. May 1, 2018. ethicalmarketingnews.com/americas-favorite-tv-doctors-of-america-are-now-on-call

O'Brien, Kyle. "Ad of the Day: TV Doctors of America Spots Feature Doogie and McDreamy for Cigna Health." The Drum. September 19, 2017. https://www.thedrum.com/news/2017/09/19/ad-the-day-tv-doctors-america-spots-feature-doogie-and-mcdreamy-cigna-health

Sederholm, Jillian. "Former TV Doctors Get Back in Their Scrubs for Cigna Commercial." CBS News. September 10, 2016. https://www.nbcnews.com/pop-culture/tv/former-tv-doctors-get-back-their-scrubs-cigna-commercial-n645986

"TV Doctors of America" Shorty Awards. 2018. https://shortyawards.com/9th/tv-doctors-of-america

With people-based services you will want to pay careful attention to the training of your employees. You will train them in how to provide the service to satisfy your customers' wants and needs. A courteous, attentive, and efficient waiter is a good example of well-trained employee that can make a real difference in the success of a restaurant.

Customer Contact

The level of customer contact a service provider has is another way to classify services. Some services, such as barbers, doctors, schools, hotels, and restaurants, have a high level of customer contact. Other services, such as equipment repair,

Want to know more about what is trending with this topic? Click on **Lesson 11.2, Marketing Decisions,** *in your MindTap.*

Connect to
MindTap

lawn maintenance, and waste collection, have a low level of customer contact.

Recognizing and responding to the level of customer contact is important if you are a service marketer. In general, the higher the level of contact, the more you must rely on personal selling as a promotional activity. With a low level of contact, it is important to provide maximum customer satisfaction because there is not much opportunity to interact with customers.

Level of Skill

Another way to categorize services is by the level of skill the provider possesses. The most common way to categorize based on skill level is to divide the

© Ministr-84/Shutterstock.com.

Apply the five service category classifications to a fast-food restaurant.

providers into professional and nonprofessional groups. Professionals include providers whose services tend to be more complex and more highly regulated than nonprofessional services. The professional category would include accountants, pharmacists, teachers, physicians, therapists, and others who are required to have high-level skills, education, and a license to practice. The nonprofessional service group would include pet sitters, personal shoppers, hotel clerks, and toll collectors.

CHECKPOINT
Identify five ways marketers categorize service businesses and organizations.

11.2.2 ▶ Evaluate Service Quality

The United States has become a service-oriented country. Businesses are continually finding new services to offer, and many consumers are spending more of their discretionary income to purchase these services. **Discretionary income** is the amount of income left after paying basic living expenses and taxes.

With the large number of service businesses in the market today, a deciding factor for whether or not a company prospers is the quality of the service provided. **Service quality** is defined as the degree to which the service meets customers' needs and expectations.

Service quality is controlled by the provider of the service and can be measured in a number of ways. It might be measured by the qualifications of the provider or by the speed of service. It also might be based on cleanliness, efficiency, safety, comfort, or any number of variables related to the type of service and customer expectations.

To improve quality, an organization must first understand how customers decide which service they want and how they will judge the quality of the service. Three types of service standards can be used to evaluate service quality—competition, performance standards, and customer satisfaction.

Competition

Marketers of services need to be aware of the nature and level of services their competitors are offering. Organizations must provide services that are at least equal in quality to what their competitors offer for the same price. As with products, services must be positioned in a way that makes them unique and sets the business apart from its competition.

Performance Standards

A service organization should set its own performance standards and communicate them to potential customers. Promotions used by airlines, car rental companies, delivery services, and telephone companies reinforce the commitment to quality service.

Each organization should have a list of standards that supports its advertising slogan. The standard should be measurable, such as: "Ninety-five percent of our arrivals will be on time" or "We will have no more than three customer complaints per month." The service should be evaluated regularly to see if it is meeting the standard. If not, the company should take corrective action.

Customer Satisfaction

The real test of service quality is customers' assessment of it. Firms use market research to find out exactly what customers think. One of the most important and useful indicators of customer satisfaction is repeat business. Do customers continue to come back to buy the service? If they do, it is a strong indication that they are satisfied with the service offered and that the organization is achieving its service standards.

> **CHECKPOINT**
> *What are the three types of standards used to evaluate service quality?*

WORKING IN TEAMS

Three types of standards can be used to evaluate service quality—competition, performance standards, and customer satisfaction. As a team, choose a service business from your community. Prepare a brief survey that a business' customers can easily complete. Develop one or more questions to evaluate each of the three types of service standards. When complete, share and discuss your questionnaire with other teams.

11.2 ASSESSMENT

What Have You Learned?

1. Define *labor intensiveness.* [11.2.1]
2. What does repeat business indicate to a service provider? [11.2.2]

Make Academic Connections

1. **Language Arts**   Select a not-for-profit service organization in your community and write a two-page report about it. Focus your report on the goals of the organization. Use library or Internet resources in preparing your report. [11.2.1]
2. **Management**   Create a brief survey that an owner of a child-care facility could use to measure customer satisfaction.

Your survey should have no more than 10 questions and should focus on topics important to customers of this service. [11.2.2]

Connect to ◇DECA

Build your Portfolio

Your team members manage a landscaping company that hopes to acquire jobs from both business and individual consumers. As a team, discuss the factors in your marketing mix that will be different for these two potential markets. Discuss how these factors will appeal to the different markets you seek. Make a three-minute team presentation of your recommended marketing mix for each type of consumer to your teacher (judge). [11.2.1]

21ST CENTURY SUCCESS SKILLS
Deal with Rude and Discourteous People

How do you feel when someone cuts in front of you in line? What is your response to someone who drives too aggressively? There are a multitude of reasons for rude behavior. Fatigue, stress, insecurity, or ignorance may cause some people to behave badly.

Rude behavior has many potential negative consequences. It angers people and diverts their energy from positive goals. It also may damage personal, social, and work relationships. Most workplaces have policies regarding expected behavior. Your behavior should conform to the business' expectations. Discussing political views or asking about coworkers' compensation is often taboo.

Courtesy and Personal Boundaries

Common courtesies help groups and organizations function cooperatively and efficiently. Courteous behavior signals that you understand and respect the needs of the people around you. Courtesies improve daily interactions. People are more inclined to respond positively when you treat them well.

Define your personal boundaries when interacting with others. If anyone asks for personal information from you, try to deflect the question. Saying "I prefer not to discuss that topic at work" is one method.

Discourteous Customers

If customers are behaving badly, consider what has made them angry. Whether it is a perceived product failure or a service error, keep in mind that they have a financial stake in the outcome of your discussion. Although it is fine to acknowledge their frustration or anger, try to focus on problem resolution. Keep your own emotions in check as you work with the customer.

You should never feel threatened because of someone's rude behavior. If their behavior has deteriorated to a level where safety becomes a concern, stop the conversation and leave the area.

Handle Rude Behavior

There are a number of nonconfrontational ways to deflect the disrespectful behavior of others. First, try to remain as calm as possible. Gently point out that the person's rude behavior is not helpful in moving to a successful resolution. Jointly define the underlying concern that caused the behavior. Establish ground rules that will be used to maintain a respectful tone while discussing the issue. If the person violates these rules, remind them of the need to be respectful and ask for their cooperation before proceeding with the discussion. If the person continues to be rude or confrontational, you have the right to stop the interaction. Tell the person you will not participate in a conversation with a discourteous tone.

Model the behavior you would like those around you to use. Thank people as much as possible. It is harder for people to be nasty to someone who's shown them kindness and appreciation.

Develop Your Skill

Think of three examples where you have encountered rude behavior. For example, someone may have interrupted you during a conversation. Prepare a nonconfrontational response for each of these situations. For example, you could say, "Please let me finish what I was saying," when interrupted.

Role-play positive responses to rude behaviors with a friend or an adult. Evaluate which nonconfrontational responses seem the most effective.

Learning Objectives

11.3.1 Explain how businesses plan and promote services.

11.3.2 Describe the importance of pricing and distribution of services.

Key Terms

endorsement
bundling

marketing matters

The unique characteristics of services make developing a marketing mix very challenging. Making a purchase decision for a tangible product is easier because customers can see, smell, touch, or taste the product. Because services are intangible, service marketers must help their customers visualize them. They do so by applying the principles of product/service planning, pricing, promotion, and distribution in ways that are suited to the nature of the services they provide. As with products, the objective is to satisfy customers.

 essential question

How do customers arrive at the decision to use a particular service rather than a competitor's service, an alternative service, or no service at all?

11.3.1 Service Planning and Promotion

When marketing services, businesses need to plan them carefully, keeping in mind the differences between services and products. Businesses also need to identify effective strategies for promoting their services.

Service Planning

When developing the service to be provided, marketers must recognize that the services cannot be defined in terms of physical attributes. Instead, companies need to shape the attributes of the service to meet the needs and wants of consumers in the most satisfactory way possible. For example, UPS sells a service and communicates its attributes: fast and reliable delivery. Banks also sell their services such as checking accounts, savings accounts, and loans. The attributes of bank services are dependability, convenience, low interest rates on loans, and high yields on savings.

Both UPS and a bank must develop favorable mental images of their services by communicating their benefits to customers.

Services are intangible, but businesses also recognize that customers pay attention to certain tangible elements associated

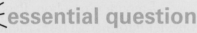

*Want to know more about what is trending with this topic? Click on **Lesson 11.3, Global Marketing,** in your MindTap.*

Connect to
MindTap

with the service. The delivery trucks for UPS are a distinctive brown color, clean, and in good repair. Banks are typically located in well-maintained offices to reinforce the idea that they are safe and responsible. Imagine how you would feel about your bank if the building were hard to find or needed major repairs, or if you could not easily identify someone to help you as you entered.

Recognizing that tangible products are important, many service organizations provide physical items for customers to take with them. Many times, these items also serve as specialty advertising. Dentists give patients toothbrushes, coffee shops give patrons mugs, banks provide checkbook covers, and professional hockey teams distribute pucks stamped with the team logo. In each case, the service business is attempting to provide a tangible symbol and reminder of the service it provides.

Promotion

Services may be difficult to promote. Something that cannot be touched is not easily described in print advertising or broadcast media. Services also are difficult to promote through personal selling because they may be difficult to demonstrate. Businesses need to appeal to the buying motives of the target market and stress the benefits derived from the use of the service.

One effective promotional strategy for services is to stress their tangible elements. The well-dressed waiter, clean and undamaged late-model rental cars, and high-quality furnishings in a law office are all tangible elements associated with intangible services.

The last part of the promotion strategy is the nature and the timing of the message. The message should create a mental image for the customer of the performance of the service. It also must foster the idea of completely meeting the customers' needs. The timing of the promotional message also must be right. It must be close enough to the potential need and/or use for the service to be memorable and influence a decision.

ENDORSEMENTS Many services use endorsements as a promotional strategy. An **endorsement** is an advertisement in which a believable person publicly expresses approval of a product or service. Sometimes endorsers are well-known role models for a target market. Celebrities and athletes often endorse products. Customers must identify with the endorser and believe what they are saying in order for the endorsement to be effective.

WORD-OF-MOUTH Service organizations rely heavily on publicity and word-of-mouth promotion. People often consider information from friends to be very credible. Service sellers encourage word-of-mouth promotion. They offer incentives to consumers who refer new customers. They also develop publicity activities and Internet or Twitter "buzz" that encourage people to talk about their business in positive ways.

PERSONAL SELLING Many marketers believe that personal selling is the most powerful promotional tool available. A well-trained sales staff can interact with customers to reduce their uncertainty, give reassurance, and promote the reputation of the service provider. Careful training and management of customer-contact personnel is crucial to the success of a service organization.

Want to know more about marketing in the information age? Click on **Lesson 11.3, Digital Marketing,** *in your MindTap.*

Connect to MindTap

CHECKPOINT

What strategies can marketers use to promote services effectively?

Price and distribution of services each play a role in meeting customer expectations. Each needs to be carefully considered when developing marketing plans for services.

Price

In the past, many service providers did not consider pricing to be important. Consumers often viewed services as unique, much like a monopoly. With increased competition and government deregulation of many industries, businesses began to see pricing strategies as a way to improve their market positions and to differentiate themselves from their competition.

Service businesses are in a good position to alter their pricing strategies because they can change prices fairly easily. A hair salon in your neighborhood can change its pricing schedule to meet competition or to create a new image. The amount or complexity of a service can be increased or decreased with the pricing strategy. For example, the hair salon can add styling specialists or offer additional services such as coloring and conditioning to justify higher prices.

One pricing strategy that many service providers use is called **bundling**. This is the practice of combining several related services for one price. If you are planning a trip to Chicago, Illinois, the travel service may offer to bundle the price of a ticket, a rental car, a hotel, and two tickets to a Cubs game into a package for which you would pay one price. Another example of bundling is a college charging one price for a student's room, board, tuition, and fees.

Bundling is a type of quantity discount. A customer can purchase more services for a lower price than if each was purchased individually. This has advantages for both the consumers and sellers of services. The consumer pays a reduced price and has the advantage of one-stop shopping. The service marketer forms mutually beneficial relationships with other service marketers to provide an appealing package for customers. The marketers are usually able to increase sales of their services using the bundling technique.

Distribution

The distribution of services is primarily concerned with offering the service at a location and time convenient for the consumer. Many services for which people once had to travel to obtain are now provided in their homes. Pet grooming, tax preparation, and elder care are examples of services that you can get at home.

An important point to remember in marketing services is that the production and consumption of services happen simultaneously. That is, you receive the service at the same time as it is performed. Therefore, the channels of distribution for a service are very short. In many cases, the channel is the producer and provider all rolled into one. A restaurant is a good example of this. The food is cooked and served at one site.

©Viktoria Gavrilina/Shutterstock.com.

Some types of services, however, make use of intermediaries. For example, you might purchase an appliance from a large appliance store. However, if your appliance needs to be repaired, the store may contract with an appliance repair business that will come to your home to make the repairs.

In planning a distribution strategy for a service, the most important element should be convenience for the consumers.

Travel agents and airlines now use the Internet, making it easier for you to buy airline tickets and make other travel plans. Automated teller machines offer convenient locations and convenient hours for a variety of banking services.

CHECKPOINT
What is the key to effective distribution of services?

11.3 ASSESSMENT

What Have You Learned?

1. Why do service providers often give customers physical items to take with them? [11.3.1]

2. Explain the pricing strategy known as bundling. [11.3.2]

Make Academic Connections

1. **Ethics** Celebrities and bloggers are often paid to endorse services. The Federal Trade Commission (FTC) has several guidelines that the endorser and business being endorsed must follow. Research the legal restrictions on endorsements and describe them in a two-page paper. In your paper, express your views on whether or not celebrities should actually use and like the services they endorse. [11.3.1]

2. **Civics** List and briefly describe five tangible elements that are associated with services your local government provides. [11.3.1]

Connect to

You have been hired by a local cleaning service to provide ideas for cleaning packages. Working with a partner, brainstorm a list of cleaning tasks. Assign individual fees for each task, and then come up with three bundling options and a fee for each option. Prepare a two-minute presentation with visual aids for the owner to describe the bundled cleaning packages. Deliver the presentation to your teacher (judge). [11.3.2]

Build your **Portfolio**

*Analyze a case study that focuses on chapter concepts. Click on **Chapter 11, Case Study,** in your MindTap.*

Review Marketing Concepts

1. Continuing economic expansion leads to prosperity, which leads households to have more discretionary income to spend on services. Why do you think Americans spend a greater percentage of their income on services and less on manufactured goods when they have more discretionary income? [11.1.1]

2. Consider the tax preparation service, popular each spring to help taxpayers complete their tax returns for the government. How is this service intangible and how is it heterogeneous? [11.1.2]

3. Compare and contrast equipment-based services with people-based services. Explain which part of the marketing mix a marketer would focus on for each. [11.1.2]

4. Which of these would be easier to change: your hairdresser/barber or your lawn service? Explain your reasoning. [11.2.1]

5. You are looking for a company to service your air conditioner. Which of these do you think is the better way to choose this service provider: conduct an Internet search or use the phone book? Explain your answer. [11.2.2]

6. Which is more likely to influence your choice of a service provider: word-of-mouth or personal selling? Explain your answer. [11.3.1]

7. Analyze the service of carpet cleaning in terms of price and distribution. How are prices for this service generally communicated and how is the service delivered? [11.3.2]

Marketing Research and Planning

1. On a separate sheet of paper create a table with three columns. Title the columns: Business Consumer Market, Final Consumer Market, and Combination of Both Markets. Conduct an Internet search to identify local service businesses that appeal to each of these markets. Write the names of the businesses in the appropriate column. Find at least three businesses for each column. Compare your table with those of your classmates. [11.2.1]

2. Though goods and services have many different characteristics, they both need to satisfy the wants and needs of the consumer. A dry-cleaning business handed out a questionnaire to all customers who brought in or picked up clothes during the month of October. Of the 1,435 questionnaires distributed, 705 were returned with the following results: [11.1.2]

Question: How often do you take items to a dry-cleaning business?

Results: At least once a week: 178; twice a month: 199; once a month: 200; less than once a month: 128

Rate the factors shown in the table (on page 320) for this business.

   a. What percentage of the surveys were returned? (Hint: Divide the number of questionnaires returned by the number distributed.)

   b. What percentage of the customers use dry cleaning services at least once a week? Twice a month? Once a month? Less than once a month?

   c. Based on the ratings of the store features and service quality (shown in the following table), make three recommendations to management to improve customer service.

	Very Satisfied	Satisfied	Not Satisfied
Location of the store	599	100	6
Hours of operation	200	300	205
Turnaround time	351	257	97
Friendliness of staff	264	254	187
Quality of service	532	101	72

3. Developing an appropriate marketing mix for a service is as important as developing the appropriate mix for a product. Develop a marketing mix for a service business that includes a description of the service, the pricing strategy, the promotional strategy, and a plan for distribution. Choose from one of the following service businesses: [11.3.1, 11.3.2]

- Tutoring and study skills
- Video arcade
- Chimney cleaning service
- Hot air balloon rides
- Golf lessons
- Coin-operated laundry

4. Bundling is an effort by service industries to sell related services in one location and for one price. Identify at least five services that can be bundled for each of the following service businesses: [11.3.2]

- Evening entertainment
- Insurance
- Automobile maintenance
- Home appliance repair
- Lawn maintenance

5. Search the Internet to find websites of 10 service businesses. Make a list of the businesses, what services they produce, their major target markets, and their major channels of distribution. How do they use their websites to market their businesses? [11.3.1]

Marketing Management and Decision Making

1. As the owner of an automobile washing and detailing business, you have noticed that although the population of your community is growing, your business is not. You believe that you provide a quality service, but you are concerned about your business volume. After discussing your problem with a marketing specialist, you decide to evaluate your service quality. Using the service quality evaluation criteria, develop at least four specific things you can do to determine your level of quality. [11.2.2]

2. As a marketing specialist, you have been asked to speak to a group of service providers about the future of the service industry and how service providers can effectively market their services. In order to do this, you have developed the following topics on which to speak: [11.1.1, 11.1.2, 11.2.1, 11.3.1, 11.3.2]

1. Future of services
2. Differences between products and services
3. Different types of services
4. Importance of the marketing mix

Using these topics, prepare a speech describing each of the items. Use as many examples as possible.

3. Services can be classified based on the following criteria:

Type of market (business-B or individual-I)
Labor intensiveness (low, medium, high)

Customer contact (low, medium, high) Level of skill (low, medium, high) Organizational goal (profit or not-for-profit)

Classify each of the following services by these criteria and create a chart, as shown below, to illustrate their appropriate classification. As an example, item a is shown in the table. [11.2.1]

a. An insurance policy protecting a professional volleyball team from loss of the team's star player

b. A new paint job for an old car

c. Three empty horses on a circus carousel

d. A manicure while the customer's hair is styled

e. Repair service on a combination copier/printer for a small business

f. An opera performed by a local community group

g. Clean uniforms provided by the employer

h. A long-distance telephone call

i. Renting a motel room

j. A golf course

k. A high school education

l. Cable television installed in a new neighborhood

Type of Market	Labor Intensiveness	Customer Contact	Level of Skill	Organizational Goal
a. Business	low	low	high	profit

Let's Start a Band! Follow-Up Discussion

Work in small teams to discuss the question posed at the end of the opening vignette. How can the band find corporate audiences for its music?

Build Your Marketing Plan

In this chapter you learned about planning the product/service element of the marketing mix. You will now apply this learning to the development of your marketing plan. To access the chapter-specific tools that you will need to complete this activity, please navigate to Chapter 11 → Build Your Marketing Plan in MindTap. Alternatively, you can access these tools online at NGLSync. Please visit www.nglsync.cengage.com, and search for the companion website that accompanies this book by entering the ISBN, author, or title. Once you locate this companion website, navigate to Build Your Marketing Plan → Chapter 11.

Hotel and Lodging Management Series Event

DECA PREP

The Hotel and Lodging Management Series Event consists of a 100-question multiple-choice Career Cluster® exam and role-plays. The role-play portion of the event requires participants to accomplish a task by translating what they have learned into effective, efficient, and spontaneous action. The performance indicators specify the distinct tasks the participant must accomplish during the role-play. Students have 10 minutes to prepare their strategy for the role-play and another 10 minutes to explain their strategy to the judge. The judge can ask questions during or after the presentation.

Hotel guests crave pampering. Some upscale hotels cater to guests by offering floors for club members only. Now, many hotels are turning club floors into retreats where members choose their pillow and have access to a free iPod and cappuccino day or night. Because most hotels are trying to boost their revenue by raising room rates 5 to 25 percent, they are increasing customer service to justify the higher room rates.

Hotels must be aware of the current trends. More business travelers are bringing their families to business meetings. These travelers demand club lounges that offer their families free breakfast. Female business travelers are requesting restricted-access floors and more exclusive lounges in place of bustling lobby bars.

The Towers Hotel chain has decided to increase its level of customer service. It now offers free wireless Internet service and allows guests to download music. The hotels also have added single-serve coffee machines and refrigerators in all rooms. In addition, the hotel offers a free lunch (sandwiches and salads) to all guests.

To make up for the additional costs of the new services, the Towers Hotel has increased room rates by 20 percent. Create a promotion strategy that emphasizes all of the new amenities and downplays the increased room rates.

Performance Indicators Evaluated

- Explain the concept of product in the hospitality and tourism industry. (Product/Service Management)

- Demonstrate a customer-service mindset. (Customer Relations)

- Explain the role of customer service in positioning/image. (Product/Service Management)

- Explain the nature and scope of the pricing function. (Pricing)

- Explain promotional methods used by the hospitality and tourism industry. (Promotion)

- Explain the relationship between promotion and brand. (Promotion)

Go to the DECA website for more detailed information. **www.deca.org**

Think Critically

1. Why are some complimentary hotel amenities actually not free?

2. Why should the Towers Hotel consider using different promotions for different target markets?

3. What type of frequent guest program could the hotel consider implementing?

CHAPTER 12

BUSINESS-TO-BUSINESS MARKETING

12.1 Business-to-Business Exchanges

12.2 Make Business Purchase Decisions

12.3 Business Purchasing Procedures

12.4 Retail Purchasing

See how effective advertising leads to successful marketing strategies.
Click on Chapter 12, Visual Focus, in your MindTap.

Let's Start a Band!

"That's not easy to find in a corporate world, somebody who cares about music."

– *Michael Penn, Singer–Songwriter, Composer*

Every once in a while I like to have a little one-on-one time with another band member to see each other outside the usual routine. I try my best to steer the conversations away from band business. So a few days after we got back from our grueling three weeks on the road, I met Layla at a coffee shop near where we both lived.

After a few minutes of casual conversation, Layla said, "I know you don't want to discuss the band, but there's something I've been wanting to talk to you about."

Sensing this was important, I said, "fire away."

"You remember Meghean? My friend who runs the cat shelter? The one we did the benefit for last summer? She works closely with a pet food manufacturer in Milton and suggested we might want to contact them."

"Sure, I remember her. But a pet food company?" I asked. "What do we do that has anything to do with pet food?"

"I'm getting there. The band has taken on animal welfare as a cause. And Meghean pointed out to me that the shelter, the band, and the company share a lot of the same values when it comes to animals. The company donates to the shelter, and she thinks they might be interested in sponsoring us. Even if they aren't, she told me they usually hire a band at their annual company picnic and their Christmas party. If you think the rest of the band will go along with this, I'll put together a pitch so they'll consider us for the gigs."

I understand Layla's passion for animals. We all, at least to some degree, share it with her. I told her I thought this was a good idea and that she should bring it up to the group. But, if they all agree, do you think we'd be getting away from what we do best? If we go down this road are we selling out?

12.1 BUSINESS-TO-BUSINESS EXCHANGES

Learning Objectives

12.1.1 Explain the reasons businesses buy things from other businesses.

12.1.2 Define the five major classifications of business consumers.

12.1.3 Describe the common characteristics typical of business markets.

Key Terms

business-to-business marketing
purchasing
derived demand

marketing matters

Any exchange of products and services involves a buyer and a seller. You probably think about businesses as sellers and individual consumers as buyers. Actually, the majority of exchanges do not involve the final consumer at all. Most take place between businesses. One business buys products and services from another business. Business-to-business marketing is a very important part of our economy.

essential question

What are the business-to-business exchanges that need to take place as consumer products are manufactured and distributed?

12.1.1 ▶ Reasons for Business Purchases

Businesses need a variety of products and services in carrying out their day-to-day operations. The exchange of products and services between businesses is known as **business-to-business marketing**. The various types of products and services businesses buy and sell are identified in the business product classification system shown in **Figure 12-1**.

Businesses purchase products and services from other businesses for many reasons. First, producers purchase the raw materials needed to develop the products they sell. They also purchase many of the component parts used in manufacturing

their products. Purchasing products to be incorporated into a production process is an important part of business-to-business marketing.

A second reason is purchasing products for direct resale to consumers. In some markets it is not efficient for the producer to sell the product or service directly to the final consumer. Therefore, other businesses facilitate the marketing and sale of products. Those businesses typically do not change the physical form of the product, but they may repackage it. They also provide a number of the marketing functions.

BUSINESS PRODUCT CLASSIFICATION SYSTEM

Categories	Description
Capital Goods	The building and major equipment of the business
Operating Equipment	Equipment used in the daily operation of the business
Supplies	Materials used in the operation of the business
Raw Materials	Unprocessed materials that are incorporated into the products the business makes
Component Parts	Partially or completely processed items that become a part of the products the business makes
Services	Tasks performed in the operation of the business or to support the production, sale, or maintenance of the products and services

FIGURE 12-1 Several types of products and services are bought and sold by businesses.

A third reason for business purchasing is to obtain products and services needed to operate the business. Companies consume a variety of supplies in their day-to-day operations. Many businesses also purchase professional services from attorneys and accountants, business services from advertising agencies and printing companies, and services that support the products they sell such as delivery and repair services.

CHECKPOINT
Name three reasons businesses purchase products and services from other businesses.

12.1.2 ▶ Purchasing as a Marketing Activity

Purchasing is an important marketing activity. **Purchasing** includes determining the products and services needed, identifying the best sources to obtain them, and completing the activities necessary to obtain and use them.

The marketing process for selling products to businesses is basically the same as that for selling to consumers. The marketer must identify the target markets, determine their characteristics and needs, and develop a marketing mix that meets their needs better than other companies. Just as all final consumers are not the same, businesses also have important differences that require different marketing strategies.

Business Customer Classifications

One way to classify business customers is by the type of organization. The major categories of businesses are producers, resellers, service businesses, governments, and nonprofit organizations. All businesses and other organizations purchase the products and services they need to operate. This includes capital equipment, operating equipment, and supplies. They make purchases appropriate for the types of activities they perform.

PRODUCERS Producers are companies that manufacture goods. They range from farms and ranches, mining companies, and oil refiners to manufacturers of business and consumer products. Producers purchase raw materials and component parts as well as the other products and services needed for business operations. Some producers are very small businesses that employ only a few people and spend less than $10,000 a year on purchases. Others employ several hundred thousand people worldwide and easily spend $10 million in one day on purchases.

RESELLERS   Wholesale and retail businesses are a part of the product distribution system connecting producers with consumers. They purchase products for resale as well as to operate their business. Resellers typically complete other marketing activities as a part of the distribution channel. They might offer distribution and storage services, promote products through advertising and personal selling, extend credit to consumers, and complete a variety of other activities to meet customer needs.

SERVICE BUSINESSES   More companies in the United States produce services than produce products for resale. Most of the purchases made by a service provider are used in the operation of the business and to develop the services it sells.

Some service businesses are rental firms and purchase products to be used by final consumers. Rather than selling the products to those consumers, they retain title and allow the consumer to use the product. You are probably familiar with rental businesses such as automobile dealerships that lease cars and stores that rent formal wear.

GOVERNMENT   Federal, state, and local government agencies provide services to citizens and develop and enforce laws and regulations. The total purchases made by the U.S. government make it the

What types of purchases would a service business such as this dry cleaner typically make?

largest single customer in the world. From a supplier's viewpoint, the government is made up of thousands of separate customers with different needs and purchasing procedures.

Government agencies and institutions purchase the full range of products, from raw materials to supplies and services. Some government organizations, such as city utilities, purchase raw materials and operate very much like privately owned producers.

NONPROFIT ORGANIZATIONS
Many organizations in our communities do not operate in the same way as private businesses. They have specific goals or clients to serve, and providing that service is the primary reason for their operations. Although they need an adequate budget to operate, profit is not their primary motive. Most have a nonprofit designation from the U.S. Department of Treasury, which exempts them from paying taxes. Common examples of these organizations are schools, museums, churches, social service organizations such as shelters and community centers, public colleges and universities, professional organizations, and some social clubs.

As with government agencies, non-profit organizations provide services to specific client groups. Therefore, they purchase what they need to offer the services. Those purchases could be only a limited number of operating supplies and products, or they could be the full range of products and services in the business products classification system.

CHECKPOINT
What are the five major classifications of business consumers?

12.1.3 ▶ Characteristics of Business Markets

Businesses that sell to other businesses need to understand how those markets differ from final consumer markets. The following section describes some common demographic characteristics and purchasing behaviors that are typical of business markets.

Derived Demand

Businesses do not buy products for final consumption. Instead, they make purchases to be used directly or indirectly in meeting the needs of final consumers. The types and quantities of products and services demanded by the business are based on the level of demand of their customers. In other words, the business's demand is based on, or derived from, its customers' demand, and so is called **derived demand**.

WORKING IN TEAMS

As a team, identify five manufacturers and one product each manufacturer would purchase and use in its operations. Identify an important customer group each business serves and discuss how the demand by that group affects the derived demand for the product purchased.

Purchase Volume

Business customers usually purchase in much greater quantities than final consumers. While final consumers may buy the same product again, their needs change much more frequently than business purchasers. Because businesses are making purchases to be incorporated into other products or for operations, they usually purchase large quantities of those products. They are less likely to change what they are purchasing unless their customers' needs change dramatically.

Similar Purchases

Businesses that produce or resell similar products and services usually have common purchasing needs. Consider two furniture stores serving the same market. They will likely purchase the same types of furniture and home accessories for resale and will buy similar capital and operating equipment for their stores. As another example, most cities have several companies that mix concrete for use in construction projects. To operate the business, they need to purchase the same raw materials, such as cement, sand, and stone, as well as similar equipment, such as mixing facilities, trucks, and concrete pumps. Also, in some business markets, the businesses that purchase similar products are in the same industry and may be located in the same geographic area of a country.

Number of Businesses

The number of business customers for specific products usually is smaller than the number of final consumers who will purchase a product. That is typically an advantage for those who sell to the business market. Having fewer customers means that it should be easier to maintain contact with the customers and understand their needs.

Buyer/Seller Relationship

Businesses that produce products for sale to final consumers often have little contact with the customer. Because customers are located throughout the country and sometimes throughout the world, it would be difficult to distribute products directly from the seller to the buyer.

In business-to-business selling, the seller typically distributes the product directly to the purchaser. The seller is responsible for contacting prospective customers, selling the product, and providing follow-up support and service.

Want to know what is trending with this topic? Click on **Lesson 12.1, Marketing Decisions,** *in your MindTap.*

Connect to MindTap

CHECKPOINT
Name five characteristics typical of business markets.

12.1 ASSESSMENT

What Have You Learned?

1. Define business-to-business marketing. [12.1.1]

2. What is the primary reason for operation of nonprofit organizations? [12.1.2]

3. What is derived demand? [12.1.3]

Make Academic Connections

1. **Economics** Visit the website of the U.S. Census Bureau. Enter "county business patterns" in the search box and locate census data on the number of businesses in your county. Prepare a pie chart that compares the number of manufacturers, wholesalers, and retailers in your county. [12.1.1]

2. **Business Writing** As a summer job, you decide to start a mowing service for companies in your area. Write a letter introducing yourself and your services to prospective customers. Keep in mind that this letter is your first step in building a relationship with the customer. [12.1.3]

Connect to ◇DECA

Build your Portfolio

A local home-cleaning business is considering expanding and focusing on cleaning schools. Develop a two-minute presentation to be presented to the superintendent of your school district on the similarities and differences between cleaning houses and cleaning schools. Give your presentation to your teacher (judge). [12.1.1]

MAKE BUSINESS PURCHASE DECISIONS

Learning Objectives

12.2.1 Describe how businesses make new purchase, modified purchase, and repeat purchase decisions.

12.2.2 Explain the roles of purchasing specialists.

12.2.3 Identify issues that often arise in international purchasing.

Key Terms

purchase specifications
reorder point
just-in-time (JIT)
reciprocal trading

marketing matters

Effective marketing requires that the seller understand the buyer and how the buyer makes purchase decisions. The business decision-making process differs from the one used by final consumers. Business buying decisions tend to be more rational and directly related to business needs. Purchasing activities frequently require the hiring of purchasing specialists and the involvement of top managers. International purchasing procedures present an additional set of issues.

 essential question

What factors should businesses consider when planning purchases?

12.2.1 ▶ The Buying Decision

Business purchasers usually follow a more rational decision-making process than consumers. The business will purchase the product or service that best meets its needs at a reasonable price. Purchases must be cost-effective in order to maximize profits.

Make or Buy

Businesses, especially manufacturers, do not always need to purchase the products and services they need. They may decide to make the product or provide the service using their own resources. For example, most businesses need a variety of printed items such as catalogs and forms. The company may be able to hire a printing company to produce the materials needed. However, if the volume of printing is large enough and printing is needed regularly, the company may save money by doing its own printing. This is referred to as *insourcing*. Purchasing the resources needed from a vendor (such as a printing company) is known as *outsourcing*.

Types of Purchases

When a business decides to buy rather than make the products it needs, it develops specific purchasing procedures. Three different types of purchasing situations determine the procedure that will be followed. Those situations are a new purchase, a modified purchase, and a repeat purchase.

NEW PURCHASE The most difficult purchasing situation is a business buying a product or service for the first time. Examples of new purchases for many companies are buildings, major pieces of equipment, and raw materials and component parts needed when manufacturers develop a new product.

Because the business has never purchased the product before, it may have little or no experience with the product or the companies that sell it. The business must carefully determine the needs it must meet with the purchase, decide on the types of products that can meet those needs, and identify the companies that offer the products.

Often the company takes a great deal of time planning for the purchase. The company may develop purchase specifications that the selling companies must meet. **Purchase specifications** are detailed requirements for the construction or performance of a product. The buyer also will have expectations in terms of the supply needed, delivery methods and schedules, and technical support required.

MODIFIED PURCHASE A company may find that the products it purchased in the past do not meet current needs and so require some changes. The company will identify the changes or improvements needed. The company will communicate the needed modifications to the company from which it has been buying the product, and that company will have the opportunity to meet the new requirements. Other companies also may be given the chance to supply the modified product if major changes are planned or if the buyer is not satisfied with the current supplier.

Retailers use modified purchasing when they have had success with a basic product and want to offer additional features and options to customers. Companies that have purchased computer systems may want to purchase additional computers that have been upgraded with current technology. A company may have contracted with an accounting firm for recordkeeping services and now may want to extend the contract to include tax preparation.

REPEAT PURCHASE Most companies purchase the same products and services over and over. The buyer is aware of the needs that are being met with the purchase and has identified the product that meets those needs. In many cases, the buyer has developed a good relationship with a seller and does not even consider buying from another company. When a new supply of the product is needed, the company just reorders from the same seller.

The purchasing process may become so routine that it can be managed by a computer program. The program monitors the inventory level of the product. As the product is used or sold, the inventory level decreases until it reaches the reorder point. The **reorder point** is the level of inventory needed to meet the usage needs of the business until the product can be resupplied. When the reorder point is reached, the program issues a purchase order to the supplier, and the product is shipped.

One way to ensure proper inventory levels is with just-in-time supply. **Just-in-time (JIT)** means that the inventory level is kept low and resupplied by vendors as it is needed.

When many companies offer the same product for sale, repeat purchasing becomes very competitive. Because the buyers realize that the same product can be purchased from several sellers, price may become an important factor. The purchasing company may pressure the suppliers to reduce the price. This situation happens regularly with companies that sell to large retailers and companies that sell common operating equipment and supplies to businesses.

CHECKPOINT
What are the three types of purchasing situations?

MATH IN MARKETING

Incremental Cost Decisions

Whenever there is an opportunity for a business-to-business exchange of products or services, both the buyer and the seller need to be aware of two measurements of cost in addition to the total cost of the exchange. *Average cost* is the cost per unit. It is found by dividing the total cost by the number of units being sold. If you buy 100 units for $2,500, the average cost is $25 per unit. Average cost can be calculated for components, raw materials, or services.

Incremental cost is a decision-making tool. It is derived by examining the costs of an exchange in increments. If 100 units cost $2,500, but 200 units cost $4,000, the average cost would be $25 or $20, respectively. More significantly, perhaps, the incremental cost of the second hundred units is only $15 each ($4,000 − $2,500 = $1,500 ÷ 100). A buyer might decide that at $15 it is better to buy a larger quantity, even if it means tying up cash in inventory.

Conversely, if a seller's incremental production costs decline for larger quantities, it might propose a long-term supply contract that benefits both parties.

Do the Math

1. If a purchaser buys 55,000 units for $27,500 what is the average cost per unit?

2. If 1,000 units cost $50,000 and 2,000 units cost $80,000, what is the incremental cost per unit of the second 1,000 units?

3. If the cost per unit up to 10,000 units is $1, and unit cost is progressively reduced by 10 percent for each additional 10,000-unit increment, what is the incremental cost of the last unit if a buyer orders 40,000 units?

12.2.2 ▶ Purchasing Requires Specialists

Purchasing in businesses occurs continuously and involves thousands and even millions of dollars each day. Many of the products purchased are unique, complex, and technical. The purchasing process involves negotiating on product specifications and costs and arranging delivery and payment schedules. Often lengthy and complex contracts are prepared between the buyer and seller.

Many businesses have departments and personnel that specialize in purchasing. The person or persons responsible for managing the purchasing procedure are members of the purchasing department. Job titles of purchasing specialists include buyer, product manager, merchandise manager, and purchasing agent. Purchasing specialists work with the purchasing department requesting the purchase, identify possible suppliers, communicate needs and specifications, gather needed information, and manage the paperwork.

Why is negotiating an important part of the purchasing process for a business?

They usually are responsible for negotiating the price and terms of the sale.

Usually several people are involved in the buying decision the first time a product or service is purchased or for particularly complex or expensive products. The department using the product plays an important role in the purchase decision. The manager and experienced employees from that department may help prepare specifications. For a very technical product or a new product, engineers or others with technical expertise also may be involved to review the specifications and evaluate and test the products of suppliers.

Financial personnel participate in purchases when the purchase is expensive or the prices of competing products are quite different. Lawyers may help develop contracts and review the documents involved in the purchase. For the most important or expensive purchases, one or more members of top management may participate in the purchasing process.

CHECKPOINT
What is the role of purchasing specialists in the purchasing process?

12.2.3 International Purchasing

Companies involved in international marketing must understand the unique purchasing procedures involved in international trade. There can be advantages to purchasing products from international suppliers. They may offer unique products or manufacturing procedures, better availability, lower prices, or higher quality. However, those advantages are lost if products are not supplied as expected or

if costs are higher than anticipated. Companies purchasing internationally must be aware of the unique customs and business practices of each country. They also must develop effective relationships with their suppliers.

Locating products from international businesses is easier today than at any time in the past. Many businesses have foreign buying offices or purchasing representatives in other countries. Manufacturers wanting to sell to other countries will be represented at international trade shows or in foreign trading offices and trade directories. Most states and many large cities now have international trade centers where buyers and sellers can meet to exchange information and negotiate purchases.

Selecting products and suppliers from other countries involves factors other than just the product to be purchased. In addition to making sure the characteristics of the product are correct, the purchaser must be assured of the product's quality. The purchaser should be able to inspect a sample of the product and talk to other businesses that have purchased or used the product.

Supplier Qualifications

The seller's qualifications are an important consideration. Problems result when the company is not reliable or financially stable. Often the purchaser's bank can help obtain financial information about the company. The stability and economic conditions of the country in which the supplier is located also must be considered. It can be risky to work with a business from a country that has a weak economy or political instability.

Pricing Considerations

One of the most important factors in international buying is negotiating price. Most countries have their own monetary system, and it may be difficult to accurately calculate rates of exchange. The exchange rate of money can change a great deal in the time it takes to negotiate a purchase and deliver the product. Also, the countries of the supplier or the buyer may impose tariffs or duties on the product, which can drastically change the price.

Reciprocal Trading

One procedure some businesses use in international trade is reciprocal trading. **Reciprocal trading** is a form of bartering in which the products or services of one company are used as payment for the products or services of another company. Reciprocal trading is used when an unsatisfactory exchange rate exists or when one of the companies does not have an adequate amount of cash to finance the purchase. As an example of a reciprocal trade agreement, a U.S. company that produces robots for use in automobile manufacturing sold a large order of equipment to a new company in Europe. Because the new company did not have enough cash to pay for the equipment, the companies negotiated a contract in which the U.S. business received a percentage of the sales of automobiles produced by the European company.

Financing

Banks that have experience in international business can provide a great deal of help in arranging financing of purchases. They can give advice on exchange rates, terms of payment, and methods of paying for purchases. Many banks that have experience in international finance have established working relationships with financial institutions in other countries. Those contacts make it easier to gather financial information and complete financial transactions with businesses in those countries.

Transportation

Transportation decisions include determining the method of shipment, selecting the transportation company, preparing the necessary transportation documents, and meeting each company's requirements for shipping, handling, and inspecting products. The time needed for transporting products between countries may be no longer than for domestic shipments in some cases. However, the timing and reliability of international shipments often is a major concern. Careful transportation planning should be done before a decision is made to purchase from an international supplier. Some companies make a small purchase or require a sample shipment before committing to a large order.

CHECKPOINT
What are important factors to consider when making international purchases?

12.2 ASSESSMENT

What Have You Learned?

1. How do new purchases, modified purchases, and repeat purchases differ? [12.2.1]

2. For first-time purchases or technologically complex or expensive products, who in the company might be involved in the buying decision? [12.2.2]

3. What is reciprocal trading, and when it is used? [12.2.3]

Make Academic Connections

1. **Communication** Locate advertisements in magazines or online for three products or services directed at business customers. Identify information in the ad that is an emotional appeal and information that is a rational appeal. What conclusions can you draw from this exercise? [12.2.1]

2. **Government** Agencies of the U.S. federal and state governments provide assistance to businesses wanting to participate in international trade. Use the Internet to locate a government agency that helps with (a) identifying international suppliers or customers, (b) financing international sales and purchases, and (c) arranging transportation services. Prepare a one-paragraph summary of the agency and the type of assistance it provides. [12.2.3]

Connect to ◇DECA

Build your portfolio

Your team members are responsible for developing a procedure for your school to follow in purchasing a new bus to be used to transport students on field trips and club activities and to athletic events. Outline the steps that should be followed, the people who should be involved, and the main factors that should be considered when choosing the company from which the bus will be purchased. Make a three-minute team presentation of your recommendations to your teacher (judge). [12.2.2]

BUSINESS PURCHASING PROCEDURES

Learning Objectives

12.3.1 Identify the steps in the business purchasing process.

12.3.2 Describe the importance of keeping accurate inventory and purchasing records.

Key Terms

vendors
total quality management (TQM)
vendor analysis
request for proposal (RFP)
bidding
inventory

physical inventory system
perpetual inventory system
purchase order
packing list
invoice
receiving record

marketing matters

The procedures businesses use to make purchase decisions are more detailed and systematic than those used by final customers. Also, they usually involve a number of people rather than just a single individual. The steps begin with identifying needs and conclude with a post-purchase evaluation to gauge how well those needs have been met. When making purchasing decisions, businesses need to consider all of the costs involved and the impact they will have on profits. Inventory and purchasing records are needed to determine what and when to purchase.

essential question

Why should business consumers consider value in addition to specific costs when making a purchase decision?

12.3.1 ▶ Steps in the Purchasing Process

The general process that business customers use in making purchasing decisions looks very much like that used by final consumers. The steps in the process for both business and consumer purchases are shown in **Figure 12-2**. For new or very expensive purchases, the business purchasing process will typically be more detailed and involve more people.

Identify Needs

With business purchasing, even the first step in the decision-making process—need identification—is complex.

Remember that the demand for business products is derived from the needs of the business's customers. In addition, the needs of many parts of the business must be considered. Those needs may not always be the same and might even conflict with one another. For example, a company with declining sales may experience a conflict regarding the purchase of training services. The sales department believes that additional training will help salespeople serve customers more effectively and increase sales. The human resources department is inclined

PURCHASING BY FINAL CONSUMERS AND BUSINESS CONSUMERS

Final Consumers	Business Consumers
1. Identify needs	1. Identify needs
2. Gather information	2. Determine alternatives
3. Evaluate alternatives	3. Search for vendors
4. Make purchase decision	4. Select appropriate vendors
5. Evaluate decision	5. Negotiate a purchase
	6. Make purchase decision
	7. Evaluate decision

FIGURE 12-2 The decision-making process used by businesses is similar to, but more detailed than, that used by final consumers.

to reduce expenses because of lower sales and to cut back on the amount spent for training. This conflict must be resolved before a purchase decision can be made.

© goodluz/Shutterstock.com.

Which do you think would be the better approach to address declining sales: train salespeople in customer service or cut back on training to lower costs? Defend your answer.

Determine Alternatives

In the second step, the business attempts to determine the types of products or services that will meet its needs. Here the business decides whether an existing product meets the needs best or whether a new product will be better. The business will develop product specifications in order to clearly describe the product it needs.

Search for Vendors

Next the business begins the search for the products and services it needs to purchase. Companies that offer products for sale to other businesses are known as **vendors** or *suppliers*. In some businesses, the purchasing department is responsible for maintaining vendor lists for various types of products and services. It selects potential vendors based on certain criteria, including availability of products, quality, reliability, delivery, service, and price. Organizations such as ISO (International Organization for Standardization) have been formed to certify businesses that meet specific standards. Purchasers can make sure vendors they are considering are on the list of certified businesses that have met the high standards of the certifying organization. Vendors that implement **total quality management (TQM)** establish specific quality standards for all procedures. TQM teams made up of employees and managers study procedures and make recommendations for improvements.

B2B customers traditionally relied on account representatives from vendors approaching and building relationships with them. Technology is changing that. Now most B2B customers locate vendors and find information about them and their products on their own: The average B2B buyer reviews 10 to 12 sources to study features and compare prices and products before making a purchase. Studies show that before contacting a supplier most B2B customers are halfway to deciding with whom they want to do business or making a purchasing decision.

Select a Vendor

After the purchasing team has identified possible suppliers, it carefully evaluates them. Often, several vendors offer acceptable products, but the vendors may vary on other factors important to the buyer. The purchasing team will have to make a decision to determine what combination of vendor characteristics best meets its needs. It may use a procedure called vendor analysis to help with the decision. **Vendor analysis** is an objective rating system that buyers use to compare potential suppliers on purchasing criteria. The purchasing team will complete a *vendor analysis form*, such as the one shown in **Figure 12-3** for the purchase of vehicles for a business.

Negotiate a Purchase

The purchasing team will determine which of the products and suppliers best meet the business's needs, and it will begin negotiations with them. Negotiations are completed in several ways. If the company is buying a standard product or one it has purchased in the past, the negotiations are simple. The buyer and seller will discuss price, quantity, and delivery, and will agree on the terms of the sale. For some products, buyers may issue a request for proposal to potential suppliers. A **request for proposal (RFP)** contains a specific description of the type of product or service needed and the criteria that are important to the buyer. Suppliers then develop proposals that contain detailed descriptions of the product or service they can supply and the way they can meet the buyer's criteria.

The company that has completely determined its needs provides product specifications to the potential suppliers, who then demonstrate how they can meet those specifications. The most restrictive type of negotiation is known as bidding. In **bidding**, several suppliers develop

Vendor	Purchasing Criteria (10 = high; 1 = low)				
	Specifications	Warranty	Service	Price	Availability
Dodge	10	8	5	6	4
Ford	9	9	6	4	5
GMC	7	7	9	8	7
Toyota	8	4	7	5	6

VENDOR ANALYSIS FORM

FIGURE 12-3 If a company is planning to buy several new vehicles, it will usually analyze potential suppliers on important criteria in order to select the best vendor.

specific prices at which they will meet detailed purchase specifications and other criteria prepared by the buyer. The supplier that is able to respond to the buyer's requirements at the lowest price usually is selected. A bidding process is a common practice in selling to government agencies.

Make a Decision

After analyzing the information available, the buying team selects a supplier. Because several people are involved, the decision may be difficult to make because each person has different needs to satisfy—both business needs (what is best for the department) and personal needs (what is best for the person's career). Businesses try to specify criteria and develop purchasing procedures to avoid those types of problems.

When a decision is made, the purchasing department prepares a detailed purchase order or contract to send to the supplier to ensure that products are supplied in the form and quantity needed at the correct time and price.

Evaluate the Purchase

After a purchase is made, the buyer determines if the product meets the needs as well as possible. If businesses develop detailed specifications, they use those specifications in evaluating purchases. They also consider their customers' needs. Sometimes businesses complete the evaluation process before using the products. When the product is received, it may be inspected to ensure that it meets requirements. For products purchased in large quantities, such as raw materials or component parts, it may not be feasible to inspect every product. The purchaser may inspect small quantities and evaluate the samples.

When purchases meet the buyer's needs, the buyer usually will continue to purchase from the same supplier unless needs change or unless the supplier is no longer able to meet the buyer's purchasing requirements. If purchasing needs remain the same, the procedure becomes a repeat purchase, and reordering is managed by the purchasing department or the user department. The purchasing procedure may even be automated so reorders can be placed by a computer that monitors inventory levels.

Want to know more about what is trending with this topic? Click on **Lesson 12.3, Global Marketing,** *in your MindTap.*

Connect to MindTap

CHECKPOINT
What are the steps in the business purchasing process?

12.3.2 ▶ Processing Purchases

From the time decisions are made to order products until the products are ready for use or resale, a business must complete a number of purchasing procedures. It must maintain a variety of records, including inventory and purchasing records, to ensure proper completion of the procedures.

Inventory Records

Inventory is the assortment of products a business maintains. Inventory includes the products and materials needed to produce other products and services, to operate the business, or to resell to customers. Inventory management allows managers to be aware of the supply of products on hand at any time. That information helps managers to control costs and to ensure that operations can continue without interruption.

Inventory records are maintained to provide information about the products on hand in the business. That information can include the type of products, their source, age, condition, and value. It should also indicate how rapidly the inventory is used, when it should be reordered, and the sources of supply.

Two types of inventory systems are typically used by businesses: physical inventory and perpetual inventory. A **physical inventory system** determines the amount of product on hand by visually inspecting and counting the items. A physical inventory count is conducted on a regular basis, often every few months or twice a year.

A **perpetual inventory system** determines the amount of a product on hand by maintaining records on purchases and sales. Daily inventory levels determined through the perpetual system are maintained on computers. When a sale is made, information from the product label is entered into a computer system (usually via sales terminals), and the inventory level is automatically adjusted. Most businesses combine the use of physical and perpetual inventory systems. There will be differences between the inventory levels of each system. The discrepancies can result from products that have been stolen, damaged, or lost or from poorly maintained records. An important task in inventory management is to reduce losses and inventory records errors.

Purchasing Records

A buyer completes a **purchase order**—a form listing the variety, quantity, and prices of products ordered—and sends it to the seller to begin the purchasing process. The seller fills the order and sends it to the buyer with a **packing list**, an itemized listing of all of the products included in the shipment. At the same time, the seller sends an invoice to the buyer. The **invoice** includes a list of items purchased along with their prices, the total amount due, and a statement of the terms of payment for the order.

When the purchaser receives the merchandise, it will be unpacked and inspected for damage. The purchase will compile a **receiving record**, which is a list of the merchandise received in the shipment and its condition. The receiving record is compared to the packing list, and any discrepancies are noted. Both are forwarded to the accounting department to be compared to the purchase order and invoice before payment is made. Finally, the products that have been received are entered into the inventory records of the company and are distributed to the departments where they will be used or sold.

 CHECKPOINT
What two purchasing records does the buyer complete and what two purchasing records does the seller complete?

What steps should be taken if the receiving record does not match the packing list?

12.3 ASSESSMENT

What Have You Learned?

1. In what situation would a buyer issue a request for proposal (RFP) to potential suppliers? [12.3.1]

2. What is the difference between a physical inventory system and a perpetual inventory system? [12.3.2]

Make Academic Connections

1. **Math**   Companies strive to keep inventories low while still generating the planned sales volume. In 2018, a company had $1.56 of inventory for every $1 of sales. By 2023, effective management reduced that to $1.26 of inventory for each $1 of sales. If the company had average monthly sales of $565,500 in 2018 and $823,750 in 2023, what would be the value of its inventory in each of those years? [12.3.2]

2. **Technology**   Use the Internet to research the advantages of using a perpetual inventory system compared to a physical system. Prepare a one-page report on your findings. Prepare a bibliography of the resources used for your report. [12.3.2]

Connect to ◊DECA

Build your Portfolio

Your marketing team has been asked to prepare complete purchasing procedures that all departments in a large manufacturing business will follow when ordering new equipment. Prepare a flow chart that illustrates the procedure you recommend including a description of each step, who is involved, and how the effectiveness of each step will be determined. Present your flowchart to your teacher (judge) for evaluation. [12.3.1]

RETAIL PURCHASING

Learning Objectives

12.4.1 Describe how retailers identify customer needs and how to satisfy them.

12.4.2 Identify the ways retailers locate the products they need to satisfy their customers.

Key Terms

merchandise plan
basic stock list
model stock list

marketing matters

Retailers buy products from selected manufacturers and wholesalers for resale to final consumers in their target markets. After studying their customers, they develop detailed merchandise plans to organize the hundreds and thousands of items they carry. They follow carefully developed procedures to get the products on their shelves as quickly and efficiently as possible. They add new products and remove old ones from their merchandise plans to respond to changing customer needs.

essential question

Why is planning an inventory to satisfy customer needs often much more difficult for retailers than for other types of businesses?

12.4.1 Plan to Satisfy Customer Needs

Retailing is very competitive, so retailers must study customer needs carefully when making purchase decisions. A retailer has an advantage if it offers customers a product they want that its competitors do not have. If a company is able to sell a similar product at a lower price than its competitors, it will usually sell a larger quantity. Retailers constantly evaluate their direct competitors to determine what products are being sold at what prices.

Determine Customer Needs

Retailers use a great deal of marketing information and research to anticipate customer needs. Most retailers collect customer and product information each time a sale is made. Many have consumer panels and focus groups that meet regularly to evaluate new products. Most businesses encourage customers to identify products they want that are not available in the store.

Retail buyers and merchandise managers study information about the economy, competition, and new products. They attend meetings and trade shows and talk with the representatives of their suppliers. They carefully track the offerings, prices, and services of competitors in order to be aware of any changes or apparent advantages of those businesses.

Track Product Sales

Retailers carefully track the sales of each product in inventory to immediately determine sales trends. Computer technology aids in that process. Scanners at checkout counters are connected to computers that store inventory information. When a purchase is made, the scanner reads the barcode on each product. The barcode provides information such as product name, product type, price, manufacturer, and the date of purchase by the business. Managers analyze the information to use in decision making. For example, it can help them determine whether special displays, mark downs, or advertising programs increase the sales volume of specific products.

For retailers with multiple locations, each store's computer system is connected to other computers in regional or national offices. This allows managers to make purchasing decisions and adjust marketing plans quickly to ensure products are sold rapidly, products that do not sell are not reordered, and new purchases respond to customers' needs.

Develop a Merchandise Plan

Retail stores must offer an adequate assortment of products to meet customers' needs. Larger department stores and discount retailers offer hundreds of different products in many merchandise categories. Specialty stores offer less variety but a complete assortment of products in specialized categories.

©Yuriy Boyko/Shutterstock.com.

Businesses prepare merchandise plans to guide decision making. A **merchandise plan** identifies the types, assortments, prices, and quantities of products that will be stocked by the business for a specific period of time. The merchandise plan is like a budget in that it provides the basis for ordering merchandise and maintaining the store's inventory. The merchandise plan is used to determine the products to order, delivery schedules, the space allocations required, initial pricing strategies, and promotional plans.

The merchandise plan may be developed for a short time period, such as one month for a specific season in which unique merchandise will be sold, or for a longer time period up to six months.

The merchandise plan is developed from a basic stock list or a model stock list. **A basic stock list** identifies the products a store must have available to meet the most important needs of its customers. The products on the basic stock list will be reordered time and time again until there are major changes in the market or economy. The basic stock list will not change a great deal over time. It includes the products customers expect to find anytime they visit the store.

A **model stock list** identifies the complete assortment of products a store would like to offer to customers. The model stock list is more extensive than the basic stock list. It is also subject to change more frequently based on economic conditions, the financial resources of the business, and the changing needs of customers. A large national retailer may have a model stock list that identifies all possible product choices for local stores to offer. Each store manager then tailors the individual location's inventory to the specific needs and conditions in that area from the model stock list.

CHECKPOINT
What is a merchandise plan and why does a retailer need to develop one?

MARKETING COMMUNICATION

Write a Purchasing Policy

Purchasing goods involves more than just getting the right product at the right price. With any company's purchasing procedures, ethical questions can arise. Most companies should set a purchasing policy to address ethical issues even if the owner is responsible for purchasing.

The ethical questions a purchasing policy should answer include the following:

- What is the business's position on conflict of interest?
- Under what circumstances, if any, can gifts be accepted or personal loans be received from suppliers?
- What types of information does the company consider confidential?
- How are legal questions that arise from purchasing situations handled?
- What is the company's position on the environmental and labor policies of its suppliers?

Think Critically

1. As purchasing manager for a large company, write a clear, one-page policy that will help purchasers and suppliers avoid ethical problems.
2. Examine the following scenarios and determine if the purchasing team member has acted within the guidelines you set in your policy: A team member has accepted a gift such as a pen from a supplier. A team member has accepted a $5,000 loan from a supplier. A team member owns stock in the supplier's company. A team member becomes close friends with the supplier's salesperson. A team member has a relative who works for the supplier.

Retail buyers make purchases from both manufacturers and wholesalers. Their first responsibility is to gather information about vendors and their products. Once suppliers are selected, procedures are completed to order merchandise and to process the orders when they are received.

Buy from Vendors

Most retail buyers receive sales calls from vendors' salespeople. For smaller businesses, vendors meet with the store owner or manager. For large regional or national retail chains, the salespeople visit buying offices where buyers make decisions for many stores. Buyers often specialize in one type of product, so a salesperson may visit with several buyers during one trip to the office.

Sometimes retail buyers travel to trading centers for specific industries. For example, many furniture manufacturers open showrooms in High Point, North Carolina, where furniture retailers from all over the world travel to see the latest product lines. In the international diamond industry, most of the world's rough diamonds pass through Antwerp, Belgium. In the United States, which is the world's largest consumer of diamonds, the major trading centers are New York City's Diamond District along with Philadelphia's Jewelers' Row and Los Angeles's Jewelry District.

© 1000SHADES/Shutterstock.com.

Trade shows also offer an opportunity for retail buyers to examine the merchandise of many manufacturers. For example, there is a large international electronics trade show sponsored by the Consumer Electronics Association each year in Las Vegas. Vendors spend thousands of dollars on exhibits, demonstrations, and advertising to attract retailers looking for new products.

Retail buyers also may purchase through vendor catalogs and websites. This buying method is particularly useful for small retailers who cannot afford to travel to trade centers or trade shows and who do not purchase large enough quantities to warrant frequent visits from salespeople. Catalogs and websites also are used to sell standardized and frequently purchased items that are sold primarily on the basis of price and availability. Most manufacturers and wholesalers are moving many of their sales and customer support functions onto websites. Many automate the online ordering process for regular customers so that routine purchases can be made and orders can be filled automatically via the Web.

Complete the Purchase Process

Retail buyers continually identify and study vendors for the many purchases they will make. Vendors must meet specific criteria in order to be considered. Each retailer will have its own criteria and will communicate them to vendors. Those criteria may vary for different products in the store's merchandise assortment. Some products may be unique and can be obtained only from one source. Others may be rather common and can be obtained from a variety of vendors.

A product may be fast-selling or perishable, requiring the retailer to quickly replace items in inventory. The retailer will want to purchase from a supplier who can guarantee rapid and reliable delivery. Some products may be very competitive and can be purchased in many stores. The retailer's customers will shop for the lowest price, so a supplier must be located that will sell at competitive prices.

For new products, fashions, or seasonal items, the retailer may not be certain of the total amount of inventory that can be sold. The buyer may want to work with a vendor who will initially ship a small amount of inventory but who will be able to rapidly provide additional quantities if sales are higher than expected.

Most businesses have a standard procedure for ordering merchandise. The order must be placed far enough in advance to be sure it is delivered before the current stock is completely sold or in time for the selling season for the product. Retailers often have difficulty with the timing of orders. If the order is placed too soon, the merchandise arrives before it is needed, taking up space and adding to storage and handling costs. If

Want to know more about marketing in the information age? Click on **Lesson 12.4, Digital Marketing,** *in your MindTap.*

Connect to
MindTap

the order is late, the merchandise is not in stock when customers want it, and sales are lost.

For retailers with many stores, the seller ships the merchandise to the buyer's distribution center. The distribution center is used to assemble product orders for local stores and then to quickly reship them. For small stores, sellers will ship orders directly to the business or rely on an intermediary who prepares and delivers shipments to smaller customers.

When orders are received at the store, they are unpacked and prepared for sale. Again, each business has specific and careful procedures to follow in receiving, unpacking, inspecting, and preparing products for sale. Those procedures may require assembly, cleaning, pricing, or other types of processing, depending on the type of products.

Some stores have large storage areas where merchandise is maintained until needed on the selling floor. Others move most of the stock immediately onto shelves or into displays for sale. Preparing

WORKING IN TEAMS

As a team, identify problems with inventory that you have encountered in retail stores, such as out-of-stock items, product damage, and incorrect or missing prices. Discuss how stores might improve purchasing, receiving, and inventory procedures to reduce each of the problems.

merchandise for sale and moving it into inventory must be done carefully and efficiently with as little disruption to customers as possible.

Merchandise can be lost, stolen, or damaged during the receiving process. Because most retail businesses have very low profit margins, any significant loss at this time can affect the business's ability to make a profit.

CHECKPOINT
What is the first step retailers take in obtaining products for resale?

12.4 ASSESSMENT

What Have You Learned?

1. What type of information does the bar-code on a product provide? [12.4.1]
2. Why do retailers often have difficulty with the timing of orders? [12.4.2]

Make Academic Connections

1. **Career Success**   Go to the employment section of a national retailer's website and gather information on retail buying jobs. If no information is provided, send an email to the company requesting information. Based on your research, write a one-page report on the company, the career, and your interest in it. [12.4.1, 12.4.2]

2. **Economics**   Review local newspapers and other information sources to identify economic information that could affect retail sales in your community in the next six months. Prepare a two-minute oral report discussing the information and how retailers should respond to it. [12.4.1]

Connect to ◇DECA

Build your Portfolio

Your friend owns a gift shop located in a strip mall in your community. She purchases a variety of products from many vendors. Many of the products she sells are holiday related. She has asked for your assistance in preparing a schedule that lists the holidays and indicates the dates by which she will need to order the items to guarantee receipt in time for holiday shopping. Assume the products will need to be ordered at least four months in advance of delivery. Present your schedule to your teacher (judge) for evaluation. [12.4.2]

Connect to MindTap

*Analyze a case study that focuses on chapter concepts. Click on **Chapter 12, Case Study,** in your MindTap.*

Just as corporations use financial statements to track and analyze their financial status, individuals use personal financial statements to measure their financial health.

Balance Sheet

An important measure of your long-term financial strength is an increasing net worth. Your net worth is determined with a balance sheet using the basic formula:

Net Worth = Total Assets − Total Liabilities

Determining net worth by preparing a balance sheet can help you assess whether you have enough assets to pay your debts.

Total assets include both current and long-term assets. Current assets include checking and savings accounts, money owed to you that will be paid in the near future, and cash on hand or in the bank. Long-term assets might include long-term savings and investments, such as certificates of deposit, stocks, bonds, and other things of value you own such as a car. Later on, long-term assets might include the cash value of life insurance, real estate, retirement plans, and other long-term investments.

Current liabilities include current bills owed, money you have borrowed, and payments on purchases. If you have a job, income taxes you will owe at the end of the year are current liabilities. Later, your rent will be a current liability. Long-term liabilities are amounts you owe that will be paid over a period longer than a year, such as a car loan. In future years, long-term liabilities may include a home mortgage or payments on loans to pay for your education.

Personal Cash Flow Statement

A personal cash flow statement shows where immediate income (cash) is coming from and how it will be used during a defined short time period, such as a month. Your monthly personal cash flow can be defined as:

Monthly Cash Flow = Monthly Income Received − Monthly Expenses Paid

Income could be money from your job, any sporadic income (from snow shoveling jobs or birthday gifts), or your allowance. Interest on savings is considered income when it is paid. Later, if you have income from investments, rental property, or loans, it would appear in your cash flow statement in the month it is received.

Expenses are payments you make for clothing, entertainment, and other things. If you borrow money, the payments you make are expenses. Later, expenses may include mortgage payments, utilities, and taxes.

You need to calculate cash flow to make sure you have enough cash to pay your bills. If not, you will have to use savings or borrow money, which hurts your overall financial position. Your goal should be to have a positive cash flow most months and a growing net worth over time. If your net worth is negative, but your current cash flow is positive, you can construct a plan to improve your net worth. People who have a negative cash flow and net worth will struggle with poor financial health.

Develop Your Skill

To analyze your financial health, use the Internet to locate forms for a personal balance sheet and cash flow statement. Using these forms, construct a sample balance sheet and cash flow statement that reflect the financial position you would like to have in 10 years. What changes will you have to make to achieve that financial position?

CHAPTER 12 ASSESSMENT

Review Marketing Concepts

1. Your school operates as a business. Cite examples of items in your classroom that were purchased as a business-to-business transaction. [12.1.1]

2. You are a salesperson who sells computer hardware. Would you concentrate your efforts on selling to producers or to government organizations? Explain your answer. [12.1.2]

3. How does the buyer/seller relationship in the business-to-business market differ from that in the consumer market? [12.1.3]

4. As a computer salesperson, which type of purchasing situation—new purchase, modified purchase, or repeat purchase—would you most value? Discuss actions you could take to preserve this purchasing situation with clients. [12.2.1]

5. You have two sales calls to make today. One is a sales presentation to an office manager at a small company and the other is to a purchasing manager at a large corporation. Explain how your two presentations will differ. [12.2.2]

6. Your company makes component parts for machines and wants to explore selling the parts in overseas markets. Why should the company establish a relationship with a bank that has experience in international finance? [12.2.3]

7. How could ISO certification benefit a computer component manufacturer? [12.3.1]

8. Why do a business's inventory and purchasing records need to be accurate? [12.3.2]

9. From an inventory perspective, explain the importance to a retailer of tracking product sales. [12.4.1]

10. Compare and contrast a basic stock list and a model stock list. [12.4.1]

11. Why do you think manufacturers and wholesalers are moving many of their sales and customer support functions onto their websites? How does this benefit both the vendors and the customers? [12.4.2]

Marketing Research and Planning

1. Use the Internet to find the website of a company engaged in each of the types of businesses listed below. Develop a table to provide the following information: company name, its URL address, major products or services it sells, and how it markets those products or services to other businesses. [12.1.2]

   a. automobile manufacturer

   b. insurance company

   c. office supplies

   d. industrial chemicals

   e. financial services

   f. work uniforms

   g. freight transportation

   h. temporary personnel

2. Identify a major purchase decision you might make within the next five years (college, new automobile, apartment, etc.). Then outline the specific steps you could follow to make the purchase. After you have outlined the steps, prepare a vendor analysis form. List the factors that you will consider when making the purchase. Develop numerical values for each factor that reflect its relative importance to you. Create the form so that it can be completed as

you evaluate several companies or organizations that provide the product or service. [12.3.2]

3. Form a team with two or three other students. As a team, select one of the following topics related to business-to-business marketing. Research the topic by reading marketing books, current business magazines, and other business resources. You might be able to identify a businessperson or other resource person in your community who is an expert on the topic to interview. Prepare a three- to five-minute oral report on the topic and include three visuals.

a. Census data on business customers [12.1.2]

b. Working with international vendors [12.2.3]

c. Using benchmarking to develop product specifications [12.3.1]

d. Manufacturers' markets and trade shows [12.4.1]

e. New technology for retail inventory management [12.4.1]

Marketing Management and Decision Making

1. A vendor wanted to determine what factors were most important to its customers when making purchase decisions. It conducted a survey of purchasing agents and asked them to assign a value from 0 to 5 for six factors they consider when purchasing products. The values ranged from 0 (not considered when making a purchase decision) to 5 (most important factor in the purchase decision). **Table 1** shows results from 140 respondents.

a. The vendor wanted to use the data to develop an average value for each of the factors. Calculate the mean value for each factor by multiplying the value by the number of respondents selecting that value, totaling the result for all six value scores for the factor, and then dividing the result by 140 (the total number of respondents).

b. The vendor asked a focus group to compare one of the vendor's products to similar products sold by two other competitors using the six factors from the research study. The focus group assigned each product a score ranging from 1 to 10 for each of the six factors, with 1 being the lowest rating and 10 being the highest rating. The results of the focus group ratings are shown in **Table 2**.

TABLE 1

| Factors | Value | | | | | |
	5	4	3	2	1	0
Price	0	40	55	32	3	0
Delivery Schedule	45	38	36	20	1	0
Vendor Reputation	0	24	38	52	18	8
Past Experience with Vendor	7	10	68	55	0	0
Vendor Service after Sale	0	5	12	22	36	65
Product Quality	110	24	6	0	0	0

TABLE 2

| Factors | Product | | |
	Vendor A	Vendor B	Vendor C
Price	6	8	10
Delivery Schedule	8	5	7
Vendor Reputation	7	7	5
Experience with Vendor	3	9	6
Service after Sale	8	4	6
Product Quality	10	7	8

The vendor then used the information from the original marketing research study to develop a product score for each company. The mean score for each factor (calculated from the research study results in Part a) was multiplied by the rating assigned to that factor by the focus group (from the second table). Then the results for each of the six factors were totaled, giving each company a final score. That procedure would predict that the company whose product received the highest score would be the one that best met the purchaser's needs. Calculate the total product score for each company using the procedure described. Then be prepared to discuss the meaning of the results in terms of customer perceptions of the three companies' products. [12.2.1]

2. May Randall is the purchasing manager for Protective Insurance Company. The company is installing a wireless network and is providing a new desktop computer or laptop for each employee. The company maintains all company records in a large mainframe computer. The new computers will need to be compatible with the wireless network and current mainframe hardware and software. Working with managers from each of the major divisions of the company, May has developed purchase specifications for the new computers and has identified four potential vendors. One of the vendors is the supplier of the current mainframe, but each of

the other vendors has assured May that their machines meet the specifications.

May is now faced with important decisions. First, should Protective Insurance buy all of the computers from one vendor or allow divisions to order from different vendors? Each division has different computing needs and vendor preferences. By choosing only one vendor, everything would be standardized, there may be a lower price, and service would be handled by one company. But if the vendor is not reliable, it will affect the entire company. Using more than one supplier allows each division to choose its preferred computer and vendor, but it can create service and support problems as well as less opportunity for price negotiations with vendors. May wonders if preference should be given to the vendor of Protective's current equipment. The company and its equipment have been very reliable, and service has been efficient and effective. However, the company has less experience with wireless systems than the other vendors. How would you recommend that May resolve the issues the company is facing? [12.2.2]

Let's Start a Band! Follow-Up Discussion

Work in small teams to discuss the question posed at the end of the opening vignette. Should the band seek a partnership with the pet food company? Brainstorm the pros and cons of doing so.

Build Your Marketing Plan

Build your **Portfolio**

In this chapter you learned about purchasing decisions and procedures. You will now apply this learning to the development of your marketing plan. To access the chapter-specific tools that you will need to complete this activity, please navigate to Chapter 12 → Build Your Marketing Plan in MindTap. Alternatively, you can access these tools online at NGLSync. Please visit www.nglsync.cengage.com, and search for the companion website that accompanies this book by entering the ISBN, author, or title. Once you locate this companion website, navigate to Build Your Marketing Plan → Chapter 12.

Retail Merchandising Series Event

Build your Portfolio

The owner of Luxury Furniture wants to increase sales. He has asked you to describe customer and sales associate incentive plans to increase sales.

The customer incentive plan must include special discounts and sales promotions when customers' annual furniture purchases reach different levels throughout the year.

The incentive plan for sales associates must reward employees for reaching different sales goals throughout the year.

You have also been asked to describe a database for customer information that will be used to communicate with customers. The owner wants to know what information will be included in the database. He is interested in information about bulk mailings that will be sent to loyal customers of Luxury Furniture.

Your plan for increasing sales must include training and development for sales associates to improve customer satisfaction. You must describe follow-up communication that sales associates will send to customers after their purchase of furniture. You must also describe a special sales event that will create excitement and increase customer traffic in the store.

You will meet with the owner of Luxury Furniture in his office to explain your plan for increasing the company's furniture sales. You

are allowed 10 minutes to describe your plan for increasing sales and maintaining a loyal customer base. During or after the presentation, the judge can ask questions.

Performance Indicators Evaluated

- Identify data monitored for marketing decision making. (Marketing-Information Management)
- Explain the types of promotion. (Promotion)
- Explain the selling process. (Selling)
- Explain the role of customer service as a component of selling relationships. (Selling)
- Plan follow-up strategies for use in retail selling. (Selling)

Go to the DECA website for more detailed information. **www.deca.org**

Think Critically

1. Why is follow-up communication so important for customer satisfaction?

2. What type of promotion would require the customer to come to the furniture store?

3. What types of credit incentives increase furniture sales?

4. Why is a customer database a good marketing tool?

CHAPTER 13

DISTRIBUTION

Connect to MindTap

See how effective advertising leads to successful marketing strategies.
Click on Chapter 13, Visual Focus, **in your MindTap.**

Let's Start a Band!

> "I had business experience.... but the music business was completely new to me. I knew nothing about distribution, or any of those things."
>
> – Greg Ginn, Singer–Songwriter, founding member of punk rock band Black Flag

You remember our first gig. It was a train wreck. What were we thinking? We just wanted to get on stage. But then what was the venue thinking, having us open for some punk rockers?

It reminded me of that old Blues Brothers movie. You know the one where they show up at a country–western venue and tell the owner they're the "Good 'ol Boys"? When they start playing blues, the audience throws bottles at them until they switch and play "Rawhide" and "Stand By Your Man." The audience would have done the same thing to us at our first gig, but Layla held us together. So, we started before a crowd that didn't want to see us and definitely didn't come to hear us. But she won them over and got us through it. I think that night really went a long way in turning us into a band rather than just a group of people who played music together.

Still it was an eye-opener for us. And while we've learned a lot about where we should be playing and who our audience is, we need to think more in terms of distribution, where the band is the product. I'm wondering if you can help us with this. Before agreeing to play somewhere, what should we consider that will give us the best chance for success?

Learning Objectives

13.1.1 Explain the importance of the distribution function to effective marketing.

13.1.2 Describe how a well-planned distribution system supports the marketing plan.

Key Terms

distribution function
supply chain

marketing matters

Distribution is concerned with matching production with consumption and is therefore considered to be the most complex and challenging marketing function. Distribution usually involves several businesses in what is known as a distribution or supply channel. Because each member of a distribution channel has its own marketing strategy, businesses must choose distribution partners wisely and manage their distribution systems carefully.

essential question

What do customers expect from an effective distribution system when they purchase a product? What do the businesses that use a distribution system to get products to customers expect from that system?

13.1.1 ▶ The Importance of Distribution Activities

Distribution is the most complex and challenging part of marketing. Many companies, activities, and people are involved in the distribution of products and services from the producer to the consumer. Large portions of marketing budgets are spent on distribution activities. For most products and services, distribution activities account for more than 50 percent of the total marketing costs.

The Distribution Function

Distribution is the oldest and most basic part of marketing. In fact, even before the term *marketing* was a part of business

language, the term *distribution* was used to describe the activities that directed the flow of goods and services between producers and consumers. Today, because marketing activities have expanded, distribution is just one of the important marketing functions. The **distribution function** involves determining the best methods and procedures to use so that prospective customers can locate, obtain, and use a business's products and services.

Consumers are not even aware of distribution when it works well—when products and services are available where and when people want them and in a usable condition. However, when distribution does not work, it is very evident. Products are out of stock, back-ordered, available only in the wrong styles or sizes, out of date, or damaged. Prices are incorrectly marked or missing. Salespeople do not have adequate product information, or products advertised in the newspaper are not available in the store. Much of the dissatisfaction consumers have with businesses results from poor distribution.

Distribution as an Economic Concept

Distribution is an important activity for the effective operation of any economic system, and it is essential in a free enterprise economy. Free enterprise is based on the matching of production and consumption decisions. When businesspeople decide to produce a product, the product will not be successful unless consumers can obtain it. When consumers have a demand for a particular type of product or service, that demand will not be satisfied until they can locate the desired product. Distribution aids in matching supply and demand.

Distribution has a major impact on economic utility. Recall that economic utility is the amount of satisfaction a consumer receives from the consumption of a particular product or service. Businesses can increase customer satisfaction by improving the form of a product or service, making it available at a more convenient time or place, or making it more affordable. As you consider the four types of economic utility, you can

Why does distribution play an important role in customer satisfaction?

see that distribution has the most direct effect on time and place utility. However, it can also affect the form of a product by making sure that products are fresh and undamaged when they are distributed. Efficient distribution also affects the final product cost, so it is a factor in possession utility.

Distribution as a Marketing Mix Element

Another way of seeing the importance of distribution is to examine the marketing mix. Distribution as a part of the marketing mix involves the locations and methods used to make the product available to customers. When a marketer develops a marketing strategy and prepares a marketing plan, distribution decisions can determine whether the customer is able to easily locate and purchase the products and services needed.

Distribution in the Supply Chain

Finally, distribution is a part of a larger process known as a supply chain. A **supply chain** is the flow of products, resources, and information through all of the organizations involved in producing and marketing a company's products. A supply chain is complex and usually involves several businesses. Those businesses must cooperate rather than compete to ensure that customer needs are satisfied and all businesses make a profit. Distribution is the part of the supply chain that facilitates the physical flow of goods.

Members of a supply chain benefit from close cooperation and sharing of information. Effective supply chains have developed secure procedures to coordinate the electronic exchange of information through their marketing information systems. They cooperate in marketing research, cost controls, and determining customer satisfaction.

CHECKPOINT
What does the distribution function involve?

13.1.2 ▶ Distribution as Part of the Marketing Plan

A well-planned distribution system supports the marketing plan. A description of how a product will be distributed is included in the marketing strategy section of the plan. The description should build on the target market information, addressing how to best reach those consumers. It will reflect the company's decision regarding whether to engage in direct selling, use a distribution partner, or both.

Companies may build a supply chain for the product. They may involve partners or intermediaries to help get the widest possible distribution for the product. For other products they may choose to be more selective in who to include in the supply chain. For example, the marketing plan may identify a target market concentrated in a specific geographical area or distribution may be limited by production. In some cases, a company may decide to give a partner exclusive distribution rights.

WORKING IN TEAMS

Share with team members personal experiences you have had with businesses that illustrate effective and ineffective distribution. Discuss how the experiences shaped your views about the companies. As a team, develop several recommendations about how companies can improve customer satisfaction through effective distribution.

This often occurs with luxury items that are only sold in specific stores.

Any time a product or service is marketed to a customer, several distribution decisions must be made for a satisfactory exchange to occur. These decisions, which should be addressed in the marketing plan, include:

- Where and when will the product be produced, sold, and used?
- What characteristics of the product or service will affect distribution?
- What services or activities must be provided in order for the product to be successfully sold?
- Is special physical handling needed?

- Who will be responsible for each of the needed distribution activities?
- When will each activity occur?
- Who is responsible for planning and managing the distribution process?

CHECKPOINT
In which section of the marketing plan is the distribution system described?

13.1 ASSESSMENT

What Have You Learned?

1. Of the four types of economic utility (form, time, place, and possession), on which two types does distribution have the most direct effect? [13.1.1]

2. Where does distribution fit into the supply chain? [13.1.2]

3. For what types of products do companies often give a distribution partner exclusive rights to sell a product? [13.1.2]

Make Academic Connections

1. **Statistics** Ask 20 people to identify a recent problem they had when shopping for a product or service at a local business. Classify each response according to the marketing mix element that seemed to be the reason for the problem—product, price, distribution, or promotion. Total the numbers for each mix element and

develop a graph that illustrates the results of your research. [13.1.1]

2. **Economics** Review newspapers, business magazines, and the Internet to locate information on a situation where there is an imbalance of supply and demand resulting from a distribution problem. Write a short report on the situation, identifying who is affected, the problems that have resulted, why the situation occurred, and what is being done to resolve the economic imbalance. [13.1.1]

Connect to ◇DECA

Build your Portfolio

Develop a two-minute presentation on the importance of distribution in implementing the marketing concept. Provide examples of effective distribution to illustrate your points. Give your presentation to your teacher (judge). [13.1.2]

Planning a Career In...
SUPPLY CHAIN MANAGEMENT

How can companies ensure that vendors understand their needs? Whether it is raw materials for manufacturing or finished goods for retailing, companies need to have a coordinated strategy for communicating and managing their needs—both within their own organizations and with their suppliers.

Job Titles

- Demand Forecasting Specialist
- Logistics Supervisor
- Materials Manager
- Supply Chain Integration Manager
- Regional Logistics Director

Needed Skills

- A bachelor's degree is usually required with specialized study an advantage. A master's degree is increasingly needed for advanced positions.
- Strong analytical, technological, interpersonal, and negotiation skills are needed.
- Professional certification or training in production and inventory management or lean manufacturing is an asset.

Connect to MindTap

Discover more about the outlook for this career and watch a video about a related career. Click on **Chapter 13, Planning a Career In...** *in your MindTap.*

What it's like to work in... Supply Chain Management

Ingrid, a distribution analyst for a large plastics manufacturer, is attending her team's monthly forecasting meeting. Demand for Ingrid's product line, the plastics used to produce laundry-detergent containers, is being reviewed. Representatives from Sales, Marketing, and the Forecasting Analysis groups are in the meeting.

Her company's forecasting software uses historical sales to project future demand. Information from sales representatives regarding the anticipated loss or growth of business can be manually entered into the forecasting system.

After the forecasts are electronically updated, Ingrid reviews their impact on the production schedule. When planning production, Ingrid needs to balance existing customer orders, forecasted customer orders, and current inventory levels against future manufacturing schedules. Her job is to make sure that each type of product is available when customers need it without excess inventory.

Rumors about raw material shortages cause Ingrid to call her counterpart at the manufacturing plant to see if there is need for concern. If shortages are anticipated, she will contact the sales manager so that she can have the sales force talk to customers about immediate needs. Order prioritization can occur after all needs are assessed.

What About You?

Would you like to use information from all areas of the supply chain—from raw materials through finished product demand—to help a company optimize its production operations?

DISTRIBUTION CHANNELS

Learning Objectives

13.2.1 Identify the differences between producers and consumers that are addressed by supply chains and distribution channels.

13.2.2 Describe the differences between direct and indirect channels of distribution.

Key Terms

channel of distribution
direct channel
indirect channel
channel captain

marketing matters

Businesses develop channels of distribution to perform the many marketing functions needed any time an exchange takes place with a final consumer. Products are sometimes distributed directly from the producer or manufacturer to the final customer. More often, other specialized businesses complete the activities needed to move products from producers to final consumers. The number and type of businesses are selected to help adjust differences in quantity, assortment, location, and timing that would otherwise prevent a satisfying exchange between the producer and the consumer.

essential question

How can the use of other businesses in a distribution channel improve the efficiency and effectiveness of the exchange process between a producer and its customers?

13.2.1 The Role of Distribution Channels

When products and services are exchanged, they move through a channel of distribution. A **channel of distribution** is made up of the organizations and individuals who participate in the movement and exchange of products and services from the producer to the final consumer. The channel can be very simple, involving only the producer and the final consumer, or it can be very complex, involving many businesses. For example, if you buy a local newspaper, it is often edited, printed, and distributed by one company. If you buy a copy of *USA Today*, it is written and edited by one company in Washington, DC, printed by one of many other companies located in various parts of the country, and then distributed and sold by other companies.

There are several reasons that channels of distribution are needed in marketing. They adjust various differences between producers and consumers, provide marketing functions, and increase market efficiency.

Adjust Differences between Producers and Consumers

What producers develop and what consumers need often differ. Channels of distribution allow for adjustments to be made in those differences so that the available products match the customers' needs. Consumers want to be able to buy a variety of products from many different companies. Adjustments usually are needed in the quantity and assortment of products, the location of the products, and the timing of production and consumption.

DIFFERENCES IN QUANTITY

Businesses sell their products to large numbers of customers. They produce thousands or even millions of those products in order to meet the total market demand. Individual consumers usually buy only a very small quantity of a product at any time. So, a channel of distribution must be able to adjust the large quantity produced by the business to match the small quantity needed by a consumer.

DIFFERENCES IN ASSORTMENT

A producer or manufacturer often specializes in production. A company typically produces a limited variety of products in one or a few product classifications. Yet consumers desire a great variety of products. A channel of distribution helps provide an assortment of products. The channel accumulates products from a number of manufacturers and makes them available in one location to give consumers adequate choice and variety.

DIFFERENCES IN LOCATION

Customers usually are not located close to where products are produced. They live throughout the country and the world. It would be nearly impossible for each manufacturer and consumer to meet to complete an exchange. A channel of distribution moves the product from the place where it is produced to the variety of places where it will be consumed.

DIFFERENCES IN TIMING OF PRODUCTION AND CONSUMPTION

For efficiency, most manufacturers operate year-round to produce an adequate supply of products. However, many of those products are not used year-round. Snow blowers, swimwear, garden tools, and children's toys are all examples of products consumers purchase in higher quantities during certain times of the year.

Producers of agricultural products may only be able to produce some products in specific growing seasons. Consumers want products such as fresh fruits and vegetables throughout the year. This presents a challenge to distributors to match seasonal agricultural production with year-round consumer demand. Making adjustments between the time of production and consumption is another responsibility of the channel of distribution.

Walk through a supermarket and study the adjustments made for the products sold there. Food has been accumulated from throughout the world. Some is fresh and some is processed. The wheat used in the bread and cereal may have been produced many months ago, processed into the products you see on the shelf, and distributed to many stores. The fruits and vegetables may have been rushed by airplane and refrigerated truck from fields in the United States or South America and delivered to the store only a few days after being harvested. Eggs and meat are evaluated and sorted so that you can purchase them in different quantities and grades. Soft drinks have been accumulated from several local and regional bottlers so that you can have a variety of choices. If the channels of distribution have worked well, the store will be stocked with all of the products you want to buy.

Provide Marketing Functions

In any exchange between producer and consumer, all of the marketing functions must be performed. If no other organizations or individuals are involved in the exchange, either the producer or consumer will need to perform the functions. Often neither of those participants is willing or able to perform some of the functions. Other organizations or individuals then have the opportunity to become part of the supply chain or channel of distribution and perform the needed functions.

Consider marketing activities such as transportation, financing, or promotion. Some businesses do not have the special equipment, technology, or personnel to complete those functions. However, the functions must be completed in order for the product to be sold to the consumer. Trucking companies, railroads, and airlines can provide transportation. Banks and finance companies provide credit to businesses and consumers. Wholesalers and retailers purchase products from manufacturers to resell at a profit. Advertising agencies, television and radio stations, magazines, newspapers, Internet websites, and search engines provide promotional assistance.

Increase Marketing Efficiency

If all exchanges of products and services occurred directly between producers and consumers, marketing activities would require a great deal of time. Consider the number of products you and your family purchase during one week. What if you had to locate and contact each producer and manufacturer, agree on a price, and find a way to get the product home? You would spend most of your time on those marketing activities, and it would be an expensive process.

A carefully planned channel of distribution results in a much more efficient exchange. When other businesses enter the channel of distribution, they take over many of the marketing responsibilities, saving you both time and money. The other businesses are convenient, purchase the products you want, and find the most efficient ways to make them available.

CHECKPOINT
Name three reasons channels of distribution are needed in marketing.

13.2.2 ▶ Plan and Manage Distribution Channels

In order to have an effective distribution system, a company must carefully plan the channels of distribution it will use. It must identify participants and consider methods for developing and managing the channel. The channel of distribution will be most effective if all participants follow the marketing concept, cooperate with one another, and direct their efforts toward satisfying customer needs.

Channel Participants

Channel members include all of the businesses in the distribution channel. There are both direct and indirect channels of distribution. In a **direct channel**, the producer sells the product to the final consumer. In a direct channel, either the producer or consumer is responsible for completing each marketing function. In an **indirect channel**, other businesses between the producer and the consumer perform one or more marketing functions. Channel members buy the product from the producer or other members and sell to consumers or other businesses. Each channel member provides one or more of the marketing functions in an indirect channel. **Figure 13-1** illustrates the flow of consumer goods in both direct and indirect distribution channels.

A business chooses between a direct channel and an indirect channel based on several factors. Indirect channels are used most often in the sale of consumer products whereas direct channels are more typical in business-to-business marketing. But there are many exceptions to that pattern. Some manufacturers use direct marketing methods such as catalogs, telephone sales, and factory outlets to reach final consumers. The Internet also allows more direct marketing for consumer products, although many businesses still use indirect channels and include sales, distribution, and customer service specialists as a part of their Internet marketing efforts. Also, manufacturers that sell to businesses across large geographic areas and in other countries often rely on other businesses to help them with selling, distribution, and other marketing functions.

Direct channels of distribution are most often selected in these cases:

- There are a small number of consumers.

- Consumers are located in a limited geographic area.

- The product is complex, developed to meet specific customer needs, or requires a great deal of service.

- The business wants to maintain close control over the marketing mix.

If the opposite market characteristics exist, an indirect channel of distribution usually will be developed.

Manufacturers often use both direct and indirect distribution, depending on the target market selected. They also may use multiple channels to distribute a product. This decision is consistent with the marketing concept because several target markets can exist for the same product. The needs and purchasing behavior of each target market can be quite different.

Think of all of the different customers and needs a carpet manufacturer must meet. The same basic product may be sold directly to a contractor who is building several large office buildings and indirectly to small businesses and individual homeowners. To reach a variety of final consumers, the carpet might be sold through department stores, home improvement centers, and specialty carpet and flooring businesses. Some of those businesses will be contacted by the company's salespeople while some very small retail businesses might buy from a

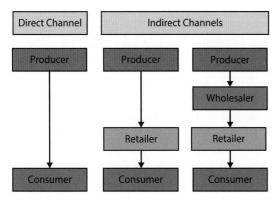

FIGURE 13-1 In direct channels of distribution, consumer goods flow from producer to consumer. In indirect channels, goods flow through other businesses such as a wholesaler and retailer before reaching the consumer.

wholesaler or another business that sells carpets for several manufacturers. The possible channels of distribution for a carpet manufacturer are illustrated in **Figure 13-2**.

Develop and Manage a Channel System

Developing an effective channel of distribution is important if a marketing strategy is going to be successful. Few products can be distributed using a direct channel. Therefore, channels must be developed carefully so that the product reaches the customers in the form they want, at the appropriate time and location, and at a price they can afford. Channel development and management is an important task for marketers.

Any business or individual can take responsibility for developing a channel of distribution. A manufacturer that develops a new product wants to find the best way to get the product to the target market. A retailer who discovers an important customer need will try to find a source of products that will satisfy that need.

COOPERATION OR CONFLICT?

Channels of distribution usually are made up of independent businesses that treat one another as suppliers and customers as products move between them. They each have their own goals and customers and cooperate only when it benefits them. This may lead to problems and conflict. For example, if a manufacturer has a very large inventory of one product and a limited supply of another, it is more likely to try to sell the first to retailers without too much concern for what the retailer will do with the product. If a retailer is competing with another business that is cutting prices, it will try to force manufacturers and wholesalers to cut their prices. The

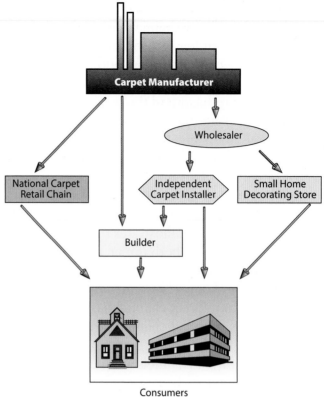

Multiple Channels of Distribution for Carpets

FIGURE 13-2 Once carpeting is produced, it may move through several channels of distribution before reaching the final consumer.

retailer usually will not worry whether those companies will make a profit. Also, it is sometimes difficult for a business that is a member of a channel of distribution but does not work directly with the final consumer to be concerned about satisfying the final consumer's needs.

CHANNEL MANAGEMENT RESPONSIBILITIES A channel of distribution must be well managed to effectively coordinate all of the activities needed to achieve a satisfying exchange. Managing a channel of distribution is the responsibility of the channel captain. The **channel captain** takes responsibility to identify channel members, assign distribution activities, help members agree on performance standards, and facilitate communication among channel members. The channel captain often is the biggest company in the channel of distribution. However, it will not be effective if it uses its size to "bully" the other companies. Instead, the captain must work to satisfy the needs of each business and allow each to make a reasonable profit.

When a company works independently to achieve its goals, effective channel management is difficult. However, when several organizations work cooperatively, they often find new opportunities and methods to successfully meet customer needs better than competitors that do not cooperate.

CHANNEL MANAGEMENT TOOLS

Technology is available to help manage a channel of distribution. *Supply-chain management (SCM) software* is used to collect and manage the information needed by each channel member. The needed information includes raw materials and finished product inventories, production and sales records, storage and shipping data, and costs of each distribution activity. Customer information is tracked using *customer-relationship management (CRM) software*. The software analyzes target market and individual customer sales records, product requests, returns, and new market opportunities.

The efficient exchange of information among departments in a company and among businesses in a supply chain has been improved with the introduction of

MATH IN MARKETING

Measuring Product Movement through the Channels

In order to gauge how well their products are doing, businesses that use intermediaries such as independent wholesalers and distributors need to distinguish between two measures of product movement. One measure is the businesses' own sales, including orders from their distributors. The other measure is the sales or deliveries that distributors make to retailers. This measure often is referred to as "depletion" because it is a measure of the rate at which distributors sell or "deplete" their product inventories.

The relationship between sales and depletions can be a good indicator of future sales trends. If sales are lower than depletions for a given time period, then the distributor's inventories will decrease. In that case, the distributor will have to buy more products to maintain inventory levels. If sales to the distributor exceed depletions, it means inventories will grow. That might indicate that sales to the distributor will have to slow to keep inventories from becoming overstocked. This may lead to a slowdown in production. In some cases, a growing inventory might be a favorable signal, indicating that distributors and retailers are building inventories because they anticipate a pickup in sales.

Do the Math

1. If sales for the just-completed quarter fall by 2,000 cases, and distributor depletions increase by 10,000 cases, what is the implied change in inventory levels at the company's distributors?

2. If a car manufacturer finds that its shipments to dealers for the past month increased by 25,000 cars while dealers' depletions increased by 15,000 cars, what is the implied change in dealers' inventory levels?

electronic data interchange (EDI). EDI allows direct computer-to-computer exchanges of information such as invoices, sales and inventory records, and product location and transportation records. Because information is converted to a standard EDI format, the information can be easily shared and analyzed in order to speed decisions and distribution activities. Also, because the information is exchanged from computer to computer, there is no need to enter information more than once, cutting costs and reducing the chance of human error.

CHECKPOINT
What is the difference between a direct and an indirect channel of distribution?

13.2 ASSESSMENT

What Have You Learned?

1. What are the four differences between producers and consumers that are adjusted by distribution channels? [13.2.1]

2. Explain the responsibilities of a channel caption. [13.2.2]

Make Academic Connections

1. **Math** A tomato farmer has used direct distribution to sell to local consumers through an area farmers' market. Last year, she sold 400 bushels of tomatoes at $2.49 a pound. (There are 53 pounds in a bushel of tomatoes.) This year she is considering using an indirect channel by selling to two area supermarkets. She estimates that she can sell 650 bushels at $1.63 a pound. What will be the difference in revenue if she makes the change? What other factors should the farmer consider before changing to indirect distribution? [13.2.1]

2. **English** Prepare a one-page written analysis of the following statement: "If there are conflicts among channel members, the channel captain should make decisions that are in the best interest of his or her business." [13.2.2]

Connect to ◇DECA

Build your Portfolio

Your team works for a manufacturer of sunglasses with a unique coating that offers better UV eye protection than existing products. Identify one method of direct distribution and two possible indirect channels. Analyze advantages and disadvantages of each and choose the one your team believes is best. Make a three-minute team presentation of your analysis and recommendation to your teacher (judge). Prepare two visuals to support your presentation. [13.2.1]

13.3 THE ROLE OF WHOLESALING

Learning Objectives

13.3.1 Describe the benefits that wholesalers provide to other members of a distribution channel and to final consumers.

13.3.2 Explain how the role of wholesalers is evolving.

Key Terms

wholesalers
wholesale member clubs

marketing matters

Wholesale businesses play an important role in many distribution channels. They perform several specialized distribution activities as products and services move from producers to their final points of use. Because of their ability to specialize and achieve economies of scale, wholesalers can provide access to new and international markets and to small and medium-sized companies and retailers.

essential question

Why is it difficult for many businesses, especially small businesses, to deal directly with producers and manufacturers to obtain the products they need?

13.3.1 Who Needs Wholesaling?

Many marketing functions occur in the exchange between a producer and consumer. They can be shifted and shared, but they cannot be eliminated. In many cases, producers or consumers are unwilling or unable to perform some of the functions. In other cases, they can and will perform the functions, but other organizations can complete those activities more effectively, in less time, or at a lower cost. In those cases, an additional organization is likely to become part of the channel of distribution.

A traditional indirect channel of distribution for consumer products would involve a producer, a retailer, and the final consumers. However, the producer may find there are so many consumers in a target market, it cannot effectively serve all the retailers needed to reach them. A retailer may find it needs to work with such a large number of producers to obtain all the products it wants to sell, that it cannot possibly work well with each one of them. In those cases, the traditional channel expands to add a wholesaler.

Wholesalers are companies that assist with distribution activities among businesses. They do not work with final consumers in any significant way. Their role is to provide needed marketing functions as products and services move through the channel of distribution between producers and other businesses.

Benefits of Wholesaling

Wholesalers provide important marketing services for the channels in which they participate. Some businesses are unable to complete the marketing tasks required because of the cost or specialized resources or skills required. Others choose not to do some tasks because they want to focus on their production or selling activities.

Wholesalers may provide one or more of the needed marketing activities better or at a lower cost. For example, a small retailer is not able to purchase most products in large quantities. Some manufacturers do not want to sell their products in small quantities. A wholesaler combines the orders of several small retailers and purchases in efficient quantities. Shipments for businesses in the same location, such as a shopping mall, can be combined, allowing less-expensive transportation methods to be utilized.

Finally, a manufacturer usually tries to produce products throughout the year, but consumer demand for the products may be seasonal. The manufacturer may not have adequate facilities to store the products until they can be sold to retailers. The manufacturer may use wholesalers who specialize in storage and inventory management, allowing it to focus on production rather than storage.

Wholesaling Activities

Typical wholesaling activities include buying, selling, transporting, storing, and financing. Wholesalers accumulate the products of many manufacturers, develop appropriate assortments for their customers, and distribute the products to them.

Farm products such as grains are examples of seasonal products that must be stored. What other examples of seasonal products can you think of?

Wholesale businesses may finance the inventories of manufacturers until they can be sold and may extend credit to retailers to enable them to make purchases.

Wholesalers also assist manufacturers in determining needs of retailers and final consumers and provide market and product information to retailers. They help collect and analyze information on sales, costs, changes in demand, and inventory levels. Some wholesalers support the promotional efforts of manufacturers and retailers.

Most wholesalers purchase products from producers and manufacturers and then resell them to their customers. They are assuming risk by investing their money. If the products are damaged or cannot be sold at the desired price, the wholesaler loses money.

Types of Wholesalers

Wholesalers fall into three categories—full-service wholesalers, limited-service wholesalers, and agents and brokers.

Full-service (or merchant) wholesalers take title to the products they sell and provide a full range of distribution activities. In addition to providing or arranging transportation services, they usually offer credit, promotional assistance, product research and information, and even product installation and repair. Full-service wholesalers may offer a broad assortment of products, such as general merchandise for supermarkets, or they may specialize in a narrow product category, such as hardware.

Limited-service (or specialized) wholesalers concentrate on one or two important functions such as warehousing and storage, product delivery, or accumulating products for sale in a convenient location such as a produce or fresh fish market for supermarkets. They may not provide services such as research, credit, or promotional support.

Agents and brokers are independent businesses that provide specialized exchange functions such as locating suppliers, selling, financing, or arranging shipments. They do not take title to products. They essentially work as an extension of the workforce of the manufacturer or retailer.

Other Wholesaling Businesses

Wholesale franchises and cooperatives are groups of small businesses that cooperate in completing marketing and distribution activities. In a *wholesale franchise,* small retailers follow the guidance of a large wholesaler in operating their businesses.

In return, they receive purchasing advantages and support from the wholesaler. They normally operate under the same business name such as IGA (Independent Grocers Alliance) and NAPA (National Automotive Parts Association).

Wholesale cooperatives are wholesale organizations owned jointly by member businesses. The wholesale businesses are owned by producers or retailers to provide distribution services to members. Farmers form wholesale cooperatives to brand and market their products, such as Sunkist Growers and Land-O-Lakes. Examples of wholesale cooperatives organized by small retailers include Ace Hardware and FTD (Florists' Transworld Delivery, Inc.).

There has been a recent increase in the popularity of **wholesale member clubs**. These are businesses that offer a variety of consumer products to members through a warehouse outlet. Many of the clubs are open to both final consumers and businesses although the membership requirements and prices may vary for each group. Products are displayed in large warehouses. Product assortments may be limited but are available in large quantities. Customers are responsible for transporting their purchased products. Well-known wholesale clubs include Sam's Club and Costco.

Wholesale clubs initially targeted small businesses. Most now offer memberships to employees of large businesses and organizations and also to individuals. Because both individuals and businesses buy products from wholesale clubs, these companies straddle the line between retailing and wholesaling.

CHECKPOINT
What are the three categories of wholesalers?

As retailers get bigger and distribution and communication methods improve, some no longer want to deal with wholesalers. They believe that they can get better service and prices if they work directly with manufacturers. To continue to participate in channels of distribution, wholesalers have adjusted their business practices and shifted their focus to serving small and medium-sized retailers. Those smaller businesses need effective purchasing and distribution methods to compete with the large businesses. Wholesalers perform those functions because they evaluate the products of many manufacturers, buy and ship in large quantities, and assist with financing and many other marketing activities.

Specialized Services

Many wholesalers provide marketing research and marketing information services to their customers. They help them gather information and provide them with data that will help the businesses improve their operations and decisions. Computer technology can process orders more rapidly and keep track of the quantity and location of products. New methods of storing and handling products reduce product damage, the cost of distribution, and the time needed to get products from the manufacturer to the customer. Wholesalers provide additional services such as marketing and promotional planning, 24-hour ordering and emergency deliveries, specialized storage facilities, and individualized branding and packaging services.

Access to Markets

Wholesalers provide access to new markets with less risk than if the retailer developed that market alone. Wholesalers help retailers become aware of new products and new manufacturers. They make products available from businesses located long distances away. For manufacturers who want to expand into new markets or sell to different types of businesses, wholesalers may already have experience in those markets. They can develop new business opportunities more effectively than if the manufacturer attempts it alone.

Wholesalers may offer specialized services including using computer technology to process orders and keep track of products. Why might a manufacturer pay a wholesaler to provide such services?

Export and import organizations are very important in building international business. They are informed of the conditions and customer needs as well as business procedures and legal requirements for operating in the international market. Without the help of wholesalers, many companies would not be successful in international markets.

Of the recent changes in wholesaling, among the most important are better communications and information, improved technology, and broader customer service.

Effective wholesalers believe in the marketing concept. They work to identify their customers and understand their needs. They learn of the problems the customers are having with products and marketing activities and help them to solve those problems.

CHECKPOINT
Why have wholesalers shifted their focus to serve smaller retailers?

13.3 ASSESSMENT

What Have You Learned?

1. What do the typical wholesaling activities include? [13.3.1]

2. How can a wholesaler benefit a manufacturer that specializes in seasonal products? [13.3.1]

3. How have wholesalers adjusted their business practices to serve small and medium-sized businesses? [13.2.2]

Make Academic Connections

1. **Research** The U.S. Census Bureau collects statistics about businesses every five years. Access the web page for the U.S. Census Bureau's Economic Surveys page. Use the search function on the page to research wholesale businesses. Find the number of wholesale businesses and their total revenues reported for the two most recent five-year periods. Construct a table and a graph that compares the changes between the two periods. [13.3.1]

2. **History** Identify and conduct research on one wholesale franchise or cooperative. Prepare a report that identifies when and how it was started, the reasons it was formed, how it has expanded and changed over the years, and future plans for the organization. Include a picture of the company's logo in your report. [13.3.1]

Connect to ◇DECA

Build your Portfolio

As a sales representative for a full-service merchant wholesaler, you are contacting a new restaurant owner that does not currently use a wholesaler. The owner purchases fresh foods from local growers and buys most other products and supplies from a local wholesale member club or through online purchases from other businesses. Prepare and deliver a three-minute sales presentation to your teacher (judge) on the benefits to the owner of using your wholesale business for all purchases rather than their current practice. [13.3.1]

Learning Objectives

13.4.1 Define retailing.

13.4.2 Distinguish between various types of retailers.

13.4.3 Describe ways that retailing is changing in response to changes in consumer preferences, the business environment, and technology.

Key Terms

retailer
inventory
 shrinkage
specialty or
 limited-line
 retailers
mixed merchandise
 retailers

superstores
service retailers
non-store retailing
online-to-offline
 retailing (O2O)
franchising
atmospherics

marketing matters

Consumers purchase most of their products and services from retailers. Retailers choose the product assortment and select the locations where consumers can make purchases, set prices, and control much of the promotion. They often provide information and customer service during and after the sale. As consumer preferences and the business environment change, retailing quickly changes in response.

essential question

What factors lead to changes in the way retailers must operate today to remain competitive?

13.4.1 ▶ What Is Retailing?

The final business organization in an indirect channel of distribution for consumer products is a **retailer**. Although some large discount retailers sell products to other businesses, their primary customers are individual consumers purchasing to meet their own needs. Retailers buy the products their customers need from manufacturers or wholesalers. They display the products and provide product information so that customers can evaluate them. Most retail businesses help customers purchase products by accepting credit cards or providing other credit or financing choices. Many retail stores provide additional services such as product assembly, installation, alterations, repairs, layaway, gift-wrapping, and delivery.

In addition to offering products and services for consumers, retailers support the marketing activities of wholesalers and manufacturers. They often finance the inventory by paying the manufacturer or wholesaler before they sell the products to consumers. Retailers also store large amounts of inventory so that customers have a variety of product choices and ready availability if they decide to make a purchase. Because of that, the retailers are reducing the storage costs of the other businesses and assuming much of the risk involved in maintaining an inventory of products. Products can be lost, damaged, or stolen or become dated before they are sold. A major cost to retailers results from inventory shrinkage. **Inventory shrinkage** is a loss of products due to theft, fraud, negligence, or error.

Promotion is an important marketing activity for retailers. Increasingly, retailers are involved in marketing research and marketing-information management. Some retailers even take responsibility for transporting products from the manufacturer to their distribution centers and on to individual stores.

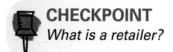

CHECKPOINT
What is a retailer?

13.4.2 ▶ Types of Retailers

Retail businesses develop to respond to the needs and purchasing behaviors of diverse consumer groups. Some consumers like to plan their purchases, gather information in advance of shopping, and complete their shopping quickly. Others might use very little planning, gather information about products in the store or mall, and enjoy the time they spend shopping. Some people prefer to do their purchasing through catalogs or online rather than travel to the stores. Retail businesses are available that serve each of these types of shopping behaviors. There are several ways to examine the various types of retailing.

Product Mix

One way to categorize stores is by the types of products they offer. Some retailers specialize in one or a few product categories. Others offer customers a wide range of products.

Specialty or limited-line retailers offer products from one category of merchandise or closely related items. Examples include food, automotive, apparel, lawn and garden, music, or travel. Some

stores in this category offer many types of products, while others may be very specialized. For example, within the category of food, it is possible to find businesses that sell only coffee, cookies, or fresh fruits and cheeses while other businesses offer many varieties of food.

Mixed merchandise retailers offer products from several categories. Common examples of mixed merchandise retailers are supermarkets in which you can buy many products other than food, department stores with many distinct departments, and drugstores that sell a variety of products other than medications and health-related items.

A recent successful example of mixed merchandise retailing is the dollar store. *Dollar stores* typically are smaller, convenience-type stores that offer a limited assortment of household and packaged food items for $1 per item or at deep discounts. The stores often target people seeking bargain prices for routine household purchases.

Another concept in retailing is the superstore. **Superstores** are very large stores that offer consumers wide choices

© Milles Studio/Shutterstock.com

What type of retailer specializes in selling gourmet cheese?

of products at lower prices. Many of today's superstores, such as Walmart and Target, began as discount stores. They have now developed much larger stores that combine groceries, home products, electronics, garden centers, and even food courts. Most superstores combine a variety of product categories so that consumers can use the store for one-stop shopping. *Limited-line superstores* sell products in a narrower product category but offer consumers many choices of products, brands, and features within that category. Two of the most popular types of limited-line superstores today are home improvement and consumer electronics and appliance stores.

A final category is **service retailers**, which have services as their primary offering with a limited number of products for sale that complement the services. Barber shops and hair salons, dry cleaners, insurance agents, movie theaters, and auto service centers are all examples of service retailers.

Location

An important characteristic of retailing is the location of the store. The location can be studied in relation to the customer or to other businesses. *Convenience stores* are located very close to their customers, offering a limited line of products that consumers use regularly. Most convenience stores sell gasoline, food, and household products. Other convenience stores are becoming popular, including snack and beverage centers and businesses that provide packing and mailing, photocopying, and printing services.

Shopping centers are a set of stores located together and planned as a unit to meet a range of customer needs. There are several types of shopping centers, based on size and types of businesses. *Shopping strips* contain about 5 to 15 stores grouped together along a street. They offer a limited number of emergency and convenience products such as fast food, gasoline, laundry services, and drug stores. *Neighborhood centers* have between 20 and 30 stores that offer a broader range of products meeting the regular and frequent shopping needs of consumers located within a few miles of the stores. *Regional shopping centers* contain 100 or more businesses. These large shopping centers attempt to meet most or all of consumers' shopping needs. The centers are developed around several large department or discount stores. They are designed and located to attract customers from 10 or more miles away.

Stand-alone stores are large businesses located in an area where there are no other retail businesses nearby. They offer either a large variety of products or unique products. Stand-alone businesses offer products that customers cannot easily find in more convenient locations or products so important or unique that consumers will make a special trip to shop there. Examples of stand-alone businesses are some auto dealerships, super-stores, home improvement stores, and lawn-and-garden centers.

Non-Store Retailing

A unique category of retail businesses is non-store retailing. **Non-store retailing** involves selling directly to the consumer at home rather than requiring the consumer to travel to a store. Two of the oldest and most common forms of non-store retailing are door-to-door selling and catalog sales. Many years ago, traveling salespeople sold many consumer products, from household supplies to potato chips. Salespeople traveled to customers' homes because consumers took infrequent shopping trips. This method is used less frequently because of cost and changing shopping behavior.

Some home sales are done through home parties, such as Pampered Chef, which offers high-end kitchen tools, and Cabi, which offers trendy fashion items for women. At these events, friends gather for food and activities as well as to see the latest products in categories from jewelry to art and even specialty foods.

The sale of general merchandise through mail-order catalogs such as the Sears' catalog once was popular, but it declined as shopping centers became more convenient and travel became easier. However, in the past decade, catalog sales have regained much of their popularity as

Why is it important for retailers to understand the purchasing behavior of customers?

Flying Colours Ltd/Photodisc/Getty Images

a result of express delivery services, strong product guarantees and warranties, and consumers' busy lifestyles. Rather than offering general merchandise, the most popular catalogs today offer specialty merchandise.

Other types of non-store retailing include vending machines and kiosks, telephone sales, televised shopping clubs, and direct mail selling. The newest and potentially the most lucrative form is Internet retailing, discussed in detail in the next section.

CHECKPOINT

What are three common ways to classify retailers?

13.4.3 ▶ How Is Retailing Changing?

Retailing has experienced many changes over the years and likely will continue to do so. Because of the large number of retailers and the choices available to consumers, it will be increasingly difficult to compete in many types of retail businesses. Consumers expect variety, quality, service, and low prices. To be profitable,

retailers will have to find the most efficient ways to operate in order to keep costs low.

Changing Types of Retailers

It is likely that there will continue to be a need for both specialty and mixed merchandise stores. Some people predicted that specialty stores would disappear as people did more one-stop shopping. Yet there are a large number of consumers willing to invest more time in shopping and are looking for a wider choice as well as unique or unusual items that are not widely available. The number and type of small specialty retail businesses is increasing again after going through a period of decline. The very large specialty businesses also continue to grow.

WORKING IN TEAMS

Select a retail business that has made a change in the way it does business. For example, perhaps the business has incorporated technology, made changes to its shopping environment, or moved into international markets. As a team, discuss why you believe the change was made and whether it has been effective.

The Expanding Internet

The growth of the Internet and an increased level of consumer comfort in making online purchases is expanding retailing opportunities. Very small businesses and even individuals have found that they can compete effectively when selling merchandise online. Easy-to-use websites and shopping-basket software and the availability of businesses that manage online stores, financial transactions, shipping, and even customer service make Internet retailing possible for almost anyone who has a product for sale. Although the first Internet retailers were usually click-only businesses, meaning they sold products online only, most major retailers today offer products for sale online as well as through their brick-and-mortar stores.

The line between traditional retailing and e-commerce is becoming blurred. Marketers know they must reach people online because they realize that most customers search online before purchasing a product. Many retailers that have a physical store are now merging their in-store retailing with an Internet presence. Referred to as "click-and-mortar" or "clicks-and-bricks," this strategy can offer customers an improved shopping experience and additional choices with more convenience, flexibility, and services.

Retailers know that customers may want to see a product before purchasing it online. This process, known as "showrooming," is often the case when consumers shop for high-end products such as electronics and designer clothing. While the practice will likely continue, marketers see an opportunity to capture some of those consumers as they are researching the product online. Closely related to click-and-mortar, this **online-to-offline retailing (O2O)** is designed to create product and service awareness by interacting with customers through websites, email, mobile ads, and mobile apps and then encouraging customers to visit the physical stores to make the purchase. The practice also involves online ordering with in-store pickup for those who don't want to wait for a package to arrive, the use of in-store kiosks for online purchases, and allowing online purchases to be returned to physical stores.

Want to know more about what is trending with this topic? Click on **Lesson 13.4, Marketing Decisions,** in your MindTap.

Connect to MindTap

Some retailers that began online also engage in O2O retailing. Warby Parker, Harry's, and Modcloth each have opened retail storefronts allowing customers to view and try products in person. Even e-commerce giant Amazon is engaged in O2O, adding physical store fronts and purchasing existing stores such as Whole Foods.

The Growth of Franchising

Franchising is a very popular type of retail ownership. **Franchising** is a business relationship in which the developer of a business idea sells others the rights to the idea and the use of the business name. In a franchise business, the owner (the *franchiser*) develops a basic business plan and operating procedures. Other people (*franchisees*) purchase the rights to open and operate the businesses according to the standard plans and operating procedures. Franchise fees are paid to the franchiser for the business idea and assistance.

Franchises allow people with limited experience to start a business that already has name and brand recognition. They are guided by the franchise plan, which can reduce the risk of failure. Popular franchise programs also increase customer awareness of a business because many businesses operate in different locations using the same franchise name and promotions. Examples of successful retail franchises include restaurants, financial services, hotels, automobile maintenance and repair, and specialty food and beverage businesses.

Increased Use of Technology

Technology is having a big impact on retailers. Not only are most business operations managed with computers, but new types of equipment also are being used in businesses to store, distribute, and display products. For example, customers can shop for products by using a computer screen on a kiosk rather than by walking around a store. When a product is selected from the description and picture on the screen, the consumer inserts a credit card into the computer. The product is packaged and available for pickup at the front of the store when the customer is finished shopping.

Technology also has enhanced the merchandising function of retailing. Starting with electronic inventory systems using barcodes or electronic tags on merchandise, products can be tracked from the point of manufacture until they are sold. Retailers use optical scanning sales terminals to instantly record sales and merchandise returns. A detailed record of each product is maintained and instantly updated so that the store can track sales, prices, merchandise shortages, damage, returns, and even detailed customer data matched to sales. That information can be shared with channel members to replenish inventory of fast-moving merchandise, cancel orders of products customers do not want, and improve pricing and promotional strategies.

The Shopping Experience

Retailers are increasingly concerned about **atmospherics**, the elements of the shopping environment that are appealing to customers, attract them to a store, and encourage them to buy. The major elements of atmospherics are the store location, exterior and interior appearance, store layout and display, and the shopping environment.

Want to know more about marketing in the information age? Click on **Lesson 13.4, Digital Marketing,** *in your MindTap.*

Connect to MindTap

Many stores have reduced product display space and widened aisles, changed interior colors and lighting, and used more visual features and appealing product presentations. Some stores have organized merchandise so that shoppers can see products displayed in the types of settings where they would be used and can participate in product demonstrations. They have product experts available to answer questions and help with purchase decisions.

The Global Marketplace

Global retailing holds a great deal of promise for the future. Although many manufacturers and wholesalers have been involved in international marketing for a number of years, retailers often are reluctant to expand into other countries.

Several types of retail businesses have successfully moved into Eastern and Western Europe and Asia. As countries of the former Soviet Union and Africa develop their economies, retail opportunities will expand there as well. Many of the U.S. fast-food businesses have been quite successful in international marketing as have businesses in the travel industry, including hotels and automobile rental agencies. U.S. fashions have wide acceptance, so specialty stores are looking at other countries as likely places to expand their businesses.

CHECKPOINT

In what ways has retailing changed in response to shifting consumer preferences and changes in the business environment?

13.4 ASSESSMENT

What Have You Learned?

1. How does inventory shrinkage occur? [13.4.1]
2. How does a specialty (limited-line) retailer differ from a mixed merchandise retailer? [13.4.2]
3. Name the four types of shopping centers in order of number of stores they have, from least to most number of stores. Include the number of stores in your answer. [13.4.2]
4. Explain online-to-offline (O2O) retailing. [13.4.3]
5. What are the major elements of a retailers' atmospherics? [13.4.3]

Make Academic Connections

1. **Research** Use the Internet or business publications to identify the five largest U.S. retailers in the following categories: [13.4.2]
   a. specialty or limited-line
   b. department stores
   c. discount stores
   d. retail franchise stores
   e. Internet retailers

2. **History** The "wheel of retailing" describes how retail businesses change over time. Use the Internet to gather information on this concept. Prepare a visual that illustrates the concept and a two-minute speech that describes it and its effect on retail businesses. [13.4.3]

 Build your Portfolio

Connect to ◇DECA

Your team has been asked to plan a neighborhood shopping center near your school. Select a location, create a drawing of the layout, and select 20 stores you think would be effective based on characteristics of local shoppers. Present and describe your plan to your teacher (judge). [13.4.2]

Learning Objectives

13.5.1 Describe the various means by which products are transported within a channel of distribution.

13.5.2 Explain the common options for storing and handling products while they are moving through the distribution channel.

13.5.3 Explain the importance of order processing and inventory control to the overall effectiveness of a physical distribution plan.

Key Terms

physical distribution (logistics)
warehouse
distribution center

marketing matters

A channel of distribution needs the right combination of businesses. Merely adding a business to complete one or more of the marketing functions does not ensure that products will move effectively from producer to consumer. An important part of channel planning is physical distribution. Businesses that specialize in physical distribution activities often are included in a channel of distribution. All activities in the physical distribution process must be carefully planned, coordinated, and controlled in order for products to reach customers on time and in good condition.

 essential question

How do the type and characteristics of a product affect the decisions made when planning physical distribution?

13.5.1 ▶ Choose Transportation Methods

When you think of physical distribution, you probably think of shipping or transportation. But it is a much more complicated process. **Physical distribution** (also known as **logistics**) is the process of efficiently and effectively moving products and materials through the distribution channel. The main physical distribution activities are transportation, storage, and product handling. Physical distribution also requires information processing to make sure accurate records are maintained throughout the process.

The Physical Distribution Process

Products usually are handled many times as they move from manufacturing through several forms of transportation and many locations to the place where they will be consumed or sold. It is likely that the products will be grouped into large units for transportation and then divided into smaller units for display, sale, storage, or use. All of these activities require further handling and packaging.

Usually products do not move continuously through the channel of distribution. They are stored as each business processes paperwork, sells to the next channel member, and determines the location of distribution. Storage facilities must be arranged to hold and protect the product. Inventory control procedures must be developed so that the product does not become lost.

Moving the Product

The first step in physical distribution planning is deciding how products will be moved from the producer to the customers. There are common transportation methods used to move most common products—railroad, truck, airplane, ship or boat, and pipeline. As you consider those alternatives, some are automatically eliminated because they are not available in certain locations or are not equipped to handle the type of product to be shipped. You would not send small packages by rail or ship, and you would not ship iron ore and coal by airplane. Other factors such as the speed of delivery needed, any special handling required, and cost enter into the choice of transportation methods.

RAILROADS Railroads are useful for carrying large quantities of heavy and bulky items. Raw materials, industrial equipment, and large shipments of consumer products from the factory to retailers often are moved by rail. The total cost to ship one or more carloads of a product is high. However, the cost of this method is relatively low if a large quantity of a product is moved. Products move quite slowly on trains compared to other methods of transportation.

Problems exist in using railroads for shipping products. Equipment is not always available where it is needed, and it takes time to move empty cars to new locations. Many areas of the country are not served by rail, so other forms of transportation will be needed to and from the closest rail site. It takes time to load and unload freight from rail cars, particularly when a carload contains shipments from several companies or for a large number of customers.

Railroads are responding to the need for improved service to customers. Railroad tracks and equipment are being upgraded, and routes are being rescheduled to improve customer service. Newer methods of product handling have been developed, including packing products into large containers or truck trailers which are then hauled on flatbed rail cars. To speed rail shipments to customers, it is now possible for a business to send several carloads of products from the production point and redirect them to customers as sales are made.

TRUCKS Trucks are the most flexible of the major transportation methods. They can handle small or large shipments, goods that are very durable or require special handling, and products going across town or across the country. Trucks reach almost any location and provide relatively rapid service. Costs are relatively low for short distances and easy-to-handle products but increase for long-distance or difficult shipments.

Many companies own their trucks. Small companies often can afford to own and maintain a delivery vehicle. Large manufacturers, wholesalers, and retailers

MARKETING COMMUNICATION

Truck-Side Ads

Selling advertising space on the side of semi-tractor trailers is a potentially profitable source of revenue for trucking companies. Traditionally, the fleets have promoted only the trucking company itself. The problem with selling truck sides as roving billboards has been the inability to gauge how many people are seeing the ads. Now there is a way to do that.

3M Graphics and Fleet Advertising, which operates a fleet of truck-side billboards, funded the development of a system that uses a global positioning satellite to track the whereabouts of trucks. It combines that information with traffic data to produce estimates of how many people are exposed to a roving truck ad.

With the high cost of billboards and with restrictions on billboards in many areas, mobile truck-side ads could find a ready market. Numerous companies specialize in this medium.

Think Critically

1. How do you think traffic data are used to estimate the number of people who see a mobile ad?
2. What are the advantages of truck-side ads compared to stationary billboard ads?

---

often own or lease fleets of trucks to be able to move products where and when needed. Trucking firms are important channel members. They provide the specialized service of transporting products to other channel members. They often have special product handling equipment, storage facilities, and well-trained drivers to ensure that products are moved rapidly and safely.

SHIPS AND BOATS   A large number of products sold internationally are transported by water. While airlines move small shipments rapidly, ships can handle large quantities and large products very well at a much lower cost than air shipments. The major problem with this form of transportation is speed.

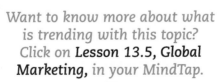

Want to know more about what is trending with this topic? Click on Lesson 13.5, Global Marketing, in your MindTap.

Connect to MindTap

Ships are relatively slow, and it may take several weeks after a product is loaded on the ship before it is delivered to the customer. Also, there is a risk of large losses if a ship is damaged by weather or other conditions. Ships usually must be used in combination with trucks or railroads, as they are limited to travel between major ocean ports with terminals that have the appropriate product handling capabilities.

Boats on inland waterways such as lakes and large rivers are another type of water transportation used for shipping. Barges and other cargo-handling boats are used to ship products such as coal, grain, and other bulky and nonperishable items. Like ships, they are rather slow, but they can handle large quantities at low prices.

AIRPLANES If a company wants products delivered rapidly and can afford a higher cost, air transportation will often be the choice. Small parcels can be carried on commercial flights while large products or quantities of a product can be moved using cargo planes.

Because of the high costs, many companies do not consider air as a transportation choice. When other factors are considered, air transportation may not be as expensive as it seems. For example, the speed of air delivery may be essential for some products and reduces the need for product storage for others. Products may need to be handled less, and the speed of distribution reduces spoilage, damage, and theft. Companies that do not regularly use air transportation may choose that method for special or emergency deliveries.

PIPELINES Gas, oil, chemicals, and water are moved in large volumes over long distances through pipelines. Pipelines are expensive to construct and can be difficult to maintain, often resulting in leaking product into the environment. Once built, though, they can be a very cost-effective method because of the large amount of product that can move through the pipeline. They also may be the only choice to deliver products from some locations, such as crude oil from oil fields.

INTERMODAL METHODS Products usually move through long distribution channels among several businesses. Many products are transported using *intermodal* (combinations of) transportation methods. A shipment of appliances may be moved from a factory to a rail site by truck, moved across the country by rail, and then loaded onto other trucks to be delivered to retailers.

Companies such as FedEx and UPS, along with the U.S. Postal Service, employ their own fleets of cargo planes and delivery trucks to move small shipments between cities throughout the world overnight. Gasoline and other petroleum products are moved from a refinery to locations across the country by pipeline. Then trucks are used to transport the products to wholesalers, retailers, and business consumers.

CHECKPOINT
What are the common transportation methods used in distribution?

WORKING IN TEAMS

As a team, identify a large industrial product and a small consumer product. Create two flowcharts that show the activities and businesses that the team believes will be required to complete the physical distribution process. Discuss the differences between the two flowcharts.

13.5.2 ▶ Storage and Product Handling

Because production and consumption seldom occur at the same time, products must be held until they can be used. This means that methods and facilities for storage must be developed as a part of marketing. Effective storage allows channel members to balance supply and demand, but it adds to the costs of products. It also adds the risk that products may be damaged or stolen or become outdated while being stored.

Warehouses

Storage of most products is usually done in warehouses. A **warehouse** is a building designed to store large amounts of raw materials or products until they can be used or sold. Warehouses can be privately owned by any of the companies in the channel of distribution. Private ownership allows the company to develop the specific type of facility it needs to handle the products at the locations where they are most needed. For companies that need limited storage space or need it less frequently, public warehouses are available. Companies often use public warehouses for overflow storage or seasonal products.

Warehouses typically are located at the edge of town near interstate highways or airports. If you enter the building, you will likely see long conveyor belts or chains that move products through the building. There may even be computer-controlled trucks and carts (robots) that move products from area to area. Special storage shelves and equipment can move products in and out without the need for handling by people. Barcodes on the shelves, containers, and packages allow computers to keep track of the location of products and the length of time they are in storage.

Distribution Centers

Another kind of storage facility is known as a **distribution center**. This is a facility used to accumulate products from several sources and then regroup, repackage, and send them quickly to the locations where they will be used. A large retailer may have a number of distribution centers

How do retailers benefit from using distribution centers?

throughout the country and the world. Thousands of products are ordered from many manufacturers and shipped in huge quantities to the distribution centers. The products are needed in various assortments and quantities in the hundreds of stores owned by the retailer. The costs of storage and transportation are high, so the distribution centers must be effective at receiving the products, combining the different products into shipments for each store, and routing those shipments quickly so that the merchandise can be sold.

The goal of the distribution center is to reduce the costs of physical distribution while increasing the availability of products to customers. That can be done by using careful and efficient product-handling methods and by reducing the time products remain in the distribution center.

Packaging

Another important part of product handling is packaging. The primary purpose of packaging is to protect the product from the time it is produced until it can be consumed. If the product is damaged or destroyed, a great deal of money invested in the product by manufacturers and other channel members will be lost. Packaging is a part of product development in that it aids in the effective transportation, storage, and use of the product. For many products, packaging also serves as a promotional tool.

Packaging materials need to protect the product and allow it to be shipped in appropriate quantities. A product being handled with a forklift and shipped in large containers by trucks and rail cars needs to be packaged differently from a product being shipped in small quantities to the consumer using a parcel service. Products sent across town require different packaging and packing than those shipped around the world.

CHECKPOINT
What are the common options for storing and handling products while they are moving through the distribution channel?

13.5.3 ▶ Information Processing

Physical distribution systems must assure that the supply matches demand. First, products must be available in adequate assortments and quantities. Then, the inventory can be matched with needs of consumers and channel members. An effective information system must be able to predict consumer demand to ensure an adequate supply is available. Products must be routed to where they are needed as quickly as possible. The two important parts of the physical distribution information system are order processing and inventory control.

Order Processing

Order processing begins when a customer places an order. The order can be placed with a salesperson, by telephone or fax, by computer using a direct connection, or by the Internet.

When the supplier receives the order, the order is sent to the department in the business where it can be filled. At the same time, the accounting department determines the terms of the sale, method of payment, and cost of the products. Other businesspeople are determining the method, cost, and timing of transportation.

When the order is filled, it must be packaged and prepared for shipment. The order is checked to make sure it is complete, and information is forwarded to the accounting department so that an invoice can be prepared. The shipper is notified so that transportation is available. The customer is informed that the order has been processed and shipped. This procedure is repeated at each stage of the channel of distribution until the product is delivered to the final consumer. Order processing is complete when payment has been received and recorded, the product has been delivered and accepted by the customer, all shipping and delivery records have been completed, and product inventory records have been updated.

Inventory Control

The level of inventory affects the cost of marketing and the degree of customer satisfaction. If too much inventory is maintained, storage costs will be too high, customer needs may change, or the product may spoil or become outdated. If not enough inventory is available, customers will not be able to buy what they need, and sales and goodwill will be lost.

An inventory control system must maintain several types of information. It must know what products are in inventory, what quantity is available, and how long each has been in inventory.

Effective inventory control methods maintain information in a computer, so a physical inventory often is not needed.

An inventory control system determines what products and quantities to order. It identifies how much of each product is being sold and how rapidly. Managers should know how long it takes to replenish the supply for each product so that an adequate inventory can be maintained to meet anticipated customer demand. They also should be aware of products that are selling more rapidly or more slowly than planned. When sales are higher than expected, the company may want to order more to be able to meet customer needs. When sales are slow, reasons for the reduced level of sales should be determined and a decision made as to whether or not to reorder.

Computerized inventory systems allow information to be exchanged instantly among channel members. For many Internet sites, and increasingly for retail stores and industrial salespeople, a request for a product can be checked instantly to determine if an adequate supply is on hand and, if not, when it will be available.

CHECKPOINT
What are the two important parts of the physical distribution system?

13.5 ASSESSMENT

What Have You Learned?

1. What is the first step in physical distribution planning? [13.5.1]

2. What is the goal of a distribution center? [13.5.2]

3. What happens if too much or not enough inventory is maintained in a physical distribution system? [13.5.3]

Make Academic Connections

1. **Communication** You are the transportation specialist for an auto manufacturer in Florida. You are asked to compare shipping new cars to dealers in Maine using auto transport trucks or rail cars. Analyze the alternatives and make a recommendation. [13.5.1]

2. **Math** A small manufacturer needs to add 20,500 square feet of storage space for additional inventory. Two warehouses are available for lease. The first rents for $.63 per square foot per month. The second rents for an annual rate of $8.50 per square foot. Calculate the annual cost for leasing each warehouse. What additional factors should the manufacturer consider when choosing which space to lease? [13.5.2]

Connect to ◇DECA

Build your Portfolio

A company is producing a new type of business card. It prints standard business card information on the card along with a barcode that clients can scan with a smartphone to access information about the business and its products through a website or a social media site. Design a package that can be used to sell sets of blank business cards in office supply stores that both protects and promotes the product. Present your design and discuss it with your teacher (judge). [13.5.2]

Connect to MindTap

*Analyze a case study that focuses on chapter concepts. Click on **Chapter 13, Case Study,** in your MindTap.*

Review Marketing Concepts

1. Why is distribution so important to effective marketing? [13.1.1]

2. You work for a company that markets snowmobiles in the United States. Write the details about "where and when the product will be produced, sold, and used" to include in the marketing plan. [13.1.2]

3. How do delivery services help adjust for differences between producers and consumers? [13.2.1]

4. You just opened a business that specializes in baking customized cookies for parties and other events. You rent a commercial kitchen for the business but do not have a retail space. Would you choose a direct or indirect channel of distribution for the cookies? Explain your answer. [13.2.2]

5. In your own words, explain why a producer would choose to add a wholesaler to its indirect channel of distribution. Why would a retailer choose to work with a wholesaler? [13.3.1]

6. Why do you think working with a wholesaler would be a less risky way for retailers to gain access to new markets and products? [13.3.2]

7. What measures can retailers take to combat inventory shrinkage due to theft? [13.4.1]

8. Compare and contrast mixed merchandise retailers, superstores, and limited-line superstores. Include an example of each in your answer. [13.4.1]

9. As related to the retail shopping experience, explain why atmospherics are very important to the success of retailing operations. [13.4.2]

10. Describe how the railroad and the trucking industries work together to move a product to its final destination. [13.5.1]

11. Compare and contrast a warehouse and a distribution center. [13.5.2]

12. In your opinion, which activity is more important to a retailer: order processing or inventory control? Explain your answer. [13.5.3]

Marketing Research and Planning

1. When products are exchanged between producers and consumers, all of the marketing functions must be performed. In a direct channel of distribution, either the producer or the final consumer is responsible for marketing functions. In an indirect channel, other channel members will perform some of the functions. For each of the examples of common exchanges in items a and b, identify the channel of distribution as either direct or indirect. Then identify which of the channel members will be responsible for each of the nine marketing functions. Prepare a brief written justification for each of your decisions. (It is likely that more than one channel member can perform some of the functions.)

   a. A consumer travels to a strawberry farm to pick and buy fresh fruit.

   b. A homebuilder orders a truckload of plywood from a building supply wholesaler to be delivered to the job site by the supplier. The supplier fills the order from a shipment of plywood delivered last month by rail car from the plywood manufacturer. [13.2.2]

2. The number of franchises is growing rapidly, with opportunities available in manufacturing, service, wholesaling, and retailing. Identify a franchise that interests you. Gather the following information about the franchise through Internet or library research, by writing to the franchiser, or by interviewing the owner of a local franchise outlet:

Build your Portfolio

a. Is the franchise a manufacturing, wholesale, retail, or service business?

b. What are the primary products and services offered?

c. Who are the customers?

d. What other businesses does the franchise work with?

e. Where is the franchise located in the channel of distribution?

f. What marketing functions does the franchise perform?

g. What types of physical distribution activities does the business perform?

Gather additional information you believe will help you understand the franchise business. Prepare a written or oral report on your findings. [13.3.1]

3. The location of a retail business is very important to its success. In general, the closer a retail business is located to consumers, the more likely those consumers are to consider purchasing from it. For each of the products listed, consider who the typical consumer would be, and then determine whether the business should be located in a shopping strip, a neighborhood shopping center, a regional shopping center, or a standalone store. Develop a written justification for each decision.

a. homeowners' and renters' insurance

b. personal computers for home and business use

c. new automobiles

d. trendy clothing

e. building materials and home improvement products [13.4.2]

4. Many e-commerce businesses have struggled to find effective ways to distribute products to customers and to accept product returns. Parcel delivery service companies such as FedEx and UPS have grown as a result of agreements with e-commerce businesses to manage their distribution activities. Visit the websites of two parcel delivery services and gather information on the physical distribution services each offers to e-commerce businesses. Prepare a table that lists at least 10 distribution activities. Develop two columns that compare the services offered by each company for the activities identified. [13.5.1]

Marketing Management and Decision Making

1. Edu Games, a new company that produces high-quality board games for children, was trying to develop an effective channel of distribution for its unique product. The company was having difficulty because its wholesalers and retailers were not implementing the marketing mix as planned. If a manufacturer is unable to get the necessary cooperation from other channel members, it will be difficult to successfully market its products.

To solve the problem Edu Games is considering three alternatives:

a. selling the games directly to customers by mail or the Internet

b. developing its own sales force to replace the wholesalers

c. finding ways to work more closely with its current wholesalers to implement the marketing plan

Prepare a written analysis of each of the three alternatives, identifying advantages and disadvantages of each. Then select the alternative you think is best and develop a rationale for your choice based on principles of effective marketing and distribution. [13.1.1, 13.2.2]

2. Using a computer spreadsheet program, compile a list of 15 to 20 household products that you and your family purchase regularly. Find the per-unit prices that these or comparable products sell for at a superstore or wholesale member club, a mixed merchandise store such as a supermarket or department store, a limited-line specialty store, and an Internet store. Use a spreadsheet program to record the prices. Select the products that are carried by each of the businesses and compute the total cost of purchasing all of those products from each type of retailer. Calculate the percentage difference in the cost of all products between each type of retailer. [13.4.2]

Let's Start a Band! Follow-Up Discussion

Work in small teams to discuss the question posed at the end of the opening vignette. Analyze the distribution element of the band's marketing mix. What factors should it consider that will give the band its best chance for success?

Build Your Marketing Plan

Build your Portfolio

In this chapter you learned about channels of distribution and distribution procedures. You will now apply this learning to the development of your marketing plan. To access the chapter-specific tools that you will need to complete this activity, please navigate to Chapter 13 → Build Your Marketing Plan in MindTap. Alternatively, you can access these tools online at NGLSync. Please visit www.nglsync.cengage.com, and search for the companion website that accompanies this book by entering the ISBN, author, or title. Once you locate this companion website, navigate to Build Your Marketing Plan → Chapter 13.

Quick-Serve Restaurant Management Series Event

DECA PREP

Build your Portfolio

Quick-Serve Restaurant Management Series Event consists of a 100-question, multiple-choice comprehensive exam and role-plays. The role-play portion of the event requires participants to accomplish a task by translating what they have learned into effective, efficient, and spontaneous action. The five performance indicators specify the distinct tasks the participant must accomplish during the role-play. Students have 10 minutes to prepare their strategy and 10 minutes to explain it to the judge. The judge can ask questions during or after the presentation.

Obesity is a serious issue in the United States. Many children and adults have unhealthy weight issues. Society has blamed much of the obesity problem in the United States on fast-food restaurants that serve food with high levels of calories and fat. Many of the fast-food restaurants are also criticized for their super-sized portions. Much of the food offered at quick-serve restaurants is fried and not very healthy.

Burger Barn has been in operation since 1960. Large juicy burgers, French fries, onion rings, malts, and sweet desserts have made Burger Barn a popular restaurant. Your marketing team has been asked to create healthy food alternatives for Burger Barn's customers. The healthy items you offer should not increase the price of the meals.

You must also develop an advertising campaign that shows how Burger Barn is helping to fight obesity by giving customers more healthy choices. The advertising campaign must give young people incentives for making healthy diet choices. Also, Burger Barn must become active in the community to promote physical fitness. You must determine an event for Burger Barn to sponsor that confirms its commitment to a healthier population.

Performance Indicators Evaluated

- Lead change. (Emotional Intelligence)
- Identify product opportunities. (Product/Service Management)
- Generate product ideas. (Product/Service Management)
- Explain the nature of effective nutritional disclosures. (Promotion)
- Explain the components of advertisements. (Promotion)

Go to the DECA website for more detailed information. **www.deca.org**

Think Critically

1. Who is the target market for a healthy diet campaign?

2. Why must quick-serve restaurants be accountable for a personal problem like obesity?

3. What kinds of commercials do some fast-food restaurants use to emphasize a healthy lifestyle?

4. What kinds of commercials should Burger Barn use to help distance itself from the obesity epidemic?

CHAPTER 14

DETERMINE THE BEST PRICE

See how effective advertising leads to successful marketing strategies.
Click on Chapter 14, Visual Focus, **in your** MindTap.

Let's Start a Band!

> ## "I'm in the music business for one purpose – to make money."
>
> *– Nat King Cole, singer and 1990 Rock and Roll Hall of Fame inductee*

Back when we started, we didn't know how much to charge for our gigs. We had a vague idea of what the other bands in the area were charging. But we mostly just figured it out as we went along.

So, when you ask me, "How do we know what to charge?," the answer is, "It depends." What's the venue? What's our time slot? Are we opening or headlining? How big is our following, or do we even have one?

Most venues and private events pay a flat fee depending on the number of players and hours you play. These fees are usually somewhat negotiable. Some venues don't pay the band directly, but let you collect donations. Others charge a fee or a cover and then give you a split.

Some venues have an "open mic" night. This is a lot like working for free, but it can help you build a fan base. Another route is a kind of "pay to play" where the venue sells us the tickets and then we resell them to the public. It's kind of like being your own StubHub. If we know we can attract a lot of fans to the venue, we consider it.

It's clear we need a better way to price our gigs. Can you help us figure out a more consistent approach to pricing for the band?

Learning Objectives

14.1.1 Explain the reasons why price is an important marketing tool.

14.1.2 Discuss how the economic concept of elasticity of demand relates to pricing decisions.

14.1.3 Describe three ways in which government influences prices.

Key Terms

price
pricing
equilibrium
elasticity of demand
inelastic demand
elastic demand

marketing matters

Price is an important part of marketing because the prices consumers pay largely determine how they value the purchase and their satisfaction with it. Sellers pay a lot of attention to prices because they typically are easier to change than the other marketing mix elements. Price also is central to the economic concepts of supply and demand. Marketers who understand the nature of the demand for a product are better able to set the optimum price for it. Government in a free enterprise economy also plays a role in pricing.

essential question

For what types of products is price one of the most important factors in the purchase decision, and for what types of products is price one of the least important factors in the purchase decision?

14.1.1 ▶ Price as a Marketing Tool

You may think of price as the amount a customer pays for a product or service. But price is much more complicated. Think of the various words used to identify the price of something. They include admission, membership fee, service charge, donation, retainer, tuition, and monthly payment. In some cases, money is not used at all. In bartering, people agree on the value of the items being exchanged rather than setting a monetary price.

As a marketing mix element, **price** is defined as the amount customers pay and the methods of conveying the value of the product to them. As one of the nine functions of marketing, **pricing** is defined as establishing and communicating the value of products and services to customers. When planning any marketing activity, businesspeople must consider the impact of the cost to the business, the price customers pay, and the value added to the product.

We know that effective marketing results in satisfaction for both the consumer and the business. A satisfactory price means that the consumer views the purchase as a value. It also means that the business makes a profit on the sale.

The Importance of Price to Consumers

People make many decisions about what to buy based on price. Their satisfaction with purchases often relates to the prices they pay. But they don't always consider the lowest price to be the best price. For example, a no-frills airline with low ticket prices may not appeal to a business traveler who needs assurance of a reliable schedule and comfort. You can probably think of many products you buy that could be purchased at a lower price. Why do you decide to pay a higher price for them?

The Importance of Price to Businesses

Prices of products and services are as important to businesses as they are to consumers. The price determines how much money a business will make to cover the costs of planning, producing, and marketing. If the price is not high enough to pay those costs and generate a profit, the business will not be able to offer that product or service for long.

Price is an important tool because it can be changed more easily than other marketing decisions. Once a product is designed and produced, it is difficult to change its form or features. When producers, wholesalers, and retailers establish a distribution channel, it will be difficult to change where consumers can purchase that product. Even promotion is not easy to adjust. Businesses must plan and produce advertisements, purchase time or space in media, and provide new information and training for salespeople. By contrast, a retailer can change the price consumers pay by printing a sale banner or changing the price label on a product. Even manufacturers can change the price by offering a coupon or a rebate to consumers.

CHECKPOINT
Define price *and* pricing.

14.1.2 ▶ Price as an Economic Concept

Price also is an important economic concept. People have unlimited wants and needs that they try to satisfy with the limited resources available to society. Price allocates available resources among people. If there is a small quantity of a product or service but a very large demand for it, the price usually will be quite high. On the other hand, if there is a very large supply of a product or if demand is low, the price will be low. When the amount of the product demanded is equal to the amount supplied, that product is said to be in **equilibrium**. **Figure 14-1** illustrates how supply and demand affect price.

Economic Utility

The value customers receive from a purchase results from more than just the product or service itself. The concept of economic utility demonstrates that value is added through changes in form, time, place, or possession. Therefore, customers believe a product is a greater value and will often

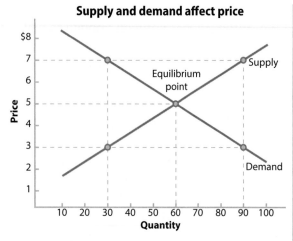

Supply and demand affect price

FIGURE 14-1 At a price of $3, demand (90) is greater than supply (30). At a price of $7, supply (90) is greater than demand (30). At a price of $5, supply equals demand (60), and the market is in equilibrium.

INELASTIC DEMAND

Price of a Dozen Eggs	Quantity Sold	Total Revenue
$1.80	284	$511.20
$1.77	288	$509.76
$1.74	291	$506.34
$1.71	296	$506.16
$1.68	300	$504.00
$1.65	305	$503.25

FIGURE 14-2 When the price is decreased for one dozen eggs, a larger quantity will be sold. The increase in quantity sold is not enough to increase the total revenue from the sales.

pay a higher price if the product is available with preferred features, if it is available at a better time or place than other choices, or if it can be purchased on credit.

Elasticity of Demand

You may think that an easy way to get consumers to buy a product would be to decrease the price. You reason that if the price decreases, more products will be sold. Many people believe that if sales increase, profits will increase as well. That is not always the result.

The table in **Figure 14-2** shows several prices a supermarket has charged for one dozen eggs. The table also shows the quantity sold and the total revenue the store received from the sales at each price. As you can see, for this product the decrease in price does not result in enough additional sales to increase the total amount of money received. A different result is shown in

Figure 14-3, which examines sales of a pint of ice cream at different prices. When the supermarket decreases the price of a pint of ice cream, the additional quantity sold increases total revenue.

The difference between these examples illustrates a key economic concept. **Elasticity of demand** describes the relationship between changes in a product's price and the demand for that product. Elasticity is based on the number of good substitutes for a product and the willingness of consumers to go without a product if the price gets too high.

Figure 14-2 shows that when the price of eggs is decreased, a larger quantity will be sold. However, the increase in quantity is not enough to increase the total revenue from sales. This occurs because there are few substitutes for consumers who purchase eggs. When consumers need to purchase eggs, they will do so even if the price is increased. If the price decreases, they will not buy many more eggs than they would have at the higher price. This is an example of inelastic

ELASTIC DEMAND		
Price of a Pint of Ice Cream	Quantity Sold	Total Revenue
$3.90	122	$475.80
$3.85	136	$523.60
$3.80	147	$558.60
$3.75	158	$592.50
$3.70	165	$610.50
$3.65	180	$657.00

FIGURE 14-3 When the price of a pint of premium ice cream decreases, the quantity sold increases. The increase in quantity sold results in higher total revenue.

demand. With **inelastic demand**, a price decrease will decrease total revenue, and price changes will have little effect on demand.

Figure 14-3 illustrates elastic demand. With **elastic demand**, a price decrease will increase total revenue, and price changes will have an effect on

*Want to know more about what is trending with this topic? Click on **Lesson 14.1, Marketing Decisions,** in your MindTap.*

demand. Demand is elastic when customers have several good substitutes for a product. Consumers view ice cream as one choice among many desserts. If the price of ice cream increases, some customers will not buy ice cream or will buy other desserts that are now a better value. If the price of ice cream decreases, people who were buying other products may switch now that ice cream seems more affordable.

If price changes are too great, the type of demand elasticity may change. If eggs become extremely expensive, people will stop buying them. There is a limit to the amount of ice cream people will buy no matter how inexpensive it is.

Therefore, marketers can apply price elasticity analysis only for price changes that consumers believe are reasonable.

CHECKPOINT
How are prices related to elasticity of demand for a product or service?

14.1.3 ▶ Government Influence on Prices

In private enterprise economies, businesses and consumers interact to determine prices and what is bought and sold. Governments play a role only when laws or regulations are needed to prevent unfair competition or to encourage activities that benefit society. When governments are involved in the economy, they often affect prices. The most important methods governments use to influence prices involve regulation of competition, controlling unfair pricing, and taxation.

Regulating Competition

A foundation of private enterprise is that competition benefits both businesses and consumers. Whenever one business becomes large enough to control a market or when a few businesses cooperate to take advantage of smaller businesses or consumers, the government may step in to regulate those businesses. Years ago, the federal government believed that AT&T had too much control over the telephone service industry. A court ruling required AT&T to divide itself into several smaller independent companies. This gave other businesses, such as Sprint, a better chance to compete.

The government also wants to encourage the development of new products and services so consumers will have additional choices. One way it helps businesses is by protecting new products from competition until they can become profitable. Patents are granted to inventors of unique products for a period of 20 years. During that time, no other business can market exactly the same thing unless the inventor grants permission or the patent is sold. People who develop artistic works such as books, films, recordings, or artwork can be protected by copyrights. The duration of a copyright can be a complex issue, but generally, it lasts the life of the author or artist plus 70 years. A company or individual that has a patent or copyright has greater control over the price charged for the product or artistic work, because there will be nothing just like it on the market for a period of time.

Regulating Prices

The federal government has enacted specific legislation to regulate the pricing practices of businesses. The most important areas regulated by laws include:

- *Price-fixing*   Competing companies at the same level in a channel of distribution (manufacturers, wholesalers, retailers) cannot cooperate in establishing prices.

- *Price discrimination*   Businesses cannot discriminate in the prices they charge to other businesses in their channel of distribution. A manufacturer must offer equivalent prices, discounts, and quantities to all wholesalers or retailers.

- *Price advertising*   Businesses cannot mislead consumers through the advertising of prices. Examples of misleading advertising include using phony list prices (prices at which the products are never sold), incorrect comparisons with competitors' prices, or continuous promotion of a sale price. Companies also must clearly communicate the terms of credit offered to customers.

- *Bait-and-switch*   Companies cannot lure customers with offers of low prices and then say the low-priced product is unavailable or inferior.

- *Unit pricing*   Many products sold in varying quantities or package sizes must list the price for a basic unit of measurement, such as a liter, ounce, or pound, so consumers can make price comparisons.

WORKING IN TEAMS

Buying concert tickets online can be frustrating. Often tickets seem to be bought up before they are available to the public and resold for higher prices. The online site adds several fees in addition to the cost of the ticket, driving the final price much higher than the published rates. As a team, discuss the reasons for and against government regulation of online ticket sales. Does your team believe regulation is needed? Present your decision and reasons to other teams in a class discussion.

Taxation

Governments also affect the products and services marketed, the prices paid, and the level of competition through taxation. An increase in the tax on a product makes it less attractive to consumers and reduces the level of sales. Taxes on products such as tobacco and liquor not only collect revenues for the government but also reduce the consumption of products believed to be harmful. Taxes or *tariffs* on imports increase the price of foreign products, making domestic products more competitive. For products considered luxuries, such as expensive automobiles and jewelry, a tax may not reduce the quantity of the products purchased, but it will increase the amount of taxes collected from people who are most able to pay.

Occasionally, the government wants to encourage a particular type of business or the development of certain products or services. Legislators use a tax reduction for that purpose. For example, to promote the use of solar panels and electric cars, the federal government and some states offer income tax credits to taxpayers who purchase these items.

CHECKPOINT
What are the three main ways that government influences prices in a private enterprise economy?

ASSESSMENT

What Have You Learned?

1. Why is price important to consumers? [14.1.1]

2. What does elasticity of demand describe? [14.1.2]

3. How does the government encourage the development of new products and services? [14.1.3]

Make Academic Connections

1. **Government**   Competition among businesses helps keep prices lower. Research a recent merger or sale between two large corporations in which the government became involved to prevent an adverse effect on competition. Write a short report describing the parties involved and the actions the government took. [14.1.3]

2. **Economics**   Select two products or services that consumers can purchase. Record three prices for each product or service—low, average, and high. Survey 20 people and ask them (1) if they would buy the items at the various price levels, and (2) how many of the items they would buy at one time at each level. Create a table like those shown in Figure 14-2 or 14-3 to determine if the demand for each item is elastic or inelastic. [14.1.2]

Connect to ◇DECA

Build your Portfolio

Many fast-food restaurants use price as a marketing tool to promote value menus, which include menu items for $1 or less. You work for a movie theater. Determine how the theater could use a similar pricing strategy to help increase its business. Present your pricing strategy to your teacher (judge). [14.1.2]

Planning a Career In...
GLOBAL SOURCING

Have you ever considered why so many companies have operations in other countries? Did you ever wonder where many of the products you purchased are manufactured? Can it really be cost effective to produce products in one country and ship them to customers in another part of the world?

The Global Sourcing field considers the most cost-effective way to manage product development while maintaining high-quality marketing and customer-service procedures. With evolving technologies that streamline communications and speed distribution, the barriers to locating manufacturing and other company activities in several different countries have decreased.

Job Titles

- Global Customer Service Specialist
- Global Logistics Specialist
- Global Sourcing Project Leader
- Strategic Sourcing Manager

Needed Skills

- A bachelor's degree is usually required with business, computer, or manufacturing specialization a plus.
- A strong knowledge of international finance, operations, and logistics is important.
- Understanding foreign cultures and proficiency in a foreign language is helpful.
- International business experience will facilitate promotions.

What it's like to work in... Global Sourcing

Perry, a global sourcing specialist for a large toy manufacturer, is compiling manufacturing specifications for a new toy. The toy's packaging will be used for storage of the toy pieces. When the specifications are completed and approved, Perry will post them on the company website and provide access to vendors from around the world. Each vendor can place its bid for the toy and the packaging according to the manufacturing specifications.

Perry set up a meeting for next week with a member of the finance department. Because many of the bidding vendors are from other countries, Perry and the financial analyst will formulate a projection of the anticipated value of the dollar relative to each of the respective foreign currencies. Fluctuations of the dollar relative to the foreign currencies will affect the long-term cost and profitability of the bids.

Perry also participates in an International Product Safety Standards meeting. Product safety is a key factor for consumers, so the meeting will focus on how each of the company's vendors ensures that safety standards are met.

What About You?

Would you like to help develop an economical and effective supply chain to produce and market your company's products?

Connect to MindTap

Discover more about the outlook for this career and watch a video about a related career. Click on **Chapter 14, Planning a Career In...** *in your MindTap.*

Learning Objectives

14.2.1 Describe three common pricing objectives for businesses.

14.2.2 Explain how businesses establish a price range for a product.

14.2.3 Identify the three components that must be considered when determining the selling price.

Key Terms

price range
breakeven point
selling price
product cost
gross margin

operating expenses
net profit
markup
markdown

marketing matters

Price planning begins with establishing price objectives. Three common objectives are maximizing profits, increasing sales, and supporting an image. The selling price must cover product costs and operating expenses and leave room for a profit. Some businesses, especially retailers, set prices by applying markups to the merchandise.

 essential question

How do companies determine if the price they set on a new product is appropriate for both the business and the customers?

14.2.1 ▶ Set Price Objectives

To begin price planning, marketers need to determine the objectives they want to accomplish with the price. Examples of possible pricing objectives are to maximize profits, increase sales, or maintain a particular company image.

Maximize Profits

Companies that seek to maximize profits carefully study consumer demand and determine what the target market is willing to pay for their products. The prices are set as high as possible while still satisfying customers. For example, Apple sets a high introductory price on new iPhone models. The company knows that many iPhone users will purchase the latest model regardless of price. Setting a high price enables a business to cover the costs of production and marketing and return a healthy profit. Companies that want to maximize profits usually select smaller target markets where unique products can be developed. Their products are quite different from competitors' and meet important customer needs in those markets.

Increase Sales

Sales-based pricing objectives result in prices that achieve the highest possible sales volume. Companies that want a greater share of the market or have high levels of inventory may choose this objective. Prices usually will be quite low to encourage customers to buy. Companies using a sales-based objective need to set the price high enough to cover costs. Also, they must have an adequate supply of the products to meet customer demand. They usually will sell their products in markets with a large number of available customers.

Maintain an Image

Companies can use the prices of products to help create a specific image for the product or the company. Many consumers believe that price and quality are related, and that higher prices mean better quality while lower prices suggest poorer quality. Therefore, companies that are building a quality image set higher prices than their competitors do. For example, high-fashion designers Louis Vuitton, Chanel, or Isaac Mizrahi know that people who are interested in high-fashion clothing are willing to pay more for their products because of the image they convey.

Some companies, such as Walmart, have built a low-price image. These companies appeal to cost-conscious customers by offering better value for less money. They need to keep their prices as low as or lower than competitors' prices. Some companies advertise that they will "meet or beat" their competitors' prices. The intention of that strategy is to convince customers that the company will always have the lowest prices.

CHECKPOINT
What are the three objectives that businesses may use in setting prices?

14.2.2 ▶ Determine a Price Range

After a company determines the basic objective that will guide pricing, the next step is to determine the possible prices for products and services. Products are sold at various prices depending on the brand, store, time of year, and other factors. To set an effective price for a product, a price range must be established. A **price range** specifies the maximum and minimum prices that can be charged for the product.

Maximum Price

The highest possible price that can be charged is determined by the target market. It is based on demand analysis. Marketing research identifies the customers in the target market and helps marketers understand their needs. Then alternative products and services that the target market will consider in satisfying its needs are identified. Finally, the customers in the target market are asked to identify what they would be willing to pay for each of the alternatives. The highest price that results from this analysis of demand is the *maximum price*.

Minimum Price

The lowest price in the price range is determined by the costs of the seller. A company can sell a product at a loss only for a short time and then only for a very few products. These products, called "loss leaders," are designed to increase customer traffic. Great deals may lure customers into stores, which will generate sales that offset the losses. Most prices must be set so that when all products are sold, the company has covered its costs. Ideally, the price set for a product will contribute profit to the company.

To determine the *minimum price*, a business needs to calculate all production, marketing, and administrative costs for the product. That is difficult because some costs cannot be directly related to specific products. Also, costs are often highest for new products and decrease as more products are sold.

One way in which companies determine the minimum price is through breakeven analysis. The **breakeven point** is the quantity of a product that must be sold for total revenues to match total costs at a specific price. The breakeven point is calculated using the following information.

- *Fixed costs*   The costs to the business that do not change no matter what quantity is produced or sold

- *Variable costs*   The costs that are directly related to the quantity of the product produced or sold

- *Total costs*   Fixed costs plus variable costs for a specific quantity of product

- *Product price*   Price at which the business plans to sell the product

- *Total revenue*   The anticipated quantity that will be sold multiplied by the product price

The breakeven point formula is:

$$\text{Breakeven point} = \frac{\text{Total fixed costs}}{\text{Price} - \text{Variable costs per unit}}$$

Figure 14-4 illustrates a breakeven analysis table for a basic nylon backpack. Using the information in Figure 14-4, you can calculate the breakeven point if the backpack sells for $14. The total fixed costs for the product are $85,000. The variable costs for each backpack are $2.80. The manufacturer wants to determine how many backpacks must be sold to break even if the price is set at $14. Use the following formula:

$$\text{Breakeven point} = \frac{85,000}{14.00 - 2.80} = \frac{85,000}{11.20}$$
$$= 7,589 \text{ units}$$

BREAKEVEN ANALYSIS FOR A NYLON BACKPACK

Units Sold	Variable Costs Per Unit	Total Variable Costs	+	Fixed Costs	=	Total Costs	Product Price	Total Revenue
5,522	$2.80	$15,462	+	$85,000	=	$100,462	$14	$77,308
6,054	$2.80	$16,951	+	$85,000	=	$101,951	$14	$84,756
6,998	$2.80	$19,594	+	$85,000	=	$104,594	$14	$97,972
7,589	$2.80	$21,249	+	$85,000	=	$106,249	$14	$106,246
8,225	$2.80	$23,030	+	$85,000	=	$108,030	$14	$115,150
9,110	$2.80	$25,508	+	$85,000	=	$110,508	$14	$127,540

FIGURE 14-4 The breakeven point is the quantity where total costs equal total revenue. Based on the figures in this table, the breakeven point for the nylon backpack would be about 7,589 units.

The company must determine if it will be able to sell this number of units. If so, they can set the price at $14. Additional calculations can be made at other possible prices to determine the relationships among prices, costs, and demand.

Price Range Example

A demand analysis for athletic shoes determined that customers in the target market would pay as much as $87 for the shoes when they are compared to all of the other choices. The company must charge at least $53 to cover fixed and variable costs. The shoes can be sold at any price between the maximum and minimum. This price range is shown in **Figure 14-5**. The company will select a price that meets its pricing objective and gives it the flexibility to change the price as market conditions change.

If the goal is to sell the greatest quantity of shoes possible, the company will set the price near $53. If the goal is to establish a high-quality image and provide a higher level of customer service, the price will be closer to $87. A goal of being competitive with the price may result in a price that is close to the prices of competing brands.

Price Range for a Pair of Shoes

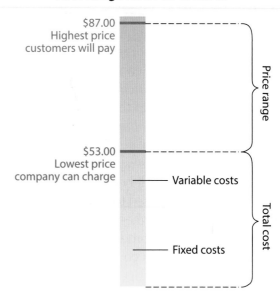

FIGURE 14-5 A company should price its product between its total cost per unit (minimum price) and the most customers are willing to pay (maximum price).

CHECKPOINT
What are the endpoints that define a price range for a product, and how are they determined?

14.2.3 ▶ Calculate a Selling Price

The price charged for a product or service is known as the **selling price**. For a successful product, the selling price has three components. The largest part of the selling price for most products is the cost of producing the product or buying it for resale. The **product cost** includes the cost of parts and raw materials (or the price paid to a supplier for finished products), labor, transportation, insurance, and an amount for damaged, lost, or stolen products. The difference between the product cost and the selling price is known as the **gross margin**. The gross margin is the amount that is available to cover the business's expenses and provide a profit on the sale of the product.

The next component of the selling price is operating expenses. **Operating expenses** are all costs associated with business operations. The costs of buildings, equipment, utilities, salaries, taxes, and other business expenses need to be calculated and added to the product cost. Marketing costs are incorporated into the operating expenses or included as a separate amount.

The final component of the selling price is profit. **Net profit** is the difference between the selling price and all costs and operating expenses associated with the product. Profit is not guaranteed to businesses when they sell products. A company's costs and expenses may be higher than anticipated, or it may have been unable to sell the item at the original price. In those cases, the business may not be able to make a profit or might even lose money on the sale. Businesses try to set selling prices high enough that reasonable profits are possible even when some costs are higher than expected or prices are reduced.

Want to know more about marketing in the information age? Click on **Lesson 14.2, Digital Marketing,** *in your MindTap.*

Connect to
MindTap

Markup can be calculated either as a percentage of the product cost or as a percentage of the selling price. For example, a box of 500 envelopes is sold at an office supply store for $3.50. The cost to the store is $2.80. The markup as a percentage of cost is 25 percent ($0.70 ÷ $2.80). The markup as a percentage of the selling price is 20 percent ($0.70 ÷ $3.50).

Some businesses use a standard markup for most products. For example, all products could be marked up by the same percentage, such as 45 percent, to determine the selling price. Other businesses determine the differences in operating and marketing costs or differences in the type of competition for various product categories. Then they develop a separate markup percentage for each product category.

When products are not selling well, a markdown will be used. A **markdown** is a reduction from the original selling price. Markdowns can be expressed as

Markups and Markdowns

To simplify the process of determining the selling prices for products, some businesses, especially retailers, use markups. A **markup** is an amount added to the cost of a product to determine the selling price. Markups are usually stated as a percentage rather than a dollar amount. Businesses determine the percentage needed to cover operating expenses and provide a profit and use that percentage to calculate the selling price.

© Denys Prykhodov/Shutterstock.com

How can markdowns affect a business's sales and profits?

specific dollar amounts or as a percentage of the original selling price. Markdowns usually reflect business mistakes because they indicate the product did not sell at the planned price. The mistakes may be a result of poor product quality or overestimating customer demand. Markdowns also can result from product and price changes made by competitors or poor marketing mix decisions involving location and promotion.

Effect of Markups and Markdowns on Profit

Businesses must consider the effect of markups and markdowns on their profit. High markups do not always mean that the business will make a larger profit on the product. Usually a high markup reduces the quantity sold or results in slower sales and higher costs to the business. On the other hand, businesspeople must be careful in using low markups. Although the lower price may result in higher sales, the markup may not cover all expenses. In some cases, expenses increase because of the costs of handling a larger quantity of products. On the other hand, markdowns usually result in lower profits, but they can help reduce inventory expenses. Marketers must carefully study the effects of different markup and markdown percentages before determining the one to use.

CHECKPOINT
What are the three components of a selling price?

14.2 ASSESSMENT

What Have You Learned?

1. What size market does a company that wants to maximize profits select, and what type of products does it typically develop? [14.2.1]

2. How does breakeven analysis help a company determine the minimum price for a product? [14.2.2]

3. When do companies decide to use markdowns in pricing products? [14.2.3]

Make Academic Connections

1. **Math**   A company manufactures and sells photo keychains for $3.50 each. Its fixed costs for the year are $40,000. The variable costs are $0.95 per unit. How many key chains will the company need to sell to break even? [14.2.2]

2. **Ethics**   Do you think it is ethical for a business to have a high markup on its products? Why or why not? How can consumers influence the markup? [14.2.3]

Connect to ◇DECA

Build your **Portfolio**

You are opening a clothing boutique that sells designer clothing and accessories. You are locating your shop in an upscale neighborhood. Write a price objective for your products. Select one product you will sell and set a price range for it. Then, calculate the selling price. Describe your price objective and explain how you determined the selling price to your teacher (judge). [14.2.1, 14.2.2]

14.3 PRICING BASED ON MARKET CONDITIONS

Learning Objectives

14.3.1 Identify two marketing tools related to competitive conditions that help marketers set prices.

14.3.2 Describe the criteria businesses use in establishing the final price a customer pays.

14.3.3 Explain why extending and managing credit is an important part of marketing.

Key Terms

skimming price
penetration price
nonprice
    competition
one-price policy
flexible pricing
    policy

price lines
FOB pricing
zone pricing
discounts and
    allowances
consumer credit
trade credit

marketing matters

Determining the best price depends as much on a company's target market as it does on its marketing objectives. Understanding product life cycles and consumer purchase classifications helps marketers tailor prices to the competitive environment. Depending on the type of market being targeted and the expectations of customers, marketers can use various criteria and tools to adjust the final price for each transaction.

essential question

What factors cause the price of a product to differ based on customer type and when it is purchased?

14.3.1 Competitive Environment

When planning the prices of products and services, marketers need to be aware of the competition in the market. If customers see many good alternatives, the prices of those products will remain very similar. If customers view a product as having few substitutes, the price of that product can be set higher than prices of competing products.

In certain types of market conditions, customers view products as very similar. Consider the difference between pure competition and monopoly. In markets with pure competition, customers see all product choices as identical. Therefore, it is almost impossible for a business to charge more for its products than other companies charge. For a business operating in a monopoly, customers have no good substitutes. Therefore, the company has more control over the price. That is why government often regulates companies operating in monopoly markets such as utility companies that provide gas and electric to homes and businesses.

Product life cycle analysis and consumer purchase classifications are two marketing tools that help businesses make pricing decisions. Some businesses also use non-price competition as a marketing strategy.

Product Life Cycle

Throughout the stages of a product life cycle, the type of competition changes. Those changes affect the prices that companies can charge. In the introductory stage, only one brand of a new product is available, allowing the business to control the price charged. Some companies enter the market with a skimming price. A **skimming price** is a very high price designed to emphasize the quality or uniqueness of the product. The business must closely study its target market to ensure customers would be willing to pay a high price for a new product. A skimming strategy usually results in higher profits for the company. Those higher profits encourage other companies to enter the market.

Other companies use a penetration price in the introductory stage of the product life cycle. A **penetration price** is a very low price designed to increase the quantity sold of a product by emphasizing value. A penetration price may result in higher total revenues, but the initial level of profit is much lower. Companies use a penetration price to attract a large share of the market early and discourage competition.

In later stages of the life cycle, competition increases, and there is an emphasis on price competition. In the maturity stage, customers see many choices that look very similar. Therefore, a small price change might encourage them to switch from one brand to another.

Consumer Purchase Classifications

Consumer purchase classifications also provide an example of different levels of price competition. Staple convenience goods and price-based shopping goods are examples of products facing intensive price competition. In each case, customers see few product differences, so they are drawn to lower prices. For products such as emergency or specialty goods, price is not as important to customers as other factors, so they are willing to pay higher prices.

Companies selling products with many similar competitors (common household products, basic clothing items, and business supplies) must pay close attention to the prices of competitors. Companies with unique products (specialty jewelry or fashion designs, expensive automobiles, and personal services) can be less concerned about the prices of competing products or services.

Nonprice Competition

When businesses emphasize price as a reason for customers to buy a product or service, two problems can result. First, the emphasis on price may encourage customers to view price as the most important reason for buying. That view causes them to see the other parts of the marketing mix (product, distribution, and promotion) as less important. Second, the emphasis on price means that businesses must keep prices as low as possible. With low prices, less profit will be made on each product sold. With lower profits, the company has less money to spend on marketing activities or new product development.

Want to know more about what is trending with this topic? Click on **Lesson 14.3, Global Marketing,** in your MindTap.

Connect to MindTap

To avoid those problems, some companies use nonprice competition. With **nonprice competition**, a business emphasizes elements of its marketing mix other than price by developing a unique offering that meets an important customer need. For example, few people with health insurance ask about the price of a visit to a physician or dentist. Price may not be the most important factor when purchasing a one-of-a-kind painting, applying for admission to an exclusive college, or planning a wedding or other special celebration.

Companies using nonprice competition need to carefully study the needs of a target market. They must examine the products and services that people in the target market view as possible alternatives. Market research can identify the things customers find dissatisfying about the competition. The company uses that information to develop a better marketing mix that is much more satisfying to those customers. If the company is successful in developing a unique marketing mix that meets important customer needs, price will not be an important factor in the purchase decision.

CHECKPOINT
Name two tools that help marketers identify the competitive environment and make better pricing decisions.

MARKETING COMMUNICATION

In-Theater Advertising

If you go to see a movie in a theater, you'll probably see several ads before the movie starts. In the past, those ads were limited to previews of other movies, but in the last decade or so, ads for other products have become part of the movie-going experience. You might see as many as five commercials before the previews begin.

Statistics show that in-theater commercials are more likely to be remembered than those on television. This may be because moviegoers are a "captive audience," meaning they aren't likely to get up and leave and can't change the channel. In this regard, they are very attractive to marketers. But many movie fans dislike in-theater commercials. They've already paid $10 or more for a movie ticket and feel they shouldn't be subjected to watching commercials. Some complain that the movie is delayed because of the ads, and others feel the theater is taking advantage of them.

When it comes to in-theater advertising, marketers must weigh these potentially negative feelings against the advantages of better brand recall.

Think Critically

1. Do you think younger audience members are more accepting of in-theater ads than older moviegoers? Why or why not? Can you think of a compromise that satisfies both marketers and moviegoers?

2. Would you be willing to pay more for a movie ticket if the theater did not run ads before the movie? How would a theater calculate the price of tickets if they decided not to run the ads?

When you go bowling or play miniature golf, you pay the price set by the business. Yet, few people expect to pay the price that is listed on the window sticker of a new automobile. Companies develop pricing strategies based on various criteria to help them establish the final prices.

Price Flexibility

Sometimes customers do not have a choice about the price they pay for a product. They either pay the price set by the business, or they do not buy. A **one-price policy** means that all customers pay the same price. In other cases, such as the purchase of a new house, the price paid by customers is based on how effectively they negotiate with the builder or real estate agent. A **flexible pricing policy** allows customers to negotiate the price within a price range.

It may seem unfair to offer different prices for the same product. In some cases, it is illegal to use flexible pricing. But consider a farmer selling fresh vegetables at a market. On days when there are a number of other farmers with the same products at the market, the farmer may need to lower the price in order to sell all of the products. On the other hand, when there are fewer products available, the demand will be higher, resulting in higher prices.

Automobile dealers traditionally have used flexible pricing to extract the highest price possible from each customer. They may agree to reduce the price if a customer is unwilling to pay the sticker price. Recently many auto dealers have begun using a one-price policy, in part because customers have access to dealer cost information on the Internet. With this policy, a lower initial price is set, and all customers are expected to pay that price for the automobile. The dealers believe they can reduce selling costs and customers will feel they are being treated more fairly under a one-price policy.

Price Lines

Many companies offer several choices of the same product to appeal to different customer groups. Appliance stores sell refrigerators, stoves, and dishwashers with several choices of options ranging from basic to full featured. To make it easier to analyze the choices, the products are grouped into two or three price lines. **Price lines** are distinct categories of prices based on differences in product quality and features. Companies must decide whether or not to offer price lines, the number of lines to offer, and the difference in prices among those lines. For example, an appliance store may sell stoves with price lines of $400, $800, and $1,200. Price lines make customers aware of the differences among products or services.

How would an appliance retailer set specific price lines for clothes dryers?

© Oleg Golovnev/Shutterstock.com

Geographic Pricing

Increasingly, companies sell products in different parts of the country and throughout the world. Costs of distribution and selling vary by location. Customer expectations of price and the level of competition are often different. Companies must determine how prices will be set in each geographic area.

Some companies keep the product price the same but charge a different amount to cover transportation costs. A method for setting transportation costs based on geographic location is known as FOB (free on board) pricing. **FOB pricing** identifies the location from which the buyer pays the transportation costs and takes title to the products purchased. For example, "FOB factory" means the customer pays all transportation costs from the point where the product is manufactured. A seller can negotiate with the customer and agree to pay some or all of the transportation costs by identifying a selected city between the buyer's and seller's locations for the FOB designation. Another type of geographic pricing is zone pricing. With **zone pricing**, different product prices or transportation costs are set for specific areas of the seller's market.

MATH IN MARKETING

Tickets or Popcorn

Theaters attract most of their customers through the movies they show. And with consumers' increasing ability to watch movies at home, theaters are under pressure to hold ticket prices down. A common pricing strategy is to charge different types of customers different amounts. It's a type of price discrimination based on willingness and ability to pay. The strategy can be viewed as one in which the customer pays a fee (the ticket price) in exchange for the right to purchase a product—popcorn, soda, and candy. Some customers exercise that right, while others won't. Customers who do purchase snacks are entering a monopoly market in which the theater charges a high price for the first few ounces of soda or popcorn, and then tries to sell them more with lower prices on the additional marginal ounces. The result is theater popcorn that costs customers more per ounce than filet mignon.

Do the Math

1. A movie theater estimates a week's attendance for a movie to be 1,500 customers, each paying $10.00 for a ticket. The theater's contract with the movie distributor says the theater must pay 70 percent of the ticket price to the distributor as rental for showing the movie or 95 percent of the profit after $4,500 in expenses, whichever is higher. However, 55 percent of the theater's customers spend an average of $12 at the concession stand, all of which contributes to profit because expenses have already been taken from the ticket income. How much profit will the theater make at the end of the week?

2. In order to increase profits, the theater can raise ticket prices by $2 or it can raise concession prices so that the average amount spent increases by $1. Assume the increases cause no drop in attendance or the percentage of customers purchasing concessions. Calculate the theater's profits if it raises only ticket prices, and then calculate profits if it raises only concession prices.

Discounts and Allowances

Sellers may choose to offer discounts and allowances to buyers. **Discounts and allowances** are reductions in a price given to the customer in exchange for performing certain marketing activities or accepting something other than what would normally be expected in the exchange. Some common discounts and allowances include the following:

- *Quantity discount* Offered to customers who buy large quantities

- *Seasonal discount* Offered to customers who buy during times of the year when sales are low

- *Cash discount* Offered to customers who pay with cash rather than credit or who pay their credit account balances off quickly

- *Trade discount* Reduction in price offered to businesses at various levels in a channel of distribution (wholesalers and retailers)

- *Trade-in allowance* Reduction in price in exchange for the customer's old product when a new one is purchased

- *Advertising allowance* Price reduction or cash payment given to channel members who participate in advertising the product

- *Coupon* Price reduction offered by a channel member through a printed promotional certificate

- *Rebate* Specific amount of money returned to the customer after a purchase is made

Added Value

© Robert Goudappel/Shutterstock.com.

Customers' perceptions of value change if the business adds value to the purchase. This is typically done through providing services during and after the sale. Another way of adding value is to provide complementary products or a larger quantity for a reduced unit price, such as "buy one, get one free." Some businesses offer prizes and premiums for purchases or use incentives for regular purchasing. Examples of such incentives are the frequent flyer programs that airlines use. Customers are given free tickets after they have traveled a certain number of miles on the airline.

CHECKPOINT
Name three strategies businesses use to determine the final price a customer pays.

14.3.3 Credit Sales

Companies that market expensive products or services may have a difficult time selling them even if customers believe the price is fair. For example, few companies have the cash to pay for a $30 million building. Few individuals are able to pay the full amount for a new car. Credit makes it possible for consumers to purchase expensive items. A company must determine if it needs to provide credit as part of its marketing mix price element.

Types of Credit

Retail or **consumer credit** is credit a retail business extends to the final consumer. The credit may be provided by the seller or it may be offered by another business that is participating in the supply chain, such as a bank, finance company, or credit card company such as Visa.

Most sales between businesses are made on credit. **Trade credit** is offered by one business to another business, often because of the time lag between when a sale is negotiated and when the products are actually delivered to the customer and used or resold. Credit sales also are a traditional business practice in many channels of distribution. Businesses rely on waiting 30 days or longer before making payment.

Credit Procedures

Credit provides a method for obtaining additional customers and sales. If a company manages credit poorly, though, costs may be high, and it may never collect from some customers. Managers responsible for credit sales must plan procedures carefully to be sure that credit is a successful part of a marketing strategy. Credit procedures include developing credit policies, approving credit customers, and developing effective collection procedures.

CREDIT POLICIES   Many companies accept credit cards which relieve them of the burden of having to manage credit policies and procedures. If a company decides to offer credit itself, one of the first decisions is whether to offer it on all products and to every customer. Next, the business develops a credit plan. It decides whether to offer its own credit plan or partner with another company such as a bank. Finally, it must develop the credit terms. The terms include the amount of credit that will be extended, the rate of interest to charge, and the length of time to give customers to pay.

CREDIT APPROVAL   Not all customers are good candidates for credit. If a customer is unable to pay for purchases, the seller loses all of the money invested in producing and marketing the product as well as the cost of extending credit. Even if the product is recovered from the customer, the company probably will not be able to resell it for an amount that will cover its costs.

A business that plans to offer credit must determine the characteristics and qualifications of the customers that will be extended credit. Those factors typically include customers' credit history, the resources they have that demonstrate their financial health, and the availability of the money with which they can make payments. Most businesses have a procedure through which customers apply for credit and provide financial references. These references include banks and other businesses from which they have obtained credit in the past. Commercial credit services such as Experian and Equifax for final consumers and Dun & Bradstreet for business customers can be used to provide information on credit history.

COLLECTIONS   Effective collection procedures are an important part of a credit plan. The procedures are needed so that customers are billed and payments are received at the appropriate time. Procedures for collecting overdue accounts are an important part of a credit system. Most businesses that offer credit have a small percentage of their accounts that are never collected. Even a small percentage of uncollected funds can make a credit plan unsuccessful. This results in losses and the need to increase prices for other customers.

This is why businesses often accept credit cards where the issuer is responsible for collection and losses rather than offering their own credit.

CHECKPOINT

Why should businesses extend credit?

14.3 ASSESSMENT

What Have You Learned?

1. What two problems may result when businesses emphasize price as the reason why customers should buy a product or service? [14.3.1]
2. What is the difference between a one-price policy and a flexible pricing policy? [14.3.2]
3. Why is trade credit useful in business-to-business sales? [14.3.3]

Make Academic Connections

1. **Geography** Research the price of a ticket for a Major League Baseball game in several cities. Why do you think the price of a ticket varies with the geographic location of the game? [14.3.2]
2. **Consumer Economics** Select a product or service that has two to three price lines.

Create a table with one column for the name of the product or service and one column for each price line. In each price line column, list the features that correspond to the price. Which price line most appeals to you? Explain your answer. [14.3.2]

Connect to ◇DECA.

Build your Portfolio

You work in the marketing department for a computer manufacturer that sells to businesses and consumers. To increase sales, you have been asked to develop a discounts and allowances program for both markets. Describe the target markets and the programs you would recommend for each to your teacher (judge). Explain why the programs will be effective and profitable. [14.3.2]

Connect to MindTap

*Analyze a case study that focuses on chapter concepts. Click on **Chapter 14, Case Study,** in your MindTap.*

CHAPTER 14 ASSESSMENT

Review Marketing Concepts

1. Why is price an important marketing tool? [14.1.1]

2. When would you knowingly pay a higher price for a product? Explain your answer using examples. [14.1.2]

3. Think of three products you purchase that have elastic demand. Explain your reasoning for your choices. [14.1.2]

4. Contrast price-fixing and bait-and-switch actions by companies. Which one of these activities poses a larger threat to consumers? [14.1.3]

5. You are opening a business that sells computer hardware and software. Which of these pricing objectives should you concentrate on for your first year in operation: maximizing profits or increasing sales? Explain your answer. [14.2.1]

6. What do you think would happen if a business operated at its breakeven point? [14.2.2]

7. Why might a business mark down an item below its cost? [14.2.3]

8. Do you think a skimming price would be a successful strategy for a product that has been on the market for several years? Why or why not? [14.3.1]

9. As a consumer, which pricing policy would you prefer: one price or flexible pricing? Explain your answer. [14.3.2]

10. Why might a large grocery store chain offer consumer credit to its customers? [14.3.3]

Marketing Research and Planning

1. Many terms are used to present the price of products and services. Also, the price or value of a product or service can be represented in a variety of ways with numbers, graphics, and pictures. Look through newspapers, magazines, direct mail advertisements, and other print materials from businesses and organizations and find examples of the many ways in which prices are communicated to consumers. Cut out examples and create a collage of price and value. [14.1.1]

2. Identify at least 10 consumers who will participate in a price study. Ask each person to respond to the following three items and record his or her answers.

   a. Identify five products or services you purchase regularly for which price is one of the important factors in the decision.

   b. Identify five products or services you purchase regularly for which price is not one of the important factors in your decision.

   c. Compare the products from the two lists and identify up to three reasons why price is more important for the first list than for the second.

   After you have collected the information, analyze the responses and develop several conclusions about the importance of price in consumer purchase decisions. [14.1.1]

3. The goal of businesses when pricing products is to set a price that provides a reasonable profit after all products are sold. Calculating the breakeven point identifies the minimum quantity that must be sold in order to cover the costs of the product. Using the following price and cost information for four products, determine the breakeven quantity. Then

construct a graph for each product that illustrates total fixed costs, total variable costs, total revenue, and total costs. Identify the breakeven point on each graph. [14.2.2]

Product	Fixed Price	Total Fixed Costs	Variable Costs Per Unit
A	$42.00	$20,000.00	$18.00
B	550.00	980,500.00	86.00
C	1.20	1,500.00	0.90
D	150.50	75,250.00	102.00

4. Identify one form of consumer credit to study. It can be a credit card from a retailer or a manufacturer, a bank credit card such as MasterCard or Visa, installment credit, a loan from a bank or finance company, or any other type of credit plan. Collect information by interviewing a credit manager or other person from the company who understands the credit system. Collect a copy of the credit application and other print information that explains the terms of credit. If possible, interview one or more people who use that particular form of credit. When you have finished your study, prepare a written report on the credit policies and procedures. Include the following information: who is offered credit, the application and approval procedure, the type of credit plan, the major credit terms, how billing is done, and the collection procedures for past due accounts. [14.3.3]

Marketing Management and Decision Making

1. Jerry Englebrecht has operated a successful dog-grooming service for 10 years. Each year the number of dogs he grooms has grown. His expenses have always been low because he is the only employee and operates the business from his home. For many years, the number of dog owners has increased in his town, but that growth has now almost stopped.

   In the past two years, three new grooming services have opened in his area. One is being offered by a veterinarian primarily to serve her customers. Another is part of a large chain of pet-grooming stores located in a larger city 15 miles away. The newest competitor is a small partnership consisting of two people who offer grooming on a part-time basis. They are open only two nights a week and on Saturdays.

   Until recently, Jerry had not been concerned about the competition. He believed he had loyal customers and had been getting inquiries from new pet owners. Recently he has noticed that fewer new people are asking about grooming services, and some of his regular customers have not returned. In talking to some of his customers, he learns that the chain store and the partnership are both offering grooming services at much lower prices than his.

   Jerry does not want to lower his price because that will decrease his profits. His goal has always been to use the profits to buy a building and expand his business.

   a. How can Jerry decide whether he should lower his price?

   b. If Jerry wants to emphasize nonprice competition, what are some recommendations you would make to him in the areas of product, distribution, and promotion to increase customer satisfaction? [14.3.1]

2. A small company has just created a new type of greeting card. It looks the same as the typical greeting card you can buy in most retail stores. The unique feature is a microchip in the card on which the sender can record a 30-second personalized message. Initially, the

cards are being produced in two categories—Valentine's Day and Mother's Day. If these cards are successful, the company may choose to expand its line of cards for other holidays, seasons, and special events.

Because of the computer technology and special envelopes needed to protect the card, the company's cost before distribution is higher than other cards—$3.40 each. The business has decided that the cards will be sold to a select set of specialty retailers throughout the world. A few wholesalers may be used for distribution if they follow a carefully developed marketing plan. The cards also will be sold to consumers who purchase in quantities of at least 50 cards. Those cards will be distributed by a parcel delivery service.

Your task is to develop a proposed set of pricing strategies for the company. Develop a specific strategy for each of the following items: price objective, price range, price flexibility, price lines, geographic pricing, discounts and allowances, and added value. The pricing strategies must be consistent with the product, its image, the type of competition that will exist, and the marketing strategies described. [14.2.1, 14.3.2]

3. A bicycle shop buys six models of bicycles for the following prices: $66, $99, $142, $180, $245, and $300. Determine the effect of various markups by designing an electronic spreadsheet that will calculate prices for the bicycle shop. Input the amounts the shop paid and develop formulas to calculate selling prices for the following markups—25%, 33%, 48%, and 60%. Then use the spreadsheet and each of the four markup percentages to calculate the total cost and total revenue for the bicycle shop if it purchased and sold three of each of the bicycle models. [14.2.3]

4. Using the information in the chart below, calculate the missing amounts. [14.2.3]

Product Cost	Gross Margin	Operating Expenses	Selling Price	Net Profit	Markup % (Selling Price)	Markup % (Cost)
$120.00	$____	$40.00	$____	$15.00	_____	_____
_____	36.00	16.00	58.00	_____	_____	_____
0.75	0.30	0.12	_____	_____	_____	_____
865.00	_____	_____	995.00	27.50	_____	_____
_____	_____	12.75	38.50	5.25	_____	_____
10.00	_____	_____	_____	2.00	_____	50
_____	25.00	25.00	80.00	_____	_____	_____
_____	_____	27.00	_____	64.00	70	_____

Let's Start a Band! Follow-Up Discussion

Work in small teams to discuss the question posed at the end of the opening vignette. What are the considerations for the band in setting more consistent pricing for its services?

Build Your Marketing Plan

Build your Portfolio

In this chapter you learned about pricing and credit procedures and setting prices. You will now apply this learning to the development of your marketing plan. To access the chapter-specific tools that you will need to complete this activity, please navigate to Chapter 14 ➔ Build Your Marketing Plan in MindTap. Alternatively, you can access these tools online at NGLSync. Please visit www.nglsync.cengage.com, and search for the companion website that accompanies this book by entering the ISBN, author, or title. Once you locate this companion website, navigate to Build Your Marketing Plan ➔ Chapter 14.

Hospitality and Tourism Operations Research Event

Build your Portfolio

The Hospitality and Tourism Operations Research Event provides an opportunity for students to demonstrate management skills. Hospitality and tourism operations include marketing and management functions in a business primarily engaged in satisfying the desire to make productive or enjoyable use of leisure time.

A customer service gap is the difference between customers' expectations of a service and the actual service they receive. The Hospitality and Tourism Operations Research Event requires participants to select a hotel or restaurant and analyze the customers' perception of service they receive from the business. Participants will survey current customers and prospective customers to determine their expectations of the hospitality business. Participants will then develop a strategic plan to expand the customer base through a promotional campaign using the most cost-effective media available.

This project can be completed by one to three members. You will have ten minutes to present your project and five minutes to answer the judge's questions. The written project consists of the following parts:

Executive Summary A one-page description of the project.

Introduction A description of the business and the community where it is located.

Research Methods Used in the Study The design of and methods used to conduct the customers' perception of the service they receive from the business.

Findings and Conclusions Analyzes the findings of the research study and provides conclusions based on the findings.

Proposed Strategic Plan Includes goals, objectives, and rationale of the institutional promotion campaign. This section includes activities, timelines, and budget for the campaign.

Bibliography and Appendix Additional sections that may be needed.

Performance Indicators Evaluated

- Explain the nature of marketing research. (Marketing-Information Management)
- Describe methods used to design marketing research studies. (Marketing-Information Management)
- Explain techniques for processing marketing data. (Marketing-Information Management)
- Coordinate activities in the promotional mix. (Promotion)
- Select placement of advertisements. (Promotion)
- Calculate media costs. (Promotion)
- Pitch marketing communications idea to client. (Selling)

Go to the DECA website for more detailed information. **www.deca.org**

Think Critically

1. Why are more hotels and restaurants emphasizing customer service in their advertisements?

2. Why should businesses be aware of the customer service gap?

3. What is the best way to survey customers about their hotel or restaurant experience?

4. What is the meaning of hospitality?

CHAPTER 15

PROMOTION

 See how effective advertising leads to successful marketing strategies. Click on Chapter 15, Visual Focus, in your MindTap.

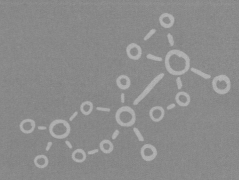

Let's Start a Band!

> "Our whole preconception will be what's going to make that kid push our button and not someone else's."
>
> – Bruce Kirkland, former President/CEO of Capitol Records

We're planning to go on the road for a while, and we need to get out in front of it with some promotion. We probably should start by updating our press kit—if you can even call what we've been sending out a press kit. If we do it right and get it to the right people ahead of time, word-of-mouth should do the rest. You know, help create a buzz. We can't depend on these gigs to promote themselves.

We need to update the bios and get some high-quality photos for it. Posed and live shots. Then we should have some flash drives made up and put the press kit on them along with some samples of our music. We'll choose music samples that will catch the listener's ear in about 30 seconds. We also need to include contact information in the press kit—and on our social media sites. Gael said we need to be sure to keep the press kit current, so it reflects where we've played and any changes in players.

We also should probably include some press reviews and interviews, but I'm not sure if we should send entire articles and reviews or just quotes from them. I want to send out a really good press kit this time, so can you help me by telling me if you agree with my ideas, what else you think we should include, and who we should send it to?

15.1 PROMOTION IS A FORM OF COMMUNICATION

Learning Objectives

15.1.1 Identify the promotion function as part of the marketing mix.

15.1.2 Identify the eight elements of the communication process.

15.1.3 Explain the three roles of promotion in marketing.

15.1.4 Identify the two types of communication that are important to marketers.

Key Terms

promotion
communication
   process
sender
message
encoding
media
vehicle
receiver
decoding
noise
feedback
interpersonal
   communication
mass
   communication

marketing matters

Most marketing messages that run on television and radio and in magazines and newspapers are lost in the clutter. For marketers to effectively reach existing and potential customers, they need to choose the right target, develop a persuasive message, and devise the right mix of advertising, public relations, sales promotion, and personal selling. With the right balance of promotions, they can deliver a consistent message that will help lead consumers to a purchase decision.

essential question

What is the key function performed by the promotion element of the marketing mix? Why is it critical for companies to understand and implement this function correctly?

15.1.1 ▶ Promotion as Part of the Marketing Mix

When you want to buy a car, you have many choices. You choose from hundreds of makes, models, and dealerships. The same is true of cheeseburgers, guitars, and toothpaste. Because you are free to choose where to spend your dollars, companies must compete for your business. They want you to believe that they offer a product or service that is superior to their competitors, and they ultimately want you to choose their product or service.

One of the most important tools for a company trying to attract customers is promotion, one of the four elements of the marketing mix. **Promotion** is any form of communication that a company uses to inform, persuade, or remind consumers about its products, services, or even itself.

As part of the marketing mix, promotion should complement the other three elements as illustrated in **Figure 15-1**. A product may be exactly what consumers want, may sell for the right price, and may be available to them because of good distribution. However, if they don't know about the product, don't know where to get it, or don't think it will fill a need or desire in their life, the product will not sell. That is why good promotion is critical. Promotion is how a company communicates with consumers.

CHECKPOINT
What is promotion?

FIGURE 15-1 Promotion is a key element of the marketing mix. It relies on and complements the other elements.

15.1.2 ▶ Promotion as a Form of Communication

Promotion is a **communication process**, or the transfer of a message from a sender to a receiver. In marketing, the communication process usually involves a company or organization sending a sales message to a potential customer. To understand how this process works, a marketer must first understand the basics of the communication process, as illustrated in **Figure 15-2**.

The Sender

The communication process originates with a sender. The **sender** is the source of the message being sent, the *who* in the communication process. This can be a person, a company, or an organization. In marketing communication, the sender typically is a company trying to send a message to consumers. When you see an advertisement, the sender is the company that planned the ad.

The Message

The **message** is *what* is being communicated. In the promotion process, there can be several messages conveyed at once, on several different levels. A simple message might be that a store is having a sale. But there may be other less explicit messages conveyed in the process. For instance, if a poster for the store's sale looks very elegant, it may send the message that the store is elegant and classy.

Encoding by the Sender

When the sender converts an idea into a message that the receiver can understand, this is called **encoding**. Encoding relies on basic units of meaning such as language, words, and symbols, but it also can include more subtle cues such as colors, design, music, and imagery. When the store having

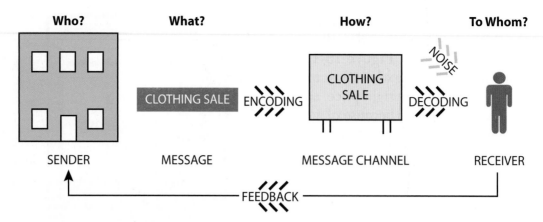

Who?   **What?**   **How?**   **To Whom?**

CLOTHING SALE   ENCODING   CLOTHING SALE   NOISE   DECODING

SENDER   MESSAGE   MESSAGE CHANNEL   RECEIVER

FEEDBACK

FIGURE 15-2 Promotion is a form of the communication process by which a company sends its message via a message channel to potential customers.

the sale creates its poster and decides what words and pictures to include, this is all part of the encoding process.

The Message Channel

The method by which the message travels is the message channel, or **media**. The message channel is *how* the message will be distributed. In marketing, the message channel can be television, radio, social media post, magazine, salesperson, text message, website, or anything else that conveys a message. The specific broadcast or print choices associated with a message channel is the **vehicle** of the message. For instance, the media choice might be a magazine advertisement, but the vehicle choice will be *Rolling Stone* magazine.

The Receiver

The message travels to the receiver. The **receiver** is the person or persons *to whom* the message is directed or any person who understands the message that is

Want to know more about what is trending with this topic? Click on Lesson 15.1, Global Marketing, in your MindTap.

Connect to MindTap

sent. In marketing, receivers are the target audience or potential customers.

Decoding by the Receiver

Before the message can be fully received, it must be decoded by the receiver. **Decoding** is the process by which the receiver interprets the transmitted language and symbols to comprehend the message. People may see a sign, but if the sign is in a language they do not understand, they will not receive the message.

Noise

Any distracting information in the transmission, the message channel, or the receiver's environment that may inhibit or distract from the message is called **noise**. Noise includes TV or radio static or interference, competing messages, unfamiliar words, or even a crying baby—anything that makes it harder to receive the message. Marketers also refer to some types of noise as "clutter."

Feedback

Sometimes there is a feedback step in the process. **Feedback** is the receiver's response to the message. It can be direct feedback, such as a letter the receiver sends back to the sender or a survey the receiver takes. It also can be indirect feedback, such as the redemption of a promotional coupon or the purchase of a company's product. Feedback helps marketers determine if their promotions work effectively and how to improve them.

 CHECKPOINT
Name the eight elements of the marketing communication process used in promotion.

What components of the communication process are represented by this simple "sale" sign?

Chad Baker/Jason Reed/Ryan McVay/Getty Images

15.1.3 The Role of Promotion in Marketing

Before marketers begin a promotion program, they must outline the program goals. Promotion fulfills three main roles for marketers. It can inform, persuade, or remind an audience, or it can involve some combination of these.

Inform

A company will often use promotion to inform people about a product. This is particularly true when a company introduces a new product or a new product feature. If a store is opening or moving to a new location, it will want to let customers know.

Sometimes a company wants to inform people of an existing product feature that people just do not know about. At other times, a certain aspect of a product will become more appealing, and the company will want to publicize that aspect. For instance, when gas prices rise, car companies often will advertise the gas

mileage of their more fuel-efficient cars because that feature has become relevant to consumers.

More complicated products and services are more likely to use promotions that inform customers about their products. When a buying decision is complicated—as when people are shopping for life insurance or a computer—consumers will want to collect as much information as possible and compare their options. The price of a product also can affect the amount of information a consumer seeks. People want more information before purchasing a big-ticket item.

Persuade

Sometimes a company will need to make a case for *why* a customer should buy its product. The company will create a promotional program with the goal of persuading customers. The company may say why its product is better than the competitor's, or it may explain how the product will fulfill a consumer need or desire. Persuasive arguments include, "Fly our airline for less" and "This car is better for the environment."

Sometimes, a promotion will both inform and persuade. For instance, if Pepsi says that people preferred Pepsi to Coke in a taste test, that information is intended to persuade you that Pepsi is better, and you should buy it instead of Coke. The message is supported by the fact that people tried both products and preferred Pepsi.

Persuasive promotions can be used throughout the life cycle of a product. However, they typically are used more after consumers are familiar with the product. A company also may change its persuasive tactics over time. Chevy may advertise the pulling power of its pickup trucks in one campaign, their longevity in another, and that they are American made in another. Chevy changes its promotional approach because different aspects of Chevy trucks appeal to different people.

Remind

The final role of promotional activities is to remind customers about existing products. These are typically familiar, mature products. Marketers may simply want to remind people a product exists, how good it tastes, or how many people enjoy it. A sign with a Snicker's logo in a football stadium is a reminder promotion. Marketers assume you are familiar with Snickers bars and how they taste. They hope that by seeing the sign, you will buy one from the concession stand.

CHECKPOINT
What three roles does promotion play in marketing?

15.1.4 ▶ Types of Communication

The types of communication marketers use depend on the product or service and the intended target market characteristics. Marketers focus on interpersonal and mass communication in delivering their messages.

Interpersonal Communication

Interpersonal communication is any person-to-person exchange. In marketing, this may be a telemarketing call, an in-person sales call, a customer service sales center call, an online chat with a company representative, or a salesperson in a store. The greatest benefit of interpersonal communication is that it is a two-way conversation. Customers can ask questions, and the salespeople can give an immediate response to the customers. They can tell if a customer is interested, bored, irritated, or confused.

Interpersonal communication is specifically targeted. For complex and high-end products, a salesperson can explain the differences between competing products and help the customer make a knowledgeable purchase decision. An experienced salesperson also can earn a customer's trust in ways other types of communication cannot.

Interpersonal communication is frequently used in business-to-business marketing. Many companies that sell to other businesses have a professional sales staff that can form relationships with clients and respond to their needs.

Weaknesses of interpersonal communication are that it can be inefficient and costly. One salesperson can only deal with one or two people at a time. And, although a knowledgeable sales force can be a great asset, it can be expensive to train and pay.

Mass Communication

Mass communication attempts to reach a wide audience, sometimes millions of people, through mass media such as radio, television, magazines, newspapers, social media, and the Web. Mass communication is a one-way flow of information. It does not provide the opportunity for immediate feedback because the receiver cannot directly respond to the sender. This limits how much the message can be tailored for the recipient. Although marketers do their best to target their messages, with mass communication they cannot be sure who will see the promotion. It may not reach all of the intended audience, and it may reach some people for whom it was not intended.

Mass communication can be much more cost-efficient than personal selling. One advertisement, for instance, can be used over and over to reach many more people in a shorter amount of time than a salesperson ever could. And although direct feedback is limited with mass communication, marketers have developed methods of gauging the effectiveness of a promotion. For example, they might issue coupons and track their use or use market research to gather consumers' reactions to ads.

CHECKPOINT
What two types of communication do marketers commonly use?

What Have You Learned?

1. Why is promotion the most critical element of the marketing mix? [15.1.1]

2. What does encoding of a message by the sender rely on? [15.1.2]

3. What does a persuasive marketing message tell the receiver? [15.1.3]

4. Why is mass communication said to be a "one-way flow of information"? [15.1.4]

Make Academic Connections

1. **Visual Art** Select an ad or other promotion you have seen or heard recently. Draw or use technology to create a picture, graphic, or other visual representation of the communication process as it pertains to that promotion. [15.1.2]

2. **Research** Use the Internet or library to research how a major brand has changed its promotions over time. Describe the changes and explain why you think they were made and whether or not the changes have been effective. [15.1.1–15.1.4]

Connect to ◇DECA
Build your Portfolio

You and your team members work for an advertising firm that has been hired by a home electronics store to create a 10-second video ad for a new type and brand of ear buds. Determine the target market for the ear buds (the receiver of the message). Write a script for the ad, and then make a video of the ad based on the script. Present the video to your teacher (judge). [15.1.2]

TYPES OF PROMOTION

Learning Objectives

15.2.1 Explain the advantages and disadvantages of advertising as a type of promotion.

15.2.2 Describe the ways public relations can be used to generate publicity.

15.2.3 Identify the benefits and drawbacks of using personal selling to promote a product or service.

15.2.4 Explain the advantages and disadvantages of using short-term incentives such as sales promotions.

Key Terms

advertising
broadcast media
print advertising
direct mail
outdoor advertising
ambient advertising

Internet advertising
publicity
public relations
personal selling
sales promotion

marketing matters

Marketers must know what to consider when deciding which types of promotion to use. The four common types of promotion are advertising, public relations, personal selling, and sales promotion. Marketers strive to find the right mix of these four ingredients. In a good promotional mix, all the elements work together, complementing one another so that consumers receive a consistent message about the product or service.

 essential question

What are the various characteristics, strengths, and weaknesses of the various forms of promotion available to marketing managers?

15.2.1 Advertising

When people hear the word *marketing*, they usually think of the various forms of advertising. But by now in this course, you know that marketing is so much more. As the most familiar form of the promotion element of the marketing mix, **advertising** is any form of paid, nonpersonal communication that uses mass media to deliver a marketer's message to an audience.

Types of Advertising

The major forms of advertising are broadcast, print, direct mail, outdoor, ambient, and the Internet.

Television and radio are known as **broadcast media**, meaning that a signal is sent from a central transmitter to receivers in a geographic area. Ads on TV and radio take the form of commercials, or "spots."

Print advertising is any paid message in a magazine or newspaper. Print advertisements can be several pages long, but they are more commonly one page or a part of a page.

Direct mail is any marketing message sent to an audience through the mail. It is sometimes referred to as "junk mail," but it can be a very effective way to target messages.

Outdoor advertising includes billboards, signs on buses or taxis, car or truck wraps, messages on the sides of buildings, posters, ads on bus shelters or benches, signage at sporting events, or any other space designed specifically for ads outside the home.

Because marketers are always looking for ways to make their message stand out and get noticed, there has been a rise in recent years of **ambient advertising**. This type of advertising includes any non-traditional medium in the environment of the audience. Stickers on bananas, messages chalked onto sidewalks, hot-air balloons, stunts or "guerilla" advertising, and messages on bathroom stall doors all fall into the category of ambient advertising.

Internet advertising is the fastest growing and most dynamic type of advertising. One benefit of Internet advertising is that it can target consumers by interest and location. Another benefit is that, unlike most other forms, Internet advertising provides marketers with instant feedback. Marketing via social media is a powerful example because it creates a dialog that enables the audience to provide immediate feedback to a company and to share the information with other consumers.

Advantages of Advertising

Because advertising is able to reach a wide audience, it is an efficient medium in terms of cost per viewer. Advertising also is a very controllable, repeatable form of promotion, delivering the same message again and again, if necessary. An ad can be run multiple times to reinforce the message as necessary.

Another advantage is that many forms of advertising are not limited by geography. Ads can reach people anywhere in the country and most places in the world.

The final advantage of advertising, particularly television advertising, is that it has great potential to move people emotionally through the film style, music, and other production factors. When it comes to building strong brands, creating an emotional tie between a consumer and a product can be invaluable.

Disadvantages of Advertising

For all the advantages of advertising, there are some disadvantages as well. First, even though advertising has a low cost per view, the overall cost can be prohibitively expensive, especially for smaller companies. A company with a national advertising plan will need to devote millions of dollars for it to be effective.

The second disadvantage is the impersonal nature of advertising. In most cases, there is no instant feedback, no ability to modify the message for the viewer, and no way to make the personal connection that face-to-face communication allows.

Finally, with so much advertising clutter and other noise, and with new

*Want to know more about marketing in the information age? Click on **Lesson 15.2, Digital Marketing,** in your MindTap.*

Connect to MindTap

technologies such as digital video recorders, it has never been easier for audiences to tune out or skip past ads. This is a major problem for marketers—one they are constantly trying to solve.

CHECKPOINT

Name several advantages and disadvantages of advertising as a type of promotion.

15.2.2 ▶ Public Relations

Marketers often try to get their message to consumers by generating publicity through existing mass media, often news outlets. **Publicity** is any nonpaid mention of a product, service, company, or cause. The effort to reach consumers by generating positive publicity is known as **public relations**, or PR.

Although the actual coverage of the product or service is nonpaid, companies often have a PR department or hire a PR firm to identify media opportunities. They will often write press releases to send to the news media about their product or service. They also may contact talk shows, magazines, and other media outlets to try to get their product mentioned.

Sometimes PR is needed to respond to negative publicity. If a product is faulty or unsafe or if there is a recall, a company may have to use public relations to control the amount of damage done to its image. The company will contact media outlets in the hope that any coverage of the issue will include the company's point of view and what it is doing to resolve the problem.

WORKING IN TEAMS

As a team, select a school event or program that needs funding or supplies. For example, perhaps the school band needs to raise money for new uniforms. Discuss how publicity might benefit the cause. Develop a public relations campaign to create community awareness.

than a commercial. When a product gets a favorable mention on a news program or a favorable review by a talk show host or celebrity, people are more likely to listen and try the product than if they had just seen a television commercial. For example, when Oprah Winfrey mentions a product or selects a book for her online book club, those products fly off the shelves because so many people trust and respect her. For that reason, many companies try to get her to endorse their products on her website or television network.

The second advantage of public relations is that it can be relatively inexpensive. If the release of a new product from a company becomes a big news story, it can be worth millions of dollars in free

Advantages of Public Relations

Publicity generated through public relations is valuable because a third-party source such as a news program is perceived as being more trustworthy

Want to know more about what is trending with this topic? Click on **Lesson 15.2, Marketing Decisions,** *in your MindTap.*

Connect to
MindTap

publicity. Apple, maker of the popular iPhone, masterfully uses the news media to create buzz anytime a new version is released, and it has helped Apple lead the industry.

Disadvantages of Public Relations

The biggest disadvantage of public relations is that it is hard to control. Because it relies on third-party media outlets, exactly what is said about a product is up to the media, not the marketer. Although coverage of a product by one media outlet may lead to more coverage, it is nearly impossible to predict or control what kind of coverage, if any, a product will get. If the news media covers a product but reviews it negatively, it can be disastrous for a company.

CHECKPOINT
What are some of the advantages and disadvantages of public relations?

MARKETING COMMUNICATION

Squealing About a Flying Pig

Game Day Communications, a Cincinnati-based firm specializing in sports and entertainment communications, was founded in 2002 by former ESPN anchor Betsy Ross and marketing expert Jackie Reau. Game Day's first major client was the city's premier race event, the Cincinnati Flying Pig Marathon. Since being involved with marketing the Flying Pig, Ross and Reau have watched it grow from a small regional road race into a multi-faceted, internationally recognized event that appeals to almost all levels of runners and walkers worldwide.

Generating awareness for the race centers on promoting a world-class marathon. It also involves promoting what has evolved into a full schedule of events and activities that make up an entire race weekend. The Flying Pig Marathon weekend includes a half marathon, a 10K, a 5K, and a four-person relay. It also offers family-friendly events, including a fun run for kids and a newly added dog walk.

Think Critically

1. Write a press release (up to one page) to target a specific type of publication, such as a family magazine, a newsletter for walkers, or a running club bulletin for the race and other events involved.
2. Leading up to and during the race weekend, how might your marketing team continue to promote the event through social media channels?

As the name suggests, **personal selling** is person-to-person communication with a potential customer in an effort to inform, persuade, or remind the customer to purchase an organization's products or services. It usually involves interaction with a salesperson.

Personal selling is most commonly used in business-to-business promotion, where salespeople from one company meet with the people in charge of making the purchasing decisions for another company. These meetings can involve elaborate presentations and follow-up meetings before a sale is made.

Other forms of personal selling include salespeople at a retail store, telemarketers, car dealers, real estate or insurance agents, or even customer service representatives available online or over the phone. All of these people help inform customers about products, answer questions, and eventually lead them to a purchase decision.

The types of products for which personal selling is appropriate are usually complicated, relatively expensive, and have many features. Business-to-business deals sometimes involve very expensive products such as manufacturing equipment. Consumer products sold with personal selling include cars, houses, and home audio systems.

Advantages of Personal Selling

An advantage of personal selling is the personal contact with customers. It can be much more informative and persuasive than advertising because of the person-to-person interaction.

Also, with person-to-person contact, feedback from the customer is immediate, and the sales presentation is flexible. For example, a salesperson in a computer store can answer questions, provide information, and even recommend a product based on a customer's needs.

Disadvantages of Personal Selling

The major disadvantage of personal selling is the per-person cost. Though the cost of advertising is high, it reaches millions of people. Personal selling reaches one customer at a time and makes one sale at a time, so the cost per customer can be extremely high. Sometimes, especially in business-to-business marketing, the selling process can go on for months and ultimately may not result in a sale.

© Iakov Filimonov/Shutterstock.com.

Why is personal selling effective in selling furniture and home décor?

CHECKPOINT
Name an advantage and a disadvantage of personal selling as a type of promotion.

Sales Promotion

Sometimes marketers will want to boost sales through the use of short-term incentives with the hope that consumers will repeat the purchase later without the incentive. Any activity or material that gives consumers a direct incentive to buy is called **sales promotion**. The use of sales promotions is a common tactic when a company introduces a new product and wants to entice consumers to try it or when a company needs to increase the short-term sales of a product. An ice cream brand may want consumers to try a new flavor. A car dealership may want to sell last year's model before the newer model arrives.

Common types of sales promotions include:

- Price promotions such as sales, coupons, or rebates

- Product incentives such as limited-time models or free product features and add-ons

- Giveaways such as sweepstakes, contests, free product samples, or free toys with purchase

- Special in-store or point-of-purchase displays sent by the manufacturer.

Advantages of Sales Promotion

The biggest advantage of sales promotion is that it reliably generates immediate, short-term sales. A company can depend on a sales promotion for a boost it hopes will create loyal customers.

Another advantage is that sales promotion results usually are measurable. Stores know how effective their coupon program is because they can count how many coupons were used, or the traffic during a sale can be compared with normal store traffic. This information can be used to plan future promotions.

Disadvantages of Sales Promotion

The biggest advantage of sales promotion also may be one of its drawbacks. Most successful businesses strive to create and rely on loyal customers. Sales promotion, on the

© Fisher Boy

How would this sales promotion stimulate short-term sales of this frozen fish product?

other hand, is all about the short term. It builds customer relationships motivated by incentives rather than a true preference for the brand. Once the promotion has ended, the business hopes that the customers will return, but often they do not. Other disadvantages of sales promotion can be the cost of providing the incentives, the loss in profit by cutting the price of products, and the cost of advertising the promotion.

CHECKPOINT
What is a sales promotion?

15.2 ASSESSMENT

What Have You Learned?

1. What are the benefits of Internet advertising? [15.2.1]

2. How is public relations used to respond to negative publicity about a company or its products? [15.2.2]

3. What are the characteristics of products for which personal selling is appropriate? [15.2.3]

4. In what two situations are sales promotions a common tactic? [15.2.4]

Make Academic Connections

1. **Language Arts** Write a one-page account of a fictional person's day. Describe how the person comes into contact with the four types of promotion and how he or she reacts to them. [15.2.1]

2. **Math** A grocery store usually makes a 10 percent profit on a box of detergent that sells for $5.00. In an average week, it sells 30 boxes of detergent. The store runs a coupon promotion for 25 cents off each box. How many boxes does it need to sell per week to break even on the promotion? [15.2.4]

Connect to  DECA

Build your Portfolio

You own a high-end clothing store in the mall. Determine how each type of promotion might be used to attract customers to your store and produce sales once they are there. Create a chart outlining the various types of promotion and how they would be applied to your store. Present the chart to your teacher (judge) and discuss your decisions. [15.2.4]

15.3 THE PROMOTIONAL PLAN

Learning Objectives

15.3.1 Explain the five major factors that affect the promotional mix.

15.3.2 Describe the seven steps in the promotional planning process.

Key Terms

promotional mix
promotional plan

marketing matters

Each type of promotion has its strengths and weaknesses. Marketers typically use several or all of the types of promotion. They fill different roles and reach consumers in different ways, but they deliver essentially the same message. The specific way in which the promotional elements are used depends on several factors: the product itself, the target market, the product price and distribution, the availability of resources, and the company's overall philosophy.

essential question

What elements should an advertiser consider when making decisions about how to compose the promotional mix?

15.3.1 The Promotional Mix

The **promotional mix** is the combination of advertising, public relations, personal selling, and sales promotion that marketers use to reach a target market. The elements of the promotional mix must complement one another. If they deliver conflicting messages, the consumer might become confused. A carefully planned promotional mix can capitalize on the strength of each type of promotion and reach customers from several different angles to deliver on the promotional objective. How marketers determine which promotional tools to use depends on several factors as shown in **Figure 15-3**.

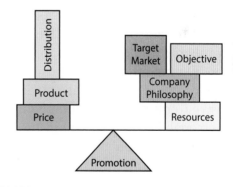

FIGURE 15-3 Many factors influence promotional plans, which makes developing the right promotional mix a balancing act.

Promotional Objective

Communication used to promote a product or business can serve three purposes for a marketer: to inform, to persuade, and to remind. Different types of promotions are better suited for certain objectives. For instance, personal selling is an excellent tool for informing customers and delivering large quantities of information. However, it wouldn't make sense to hire salespeople to remind people to buy milk at the store.

Target Market

It is critical to consider the target market in formulating a promotional mix. Who are the people the company is trying to reach, and what do they find compelling? If your target market is upper-income, health-conscious women, offering coupons for 25 cents off a nutritional supplement may not be as effective as advertising the product's health benefits. You also need to consider where the target market lives. For example, a target market that is dispersed across the country might make television advertising a better approach than a billboard.

Marketing Mix

The type of product, the price, and its distribution channel also affect the promotional mix. Certain products are better served by certain types of promotions. A low-priced product such as bar soap, for instance, is not a good candidate for personal selling. However, soap probably would benefit from a coupon. On the other hand, consumers want more information before buying expensive items such as a guitar, which is why personal selling is a good fit for that product. Distribution also plays a role. Internet advertising works particularly well for products promoted and sold online because of its ability to link to websites selling the item.

Company Philosophy

Some companies believe in certain principles and build their promotional mix based on those principles. For example, a hiking boot company may feel that outdoor billboards clutter the landscape and, therefore, will not use billboards.

© Monkey Business Images/Shutterstock.com

Do you think television commercials would be an effective way of advertising products geared to health-conscious women? Why or why not?

Resources

The final factor to consider is the company's financial situation. Promotion can be expensive, and the marketer must determine which elements will have the greatest chance of achieving the company's objectives for the least amount of money. Small companies may not have the budget to use all the promotional tools available.

CHECKPOINT

What five major factors affect marketers' choices when developing the promotional mix?

Each type of promotion serves a different function in the promotional mix and should be used to complement the other methods of promotion. Advertisements, for example, reach larger audiences and create awareness. Without them, the personal sales effort would be much more difficult, time-consuming, and expensive. Public relations lends credibility to the message, but it is difficult to control. Personal selling, on the other hand, offers person-to-person contact, can provide any extra information the customer needs, and can close a sale. Without personal selling, the initial interest generated by advertising might be wasted. Sales promotion supplements the other methods and fills in the gaps by stimulating short-term sales efforts.

The promotional mix must be carefully planned around a common theme so that all the elements work together, and, when viewed as a whole, deliver the message to the consumer. The blueprint for how the elements of the promotional mix will work together is called the **promotional plan**.

Steps in Promotional Planning

Creating an effective promotional plan takes time. Most large companies plan years in advance to ensure they use their promotion budget as efficiently as possible. Companies of all sizes follow a basic process for developing their promotional mix. They carefully analyze the current situation and identify opportunities. Then they formulate a promotional plan to take advantage of those opportunities. After the plan is implemented, marketers study the results and use what they learn to guide future efforts. The steps in the promotional planning process are shown in **Figure 15-4**.

1. **Research and Analyze the Market** Marketers can conduct market research or use existing research to gain an understanding of the market. They then analyze the research and identify the strengths and weaknesses of their product, opportunities in the market, and competitive threats.

2. **Select the Target Market** Based on the opportunities identified, the marketer can select a specific target market. In this step, the marketer should identify key characteristics of the target market and fully understand what might motivate consumers to buy the product. This allows the marketer to create an informed promotional strategy.

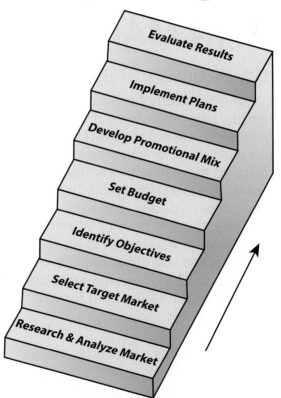

Promotional Planning Steps

FIGURE 15-4 Marketers follow a step-by-step process to develop a promotional plan that is focused, efficient, and based on achievable goals.

3. **Identify Promotional Objectives**   With an understanding of the market, the marketer can then define the objective of the promotion. What does the company want to achieve with its promotional plan? The objective should be realistic and measurable.

4. **Set the Promotional Budget**   At this point, the marketer determines what it will cost to meet the proposed objectives. Although in reality budgets are sometimes dictated by the funds available, the ideal promotional budget is set to fit the plan, not the other way around. Previous annual budgets or predicted sales often are used to help determine a reasonable promotional budget.

5. **Develop the Promotional Mix**   With the budget set, the marketer can then decide the appropriate mix of advertising, public relations, personal selling, and sales promotion, balancing all the factors that affect the mix.

   Once the promotional mix is set, the company can begin to make decisions about the media to use and what vehicles in those media are best suited to the objectives and budget.

6. **Implement the Promotional Plan**   The company allocates money from the total promotional budget to each promotional mix element. It develops a schedule and makes decisions about when the various

MATH IN MARKETING

Gauging Effectiveness

The success of most promotions ultimately depends on the effect they have on business profits. The tricky part is figuring out which parts of a complex promotional mix are responsible for what portion of subsequent changes in revenue and profits. In most cases, there is no way to tie changes in revenue directly to a specific promotion, so marketers have to use indirect means to estimate a promotion's effectiveness. Magazines and newspapers track paid circulation and total circulation. They also provide readership estimates, which factor in how many people typically read each copy.

Electronic media have developed new ways of measuring success. Website *hits* are the number of people who log on to a site. *Click-through rates* are the portion of viewers who click on an ad to see the sponsor's site, where the amount of time each spends at the site also is tracked. *Conversion rates* are the portion of viewers who follow through by buying something or registering for whatever is being promoted.

Do the Math

1. The weekly *Rabbit Hash Business Journal* has a paid circulation of 5,000, gives out 800 free copies, and estimates that for each copy of the newspaper printed, 5.5 people read it. How many people read the paper each week?

2. If a popular website averages 10 million hits a day, and an advertising agency estimates that a banner ad for a contest promotion on the site will yield a click-through rate of 3 percent and a conversion rate of 22 percent, how many people per day can it expect to register for the promotion?

promotional efforts take place. Then the promotional materials are created, and the plan goes into effect.

7. **Evaluate the Results**   Marketers evaluate their promotional plan during and after the promotions, comparing the results with the objectives. They may change the promotional mix or certain elements of it based

on what they learn. They can use the results to help plan future promotional efforts.

 CHECKPOINT
What are the seven steps in the promotional planning process?

15.3 ASSESSMENT

What Have You Learned?

1. How do a company's financial resources affect the types of promotion it uses? [15.3.1]

2. What is a promotional plan? [15.3.2]

Make Academic Connections

1. **Technology**   Some people say the Internet should be counted as a fifth element in the promotional mix. Do you agree? How many elements of the promotional mix can be fulfilled via the Internet? [15.3.1]

2. **Management**   You are the marketing manager for a designer shoe company. You have spent weeks developing the perfect promotional mix that involves

all four elements. Today you found out that your budget has been cut in half and you must cut two of the elements. Which two elements would you cut? Why? [15.3.1, 15.3.2]

Connect to ◇DECA   *Build your Portfolio*

Ben & Jerry's Homemade Ice Cream has hired your team to create a promotional mix for its company. Research Ben & Jerry's and consider what elements of the promotional mix would be the right fit for the company. Present a proposed promotional mix, with specific media recommendations when appropriate, to your teacher (judge). [15.3.1, 15.3.2]

 Connect to MindTap

*Analyze a case study that focuses on chapter concepts. Click on **Chapter 15, Case Study,** in your MindTap.*

A *press release* is a communications tool organizations and companies use to inform the media about exciting new developments. The purpose of a press release is to "sell" the media outlet on the newsworthiness of whatever the press release is seeking to promote so that it will provide media coverage to inform the public.

Press Release Contents

To catch the reader's attention, a press release should lead with a thought-provoking, attention-grabbing headline. Effective press releases have a tantalizing tone that motivates the reader to finish reading the entire release.

A press release should use language and content that evokes an emotional response. Quotations from an expert can be used effectively to express enthusiasm and can add credibility. A quote from a typical "person on the street" can make the product or event seem relevant to a mass audience.

Answer the "who, what, when, where, and why" questions in a press release, just as you would for a journalism article. Other types of information are essential as well. When promoting an event, include a description of the sponsoring organization and the cost of attending the event. For people who might have questions, provide as much contact information as possible, including phone numbers, website URLs, and email addresses. Decide who in your organization will be responsible for answering inquiries.

A variety of press release templates are available online and in commonly used software programs.

Media Outlets

A variety of media outlets are available for press release distribution, including newspapers, magazines, radio, and websites. Press releases are distributed to the decision makers in media organizations. These organizations are bombarded by competing press releases, so concise, well-written, professional copy is crucial. A press release should be written with a particular media outlet in mind.

When choosing the media outlet, consider the target audience of the issue or event that the press release is promoting. For example, if your school drama club is trying to raise money by performing as clowns at children's birthday parties, you could send a press release to a local magazine that focuses on children's activities.

Distribution and Follow Up

Carefully think about when to distribute the press release. To provide adequate lead time, consider the time each media outlet will take to make a decision, prepare the news feature, and run it before the event.

Follow up on the press release by calling the decision maker who received it. Prepare a brief outline of points you want to make prior to the call. When you have the decision maker on the phone, engage him or her in a brief conversation to "sell" the importance of your press release.

Develop Your Skill

Build your Portfolio

Volunteer to write a press release for an upcoming school event. Work with an advisor to clarify the target audience of the release and the key information to include. Develop the content of the release using the guidelines described.

After distributing the press release to the appropriate media outlet, follow up with the decision maker and review the results with your advisor.

Save copies of your press release and any media reports that resulted. They provide a good addition to your educational and career portfolio.

Review Marketing Concepts

1. You are starting an auto detailing business. Why would you want to prepare some sort of promotion in advance of your opening day? [15.1.1]

2. You receive many promotions during your day-to-day activities. Which message channel is most effective in reaching you? [15.1.2]

3. You need a new computer. Would a promotion program that informs or one that persuades be more likely to affect your buying decision? Explain your answer. [15.1.3]

4. To reach clients, interpersonal communication is more expensive than mass communication. Explain why a company would prefer interpersonal communication to promote its products. [15.1.4]

5. You are opening a take-out pizza shop in your neighborhood and don't have much money to spend on advertising. Of the types of advertising discussed in section 15.2.1, which would be your best choice to get the word out about your new business? [15.2.1]

6. You decide to write a press release to send to local media outlets to help get the word out about your pizza shop. What kinds of information would you include in the press release? (Information about writing a press release is found in the 21st Century Success Skills feature in this chapter.) [15.2.2]

7. Many clients do not like the personal selling experience. Explain why clients might be put off by this type of selling. [15.2.3]

8. As a consumer, you often receive coupons in the mail, newspapers, or online. Explain why you take advantage of some coupon offers but not others. [15.2.4]

9. Your company is introducing a new pet food product. The company philosophy is that pets are family members to be loved and cared for. What kind of promotion would foster your company philosophy and also persuade pet owners to purchase your product? Explain your answer. [15.3.1]

10. There are many steps in promotional planning. Which step do you think is the most important? [15.3.2]

11. Why is it important to carry out each step in the promotional planning process? [15.3.2]

Marketing Research and Planning

1. Choose a national brand and research how it uses advertising, public relations, personal selling, and sales promotion to effectively grow its business. Prepare a report on the specific promotional efforts of the brand and why they have worked for that company. [15.2.1–15.2.4]

2. You encounter many types of promotions each day. For each of the following promotions, make a list of five examples. Write a sentence describing each item on each list.

   a. five different types of advertisements [15.2.1]

   b. five public relations activities related to companies, products, or services [15.2.2]

   c. five examples of personal selling you have witnessed or know about [15.2.3]

   d. five promotions in a local store [15.2.4]

3. Select an advertisement from a magazine, newspaper, or online. Show the ad to eight people and ask them the following questions:

   a. What is the central message of this ad?

   b. What does it tell you about the company that is running it?

c. Does it make you want to buy this product or use this service?

d. What other promotions are you aware of from this company?

When you have completed the interview, write a summary of your findings. Do the people agree in their interpretation of the ad's meaning? If there are any differences in opinion, speculate as to what might cause those differences. [15.2.1]

4. Companies benefit greatly from promotional elements that work together and complement one another. Give specific examples that illustrate how the following promotional elements can work together. [15.3.1]

   a. advertising and public relations

   b. sales promotion and personal selling

   c. advertising and personal selling

5. Search the Internet for product sites that have sales promotions related to the products listed in items a–f. Write a half-page summary for each product site, indicating the address (URL) of the website, the operator of the site, and the kinds of sales promotions offered. Select the one you think is the most effective and explain why. [15.2.4]

   a. boat

   b. organic food

   c. pet care products

   d. lawn and garden supplies

   e. computer

   f. home decor products

6. Select a product or service with which you are familiar. Walk through the promotional planning process using the product or service you have selected and answer the questions you think the company had to answer to create its promotional plan. Use the Internet to research anything you do not know. Outline your findings in a written report. [15.3.2]

Marketing Management and Decision Making

1. Marketing managers are responsible for meeting the promotional objectives they set for their products or services. They also understand that thoughtful, well-written objectives can help focus and direct a promotional effort.

The following list contains several products and services. Develop two promotional objectives that are appropriate for each of these products or services. Consider whether the objectives would be achievable through promotion. You may want to focus on a specific role of promotion (to inform, persuade, or remind). [15.3.1]

   a. amusement/theme park

   b. a local used car dealer

   c. fat-free frozen yogurt

   d. a national car rental company

2. A marketing manager oversees the development of the promotional mix based on the objectives set forth. For each objective you developed in the previous activity, create a promotional mix that describes at least one element from each type of promotion that might be used to help achieve the objectives. [15.3.1]

3. Marketing managers need to evaluate the results of their promotional plans and analyze what worked and what could be improved. This analysis helps them prepare future objectives and create promotional plans in upcoming years.

Select one of the promotional mixes you developed in the previous activity. Assume that your promotional plan was a success and that your company wants to be even more aggressive next year. If your plan calls for it, the company is willing to double the money allocated for your promotional efforts. Write a new promotional objective and develop a new promotional mix that will aggressively grow your business. Be prepared to defend and support your decisions. [15.3.2]

4. Promotional displays inform prospective customers about a product, entice them to look at it, and stimulate their buying impulse. The display reflects not only the product being promoted but also the spirit of the sponsoring organization. Some guidelines for creating a display include: (1) Make sure displays are well-balanced and proportional. (2) Decide what feelings the display is trying to evoke and choose colors accordingly. (3) Tailor the design to attract the target audience of the display. (4) Make sure each item in the display supports its overall theme.

Using poster board, draft two designs for a display promoting a school event. Ask several people for feedback to determine which design is the most appealing. Refine the display that received the strongest feedback. Develop a layout of all the elements you would include in the display. On a chart, outline why each element was included and how it supports the overall goals of the display. [15.2.4]

Let's Start a Band! Follow-Up Discussion

Work in small teams to discuss the question posed at the end of the opening vignette. What should the band include in its press kit and who should receive the kits?

Build Your Marketing Plan

Build your
Portfolio

In this chapter you studied the promotion element of the marketing mix and how to develop a promotional plan. You will now apply this learning to the development of your marketing plan. To access the chapter-specific tools that you will need to complete this activity, please navigate to Chapter 15 ➔ Build Your Marketing Plan in MindTap. Alternatively, you can access these tools online at NGLSync. Please visit www.nglsync.cengage.com, and search for the companion website that accompanies this book by entering the ISBN, author, or title. Once you locate this companion website, navigate to Build Your Marketing Plan ➔ Chapter 15.

Community Giving Project

Build your Portfolio

The Community Giving Project provides an opportunity for DECA members to develop a better understanding of the role community giving activities have in society, to make a contribution to a community service or charity, and to learn and apply the principles of marketing management.

One to three members can participate in the Community Giving Project. Participants are required to develop a written entry on the procedures for initiating, planning and organizing, executing, monitoring and controlling, and closing the project.

The project consists of the written document and oral presentation. The body of the written entry is limited to 20 numbered pages, including an appendix but excluding the title page and the table of contents. The oral presentation will consist of 15 minutes for participants to explain and describe the project and answer the judge's questions.

The written entry will consist of the following parts:

Executive Summary is a one-page description of the project.

Initiating provides a historic background of the selected community service or charity. This section includes the description and purpose of the project, rationale for selecting the project, and description of the benefits of the project.

Planning and Organizing includes an organizational chart, member involvement, and job descriptions. This section includes the schedule, quality management plan, risk management plan, and proposed projected budget.

Execution, Monitoring, and Controlling describes the project implementation, unusual or unforeseen challenges or successes, and methods of handling them.

Evaluation and Recommendations includes an evaluation of the project, the impact of the community giving project, and recommendations for future projects.

Bibliography and Appendix are additional sections that may be used.

Performance Indicators Evaluated

- Explain the importance of company involvement in community activities. (Promotion)
- Propose community issues for company involvement. (Promotion)
- Utilize project management skills to start, run, and end projects. (Project Management)
- Monitor project and take corrective actions. (Operations)
- Evaluate project success. (Operations)
- Organize and prioritize work. (Operations)

Go to the DECA website for more detailed information. **www.deca.org**

Think Critically

1. What are some of the personal benefits from participating in community service?
2. What kind of publicity does an organization receive from participating in community service?
3. What strategy can be used to rally members of an organization to participate in a community service project?
4. Why are committees important for completing community service projects?

CHAPTER 16

ADVERTISING

See how effective advertising leads to successful marketing strategies. Click on Chapter 16, Visual Focus, in your MindTap.

Let's Start a Band!

> "A brand is a voice and a product is
> a souvenir."
>
> – Lisa Gansky, *Entrepreneur and Author of* The Mesh

Naomi walked into rehearsal waving a card above her head. On it was our logo. I can't believe we just got around to having someone design it. We really needed something that represents us and catches people's attention.

Everyone dropped what they were doing and rushed over as she handed out copies. I know it isn't as eye catching as the Rolling Stones' logo. Nobody in our group can compete with Mick Jagger's mouth. And it wasn't as simple as just finding the right font design. Run DMC and the Beatles already did that. But I think what the designers came up with will set us apart. It will grab people's attention, and in time will become something that identifies us.

Everybody in the band has ideas on how to use it. You know, T-shirts and that kind of thing. Gael even wanted it on his drum. Layla said it would help with our image, but Eddie said, "It will do more than that. We created a band, now we're creating a brand."

I have to agree with Eddie. And now that we have a logo, I think we need to update our advertising. What else do you think we should do with it?

WHAT IS ADVERTISING?

Learning Objectives

16.1.1 Distinguish between product advertising and brand advertising.

16.1.2 Describe the major roles at an advertising agency.

Key Terms

product advertising
brand advertising
corporate
    advertising
advertising agency
account executive
account planner

media plan
media planner
art director
copywriter
creative director
producer

marketing matters

Advertising is any paid, one-way communication delivered through a mass medium. Companies advertise in order to inform, persuade, or remind their customers. They use a mix of product advertising and brand advertising to deliver specific product messages to their audience and to help build their brands. A company often hires an advertising agency to help develop the communication strategy and marketing message and then to create advertisements that communicate that message.

essential question

What are the major differences between brand advertising and product advertising?

16.1.1 ▶ Two Approaches to Advertising

U.S. companies spend billions of dollars each year on advertising. Much of the growth in the advertising market is driven by digital marketing. Companies rely heavily on advertising to drive demand for their products and services. Developing targeted, effective ads is a lengthy and expensive process. Successful advertising requires knowledge of marketing and psychology, markets and cultural trends, and an ability to communicate clearly, artfully, and persuasively.

Marketers determine what the most persuasive advertising message will be for their business. Then they ensure the message is delivered to their target audience in a clear and convincing manner. Advertising targets everyday people. It speaks their language and touches their emotions.

Advertising is used not only by corporations, but also by non-profit groups, politicians, and other organizations. Advertising typically aims to sell a specific product, build a brand or, most often, achieve a combination of the two.

Product Advertising

Product advertising relays the benefits of a specific product or service and uses rational arguments or emotional appeals to explain why a customer should buy it.

Product advertising may include product information, prices, or comparisons with competitors.

Product advertising includes at least one product attribute and accompanying benefit to convince consumers to purchase a product. For example, "Phillips energy-saving light bulbs help you save money on your power bill."

Brand Advertising

A *brand* is the accumulation of all the tangible and intangible qualities of a company, product, or product line. It includes elements such as the name, logo, slogan, and designs associated with the brand. It also includes associations such as attitude and personality. These rational and emotional elements comprise the *brand character*.

If you were to describe Coca-Cola, for example, you might offer a product attribute such as the taste, or you might give a brand attribute such as the colors red and white. You might also mention a less tangible attribute, such as "young" or "fun." These are all part of the brand.

One reason that brands are important is that consumers' purchasing decisions contribute to their self-image. In other words, the things you purchase say something about you. Certain brands are cool or rebellious. Others are classic or dependable. The character of a brand is transferred to the product owner. If this surprises you, consider your perceptions of the sorts of people you would expect to drive certain vehicles. Do you picture a difference between a

Prius driver and a pick-up truck driver? Would you expect to encounter the same types of consumers driving Buicks as you would find driving Mustangs? Consider why consumers choose the cars they do.

Brand advertising is advertising that aims to build an image. It uses common elements to define what a product or company stands for and to give it a personality in the minds of consumers. Brand advertising may be done for a company brand, such as Nike, or for vacation destinations, such as the Cayman Islands.

© American Express/Cayman Islands Tourism

Brand advertising can be used for vacation destinations, such as the Cayman Islands, to help build an image. What elements in the ad help to convey the brand image of this destination?

Sometimes, the brand that is being advertised is the company or corporation itself. Brand advertising of this nature is called **corporate advertising**. Examples of corporate advertising are the ads you see along the perimeter of arenas at sporting events. Brand advertising may also be done for a branded line of products, such as Swanson frozen dinners.

Almost all advertising is a mix of product and brand advertising. An advertisement for Snickers, for instance, will sometimes deliver a message about the candy bar—that it satisfies hunger—but it will also make you feel something about the brand. Perhaps the ad makes you laugh or makes you think that Snickers is for young, energetic people. Those associations are brand associations.

 CHECKPOINT
Explain the difference between product advertising and brand advertising.

Why do you think companies choose sporting events to conduct corporate advertising?

© Anton_Ivanov/Shutterstock.com.

16.1.2 ▶ The Advertising Agency

A business will often hire an **advertising agency**, a company that specializes in creating advertising. Many people within an advertising agency work together to create an ad from start to finish. These people all bring different expertise to the process.

An **account executive** is the key liaison between the client and the agency. Account executives help clients plan the advertising and relay information from the clients to other people in the agency.

To learn about the target market, the agency looks to its **account planner**. Account planners spend a lot of time talking to the target markets. Sometimes they conduct research in *focus groups*, where a moderator leads a discussion about the advertising with a small group of people. At other times, they travel to the homes of the people in the target markets to see how they live, work, and think.

Some ad agencies develop a media plan for the business. A **media plan** is a detailed listing of where and when ads will run. It is designed to give the business the best coverage of its target market for the least amount of money. The person who develops the media plan is the **media planner**.

The team that actually creates the advertising is typically made up of an art director and a copywriter. Generally speaking, the **art director** has a background in design or fine art and is responsible for how the ad will look. **Copywriters**, who have various backgrounds and a strong command of language, write the words in the ad. Good creative teams work together, and their roles are not so rigid.

Sometimes, a creative director oversees the creative team. The **creative director** helps guide the creative process and ensures that the creative team's work conveys the right message and is in line with the client's needs.

An advertising agency also may have a production department. The job of the **producer** is to facilitate everything that happens after the client agrees to develop an ad or campaign. This includes hiring a director and editor to make a television commercial or a photographer for an ad in social media. The producer also is responsible for ensuring that an ad does not exceed the client's budget.

CHECKPOINT
Name the major roles at an advertising agency.

16.1 ASSESSMENT

What Have You Learned?

1. What is corporate advertising? [16.1.1]
2. What is a media plan designed to do? [16.1.2]

Make Academic Connections

1. **Visual Art**   Pick a brand that you like. Create a collage or "mood board" with pictures, words, colors, symbols, or other elements that you associate with the brand you selected. [16.1.1]
2. **Writing**   Carry a notebook with you throughout your day. Write down the brands that you encounter. Make a note of how they make you feel and any associations you might have with them. Write a one-page summary of your findings. [16.1.1]

Connect to ◇DECA

Build your Portfolio

Your advertising agency has been given a new assignment: to create brand advertising for a new soda called Silver Cola. Develop a two-minute presentation on the elements you would use to create a brand for Silver Cola. What colors, designs, and music would you use? What kinds of people would you use in your commercials? How would you want your target audience to think of your cola? What would be its "personality"? Give your presentation to your teacher (judge). [16.1.1, 16.1.2]

Learning Objectives

16.2.1 Describe the process of setting objectives, determining the budget, and developing the creative strategy.

16.2.2 Describe the different types of media and the factors that must be considered when selecting which media to use.

Key Terms

advertising plan
advertising campaign
creative strategy
strategic brief
reach
pass-along rate
frequency
lead time

marketing matters

When a company decides to include advertising as part of its promotional mix, it must develop an advertising plan. The first steps in developing this plan are to set the advertising objectives and work out a budget. A creative strategy that will guide the creative message of the advertising is then written. As the project moves through the production process, the media planner begins to select the media types and vehicles.

essential question

What are the key elements of the advertising plan and how do they fit together?

16.2.1 The Planning Process

An **advertising plan** is a document that outlines the activities to be completed and resources needed to create advertising. It specifies objectives and a budget and includes the basis for creating and evaluating the advertising strategy and creative strategy. An advertising plan may be for a single advertisement, but it is most often written for an advertising campaign.

An **advertising campaign** is a series of related advertisements with a similar look, feel, and theme that centers on a specific product, service, or brand. Because advertising involves large sums of money, advertisers follow a specific process to create the advertising plan and develop the most effective, cost-efficient campaign. Steps in developing an advertising campaign include the following:

1. Set objectives
2. Determine the budget
3. Develop the creative strategy
4. Select and schedule the media
5. Develop the creative concept
6. Produce the advertising
7. Evaluate the plan's effectiveness

Set Objectives

The first step in the development of an advertising plan is to determine the advertising objectives. Objectives are the desired results to be accomplished within a certain time period. Objectives may be to increase sales, to increase awareness, or to communicate an idea to an audience. It is important for objectives to be specific and measurable. As part of the objectives, advertisers specify the main message of the advertising, the target audience, and the time frame.

Objectives for a specific advertising plan will vary from organization to organization and from product to product. For example, an advertising plan for a municipal library might have as its objective to attract 1,000 new library cardholders between the ages of 5 and 10 during the next month. An advertising plan for the Nissan Xterra might have as its objective visits to Nissan dealerships by 9,000 Hispanic residents of West Texas, Arizona, and New Mexico during the months of June and July. **Figure 16-1** presents objectives for the advertising plan of Seaside Resorts.

Determine the Budget

Once the advertising objectives are defined, the budget can be developed. Managers identify a total advertising budget early in the planning process. They prepare a more detailed budget as planning is completed. There are four common methods of determining budgets for advertising.

WHAT YOU CAN AFFORD   In this method of determining the ad budget, organizations account for all of their other expenses, and whatever is left over is budgeted for advertising. This is not the ideal method, but sometimes, especially with smaller companies, it is the reality.

PERCENTAGE OF SALES   The percentage of sales approach budgets a percentage of past, current, or projected future sales for advertising. For example, a firm that sold $50 million in tractors last year might allocate 5 percent of sales to advertising, for an ad budget of $2.5 million.

One drawback of this method is that advertising varies directly with sales. If sales drop, more advertising, not less, may be what the company needs to bring sales back up. In addition, past sales are not always the best predictor of future sales. Markets are volatile, and changes such as increased competition, evolving customer tastes, or new technology can impact sales drastically. Companies are better off using a percentage of predicted future sales when calculating the budget.

COMPETITION MATCHING   The competition matching approach suggests that an organization should have an ad budget similar to its competitors. However,

OBJECTIVES FOR SEASIDE RESORT'S ADVERTISING PLAN	
Sales objective	Increase reserved summer rentals by 10% by February 15
Message	Make reservations by February 15 and save $100 off the weekly rental rate
Target market	Families living in California who spend one week or more at the beach every year

FIGURE 16-1 Objectives are the results the advertising plan sets out to attain.

this approach can be problematic because competitors may have different advertising objectives and different resources and it is difficult to know how much they spend.

OBJECTIVE AND TASK The best method of determining an advertising budget is to base it on the objectives to be achieved. The advertising team determines the desired goals of the advertising effort and outlines the activities needed to accomplish those goals. Then it calculates the cost of completing each necessary task in order to determine the advertising budget.

Develop the Creative Strategy

Effective advertising campaigns are targeted to deliver a clear message to a defined target audience. The process of deciding what to say and how to say it starts with the creative strategy.

The **creative strategy** is how a company positions its brand or product in its advertising. At this phase of the process, an advertising agency's account executive works with the client to define certain parameters for the advertising. They determine the target market for the advertisement and what to communicate to it.

Members of the account team then write a **strategic brief**, also known as a *creative brief*, which is a short document that defines the target market and conveys the main message of the advertising. The strategic brief guides the remainder of the advertising process.

CHECKPOINT
What are the four common methods of determining an advertising budget, and which one is usually the most effective?

16.2.2 ▶ Select the Media

As an agency's creative department begins work on developing the advertising, media planners simultaneously work on where and when to place it. The media plan answers questions regarding what types of media, which vehicles, in what units, and at what time.

The media type refers to the format, such as TV, radio, print, or digital. The vehicle is the programming, publication, or digital medium in which the advertising appears, such as the TV show *60 Minutes*, the magazine *Sports Illustrated*, the newspaper *USA TODAY*, and digital apps like YouTube, Snapchat, and Waze. The unit refers to the length or size of the

advertisement, such as a 15- or 30-second commercial or quarter-page print ad.

The timing of an ad campaign might be *continuous*, which means that it runs continually over a period of time. Or it might be *pulsing*, which means that the campaign runs more often during specific times, such as holidays.

Each type of media has its strengths and weaknesses (**Figure 16-2**). The job of the media planner is to create a plan that takes advantage of the strengths of the media vehicles and reaches the target market with just the right frequency. The goal is to reach the most people in the target market for the

*Want to know more about marketing in the information age? Click on **Lesson 16.2, Digital Marketing,** in your MindTap.*
Connect to
MindTap

ADVANTAGES AND DISADVANTAGES OF MAJOR ADVERTISING MEDIA

Media	Advantages	Disadvantages
Television	Reaches large audiences Low cost per viewer Has emotional impact Highly segmented markets	High total cost Long lead time Strong potential for interference from other sources
Radio	Highly mobile Relatively low cost Short lead time Highly segmented markets	Message limited to audio Strong potential for interference from other sources
Outdoor	Low cost High visibility Short lead time	Increasingly regulated Message length is limited Strong potential for interference from other sources
Direct Mail	Highly segmented Easy to measure effectiveness Stimulates action Hidden from competition	Often considered junk mail Expensive High clutter
Magazines	Long life span Can carry response vehicles (coupons, response cards) High pass-along rate Highly segmented	High cost Long lead time High clutter
Newspapers	Short lead time Large circulation Can carry response vehicles (coupons) Inexpensive	Lower print quality Short life Limited segmentation High clutter (competing ads)
Digital – General	Highly targeted Instantly measurable Built-in response vehicles Interactive	Limited audience High clutter (competing ads) Security and privacy concerns
Digital – Social media	Develop customer relationships Can be very targeted Comparatively low-cost	Low return on investment Appeals to viewers not interested in traditional advertising Traffic typically occurs in the early stages of the buying process
Digital – Pay per click	Pay only for results Quick, easy tracking Ability to select where ads will be shown Ads can be easily modified	Bidding war with competitors over keywords Using widely searched terms and keywords can result in irrelevant results Requires constant monitoring
Digital – Banner ads	Prices are decreasing Good for branding Easy to track	Often viewed as annoying and intrusive Growing use of ad blockers Declining click-through rate Oversaturation leading to "ad blindness"

FIGURE 16-2 Each advertising medium has advantages and disadvantages. It is up to the media planner to determine the right balance for the advertising.

least amount of money. Media planning is a balancing act of many factors, and advertisers are constantly looking for new ways to break through the clutter of traditional media.

While traditional media (led by television, then print, then radio), remains an enormous industry, it has been surpassed in worth by advertising on digital media. Digital advertising includes online display ads (banner and pop-up ads), search engine marketing (SEM), video ads, email marketing, mobile advertising, blogs, as well as advertising on social media on sites such as Instagram.

Each type of media has characteristics that marketers should analyze before making a choice (**Figure 16-3**). They must consider the cost, reach, frequency, lead time, and fit of each format.

COST   Media costs depend on the type of media, the specific vehicle, and the unit. The media planner tries to balance these factors to reach the most people for the least expense. The planner must figure out whether the total cost of a specific medium is affordable for the budget and whether it is cost efficient. Efficiency is measured by the per-reader or per-viewer cost. The total cost of an ad in a national magazine might be $250,000. The per-reader cost of magazines or impressions is expressed as the cost per thousand readers, or CPM. The CPM for an ad that costs $250,000 and reaches 1,000,000 people is $0.25 ($250,000 ÷ 1,000,000 = $0.25).

REACH   The **reach** is the total number of people who see an ad. In TV advertising, it is based on the number of people watching the programming. In outdoor advertising, traffic statistics help estimate the number of viewers. In online advertising, reach refers to the number of unique users who view the ad.

Questions to Consider When Selecting Media	
Cost	What is the total cost of the medium? What is the cost per viewer? Does the cost fit into the advertising budget? Is it the most effective use of advertising dollars?
Reach	What is the overall circulation or viewership? Will it reach the target audience? Is there a strong pass-along rate?
Frequency	How often will the target audience see the advertising message? How many viewings does it take for the message to "stick"? After how many viewings does "wear-out" occur?
Lead Time	How long before running the advertising does the medium outlet require the ad materials? How flexible is this medium? Can the ad materials be ready by the medium's deadline?
Creative, Brand, and Corporate Fit	Does the medium fit the message? Is the medium a good fit for the brand? Does the medium fit the company philosophy?

FIGURE 16-3 Marketers consider several factors when determining which advertising medium to use.

For a magazine or newspaper, the number of copies distributed is called the *circulation*. But with those media, there is also the **pass-along rate**, which is the number of people who read a single printed copy of a magazine or newspaper. A printed issue of *Newsweek*, for example, is read on average by about six people. Therefore, its reach is much higher than its actual circulation.

FREQUENCY   The number of times a member of the target audience is exposed to the advertising message is the **frequency**. Advertisers can run the same message daily or, in the case of radio and television, even hourly. A message loses effectiveness after a certain number of exposures, however. This is called *wear-out*.

For example, if you see a commercial once or twice, you will get much more out of it than when you see the commercial the tenth time. By then, you will stop paying attention to it.

LEAD TIME   The amount of time required to place an ad is the **lead time**, which varies greatly among media types. The lead time for a newspaper ad might only be a day compared to several months for a magazine ad. The timeline for the production of the ads must be considered to ensure the ads will be finished by the media deadline.

MARKETING COMMUNICATION

Reducing Ad Clutter

The emergence of streaming devices and video-on-demand services allows millions of people to watch their favorite network shows anytime within a week of their initial airing. Watching a program on such a delay allows viewers to skip commercials. While television viewers may still be seeing some commercials, they are seeing fewer. Viewers, especially millennials (who have adapted to viewing on digital devices more quickly than people in earlier generations), expect fewer commercials.

In response to this trend, traditional networks are reducing the amount of time devoted to commercials during their programming. However, a network that airs fewer commercials risks making less money. Networks hope to convince advertisers that a spot in a shorter commercial break is more valuable than a spot in a longer one. They argue that by offering advertisers the chance to run messages in a less-cluttered environment, the ads will reach a more attentive audience. "I absolutely think a shorter commercial pod is better for the advertiser," said David Campanelli, senior vice president and managing director of video investment for the ad-buying firm Horizon Media. "How much better will it be versus how much more they charge for it? That's a big outstanding question."

Think Critically

Despite a declining audience, why might advertisers still pay the higher advertising prices charged by traditional TV channels?

Source: Battaglio, Stephen. "TV Networks Shed Ad Time as Consumers Skip Commercials." *LA Times.* March 27, 2018. https://www.latimes.com/business/hollywood/la-fi-ct-commercials-clutter-20180327-story.html

CREATIVE, BRAND, AND CORPORATE FIT Marketers also must consider whether or not a medium is appropriate for the advertising, the brand, or even the company running the ad. For example, if the creative message is long and complex, an outdoor billboard on a highway would not be a good fit. It is hard to read a long message when you are driving past at 65 miles per hour. Likewise, a brand or company may not wish to associate itself with certain media vehicles or types of programming. Family companies such as Disney are very sensitive to the types of media vehicles they use to advertise. For example, Disney may not want to advertise on a television show if it contains material that does not reflect the company's values.

> *Want to know more about what is trending with this topic? Click on **Lesson 16.2, Global Marketing,** in your MindTap.*

Connect to
MindTap

CHECKPOINT
What are the five primary considerations in selecting the types of media in which to run an advertisement?

16.2 ASSESSMENT

What Have You Learned?

1. How does the creative team start the process of deciding what to say in an advertisement? [16.2.1]
2. When selecting media, what is the media planner's goal? [16.2.2]

Make Academic Connections

1. **Communication** Choose an advertisement you saw or heard today. Write a strategic brief defining the target market for the ad and spelling out its main message. [16.2.1]
2. **Research** Pick an advertising campaign that you particularly like. Conduct Internet research to learn the company and ad agency responsible for the campaign. Write a one-page report about the campaign. In your report, identify the brand or company being advertised and the type of media and vehicles used. Also explain why you like the advertising. [16.2.2]

Connect to ◇DECA

Build your Portfolio

You have been hired as a media consultant for a grocery store. The store manager wants to advertise on social media. Prepare a digital media plan for the store addressing the four types of digital media described in Figure 16-2 and the questions to consider in Figure 16-3. Present your digital media plan to your teacher (judge) with any necessary visual aids. Be prepared to explain why you chose those vehicles. [16.2.2]

CREATE AND EVALUATE ADVERTISING

Learning Objectives

16.3.1 Identify common creative advertising formats.

16.3.2 Explain what happens during the production phase of the advertising process.

16.3.3 Differentiate between quantitative and qualitative research.

16.3.4 Name the four types of advertising regulation.

Key Terms

quantitative research
qualitative research
cease-and-desist order
corrective ads
fine

marketing matters

After the advertising plan is created, the budget set, and the creative strategy developed, the creative team prepares the strategic brief, which guides the development of the creative concept. The creative concept for advertising utilizes several common formats, all with the goal of standing out among the clutter and delivering the message in a memorable way. After the client approves the creative concept, the advertisement is produced. Once the advertising has run, several research techniques are used to gauge its effectiveness. Various review boards and other individuals oversee advertising to help ensure it is fair, honest, and not deceptive or harmful to the public.

essential question

What are the different types of creative formats, and how are they used in advertising?

16.3.1 ▶ Creative Development

After the media decisions are made, the creative work begins. This is the step during which the advertising is created. The advertising must reach the target audience, be consistent with the objectives set, and fit within the budget.

Creative Formats

Because advertising aims to stand out, the creative team tries to develop a completely original concept. Common creative formats they might use, alone or in combination, include a musical format, dramatization, testimonial, comedy, image, demonstration, or competitive advertising.

MUSICAL Some commercials revolve around a song: a jingle, characters or famous musicians singing, or simply background music. Over the years, Pepsi has used many different musicians from

Beyoncé to One Direction. Jingles like "I wish I were an Oscar Mayer wiener" can stay in your mind for life, creating strong brand awareness.

DRAMATIZATION Sometimes commercials present a realistic scene played by actors, often with the product solving a problem of some sort. Dramatizations are supposed to give us the feeling that we are watching or hearing a real event.

TESTIMONIAL Celebrities, knowledgeable professionals, or everyday people sometimes endorse a product by giving a testimonial. Whether it is Taylor Swift drinking Coke, a doctor recommending a medicine, or an everyday person talking about the Jeep Wrangler, the idea is that an audience is more likely to trust a message from a third party than one directly from a company. In the latest twist on testimonials, *influencers* spread branded messages through their personal social media channels. The use of influencers has proven especially effective with younger consumers who are active on social media.

COMEDY One way of giving a brand personality is to make the audience feel an emotion, and humor is a popular way to do that. Even if they don't want to buy your product, viewers who laugh at a commercial will have positive associations with that brand.

IMAGE ADVERTISING
Image ads evoke some sort of mood or attitude for a brand or product. For example, an ad for the iPod and nearly all fashion is pure image advertising.

PRODUCT DEMONSTRATION This creative format shows the product in action. It may be a simple demonstration of a cleaning product removing soap scum or something exaggerated like a Chevy truck pulling a spaceship.

COMPETITIVE ADVERTISING
Competitive advertising makes a claim of superiority over the competition. It may show competing products side by side, or it may just refer to some aspect of the competition.

The Creative Concept

Once the creative team has developed the creative concepts and the creative director has approved them, they are drawn up in rough form and presented to the client. At the client presentation, the agency may act out ideas for TV commercials, read scripts, or show rough versions of print ads to help bring the creative ideas to life.

Because advertising is expensive, and because creative concepts sometimes fail, clients may conduct research on

*Want to know more about what is trending with this topic? Click on **Lesson 16.3, Marketing Decisions,** in your MindTap.*

Connect to MindTap

a concept to make sure it will be effective. They may present the concept to focus groups for quick feedback. Or, they may use more extensive testing techniques that require them to produce a rough version of the ad and then ask an audience some questions about it. Research helps gauge if an audience will like an ad and understand its main message. If the advertising concept passes these tests, the client will approve it for production.

CHECKPOINT
Name seven formats for creative concepts.

16.3.2 ▶ Production

Once the client feels comfortable with the creative concepts, the agency will start the production phase. For a print or Internet ad, this may involve hiring a photographer, selecting models for the ad, and finalizing the design and layout.

For a television commercial, the process is more involved. The producer and creative team hire a director, cast the actors, select locations, and work with a crew of as many as 100 people to shoot the commercial. After the commercial is filmed, the creative team works with a variety of people—an editor, a sound engineer, and possibly special effects artists—to finish the project, sometimes adding music, sound effects, and an announcer.

The agency then presents the advertising to the client and continues to work on the commercial until the client is confident it will be effective. The final step is to send the ads to the TV stations, magazines or newspapers, or online outlets that will run them. **Figure 16-4** shows the steps in the creative development and production processes.

Creative Development and Production Process

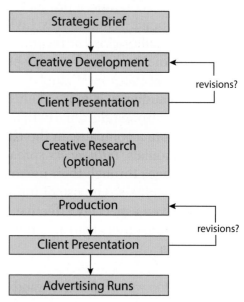

FIGURE 16-4 Executing the advertising begins when the creative team receives the strategic brief.

CHECKPOINT
At what point in the process of creating an ad does the agency start the production phase?

Gauge Advertising Effectiveness

Advertisers must evaluate ad campaigns to measure how well they meet the objectives of the advertising plan. Sometimes the impact of advertising is difficult to measure because there are many other variables that can affect sales. Evaluation is an important step that helps the advertiser collect data to improve future efforts.

Evaluation Techniques

If the advertising has a built-in evaluator, such as a redeemable coupon or a rebate offer, then the advertisement's effectiveness can be determined from the number of coupons or rebates redeemed for these promotional items. However, many advertisements do not have built-in measures and need to be evaluated using other techniques.

Advertising is sometimes evaluated *before* it is run. This is especially common with television commercials due to their expense. After the advertising has run, it also is evaluated to see how effective it was. There are various methods to evaluate advertising, including both quantitative and qualitative research. Advertisers choose which type of research and specifically what method they will use based on their budget and what they hope to learn. They may perform the research in carefully selected test markets, which they believe best represent the demographic they are targeting with the advertising.

QUANTITATIVE RESEARCH Sometimes advertisers want to ask a large number of people simple questions. Surveys about the advertising, recall tests that see if people remember the ads, and other types of testing that ask questions and allow respondents to pick from a set of answers are all types of quantitative testing. **Quantitative research** involves collecting data that can be interpreted into meaningful numerical values. It can give advertisers valuable information such as the increase in brand awareness during an ad campaign or a comparison of how respondents who have seen a commercial and those who have not would rate a product.

QUALITATIVE RESEARCH On the other hand, research that looks deeper into the *why* and *how* of people's opinions is called **qualitative research**. This method includes such techniques as focus groups. It also may include one-on-one interviews or other types of face-to-face discussions. Qualitative research typically has a much smaller number of respondents than quantitative research. However, its advantage is that it allows the researcher to deeply probe the issues and ask follow-up questions. "Tell me why you like the commercial." "How could we make it better?"

CHECKPOINT
Describe the difference between quantitative and qualitative research.

Advertising Regulation

Although it ultimately is in marketers' best interest to be truthful in their advertising, a number of systems are in place to protect consumers and ensure that advertisers are honest and ethical.

MATH IN MARKETING

Advertising as a Game of Chance

It can be difficult to accurately predict the effectiveness of an advertising plan due to the number of variables and calculations involved. Most plans rely on getting a message out to many people, hoping a few will buy the product. But a few small changes can seriously affect the plan.

Consider a company that buys a TV spot during the World Series expecting to reach 30 million baseball fans with a pitch for a credit card. Based on prior experience, the plan estimates that 1 in every 200 people (0.5 percent) will apply for a card. That number of people yields 150,000 applications, of which 120,000 (80 percent) can be expected to qualify, which satisfies the objective of 100,000 new cards.

What happens if the game is a blowout by the end of the second inning, and the ad runs in the fifth inning when only 60 percent of the viewers are still watching? And what if 25 percent of them drift out of the room during the break? The audience has now shrunk to 13.5 million. Now suppose that because of overexposure to prior promotions, the response rate is weak, and only 1 in 500 (0.2 percent) apply. And suppose those still watching have below-average credit, so only 67 percent qualify. All of these factors leave the company with only 18,000 new credit cards. How could it have been so far off? It is the result of cumulative changes in a long series of variables.

Do the Math

1. A banner ad is seen by 20 million Internet users, and 0.4 percent of them click through to the sponsor's site, at which point 2 percent buy the product being promoted. How many sales result?

2. By what percentage do product sales decrease if the click-through rate is reduced to 0.2 percent?

GOVERNMENT REGULATION The Federal Trade Commission (FTC) and the Federal Communications Commission (FCC) oversee all commerce and commercial communications in the United States. They uphold laws, decide cases, and enforce standards to prevent misleading and deceptive advertising. If they deem the advertising deceptive, these government bodies have the power to enforce corrective measures.

REGULATORY BOARDS There are a number of regulatory boards that oversee truthfulness in advertising. These boards usually are organized by consumer groups, business associations, or the advertising industry itself. The National Advertising Review Council, the National Advertising Review Board, and the Children's Advertising Review Unit all oversee various aspects of advertising to protect consumers.

MEDIA OUTLET REGULATIOᵒN Because networks and publications are ultimately responsible for everything they air or publish, they have standards and guidelines regarding advertising claims and content. Advertisers must follow these regulations, or the outlets can reject their advertising. According to the Federal Trade Commission's (FTC) published guidelines, the general principles of advertising law also apply to online outlets, but new issues in this area arise almost as fast as technology develops.

COMPETITIVE REGULATION A large part of regulation actually comes from competing companies. Companies watch one another closely to ensure that competitors are not gaining an unfair advantage by making untruthful claims. They may file complaints or lawsuits if a competitor makes a claim that it cannot adequately validate.

CORRECTIVE ACTIONS The regulatory forces work together to make sure that advertisers can support any product claim and that they disclose all information necessary for a customer to make an informed decision.

When advertisers fail to meet the guidelines, they may face a number of corrective measures. Advertisers may receive a **cease-and-desist order**, which is a legal order to discontinue the deceptive advertising. The company may be forced to run **corrective ads** that amend any false impressions left by the deceptive ads. There also may be a monetary penalty, or **fine**, imposed on the offending company. Depending on the violation, those fines can be large amounts.

All of these corrective measures are intended to keep advertising honest, keep competition fair, and protect the public. Upholding these standards is in everyone's best interest.

> **CHECKPOINT**
> *What are the four forces working to regulate advertising?*

16.3 ASSESSMENT

What Have You Learned?

1. Why is it important for creative concepts to be unique and original? [16.3.1]

2. What is the final step in the production phase for an advertisement? [16.3.2]

3. What federal agencies oversee commerce and commercial communications in the United States? [16.3.4]

Make Academic Connections

1. **Writing** Write a script for a 15-second ad for a new energy beverage to be delivered via online gaming. Determine the creative format, the main message to communicate about the beverage, and the visuals you will use. [16.3.1]

2. **Research** Use the Internet to learn more about focus groups. Locate a company that is using a focus group to conduct research related to advertising. Prepare a one-page report on the company and the purpose of the focus group. [16.3.3]

Connect to ◇DECA

Build your portfolio

Select a product and create an advertising campaign for it. Write a strategy that outlines your target market and main message. Then, create ads in at least three different media for the product. As necessary, make video or audio recordings for the ads, and draw or create any print or outdoor ads on a computer. Present your campaign to your teacher (judge). [16.3.1]

Connect to MindTap

*Analyze a case study that focuses on chapter concepts. Click on **Chapter 16, Case Study,** in your MindTap.*

Planning a Career In...
VIRTUAL CREATIVE SERVICES

How do companies decide on the best advertising content to inform and excite consumers about their products? How are messages customized for various audiences?

Creative services is a field that focuses on the thematic content, graphics, and presentation of advertising. Selecting the mass media distribution channel—from billboards, radio, TV, or the Internet—is also within the realm of creative services.

Job Titles

• Web Content Manager

• Content Strategy Director

• Lead Web Content Editor

• Director of Content

• E-Communications Editor

Needed Skills

• A bachelor's degree including liberal arts, writing, and business courses with an emphasis on marketing is recommended.

• Excellent writing, communication, and computer skills are needed.

• Experience with web content management tools and web publishing tools is important.

What it's like to work in... Virtual Creative Services?

Bashir, a web content editor for an online mortgage company, just finished a presentation to the product management team about an addition to the company's website.

During the development process, Bashir held group meetings with representatives from product management and marketing to ensure that the content was aligned with brand objectives. He also received input from a focus group of prospective customers who matched the target market.

Now that the copy has been approved, Bashir is meeting with his company's website designer. Bashir wants to be sure that the website design provides an easy way for customers to navigate the website and review all of the mortgage materials in order to make the best product choice.

At the end of the day, Bashir prepares for tomorrow's meeting with the media communications manager. The meeting objective is to review the editorial style guides for both print and electronic media to ensure a consistent look, feel, and voice for all published materials.

What About You?

Would you like to be part of the creative process, helping a company develop customer-focused product information for new electronic media?

Connect to **MindTap**

*Discover more about the outlook for this career and watch a video about a related career. Click on **Chapter 16, Planning a Career In...** in your MindTap.*

CHAPTER 16 ASSESSMENT

Review Marketing Concepts

1. Think of a brand that you like and purchase repeatedly. Explain how this brand contributes to or reinforces your self-image. [16.1.1]

2. You are the vice president of marketing for a relatively new company. You have decided to work with an advertising agency for help with creating ads. What will be your main deciding factor in choosing an agency? [16.1.2]

3. Your company has created and implemented an advertising plan. How would you analyze the effectiveness of the plan? [16.2.1]

4. If you were a media planner selecting media for advertisements geared to high school students, which media type would you choose, and why? [16.2.2]

5. What do you think is the benefit of using a musical format in an advertisement? [16.3.1]

6. The TV station you work for wants to sell more commercials. However, the expense of production limits some potential customers from advertising. What can the TV station do to lower the production expense for customers? [16.3.2]

7. In comparing quantitative and qualitative research, which type do you think would be more effective in evaluating an advertising campaign? Explain your answer. [16.3.3]

8. Your competitor provided misleading information about the capability of its product, and the government caught this deception. In comparing corrective actions of cease and desist, corrective ads, or fines, which do you think would be the best way to deter this deceptive practice in the future? [16.3.4]

Marketing Research and Planning

1. Marketers annually spend a great deal of money on advertising. Your task in this activity is to become acquainted with advertising costs in a local market. Select an advertising medium used by marketers in your community, such as a radio station, a newspaper, a website, an outdoor advertising agency, or a television station.

   Contact the organization or use reference materials to obtain information regarding its advertising rates. Be prepared to report to your class regarding the cost of advertising per minute, per inch, per week, per day, or whatever measurement is used. [16.2.2]

2. One of the major concerns of organizations that advertise is how to use their advertising dollars effectively. A recent survey of 259 successful companies asked what type of evaluation techniques they use. The responses are summarized in the following table.

(Respondents could select more than one type of approach.) [16.3.3]

Type of Approach	Number of Respondents
Coupon redemption	179
Toll-free customer line	114
Focus groups	114
Customer survey	44
Rebate redemption	41
Recognition tests	26

a. Calculate the percentage of each of the response types and create a bar graph to illustrate the results.

b. Based on these results, how have the companies decided to allocate evaluation dollars? Do you think this is the best approach for all companies? Explain your answer.

3. You are the owner of the only hardware store in a city of 100,000 people. You have been able to reduce your promotional efforts because of the lack of competition.

   Recently, however, a large hardware store chain has purchased land on which to build a new store. You have decided to increase the amount of advertising you do and decide you need an advertising plan. Write the objectives for the plan. Specify the main message of the advertising, the target audience, and the time frame for the advertising. [16.2.1]

4. New companies, or companies with new products, often use very different advertising strategies than do established and trusted companies with established products. For each example below, explain how the advertising for a new product or company might differ from an established one. [16.2.1]

   a. Family restaurant

   b. SUV

   c. Energy drink

5. Many businesses experience seasonal fluctuations in sales. Listed below are three products or services that often experience high and low sales periods. Suggest two advertising strategies for each product/service that could help reduce these sales fluctuations. [16.2.1]

   a. Lawn maintenance

   b. Ski resort

   c. Toy manufacturing

Marketing Management and Decision Making

1. You are the chief executive officer of a company that manufactures golf equipment. Your marketing research determines that there is a large market for an oversized driver golf club. Your company invests heavily in designing and manufacturing this new driver.

   The advertising agency you have hired is developing an advertising plan for the new golf club. As CEO, list five factors you will be looking for in the advertising. List five questions you will want to ask the agency to ensure its ideas will help your sales. [16.1.2]

2. Not all advertising is done by companies selling products and services. Find an example of advertising for a charity, cause, or political campaign and prepare a short report describing the advertising, the strategy, and how it differs from product advertising. Be prepared to present your findings to the class. [16.2.1]

3. Research one of the laws or agencies that deal with illegal advertising and prepare a short report. Be prepared to present your findings to the class. [16.3.4]

4. Log on to the website of the Interactive Advertising Bureau and prepare a one-page report of the services it offers to its members and the kinds of information available on its site. Be prepared to give a presentation to the class. [16.2.2]

5. Search the Internet for a website that carries a lot of online advertising. Browse the site for 15 minutes and count the number of different ads that you see. Write a one-page report on the ad content of the site, including the types of advertisers you see, the formats of the ads displayed on the site, and any notable ads that stood out in the clutter. Explain why the ads captured your attention. [16.2.2]

6. Though you usually think of brands in relation to a company, a product, or a product line, marketers often consider how people brand themselves. You brand yourself in the way you dress, speak, and approach different situations. What kind of brand would you like to put forth in a job interview for a professional job, and how would you demonstrate that brand? [16.1.1]

Let's Start a Band Follow-Up Discussion

Work in small teams to discuss the question posed at the end of the opening vignette. What can the band do to maximize the value of its new logo?

Build Your Marketing Plan

Build your Portfolio In this chapter you learned about the advertising element of the promotional mix. You will now apply this learning to the development of your marketing plan. To access the chapter-specific tools that you will need to complete this activity, please navigate to Chapter 16 ➔ Build Your Marketing Plan in MindTap. Alternatively, you can access these tools online at NGLSync. Please visit www.nglsync.cengage.com, and search for the companion website that accompanies this book by entering the ISBN, author, or title. Once you locate this companion website, navigate to Build Your Marketing Plan ➔ Chapter 16.

Integrated Marketing Campaign Event

DECA PREP

Build your Portfolio The purpose of this event (for one to three students) is to prepare an integrated marketing campaign of no more than 45 days in length for a real event, product, or service for a prospective client/advertiser. Students also must present the campaign in a role-play situation to a prospective client/advertiser.

You will prepare a 10-page written document. All members of the team must participate during the 15-minute presentation to the client/advertiser. The written document must include:

Executive Summary One-page description of the campaign.

Description Description of the event, product, or service; description of the client/advertiser.

Campaign Objectives Major reasons for the integrated marketing campaign.

Campaign Target Marketing Description of the primary and secondary markets of the integrated marketing campaign.

Campaign Activities and Schedule List of the types of media, the schedule and creative samples.

Budget Detailed projections of actual costs.

Key Metrics Methods to evaluate the effectiveness of the campaign.

Bibliography List all sources used.

You will assume the role of a marketer who has the goal of pitching your campaign to the judge (client/advertiser).

Performance Indicators Evaluated

- Gather brand information. (Marketing-Information Management)
- Explain the nature of marketing research. (Marketing-Information Management)
- Compare business objectives with the expected use of the marketing-research outcomes. (Marketing-Information Management)
- Explain the concept of market and market identification. (Market Planning)
- Identify the elements of the promotional mix. (Promotion)
- Understand promotional channels used to communicate with targeted audiences. (Promotion)
- Calculate media costs. (Promotion)
- Make client presentations (includes strategies and research findings). (Communication Skills)

Go to the DECA website for more detailed information. **www.deca.org**

Think Critically

1. Why is the budget an important part of the marketing campaign?

2. Why must the marketing campaign understand buying behavior of primary and secondary markets?

3. How can the scheduled events for a marketing campaign stimulate sales?

4. What is the bottom line for a client considering a marketing campaign?

CHAPTER 17

SELLING

See how effective advertising leads to successful marketing strategies.
Click on Chapter 17, Visual Focus, in your MindTap.

Let's Start a Band!

"Don't try to explain it, just sell it."

– Colonel Tom Parker, Elvis Presley's manager

Now that we have T-shirts, I asked everybody if we should just put them on a folding table at the gigs or if we really want to try to sell them. Everyone thought that since we had them to sell, we should put forth the effort.

Malik said that while we're at it, maybe we should offer a few other "merch" items. Eddie brought up things like stickers, posters, and patches. Naomi suggested hats, buttons, and hoodies. I said we could try selling flash drives like the ones we made up for our press kit. Besides our music we can add photos, interviews, stories—anything the fans might be interested in.

I pointed out that some of those things are cheap, so we can easily afford to buy and then resell them. But if we go for hats and hoodies, we'd better get it right. Those items aren't cheap, and we don't want to be stuck with a lot of expensive stuff we can't sell.

"I'll get them to the table," Layla announced. "Before the encore I'll tell the audience that if they give us ten minutes, we'll be there to sign whatever and pose for pictures."

"Don't forget," Gael said, "We can offer these things on our website, too."

Selling merch is new to all of us. What do you think of our plan? Do you have any suggestions for improving it?

THE VALUE OF SELLING

Learning Objectives

17.1.1 Define selling.

17.1.2 Explain the advantages and disadvantages of personal selling.

17.1.3 Describe the need for salespeople to manage themselves, their customers, and marketing information.

Key Term

selling

marketing matters

Personal selling allows a company to respond to the unique needs of customers with specific messages designed to help customers make purchasing decisions. Selling is not the best promotional method for every situation. Marketers must weigh the distinct advantages and disadvantages of personal selling to determine if it fits a business's needs, either alone or in conjunction with other promotional methods. Salespeople need to develop skills to manage themselves, customers, and information.

essential question

What is personal selling, and how do marketers go about deciding whether or not personal selling is appropriate for their products?

The Personal Selling Process

The ultimate goal of any business is to sell its products and services profitably. Selling is a part of the promotion element of the marketing mix. Recall that *promotion* includes the methods used and information communicated to customers to encourage purchases and increase their satisfaction. Businesses use a variety of promotional methods, and each has a specific purpose. **Selling** is direct, personal communication with prospective customers in order to assess needs and satisfy those needs with appropriate products and services.

Direct and Personal Communication

All promotional methods involve communication with customers. Most are targeted toward large groups of customers and are generalized to appeal to their common needs. The larger and more diverse the audience, the less specific and individualized the promotional messages can be.

Personal selling is used to communicate with one or a few customers. Salespeople work directly with customers. They devote time and effort to getting to know the customer so they can tailor the information to meet that person's needs.

Direct communication means that the salesperson meets and talks with the customer. Usually the meeting is face to face, but it also may be completed via telephone, video conferencing, or Web conferencing. Based on the discussions, the salesperson provides additional, specific information as needed. If a customer has concerns or asks questions, the salesperson is able to respond. By listening to the tone of voice or observing body language, the salesperson may determine that the customer is still uncertain about a decision. Based on that feedback, the salesperson personalizes the communication to address the customer's doubts and resolve concerns.

Assess and Satisfy Needs

Effective marketing matches the most appropriate products and services to customer needs. Salespeople can tailor the choices of a business's products to individual customer needs and preferences. They also can determine where each customer is in the decision-making process. Some people may be ready to buy while others need more information. Some may not have fully clarified their needs, so they are not ready to choose a specific product.

Salespeople should assess a customer's needs and try to sell the product that best fits those needs. It is appropriate to offer an alternate product if it is the best match to the customer's needs. It is not appropriate to try to substitute an alternate product if

- The product is not the one that is best for the customer
- Customers do not understand their options
- The salesperson's goal is to make a bigger commission
- The salesperson is instructed to encourage customers to purchase certain products

The salesperson should discuss the purchase decision with each customer to make sure that specific needs and concerns are addressed. The salesperson should then offer each customer the best possible solution the company can provide to meet those needs.

If a company's products will not meet a customer's needs, there is no benefit in making the sale. The customer will realize quickly that the purchase was not appropriate and may return the product to the company, resulting in a lost sale and wasted selling expenses. Even if the product is

How might this jewelry salesperson assess this customer's needs?

Digital Vision/Getty Images

not returned, the customer likely will be unhappy with the company and salesperson and may be unlikely to make another purchase from the company in the future.

CHECKPOINT
How does selling differ from other promotional methods?

17.1.2 ▶ Advantages and Disadvantages of Personal Selling

Personal selling is the appropriate promotional method for some but not all products. There are advantages and disadvantages to consider in determining where and when personal selling fits a business's needs. The advantages and disadvantages of personal selling are listed in **Figure 17-1** and discussed below.

PERSONAL SELLING	
Advantages	**Disadvantages**
More information	Cost per customer
More time	Time required
Flexible	Less control
Uses feedback	Requires skilled
Persuasive	personnel
Follow-up	

FIGURE 17-1 Organizations need to consider the advantages and disadvantages of personal selling when deciding whether to include it in their marketing mix.

Advantages

Personal selling offers many advantages that other forms of promotion do not.

INFORMATION More product information can be provided through personal selling than through other forms of promotion. When a business offers information through an advertisement, only a limited amount of information can be included. An outdoor billboard or electronic display usually is restricted to fewer than 10 words because viewers pass by very quickly. Although newspaper and magazine advertisements can be longer, few people will spend more than a minute or two reading a print advertisement. Television advertisers typically only have 15 seconds to convey their message, and advertisers in online games have between 11 and 20 seconds to get their message across.

TIME Salespeople spend a considerable amount of time with customers. Even in the very shortest sales presentation, the conversation may last several minutes. Effective salespeople often meet with customers several times. Each meeting may last from 10 minutes to one hour. With that amount of time, a great deal of information can be exchanged.

FLEXIBILITY Personal selling is very flexible. The sales presentation is typically scheduled at a time and place that is convenient for the customer. During the meeting, if it is clear that a customer understands certain information or if that information is not important to the customer, the salesperson can move on to another topic.

FEEDBACK Because personal selling is two-way communication, the customer provides feedback. An effective salesperson asks questions, listens to customers' concerns, and determines if additional information is needed. That feedback is used to make the information even more specific to the individual needs of the customer. In addition to obtaining feedback from the customer, the salesperson provides feedback to the company. If the customer is dissatisfied with any part of the marketing mix or if competing products appear to meet customer needs better, the salesperson can inform the company so that changes and improvements can be made.

PERSUASION   Salespeople typically use persuasion near the end of the consumer decision-making process, when the customer is deciding whether or not to make the purchase. The customer may compare one or two very similar products before making a final decision. The salesperson can match the customer's needs with the features of the company's product and compare them to those of competitors. If the product will satisfy the customer, the salesperson is in a position to persuade the customer to make the decision to purchase.

The salesperson also may be able to offer adjustments in the marketing mix such as offering credit, delivery service, or even a modification in the product, if needed. By knowing what changes are possible and matching them with specific customer needs, the salesperson can be very effective in making a sale.

FOLLOW-UP   A sale is not completed at the time the customer makes a purchase. Customers must use the product and decide if it meets their needs. If they are dissatisfied with the product, they may return it and not want to buy other products from the company.

An important responsibility of a salesperson is to follow up with the customer after the sale. The follow-up provides an opportunity to ensure that the customer is able to use the product correctly,

How can salespeople follow up with customers?

© Pressmaster/Shutterstock.com

has everything needed, and is satisfied. Often a customer needs additional product information or reassurance to be fully satisfied with the purchase. If, however, the product does not work as expected or does not fully meet the customer's needs, a salesperson who is willing to make adjustments or accept a product return and replacement can usually turn a negative situation into a positive one.

Disadvantages

While there are many advantages of personal selling, there also are some disadvantages.

COST PER CUSTOMER   If an advertisement reaches thousands of potential customers, the cost per person might be as low as one dollar or often even less. In contrast, because a salesperson may talk to only a few customers each day, the cost per person for personal selling can be very expensive. A salesperson's expenses can include the cost of salary, travel, time spent with a customer, and equipment and materials needed for sales presentations. For sales of products to businesses, the cost of selling to each customer can easily be several hundred dollars. For very high-value products requiring months of negotiations and often involving several people as a part of a sales team, the cost of personal selling can be tens of thousands of dollars. However, if the process results in a multimillion-dollar sale, that cost is well worth it.

TIME Because a salesperson meets with relatively few customers per day, it takes a great deal of time to contact a large number of customers. Compare that to an advertisement that reaches millions of people at once. The length of time needed to reach a large number of customers is a disadvantage of personal selling. A company can solve that problem by employing a large number of salespeople, but that adds to the costs of selling. Usually personal selling is used when the number of customers

Want to know more about what is trending with this topic? Click on **Lesson 17.1, Marketing Decisions,** *in your MindTap.*

Connect to
MindTap

in the target market is small.

CONTROL The salesperson is responsible for deciding what information to provide as well as how and when activities are completed. Therefore, the company's managers have limited control over the sales process.

SKILL Salespeople need to understand selling procedures, communications, psychology, accounting, and management. They also need a great deal of knowledge about their products and services and those of their competitors. The selling process requires people who are outgoing, creative, able to adjust to different people and situations, and good at solving problems. The job often requires long work hours and travel. It is not easy for companies to find salespeople who have all of these characteristics.

© auremar/Shutterstock.com

Salespeople need to be outgoing, creative, flexible, and good problem solvers. Do you have the qualities needed to be a good salesperson?

Choose Personal Selling

Personal selling should be used when it improves the company's marketing efforts. It can be the only method of promotion a company uses. Usually it is combined with other methods as a part of a promotional plan. Characteristics of products and markets that indicate the need for personal selling include

- Complex or expensive products
- Markets made up of a few large customers
- New or very unique products with which customers are unfamiliar
- Customers located in a limited geographic area
- Complicated or long decision-making process
- Customers who expect personal attention and help with decision making

CHECKPOINT
What are the advantages of personal selling over other forms of promotion?

17.1.3 ▶ Personal Sales Management

Personal selling is a demanding career. Most salespeople are responsible for their own time, with limited direction from their managers. Often they are paid on commission. This means they are not paid unless they sell something.

A sales career may be very rewarding. Highly skilled salespeople are in high demand in business because their customers are loyal and return again and again to buy. Professional salespeople who do their jobs well earn more than many other businesspeople because they help a company sell products profitably. Because salespeople are responsible for the sales presentation, they typically have a great deal of satisfaction when they make a sale and satisfy the customer. Even though they may not manage other people, successful professional salespeople possess the qualities of good managers. The important areas of personal sales management are self-management, customer management, and information management.

Self-Management

Selling requires motivation and an effective use of time. It is difficult to call on yet another customer at the end of a long day. It is demanding to complete the necessary research needed to plan a personalized sales presentation. Much of a salesperson's time is spent on non-selling activities—paperwork, research, studying customer needs, and solving customer problems. A salesperson must be able to determine what needs to be done, set an efficient work schedule, and devote the necessary time until the work is completed. At times, it may require more than an eight-hour day or 40-hour week.

Salespeople need to be emotionally and physically healthy. They may feel stress because their success depends on customers deciding what to purchase and when they will purchase. They may be expected to achieve specific levels of sales for the company in a given time. Long hours of work may leave little time for exercise and relaxation.

An important part of self-management is personal development. Salespeople must be well educated and informed. They need to continue to learn about new selling procedures, the applications of technology, and information about products, customers, and competitors. Although they may feel their time is better spent with customers, salespeople must schedule time for personal and professional development as well.

Customer Management

Selecting and scheduling customers is a difficult challenge for salespeople. Some customers offer a greater potential for sales because they purchase more frequently or in larger quantities. Certain customers require more time because they are at an earlier decision-making stage. Some customers require more time because their needs are not well identified or they ask for a great deal of information. Salespeople must be able to decide how much time to spend with each customer to maximize their sales.

When salespeople travel to meet customers, they must schedule their time carefully. They need to limit travel time in order to spend more time selling. Also, they need to keep their travel costs as low as possible to help with the company's profitability.

Information Management

Think about what it might be like to buy a house or a car or maybe even a new musical instrument. Then, think about the types

MATH IN MARKETING

Pay-for-Performance Incentives

Salespeople are paid to sell, and many have compensation packages that provide incentives based on their sales. Some receive base salaries plus incentives. Others are compensated solely on what they sell. These incentive packages are designed to motivate the salespeople and keep them hungry for more sales.

Common forms of incentives include quotas, commissions, bonuses, long-term incentives, contests, or a combination of these. For example, car salespeople are commonly paid a flat fee for each car they sell plus a commission based on a percentage of the gross profit from each sale. If they reach a certain level—say, 20 cars in a month—their percentage of the profit is increased.

That kind of pay structure might explain why car salespeople are notorious for high-pressure sales tactics. Many businesses have found that such compensation systems hurt customer relationships. They try to balance compensation packages with long-term incentives and management systems that rein in overly aggressive salespeople.

Do the Math

1. A salesperson is paid $100 for every car she sells plus 10 percent of the gross profit from each sale. She also receives a bonus of $100 for each car in excess of 20 in a given month plus an additional 1 percent of her total gross profits for each car she sells in excess of 25 cars in a month. How much will she be paid if she sells 28 cars for a total gross profit of $65,000?

2. A salesperson is paid $2,000 per month plus a 5 percent commission on sales in excess of $40,000 in a month. If he already has booked sales of $31,000 by the last day of the month, how much is it worth to him if he can close on a $10,000 order by the end of the day?

of information salespeople need to convey to customers with each of these purchases. For example, real estate salespeople need to convey information such as the number of bedrooms and bathrooms, the property tax rate, the school district, the municipality, and the asking price for the house. In addition to identifying needed information, salespeople also must develop effective record-keeping systems and use the company's information system. They must complete orders and other sales records

 Want to know more about marketing in the information age? Click on Lesson 17.1, Digital Marketing, in your MindTap.

 Connect to MindTap

carefully and completely. If a salesperson makes an error in the price or quantity of an order or other required information, it can result in problems for the company, such as added expenses or lost profits. It may even open the company up to a possible lawsuit.

CHECKPOINT
Identify three important elements of personal sales management.

17.1 ASSESSMENT

What Have You Learned?

1. When is it appropriate to offer a customer a product they did not originally intend to buy? [17.1.1]
2. What are the disadvantages of personal selling compared to the other forms of promotion? [17.1.2]
3. Name some non-selling activities salespeople do in performing their job. [17.1.3]

Make Academic Connections

1. **Math**   A top business magazine has a total readership of 971,435, and 57 percent of readers report seeing a company's advertisement in one issue. The cost of the ad was $104,300. The company's salespeople have a prospective client list of 8,327 businesspeople and are able to arrange a meeting with 93 percent of them. The total sales budget for those calls was $37,280. Calculate the cost per customer of each method. [17.1.2]

2. **Career Success**   Use Internet career boards or the employment section of a large-circulation newspaper to identify four different personal selling job opportunities in business-to-business and retail sales. Study each job and prepare a table that compares the jobs, identifying things that are similar and things that are different. Based on the analysis, write a one-paragraph statement identifying which of the jobs you would prefer and why. [17.1.3]

Connect to ◇DECA

Build your Portfolio

You are the sales manager of a neighborhood office for a major cell phone service provider. Your goal is to make sure the company's service plans are well matched to the needs of each customer. Prepare a list of five questions you want each salesperson to ask new customers to gather information about their needs. Present your list of questions to your teacher (judge) and discuss the reasons for each question. [17.1.1]

Many times, the most efficient way to move an issue or sale forward is by making a persuasive presentation. This requires a great deal of preparation. First, you should define specifically what you want to accomplish with your presentation. What actions are you trying to motivate your audience to take? Do you want them to become active supporters of a cause? Do you want them to purchase the product or service you are selling?

Adapt to Your Audience

The presentation should be tailored to your specific audience members. If you do a presentation on the same topic to different audiences, you should adapt the presentation to effectively influence each audience. You need to "sell" yourself and your knowledge base, so the audience will believe you are a credible source on the information being presented. Making comments and providing information that demonstrate you have thoroughly researched your topic is one way to do this. You also should be sure to address any issues related to your topic that are important to the audience. This way your audience members will know that you studied not only the topic you are presenting, but also other factors that could impact them.

Dress in a manner that is appropriate for your audience. If you are making a pitch for new sports equipment, you could dress in neat, crisp athletic wear. If presenting a business proposal for which you are seeking funding, you should dress in professional business attire.

Present the Content

Carefully consider the presentation content. Describe or define the product, service, or issue clearly. Support the points you make with simple, understandable facts and reasons.

Give the audience a clear understanding of how they will benefit from what you propose. Define how your idea or proposal is superior to existing items. That superiority might arise from an improvement on existing technology or from an entirely new innovation in the field.

Use visual tools in the presentation that are attention-getting, easy to understand, and memorable. Determine the most effective way to present your ideas visually and make sure you are comfortable with the technology.

Engage the audience in the presentation. Meaningful examples and experiences as well as language that evokes an emotional response are ways to accomplish this. Compelling endorsements from others that the audience identifies with are an effective way to sway an audience. Let your passion for the product show through in your tone, mannerisms, and presentation style.

Construct your closing to move your idea forward. Whether you are asking for a sale or asking for support, your goal is to persuade the audience. Address any questions or concerns.

Finally, define the next steps and make it easy for people to take action. End with enthusiasm, conviction, and a positive tone.

Develop Your Skill

Think of a social issue you are passionate about. Decide what action you would like people to take in support of the issue. Using the methods noted above, prepare a persuasive presentation. Practice the presentation several times to become comfortable. Then deliver it to a close friend, family member, or adult mentor to get feedback before presenting it to your class.

Learning Objectives

17.2.1 Explain the ways by which salespeople come to understand their customers.

17.2.2 Discuss why salespeople need to know their product thoroughly.

17.2.3 Explain why it is important to understand the competition's products and marketing plans.

Key Terms

lead
cold calling
qualifying

prospect
feature
benefit

marketing matters

Success for salespeople is typically measured by the sales they make and the satisfaction of their customers. That success often is determined well before they ever meet with the customer. Many salespeople spend more time preparing for sales than they do in actual contact with customers. In addition to developing effective selling skills, three areas are important: understanding the customer, understanding the product, and understanding the competition.

 essential question

Why do salespeople need to develop an understanding of their customers, and how do they go about developing an understanding of products those customers might want?

17.2.1 ▶ Understand Customers

Marketing is responsible for creating satisfying exchanges between a business and its customers. Because salespeople negotiate the sale of products and services with the customer, they need to ensure that the customer is satisfied with the purchase. Understanding each customer helps a salesperson organize the presentation to meet that customer's needs. Effective selling requires a great deal of preparation.

Identify Potential Customers

Just as a business identifies its target market, salespeople need to identify potential customers. A potential customer is called a **lead**. Not every lead a salesperson comes across is an appropriate customer or results in a sale. Even after identifying high-potential customers, a salesperson needs additional information to tailor the best possible match of products and services for each one. Leads can come from a variety of sources.

COLD CALLING   Some salespeople use a process called cold calling to generate leads. With **cold calling**, a salesperson contacts a large number of people without knowing a great deal about each one. Examples of cold calls include a salesperson for business products who plans to call on every business listed in a city business directory with annual sales of more than $1 million. A telemarketer selling family health insurance plans may use a computer dialing system programmed to randomly call all unrestricted residential telephone numbers. A salesperson for a carpet-cleaning business may knock on the door of every home on a block to locate prospective customers.

You can imagine how salespeople might find cold calling both difficult and discouraging. They most likely have to contact a large number of customers before finding one who is interested in their products. They also may have a difficult time beginning the selling process if they know almost nothing about the prospective customer, whom they have just met. Further, people on the receiving end of the cold call may not appreciate the intrusion if they are not interested in the products being sold.

OTHER SOURCES OF LEADS
A marketing-oriented business typically does not use cold calling as a part of personal selling. Salespeople gather information on possible customers and determine if they fit the characteristics of the company's target market before reaching out to them. Often, through the company's marketing information system or marketing research, information on prospective customers already is available to assist the salesperson.

Referrals from other people are a frequent way of generating leads. Networking also is a common technique for obtaining leads, especially in the real estate and insurance industries. Other common techniques include trade shows, direct mail, and website contact forms.

Promotional or marketing efforts such as coupons and product registration cards are frequently used to generate leads and gather other information before the salesperson makes the first face-to-face contact. When the salesperson knows who prospective customers are, where they are located, some of their important needs, and when and how each customer prefers to be contacted, the selling process is a much more positive experience for both the customer and the salesperson.

Qualify Prospective Customers

Not all prospective customers are prepared or able to purchase a product at a particular time. Salespeople gather information to determine which people are most likely to buy in a process called **qualifying**. A lead that has been qualified becomes a **prospect**.

Three identifying characteristics qualify a person as a prospective customer. Without all three characteristics present, the person will not purchase the product. The characteristics include:

* A need for the product
* The resources to purchase the product
* The authority to make a decision to purchase

Although everyone in a target market has a general need for the product being marketed, that need may not be as important as other needs. Salespeople identify customers who have the strongest need and who are ready to make a purchasing decision. Most people have many more needs than they can satisfy at a given time.

A common limitation for customers is a lack of resources to buy the product. A customer may not have the money or adequate financing to make a purchase. No matter how hard the salesperson works or how effective the sales presentation is, a sale is not possible if the customer cannot afford to purchase the product. Part of the information-gathering process is determining if the customer has adequate resources or if financing will make resources available.

Many times one person in an organization wants to buy a product but does not have the authority to make the decision. For example, a manager may need to get approval from the purchasing department, or a partner in a business may need to have the agreement of the other partners. Salespeople often need to work with multiple people before a purchase decision is made. It is important to determine early on which person or people will make the final decision and to make sure they are included in the selling process at the appropriate time.

Understand Customer Decisions

In order to further understand their customers, salespeople need to understand the steps in the consumer decision-making process. Those steps include identifying a problem or need, gathering information, evaluating alternatives, making a decision, and evaluating the decision. Consumers need specific types of information as they move through each step. If the consumer is gathering information on possible products to satisfy a need, information on financing alternatives will not be helpful. On the other hand, if the customer has narrowed the choice to two products and is comparing them, it will not help to provide general

Why is it important to identify decision makers early in the selling process?

© fizkes/Shutterstock.com.

information on the needs a product satisfies. Salespeople often translate the consumer decision-making steps into a series of mental stages that lead to a sale. Those mental stages are summarized with the letters AIDCA. The meaning of each letter is shown in **Figure 17-2**.

A salesperson knows that the customer must first focus *attention* on the salesperson and the sales presentation. It is important to get the customer's *interest* in the product early in the presentation. A customer moves from interest to *desire* when it is clear that the product meets important needs. The desire turns to *conviction* when the customer determines that the product is a good value and the best choice. That leads to *action*, or the purchase of the product.

A salesperson who understands consumer decision making and is able to determine which of the AIDCA stages each customer is in will be able to provide the specific information that each customer needs at a particular time to assist with an appropriate decision. An important advantage of personal selling is the capability of providing specific information to each customer when it is needed.

Mental Stages of Consumer Decision Making

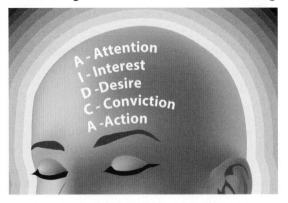

A - Attention
I - Interest
D - Desire
C - Conviction
A - Action

FIGURE 17-2 Salespeople need to understand the mental stages of consumer decision making in order to plan each sales presentation.

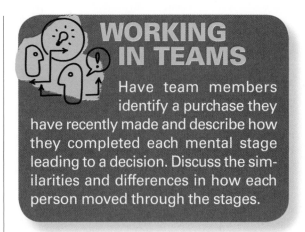

WORKING IN TEAMS

Have team members identify a purchase they have recently made and describe how they completed each mental stage leading to a decision. Discuss the similarities and differences in how each person moved through the stages.

CHECKPOINT

Name the three ways by which salespeople come to understand their customers.

17.2.2 ▶ Understand the Product

The salesperson is responsible for providing the information the customer needs to make a good decision. There are two parts to that responsibility. The salesperson must have adequate product knowledge and the ability to communicate the information effectively to the customer.

Product Knowledge

Choosing the best product to satisfy a customer's needs often is not an easy task. Customers may not be able to determine by examining a product, or even by reviewing the information that accompanies a product, whether it is the one they should buy. Salespeople need to know a great deal about the products they represent. They also must be able to quickly access additional information when needed to answer customers' unique questions.

MARKETING MIX INFORMATION

Effective salespeople are familiar with all parts of the marketing mix for the products they sell. Customers are concerned not only about the product but also about the price and availability. They may have seen other company promotions and have questions about that information. Although an individual customer may not be interested in all of the marketing mix information, the salesperson must be able to tailor a sales presentation to the needs of each customer.

One customer may want to know about the construction and durability of a product. Another may be concerned about the warranty and repair services. Still another may need to know about financing. A salesperson who does not have that information or who is unable to obtain it quickly will not be able to satisfy potential customers and will lose their confidence and respect. Sales will be lost to other salespeople who can provide the needed information.

INFORMATION SOURCES Salespeople have a variety of sources of product information available. Their companies prepare information sheets, product manuals, and online videos. Advertisements and other types of promotions often contain valuable information, including price changes and special incentives. The product's marketing plan and marketing research reports are sources of useful information, as are other salespeople and company personnel including engineers, production people, and other marketers.

Many companies offer frequent training for salespeople that emphasizes important and up-to-date product information. They also prepare sales aids and other materials for salespeople to use as a part of their sales presentations. Effective salespeople regularly read business publications, attend conferences and trade shows, and study other information sources to keep up to date on the products and services they sell. Being well prepared and having a great deal of product knowledge makes salespeople confident they can answer customer questions and provide the marketing mix each customer needs.

Communicate Product Information

Which statement is more effective as a part of a sales presentation?

- The standard engine in this vehicle is a 3.5-liter V6.

- Our standard engine offers the best combination of efficiency and power. You will average 29 miles per gallon, but it will also give you immediate acceleration, so you won't have trouble merging into faster traffic when entering the freeway.

The statements provide examples of features and benefits. A **feature** is a description of a product characteristic. The first statement describes a feature—the standard 3.5-liter V6 engine. A **benefit** is the advantage provided to a customer as a result of the feature. Stating the benefit tells the customer what the feature will do for them. The second statement is more effective because it describes how the customer will benefit from the engine—fuel efficiency and adequate acceleration when needed. Salespeople communicate most effectively when they can describe the benefits of a product for a customer in terms of important needs.

Frequently a product's features are similar to those of competitors. Other features are different, and a few may be unique. Customers want to know how various products and brands are similar and how they are different. The salesperson needs to understand the features, compare them to competitors, translate them into customer benefits, and communicate the important benefits in an understandable way to each customer.

 CHECKPOINT
Why do salespeople need to tell customers about the benefit of a product feature?

MARKETING COMMUNICATION
Websites for Distributor Communication

For many industrial supply distributors, the Internet or World Wide Web (WWW) is evolving into the key medium for getting their message out to prospective customers. Because they are dealing with standard parts and supplies that customers usually can obtain through a number of distribution channels, successful selling frequently hinges on price, availability, and reliability. Providing up-to-date information to customers is vital to staying competitive in what many believe has become an "information transfer" business.

Even for small distributors, the Web opens the door to a potential worldwide market for products, particularly those for which shipping is not a big expense. The big advantages of communicating via the Web are cost-effectiveness and timeliness. A distributor's online catalog is available 24 hours a day, seven days a week, and is available to anyone with Internet access. Unlike print catalogs, online information can be updated continuously, so product listings and prices are always current.

From a buyer's perspective, online catalogs allow a business to query dozens of suppliers by email with just a few keystrokes. Distributors have learned to reply promptly or risk losing an order to a competitor.

Think Critically

1. What role does personal selling have in an "information transfer" business that relies heavily on a website to generate sales?
2. What are the advantages and disadvantages of Web-based catalogs versus printed catalogs?

17.2.3 ▶ Understand the Competition

Customers usually choose among several options before making a purchase. The consumer wants to buy the most appropriate product with the best value. With products that are similar, quite complex, or for which little information is available, consumers may have a difficult time determining which is best. It is not unusual for a customer to buy one product only to realize later that another choice would have been better.

Salespeople who are familiar with competitors' products can help the customer understand the differences among the choices they have. They should incorporate the information they have about competitors' products into their sales presentations. Salespeople should avoid making negative comments about competitors and their product. Customers are deciding among two or three alternatives and may be offended if the salesperson makes negative comments about one of their final choices. Customers will have a better attitude toward a salesperson who demonstrates an understanding of the competition and carefully helps them compare advantages and disadvantages so that they can make the most informed choice.

Customers may study several brands or similar products before making a decision. A knowledgeable salesperson can explain important differences to customers to assist them with the comparison. The customer may not make a final decision immediately but may spend additional time comparing competing products. The customer will be able to use the information the salesperson provided when examining a competitor's product and see the advantages of salesperson's brand. Just as with their company's products, salespeople need to study the important parts of the marketing mix for competitors' products and call attention to the benefits of each of the mix elements when appropriate. Online reviews of the competitors' products, as well as of their own products, also can provide insight into specific issues customers have.

*Want to know more about what is trending with this topic? Click on **Lesson 17.2, Global Marketing,** in your MindTap.*

Connect to **MindTap**

CHECKPOINT

Why is it necessary for a salesperson to understand competitors' products?

17.2 ASSESSMENT

What Have You Learned?

1. Why is it important to qualify prospective customers before engaging them in a sales presentation? [17.2.1]

2. What is the difference between a lead and a prospect? [17.2.2]

3. Why do salespeople need to tell customers about the benefit of a product feature? [17.2.2]

4. Why should a salesperson avoid making negative comments about competitors and their products in a sales presentation? [17.2.3]

Make Academic Connections

1. **Research**   You are a salesperson for an athletic uniform company. Your assigned market is all public and private schools within 200 miles of your community. Locate two resources you can use to identify all of your potential customers. Describe the information in each resource that will help you qualify the customer. List additional information you will need to fully qualify each school that is not available in the resources. [17.2.1]

2. **Ethics**   As an automobile salesperson, you know you can often sell customers expensive cars by offering lower monthly payments and allowing six years to pay. It increases your current commissions, but it means customers may struggle to make monthly payments for many years. Write a three-paragraph analysis of your responsibility to the customer, to your business, and to yourself. [17.2.1]

Connect to ◇DECA

Build your Portfolio

Choose a product you are familiar with that has multiple features, such as a cell phone. Develop a chart that identifies five important product features and a specific customer benefit statement for each feature. Put the benefit statements in your own words. Present the chart to your teacher (judge). [17.2.2]

17.3 THE SELLING PROCESS AND SALES SUPPORT

Learning Objectives

17.3.1 Identify the seven steps of the selling process.

17.3.2 Explain why salespeople need support from other areas of the business.

Key Terms

approach
preapproach
demonstration
close

trial close
suggestion selling
follow-up

marketing matters

A salesperson carefully assesses customer needs and uses the company's resources to design an effective marketing mix. The salesperson then presents that mix and describes how it meets the customer's needs. The salesperson asks questions to determine if the mix is satisfactory or if adjustments must be made and helps the customer make the best decision. Good salespeople follow up with customers to make sure they are satisfied and to provide any additional support needed.

essential question

What are the key steps in the selling process?

17.3.1 ▶ Steps in the Selling Process

When a company aligns its selling process with the marketing concept, the salesperson represents the company to the customer and is responsible for making sure customer needs are satisfied. The selling process is a cooperative process. The salesperson helps the customer through the decision-making steps to ensure that the final decision is the best choice. Sales involves persuasion, and it is easier to persuade people to buy if they think you understand their needs and have their best interests in mind.

The activities of effective salespeople can be summarized in the seven steps

of the selling process. Those steps are listed in **Figure 17-3** and discussed below.

Approach

The **approach** is the first contact with the customer when the salesperson gets the customer's attention and creates interest in the product. The approach may be initiated by the customer or by the salesperson. In either case, the salesperson is responsible for the result. The approach used in retail selling differs from that in business-to-business selling.

STEPS IN THE SELLING PROCESS

Step	Purpose
Approach	Contact customers, gain their attention and interest, and create a favorable first impression
Determine needs	Gather information to determine customers' needs and how they can be met
Demonstrate	Present the product in a way that emphasizes customer benefits
Answer questions	Overcome objections and ensure the marketing mix meets customers' needs
Close	Obtain a decision to purchase
Suggestion selling	Suggest other products customers may see as valuable
Follow-up	Continue contact to ensure satisfaction, determine other needs, and build rapport

FIGURE 17-3 Effective salespeople follow a specific procedure to match customer needs with the company's products and services.

RETAIL SELLING When a customer enters a retail store, the salesperson must decide whether to approach and greet them or to allow the customer to look around the store. Some customers have a particular product in mind. Others are making initial judgments about whether the store offers products that interest them. Still others are simply spending time in the store without any real interest in making a purchase. A salesperson who approaches the customer in a pleasant way can quickly determine if the customer wants assistance.

For the customer who is just beginning to search for a product, the salesperson provides information on the basic characteristics of products that might meet the customer's needs. The salesperson allows the customer to examine several choices but will step in if the customer appears to need help or has a question. By observing and talking to the customer, the salesperson can offer information on the products that appear to meet the customer's needs.

As the customer is nearing a decision, the salesperson might review advantages of certain product features, payment options, or any final important factors that will help the customer decide to buy. Even if the customer does not buy, the salesperson should be courteous and remind the customer of important features and benefits of the items they were considering. That will usually impress the customer and encourage a return visit.

BUSINESS-TO-BUSINESS SELLING Salespeople who call on business customers have different considerations when planning an approach. Because several people may be involved in making a purchase decision, the salesperson must decide whom to contact. Businesspeople receive frequent visits from many salespeople. They do not have time to meet with all of them, so they select only those whom they think can be of help. Telephone calls, letters of introduction, or special promotional materials sent to the prospective customer can be used to make the customer aware of the salesperson, the company, and its products.

When an appointment is set with a business customer, the salesperson needs to be on time and well prepared with all materials required to discuss products and services with the customer. The salesperson needs to clarify who will participate in the initial meeting and whether others are involved in the final purchase decision. The initial call may be used to acquaint the customer with the business and its products and to gather information in order to facilitate follow-up meetings. Many business-to-business sales are completed in one sales call, so the salesperson needs to be well prepared with customer information and the capability to negotiate an order. It helps if both the salesperson and the customer agree on the purpose and goals of the first meeting.

Determine Needs

Determining needs is central to the marketing concept and the selling process. This step can be performed both before and after the initial customer contact. Whenever possible, salespeople should gather information about customers and their needs before the first meeting. Based on that information, they can outline and practice their sales presentation.

Efforts to prepare for a sales presentation in advance of the first customer contact are called the preapproach. The **preapproach** includes gathering preliminary information and preparing a preliminary sales presentation for a customer. Salespeople study information available on the specific customer. They also review information about their own company, its products, and the marketing mix. Preparation and practice help the salesperson to be more comfortable and to focus on the customer during the meeting.

Once customers are contacted, salespeople confirm and fine-tune the information they have and then zero-in on determining the customer's specific needs by direct questioning. The goal is to find the best way to satisfy those needs and lead the customer effectively to a decision through a sales presentation. Preapproach work with a customer may be done through surveys and questionnaires, email and telephone contacts, or even a meeting with the stated goal of gathering information.

Demonstrate

The main part of the sales presentation is the demonstration. The **demonstration** is a personalized presentation of the product features in a way that emphasizes the benefits and value to the customer. The salesperson tailors the product information to the customer and emphasizes the parts of the marketing mix that best meet the customer's needs. The demonstration aims to turn the customer's interest into desire.

As the salesperson moves from the approach to the demonstration, the main needs of the customer should be identified. The salesperson confirms those needs and determines the information that will help the customer make a decision by asking questions and listening carefully to the answers.

The most effective demonstrations are based on a feature–benefit presentation. The salesperson must identify the features of the marketing mix that are most important to the customer and describe how the customer will benefit from each of the features.

To conduct an effective demonstration, a salesperson needs to

- Use active, descriptive language that is understandable and meaningful.
- Direct the customer's attention to a feature and explain its benefit.
- Observe reactions and listen to comments to focus on customer needs.
- Demonstrate the feature rather than just describing it when possible.
- Involve the customer. Let the customer handle and test the product.
- Be animated and enthusiastic so the customer remains interested and remembers important features.

- Use sales aids such as pictures, charts, and computer demonstrations to enhance understanding.

- Review the benefits that seem to be most meaningful to the customer.

Answer Questions/ Overcome Objections

Customer's questions help a salesperson resolve concerns and provide additional information. As a salesperson successfully responds to each question, the customer is mentally moving from desire to conviction.

This step in the selling process is often referred to as *overcoming objections*. In the traditional view of selling, it was believed that customers raised objections to avoid making a purchase decision. Salespeople had to overcome that resistance by handling the objection. That approach set up the selling process as a competition between the customer and the salesperson.

When the salesperson has consumer interests in mind and is presenting a product or service that meets customer needs, there is less reason for the customer to resist. Customers want to be certain they are making the correct decision. They ask questions to gather information and clarify their understanding.

A salesperson should welcome and encourage questions. Questions often will help the salesperson identify the most important needs of the customer. They indicate the parts of the marketing mix that the customer does not yet understand. By answering each question well, the salesperson demonstrates an interest in the customer's needs and the customer's understanding of the product. An effective procedure for answering questions is shown in **Figure 17-4**.

Close the Sale

The **close** is the step in the sales process when the customer makes a decision to purchase. A well-planned sales presentation helps the customer move from attention to interest to desire and then to conviction. A customer must be confident that a product or service will meet important needs and that it offers the best value.

A salesperson needs to be skillful in closing the sale. A customer who feels pressured will resist buying the product. On the other hand, some customers need encouragement. If the salesperson does not ask for the order, the customer may postpone the decision and buy something later. The salesperson must provide opportunities for the customer to purchase the product and be willing to continue the sales presentation if the customer is not ready to buy.

Providing the customer with the opportunity to buy during the sales presentation is known as a **trial close**. A customer who repeatedly handles the product, appears satisfied with answers to questions, or responds favorably to a feature–benefit description or demonstration may be ready to buy. The salesperson should take that opportunity to ask for the order.

Answering a Customer's Questions

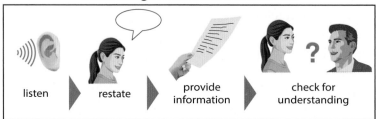

listen ▶ restate ▶ provide information ▶ check for understanding

FIGURE 17-4 Answering questions requires effective communication skills.

There are several ways a salesperson can close a sale. The goal is to make the decision easy for the customer. **Figure 17-5** identifies six methods of closing a sale.

As soon as the customer decides to buy, the salesperson should reinforce that decision. Customers want to believe they made the right choice, but they often have concerns after the decision is made. The salesperson should then re-emphasize the value and summarize the benefits the customer will receive from the purchase.

Suggestion Selling

One of the responsibilities of the salesperson at the completion of a sale is to be certain the customer's needs are satisfied as fully as possible. Frequently, a product can be used more effectively if the customer purchases related merchandise. A bicycle rider needs a helmet. An office chair may be useful for a businessperson who just purchased a desk and file cabinets. If customers leave without all of the things they need to use the product, they may be dissatisfied. Offering additional products and services after an initial sale in order to increase customer satisfaction is known as **suggestion selling**. Products offered after a sale should be clearly related to the product purchased and beneficial to the customer. A customer who believes that the salesperson is just trying to add to the sale or is pushing products that the business is currently promoting will no longer have a positive attitude toward the salesperson.

Follow-Up

Customers who purchase products and services from a company and are satisfied with their purchases are likely to buy from that company again. Making contact with the customer after the sale to ensure satisfaction is known as **follow-up**. Follow-up also provides another opportunity to reinforce the customer's decision and determine if the customer has additional needs that the business can meet. Following up each sale is an important part of relationship building that can lead to repeat sales and referrals to additional customers.

METHODS FOR CLOSING A SALE	
Closing Method	**Example**
Close on an important benefit	"You obviously are concerned about safety. This automobile not only has front and side air bags but also has built-in child safety seats in the rear. You can't find a safer family automobile."
Offer the customer a choice	"We have both the green and blue in stock. Which would you prefer?"
Provide an extra value	"This month we are offering a 3 percent discount if you decide to order 500 or more units."
Ask about the method of payment	"Will you pay cash, or would you like to use the 6-month financing plan we discussed?"
Emphasize availability	"If you place the order today, we can have it delivered and installed by Friday."
Guarantee satisfaction	"You can try it for two weeks. If you are not satisfied for any reason, we will gladly replace it or offer a full refund."

FIGURE 17-5 Salespeople use various methods to close a sale.

Part of the follow-up responsibility may include checking on delivery schedules, making sure warranty or product registration information is accurate, scheduling product installation and maintenance, or making sure financing paperwork is complete and accurate. If the customer has any problems, the salesperson should arrange to resolve them quickly. Following up on the sale also will make the customer feel important.

CHECKPOINT
Identify and describe each of the seven steps in the selling process.

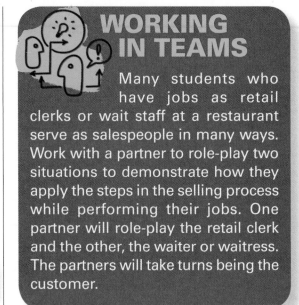

WORKING IN TEAMS

Many students who have jobs as retail clerks or wait staff at a restaurant serve as salespeople in many ways. Work with a partner to role-play two situations to demonstrate how they apply the steps in the selling process while performing their jobs. One partner will role-play the retail clerk and the other, the waiter or waitress. The partners will take turns being the customer.

17.3.2 ▶ Sales Support

For selling to be effective, the salesperson must receive support from many parts of the business, including other marketing personnel. To meet customer needs, the salesperson must have products and services that are well designed, readily available, and priced competitively. People in production, finance, and management need to coordinate their work with salespeople to match the supply of products with sales. Order processing, customer service, and many other business activities are required.

Each of the following descriptions of important marketing activities demonstrates how they support the work of salespeople:

- *Marketing-Information Management* Salespeople need access to a wide variety of information throughout the selling process. In the preapproach, the salesperson needs information on customers and their needs. During the sales presentation, the salesperson may need to gather additional information about products, competitors, or the customer that should be maintained in the company's marketing information system (MkIS).

- *Financing* Many customers need to finance their purchases. Salespeople must have access to credit services to offer their customers. They also may need assistance in explaining financing and completing the paperwork.

- *Pricing* Many prices can be negotiated. Offering discounts, accepting trade-ins, and other methods can be used to adjust the price. A salesperson must have the authority to negotiate the price or must be able to get pricing information quickly.

- *Promotion* Customers may obtain information from sources other than the salesperson to aid in making a buying decision. Promotion, including advertising and publicity, can create interest, inform customers of product choices, or reinforce a purchase decision.

- *Product/Service Management* Salespeople can provide information on customer needs and customer reactions to the current products and services offered by the business. That information should be used to improve existing products and develop new ones.

- *Distribution* Products and services often need to be delivered to customers. Salespeople rely on transportation services to get the products delivered at the time the customers want them. Salespeople need to have information on transportation schedules and costs when they work with their customers.

CHECKPOINT
Why do salespeople need support from other areas of the business including other marketing personnel?

17.3 ASSESSMENT

What Have You Learned?

1. What is the goal of the preapproach? [17.3.1]
2. How does promotion support the selling process? [17.3.2]

Make Academic Connections

1. **Communication** Choose a partner and together select a product that each of you is familiar with and would be comfortable selling. For each of the methods of closing a sale, write a short script that a salesperson could use to sell the product. Use the script to role-play each closing method for the class. In your role-play, make sure that when you introduce yourself to the customer, you make eye contact with him or her and extend a firm handshake. [17.3.1]

2. **Finance** People who sell new cars typically have three payment options to offer customers: cash, loan, or leasing. Imagine you have chosen a new car with a selling price of $25,000. Conduct research online to determine the pros and cons of each payment option. To get started with your research, use the search term "leasing vs. buying a new car." [17.3.2]

Connect to ◇DECA

Build your Portfolio

You are a salesperson meeting with a prospective customer to sell a new tablet computer. Select the brand and model of computer you want to sell, gather product information, and prepare a five-minute sales presentation that includes the appropriate approach, demonstration, trial close, close, and suggestion selling. Meet with your teacher (judge) to give your sales presentation. [17.3.1]

Connect to MindTap

Analyze a case study that focuses on chapter concepts. Click on **Chapter 17, Case Study,** *in your MindTap.*

Review Marketing Concepts

1. Explain why personal selling would be helpful to customers who are in the market for technology products such as computers and cell phones. [17.1.1]

2. How can time be both an advantage and a disadvantage of personal selling? [17.1.2]

3. What do you think is the main cause of stress in personal selling? [17.1.3]

4. Which of these is more important: identifying customers or qualifying them? Explain your answer. [17.2.1]

5. Why is merely describing a product's features not enough for an effective sales presentation? [17.2.2]

6. You sell multifunction printers to small businesses. Your competition sells a different brand, but its products are nearly identical to yours. How do you separate yourself and your products from the competition? [17.2.3]

7. Which of these closing techniques do you think is more effective: close on an important benefit or guarantee satisfaction? [17.3.1]

8. You sell new cars. Describe how you would use financing as a method to assist clients with their buying decision. [17.3.2]

Marketing Research and Planning

1. The following is a list of important personal selling concepts. Match each concept with the correct example or description. [17.1.1, 17.1.2, 17.2.1, 17.2.2]

   a. assess and satisfy needs

   b. customer decision-making process

   c. feedback

   d. flexibility

   e. follow-up

   f. qualifying

   g. time

   _____ During a sales presentation, the salesperson can respond to the customer's questions or determine if specific information is needed.

   _____ Salespeople listen and ask questions to respond to the needs of each customer.

   _____ Customers get more detailed product information than they can with other methods of promotion.

   _____ Lin Chung estimates that she spends about one-third of her time with customers to help them with products they have purchased.

   _____ Rosa Garcia likes to make sure her customers get the best products possible to solve their problems.

   _____ Salespeople use marketing research information to determine the customers who are interested in and able to buy the company's products or services.

   _____ Fred March works closely with his customers so that he can understand when they are ready to make decisions to purchase.

2. Effective salespeople help to solve customer problems by explaining how a product or service will benefit the consumer. It is helpful to prepare a feature–benefit chart for each product a salesperson represents. Assume you are a salesperson selling a video camera. For each of the following features, describe a customer benefit using descriptive, meaningful language. [17.2.2]

a. automatic focus

b. date and event imprinter

c. case with carrying strap and ID tag

d. removable flash memory storage

e. six-hour battery

f. low-light lens

g. detachable microphone

h. image stabilization system

3. Before making a sales call, the salesperson should be armed with information about the customer, the product, and the competition. Assume you are a salesperson of vehicle tires to be sold to automobile manufacturers. List three pieces of information that would be helpful to know about your customer, your product, and the competition. List three methods or sources you can use to find the necessary information. [17.2.1, 17.2.2, 17.2.3]

4. Salespeople are often paid bonuses or commissions on their total sales. Each of the salespeople shown in the table earns $60,000 per year and, in addition, earns 2 percent commission on all sales that exceed $250,000 per year. [17.1.3]

a. What is each salesperson's total income for the year?

b. What is the average amount of each salesperson's sale?

c. What percentage of calls resulted in a sale for each salesperson?

Salesperson	Total Sales	Number of Sales Calls Per Year	Number of Sales Per Year
Chin Miller	$2,345,200	250	107
Jane Brown	$3,395,200	350	120
Marcus Gonzalez	$2,930,400	400	99

Marketing Management and Decision Making

1. As the CEO of a company that offers website design and Web hosting services to other businesses, you understand how important it is to provide support to your salespeople as they plan sales presentations and work with prospective and current customers. For each of the marketing activities listed below, specify one way that the people working in these areas can provide the necessary support for the salespeople. [17.3.2]

a. Distribution

b. Financing

c. Marketing-Information Management

d. Pricing

e. Product/Service Management

f. Promotion

2. Search the Internet for six full-time job openings in sales. Prepare a table that compares the industry and product/service to be sold, job duties, qualifications (education and experience), and type of compensation (wage, salary, commission). Add notes from the job announcement that identify whether or not it seems the company expects the salesperson to understand and follow the principles of the marketing concept. [17.1.3]

3. Choose one of the following products and go comparison shopping for a particular brand and model of that product at three different retailers. Obtain data on the list or sticker price, the prices of features or options you prefer, and the final price offered by the salesperson. Input the data into a computer spreadsheet program and calculate the average list price, the average price of each option, and the average final price. Calculate the difference between each list and offered price. Using a word processing program, write a one-page report of the actions taken by salespeople you encountered to determine your needs and help you make a good purchase decision. [17.2.2]

a. motor scooter

b. set of golf clubs

c. smart HDTV

d. newest full-featured cell phone

e. work desk and chair for your room

f. musical instrument

4. Form a three-person sales team with two classmates. Your team represents a local vending company that wants to enter into an exclusive contract with your school to supply vending machines that will offer healthy beverages and snack foods. You hope to be the only vendor, place 10 machines in the school, and offer the school 20 percent of all revenues from the machines. Your company is willing to negotiate on the types of items in the machines, the number of machines, and the percentage of revenue shared. As a team, identify the person in the school who will be your initial contact, the other school personnel you expect to be involved in the final decision, and how you will make your initial contact. Prepare a team sales presentation following the steps in the selling process. Prepare visuals to support your sales presentation. Practice the presentation as a team, and then give the presentation to a group of your classmates who will role-play the school's decision makers. [17.2.1, 17.3.1]

Let's Start a Band Follow-Up Discussion

Work in small teams to discuss the question posed at the end of the opening vignette. What suggestions do you have for the band for selling their merch? What items should they sell and how should they sell them?

Build Your Marketing Plan

In this chapter you learned about the selling element of the promotional mix. You will now apply this learning to the development of your marketing plan. To access the chapter-specific tools that you will need to complete this activity, please navigate to Chapter 17 ➜ Build Your Marketing Plan in MindTap. Alternatively, you can access these tools online at NGLSync. Please visit www.nglsync.cengage.com, and search for the companion website that accompanies this book by entering the ISBN, author, or title. Once you locate this companion website, navigate to Build Your Marketing Plan ➜ Chapter 17.

Professional Selling Event

DECA PREP

Build your Portfolio

The Professional Selling Event provides an opportunity for participants to demonstrate knowledge and skills for a career in sales. Participants will organize and deliver a sales presentation for one or more products and/or services. New products, services, and target market customers (prospects) will be identified annually by DECA. Participants will research the company and the product or service they represent. The participant will present the product or service to meet the needs of the customer (prospect).

Society is becoming increasingly concerned with the number of young people being abducted each day. You have been asked to do an analysis of the Student Tracker—an electronic device that allows parents to know the location of their children at all times. First Alert sells a broad line of security products, ranging from home security systems to GPS tracking devices frequently used by business travelers.

You must convince the First Alert CEO that the Student Tracker is an important product with great potential for profitability. You must analyze Student Tracker features and benefits. The Student Tracker must be inconspicuous, easy to wear, and dependable with a long battery life. You must explain a strategy to convince students to wear the Student Tracker. Your presentation must explain how easy it is to monitor people wearing the Student Tracker.

You must organize appropriate information and present/defend a sales presentation. The 15-minute oral presentation will consist of the sales presentation and judge's questions. Your presentation will be evaluated for effectiveness of public speaking and presentation skills and how well you respond to the judge's questions.

Acceptable visual aids include three standard-sized posters not to exceed 22 ½" × 30 ½" each and one standard-sized presentation display board not to exceed 36 ½" × 48 ½" to be placed on chairs or free-standing easels. Cell phones/smartphones, iPods/MP3 players, iPads/tablets or any type of a handheld, information-sharing device will be allowed in written events if applicable to the presentation. Sound, as long as the volume is not too loud, also may be used.

Performance Indicators Evaluated

- Explain the nature of professional selling. (Professional Development)
- Describe the use of target marketing in professional selling. (Marketing-Information Management)
- Assess prospect's needs in relation to product offering. (Selling)
- Demonstrate product solution for prospect's needs. (Selling)
- Close the sale. (Selling)

Go to the DECA website for more detailed information. **www.deca.org**

Think Critically

1. How has the media been a driving force behind the need for the Student Tracker?
2. Why must the Student Tracker be small and inconspicuous?
3. Where are the best opportunities for First Alert to present the Student Tracker to its target markets?
4. Why might students resist wearing the Student Tracker?

CHAPTER 18

MARKETING IN A GLOBAL ECONOMY

Connect to MindTap

See how effective advertising leads to successful marketing strategies.
Click on Chapter 18, Visual Focus, *in your MindTap.*

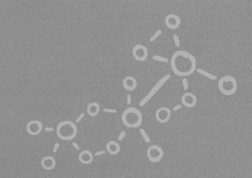

Let's Start a Band!

"American music is something the rest of the world wants to listen to. Our job is to make sure they pay for it."

– Jason Berman, Music Industry Executive

We met the other day to get a start on our plans for the summer. I knew we wanted to do a couple of tours. You know, hit the festival circuit, do a few clubs. I told the band about an opportunity we have to play in Canada. They want us there July 1st for Canada Day weekend.

That got their interest. Gael asked if that meant we'd do a Fourth of July concert in Canada. "Sure," I told him. "But remember that Fourth of July isn't a holiday there."

Next Jake asked about the money. He knew they used the dollar but thought it wasn't worth as much as a dollar in the United States. "So," he went on, "If we play in Canada, we won't be paid in American money, will we?"

"I don't know," Naomi answered him. "But if we aren't, we just have to figure out the exchange rate to see if it's worth it."

Jake said, "That's fine, but if we settle on a price now, what assurance do we have that what we get will be worth it? The exchange rate is sure to change between now and then."

"That's probably a risk we have to take if we're going to play there," I replied.

"Same thing about the merch," Eddie pointed out. "We know what the t-shirts cost us, but what do we sell them for there in order to make a profit?"

"If we go," I told them, "We'll have some time to decide if it's worth bringing the stuff over." Like everything else, it's complicated.

Can you help us sort this out? What are the pros and cons of bringing the show to Canada?

Learning Objectives

18.1.1 Describe the mechanics of international trade.

18.1.2 Explain why businesses expand into international markets and how governments assist in this expansion.

Key Terms

international trade
imports
exports

balance of trade
indirect exporting
direct exporting

marketing matters

Businesses often reach out to international markets when they run out of new customers in their home markets. They also reach out to customers in other countries to try to counteract competition from foreign firms that have entered their home markets. Their goal is to be able to satisfy a growing demand from foreign consumers for a greater variety of products.

essential question

What can U.S. producers and manufacturers do to compete successfully with foreign businesses?

18.1.1 ▶ How International Trade Works

The sale of products and services to people in other countries is known as **international trade**. Participation in international trade has been increasing in importance to companies worldwide. U.S. companies of all sizes and in all industries have expanded into the global marketplace. Today, American brands such as Nike, McDonald's, General Electric, and Boeing are recognized around the world. Likewise, foreign-based companies have increased their presence in the United States. Non-American brands such as Subaru, BMW, IKEA, Samsung, and Panasonic are as well known in the United States as most domestic brands. Many

companies that engage in international trade are not well-known but are local suppliers that sell their products in other countries. This section examines the mechanics of international trade.

Imports and Exports

Spend a short time looking at all the products and services you consume, use, and wear during just one day to determine where they were produced. You will quickly see that many were produced in countries around the world. Products or services brought in from another country are known as **imports**.

You may not realize it, but you and the people in your community are international consumers. You consume products that were imported from other countries. You may start your morning with fruit grown in El Salvador and transported here in ships from Panama. Your clothes may have been manufactured in Taiwan, and you may ride to school on a bus that was assembled in Canada. Your textbooks may have been published by a company that is part of a British corporation. After school, you may call your classmates about homework on a phone that was produced in Japan. In the evening you may watch a movie that was filmed in Kenya on a tablet assembled in South Korea.

International business also is important to other countries. Just as you use products manufactured in foreign countries, consumers in those countries use products made in the United States by U.S. businesses. Products and services produced in one country and shipped to and sold in another country are known as **exports**. Important consumer products exported from the United States to other countries include music, movies, automobiles, and food products. U.S. manufacturers of airplanes, medical equipment, and electronics also have a large number of international customers.

How do you participate in international trade?

© Monkey Business Images/Shutterstock.com.

The Balance of Trade

The difference between the amount of a country's imports and exports is known as its **balance of trade**. Countries generally try to maintain a *positive balance of trade*. This means the products a country exports to other countries are worth more than the products it imports. A *negative balance of trade* shows that the products a country imports are worth more than the products it exports. In the short run, the balance of trade may not have an effect on a country. However, many economists believe that continual negative balances can create problems. They also demonstrate that businesses from other countries are satisfying the needs of consumers better than the country's own businesses. Since 1975 the United States has had a negative balance of trade. It has been importing more goods and services to other countries than it has been exporting.

WORKING IN TEAMS

As a team, identify three products made by U.S. companies you think are popular worldwide. Now think of another country and identify three products it produces that you think are popular globally. Use the Internet to determine whether or not you are correct.

Indirect vs. Direct International Trade

There are many forms of international trade. Most businesses first get involved through exporting or selling their existing products in other countries. When businesses have been successful selling products in their own country, they may begin to look for markets in other countries. Or customers from other countries may become aware of the products and seek to purchase them.

Companies new to international marketing engage in indirect exporting. **Indirect exporting** is the process in which the exporting company is represented by a marketing business that has exporting experience and arranges for the sale of the company's products in other countries. The company will not be directly involved in exporting activities but will rely on the exporting business to serve the international markets. With more experience, a company may try **direct exporting**, which involves taking complete responsibility for marketing products in other countries.

The Changing Nature of International Trade

The type of products and services countries exchange is changing. Years ago, a great deal of international trade was devoted to obtaining raw materials. Some countries had an abundance of raw materials (timber, iron ore, petroleum) but had not developed their manufacturing capabilities. Other countries were heavily involved in manufacturing but did not have adequate supplies of needed resources to operate their factories.

Therefore, they purchased the raw materials from other countries. At that time, raw materials made up almost all of the products traded among countries. Today, raw materials comprise fewer than one-third of the world's exports. Most exports now consist of manufactured goods and services.

The amount of services relative to the amount of merchandise exported also is changing. International trade in services has grown and continues to grow more rapidly than trade in products. Service trade now accounts for more economic production internationally than does trade in merchandise. Common types of services exchanged among countries include communications, travel, education, financial services, and information. One interesting example of the exchange of services is in the area of data management. Banks and other financial institutions in the United States are using companies in India, Ireland, and South Africa to complete the data processing for their businesses. At the end of the business day in the United States, companies transfer the data to another country. Data processing companies in the other country complete work on the information, update the customers' accounts, and transfer the data back to the U.S. location in time to be used the next business day.

> *Want to know more about marketing in the information age? Click on* **Lesson 18.1, Digital Marketing,** *in your MindTap.*

Connect to MindTap

CHECKPOINT
What is the difference between imports and exports?

MATH IN MARKETING

Currency Exchange Rates

Most people think a strong domestic currency is a good thing because it makes imported products cheaper. However, that is not entirely true. A strong currency may reduce export competitiveness. But, cheap imports that cause the trade deficit to widen can severely hurt domestic industries that rely on exporting. A strong dollar makes other currencies appear inexpensive, so the country's products appear to be priced lower.

When people in one country demand products from companies in another country, they first must enter the currency market to buy that country's currency. Just as supply and demand for products shift prices of those products, so does the supply and demand for a currency result in currency price fluctuations.

Do the Math

1. You can purchase a product from any of four countries. Listed below is the price (including shipping) of the product in each country's currency: Mexico, 6,500 pesos; Canada, 550 Canadian dollars; France, 360 euros; Great Britain, 295 pounds. The exchange rate of $1 U.S. equals 13.02 Mexican pesos; 1.10 Canadian dollars; .72 euros; .59 British pounds. From which of the four countries would the product you want be least expensive?

2. A month later you want to purchase the same product. Although the price remains the same, you find the dollar has strengthened against the four currencies. The exchange rate is now $1 U.S. equals 12.85 Mexican pesos; 1.09 Canadian dollars; .69 euros; .57 British pounds. From which of the four countries is the product you want now the least expensive?

18.1.2 ▶ Why Businesses Are Going Global

Businesses engage in international trade to maintain or increase their profits. They may look for new markets overseas in the face of increased competition. Or they may decide to enter overseas markets in response to the increased demand for their products there. The availability of assistance with exporting makes entering overseas markets a viable option for businesses.

Changing Markets and Competition

Some businesses decide to market products in other countries out of necessity. They find that competition in their current markets is becoming very intense and their sales and profits are declining. To gain sales and increase profits, companies look at other countries for potential markets.

When the birth rate declined in the United States, companies that manufactured products for babies (such as formula, baby food, and diapers) looked for markets in other countries. When attendance at U.S. movie theaters declined for several years, film distributors increased their efforts to market them abroad.

Other companies consider international markets when they see companies from other countries entering their own markets.

Rather than just competing with the foreign companies in their own country, they decide to enter international markets to keep the competition more balanced. In the 1970s, automobile manufacturers from Japan and Germany moved into the U.S. market to take advantage of the need for smaller, more fuel-efficient cars. The first Volkswagen Beetles were quite different from the popular U.S. brands and quickly drew a small but loyal following.

With the success of foreign auto manufacturers in U.S. markets, American firms increased their efforts to sell their brands in other countries. As a result, automobile marketing has become truly global. Today, only China produces more automobiles for the world market than U.S. manufacturers.

A third reason for global marketing is the increasing worldwide demand for products. Consumers in many countries look to the United States for product and service ideas. As economies expand throughout the world and standards of living increase, consumers in those countries are willing to spend money for a variety of products. Businesses that recognize the increasing demand offer their products for sale wherever customers are willing to buy, including internationally. Manufacturers of products ranging from blue jeans to music and hamburgers are finding success in world markets.

To some businesses, the idea of selling products or services internationally seems too complicated, so they may decide not to become involved. But with improvements in transportation, communication, banking and finance, and other business processes, it is often as easy to serve markets in other countries as it is to sell in markets several states away.

Assistance with International Trade

Because of international business, consumers have a greater variety of products and services to choose from, and businesses have the opportunity to earn higher profits from exporting products. Most governments support companies that want to increase the business they conduct in other countries.

© Fedor Selivanov/Shutterstock.com

Why do you think U.S. consumers were so receptive to automobiles imported from German and Japanese automobile companies in the 1970s?

The U.S. government supports the exporting efforts of businesses in several ways. The U.S. Department of State maintains embassies in most countries that can help with passports, documents, and laws. The U.S. Department of Commerce maintains the Trade Information Center and Export Assistance Centers to provide support for U.S. businesses involved in international trade. Even the Small Business Administration has an office to assist small U.S. businesses wanting to expand into foreign markets. Most U.S. government export-support services can be accessed through a central website, export.gov. Many states have trade promotion offices to help businesses develop markets in other countries.

In addition to government support, an increasing number of other sources, such as banks and other financial services companies, insurance businesses, accounting firms, transportation companies, and communications services firms, provide assistance to their customers.

CHECKPOINT
Why do businesses engage in international trade?

18.1 ASSESSMENT

What Have You Learned?

1. What does a negative balance of trade indicate? [18.1.1]
2. What is the difference between indirect and direct exporting? [18.1.1]
3. What U.S. government agencies assist companies with international trade? [18.1.2]

Make Academic Connections

1. **Research** Use the Internet to access the latest *World Trade Statistical Review* report compiled by the World Trade Organization. Review the different parts of the report—Introduction, Highlights, Trends, Goods and Services, etc. How might this information be important to marketing departments of companies involved in international trade? [18.1.1]

2. **Government** Use the Internet to identify one federal agency or office and one agency or office from your state that provides information and support for businesses seeking to become involved in international marketing. Based on your research, prepare a two- to three-paragraph description of each agency or office. Identify the types of businesses they support, the services they provide, and contact information. [18.1.2]

Connect to ◇DECA

Build your Portfolio

Your employer manufactures electric-powered scooters that have been very popular among U.S. teenagers and young adults as well as commuters. The company is deciding whether to begin selling the scooters internationally. Prepare a two-minute presentation with at least one chart or handout describing the advantages and disadvantages of international marketing for the company. Give your presentation to your teacher (judge). [18.1.2]

Planning a Career In...
INTERNATIONAL HOSPITALITY

How do corporations conduct business in foreign countries? How do tourists manage daily life needs while abroad? International hospitality coordinators work to ensure successful, stress-free experiences for international travelers. Because businesspeople may need help with writing and speaking in other languages, both interpreters and translators need to be available in the host countries. Interpreters focus on verbal language translations. Converting words from one language to another is the role of translators. Concierges and coordinators are familiar with local customs and resources and can provide specialized information as well as access needed for personal and business services at a moment's notice.

Job Titles

- International Travel Coordinator
- Hotel Concierge
- Translator and Interpreter
- Cruise Line Guest Services Director
- International Convention Planner

Needed Skills

- Interpreters and translators must be fluent in multiple languages.
- A bachelor's degree in Hospitality Management is beneficial.
- An understanding of and experience with varied cultures is an advantage.

Discover more about the outlook for this career and watch a video about a related career. Click on **Chapter 18, Planning a Career In...** *in your MindTap.*

- High school students may participate in a two-year program developed by the Hotel and Lodging Association. Program completion results in a professional certification in hospitality.

What it's like to work in... International Hospitality

Arden, an international sales agent for a hotel chain, is preparing a sales proposal. Tomorrow she will be calling on the conference coordinator for an international professional society. The society has booked the local convention center for its annual conference. Although the conference will not occur for two years, the organizers want to ensure that the hotel they use responds to the needs of international visitors.

Arden has arranged the services of several international language specialists for the entire conference. Given the variety of countries represented by conference attendees, Arden needs to secure a broad spectrum of interpreters and translators.

Arden's sales plan incorporates recommendations from the hotel staff that focus on accommodating the cultural needs of guests from various countries. The entire hotel's staff receives extensive training about cultural differences. Proactively catering to the needs of international travelers should give Arden's hotel a competitive edge.

What About You?

Would you like to work with international travelers to help make their visit to your country more enjoyable and successful? Why or why not?

18.2 INTERNATIONAL VENTURES

Learning Objectives

18.2.1 Explain how foreign production, foreign investment, and foreign joint ventures operate.

18.2.2 Describe the way in which multinational companies compete by thinking globally.

Key Terms

foreign production
foreign direct investment (FDI)
joint venture
multinational companies

marketing matters

International trade is important to the U.S. economy because it gives companies access to a larger market, which could lead to more sales and profit. Beyond importing and exporting, companies' options for participating in international trade include producing goods in other countries, investing in foreign companies, and forming joint ventures with foreign firms. Companies involved in international trade for a long time may become multinational companies.

 essential question

What is a company's best option for participating in international trade?

18.2.1 ▶ Foreign Production, Investment, and Joint Venture

In addition to exporting and importing, businesses participate in international trade through foreign production, foreign investment, and joint ventures.

Foreign Production

With **foreign production**, a company owns and operates production facilities in another country. As companies expand internationally, they find it difficult to maintain manufacturing in only one country and meet all of the new market demands. With foreign production, manufacturing occurs where products are needed or produced more efficiently. Raw materials and resources often can be purchased inexpensively close to the markets where the products will be sold.

In the past, all of the production activities for a product would be completed in a country in the region where the product would be sold. Today it is not unusual for the production process to occur in more than one location. Computers, automobiles, and medical equipment are manufactured using parts produced in one country and then shipped to another country for final assembly. Multi-country production requires effective planning and distribution systems.

There is a concern that moving production overseas can have a negative effect on a country. If a company closes a U.S. factory to open a foreign facility, U.S. jobs and wages are lost. When this happens, the U.S. workers who lose their jobs are not able to purchase as many goods and services. This leads to an overall reduction in consumer purchasing power in the economy.

What are the benefits and drawbacks for a country when a domestic company decides to produce its products overseas?

Companies from other countries with U.S. markets may invest in production facilities in this country, and this has a positive effect on the economy. As more U.S. consumers purchase Toyotas, BMWs, and other foreign brands of automobiles, those companies have opened automobile plants in the United States. Those companies hire employees from the area and attract other businesses that produce component parts used in the production of the vehicles. For example, Chinese computer manufacturer Lenovo builds new models of tablet computers as well as some laptop and desktop models in the United States.

Foreign Investment

Rather than entering the country and starting a new business, companies may purchase existing business in other countries that already have production or marketing capabilities. Owning all or part of an existing business in another country is known as **foreign direct investment (FDI)**. Businesses can move more quickly into another country through FDI. They also can use the past financial performance of the purchased business to determine whether it is a good investment. The new owners may decide to change the business or continue to operate it in the same way as the previous owners. That decision will be based on the past success of the business and the needs of the company making the foreign investment.

The United States is both the largest investor as well as the largest recipient of FDI in the global economy. More than half of the United States' direct investment abroad is in Europe.

Joint Ventures

When two or more companies in different countries have common interests, they may form a joint venture. In a **joint venture**, independent companies develop a relationship to cooperate in common business activities. The agreement may be in the form of a contract where the companies agree to a specific set of activities for a set period of time. In another form of joint venture, each company agrees to purchase a portion of the other company to create joint ownership. They then have a continuing relationship based on that ownership.

One of the largest joint ventures involves 13 of the biggest international airlines that have signed agreements to cooperate in coordinating flight schedules, marketing activities, travel reward programs, and airport resources. Called **one-world®**, the companies believe the cooperative activities make them more competitive for the international traveler. It also offers ways to reduce costs and increase customer service. Problems may arise because each of the cooperating airlines is still an independent company with its own procedures and own markets and customers to serve.

> *Want to know more about what is trending with this topic?* Click on **Lesson 18.2, Global Marketing,** *in your MindTap.*
>
> Connect to **MindTap**

CHECKPOINT

If a U.S. company wants to expand its manufacturing operations in other countries, what options does it have?

Some companies have been involved in international business for a long time. They may use several of the strategies described above and sell services and products in a large number of countries throughout the world. They probably are purchasing products and services from companies in many countries to use in production and operations. Companies heavily involved in international business usually develop factories and offices in several countries in order to keep operations closer to the customers. Businesses that have operations throughout the world and that conduct planning for worldwide markets are **multinational companies**. Multinational businesses no longer think of themselves as being located in one country selling to customers in other countries. They think globally.

Many businesses you may think of as U.S. companies are really multinational. They operate throughout the world and derive a large part of their sales and profits from countries other than the United States. McDonald's is an example of a multinational company. Other examples of well-known multinational companies that started in the United States are Coca-Cola, Microsoft, John Deere, 3M, Nike, and IBM. There also are many multinational firms that started in other countries. Some familiar examples include Nestlé S.A., Panasonic, Hyundai, L'Oreal, and Royal Dutch Shell.

Multinational companies have advantages over firms operating in only one country. When a company views the world as one market, it can more easily develop global brands and enter global markets. It can manufacture its goods wherever conditions are best. Competitors for multinational businesses come from many different locations. A business may compete with one set of companies in Australia and another in Africa or South America. An increasing number of large multinationals compete for customers worldwide.

> **CHECKPOINT**
> *What is a multinational company?*

18.2 ASSESSMENT

What Have You Learned?

1. What is foreign direct investment (FDI)? [18.2.1]

2. What are the advantages for a multinational company of viewing the world as one market? [18.2.2]

Make Academic Connections

1. **Geography** Select a large retail business that operates in countries around the world (McDonald's, Walmart, Starbucks, Holiday Inn, and others). Visit the company's website and determine the countries in which the business operates and the number of locations it has in each country. Locate and print a map of the world. Identify the countries and number of locations for the business on the map. [18.2.2]

Connect to  DECA

You have been asked by a local citizens group to speak to the organization on how the local community benefits from international trade. Prepare a two-minute informational speech. Deliver the speech to your teacher (judge). [18.2.1]

18.3 UNDERSTAND INTERNATIONAL MARKETS

Learning Objectives

18.3.1 Explain the effects international economic conditions have on marketing opportunities within a country.

18.3.2 Describe the factors that determine the best marketing mix for particular countries.

18.3.3 Explain the procedures a company follows to gather and analyze international marketing information.

Key Terms

preindustrial economy
industrial economy
postindustrial economy
business cycles
gross domestic product (GDP)
gross national product (GNP)

standard of living
productivity
purchasing power
inflation
consumer price index (CPI)
quotas
tariffs
subsidy

marketing matters

Companies doing business internationally must apply the marketing concept in other countries' markets just as they do in their home market. Although the same marketing functions are needed in international business, there may be differences in how they complete specific marketing activities from one country to another. Businesspeople involved in international business often work with marketing experts from the foreign country in which they are operating to be sure they use the most effective procedures possible.

essential question

Why can products that are in high demand in many countries be unpopular in the United States? Are most products that are successful in the United States likely to be popular in other countries? Why or why not?

18.3.1 ▶ The International Economic Environment

The concept of a market is the same in all countries. A *market* refers to the prospective customers a business wants to serve and their location. Businesspeople should not assume that all countries have the same kinds of markets or that all people in a country have the same characteristics, needs, and interests (**Figure 18-1**). Just as it would be a mistake in the United States to market to all consumers as if they were the same, businesses need to recognize important differences among prospective customers in other countries.

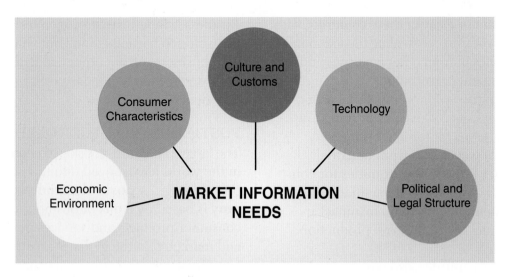

FIGURE 18-1 Businesses must gather a great deal of information in order to determine if they can successfully market their products and services in another country.

There are many similarities but also some differences between marketing internationally and marketing within one country. The idea of identifying markets and developing a marketing mix remains the same. So does the need to complete each of the major marketing functions. The characteristics of markets, the information needed and how it is obtained, and the procedures used to develop each marketing mix element will change as companies concentrate on target markets in other countries. Companies also face higher costs and more risk when marketing products internationally.

The level of economic development of a country and the current condition of the economy must be understood for effective marketing. A country that has a high standard of living will have well-established businesses that manufacture and sell a variety of both consumer and business products. That country will offer very different marketing opportunities than a country struggling to meet citizens' basic social and economic needs.

Level of Economic Development

Economies of the world's countries can be grouped into three broad categories: pre-industrial, industrial, and postindustrial.

PREINDUSTRIAL ECONOMIES The **preindustrial economy** is based on agriculture and raw material development through activities such as mining, oil production, and cutting timber. In this type of economy, many of the country's citizens provide for all of their own needs and have a very low standard of living. Manufacturing, distribution, and retail systems are just beginning to develop. This makes it difficult for businesses to produce, distribute, or sell products until the economy is further developed.

Leaders in a country at the preindustrial stage recognize the importance of moving to the next stage. They see their natural resources being consumed and few job choices for their citizens. Those countries are unable to participate in the international economy except through the sale of raw materials. The leaders of the countries are looking for help in developing their economies. Unfortunately, corruption is rampant in many of these countries, with leaders misusing or stealing the aid money that comes in from other countries and development organizations.

Countries with preindustrial economies were once viewed as offering few opportunities for foreign businesses. Today, however, many preindustrial countries provide opportunities for companies that want to sell manufacturing equipment, help develop manufacturing businesses, or improve production processes.

Many countries also seek assistance in developing distribution systems. They need effective methods of getting products to customers and places for the products to be sold. Roads, railroads, river systems, and airports are needed to distribute products as manufacturing develops. Developing distribution systems and organizing wholesale and retail businesses will make it possible to sell products.

INDUSTRIAL ECONOMIES Today, most developed countries have industrial economies. In an **industrial economy**, the primary business activity is the manufacturing of products. Much of the manufacturing in the early stages of an industrial economy is devoted to the production of equipment and materials for businesses and the development of marketing systems. Later, as people work in the factories and other businesses, wages increase, and the standard of living improves. There is greater demand for a variety of consumer products, and businesses develop to meet those needs.

There are many opportunities for international businesses in industrial economies. There is demand for both business and consumer products. Often, products and services that are successful in countries with more developed economies can be sold in the industrial economies as those countries develop.

Businesses in industrial economies may be willing to participate in joint ventures with businesses from other countries in order to develop needed expertise and experience.

POSTINDUSTRIAL ECONOMIES

The largest and most-developed economies in the world have moved into the postindustrial stage. A **postindustrial economy** is based on a mix of business and consumer products and services produced and marketed in the global marketplace. Countries with postindustrial economies have very high standards of living with many international business opportunities. Companies use current technologies and effective business procedures. Countries with postindustrial economies work with other countries to develop laws and procedures that encourage and support international trade.

People living in postindustrial economies are very aware that products and services are available from other countries. They expect the businesses in their country to produce similar products of equal or higher quality at a reasonable price, or they will buy from companies in other countries.

WORKING IN TEAMS

Use the library or Internet to identify three countries, each representing one of the economic categories. A good source of information is the *CIA World Factbook*. As a team, prepare a chart that compares the three economies to illustrate the reasons for your classification.

Condition of the Economy

A country's stage of economic development relates to the long-term outlook for its economy. Current conditions are important as well. If a country's economy is strong and growing, citizens will have more job opportunities and money to spend. Businesses will have a better environment for sales and profits. The government will have more resources for roads, schools, education, and other services. If a country's economy is not healthy, the number of jobs and business profits will suffer, and fewer resources will be available to meet the needs of citizens.

BUSINESS CYCLES   Even while economies grow, they go through periods of expansion and decline. Those recurring changes in an economy are called **business cycles**. One phase of a business cycle is *expansion,* where the economy as measured by GDP is growing. This phase eventually reaches a peak, and economic output begins to decline or contract. If the contraction lasts two quarters, the economy is in *recession.* While there is no agreed-upon definition, a severe, sustained recession where the GDP declines more than 10 percent and lasts more than three years is called a *depression.* The lowest point of the decline is the *trough.* As the economy begins to grow again, it enters the recovery phase.

ECONOMIC MEASURES   There are several important measures of a country's economy. One of the most-used measures is gross domestic product. **Gross domestic product (GDP)** is the total value of goods and services produced within a country during the year. A lesser known calculation, *gross domestic income (GDI),* measures all income earned while producing goods and services within a country. Another related measure is gross national product. **Gross national product (GNP)** is the total value of all goods and services produced by a country during the year, including foreign investments. GNP is a broader measure and includes the production of multinational companies that occurs outside a country's borders. A growing GDP and GNP is a sign of a strong economy.

A country's **standard of living** is a measure of the quality of life for its citizens. It is based on areas such as housing, food, education, clothing, transportation, and employment opportunities. A country's standard of living is calculated by dividing the total income of the country (GDP) by its population. This figure is referred to as *GDP per capita.* A country with a high standard of living produces and sells larger quantities of goods and services. A place with a high standard of living has more jobs, higher wage rates, and better markets for businesses than a place with a low standard of living.

A fourth measure, **productivity**, is the average output by workers for a specific period of time. For example, if a business

Photodisc/Getty Images

Why is education a factor in a country's standard of living?

has 20 employees working 40 hours a week and produces 80,000 units of a product during the week, the productivity is 100 units (80,000 units/800 work hours per week). If the same employees produce a larger number of units working the same number of hours, this business has increased its productivity. Productivity shows the efficiency of a country's work force and technology used in production. Productivity can increase as a result of a more educated and skilled workforce, more efficient operations, and increased use of technology to support work procedures.

A final measure of the condition of an economy is purchasing power. **Purchasing power** is the amount of goods and services that can be purchased with a specific amount of money. Purchasing power declines with **inflation**, where prices increase faster than the value of goods and services. A specific measure of purchasing power, and therefore inflation, is the consumer price index. The **consumer price index (CPI)** is the change in the cost of a specified set of goods and services over time. If a country's CPI increases, consumers' purchasing power declines: they can make fewer purchases with the same amount of money.

CHECKPOINT
What are the three stages of economic development that can affect a country's receptiveness to international trade?

18.3.2 ▶ Find the Right Mix for Foreign Markets

Each international market can be very different and may require changes in the marketing mix. Companies should study the markets to identify unique characteristics. They can then begin to design an appropriate product or service, determine how the product will be distributed, establish pricing policies, and develop promotion strategies appropriate for each country's market.

Consumer Characteristics

Companies first need to gather information about the people in a country and determine if there are enough prospective customers. They need to know the amount of money the people have to spend and other demographic characteristics such as age, income, employment, and education. They also must determine where prospective customers are located in the country, where and how they typically buy products, what methods of transportation will work best, and which communications media are available.

Culture and Customs

The culture and customs of a country may determine whether certain products or marketing methods will be appropriate or acceptable. *Culture* is the common beliefs and behaviors of a group of people who have a similar heritage and experience. *Customs* are accepted or habitual practices. Family structures, religion, beliefs and values, language, personal habits, and daily activities may be quite different from those in the marketers' own culture. Failure to recognize differences may result in misunderstanding and

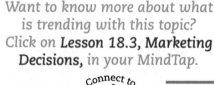
Want to know more about what is trending with this topic?
Click on **Lesson 18.3, Marketing Decisions,** *in your MindTap.*

Connect to
MindTap

mistrust. Businesses moving into countries that have different cultures should seek advice and assistance from people who are knowledgeable about the country's cultures and customs. Many multinational companies employ people from the countries they are entering to provide the needed expertise.

Technology

The technology of business and marketing is changing rapidly. Businesses are adopting new methods of manufacturing, transportation, product handling, and communication. Consumers have access to computers and the Internet, new types of products for their home and work, and changing technology for work and leisure time.

Once these new products and technologies are developed in one country, they usually are rapidly distributed and accepted in many other countries. Businesses cannot assume, though, that the same technology used in their home country is available or used in other countries. Even if the technology is used, there might be important differences. Take systems of measurement, for example. The International Systems of Units (SI), known as the metric system, is in use in most of the world. Only the United States, Liberia, and Myanmar have not adopted SI and use the Customary System of measurement instead.

Another example of conflicting technologies among countries are the differing voltage requirements and power supplies used for their electrical systems. Further, cell phone communication networks and frequencies used in most other countries differ from those used in the United States.

Political and Legal Structure

Other important factors that affect the success of international marketing are a country's political and legal systems. The types of political systems range from democratic, in which the citizens of the country control the decisions of the government, to autocratic, where power is in the hands of a very small group of people. In the recent past, one of the major political structures, communism, was rejected in many Central European countries and in the former Soviet Union. Those countries reorganized their political systems to adopt more democratic principles.

A stable political system is important for businesses. If a country is politically unstable, business ownership and operating procedures may be threatened. There have been many examples of countries in which the government was overthrown, and the businesses owned by people from

Why would U.S. businesses be concerned about the political structure and stability in other countries?

© Radu Bercan/Shutterstock.com

other countries were destroyed or taken over by the new government.

Countries develop laws to regulate business. Many of those laws affect international business operations. Some countries have laws that provide strong support for their businesses in the sale of products and services in other countries or protect the country's businesses from foreign competition.

Because the governments of industrial economies want the businesses in their countries to be successful, they may try to restrict the amount of imports through the use of quotas or tariffs. **Quotas** are limits a government sets on the numbers of specific types of products that foreign companies can sell in the country. **Tariffs** are taxes a government places on imported products to increase the price for which they are sold. Countries also may support their businesses through subsidies. A **subsidy** is money a government provides to a business to assist in the development and sale of its products. International free trade efforts attempt to reduce these types of restrictions and protections. When countries use these tools to regulate trade, they are said to be engaging in *protectionism*.

> ### CHECKPOINT
> *Name four factors that can affect the success of a marketing plan in an international market.*

18.3.3 ▶ International Marketing Activities

Before a business can begin to plan the marketing mix for an international market, it needs reliable information about that market. The procedures a company follows for gathering and analyzing international market information are quite similar to those it follows in its home country. The business needs to develop a marketing information system to collect and analyze information. It also may need to complete marketing research or work with local or international research companies to answer specific questions about customers and competitors.

Gather Market Information

International marketers must pay special attention to both marketing-information management and marketing research. The sources of information, the types of technology and research capabilities, the ways that people respond to research procedures, and the laws relating to information collection likely will be quite different. For example, in the United States, much of today's consumer research is completed using Internet or telephone surveys, or data is collected using technology at the time of sale. In some countries, technology is not as well developed, eliminating those options. And in some cultures, asking personal questions is considered discourteous.

Companies often work with businesses and businesspeople from the country in which they hope to market products to gather needed information. This helps to ensure that those doing the research understand

> *Want to know more about marketing in the information age? Click on **Lesson 18.3, Digital Marketing,** in your MindTap.*

Connect to
MindTap

the unique characteristics of the country and that the research will be completed in a way that does not harm the image of the business. People in international business need to listen carefully to people from the countries they want to serve in order to avoid biases and stereotypes.

Adjust the Marketing Mix and Marketing Functions

After marketers have gathered the necessary information to understand the new market, they can develop the marketing mix. With this information, the mix can be specifically designed to meet the needs of the international market. The types of marketing activities often will be the same or similar to those previously used by the company. However, there may be some important differences in the marketing functions, as shown with the following examples.

PRODUCT/SERVICE MANAGEMENT

Products and services must be developed to meet the needs of customers and market conditions. Important activities for international markets include packaging for protection and for easy use by customers. In addition, brand names must be carefully selected to fit the language and

MARKETING COMMUNICATION
Cultural Differences in Consumer Preferences

In a world with more than 3,000 languages and countless cultural differences, companies must consider cultural diversity when marketing products internationally. Cultural preferences regarding color, concepts of beauty and good taste, and religious beliefs can impact consumers' shopping patterns. Green is unacceptable for packaging in Egypt because religious leaders once wore it. Purple is unacceptable in Hispanic nations because of its association with death. Toothpaste promising white teeth does not work in parts of Southeast Asia because having black or yellow teeth is a symbol of prestige.

Among Mexican apparel shoppers, image and status are important so brand names are very popular. Mexicans tend to purchase clothing more from desire than need and are willing to pay higher prices for higher-quality items. Nearly two-thirds of Mexican consumers favor domestic clothing stores and are more store loyal than their U.S. counterparts.

Although apparel for the Chinese consumer is a favorite shopping choice, they tend to be conservative spenders who mostly buy clothing out of need. Fit and style are important factors for consumers who purchase clothing throughout China. However, it is still a diverse market with regional differences as to desire for name brands and price promotions.

Think Critically

1. What aspects of marketing should a clothing producer emphasize in China?
2. Which would be the best way for a foreign-owned company to be successful in selling products in your community—under its own brand or by purchasing a known American brand? Explain your answer.

culture of the country. Finally, any product information must be written to meet the country's laws and to clearly communicate information needed by customers in order to buy and use the product.

DISTRIBUTION Effective distribution of products to and within other countries often is one of the most challenging marketing functions. Companies need to make decisions on the appropriate shipping method from country to country and within the new markets.

Selection of the types of businesses in which the product will be sold is part of distribution. It is important to know the amount of time it will take from processing an order until the product is available to customers. Also, laws regulating distribution, including taxes, tariffs, and quotas, must be understood and observed. Most countries also require inspection of imported products.

SELLING A country's customs play an important role in successful selling. Salespeople must be aware of the need to be formal or informal, who initiates conversations, how a business card is presented, and whether it is appropriate to conduct business during a meal. In some cultures, salespeople are expected to present a gift to a prospective customer, whereas in other countries the gift would be seen as a bribe and considered illegal or offensive.

FINANCING In most cases, the company will need to extend credit to the businesses that will distribute its products in the other country. It also will need to consider the accepted credit practices for consumers, and the procedures used to assist customers in purchasing will need to conform to the country's laws and customs. The types of contracts and forms used, as well as the monetary system, may be different. Although some credit cards are used internationally, they may not be the form of payment consumers in each country commonly use. The business also will need to develop relationships with banks and other financial organizations in the new country.

PRICING The customs of the new country may require a new approach to deciding how prices are set, changed, and communicated to the customer. Customers from another country likely will have different perceptions of value than those in the business's home country. Even if that perception is similar, the costs of marketing may be higher or lower, so prices may have to be changed. Prices also need to be expressed in the country's own currency.

PROMOTION A country's customs and culture are particularly important with the promotion element of the marketing mix. Promotion relies on effective communication. Language and pictures communicate a business's message to customers. There are many examples of promotional mistakes where words were not translated correctly or had very different meanings. Promotional planning for international markets includes careful selection of the media to be used. Mass media may not be as available in some countries or may not be used for promotion. In many countries,

© imtmphoto/Shutterstock.com.

television is not used extensively for advertising. Use of the Internet is growing rapidly in many countries, but it may not be used in the same ways for communication between businesses and customers.

CHECKPOINT

What must a company do before developing a marketing mix for a targeted international market?

18.3 ASSESSMENT

What Have You Learned?

1. What are the measures of the condition of a country's economy? [18.3.1]

2. Describe the tools governments use to restrict the amount of imports into their countries. [18.3.2]

3. For which element of the marketing mix is a country's customs and culture particularly important? [18.3.3]

Make Academic Connections

1. **Math**   A method to calculate a country's standard of living is to divide its GDP by its population. Use the Internet to determine the GDP for the top 10 countries in the world and the population for each country. Use the information to calculate the standard of living for each country. Prepare a table that compares the GDP and standard of living rankings of the 10 countries. [18.3.1]

2. **Research**   Choose a foreign country in which you would like to live and work. Use the library or Internet to gather information about the country's population, economy, culture, political and legal system, and business environment. Prepare a two-page report discussing what you learned. [18.3.2]

Connect to ◇DECA.

Build your Portfolio

A Chinese bicycle manufacturer wants to begin selling its most popular model in the United States and has asked your marketing team for advice on effective marketing. Prepare one important recommendation on selecting a target market and on each marketing mix element that will help the manufacturer understand the U.S. market for bicycles. Make a team presentation of your recommendations to your teacher (judge). [18.3.2]

Connect to MindTap

Analyze a case study that focuses on chapter concepts. Click on Chapter 18, Case Study, in your MindTap.

CHAPTER 18 ASSESSMENT

Review Marketing Concepts

1. Make a list of three or four products you and your family have purchased that have been imported from other countries. Why did you purchase those particular products rather than products produced in the United States? [18.1.1]

2. Explain the effect a weak dollar has on U.S. companies who are exporting to other nations. [18.1.2]

3. Why would a business choose to use indirect exporting to enter a foreign market? [18.2.1]

4. What are the benefits for a U.S. company of manufacturing products in other nations? [18.2.2]

5. In your own words, how can a company "think globally"? [18.2.2]

6. Your company is considering entering a foreign market. Which factor would be more important in your decision making: standard of living or productivity? [18.3.1]

7. Why would U.S. businesses be concerned about the political structure and stability in other countries? [18.3.2]

8. You are considering opening a McDonald's in India. Why would the menu there need to be different from the menu in the United States? [18.3.3]

Marketing Research and Planning

1. In order to be successful, businesses that sell their products in other countries must be able to offer a product that has advantages compared to the competing products in the country.

   Look at several products you own or use regularly, including at least one item of clothing, and identify five that were manufactured outside the United States. For each product, identify the part of the marketing mix that was the most important reason you decided to purchase the product. Then make a recommendation for U.S. manufacturers on how they can improve their marketing mix to be more competitive.

   Next, identify five products you own or use that were manufactured by U.S. companies. For each product, identify the part of the marketing mix that was the primary reason you selected that product rather than one manufactured in another country. Make a recommendation to foreign manufacturers on how they could offer a more competitive marketing mix. [18.3.2]

2. Choose one of the following:

   a. Large piece of equipment used for road construction

   b. Vitamins and mineral supplements for use by consumers

   c. Movies

   d. Fresh flowers

   e. Auto repair service

   Assume you are deciding how to market the product or service to another country. For each of the nine marketing functions (Chapter 1), describe a specific marketing activity that must be completed in order to market that product internationally. [18.3.3]

3. Search the Internet for a site that contains economic and demographic statistics for various countries. Pick a continent or region with at least 10 different countries. Using a computer database or spreadsheet program,

compile a database of statistics for each country, including population, GDP, and GDP per capita. Sort and rank the countries by each of the statistics. [18.3.1]

4. Use the Internet to search the U.S. Department of Commerce website or another source for statistics on U.S. exports for the latest full year that has been reported. List the top 10 countries for U.S. exports and the main types of goods and services they purchase. Now, complete the same activity for U.S. imports. Identify the top 10 countries that sell goods and services to the United States and the main types of goods and services the United States imports from each country. Prepare two tables to illustrate your results. [18.1.2]

Marketing Management and Decision Making

1. Businesses must make decisions that are ethical and socially responsible. When marketing products internationally, the cultures and values of countries may conflict. Businesspeople may be criticized for decisions that seem to be positive and acceptable in another country but are not viewed as appropriate in their home country—and vice versa.

   The following scenarios describe ethical decisions U.S. businesses face when marketing in other countries. Read each scenario carefully and consider the effects of the decisions on the company, its customers, and the country in which it plans to market the products. Also, consider the business's social responsibility in the United States and internationally. For each scenario, write two paragraphs that describe how you would respond to the ethical situation facing the company and provide reasons for your decision.

   a. A prescription drug manufacturer has spent more than five years of research to develop a new medication to help young children with asthma. The company is certain the medication is safe although there have been minor side effects in some who used it during testing. The company has spent more than $40 million developing the medication and wants to begin selling it as quickly as possible to begin to recover those costs and return a profit. The U.S. Food and Drug Administration (FDA) requires an additional three years of testing before the medication can be approved for sale in the United States. A large international wholesaler is willing to purchase the drug and sell it over the Internet from its distribution facilities in another country that does not require the lengthy testing period. The procedure would allow people from any country, including the United States, to order the medication online as long as they could fax a letter from their physician certifying that the patient was under treatment for asthma. [18.3.3]

   b. A U.S. airline recognized that the number of businesspeople and vacationers traveling to the United States from a Southeast Asian country was growing faster each year than from any other country in that region. It wanted to enter the market and capture a large percentage of that growing business. However, it had to compete with a successful smaller airline based in the Asian country that already had many flights into the United States. The U.S. company's advertising agency suggested it could find former employees of the smaller airline who would say that they were concerned about the safety and quality of the airline's service. The statements would all be true, but they clearly did not represent the beliefs of most of the company's employees. The goal would be to raise questions in the media about the airline, causing travelers to question whether they would fly with that airline. At the same time, the U.S. airline would begin an ad campaign promoting its expanded service to the United States as well as its quality and safety record. [18.3.3]

c. A hotel chain was considering a joint venture with a company in another country. The plan was to build five new hotels in resort areas that were growing rapidly. The businesses already located in the resorts were experiencing a great deal of success, and it was clear that other hotels would be built in the resorts as soon as companies could purchase the land and obtain financing. The advantage of the joint venture for the hotel chain was that the company it was working with already owned land in several of the resort areas and had available cash to begin hotel construction while additional financing was being arranged. As the hotel company management was preparing the paperwork to finalize the joint venture, it received a letter from a civil rights group providing evidence that the company with which it was planning to cooperate had an unwritten but clear policy to discriminate in its hiring practices. A check of the company's employment records showed that the employees were 96 percent white in a country that had a 35 percent nonwhite population. Also, no women had ever been promoted beyond the level of supervisor in the company. The management knew that if the joint venture was not successful, it was unlikely that they would find a similar company with which to work. [18.2.1]

2. In an attempt to protect its industries from international competition, a government may take action to restrict another country's imports. When the other country retaliates, the two countries are said to be engaged in a "trade war." Trade wars often begin because of what a country considers to be unfair trading practices. They are started with the objectives of protecting domestic businesses from cheaper imported goods, protecting intellectual property rights, or reaching a more favorable balance of trade. The most common weapon in a trade war is imposing tariffs, which are taxes on another country's imports. Besides tariffs, countries also may make it difficult for the opposing countries' businesses to operate within its borders.

In the early stages of a trade war the increased cost of imports may be absorbed by domestic businesses. However, the effect of a longer trade war is an increase in the prices consumers will pay, which over time may lead to inflation. Trade wars also can hurt rather than help domestic businesses that rely on international markets to maintain profitability. Not only will these domestic companies lose some of their international markets during the period of high tariffs, but foreign countries may be forced to seek new sources or develop their own goods to meet the demand for them. In today's global economy with its globalized supply chains, the effects of a trade war between major economies may be felt by producers and consumers throughout the world.

Research examples of trade wars that the United States has participated in over the years. Choose one example, and write a one-or two-page paper that includes the following information:

a. Which countries were involved in the trade war, which country started it, and when did it occur?

b. What was the purpose of the trade war?

c. Did the country that started it achieve its objective? Why or why not?

d. What was the effect of the trade war on the industry or industries involved?

Let's Start a Band Follow-Up Discussion

Work in small teams to discuss the question posed at the end of the opening vignette. What are the pros and cons of bringing the show to Canada?

Build Your Marketing Plan

In this chapter you learned about identifying opportunities in global markets. You will now apply this learning to the development of your marketing plan. To access the chapter-specific tools that you will need to complete this activity, please navigate to Chapter 18 ➔ Build Your Marketing Plan in MindTap. Alternatively, you can access these tools online at NGLSync. Please visit www.nglsync.cengage.com, and search for the companion website that accompanies this book by entering the ISBN, author, or title. Once you locate this companion website, navigate to Build Your Marketing Plan ➔ Chapter 18.

Food Marketing Series Event

DECA PREP

The Food Marketing Series Event consists of a 100-question multiple-choice Career Cluster® exam and role-plays. The role-play portion of the event requires participants to accomplish a task by translating what they have learned into effective, efficient, and spontaneous action. The four performance indicators specify the distinct tasks the participant must accomplish during the role-play. Students have 10 minutes to prepare their strategy for the role-play and an additional 10 minutes to explain their strategy to the judge. The judge can ask questions during or after the presentation.

The highly competitive supermarket industry has tried new strategies to market and distribute products to consumers. Many of the smaller grocery stores have closed due to the competition from larger supermarkets. Larger supermarkets offer customers a wide array of goods and services. Because grocery store customers are usually price-conscious, their loyalty can be fickle.

Fresh Produce is an independent neighborhood grocery store. It is known for its fresh meats, vegetables, and fruits. Customer service is a top priority that has kept the local grocer in business. Fresh Produce employees carefully bag groceries and carry them to the customers' vehicles. Fresh Produce also excels at fulfilling and delivering telephone orders. This service is greatly appreciated by senior citizens in the community. Employees at Fresh Produce know customers by name.

Some major supermarkets have unsuccessfully tried to sell groceries online. Fresh Produce believes that a website showcasing its unique qualities could be a successful promotional tool.

You are a web designer who must design an attractive website for Fresh Produce. You must explain how the website will emphasize the grocery store's uniqueness and contribute to this image by offering features such as an online newsletter and recipes for healthy living. You must present a plan for collecting the email addresses of Fresh Produce's loyal customers. The website should provide clear instructions on how to order online and how to access coupons for items offered at Fresh Produce.

Performance Indicators Evaluated

- Identify ways that technology impacts business. (Information Management)
- Describe current business trends. (Information Management)
- Describe the use of technology in the product/service management function. (Product/Service Management)
- Explain issues and trends in the food marketing industry. (Information Management)

Go to the DECA website for more detailed information. **www.deca.org**

Think Critically

1. How will senior citizens react to using Fresh Produce's website? How can you overcome any objections they have about using the website?
2. How can the website make Fresh Produce more efficient?
3. What type of contest could the website offer customers?
4. Why must the website be user-friendly?

CHAPTER 19

MANAGE RISK

See how effective advertising leads to successful marketing strategies.
Click on Chapter 19, Visual Focus, **in your MindTap.**

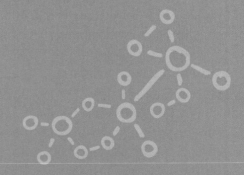

Let's Start a Band!

"Make sure you know what you are signing when you sign a recording contract."

– Tommy Shaw, Singer–Songwriter and Member of the Band STYX

You know how I said we wanted a recording contract? Now we're not so sure. We talked with an entertainment lawyer and found out the only thing we really understood is that we'd be bound by it.

We knew that if we had a contract, the label would produce, record, master, and distribute the album, and we would get a percentage—a royalty of at least 10 percent, maybe 15.

The lawyer said we probably could get an advance to cover the costs of production, but we would have to pay it back before we'd see any royalties. He called this *recoupment*. Besides the recording costs, the record company may want to recoup other costs before writing us a check.

We learned that any contract offered will require us to record a number of albums. Once we record an album or song it becomes the property of the label forever. We can't re-record any of the songs for at least five years and most likely 10, even if the company shelves the album and never releases it.

So, say we're wildly successful and the album makes $1.2 million dollars. We get 10 percent, or $120,000, but the recoupable expenses are $200,000. It may look like we've made money but we're actually $80,000 in the hole. We don't get a check, and the record company probably made about $330,000. And we've got to make a second album to cover the $80,000, plus the cost of producing it. I'm not sure how much success it would take to get us out of the hole, but we'd be doing more albums before seeing any money.

I asked the lawyer if there was any upside to a recording contract. He said we might get lucky and be one of the 5% who sell enough music to make money, but the odds are against that. Exposure and prestige are probably the best reasons he gave for signing a recording contract.

I need some help here. We all want to record, but do you think it is worth the risk? Do we have alternatives if we want to record?

19.1 ASSESS BUSINESS RISKS

Learning Objectives

19.1.1 Explain the nature of business risk.

19.1.2 Describe the four ways businesses manage risk.

Key Terms

risk
opportunity
natural risk
human risk
economic risk
pure risk

speculative risk
controllable risk
uncontrollable risk
insurable risk
uninsurable risk

marketing matters

Risk is a part of most marketing activities and affects both businesses and consumers. Each decision involved in developing and implementing a marketing strategy involves some amount of risk. Risks can be classified based on the source of the risk, result of the risk, control of the risk, and insurability of the risk. Marketers can avoid a risk by choosing an alternative that does not involve that risk. They can transfer a risk to someone else, usually at a cost. They can insure the potential loss from a risk. Or they can assume the risk and accept the consequences.

essential question

Why do marketing decision makers need to be concerned about possible risks they face? What are the possible consequences to a business of failing to identify or ignoring potential risks?

19.1.1 ▶ The Nature of Business Risk

Every year thousands of people decide to open their own businesses. Most first-time entrepreneurs will use all of the money they have saved and borrow thousands of additional dollars. They may quit their current jobs to devote all their time to the new business. Each believes he or she has an idea that will attract customers and eventually make a lot of money.

At the same time that thousands of entrepreneurs open new businesses, many others close their doors. Their dreams did not come true. Most lost the money they

invested in the business. Many will never attempt to start a new business again.

When a person decides to open a business or a company decides to develop a new product or service or enter a new market, there is a chance for success and a chance for failure. The possibility that a loss can occur as the result of a decision or activity is known as **risk**. Why do people invest a great deal of time and money in new businesses or products when there is a risk of loss? Because although there is a chance of loss, there is also an **opportunity**, or the possibility for success.

Success takes many forms. For both individuals and businesses, it can mean recognition, being viewed as a leader, or satisfaction for oneself and others. An important measure of success in business is profit. People invest money and take risks in business to make a profit.

Each of us takes risks every day. You might decide whether to speak to a new person you meet. The risk is that the person might not respond in a positive way. The opportunity is that you will gain a new friend. You may have spent a great deal of time and effort in the past few years selecting difficult courses, completing homework, and preparing yourself for college. Nevertheless, there is a risk that your effort will not pay off. Your grades might not be high enough, or you may not have the money needed to attend the college of your choice. But you have chosen to assume these risks for the opportunities a college education provides.

Classification of Risk

Marketers need to understand the risks involved in order to deal with them. There are four classifications of risk. They are based on the source, result, control, and insurability of the risk.

SOURCE OF THE RISK Business risks generally arise from one of three things. A **natural risk** is caused by the unpredictability of nature, such as the weather or an earthquake. **Human risk** arises because of the potential actions of individuals, groups, or organizations. The uncertainty associated with market forces, economic trends, and politics creates **economic risk**.

RESULT OF THE RISK A risk that presents the chance of complete loss or no loss at all and is beyond human control is

known as a **pure risk**. Examples of pure risk include premature death and natural disasters that result in fire, wind damage, and flooding.

For other risks, you have the chance to gain as well as lose from the risk. This is known as a **speculative risk**. If you invest in the stock market, you could lose money if the value of the stock goes down. On the other hand, you have an opportunity to make money if the stock price increases.

CONTROL OF THE RISK A risk that can be reduced or even avoided by actions you take is a **controllable risk**. If you are concerned about losing jewelry or cash, you might decide to put it in a home safe or a safe deposit box in a bank. If the roads are slippery, you can avoid driving or drive carefully to reduce the chance of an accident.

If your actions do not affect the result of a risk, it is an **uncontrollable risk**. The weather cannot be controlled even though the type of weather has a big impact on businesses such as farms. If the weather is favorable, farmers have the opportunity to grow and harvest crops. In poor weather, healthy crops will not develop. Weather affects many other types of businesses as well, from vacation resorts to airlines and construction companies. Other uncontrollable risks facing most businesses are changes in the economy and laws, the actions of competitors, and consumer preferences.

INSURABILITY OF THE RISK If a large number of people face a risk, if the risk is pure rather than speculative, and if the amount of the loss can be predicted, it is an **insurable risk**. For example, many people who own homes or buildings face the risk that their property could be destroyed by fire or severe storms. Insurance companies look at the amount of losses from those risks in past years and sell insurance that would pay to repair or replace the buildings and property that could be damaged.

For an **uninsurable risk**, it is not possible to predict if a loss will occur or the amount of the loss. Speculative risks usually are not insurable. A business is not able to buy insurance that will pay for losses suffered because customers did not buy a new product. People who invest in the stock market must accept any losses or gains because it is not possible to accurately predict the result of that type of investment.

CHECKPOINT

What is the difference between a natural risk and a human risk?

19.1.2 ▶ Dealing with Risk

Marketing activities are subject to many risks. Every activity performed has the chance of success or failure. Each target market presents the possibility of a profit or loss for the company. Marketers need to be familiar with ways to deal with risks.

People responsible for risk management go through a careful process to decide the best way to deal with each risk faced by the business. Four methods can be considered (**Figure 19-1**).

AVOID THE RISK   It is possible to avoid some risks. For example, some shipping methods are more likely to result in lost or damaged products. To avoid that risk, the marketer would choose another shipping method. If a business has evidence it will be difficult to enter a market to compete with several larger businesses, it can avoid that market. Conducting market research can be a good way for a business to anticipate such risks.

TRANSFER THE RISK   A common method of dealing with risk in marketing is to transfer the risk to others. A business that believes it will have difficulty collecting money from credit customers does not offer its own credit. Instead, it accepts several national credit cards. The credit card companies accept the risk for the opportunity to make a profit.

METHODS OF DEALING WITH RISK

Management Strategy	Result
Avoid the Risk	Business chooses a different strategy that doesn't involve risk.
Transfer the Risk	Business lets another business complete the risky activity.
Insure the Risk	Business pays insurer to reimburse the amount of any losses from the risk.
Assume the Risk	Business proceeds with the decisions made and takes full responsibility for the results.

FIGURE 19-1 When facing a risk, managers have several choices of how to respond.

INSURE THE RISK   If a financial loss is possible from the risk and that loss can be predicted, the risk can be insured. The company facing the risk pays a small amount of the potential loss to an insurer. If the loss occurs, the insurer guarantees payment to the company. The company accepts a small, certain loss (the cost of the insurance policy) for protection from a larger, uncertain loss. Remember that many risks are not insurable because they are speculative. Some insurance may be very expensive if the risk or potential loss is great.

ASSUME THE RISK A company that assumes a risk must deal with any result of that risk. This strategy is sometimes referred to as *risk retention*. Some risks are unlikely to occur. Other risks have relatively small losses compared to the opportunities. And some risks are simply a normal part of doing business. In each case, it may be best to assume the risk because it will not have a serious negative effect on the business.

Sometimes a business *must* adopt a risk retention strategy because it cannot

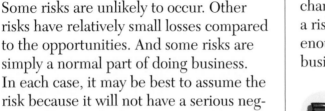

Want to know more about what is trending with this topic? Click on **Lesson 19.1, Global Marketing**, in your MindTap.

Connect to MindTap

avoid, transfer, or insure a risk. For example, once a product is in the market, many things can happen that may result in much lower sales than expected. The business accepts that possibility and attempts to make the product as successful as possible. Economic conditions sometimes change rapidly, and the business faces a risk it did not anticipate. There is not enough time to make changes, so the business must assume the risk.

CHECKPOINT
In what four ways do managers deal with business risks?

19.1 ASSESSMENT

What Have You Learned?

1. When is a risk considered uninsurable? [19.1.1]

2. Why would a company choose risk retention as a strategy to deal with risk? [19.1.2]

Make Academic Connections

1. **Visual Art** Working as a group, create a picture, graphic, or other visual representation of the different types of risks. Present your visual to the class and explain how each image represents a risk. [19.1.1]

2. **Communication** How might the formation of a joint venture between two companies be a way of dealing with risk?

What method of dealing with risk does it represent? Explain your answer in a short report. [19.1.2]

Connect to ◇DECA

Build your Portfolio

Because many employees have trouble finding day care for their children, your company is considering opening an on-site day-care facility. You have been asked to develop a report that outlines the potential risks involved. You also must describe the four management strategies the company could use to handle the risk, weighing the pros and cons of each. Present your report to your teacher (judge) and recommend a strategy, explaining your choice. [19.1.1, 19.1.2]

IDENTIFY MARKETING RISKS

Learning Objectives

19.2.1 Explain how changes in the economic, regulatory, and competitive environment create marketing risks.

19.2.2 Describe the marketing risks associated with each of the marketing mix elements.

Key Terms

risk management
liability
brand cannibalization

marketing matters

Many factors combine to determine whether or not a business is successful. These factors include the economy, laws and regulations, competition, technology, and customer needs. As factors change in unpredictable ways and market conditions shift, each one presents both risks and opportunities. Choices made for each of the marketing mix elements—product, distribution, price, and promotion—also may lead to certain risks. Marketers consider those risks as well when planning and implementing marketing decisions.

essential question

What changes might a business face that pose both risks and opportunities for marketers?

19.2.1 ▶ The Risk of Change

Each aspect of marketing carries its own set of risks and challenges. This reality means that managing risk is an important marketing function. **Risk management** in marketing includes providing security and safety for products, personnel, and customers and reducing the risk associated with marketing decisions and activities. It is possible to analyze the marketing environment and marketing mix to identify the areas where risks are likely to occur.

Many factors influence whether or not a business will be successful. These factors include the economy, laws and regulations, competition, technology, and customer needs. Each factor poses risks and also offers opportunities. Marketers are willing to take a risk if there is a real possibility of

*Want to know more about what is trending with this topic? Click on **Lesson 19.2, Marketing Decisions**, in your MindTap.*

Connect to MindTap

How can a business provide security for its personnel and customers?

success. They evaluate opportunities to determine which provide the greatest opportunities with the least risk.

ECONOMY Businesses regularly face the risk of a change in the economy. Sales may be high, and customers may value the product until faced with a recession. Suddenly, the business is unable to maintain sales, and profits fall. High unemployment rates or an increase in tax rates could have similar effects on a business.

LAWS AND REGULATIONS Failure to follow laws and regulations can put a company at risk. For example, if a restaurant does not follow the proper health regulations, it could be shut down. Implementation of new laws or a court ruling can require a major change in operations. Even inadvertently breaking the law could create

problems for a business. The laws and regulations a business must follow may be federal, state, or local. An example of laws and regulations are minimum wage laws, which set the lowest hourly amount an employee may be paid.

COMPETITION A company can lose market share by failing to consider the actions of its competitors. New products can enter the market at any time and can pull market share away from a company. The company needs to be aware of what its competition is doing at all times by gathering information on competitors' marketing mix elements. It must respond promptly to any changes it identifies.

TECHNOLOGY Many new products are introduced as a result of new technology. Those changes in the market can have an immediate effect on a business. Consider how quickly a new cell phone design or a new television screen technology can cause existing products to become outdated. Changes in business practices due to new technology also have an effect. For example, when a few supermarkets and retail stores converted

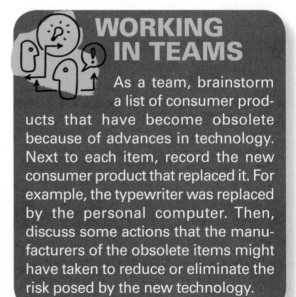

WORKING IN TEAMS

As a team, brainstorm a list of consumer products that have become obsolete because of advances in technology. Next to each item, record the new consumer product that replaced it. For example, the typewriter was replaced by the personal computer. Then, discuss some actions that the manufacturers of the obsolete items might have taken to reduce or eliminate the risk posed by the new technology.

to scanner technology they were able to check customers out more quickly. Other stores had to install the equipment or risk losing customers.

CUSTOMER NEEDS   Customer needs can change with little notice. Marketing must respond to customers' needs and be alert to anything that changes how customers view a product or a business. Product life cycles illustrate how demand changes for products. Some life-cycle stages last a short time and require the business to make rapid changes to maintain sales and profits.

CHECKPOINT
What risk-related factors influence whether or not a business will be successful?

19.2.2 ▶ Risks to Elements of the Marketing Mix

When selecting from among several target markets, a company reduces its risk if it works with markets it can clearly identify and locate. The company should choose a market for which adequate information is available. A group of customers that has purchased and been satisfied with a company's products presents a better opportunity for introducing a new product than a group that has no previous experience with the company. When a company has choices of marketing mixes, it often will select the one that emphasizes its strengths and that can be completed successfully.

Each marketing mix element is subject to some risks. Marketers should consider those risks when planning and implementing marketing decisions.

Product

The product itself faces several risks including those associated with damage, product design, and liability.

RISK OF DAMAGE   Probably the most obvious is the risk of damage before the product is sold or used. The product needs to be designed so it is sturdy and durable. Packaging needs to protect the product while it is transported and stored.

You probably have purchased a product and opened the package only to find it was damaged or broken This may have caused you to lose confidence in the product and others with the same brand name. You may even have returned the product for a refund. A company risks a great deal with a fragile or poorly packaged product.

PRODUCT DESIGN RISKS
Businesses must study how the consumer will use the product. They must be sure it is designed to meet consumer expectations for use. The product must perform the way customers expect when they use it. The product must not spoil or deteriorate before it is used if it will not be consumed immediately. Many food products are dated to tell consumers when they were processed. They may have an expiration date after which the product should not be used due to a decline in quality or effectiveness. Restaurants that prepare foods in advance must discard food if it sits too long before being ordered, resulting in increasing costs.

The product design must be up to date. If competing products have improvements or incorporate new technology, customers will quickly see the differences and switch to those brands.

There are many examples of businesses that failed because their products did not change with the times. Even the most loyal customers will not continue to buy the same product when they see that a superior design is available. However, changing or updating a product is risky as consumers must see the benefits in order to accept the change. As shown in the advertisement, French's used promotion and price incentives to introduce new mustard flavors.

LIABILITY RISKS The product risk that concerns businesses most is liability. **Liability** is a legal responsibility for loss or damage. Companies are responsible for the design and use of their products. When a consumer or end user suffers an injury, death, or financial loss that involves a company's product in any way, the company may be held legally liable. In these cases, a court may order the company to pay up to millions of dollars in compensation to the injured party.

Even services are subject to liability risk. For example, if the dry-cleaning process damages a suit, the dry cleaner will be required to pay the customer for a replacement.

Careful product design and testing, providing understandable information to customers on effective product handling and use, and well-trained service employees are important company investments to reduce the likelihood of liability claims.

Distribution

When planning for the distribution of products, businesses need to be concerned about safety, security, and performance of distribution activities.

Why do you think French's used a coupon and a contest in its advertising to introduce new mustard flavors?

SAFETY RISKS Distribution safety risks involve the safety of products, buildings, and equipment. They also involve the safety of people involved in distribution activities and customer safety. Whenever products are moved from one location to another, there are opportunities for damage or injury. Companies must carefully plan product handling, storage, and transportation procedures to reduce that possibility. They must train employees in proper handling procedures and set safety standards for the design of facilities and equipment.

SECURITY RISKS As products move through a channel of distribution, there are many opportunities for theft. Products can be stolen by burglars, by customers who shoplift, and by employees. Surveillance equipment and security procedures and personnel are used to protect against theft.

You can see the importance retail stores place on security when you shop. Well-designed merchandise displays, security tags, video monitors, security personnel, and electronic sensors at all exits are used to reduce shoplifting and employee theft. The loss due to shoplifting and theft adds tremendously to the price of products. It also requires special product-handling procedures that inconvenience customers and add expense for the business.

Companies that deliver products and services online, such as computer apps and banking services, face the risks of unlawful access to the products or accounts. These companies must put Internet security measures in place, such as requiring the input of access codes and passwords, to prevent theft by hackers. These are people who use their technical skills to gain unauthorized access to systems or networks in order to commit crimes.

PERFORMANCE RISKS The final area of business risk related to distribution is the performance of the distribution system. Products need to be available to the customer at the place and time they are needed, or a sale may be missed. Products must move through the distribution system efficiently. Ordering and order processing, inventory control, materials handling, and transportation must all work effectively. If an order is misplaced, a shipment is sent to the wrong location, or inventory levels are not maintained correctly, customers cannot obtain the products they want. Product damage is another concern in the distribution system. Procedures and equipment are used that protect the products while they move through the channel of distribution.

It is even possible for factors outside the control of a business to interfere with distribution. Poor weather conditions can slow transportation or damage or destroy buildings, equipment, and inventory. Rising oil prices can increase the cost of fuel to the business and to other companies involved in the transportation of raw materials, supplies, and finished products.

To reduce costs, companies have outsourced some logistics operations to foreign companies. However, the risks involved have led some companies to relocate the outsourced operations closer to the United States (*nearshoring*) and, in some cases, resume operating within U.S. borders (*reshoring*).

Price

Customers must see the product price as a value. They also must be able to afford the product. Companies face two risks when pricing products and services. Setting the price too high reduces demand and causes products to remain unsold. At the other extreme, if products are priced too low, the company will not make a profit.

A number of factors enter into setting the price, including the costs of production, marketing, and operations. Any services offered, discounts, markdowns, and the cost of credit also must be considered in order for a profit to be earned. Every business in a channel of distribution must be able to make a profit after paying its costs. Finally, customers usually will compare the price of a product with those of competitors.

Promotion

The goal of promotion is to communicate with consumers to influence them to purchase the company's products. Anything that interferes with that goal is a business risk. The media need to perform as planned. If a radio or television commercial is not aired as planned, or if a newspaper or magazine is not distributed on schedule, the promotional plan is less effective. If a salesperson cannot meet with a customer or does not communicate effectively, sales are lost.

If a promotion of a specific brand is designed to bring in new customers, then there is a risk of **brand cannibalization**. This occurs when the promotion results in customers shifting from an established brand to a new brand made by the same producer. An example is the Coca-Cola Company promoting the launch of a new beverage that competes with its original cola beverage.

Companies also have legal responsibilities related to promotion. Information must be honest and accurate, or the company may be liable for the harm caused by inappropriate or illegal promotion.

Another area of risk is the damage that can result from competitors' promotions. These promotions may contain misleading or incorrect information about a company's products. Although it may be possible to get the company to stop using those promotions, the damage already may be done. It is difficult to correct misinformation. Lastly, damage may result when customers who have had a negative experience with a product tell many other people about their experiences. That negative word-of-mouth publicity can be very damaging.

CHECKPOINT

For most businesses, what is the most serious product risk?

ASSESSMENT

What Have You Learned?

1. What does risk management in marketing include? [19.2.1]
2. What risks can laws and regulations pose for a business? [19.2.1]
3. What are the three categories of product risk? [19.2.2]
4. What are the risks associated with setting a price too high or too low? [19.2.2]

Make Academic Connections

1. **Ethics** To minimize competition risk, employees from a local restaurant regularly "keep tabs" on competitors by posing as potential customers. Do you think this is ethical? Why or why not? What are some ways a business can legitimately research the competition? [19.2.1]
2. **Economics** The economy can be a contributing factor to the success or failure of a business. Examine the current state of the U.S. economy. Identify three potential risks a business faces today based on current economic conditions. Summarize these risks in a one-page report. [19.2.1]

Connect to ◇DECA

Build your Portfolio

Your team members manage a wholesale company that purchases fresh fruits and vegetables from farmers and sells them to local grocery stores. As a team, talk about the types of distribution risks your business faces. Discuss some procedures your business can take to minimize performance errors in the distribution system. Develop a plan to implement those procedures. Make a three-minute team presentation of your plan to your teacher (judge). [19.2.2]

21ST CENTURY SUCCESS SKILLS
Evaluate Information Sources

Modern society bombards us with information. Electronic information is available through social media apps, text messages, email, blogs, interest groups, pop-up ads, and more. Traditional information outlets such as radio, TV, newspapers, magazines, and billboards also remain significant information sources.

The Internet provides an inexpensive and instantaneous distribution channel for information. It has enabled everyone—from individuals to special interest groups to large corporations—to distribute messages widely and quickly. However, the quality of that information can sometimes be questionable.

Traditional information outlets typically employ people to check the accuracy of data before it is published. In contrast, bloggers and other online information content providers often work independently with no one monitoring them for accuracy before they post. Inaccurate information is frequently published online, and the speed of distribution and reposting simply compounds the problem.

Informed readers can use a variety of strategies to evaluate the accuracy of information. These strategies are appropriate for both electronic and traditional media.

1. Consider the source of the information.
   - Where did it come from?
   - Who published it?
   - What qualifications does this person or organization have?
   - Is the person or organization widely recognized as a source of reliable information?
   - What other information can you find about the author or organization responsible for this information?

2. Determine the objectivity of the information.
   - Does the author have an obvious bias concerning the topic?
   - Are all sides of the issue presented, and evaluated?
   - Is the language objective and reasoned or emotional and inflammatory?
   - Are the statements factual? Are sources and references noted?

3. Identify the purpose for the information.
   - To whom is the information directed?
   - Is someone trying to sell you something or have another motive for the information?
   - Do opinions seem to be stated as facts?
   - Does the presenter express a preference for a person, group, or point of view?

4. Is the information current?
   - Is this a topic on which up-to-date information is important?
   - Is there copyright or footnote information that will help you determine when the content was created?

Develop Your Skill

Pick a topic you know is controversial. Research a claim within that topic. Look for information that will support both sides of the claim. Gather information from both electronic sources and traditional sources.

After you have located a number of sources, compare and evaluate their accuracy, timeliness, and reliability using the above strategies. Prepare a table listing the sources and assign each one a "credibility rating" of 0 to 5. Explain how you arrived at that rating.

MANAGE MARKETING RISKS

Learning Objectives

19.3.1 Explain how to use the various sections of the marketing plan to identify and develop plans for managing risk.

19.3.2 Describe additional ways to eliminate or control marketing-related risks.

Key Terms

surety bond
product liability insurance
professional liability insurance

marketing matters

Businesses need to find ways to prevent risks from interfering with marketing plans. They can either eliminate risks or minimize their effects. The marketing plan provides an excellent tool for developing risk management strategies. Each of the three sections of the marketing plan includes elements related to risk management. In addition to managing risks through the marketing planning process, businesses can effectively manage risks by implementing safety and security policies, by purchasing insurance to cover damages that arise from risks, and by using risk reduction measures.

essential question

How can a well-developed marketing plan reduce the amount and cost of insurance a business needs to manage risks?

19.3.1 ▶ Handle Risks with Marketing Planning

With the large number of risks in marketing, a business must find ways that prevent those risks from interfering with the marketing plans. The first goal should be to prevent risks. If it is not possible to prevent a risk, the business should make plans to reduce the negative effects of a risk on the business and its customers. Remember there are four ways to deal with risks: to avoid the risk, transfer the risk, insure the risk, or assume the risk. Careful planning is needed for each of these methods. Risk management is so important to the success of a business that a company should incorporate it into its marketing plan.

Developing a marketing plan provides an ideal opportunity for a business to identify potential risks and make plans to avoid or reduce those risks. Each of the three sections of a marketing plan provides opportunities to identify and develop plans for managing risks (**Figure 19-2**).

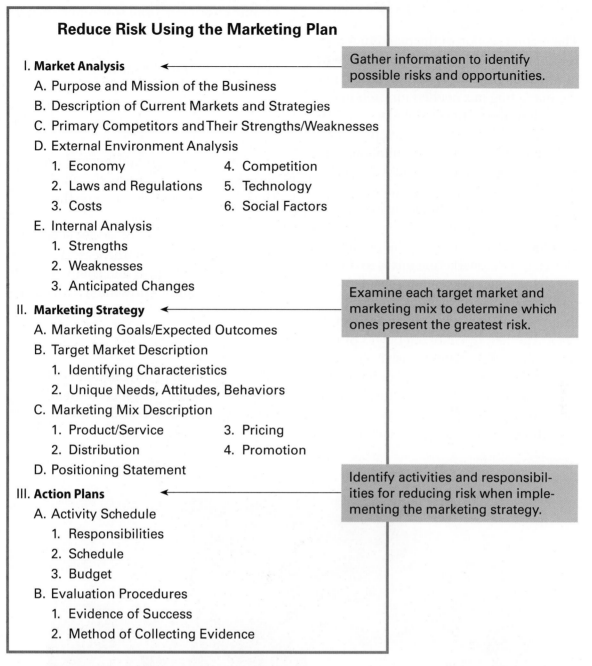

Reduce Risk Using the Marketing Plan

I. **Market Analysis**
   A. Purpose and Mission of the Business
   B. Description of Current Markets and Strategies
   C. Primary Competitors and Their Strengths/Weaknesses
   D. External Environment Analysis
      1. Economy
      2. Laws and Regulations
      3. Costs
      4. Competition
      5. Technology
      6. Social Factors
   E. Internal Analysis
      1. Strengths
      2. Weaknesses
      3. Anticipated Changes

II. **Marketing Strategy**
   A. Marketing Goals/Expected Outcomes
   B. Target Market Description
      1. Identifying Characteristics
      2. Unique Needs, Attitudes, Behaviors
   C. Marketing Mix Description
      1. Product/Service
      2. Distribution
      3. Pricing
      4. Promotion
   D. Positioning Statement

III. **Action Plans**
   A. Activity Schedule
      1. Responsibilities
      2. Schedule
      3. Budget
   B. Evaluation Procedures
      1. Evidence of Success
      2. Method of Collecting Evidence

Gather information to identify possible risks and opportunities.

Examine each target market and marketing mix to determine which ones present the greatest risk.

Identify activities and responsibilities for reducing risk when implementing the marketing strategy.

FIGURE 19-2 The marketing plan is a tool that can be used to reduce and manage risk. Risk management should be addressed in each section of the marketing plan document.

Market Analysis

When completing a market analysis, a company gathers information on current marketing strategies, competitors, the marketing environment, and its own strengths and weaknesses. It can study each of these areas to determine risks and opportunities. Changes in the economy, new technology, and competitors' actions that can affect a business should be identified as part of the market analysis.

Marketing Strategy

The second section of the marketing plan is used to develop the marketing strategy, in which target markets are identified and the marketing mix needed for each market is described. (Recall the elements of the marketing mix are product, place or distribution, pricing, and promotion.) This section of the marketing plan will likely offer the business a choice of marketing mix alternatives and should include a review of the possible risks.

One strategy related to the product element of the marketing mix is to diversify the product mix (rather than depend on sales of one or two items) in order to spread the risk across many product lines. Another aspect of a retailer's pricing strategy that relates to risk is deciding whether to accept credit and debit cards. Credit cards add expense for the business and some additional risk. However, accepting credit cards may result in gaining customers from stores that do not accept credit cards.

A strategy relating to the distribution element is to transfer much of the risk to a wholesaler. The wholesaler takes title of the product and assumes the responsibility for the possible costs associated with theft, damage, spoilage, and obsolescence. The risks involved in warehousing and transportation are also borne by the wholesaler. The wholesaler will also assume the risks involved with financing.

The business will not always choose the marketing mix with the least risk. It will analyze the risks and compare them to the opportunities presented with each choice.

Action Plan

The final section of the marketing plan is the action plan. This section identifies the activities and responsibilities for the marketing strategy. Some of the activities

Why is planning an important component of risk management?

MARKETING COMMUNICATION

Customer Risk

When customers make a purchase, they take the risk that the purchase may have negative consequences for them. These risks may take the form of financial risk, social risk, and/or psychological risk. Marketers need to be aware of these risks, because the more risk customers perceive, the higher their involvement will be in the selling process.

The higher the cost of a product or service, the more financial risk the customer will have. When buying expensive products, consumers are more likely to research and solicit the opinions of others. Purchases such as homes and automobiles fall into this category. For an involved customer, successful marketing interaction requires personal selling from a knowledgeable salesperson with good communication skills.

Purchases with a financial risk also may contain a social risk: the product or service may affect other people's opinions of the buyer. Still, many purchases that have a social risk are relatively inexpensive. Items such as jewelry and clothes are highly visible: purchasers run the risk of being judged by the choices they make. In such cases, purchasers may consult with sources such as friends, family, or other trusted influencers to gain approval before making their choice.

Nearly any purchase can cause psychological risk for a consumer. This occurs when the consumer believes that the wrong purchase decision may cause some concern or anxiety. Food choices often fall into this risk category. For example, some people may have anxiety when purchasing produce because they are unsure about whether it has been treated with harmful pesticides. Further, ethical concerns about sustainability and sourcing often provoke psychological risk. The expensive purchases associated with financial social risk also may contain a psychological risk for consumers: consumers may worry about the expense as well as the social impact of their purchases.

Think Critically

1. What type of message should marketers convey when promoting products that might involve a great amount of social risk for consumers?
2. How would a consumer's income level affect his or her tolerance for financial, social, and psychological risk?

Source: Lamb, Charles W., Joe F. Hair, and Carl McDaniel. *MKTG*[12]*: Principles of Marketing*. Cengage Learning. 2019. pp. 108–109.

and responsibilities will relate to risk reduction. For example, employees are given responsibility for controlling quality, scheduling and coordinating distribution activities, checking promotional plans to make sure they meet all legal requirements, and performing the many other activities that deal with the risks in marketing. A responsibility of the marketing manager is to carefully review each part of the action plan to determine if risks are adequately addressed.

CHECKPOINT
How can the market analysis section of the marketing plan address risk?

In addition to planning, most businesses implement specific security and safety plans, purchase insurance to protect against financial loss, and regularly review marketing activities and operations to identify and reduce risks.

Security and Safety

Because of its importance, planning security and safety is often a responsibility of people specifically trained in that area. In many businesses, security and safety management is part of the operations area. It must be coordinated throughout all business functions, including marketing activities. Marketers will work with security and safety experts to identify areas needing attention and procedures to use that will reduce those problems.

All marketing personnel should receive special training in safety and security procedures. They should

- be able to recognize security problems and safety issues

- know how to prevent accidents and injuries

- be aware of company policies regarding surveillance, shoplifting, and theft prevention

Salespeople and customer service personnel need to discuss risks and safety concerns related to product use with customers. Products and packaging should be analyzed to ensure they meet all safety and health requirements. Information should be supplied with all products informing customers about safe handling and use of the products.

Insurance

One method of transferring risk is to purchase insurance. The payment of insurance premiums transfers some or all of

© sirtravelalot/Shutterstock.com

How would assigning specific responsibilities to employees help a business reduce risk?

the financial loss for the insured risk to the insurance company. There are some common areas of marketing in which businesses purchase insurance.

Insurance on marketing personnel includes health and life insurance as well as surety bonds. A **surety bond** provides insurance for the failure of a person to perform his or her duties or for losses resulting from employee theft or dishonesty.

Property insurance protects the buildings, equipment, and in some cases, the inventory of the business. Liability insurance pays for damage caused to other people or their property. Theft insurance provides an additional form of property loss protection. There are several types of insurance available to protect against damaged and lost merchandise while it is being transported. Another important type of insurance is **product liability insurance**, which provides protection from consumer claims arising from the use of the company's products. Similar insurance is available for service businesses. **Professional liability insurance** protects against claims of negligent or harmful actions by business professionals. Examples of professional liability insurance include malpractice insurance for physicians and errors and omissions insurance for financial advisors, attorneys, and accountants.

Risk Reduction

Marketers constantly search for opportunities. Those opportunities include new target markets and improved marketing mixes. With every opportunity comes a certain amount of risk. Risks can never be eliminated entirely. However, careful planning and effective marketing management can help companies avoid some risks and limit damages.

> *Want to know more about marketing in the information age? Click on* **Lesson 19.3, Digital Marketing,** *in your MindTap.*

Connect to
MindTap

MATH IN MARKETING

Risks, Rewards, Expected Value

With almost any business or investment activity, the results are uncertain but not wholly unpredictable. In most cases, there is a known range of possible outcomes. For example, investing in a company's stock will result in a complete loss if the company goes bankrupt. On the other hand, if it does very well, the value of the stock might double or triple over a period of time.

Through detailed analysis, reasonably accurate estimates can be made of the likelihood of the various outcomes. Those estimates, expressed as probabilities, can be used to derive what is known as the expected value of a course of action. *Expected value* is calculated by multiplying each possible outcome by the probability of its occurrence and then adding all of the subtotals. That final sum is the expected value. The expected value can be used to determine whether a course of action is a worthwhile risk. For a large number of actions, the average outcome should approximate the average expected value.

Businesspeople need to keep in mind that an expected value is only as good as the probability estimates it is based on. If a highly favorable outcome is given an unreasonably optimistic (high) probability, a risk might seem well worth taking when it actually is not.

Do the Math

1. In a game of chance played by flipping a coin, if a coin comes up heads the player wins $5, and if it comes up tails the player pays $5. If there is a 50 percent chance of getting heads or tails, what is the expected value of each flip?

2. What would the expected value be if the player had to pay $6 when the coin came up tails?

The marketing plan provides a useful structure to identify risks and develop ways to deal with them. Another important method of reducing risk is with the careful selection and training of marketing personnel. Employees should be selected based on their concern about customers and their needs. Employees should want to perform their jobs effectively. Then they should be trained to follow safety and security procedures. Finally, all marketing employees should be constantly alert to possible risks that can cause problems for the business or harm to customers or other people. When problems are identified, changes should be made to reduce the risk and avoid damage or loss.

 CHECKPOINT
Which marketing personnel should receive special training in dealing with surveillance techniques and safety and security risks?

19.3 ASSESSMENT

What Have You Learned?

1. Why would a company develop a marketing mix that does not present the least risk? [19.3.1]

2. What are the marketing-related areas for which businesses purchase insurance? [19.3.2]

Make Academic Connections

1. **Government** The Occupational Safety and Health Administration (OSHA) aims to ensure employee safety and health in the United States by working with employers and employees to create better working environments. Prepare a two-page report about OSHA focusing on its mission, history, and impact on workplace safety. Explain how compliance with OSHA regulations can help a business reduce workplace risks. [19.3.2]

2. **Social Studies** Doctors' groups, patients, and insurance companies have criticized medical malpractice litigation as expensive, unpredictable, and inefficient. These critics claim that the cost of malpractice insurance has forced many doctors to go out of business. Others claim that the "malpractice crisis" is a myth. Research the issues surrounding medical malpractice litigation, including potential solutions to the problems. Present your findings in a three-page report. [19.3.2]

Connect to ◇DECA

Build your Portfolio

You manage a clothing store. The owner has asked you to prepare a presentation about the types of insurance your company should purchase to reduce risks. Develop a three-minute presentation using visual aids for your teacher (judge) in which you describe the types of insurance your company should have and explain why the company needs this type of insurance. [19.3.1]

Connect to MindTap

*Analyze a case study that focuses on chapter concepts. Click on **Chapter 19, Case Study,** in your MindTap.*

CHAPTER 19 ASSESSMENT

Review Marketing Concepts

1. Why do businesses take risks even when failure and financial losses may result? [19.1.1]

2. Why are some insurable risks more expensive than others to cover under an insurance policy? [19.1.2]

3. As a business owner, which of these risks would be more difficult to handle: laws and regulations or competition? Explain your answer. [19.2.1]

4. How do changes in the economic environment affect marketing risks? [19.2.1]

5. Both products and services are subject to liability risks. Think of an example of a liability risk a service might face. Explain the nature of the risk and what a company can do to reduce the likelihood of a liability claim. [19.2.2]

6. Give an example of a risk associated with the promotion element of the marketing mix. [19.3.1]

7. Give an example of when a business owner might purchase a surety bond on one of its employees. [19.3.2]

Marketing Research and Planning

1. The management of a local drug store has just received the monthly figures for gross sales and losses due to shoplifting for the past year (see the table, below). [19.2.2]

   a. Calculate the percentage of gross sales lost to shoplifting each month.

   b. Calculate the total gross sales and the total dollars and percentage of sales lost to shoplifting for the year.

   c. Develop a bar graph by month showing the dollar amount lost to shoplifting.

2. Interview a local businessperson concerning the types of risk his or her business faces. Use the following questions as a guide for your discussion, but do not limit yourself to these questions.

   - What industry is your business in?
   - What types of risk does your business face?
   - How can you prevent, reduce, or avoid these risks?

   After you have completed your interview, bring your results to class and share them with your classmates. Tabulate the class results and answer the following questions. [19.1.1, 19.2.1, 19.2.2]

Month	Gross Sales	Dollar Losses Due to Shoplifting
January	$200,356	$2,004
February	237,595	4,039
March	377,920	7,558
April	394,395	9,860
May	420,400	4,204
June	310,497	7,752
July	292,304	2,923
August	230,422	5,761
September	379,295	11,379
October	599,395	29,970
November	735,284	40,441
December	923,502	55,410

a. What types of risks did each business name?

b. Are there similarities and/or differences in the types of risks various businesses face?

c. What types of solutions or remedies did the businesses employ to prevent, reduce, or avoid their risks?

3. The best method of reducing risk is to be an informed marketer. The information a marketer needs usually is gained by maintaining a marketing information system and doing specific market research. Marketers cannot make good decisions without knowing as much as possible about all internal and external influences on their products or services. Using your knowledge of marketing information, describe a marketing risk associated with each of the following areas. Explain how a marketing information system can reduce the risk. [19.3.1]

a. New tax laws

b. Increased cost of raw materials needed to manufacture your product

c. Possible strike of transportation workers

d. A major competitor's price-cutting tactic

4. You are a marketing student and work part-time in a local ice cream store. You decide you need to explain to your manager the value of the competitive positioning of a business as a strategy to reduce the risks associated with operating the business (see Lessons 4.1, 7.2, and 7.3). Recently, a franchised ice cream store has opened in your town, and it threatens to take many of your customers away. Your manager is unsure of how to respond to these problems. In your discussion, explain how to turn problems into marketing opportunities using competitive positioning. [19.2.1]

Marketing Management and Decision Making

1. The Internet is rapidly changing the way people watch television. No longer are viewers willing to fit their schedules to the choices made by a few network executives. Internet streaming now makes that possible. But the competition to deliver content via Internet streaming is intense. Netflix, Hulu, Amazon, Apple TV, and others are spending large sums of money to develop agreements with the creators of television series, special features, and movies. They each must find the right mix of product, prices, promotion, and distribution to build a profitable customer base. Using your knowledge of risk management and the marketing planning process, answer the following questions:

a. What type of risks will a company that wants to compete in the growing Internet streaming service market face?

b. How can a company attempt to minimize these risks? Can it avoid these risks completely?

c. Use the three-step approach in marketing planning to show how it can help a company minimize risk. [19.1.1, 19.2.1, 19.2.2]

2. Using correct pricing strategies is an effective way of managing risk. Refer to Lesson 14.3 to review the pricing strategies. Explain how the following pricing strategies are used in effective risk management: [19.3.1]

a. Penetration pricing

b. Price skimming

c. Nonprice competition

d. Discounts

e. Price lining

3. Search the Internet for the website of an insurance company that specializes in insuring business risks. Write a one-page report on the types of services it offers, the types of business risks it insures, and how it uses its website to market insurance coverage to businesses. [19.3.2]

4. Search the Internet for a news article describing a corporate bankruptcy filing or financial reorganization. Describe the circumstances that led to the company's financial problems and explain how it failed to successfully manage the risks it faced. What could it have done differently to avoid those risks or minimize the damage it suffered? [19.1.2]

Let's Start a Band Follow-Up Discussion

Work in small teams to discuss the question posed at the end of the opening vignette. What are the risks involved for the band of signing a recording contract? Is signing with a record label worth the risk? What alternatives does the band have if they want to record?

Build Your Marketing Plan

Build your Portfolio

In this chapter you learned how to identify risks that can affect marketing and develop plans to reduce risks. You will now apply this learning to the development of your marketing plan. To access the chapter-specific tools that you will need to complete this activity, please navigate to Chapter 19 ➔ Build Your Marketing Plan in MindTap. Alternatively, you can access these tools online at NGLSync. Please visit www.nglsync. cengage.com, and search for the companion website that accompanies this book by entering the ISBN, author, or title. Once you locate this companion website, navigate to Build Your Marketing Plan ➔ Chapter 19.

Business Services Marketing Series Event

DECA PREP

The Business Services Marketing Series Event consists of a 100-question multiple-choice Career Cluster® exam and role-plays. The role-play portion of the event requires participants to translate what they have learned into effective, efficient, and spontaneous action. The five performance indicators specify the distinct tasks participants must accomplish. Students have 10 minutes to prepare their strategy for the role-play and 10 additional minutes to explain their strategy to the judge. The judge can ask questions during or after the presentation.

Some of the nation's largest banks are offering mobile banking through the use of cell phones. Banks send customers a text message when their account balance falls below a certain level or unusual activity occurs in their account.

Young consumers who are comfortable using their cell phones to browse the Internet are the most likely users of the newest bank services. Banks do not charge for mobile banking services, but this does not mean that the service is free. The mobile banking services can increase the customer's cell phone bill because of charges for text messages and data usage. Users may also may incur extra charges for time spent online monitoring their account balance.

Banks that offer mobile banking take security measures to protect customers. Banks require customers to use a six-digit access code to use the banking service. Customers will not be liable for losses caused by fraud, but they may find it difficult to get their money back if the account is compromised. Customers who choose to use mobile banking should make sure the bank requires the use of a password or PIN (personal identification number) to access cell phone accounts and should contact the bank immediately if the cell phone is lost or stolen.

Prepare a presentation to persuade customers to use mobile banking and present it to the bank's CEO (judge).

Performance Indicators Evaluated

- Describe the use of technology in the product/service management function. (Product/Service Management)
- Identify consumer protection provisions of appropriate agencies. (Product/Service Management)
- Explain the concept of product in business services. (Product/Service Management)
- Describe the concept of promotion in business services. (Promotion)
- Analyze product information to identify product features and benefits. (Selling)

Go to the DECA website for more detailed information. **www.deca.org**

Think Critically

1. Which age groups should be targeted first for mobile banking?
2. Why might customers hesitate to use mobile banking?
3. What joint venture opportunities exist for the banks and cell phone providers?
4. Will the growth of mobile banking be gradual or rapid?

CHAPTER 20

MARKETING AND FINANCE

See how effective advertising leads to successful marketing strategies. Click on Chapter 20, Visual Focus, in your MindTap.

Let's Start a Band!

> "In this business, the first rule is, never act out of desperation, because there is always someone out there looking to sucker you."
>
> – *Kevin Czinger, Volcano Entertainment Founder*

Remember when the band was just starting out? We thought all we had to do was practice, perform, and then pack up and move on to the next gig. We were doing it because we wanted to play and entertain and didn't give the business aspects much thought.

We found we all had to be promoters, and we got a pretty good handle on marketing and advertising. But now that we're doing well and making some money, it's also costing us more. We have lots of expenses when we're on tour, and the venues are often bigger, so it costs more to attract the crowds. And every venue does a different amount of promotion and offers us a different amount of help.

The band elected me to handle our finances, which basically amounts to depositing our earnings, writing checks to band members, and paying our expenses. But how do we pay expenses when we go on tour? And how do we cover them when we want to record and don't have time for gigs? Can we take out a loan to pay expenses or can we just put them on a credit card? I think we could benefit from some financial planning, but I don't really know where to start. Can you help me sort this out?

20.1 MARKETING AFFECTS BUSINESS FINANCES

Learning Objectives

20.1.1 Explain how marketing affects a business's financial planning.

20.1.2 Categorize marketing expenses in terms of the time it takes to use and pay for them and the type of purchase involved.

Key Terms

revenue
capital expenses
operating expenses

marketing matters

Marketing can be expensive. Marketing costs include capital expenses, inventory costs, and operating costs. A business needs to develop sources of financing for each category of costs. Those sources may include investor capital, loans from financial institutions, credit offered by sellers, cash available in the business, and money obtained from the sale of products and services. Marketing activities also affect the amount of revenue a company earns. To control costs and increase revenue, thus profits, the company needs to study the potential revenues available from target markets and the costs of marketing mixes.

essential question

Why does a business need to monitor both revenues and expenses when planning and implementing marketing activities?

20.1.1 ▶ Marketing Costs Affect Business Success

Marketing costs money, so in order for a company to be profitable, it must do a good job of managing marketing expenses. If marketing costs are carefully controlled, the company has more money available to use for important activities such as marketing research, product improvement, and customer services. The result should be greater customer satisfaction. On the other hand, if marketing costs are not well managed, the company does not have the money to improve the marketing mix. Production costs may need to be reduced, marketing activities cut back, or prices to

customers increased. The result is a product or service that is less satisfying to customers and not as competitive with other brands. In the end, there will be reduced profits for the company.

The Importance of Finances

The goal of every business is to generate **revenue**—the money received from the sale of products and services. In order to sell products, money must be spent to pay the costs of producing or obtaining the products and services to be sold. The cost of operating and managing the business must be covered. When all of those costs are subtracted from the revenue, the result is a profit or loss for the business. This basic financial equation is:

Revenue − Costs = Profit or Loss

Finances are important in both for-profit and nonprofit organizations, and revenue must exceed expenses, even for nonprofits. For example, a health care center might operate as a nonprofit organization, but it still performs marketing activities. The center must offer the appropriate services in a safe and comfortable facility. It must be open when clients need health care services, and it must offer prices the patients can afford. The organization needs to communicate with current and prospective clients about the center's services. If the revenue collected from the clients and other sources is not adequate to support the marketing mix, the center will not be able to continue to operate. Therefore, the manager of the health care center must carefully plan and control both revenues and expenses in order to keep the center open and available to families in the community.

The Role of Marketing in Financial Planning

Most large organizations have departments that deal specifically with financial planning and management. Experts in finance and accounting are responsible for maintaining the best financial position for their company. These experts assist other managers with planning. They maintain financial resources and records and provide information on revenue and expenses. A business may employ an accountant full- or part-time, use an accounting service, or consult a financial planner. Computer software

programs can help even new and small organizations with record keeping and financial decisions.

Although marketers may rely on experts to help with financial planning, they are responsible for the revenue and expenses related to marketing activities. Marketers need to identify ways to increase revenues while controlling marketing costs. They must decide which markets present the most profitable opportunities and which choices in a marketing mix are most cost effective.

TARGET MARKETS Decisions about which target markets to serve determine the amount of sales and revenue a company can earn. Suppose a company has a choice between two markets. One market has a smaller number of potential customers, but those customers spend a higher percentage of their income on the product. This market also has fewer competitors. Would this be a good fit for the company?

What about competing in international markets? On one hand, it may be difficult and expensive for the business to enter a distant market with which it has no experience. If the business is not successful in the market, it could lose a great deal of money. On the other hand, successful entry could mean substantial profits for many years to come and opportunities to enter adjoining markets in other countries.

MARKETING MIX Decisions about the marketing mix also have an important impact on the company's financial resources. As the product element of the marketing mix is developed, marketers may decide that additional customer services or improved packaging to prevent product damage is needed. Each of those choices increases the cost of the product. The changes also may result in increased sales or customers who are willing to pay more because of the improvements.

Distribution decisions also can increase expenses. Examples include using several channels for distribution or operating regional warehouses to reduce the time needed to get products to customers. Expenses involved with the pricing element include offering credit, coupons, or rebates. Expenses associated with the promotion mix element include more frequent advertising, direct marketing efforts such as telemarketing, or additional training for salespeople. Each time marketers consider changes in the marketing mix, they need to study the costs of those changes and predict the effect of the change on sales.

CHECKPOINT
What is the basic financial equation?

MARKETING COMMUNICATION

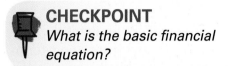

Marketing vs. Finance?

In many businesses, tension exists between the marketing and finance departments. While both departments are working for the same goal, their relationship often is adversarial. Those in finance may view marketers as employees who spend the company's money ineffectively and are always asking for more. Marketers may perceive that those in finance are only concerned with cash flow and scrutinizing the budget for where to cut.

Successful companies find ways for the two departments to work together. The basis for a productive working relationship begins with effective lines of communication between the two departments. Marketers need to communicate to the finance department how the money budgeted to them is being used productively. When the finance department understands how a particular marketing expenditure brings in traffic or aids in brand positioning, it is more likely to approve future marketing requests.

Think Critically

Should marketing departments be given a budget and then left alone to develop their marketing campaigns as they see fit, or should finance departments oversee marketing expenditures to ensure the desired results are produced? Explain your answer.

Sources:

Fripp, Geoff. "Difference between Marketing and Financial Goals." Marketing Study Guide. 2019. https://www.marketingstudyguide.com/difference-marketing-financial-goals/

Olenski, Steve. "5 Ways to Improve the Alliance Between Finance and Marketing." *Forbes.* April 7, 2015. https://www.forbes.com/sites/steveolenski/2015/04/07/5-ways-to-improve-the-alliance-between-finance-and-marketing/#9370e7470f99

Expenses involved in producing goods or services are categorized both by the amount of time it takes to use and or pay for the items and also by type of purchase.

Long- vs. Short-Term Expenses

Long-term expenses are for items the company can use for several years. Short-term expenses are for current activities or items used within a short time, typically less than one year. Long-term expenses are usually paid over an extended period of time. They often are financed by borrowing money from a bank or other financial institution. Normally, short-term expenses must be paid when purchases are made. Sometimes they are financed with credit from the seller and must be paid within one or a few months.

LONG-TERM EXPENSES Most long-term business costs apply to production or operations rather than marketing. The costs of land, buildings, and equipment are the typical expenses in this category. Some marketing plans identify land and building needs. A company that distributes products may need buildings, vehicles, and equipment for product storage and handling. Manufacturers who sell directly to customers through factory outlet stores need to build or rent facilities and equipment for retail operations. The increased use of technology in other parts of marketing requires investments in special equipment. For example, computers are essential for effective marketing research and marketing information management. Companies also must invest in high-speed Internet access, telephone and computer systems, and other office equipment as well as the personnel to manage the technology.

SHORT-TERM EXPENSES Most marketing expenses result from performing specific marketing activities that are completed in a short period of time. The specific types of expenses depend on the marketing mix, but most businesses commonly incur short-term expenses in areas such as salaries and wages, administrative costs, operating expenses, order processing, customer services, advertising and promotion, and transportation costs.

Types of Expenses

The three main types of marketing expenses are capital expenses, inventory expenses, and operating expenses. Marketers work with a company's executives and financial managers to identify how these expenses will be financed.

CAPITAL EXPENSES Long-term investments in land, buildings, and equipment are **capital expenses**. They usually are financed by money borrowed from a financial institution. Some manufacturers provide long-term loans to their customers to help finance a major equipment purchase. Companies also may lease equipment and buildings instead of buying them. The financial personnel of an organization usually are responsible to arrange for financing capital purchases.

INVENTORY EXPENSES The assortment and quantities of products that a company maintains for sale to customers is inventory. Inventories for manufacturers are produced with the anticipation that they will be sold to customers. For other channel members, inventories are purchased and then resold to their customers. The cost of the inventory is not recovered until the products are sold and the customer pays for the purchase.

Companies usually finance inventories in one of two ways. A company may obtain a short-term loan from a financial institution. Most banks will not loan the full value of the inventory because it may not sell as planned. A company also may finance its inventory through credit extended by the seller. Most sellers will finance the sale for only a short period, often 30 to 60 days, so the purchasing company must be able to sell the inventory quickly to pay for the order on time. In both cases, the purchaser pays interest on the money borrowed and factors the cost of financing into the price of the products.

OPERATING EXPENSES The final category of marketing expenses is operating expenses. **Operating expenses** are the costs of day-to-day marketing activities. They include salaries and wages, materials and supplies, advertising and other promotions, and customer services. Marketing expenses include the variety of other marketing activities completed regularly to sell products and services and to meet customer needs. These types of expenses normally are paid as they are incurred or shortly thereafter. The money for payment of operating expenses comes from the cash on hand in the business and the income from sales. Monthly and weekly budgets and financial reports monitor operating expenses and income to ensure that money is available to pay the expenses. Marketing managers pay careful attention to operating budgets and make changes rapidly if it appears that operating expenses are too high or revenues are too low.

CHECKPOINT
What is the difference in how capital expenses and operating expenses are typically financed?

20.1 ASSESSMENT

What Have You Learned?

1. What are some expenses related to the pricing element of the marketing mix? [20.1.1]

2. What is the difference between long-term and short-term expenses? [20.1.2]

Make Academic Connections

1. **Economics** Find at least one story related to a company's capital expenses in the newspaper or online. Find a second story related to another company's operating expenses. Summarize each article and explain why you classified each as relating to capital or operating expenses. [20.1.1]

2. **Math** Suppose your company takes a $25,000 loan for one year at 8 percent interest with equal monthly payments. Assuming the principal and interest will be paid at the end of the year, calculate the monthly payment on this loan. [20.1.2]

Connect to ◇DECA

Build your Portfolio

You work as a classroom aide at a nonprofit day-care center. Today, the director of the center remarked that a board member told her not to worry about watching expenses and revenues because the day-care center is a nonprofit organization. She asked you to prepare a brief but tactful report explaining to the board member why this perception is incorrect. Present your report to your teacher (judge). [20.1.1]

Learning Objectives

20.2.1 Describe the planning and operating tools businesses use.

20.2.2 Detail how marketers develop forecasts, budgets, and financial statements.

20.2.3 Explain the kinds of financial analyses marketers perform to increase profits.

Key Terms

financial forecast
budget
financial statement
income statement

balance sheet
assets
liabilities
owner's equity

marketing matters

Three factors contribute to the financial performance of a business—revenue, costs, and results (profit or loss). Managers are responsible for operating the business so that customers are satisfied, and the business makes a profit. Financial planning and operating tools help managers meet that responsibility. The primary planning tools are forecasts and budgets. Forecasts predict long-term financial performance, generally for periods of a year or longer. Budgets are shorter-term tools used to develop detailed plans for specific activities. The primary operating tools are income statements and balance sheets. Managers use these summaries of financial performance to develop marketing plans, improve decision making, and determine the effectiveness of business operations.

essential question

Why do both managers and investors need to understand a company's financial statements and reports?

20.2.1 ▶ Planning and Operating Tools

Businesses use a number of tools for planning and operating the company including forecasts, budgets, and financial statements.

Planning Tools

Businesses operate from plans. Plans identify the goals of the business and determine the best ways to achieve those goals. They guide the activities of employees. Plans are used to evaluate the progress of the business in meeting its goals. Two important types of financial plans are forecasts and budgets.

FORECASTS Financial plans are based on estimates of future events. Managers want those estimates to be as accurate as possible. They prepare forecasts to aid in planning. A **financial forecast** is a prediction of future performance related to revenue and expenses. Forecasts usually are made for a period of at least one year or longer. Some companies develop forecasts for as long as five years. However, because conditions can change, long-range forecasts usually are not as accurate as shorter forecasts. Software simulations are available that allow companies to integrate their own customer relationship management (CRM) data with Big Data, artificial intelligence, and learning algorithms to prepare forecasts.

The most important financial forecasts for marketing are sales, market share, and marketing expenses. Sales forecasts predict the quantity of sales (unit volume) or the amount of sales (dollar volume) for a product or a specific market. For example, a sales forecast may predict the sales of a product to increase by 6 percent for each of the next two years. Forecasts of market share anticipate the percentage of sales in a market that will be made by each of the major competitors. An appliance store that currently has 14 percent of the market in a city will need to determine how to respond to a forecast that projects its share dropping to 10 percent in two years. Expense forecasts project changes in the amount a company will need to spend for specific operations or activities. A forecast for an office supplies company that uses trucks to make deliveries to customers might project that transportation costs will increase by 24 percent over the next five years due to increased energy costs.

BUDGETS When planning for a shorter time period, managers use budgets. A **budget** is a detailed forecast of financial performance for a specific time period, usually one year or less. When managers identify the activities that must be completed to accomplish the goals of the business, they develop budgets to anticipate the costs of those activities and the revenue that can be expected to be generated by them. Two common examples of budgets used in marketing are sales and advertising budgets. Separate budgets are usually developed for each product, market, and major marketing activity.

Why do marketing managers need to develop several types of financial forecasts?

© wavebreakmedia/Shutterstock.com

Operating Tools

Managers use financial statements to gauge the effectiveness of operations. A **financial statement** is a detailed summary of the specific financial performance for a business or a part of the business. The important financial statements for marketers are income statements and balance sheets.

INCOME STATEMENT An **income statement** reports on the amount and sources of revenue and the amount and type of expenses for a specific period of time. Its purpose is to determine if the business earned a profit or loss on operations. A sample income statement is shown in **Figure 20-1**.

An income statement can be developed to analyze the profitability of the entire company or just one operating unit of the company. For example, Starbucks operates stores in many different countries. It can develop an income statement for the entire corporation, which includes the income and expenses of all stores in every country. It can also analyze the performance of all of the stores operating in a specific country or

region of a country. Additionally, each store will have its own income statement.

Managers also may want to determine the profitability of specific parts of the business operations. An income statement can be developed for a specific market, a category of

---

Dendum Products, Inc.
Income Statement
for the Six-Month Period Ending June 30, 20—

Revenues:

Gross Sales:

NE region	$123,528	
NW region	195,426	
SE region	232,965	
SW region	148,258	
Total Gross Sales		$700,177

Less Sales Returns:

NE region	$ 6,123	
NW region	5,896	
SE region	8,344	
SW region	7,421	
Total Sales Returns		27,784
Net Sales		$672,393

Cost of Products Sold:

Inventory, Jan. 1, 20—		$86,593	
Purchases	$583,226		
Less: Purchase Returns	−6,048		
Purchase Discounts	−3,582		
Net Purchases		573,596	
Total Cost of Products For Sale		$660,189	
Inventory, June 30, 20—		−78,190	
Net Cost of Products Sold			581,999
Gross Margin			$ 90,394

Operating Expenses:

Rent Expense	$ 8,225	
Bad Debts Expense	695	
Credit Card Fee Expense	1,200	
Transportation Expense	10,150	
Equipment Purchases	860	
Equipment Depreciation	620	
Insurance Expense	1,050	
Salaries and Wages	12,845	
Payroll Taxes	1,926	
Supplies Expense	734	
Advertising Expense	18,040	
Total Operating Expenses		$56,345
Net Income Before Taxes		$34,049

FIGURE 20-1 An income statement shows the relationship between sales and expenses in order to determine if operations are profitable.

customers, or a product or product category. The income statement in Figure 20-1 analyzes the financial performance of a company for a six-month period, with sales figures for four different regions of the country.

Marketers use income statements to determine if marketing activities are achieving an adequate sales volume. Income statements are also used to identify the costs of the activities needed to attain that sales volume.

BALANCE SHEET A **balance sheet** describes the type and amount of assets, liabilities, and owner's equity in a business on a specific date. **Assets** include the things the business owns. **Liabilities** are the amounts the business owes. The difference between the amount of assets and the amount of liabilities is the **owner's equity**. Managers must be able to identify changes in each of those amounts to determine if the financial condition of the business is improving or declining. **Figure 20-2** shows an example of a balance sheet for a corporation. Note that owners' equity for a corporation is reported as stockholders' equity, which includes two components: capital stock and retained earnings.

Important information that marketers obtain from balance sheets includes the value of assets used for marketing activities, the levels of inventory of products for sale, the amount owed by customers who have been offered credit, and the

amount owed by the company to its creditors. A balance sheet also identifies whether the company has money available to spend on items such as new product development, buildings, equipment, and other resources needed to improve marketing activities.

CHECKPOINT
What kinds of financial information do income statements contain?

Froerich Fundamentals, Inc.
Balance Sheet
December 31, 20—

Assets

Current Assets:

Cash	$ 95,436	
Accounts Receivable	42,827	
Product Inventory	135,673	
Supplies	21,128	
Prepaid Insurance	2,442	
Total Current Assets		$ 297,506

Noncurrent Assets:

Buildings	$ 647,545	
Vehicles	97,221	
Equipment	228,322	
Noncurrent Assets $973,088		
Less: Depreciation of Capital Assets	13,286	
Total Noncurrent Assets		959,802
Total Assets		$1,257,308

Liabilities

Current Liabilities:

Accounts Payable	$ 92,286	
Mortgage Payable	296,243	
Notes Payable	63,552	
Payroll Taxes Payable	71,074	
Insurance Payable	6,995	
Total Liabilities		$ 530,150

Stockholder's Equity

Capital Stock	$440,478	
Retained Earnings	$286,680	
Total Stockholder's Equity		727,158
Total Liabilities and Stockholder's Equity		$1,257,308

FIGURE 20-2 A balance sheet shows the relationship between the assets and liabilities of a business.

Marketers work with finance and accounting experts to develop and use financial tools such as forecasts, budgets, and financial statements. Some of the information they use to prepare these tools comes from the marketing department and its operations. The reports are prepared in accounting and finance and then distributed to marketing managers for use in decision making. Marketers must be able to understand and interpret forecasts, budgets, and financial statements. Marketers use the information to develop marketing plans and to make changes and improvements in marketing operations.

© Leah-Anne Thompson/Shutterstock.com.

Develop Forecasts and Budgets

Planners use several methods to develop accurate forecasts and budgets.

PAST PERFORMANCE   Financial plans are most commonly based on past performance. By comparing the forecasts and budgets from previous years with the actual results, planners can see which ones were accurate and which were not.

INDUSTRY PERFORMANCE   Another method is to use information from comparable businesses and markets to develop plans. New businesses frequently rely on this method to develop forecasts and budgets because they have limited past performance on which to base projections. Often, trade associations or private information services companies collect and report the financial performance of businesses in a particular industry. Some federal and state government agencies, such as the U.S. Department of Commerce, gather and report financial information.

MARKETING-RELATED DATA   Planners also can look for data that help to predict performance. For example, the number of tires an auto service business might sell can be based on the number of cars in a market and the age of those cars. The original tires on a car will normally need to be replaced between three and four years after the car is sold. Identifying those cars in the business's target market will help in developing a forecast for tire sales.

MARKETING PLAN   The most effective way to develop a budget for marketing expenses is to calculate the costs of performing the necessary marketing tasks. The marketing plan describes the marketing activities necessary to implement the marketing mix. The marketing manager analyzes each of the planned activities to determine what personnel and resources will be needed. Then the wages, costs of resources, and the amounts of all other expenses are matched with each activity. When all of those items are totaled, the marketing manager has a specific estimate of the amount to budget for that activity **(Figure 20-3)**.

Gather Information for Financial Statements

The information used to prepare income statements and balance sheets is the actual financial performance of the business.

Therefore, the marketing department is responsible for maintaining accurate records on sales, expenses, inventory levels, customer accounts, and equipment.

For most businesses, when a sale is made, information about the customer, product, and terms of the sale is captured electronically. Information is entered using a cash register or point of purchase terminal, a keyboard, a touchscreen, an electronic pen, or a scanner. Scanners read barcodes on products and then send the data to a computer database. Scanners also may be used to keep track of inventory as products move through the manufacturing and distribution process.

 CHECKPOINT
Where do businesses obtain the information they need to develop financial statements, forecasts, and budgets?

DEVELOPING A BUDGET FOR A MARKETING ACTIVITY

Planned Monthly Customer Service Department Expenses

Management Salary	$ 4,028
Personnel Wages	18,840
Facility Expense (space and utilities)	3,526
Office Equipment	305
Telephone Expense	498
Computer Expense	295
Postage	86
Supplies	175
Travel Expense	830
Product Returns and Replacements	644
Total Budgeted Expenses	$29,227

FIGURE 20-3 This budget helps managers analyze the costs and benefits of operating a customer service department.

20.2.3 ▶ Analyze Financial Information

Information available from financial tools can be valuable in improving marketing decisions. Forecasts and budgets are evaluated to determine their accuracy. The projections are compared with actual performance. Any differences are studied to determine why they occurred. If projections proved inaccurate, the methods used to develop forecasts and budgets may need to be modified or the marketing activities improved.

Use Financial Information

Marketing managers evaluate financial statements to determine the changes that occur from one period of operations to the next. They study various markets to determine if sales are increasing or decreasing.

Inventory levels can be compared from year to year as can the amounts owed by customers. If the information shows that the financial performance is improving, a marketing manager will want to continue with the same activities. If sales are decreasing or inventories are increasing too quickly, marketing activities may need to be changed.

Another method of analysis is to compare one type of financial performance to another. For example, sales volume can be compared to advertising expenses. If expenses are going up at a faster rate than sales, a problem may be developing. Other important comparisons in marketing are the level of inventory to sales, costs of transportation compared to costs of product handling and storage, and product cost compared to marketing expenses.

Marketers need many types of information for their efforts to be effective. Marketing research provides information to aid in understanding customers. Financial information is needed to determine what marketing activities the organization can afford to complete and the impact of those activities on profits.

Marketers use financial information to identify how to increase revenue and reduce costs. As shown in **Figure 20-4**, if a greater volume of sales can be achieved while controlling expenses, profits will increase. If sales can be maintained while reducing the costs of marketing, the company also will be able to increase profits.

Increase Revenues

Increased revenue results from selling more products and services. Marketers analyze financial information to

Want to know more about what is trending with this topic? Click on **Lesson 20.2, Marketing Decisions,** *in your MindTap.*

Connect to MindTap

determine the products that sell the best and the customer groups that buy the most products. They concentrate their efforts on the best products and markets and either improve or remove poorly performing products and markets. Each time they develop a new marketing plan, they identify the most important products and markets.

Marketers also need to be sure the product is priced correctly. The company may be able to sell more units to customers if it offers discounts or reduces the price. Yet the lower price may reduce revenue to the point where a profit cannot be made. Salespeople who understand customer needs make an effective presentation of the entire marketing mix in response to those needs. They know that customers look for the best value, not the lowest price.

Control Costs

Marketing managers are very concerned about reducing and controlling the costs of marketing activities. When businesses are in competitive markets, the company that operates most efficiently is more likely to make a profit. Businesses that are concerned about satisfying customer needs must be very careful in cutting costs. Marketing activities that are important to customers cannot be eliminated without considering the impact on customer satisfaction. It is often possible to find ways to perform marketing activities in a less costly

Marketing Strategies to Increase Profits

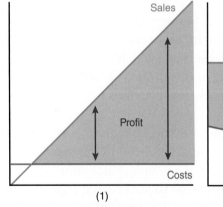 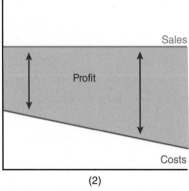

FIGURE 20-4 When the goal of a business is increased profits, marketers have two basic choices related to managing costs: (1) They can increase sales while holding costs steady. (2) If sales are not increasing, they can reduce the cost of achieving those sales.

way while keeping the same level of customer service.

As an example, an insurance company provided its salespeople with personal computers to reduce the number of forms to be completed. The company also wanted to cut the time it took for information to be exchanged between the salesperson and the company. With the technology, salespeople entered information directly into forms on the computer rather than completing printed copies of the form to be processed by data entry personnel. The company found that even with the cost of laptops, the new procedure not only reduced expenses by more than 15 percent but also cut the number of errors on insurance applications by nearly 5 percent.

Another example of reducing marketing expenses comes from a large supermarket in the Southeast. It operates a large fleet of trucks to deliver products from its warehouses to its stores. The trucks would deliver the products and return to the warehouse empty. The transportation manager started to identify suppliers of products that were located in the towns where the supermarket had stores. When a truck was delivering a load from the warehouse to a store, the manager would determine if a nearby supplier had an order to be sent to the warehouse. If so, the supermarket's truck would pick up the order rather than driving back empty. This procedure saved the company thousands of dollars each month in transportation costs.

© Goodluz/Shutterstock.com

How does providing up-to-date technology to salespeople help a business control costs?

Both marketing employees and managers need to be aware of the costs of marketing activities and identify ways to reduce expenses. It is often possible to identify ways to perform marketing activities more efficiently to reduce the amount of supplies or materials or eliminate waste.

Many companies provide incentives for employees who identify cost savings.

CHECKPOINT
What are the two basic ways that businesses can increase profits?

20.2 ASSESSMENT

What Have You Learned?

1. What kinds of financial information do balance sheets contain? [20.2.1]

2. What is the most effective way to develop a budget for marketing expenses? [20.2.2]

3. For businesses concerned with satisfying customer needs, what types of costs must they be careful about cutting? [20.2.3]

Make Academic Connections

1. **Finance**   Use the Internet to locate the financial statements of a business you admire and find (a) the company's net income before taxes last year, and (b) the dollar amount of the company's value (capital). Record these figures and explain which financial statement you used to find the information. [20.2.1]

2. **Ethics**   Suppose a cell phone manufacturer decides to cut costs by reducing the terms of its product warranties from two years to one year. Do you think this decision is ethical? Why or why not? What would you think if data shows that about 8 percent of the company's best-selling model becomes defective after about 18 months of use? [20.2.3]

Connect to ◇DECA

Build your Portfolio

You and a friend have decided to start a small computer repair shop. You are new entrepreneurs, so your business has no past performance on which to base a budget. Using the library or Internet, compile a list of resources you can use to help you prepare the first budget for your business. Estimate revenues and expenses and create a startup budget for your new business. Present it to your teacher (judge) and explain how you arrived at the amounts in your budget. [20.2.2]

How do credit card companies obtain new card holders? How do they approach existing card holders who don't use their cards? Credit marketing managers work to increase the use of credit cards among consumers. Encouraging potential customers to obtain credit cards through various promotional efforts and determining the appropriate target groups for direct-mail marketing campaigns are among the strategies they employ.

Job Titles

- Online Marketing Manager
- Co-Branding Credit Card Marketer
- Direct Mail Credit Manager
- Credit Card Portfolio Manager
- Credit Sales Manager

Needed Skills

- A bachelor's degree with a major in a quantitative business discipline (such as accounting or finance) usually is required.
- A thorough knowledge of laws, regulations, and tax implications specific to the credit card industry is necessary.
- Continuing education, either through a university or professional society, is needed to remain current with changes affecting the industry.

What it's like to work in...
Credit Marketing Management

As a credit marketing manager at a large department store, Miguel is responsible for expanding the use of credit cards within each division of the company. This morning he analyzed the effectiveness of a direct mail campaign to prospective customers that he had initiated. By comparing the forecasted growth of credit cards to the actual growth of credit cards for each division, Miguel could gauge the campaign's effectiveness. Miguel needed to follow up with representatives from each of the two divisions that had not met their forecast. He wants to understand why the forecasts were not met in order to develop a new, more effective campaign.

Tomorrow Miguel will teach a course for recently hired credit marketing representatives. Miguel wants to ensure that each representative is well versed in the incentives offered to credit card holders. For example, many consumers were eager to sign up for a store credit card when they learned that they would receive an additional 10 percent off all store purchases made with the store credit card.

What About You?

Would you like to help a corporation increase the use of its credit cards among its customers? Why or why not?

Connect to MindTap

Discover more about the outlook for this career and watch a video about a related career. Click on **Chapter 20, Planning a Career In...** *in your MindTap.*

Learning Objectives

20.3.1 Explain the various ways businesses raise revenue through marketing activities.

20.3.2 Describe the marketing expenses that arise with each element of the marketing mix.

Key Term

accounts receivable

marketing matters

Marketing managers need to decide on the best way to use the marketing budget. They do that by analyzing the revenues expected and expenses involved in marketing. Most of the revenue comes from the sale of primary products and services. Secondary and after-sale products and services also may contribute substantially to revenues and profits. Offering credit can generate revenues from interest earned as well as from sales to customers who otherwise could not buy. Completing marketing activities also incurs costs associated with each of the four marketing mix elements.

essential question

Why should a business that is having difficulty making a profit focus on both increasing revenues and reducing costs rather than just cutting costs?

20.3.1 ▶ Effects of Marketing on Revenue

A marketing strategy provides the basis for developing the marketing budget. The marketing strategy identifies the target markets the business intends to serve and the marketing mixes to be used for each market. Marketers prepare a written marketing plan to show how the business will implement the marketing strategy. The plan describes the activities to be completed and the resources needed.

Managers who develop a marketing plan often find they do not have adequate resources to develop the most effective marketing mix. For example, research might show that customers prefer a product with several options they can purchase from a large number of outlets. Yet the company cannot afford to spend money on both product improvements and more extensive distribution. It needs to decide between putting more money into the product or more money into distribution. That decision often is based on which of the mix elements is most important to the customer, the type of mix offered by the competition, and the actual costs of each choice to the company.

The marketing mix and budget also are affected by the way the company has spent money in the past. If the company was responsible for the transportation of its products, it may have invested in trucks or other equipment needed to move products from the business to customers. Warehouses or distribution centers may have been built to handle the inventory.

Marketing activities are completed in order to generate revenue. Most of the revenue for a business results from the sale of products and services. The marketing plan identifies the markets the company plans to serve. Marketing activities are developed to meet the needs of customers in the market so they will purchase the products or services offered by the company. There are several parts of the marketing mix that can affect the amount of revenue. Sources of revenue affected by mix elements include sales, after-sale products and services, and interest earned on credit services.

Sales of Products and Services

The primary objective of a marketing strategy is for the business to obtain the most profitable level of sales possible while satisfying a target market. The marketing mix is developed to increase customer satisfaction by offering a product or service that is different from and better than the competition. The most important source of revenue for an organization is from the sale of its primary products and services. A company can improve a product and increase revenue by offering additional features and options, better packaging, or customer services. It can make the product available

A company has always relied on other businesses to store and transport its products. Will it be more or less costly for this company to make changes in distribution strategies than if it owned those resources?

in a more convenient or appropriate location. It also can offer credit to make the product more affordable.

Promotion and other types of communication show the customer the value of the product and how it can be used most effectively. Marketers need to study the likely impact of each mix choice on sales and profits and then select the mix that achieves the best combination for the company.

Several factors can reduce the level of sales. Customers may not be satisfied with a product because it is damaged, is not what the seller promised, or does not meet customer needs. In those cases,

Want to know more about marketing in the information age? Click on **Lesson 20.3, Digital Marketing,** in your MindTap.

Connect to MindTap

MATH IN MARKETING

Unit Sales Provide Another Perspective

One way in which marketers analyze sales is to distinguish between the dollar volume and unit volume. Dollar volume is measured by the revenue derived from sales. Unit volume is the number of products or services that are sold. Regardless of the dollar volume on an income statement for a given period, the number of units sold can be a good indication of where the business is headed.

Marketers can quickly derive unit sales from dollar volume by dividing sales revenue by the price per unit or by the average price per unit. Conversely, the average price per unit sold can be calculated by dividing dollar volume by the number of units sold.

Flat or declining unit sales usually are a sign of trouble. Perhaps one of the target markets for a product or service is maturing, and new markets need to be developed to stimulate growth. Or maybe competitors have grabbed a larger share of the market. A decline in unit sales accompanied by increasing revenues might indicate that prices are too high. Often, price increases will boost dollar volume initially. Customers may continue to buy the product, but as time goes by, they begin to search for and find cheaper, equally effective alternatives.

Do the Math

1. The dollar volume of sales for a product increases 4.5 percent, and the number of units sold increases 10 percent. What happens to the average price per unit?

2. An income statement indicates that total revenue for a product line was $10 million. The basic model costs $250, and a new advanced model costs $400. The unit volume of basic models was 30,000. How many advanced models were sold?

---

customers will return the product to the seller and expect a replacement or a refund. Returned and replacement products reduce the level of sales and add to the seller's costs.

The seller may offer the customer a discount on the price charged if the customer is not satisfied or receives less than promised. Again, the discounts reduce the sales revenue. If the company offers a rebate to customers, the amount of the rebate must be subtracted from the original sales amount.

After-Sale Revenue

It has been said that a current customer can be more profitable than a prospective customer. Therefore, marketers may attempt to increase sales to existing customers while satisfying their needs. Automobile dealers and movie theaters provide two examples of this marketing strategy.

Automobile sales is a very competitive business. Customers carefully shop for the best price, so dealerships often have to cut prices so low that they make little profit on the sale of the automobiles. Profit for the business comes from activities that occur after the sale. A very important source of revenue and profit for automobile dealers comes from servicing and repairing automobiles they have sold. They work very hard to encourage customers to return to the dealership for service.

Similarly, many movie theaters rely on the sale of other products to operate profitably. Most movies are shown several times a day for many weeks. The first few times a new movie is shown, the theater may be full of customers, and the sale of tickets itself will generate profit. Later on, however, fewer customers will come to see the movie. The sale of concession items (pop-corn, soft drinks, candy) provides the opportunity for the theater to make a profit when ticket sales alone do not.

What kinds of products and services might a garden store offer to generate after-sale revenue?

Sometimes businesses identify other ways of generating revenues in addition to the sale of the primary products and services. Restaurants may sell T-shirts, coffee mugs, or packaged popular menu items such as pasta sauce or baked goods. Those sales are both effective promotional tools and another source of revenue. In the northern states, landscaping and grass-cutting businesses often see their profits reduced during winter months because of cold weather. People do not need to have much yard work done in the late fall and winter. However, some of these companies may contract with cities, large businesses, and even homeowners to clean the snow from streets, parking lots, and driveways. This provides revenue during a time when they otherwise would not be able to operate.

Credit and Interest

Many purchases are made with cash, and the seller receives payment as soon as the sale is made. If credit is offered to customers, the sale is not complete. A company's balance sheet often includes an item called accounts receivable. **Accounts receivable** are sales for which the company has not yet been paid. Credit often is offered to increase sales beyond the amount that is possible if customers had to pay cash.

CREDIT CARDS Many businesses use credit services offered by other companies rather than developing and managing a credit department. For example, a retail store may accept credit cards such as MasterCard, Visa, or American Express. The credit card company pays the retailer the amount of the purchase. It is then the credit card company's responsibility to collect the money from the customer. In return for using the credit card company, the retail business is charged a fee that usually amounts to 2 percent or more of the total amount of its credit sales.

Some companies have their own credit systems that can be used only for the purchase of products from their business. There are several costs for companies that choose to manage their own credit services. The company needs to determine the terms that will be offered to customers. It must then hire and train personnel to manage the credit system. Computers and other equipment are needed to maintain the credit records, billing, payments, and other information. Businesses offering credit usually charge interest to their customers who do not pay their account balance in a reasonable time. If those accounts are ultimately paid in full, it is possible that the interest charges will provide a profit for the company.

UNPAID CREDIT   Even with the most careful and effective credit system, some customers do not pay their accounts when billed. Even a small amount that remains unpaid can eliminate any profit the company makes on credit sales and reduces the total dollar amount of sales. Companies offering credit to customers work to develop effective credit procedures to reduce the amount of unpaid accounts. If an account remains unpaid for several months beyond its due date, it likely will never be paid.

No matter how carefully a company manages credit accounts, it likely will have at least a small percentage of credit sales that are uncollectible. Those uncollected accounts and the cost of collection activities are a significant business expense. Businesses must carefully study whether the increases in sales resulting from credit actually add to or reduce their profits.

REGULATION   Companies that offer credit need to be aware of laws that regulate credit activity. Among the important federal laws is the Equal Credit Opportunity Act, which prevents companies from discriminating among the people to whom they offer credit. The Truth-in-Lending Act specifies the type of information businesses must provide to credit customers. The Fair Credit Reporting Act regulates

WORKING IN TEAMS

As a team, locate several advertisements in which a company is offering credit or leasing terms to customers. Study the leasing or credit disclosure information in the ads that businesses are required to include by federal and state regulation. (The information is usually in small print at the bottom of the ad.) How do the terms or the offers differ? Do you think the disclosure requirement and how it is presented are helpful to customers? Why or why not?

the use of the credit information that businesses gather about individual customers. Also, the methods companies use to collect money owed by customers are controlled under the Fair Debt Collection Practices Act.

CHECKPOINT
What activity has the biggest impact on the amount of revenue a business generates?

20.3.2 ▶ Expenses and the Marketing Mix

Each marketing mix element has associated expenses.

Product Expenses

The majority of expenses related to product development for manufacturers is a part of the production budget. Those expenses include the cost of materials, equipment, and personnel needed to produce the product. Also, the cost of packaging is considered a production cost. For wholesale and retail businesses, product expenses include the prices they pay to purchase the merchandise.

Other product expenses include those related to offering a guarantee or warranty, as well as the costs of repairing items that are damaged or fail. In addition, many businesses offer customer services, some of which can be very expensive.

Some services, such as delivery and setup or training, are offered as part of the actual sale. Other services are provided for a long time after the sale while the customer is using the product. For example, KitchenAid has a toll-free telephone number that customers can call to get information about the use of any product the company manufactures, ranging from small appliances to large industrial equipment. Several automobile manufacturers offer 24-hour-a-day roadside repair service for their customers.

Distribution Expenses

Distribution costs are a major area of marketing expenses. Companies must pay to transport, store, and display their products. These costs include long-term expenses, such as buildings and equipment, and short-term expenses, such as wages and supplies. Even service businesses have expenses associated with delivering the services to customers or operating the location where customers come to purchase the services. In addition to the obvious costs of distribution, other expenses for most businesses include the costs of developing and managing the channels of distribution, inventory control costs, materials handling expenses, the costs of order processing, and even government-imposed expenses such as operating licenses and local, state, and federal taxes.

Price Expenses

The major expense related to the price mix element is the cost of offering credit. Another price expense item is the cost of communicating prices to customers.

Although this may seem like an unimportant item, consider the thousands of items that a business stocks and sells during one year. If each item needs a price tag, the cost of printing the stickers or tags and the expense of placing them on the products can be high. This cost increases if a price change needs to be made. Many retail businesses have introduced other methods to control the expense of pricing products. For example, instead of attaching a price sticker to products, the price is posted on the display shelf. The price is stored in the company's computer and is identified through a barcode on the product package. The price is changed by changing the amount in the computer and updating the price on the product display shelf.

Promotion Expenses

Many costs are associated with promotion, and most methods of communicating with customers are expensive. Each type of promotion has its own set of expenses.

Advertising is the most common type of promotion. The major cost of advertising is buying time on television or radio or purchasing space for ads in newspapers, magazines, or online. It also is expensive to create and produce the advertisements. These expenses include the salaries of a variety of creative people as well as the equipment and materials they need for their work. For online advertising, Web pages need to be designed and updated frequently, computers and servers must be maintained, and customer service personnel must be available whenever customers

*Want to know more about what is trending with this topic? Click on **Lesson 20.3, Global Marketing,** in your MindTap.*

Connect to
MindTap

contact the company to answer questions via chat, email, or telephone.

Personal selling also is an expensive promotional method with the biggest cost being the salaries of salespeople. Additional costs include training and management as well as the equipment, materials, and product samples salespeople use. Salespeople for manufacturers often travel regularly to meet with customers. Their sales territories can cover several states or countries. Transportation costs, hotel rooms, meals, and other expenses can amount to hundreds of dollars each day.

It is said that the most inexpensive form of promotion is word-of-mouth. But companies that want customers to help sell their products often spend money to ensure that it is done well. When a customer buys a product, the company may make a follow-up phone call or send letters and gifts to show that it appreciates the customer's business. Some companies offer satisfied customers money or other incentives if they identify a prospective customer who then buys a product.

CHECKPOINT
Which elements of the marketing mix give rise to related marketing expenses?

20.3 ASSESSMENT

What Have You Learned?

1. Name the sources of revenue affected by marketing mix elements. [20.3.1]

2. What are some of the expenses associated with the product element of the marketing mix? [20.3.2]

Make Academic Connections

1. **Research**   Conduct online research to find the costs of at least five different advertising media (radio, television, newspaper, digital, etc.). Prepare a table listing each media type and its costs. [20.3.2]

2. **Government**   Use the library or Internet to find information about the Fair Debt Collection Practices Act. When was it passed? What are its major provisions? What effect has it had on the debt-collection industry? Report your findings in a two- to three-page paper. [20.3.1]

Connect to ◇DECA.
Build your Portfolio

You work in the marketing department for a local coffee shop chain. To increase revenue, you have been asked for some ideas about products to sell other than hot coffee, the stores' primary product. Describe the target markets and the types of products you would recommend to your teacher (judge). Explain why your ideas would be effective and profitable. [20.3.1]

Connect to MindTap

*Analyze a case study that focuses on chapter concepts. Click on **Chapter 20, Case Study,** in your MindTap.*

CHAPTER 20 **ASSESSMENT**

Review Marketing Concepts

1. Why is effective marketing so important to an organization's financial planning process? [20.1.1]

2. Marketing expenses are categorized as capital expenses, inventory expenses, and operating expenses. Which of these do you think represents the highest priority and which represents the lowest priority for a business? [20.1.2]

3. Compare and contrast financial forecasts and budgets. Give examples of each. [20.2.1]

4. Managers use information about past performance to develop forecasts and budgets. Provide three examples of events or situations that would make past performance an invalid indicator of future performance. [20.2.2]

5. To increase profits, companies can either try to increase revenues or control costs. Which of these do you think would be more effective? [20.2.3]

6. You are the marketing manager for a popular online video game. Suggest ways you can increase after-sale revenue. [20.3.1]

7. Your local drug store doesn't put a visible price tag on the items it sells. Instead it lists the prices on the shelf below the product and embeds the price in a barcode on the items. What are the benefits for the store of this pricing practice? [20.3.2]

Marketing Research and Planning

1. Two important methods of planning and analyzing financial information are (1) comparable information from similar businesses, and (2) the costs of performing specific marketing tasks and activities.

   A number of reference books published by the federal government, trade and professional associations, and private businesses contain this information. Using the library, a business information encyclopedia, business reference books, the Internet, or the resources of a businessperson you know, identify at least two sources of financial information available to marketers. Review one of the sources and prepare a written summary of the information the reference contains. Provide examples of the specific information. [20.2.2]

2. You are the marketing manager for Enviro-Safe, a company that has developed a new type of lawn care product that controls weeds and insects without chemicals. The product is currently sold through garden centers in eight states in the northwestern United States. You are responsible for all distribution and promotional activities and for completing marketing research. You work with other managers to set product prices, to develop and provide customer services, and to complete new product planning. You believe that you can make the most effective decisions if you have financial information available related to the marketing activities you control.

   Write a one-page memo to Frances Payton, chief financial officer of EnviroSafe. Identify the types of financial information you need, list the financial tools that will help with planning and operations, and explain why it is important for the marketing manager to be involved in financial planning for the business. Use information from the chapter to help you prepare the memo. [20.1.1, 20.1.2, 20.2.1, 20.2.2, 20.2.3, 20.3.1, 20.3.2]

3. One of the methods of forecasting sales for products and services is to identify relationships between two products or services. The example in the chapter suggested that the volume of automobile sales can be used to predict the sale of automobile tires. If businesspeople can identify similar relationships among products and services, they can increase the effectiveness of their forecasts. List at least 10 other product/service relationships where you think the sale of one affects the sale of the other. Two more examples are given to help you. [20.2.1]

The sale of	Is related to the sale of
computers	computer software
winter coats	gloves and hats

Marketing Management and Decision Making

1. A school club needs to raise funds to pay for a trip to a state conference. The members want to plan a fundraiser that will be fun, provide a community service, and result in a reasonable profit for the club. The idea being considered is an international food celebration. The club would be responsible for contacting community groups to staff a booth in which a specific type of food would be sold. The group also would develop a display representing each country's culture or provide a short presentation (dance, historical story, and so on) about each culture. The event would be held on a Saturday afternoon for three hours in the school's gymnasium. People would come to sample the food and to enjoy the presentations. For financial planning, some of the anticipated costs are shown in the table.

The plan is to sell booths for the celebration. There is space for up to 40 booths in the gymnasium if three tables are used per booth. The groups would be able to sell their food and keep all revenues from the sale after paying the booth fee. An admission fee could be charged, and other products, such as T-shirts and souvenir cups, could be sold.

Develop a plan of activities the club should follow in planning and managing the celebration. Include all aspects of a marketing mix (product development, distribution, pricing, promotion). Based on the plan of activities, prepare a budget for the celebration using the income statement format illustrated in the chapter. Include projections of all types of revenues and reasonable expenses. Estimate those expenses for which no costs are given. Develop at least three projections of revenues using alternative prices charged for the booths, varying admission prices, or different attendance levels.

Expense Category	Cost
Gymnasium rental	$300
Table rental for booths (minimum of 50 tables)	$3 per table
Security	$45 per hour
Insurance	$80
Labor costs (Set up, tear down, cleaning)	$6 per hour
Possible Promotional Materials	
Flyers	$0.08 each
Posters	$0.45 each
Envelopes and postage	$0.32 each
30-second radio ad	$58 each (10 for $500) + $80 production costs (fixed)
Salesperson commission	$8/booth sold

Calculate the impact on profit or loss. [20.1.1, 20.1.2, 20.2.1]

2. A hardware store has decided to add free delivery as a service for customers who purchase more than $250 of merchandise in one order. Delivery also will be available to other customers, but a delivery fee will be charged. The store can purchase a delivery van for $18,000. Three methods of financing the van are being considered.

   a. The store's bank will provide a one-year capital improvement loan at 9 percent interest. To qualify for the loan, the company must maintain 150 percent of the value of the vehicle in checking or savings accounts with the bank.

   b. A finance company will purchase all of the company's accounts receivable for 86 percent of their value. The store's accounts receivable currently are valued at $26,000.

   c. The store can use cash on hand to make the purchase. The current balance sheet for the store shows the cash balance is $31,800. The cash budget for the coming 12 months shows that the highest projected cash total during that time is $38,000 and the lowest projected cash total is $12,200.

   Analyze the three sources of financing to determine the direct cost of each to the business and the possible advantages and disadvantages of each method. Prepare a written recommendation of the method you think the store should use to finance the delivery van. [20.1.2, 20.3.2]

3. Search the Internet for a public corporation's annual report and find the section that discloses its revenues, costs, and results for three or more years. Using a spreadsheet program, calculate the percentage increase in sales revenue for each year. Also, calculate the ratio of sales revenue to earnings or net income. Print the results of your calculations. [20.2.1]

Let's Start a Band! Follow-Up Discussion

Work in small teams to discuss the question posed at the end of the opening vignette. What advice can you give the band about handling its finances and developing a financial plan?

Build Your Marketing Plan

Build your Portfolio

In this chapter you learned how to finance and budget for marketing activities. You will now apply this learning to the development of your marketing plan. To access the chapter-specific tools that you will need to complete this activity, please navigate to Chapter 19 ➜ Build Your Marketing Plan in MindTap. Alternatively, you can access these tools online at NGLSync. Please visit www.nglsync.cengage.com, and search for the companion website that accompanies this book by entering the ISBN, author, or title. Once you locate this companion website, navigate to Build Your Marketing Plan ➜ Chapter 19.

Financial Services Team Decision Making Event

DECA PREP

Student Lawn Services has been a successful lawn service operation for the past two years. It is located in a growing suburb of a large city that has a mild climate year-round.

The owner of Student Lawn Services started the business by maintaining the yards for five customers. He gives satisfied customers poinsettias in December as an expression of customer appreciation. The business has grown rapidly through word-of-mouth advertising from satisfied customers. It has expanded to 50 customers who require weekly lawn services. Profits from the business operation allowed him to upgrade his lawn equipment.

The owner has become overwhelmed with the growth of the business. Competitors have entered the market in hopes of winning over some of his business. However, customers still prefer the personal touch Student Lawn Services provides, and the prices are reasonable compared to the competition.

The owner of Student Lawn Services has called upon your financial management team to suggest strategies for the business to keep up with increasing demand for personalized lawn service. Much of this demand is due to an expanding community and numerous new housing developments.

The owner began the business as a sole proprietorship. He is considering partnering with some of the competing lawn service businesses in the community.

Your team must outline a strategy for Student Lawn Services to successfully stay in business. Your team must explain the advantages and disadvantages of partnering with another business. Your team must also explain pricing strategies for lawn services.

You have 30 minutes to prepare your presentation, 10 minutes to present your plan to the owner of Student Lawn Services (judge), and 5 minutes to answer the judge's questions about your plan.

Performance Indicators Evaluated

- Explain the concept of productivity. (Economics)
- Explain the concept of economic resources. (Economics)
- Describe the concepts of economics and economic activities. (Economics)
- Explain the principles of supply and demand. (Economics)
- Determine factors affecting business risk. (Economics)
- Establish relationship with customer/client. (Selling)
- Explain the types of business ownership. (Business Law)

Go to the DECA website for more detailed information. **www.deca.com**

Think Critically

1. Why is financial management important for a growing business?

2. How does this case involve supply and demand?

3. What is the advantage of partnering with a competitor?

4. What public relations campaign can Student Lawn Services use to maintain positive relationships with customers?

CHAPTER 21

ENTREPRENEURSHIP AND MARKETING

See how effective advertising leads to successful marketing strategies.
Click on Chapter 21, Visual Focus, **in your MindTap.**

Let's Start a Band!

"I came to music knowing a little bit about life, and I came to music knowing a lot about business—and that's a real advantage."

– *Mary Gauthier, Grammy-Nominated Folksinger–Songwriter*

I know you told me once that we were entrepreneurs. I never thought of us that way. We were just a band. But the other day before rehearsal we were talking about the money we're bringing in now that we've become a regional act. Some of us thought we should have a better understanding of the band as a business. We all agreed we need some kind of business structure.

I told them I've been consulting with you on business matters, and you'd mentioned several options we had for organizing the band as a business. I told them I would look into this and do my best to lay out the advantages and disadvantages of each option. Can you help us decide which form of legal ownership would be best for the band?

UNDERSTAND ENTREPRENEURSHIP

Learning Objectives

21.1.1 Define *entrepreneur* and *entrepreneurship*.

21.1.2 Describe the importance of entrepreneurship to the U.S. economy.

21.1.3 Identify personal characteristics of entrepreneurs.

21.1.4 Describe the education needed to prepare for entrepreneurship.

Key Terms

entrepreneur
entrepreneurship
risk-taking
self-confidence
creativity
netiquette

marketing matters

Entrepreneurs are willing to take risks to start businesses. Successful entrepreneurs often start several companies during their business careers. Once the business is established, however, many entrepreneurs do not succeed when they are required to make the transition to the role of manager. Creativity, determination, risk-taking, and willingness to take responsibility and make decisions are all important characteristics for entrepreneurs to have.

essential question

Why is it important in a free enterprise economy to have people who are willing to take risks to start new businesses?

21.1.1 ▶ What Is an Entrepreneur?

You may have heard the story of Henry Ford, who created Ford Motor Company. Today, Ford Motor Company is a giant international corporation. But it had its beginnings in 1896 when Henry Ford produced his first automobile in a Michigan garage. Bill Gates provides another example of a person who started with an idea and developed a successful large business, the Microsoft Corporation. The idea for the company began when, as college students, Bill and his friend Paul Allen developed a computer program to operate the first personal computers. Many other people have put their personal stamps on the U.S. economy with business ideas and the commitment to bring the ideas to life in new companies.

People go into business to make a profit, but they also start their own businesses to have the freedom to do work they enjoy and to take responsibility for the success or failure of the business. Few things are more rewarding than seeing your ideas and efforts grow into a profitable business, offering jobs to others, and providing products and services that satisfy customers. On the other hand, being a business owner presents a continuing challenge to meet a payroll, pay the bills, and find ways to compete successfully.

An **entrepreneur** is someone who takes the risk to start a new business. That risk involves investing his or her money in the business. **Entrepreneurship** is the process of planning, creating, and managing a new business. Entrepreneurship requires both innovation and business savvy.

An entrepreneur is different from a business manager. A manager is responsible for a business created and owned by others. The manager is an employee and so takes direction from the owners of the business. The owners must approve any major change in the business.

WORKING IN TEAMS

Team members should think about the work of entrepreneurs and of business managers and prepare one list of differences between them and one list of similarities they share. Compare the items in the two lists and discuss whether entrepreneurs and managers are more alike or more different.

The manager does not take on the financial risks faced by owners. If the business fails, the manager will lose a job but will not have lost any money invested in the business.

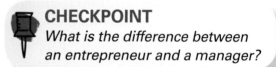

CHECKPOINT
What is the difference between an entrepreneur and a manager?

21.1.2 ▶ The Importance of Entrepreneurship

Small business and entrepreneurship are not the same thing. Not all small businesses are owned and operated by entrepreneurs. Many people buy and operate an existing small business or a franchise and so may not be considered entrepreneurs. Nevertheless, almost all businesses developed by entrepreneurs start out as small businesses.

Economic Role

Entrepreneurs develop small businesses, and small businesses are important to the U.S. economy because they create jobs. According to a Small Business Administration (SBA) report, small businesses—those with fewer than 500 employees—account for 99.9 percent of U.S. businesses. Almost half of U.S. employees (excluding government employees) work in a small business.

Small businesses are more likely to hire younger and older workers and workers who need part-time jobs. Small businesses have historically been the source of the initial job training for many people. A first part-time or full-time job working for a small business teaches important lessons such as time management, human relations, and good work habits as well as the knowledge and skills to perform the job.

Personal Benefits

Entrepreneurs work long hours to make their businesses successful. They sacrifice to invest their savings and often have little or no income for the first few years of operations. They are responsible for the success of the business, so they have to handle complaints and solve problems. With all of those difficulties, why would anyone want to be an entrepreneur?

Owning a small business offers many personal benefits. Many people are able to add to their income by operating a part-time business in addition to having a full-time job. Most entrepreneurs start their first business while they are still working for another company. They often start the business at home on a part-time basis and expand it to a full-time business if it is successful.

Entrepreneurs receive personal satisfaction from developing an idea into a business and completing work that is interesting and uses their skills. Watching a business grow, providing jobs for people in the community, and being able to control the profits from the company are reasons why entrepreneurs are drawn to business ownership.

CHECKPOINT
Why are small businesses an important part of the U.S. economy?

21.1.3 ▶ What Does It Take to Be an Entrepreneur?

Why do some people start several successful businesses, often when they are still quite young, whereas others never consider starting one? What makes one person suited to be a business owner and other people suited to be managers or employees? Researchers have studied successful entrepreneurs and have identified qualities they have that others do not.

Characteristics of Entrepreneurs

Almost anyone can be an entrepreneur given a strong desire to do so. Women and men of all races, ages, and educational backgrounds have become successful entrepreneurs. People are not born with entrepreneurship skills. They develop them if they want to start their own business.

Studies of successful entrepreneurs show that they usually possess the following characteristics:

- *Entrepreneurs are focused and goal-oriented.* Many successful entrepreneurs thought about and planned their business for many years. Often they dreamed of starting their own business when they were very young. They may have faced a number of obstacles before they were able to succeed, but they did not give up.

- *Entrepreneurs are risk-takers.* **Risk-taking** is a willingness to accept the chance of failure in order to be successful. Entrepreneurs invest time and money in ideas that others may not have tried. They carefully consider the risks associated with the idea and work hard to reduce them.

- *Entrepreneurs want to achieve.* They set ambitious personal goals, and then do everything they can to meet those goals. They will be unhappy if they do not achieve what they want and may keep working even when success does not seem likely.

- *Entrepreneurs are independent.* They often are not involved in team activities and may not do well when asked to cooperate with others. They are more comfortable when they are in charge and responsible for results, so they may seek activities where their individual skills are important.

- *Entrepreneurs have a high level of self-confidence.* When people have **self-confidence**, they believe in themselves and their abilities and expect to be successful. If they do not succeed at an activity, they will either decide it was not important or work hard to improve so that they will succeed the next time.

- *Entrepreneurs are creative.* **Creativity** is the ability to use imagination to find unique ways to solve problems. Creative people often approach problem solving differently than others and are likely to develop original ideas and solutions. That creativity often inspires entrepreneurs to develop products and services others have not considered.

Often, a business started by an entrepreneur will fail when it begins to grow and the owner has to spend time managing it. The entrepreneur may not have the patience nor the interpersonal skills needed to successfully manage the business. Sometimes an entrepreneur will sell the business after several years and then begin the process of starting a new business all over again.

Do You Want to Be an Entrepreneur?

If you have thought about starting your own business, you should assess your potential. Determining whether you have what it takes to be a successful entrepreneur is an important step. If your desire to start a business is strong, you can develop the characteristics and skills that are necessary.

Answer the questions in **Figure 21-1** to determine if you have the characteristics needed to successfully start your

Characteristics of Entrepreneurs: How Many Do You Have?	Yes	No
I usually set realistic and achievable goals for myself.		
I like to take responsibility for my own actions.		
I like to solve problems and identify new ways to do things.		
I'm willing to take risks when I know there is a chance to be successful.		
I am able to manage my time well and usually complete the tasks I start.		
When I am doing something I enjoy, I will commit long hours to the work.		
I like challenges and don't mind the pressure.		
I can manage several things at one time.		
I usually have confidence in the things I choose to do.		
I often put personal activities ahead of socializing.		
I would rather do things where I can control the results rather than relying on others.		
When I don't have the answer to something, I will go out and find it.		
I understand my strengths and weaknesses.		
When I have accomplished an important goal, I often want to move on to something else.		

FIGURE 21-1 Do you have what it takes to be an entrepreneur?

own business. For the items to which you answer "No," make a plan to develop the quality so that you can improve your chances for success as an entrepreneur.

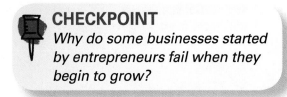

CHECKPOINT

Why do some businesses started by entrepreneurs fail when they begin to grow?

21.1.4 ▶ Prepare for Entrepreneurship

You may know others your age who have started successful businesses on a part-time basis, or you may have done so yourself. If you have not, but you have the desire, you should begin planning now if you want to become an entrepreneur. When you begin planning, you may find that you already have done several things that will improve your chances for starting a successful business. You will need to prepare yourself academically, develop the necessary technology skills, and acquire the business skills needed for the field you choose.

Academic Preparation

To plan and start a business, you will need to work with many people, develop and communicate your business plans, seek financing, prepare and review financial documents, make decisions, and solve problems. A strong academic preparation in the following disciplines will provide the knowledge and skills needed for these tasks.

COMMUNICATION Writing and speaking are essential entrepreneurial skills. You will write business letters, memos, and reports. You will prepare written materials such as employment advertisements, job descriptions, and product information. Classes in English and composition will help you develop your ability to write clearly and efficiently using the form and style the reader expects.

Oral communication is especially important to entrepreneurs. You will make presentations to investors, bankers, lawyers, other businesspeople who will provide products and services for your business, and prospective customers. You also must communicate effectively with employees to conduct meetings, give directions, and explain procedures.

Public speaking, speech, and other oral communication courses are important if you plan to be an entrepreneur. In addition, find leadership roles in class projects, become an officer in a club, and practice giving formal and informal presentations.

MATH Basic math skills are used to develop financial plans for the business as well as to perform day-to-day business operations. You will need to make calculations quickly and accurately involving the mathematical functions of addition, subtraction, multiplication, and division. You will frequently calculate percentages and use fractions and decimals. The ability to estimate the accuracy of a calculation will allow you to quickly check a budget, an invoice, or a sales estimate.

Advanced math skills will be useful in conducting research and in preparing and analyzing financial reports. You will be able to select the best investment opportunities, negotiate favorable loan terms, and compare the performance of your business with similar businesses. To develop the needed skills, you should take a number of mathematics classes, including algebra and statistics. You also should take business classes that apply basic math

What kinds of math skills would be valuable for entrepreneurs? Why?

and accurately using a computer and available software. Business records—including payroll, taxes, budgets, accounts payable and receivable, and others—can be developed, maintained, and analyzed using a computer.

Entrepreneurs need to be able to use a variety of business software programs including word processing, spreadsheet, database, graphics and presentation design, Web design, accounting, and statistics programs. Other technology businesspeople use includes printers, copiers, and smart phones.

The Internet is an essential personal and business communication medium and information resource. Entrepreneurs need to be able to use the Internet to quickly gather information, analyze competition, and communicate via email with vendors, investors, bankers, customers, and employees. They also need to develop a social media presence to promote themselves and their business.

Understanding search engines, website design, and communication resources also are important. Understanding and following security procedures and following netiquette principles helps an entrepreneur communicate in a professional manner. **Netiquette**, short for *Internet etiquette*, is the informal code of conduct regarding acceptable online behavior.

You can learn to use business technology in a number of ways. Most of your classes will help you develop computer skills. Business classes will introduce you to common business software. Part-time jobs and internships also provide opportunities to use technology. Many of your hobbies and activities will help you develop technology skills.

skills, such as accounting, finance, business statistics, and marketing research.

SCIENCE Taking science classes is an important way to learn to solve problems, conduct research, and make decisions based on careful and objective analytical procedures. Scientific skills include identifying problems, reviewing information, considering alternative solutions, and basing decisions on objective information. Science classes also teach careful observation skills, note taking, and report writing.

Use Technology

Many tools are available to help entrepreneurs plan and manage their businesses. The most common and important business tool is a computer. Business planning can be completed much more easily

Want to know more about marketing in the information age? Click on **Lesson 21.1, Digital Marketing,** *in your MindTap.*

Connect to MindTap

Business Skills

Many entrepreneurs develop business skills through experience. They often work in another business for many years and advance to become managers before deciding to start their own business. Others learn from the mistakes they made when starting a business. If they are lucky, they are able to correct the mistakes, but many entrepreneurs fail before succeeding.

There are many opportunities to learn about business and develop the knowledge you will need as an entrepreneur. High schools and colleges offer many business classes. Often, you can take courses in entrepreneurship that help you develop your business idea and business plan.

Important business classes for entrepreneurs are accounting, business communications, business law, finance, business management, and marketing as well as computer classes. Because many new businesses are using the Internet, e-commerce is an increasingly important business class.

*Want to know more about what is trending with this topic? Click on **Lesson 21.1, Global Marketing,** in your MindTap.*

Connect to MindTap

You also should participate in cooperative education or internship programs and become a member of a student business organization such as DECA or Key Club. These activities will give you practical experience, allow you to identify and work with business mentors, and develop important leadership, interpersonal, and teamwork skills.

CHECKPOINT
What academic skills are important for entrepreneurs to have?

21.1 ASSESSMENT

What Have You Learned?

1. Define entrepreneurship. [21.1.1]
2. What type of personal satisfaction do entrepreneurs receive from starting a business? [21.1.2]
3. Why is creativity an important characteristic for entrepreneurs? [21.1.3]
4. Explain how using the Internet is an essential skill for entrepreneurs. [21.1.4]

Make Academic Connections

1. **Technology**   Gather additional or more recent information on the role of small businesses in the U.S. economy. Use a computer and graphing software to prepare bar or pie charts that illustrate that role. Make sure to prepare specific and meaningful titles and labels for each chart. [21.1.2]

2. **Reading**   Use the Internet to find articles that have been written about a well-known entrepreneur. Based on your reading, how do the personal characteristics of the entrepreneur compare to those discussed in the lesson? Make a list of the characteristics you were able to identify. [21.1.3]

Connect to ◇ DECA

Build your Portfolio

Your team has been asked to prepare a presentation for a local community television channel to promote the importance of entrepreneurship. Develop a five-minute presentation that uses an informational poster as a visual aid. Record your team presentation so that it can be viewed by your teacher (judge). [21.1.1]

Do you ever find yourself struggling to accomplish everything you need to do during the day? Do you procrastinate or focus only on the things you enjoy while avoiding activities you find difficult, challenging, or boring? Effective time management helps you accomplish more things while increasing your efficiency and your mental attitude. By using effective time-management principles, you will actually find more time in your day for the things you enjoy. Effective time managers are in demand in every business and organization.

To become an effective time manager, practice these principles:

• Identify everything that needs to be done. Don't rely on your memory alone. Make a list on your phone, tablet computer, sticky note, or notebook. List work, social, family, and personal tasks and responsibilities.

• Prioritize. Determine what is most and least important. How much time do you expect each will take?

• Determine when you will accomplish each task based on your schedule. When will you be at school, work, and in clubs, organizations, and other groups? Fit tasks into your schedule as appropriate. If things need to be done in advance to prepare for school, work, or organizations, what times are available for those tasks?

• Mix tasks between most and least enjoyable, time-consuming and quick, difficult and easy. Don't try to do all the difficult and least enjoyable tasks at once, but don't put them off, either.

• Get cooperation, support, and assistance. Find others who have similar work to do, have specific skills they can provide, and are willing to share or exchange work when appropriate to speed completion or get tasks done more effectively. Working together can make many tasks more enjoyable and even result in faster and better results.

• Take a few minutes to clear your mind, relax, and refocus. A short break can lead to higher quality and better productivity.

• Check your work, get feedback from others, and correct errors. Don't try to get by with less than your best work in order to save time. Don't wait for others to discover errors when you can correct your work immediately.

• Help others improve their time-management skills. Don't let team members slow your progress through poor use of time. Pass on and demonstrate the skills you learn, provide encouragement, and share tasks. Effective leadership and cooperation make work more enjoyable and successful.

Develop Your Skill

Select an upcoming day that will be busy and challenging. Make a list of all activities you need to complete during the day. Prioritize and develop a work order for the activities. Determine if there are things you can do in advance to make the day run smoothly. Outline a work plan for the day making sure to mix the tasks and allow some time to relax. At three points during the day, mentally review your progress. Note what you did well and what you might do differently the next time. At the end of the day, review your plan to see how well you did. Use what you learned to improve your time-management skills in the future.

21.2 BUSINESS OWNERSHIP

Learning Objectives

21.2.1 Identify business opportunities related to marketing.

21.2.2 Explain the two-step process for creating a competitive market offering.

21.2.3 Describe the legal forms of ownership for a business.

21.2.4 Discuss legal steps to follow in starting a new business.

Key Terms

microcredit
sole proprietorship
proprietor
partnership
partnership agreement
corporation
charter

marketing matters

Entrepreneurs start businesses for various reasons. Many will open a business that allows them to use special skills they have. Others start a business related to a hobby or interest or to the business experience they have. People with marketing experience and skills have many entrepreneurial opportunities. Whatever the reason they decide to start a business, all entrepreneurs need to choose a legal form of ownership and fulfill the legal requirements associated with it.

essential questions

What are some entrepreneurial opportunities for marketers? What are the legal forms of ownership they can choose in organizing their business?

21.2.1 Marketing and Business Ownership Opportunities

Entrepreneurs start all types of businesses. Manufacturing businesses tend to be the most recognized, but marketing-related opportunities abound for entrepreneurs.

Opportunities Related to Marketing Functions

Some entrepreneurs may choose to start retailing and wholesaling companies, which are marketing businesses that accumulate products from manufacturers and make them available to consumers. All businesses must perform marketing functions as products and services are exchanged between producers and consumers, and those functions can be used as the basis for an entrepreneurial venture.

PROMOTION Many types of businesses offer promotional services. Advertising agencies, public relations firms, graphic design, copywriting, and printing companies are examples. Other companies build displays or design billboards and electronic signs to promote businesses and products. The explosion in advertising via social media provides the opportunity to offer unique promotional services to other businesses. Social media marketing agencies assist companies with social media strategy development as well as content creation.

SELLING   A company may hire a sales agency to sell its products and services. This often is done when it is not profitable for a company to employ its own sales force. Offering sales training or developing resources that are used by salespeople, such as computer programs or product models, are other business opportunities related to selling.

DISTRIBUTION   Many types of companies are involved in storing and distributing products from producer to consumer. Trucking companies, express delivery businesses, and couriers handle thousands of products each day. Warehouses and storage centers are distribution businesses

that ensure products are held safely until needed.

PRICING   A number of companies provide services related to the pricing function. Some help determine the value of products and negotiate agreements between the buyer and seller. An example is an auction house, where products are presented and sold to the highest bidder. One Internet business that helps buyers and sellers negotiate a fair price for products is eBay. Other companies provide pricing information to prospective buyers so they know how much they should pay for products such as cars, real estate, or travel.

FINANCING   Banks and credit card companies provide financial services to businesses and consumers. Financial advisors help in obtaining credit and making investments. **Microcredit** provides low-value loans to people who cannot qualify for traditional bank loans. Microcredit has become a way of increasing the number of

MATH IN MARKETING

Return on Investment

To finance a new business, an entrepreneur invested $75,000 of her own money. She also obtained $490,000 from a venture capital company. These companies look for attractive new business ideas where they can get a good return on the money they invest. The table shows the total amount of money invested and the net profit received at the end of three years of operation.

	Entrepreneur	Investors
Total Investment	$75,000	$490,000
3-Year Net Profit	$ 9,500	$112,000

Do the Math

1. What was the three-year return on investment for the entrepreneur and the investors [ROI = (Net Profit ÷ Total Investment) × 100]?

2. What was the total amount invested in the business and the total amount of profit?

3. Why would an entrepreneur be willing to accept a smaller return on investment after three years than the venture capital group is willing to accept?

small businesses in rural and high-poverty areas that can benefit from economic development and in countries just starting to develop their economies.

RISK MANAGEMENT   Entrepreneurship opportunities exist for experts in security, safety, and using technology to help businesses anticipate, manage, and reduce their risks. All businesses must maintain the privacy and security of business and customer information. They often rely on experts for help in responding to those issues.

MARKETING-INFORMATION MANAGEMENT   Gathering and analyzing information and conducting marketing research are important marketing activities. Many types of businesses perform this marketing function. Some companies pay consumers to test products, conduct surveys in malls, or send shoppers into businesses to determine the effectiveness of customer service. Businesses gather information, prepare reports for businesses, or provide data security services.

PRODUCT AND SERVICE MANAGEMENT   Some companies provide assistance to other businesses in product research and design. Others provide testing to ensure the quality or to compare the strengths and weaknesses of competing products. One new area related to product and service management is product disposal. Many marketers forget about the product once it is sold to the customer, but

WORKING IN TEAMS

As a team, choose one of the marketing functions. Have each member in turn identify a product or service idea related to that function that could result in a new business. Be creative and do not criticize any idea suggested. When the team runs out of ideas for a function, select another function and repeat the process.

when the product wears out or becomes obsolete, what happens to it? There are opportunities in recovering raw materials from landfills, recycling building materials, developing new ideas for obsolete products, and many others.

MARKET PLANNING   Many companies need assistance in identifying new markets and determining the feasibility of entering those markets. Entrepreneurs with expertise in underserved markets (such as ethnic groups and international markets) can offer specialized services to other businesses.

CHECKPOINT

Why is each marketing function a source of opportunities for entrepreneurship?

21.2.2 ▶ Two-Step Process to Develop a Competitive Product

In deciding whether to pursue a business opportunity, entrepreneurs need to develop a unique offering that will satisfy customer needs. Successful marketers and entrepreneurs use a two-step process. The first step is to identify customers and their needs. The second step is to develop a marketing mix to meet the customer needs.

Step 1: Identify Customers and Their Needs

Before you decide to start a business, you should determine if a target market exists for the business. Who are the possible customers and where are they located? What are their specific needs? Are those needs generally satisfied by existing products and services or are they unsatisfied with current choices?

A new business will have difficulty competing with an existing business unless the existing business has a weakness. Identify companies offering similar products. Determine the prices they charge and services they offer. Find out what customers in your target market like and dislike about each competitor.

Step 2: Develop a Marketing Mix

Based on a study of the customers and competitors, determine if you can provide a unique product or service that customers will view as satisfying their important needs better than what is being offered by your competitors. Your understanding of marketing planning will help you develop the marketing mix elements—the product, and the distribution, pricing, and promotion activities that will be used to satisfy your customers' needs.

CHECKPOINT
Explain the two-step process entrepreneurs and marketers use to identify a competitive product.

21.2.3 ▶ The Ownership Decision

One of the first decisions made by an entrepreneur is the legal form of ownership for the new business. There are three common ownership choices. They are sole proprietorship, partnership, or corporation. Each form of ownership offers advantages and disadvantages.

Sole Proprietorship

A business owned and managed by one person is a **sole proprietorship** (also simply called *proprietorship*). A **proprietor** is a person who has sole ownership of a business. Sole proprietorship is the most common form of business ownership, with nearly three-quarters of all businesses organized in this way.

Under the sole proprietorship form of organization, the owner is responsible for the money needed to start and operate the business as well as all business planning and management. As a result of being the sole owner, the proprietor is entitled to all profits the business earns. If there are no debts, a proprietor has full claim to all of the business's assets. If there are debts, people to whom the business owes money have the first claim against the assets if the business is sold or fails.

ADVANTAGES OF PROPRIETORSHIPS
The sole owner of the business is the boss and can make all decisions. That feature suits many entrepreneurs, who generally are quite independent.

The proprietor receives all profits of the business. Because of the profit motive, entrepreneurs work very hard to make their businesses successful.

The owner can make decisions without consulting others, so he or she can act quickly when needed. As a result, sole proprietorships are flexible and can adjust rapidly to changing conditions.

Forming a sole proprietorship also is relatively easy. There are few legal requirements to start the business or to end it. As a result, people who are trying to form their first business are drawn to this form of business ownership.

DISADVANTAGES OF PROPRIETORSHIPS Running a business successfully requires many skills. A proprietor is totally responsible for the business and may not have all of the skills needed. There is a greater chance that the business will fail due to lack of planning and management skills or other areas where the proprietor is not well prepared.

Although a few businesses can be started without a lot of money, most new businesses are expensive to form. One person may not have the needed funds. Many business ideas are not developed due to the entrepreneur's lack of funds.

In a sole proprietorship, the owner assumes a great deal of risk. Although the owner receives all the profits of the business, that person also suffers all the losses if the business is not profitable. Creditors can make claims on everything the entrepreneur owns, not just the assets of the business if it fails.

The business will not be able to continue to operate for long if the owner becomes ill or dies. The business will either have to be sold or close. Sometimes an entrepreneur loses interest in the business or does not have adequate time to devote to developing and managing it. With no other owners, the business is likely to fail.

Why is a sole proprietorship a popular form of ownership for entrepreneurs?

© iStock.com/PeopleImages

Partnership

A **partnership** is a business that is owned and operated by two or more people who share in the decision making and profitability of the company. A partnership is formed using a **partnership agreement**, a legal document that specifies the responsibilities and financial relationships of the partners. Some research indicates that the most successful startups have two founders.

ADVANTAGES OF PARTNERSHIPS Partnerships pool the knowledge and skills of all the owners. There are more people available to manage the business.

Because more than one person owns the business, there usually is more money available. Also, banks are more likely to loan money to companies when more than one person is responsible for repaying the loan.

What are the advantages of the partnership form of business?

company. Corporations are granted a charter by the state in which they are formed. A **charter** is a legal document allowing the corporation to operate as if it were a person. That means the business can borrow money, enter into contracts, and be liable for its decisions and actions.

ADVANTAGES OF CORPORATIONS

A corporation is most often formed by an entrepreneur to raise money and to limit the liability faced by the owners. Because an owner invests in stock, the losses suffered by the business in case of failure are limited to the amount of the investment.

The life of a corporation does not depend on any one owner. If an owner decides to sell his or her stock, another person can buy it, and the business continues to operate.

As a corporation grows, it is easier for the owner to turn day-to-day management responsibilities over to managers. Policies and direction of a corporation are controlled by a board of directors who hire well-prepared executives to manage the business.

DISADVANTAGES OF CORPORATIONS

Because corporations operate based on a charter, they face more rules and regulations than other forms of businesses. They are watched carefully by the states in which they operate and must file regular reports.

If one person decides to leave the business or dies, the business does not have to close. Partnership agreements specify how a partner can be replaced. The remaining partners can continue to operate the business until a new partner is located.

DISADVANTAGES OF PARTNERSHIPS

Disagreements on important decisions can occur among partners. It may take time for partners to discuss issues and agree on the best solution. Many partnerships fail due to disagreements among the partners that cannot be resolved.

In a partnership, all partners are generally responsible for any actions and decisions made by another partner. If money is owed, each partner is liable for the debt.

Corporation

A **corporation** is a business owned by people who purchase stock in the

The people who own the company's stock usually do not have as much interest in the business as the entrepreneur. They may be more concerned about the profits the company earns than they are about the day-to-day operations. No one individual has to take responsibility for business operations and decisions.

Corporations usually are taxed at a higher rate than the other forms of business. Also, individual investors must pay taxes on any profits distributed to them.

CHECKPOINT
How does ownership differ in each of the three legal forms of business ownership?

21.2.4 ▶ Start Your Business

Once you have decided to start a business, you would need to complete several legal steps before you could open for business.

- Select the form of ownership. Decide if your business will be a sole proprietorship, partnership, or corporation. If it is a partnership, prepare and sign the partnership agreement. If it is a corporation, prepare and file a charter and complete the other forms required by the state.

- Decide on a business name and register it with the state and local government.

- Determine the licenses and permits needed to operate your business. Complete the procedures to obtain each one.

- If you are creating a new product, you would need to address issues relating to intellectual property. First you would determine if a patent, copyright, or trademark is needed. If so, you would need to file an application with the U.S. Copyright Office or U.S. Patent and Trademark office to obtain it.

- Purchase or lease buildings and equipment. Obtain necessary financing for the purchases and for business operations. Complete mortgage, lease, and loan applications and financial documents.

Stockbyte/Getty Images

Which of the legal steps for starting a business would an entrepreneur who opens a comic shop *not* be required to take?

- Create necessary business records.
- Identify insurance needs and purchase the necessary policies.
- Prepare personnel policies and procedures if employees will be hired. Identify and comply with all employment and tax laws.
- Develop procedures and prepare forms you will use to sell products to customers and make sure they meet all legal requirements. Be prepared to collect and report all local, state, and federal taxes.

You can see that starting a business involves many steps and requires a great

Want to know more about what is trending with this topic? Click on Lesson 21.2, Marketing Decisions, in your MindTap.

deal of legal information. An entrepreneur should work with a lawyer skilled in business startups and should seek assistance from experienced businesspeople, business associations, and government offices to make sure all procedures are followed and all legal requirements are met.

CHECKPOINT

Why should an entrepreneur seek legal assistance when starting a new business?

21.2 ASSESSMENT

What Have You Learned?

1. Why are retailing and wholesaling companies considered marketing businesses? [21.2.1]
2. In studying a potential competitor, how would you go about identifying a weakness in its offering? [21.2.2]
3. Why would an entrepreneur choose the corporate form of organization? [21.2.3]
4. What legal matters would you need to address if you are creating a new product? [21.2.4]

Make Academic Connections

1. **Math**   A community has 5,789 fitness center customers. Research shows 18% are dissatisfied with their current fitness center. If a new business can enroll 25% of the dissatisfied customers, how many members will it have? What percentage of the total market will the fitness center enroll? [21.2.2]

2. **Government**   Use the Internet to identify the procedures that must be followed to form a corporation in your state. Prepare a written list of the procedures including the name of the state department or office that administers the process. [21.2.4]

Connect to ◇DECA

Build your Portfolio

A family friend has worked for a large advertising agency and now wants to start a new business to provide social media management services to other small businesses. He plans to form the business as a sole proprietorship because it is easy to start. You want to convince him that the business will be more successful organized as a partnership or corporation. Participate in a role-play with your teacher (judge) to present the reasons for your beliefs and to answer questions. [21.2.4]

21.3 THE BUSINESS PLAN

Learning Objectives

21.3.1 Discuss why a new business should have a business plan.

21.3.2 Explain the parts of a business plan.

Key Terms

business plan
executive summary

marketing matters

Taking the time to carefully plan for a business will help an entrepreneur increase the chances for success. One of the most important tools to the success of a new business is a carefully developed, written business plan. The business plan will guide the entrepreneur in decision making before opening the business and after the business begins operations.

essential question

Why is developing a business plan an important step in starting a business?

21.3.1 The Purpose of a Business Plan

A **business plan** is a written document prepared to guide the development and operation of a new business. It contains the information used and the initial decisions made to manage each of the major areas of the business.

Gathering and studying information in preparing a business plan will help the entrepreneur think through the issues involved in operating the business. The business plan will become a ready reference when the entrepreneur needs to make careful and objective decisions about the business.

Each new business will have a slightly different plan. The business plan should be prepared by the business owner and should reflect the owner's knowledge, ideas, and experience. All business plans must communicate:

- The purpose of the business and the types of products and services it plans to offer

- Descriptions of the business's customers and their important needs

- Major business activities that will be completed

- Resources needed, including materials, equipment, and people

- Sources of financing and the amount of money needed to start and operate the business

- The type of competition to be faced and major competitors

- Financial requirements and profit projections

Use the Business Plan

The business plan is an important guide for starting and operating the business. Because of the detailed planning, the entrepreneur can use it to determine if the business is developing according to the plan and if changes need to be made.

In addition to the value of the plan to the business owner, other people who are involved in starting the business also benefit from a well-prepared business plan.

PROSPECTIVE PARTNERS AND STOCKHOLDERS

If the entrepreneur wants to organize the business as a partnership or a corporation, potential owners will want information about the business to determine if they want to participate.

BANKERS AND INVESTORS

Many new businesses will need to borrow money to finance buildings, equipment, product purchases, and several months of operations. Bankers and other people who might consider making loans will need detailed information to make sure the business is a solid investment. Most investors and financial institutions insist that entrepreneurs provide a well-developed business plan.

EMPLOYEES OF THE BUSINESS

The owner of a new business works many hours each week and is very busy making sure the business is successful. Employees are an important part of operations. The business plan provides information to employees so the owner will not have to orally communicate the information to them when they need it or when the owner is not available.

MARKETING COMMUNICATION

Present Your Business Plan

A new business needs money to be able to purchase or lease buildings, equipment, and materials used in operating the business. An entrepreneur can obtain funding from investors, loans from banks, or financing from other companies.

An entrepreneur prepares a business plan to provide the information others need to decide whether to invest or provide financing. He or she must be able to make a short oral presentation when meeting with potential investors and businesspeople that will spark their interest in the new company. For the presentation to be successful, it must get investors' attention in the first minute and present two or three meaningful points and supporting information shortly thereafter.

This presentation is your opportunity to market yourself and your brand. You will need to make sure that you develop your own brand in a way that suits the audience you are addressing. You would need to dress appropriately and speak in a way that is confident and informative but not too aggressive. In other words, you market yourself in a suitable fashion.

Think Critically

1. Why do prospective investors want to hear a short presentation from the entrepreneur who is seeking funding?
2. Create a presentation outlining the major topics you would cover in three to five minutes to interest investors in a new business.

OTHER BUSINESSPEOPLE People who work in other businesses will be a part of the success of the new business. If the new business manufactures products, it will need cooperation from retailers to sell products. It will need to purchase raw materials, supplies, and equipment and usually will want credit from suppliers. The new business may need the help of lawyers, accountants, advertising agencies, and others. A business plan assures the cooperating businesses that the owner is well prepared to work with them.

CHECKPOINT
Why is it important for a new entrepreneur to have a written business plan?

21.3.2 ▶ Develop a Business Plan

A business plan is used to make important decisions about business operations, to communicate those decisions to others, and to serve as a guide for business operations. The major sections of a business plan are illustrated in **Figure 21-2**.

The sections of the business plan present the specific decisions that have been made and describe how the business will be organized and managed. The written plan identifies the resources that will be needed to operate the business successfully. Financial plans describe the money that will be needed to operate the business and how the money will be used. Detailed financial projections are made

---

Outline of a Business Plan for a New Business

I. Introduction to the Business
   A. Description of products and services
   B. Owners and form of ownership
   C. Business organization
   D. Long- and short-term objectives
   E. Strengths and weaknesses

II. Description of the Industry
   A. Economic conditions
   B. Types of competition
   C. Strengths and weaknesses of competitors
   D. Anticipated changes in the industry

III. Market Analysis
   A. Description of target markets
   B. Analysis of needs and purchase behavior
   C. Sales forecasts for major markets

IV. Operations
   A. Organization of operations and departments

   B. Descriptions of major activities
   C. Identification of equipment, materials, and other operating resources needed
   D. Staffing requirements and management plans

V. Marketing
   A. Description of marketing mix
   B. Procedures for implementing marketing activities
   C. Resources needed for marketing

VI. Financial Plans
   A. Startup costs
   B. Semiannual income and expense projections
   C. Monthly cash flow budgets
   D. Annual balance sheet projections
   E. Analysis of financial plan
   F. Sources of financial and funding requests

FIGURE 21-2 Each section of a business plan provides detailed information on decisions made for that part of the new business.

to show income, expenses, profit, and the return on investment that investors, including the entrepreneur, can expect from the financing they provide.

After the business plan is complete, the owner should prepare a one- or two-page summary of the plan. The **executive summary** provides an overview of the business concept and the important points in the business plan. It highlights the major planning decisions made by the business owner. The written summary is useful when the owner needs to present the plan to others in order to build understanding and support for the new business.

 CHECKPOINT
What are the major sections of a business plan?

21.3 ASSESSMENT

What Have You Learned?

1. Why is a business plan helpful to bankers for and investors in a business? [21.3.1]
2. What is the purpose of a business plan's executive summary? [21.3.2]

Make Academic Connections

1. **Communication**   Plan and practice a persuasive speech to convince new business owners they can benefit from preparing a detailed written business plan. The speech should include at least four specific benefits of the written business plan. Present your speech to other students. [21.3.1]
2. **Reading**   Use the library or Internet to locate a sample business plan for a new business. Read the plan as if you were a prospective investor to determine if it provides the information you need to understand the business and make a financing decision. Write a three-paragraph analysis of the strengths, weaknesses, and effectiveness of the plan. [21.3.2]

Connect to ◇DECA.

Build your Portfolio

Identify a target market and an idea for a small business to serve that market. Use the outline of a business plan shown in Figure 21-2 to prepare a one- or two-page executive summary of the planning decisions for your small business. Use the executive summary to present your business idea and plans to your teacher (judge). [21.3.2]

 Connect to MindTap

*Analyze a case study that focuses on chapter concepts. Click on **Chapter 21, Case Study,** in your MindTap.*

CHAPTER 21 ASSESSMENT

Review Marketing Concepts

1. Why do you think many entrepreneurs decide to start marketing-related businesses? [21.1.1]

2. Explain why the success of entrepreneurs is important to the country's economic well-being. [21.1.2]

3. Of the characteristics of entrepreneurs discussed in the book, which characteristic do you think is the most important to have in order to build a successful business? Justify your response. [21.1.3]

4. Which educational skill—communication or math—do you think is more important to the success of an entrepreneur? Explain your answer. [21.1.4]

5. Why do you think the field of market research (marketing-information management) would be suited to the skills of an entrepreneur? [21.2.1]

6. Why is developing a unique offering in a market so important to an entrepreneur? [21.2.2]

7. If you were to start a new business, would the sole proprietorship or partnership form of business be more attractive to you? Explain your answer. [21.2.3]

8. Explain why setting up the business might be difficult for an entrepreneur. [21.2.4]

9. From the entrepreneur's perspective is the business plan more important for bankers and investors or for their employees? Explain your answer. [21.3.1]

10. Explain why the financial plan section of the business plan is important to the success of a new business. [21.3.2]

Marketing Research and Planning

1. Identify a small business you would be interested in starting as an entrepreneur. Use the Internet to locate the following information about that type of business:
   - Two existing businesses that offer the same type of product or service
   - Two businesses that could supply products or services needed by the business for its operations
   - Two sources of small business assistance available to a new entrepreneur
   - Two financial institutions in your area that may provide startup financial support for the new business

   Write a report based on your findings. [21.2.2, 21.3.1]

2. Use a word processing program to develop a questionnaire using the items in Figure 21-1. Add three additional items asking respondents to identify their age and number of years of education.

   Give a copy of the questionnaire to five people and ask them to complete it. When you have all of the completed questionnaires, enter the items into a spreadsheet. Calculate the totals for each item. Prepare a report of your findings.

   Working with other students in your class, enter the information from all questionnaires into one electronic spreadsheet and calculate the class totals for each item. Discuss the results. Identify any differences in responses that seem to relate to age and education. [21.1.3]

3. The number of businesses formed as sole proprietorships, partnerships, and corporations is identified and reported by state and federal governments each year. Use the Internet to obtain the most recent information on the number and type of businesses for the United States and for your state.

Develop a spreadsheet to report the information you obtained. Use the spreadsheet to calculate the total number of businesses in the country and in your state. Calculate the percentage of U.S. businesses in each category, the percentage of the total number of businesses in your state in each category, and the percentage of the U.S. totals represented by the businesses in your state. Prepare national and state pie charts to illustrate the results. Make sure to label the charts and all data presented. [21.2.3]

Marketing Management and Decision Making

1. Becoming a successful entrepreneur requires a person who has the necessary personal characteristics, education, and experience, as well as the financial resources to be able to provide some of the initial financing of a new business.

Prepare a personal analysis of your current status as a possible entrepreneur and a plan to improve your preparation. Using a word-processing program, prepare a two-column table titled "My Entrepreneurship Preparation." Write *What I Have* at the top of the left column and *What I Need* at the top of the right column.

Using information from the chapter, complete the table to describe what you have already done to prepare to be an entrepreneur and what you need to do to continue your preparation. Use the following headings as rows in your tables:

    Entrepreneurship Characteristics
    Academic Preparation
        Communication Skills
        Math Skills
        Scientific Skills
    Technology Skills
    Business Skills
    Work Experience [21.1.3, 21.1.4]

2. Entrepreneurship opportunities often result from the design of new products or the development of improvements in existing products. Select one of the following products or identify another product category approved by your teacher:

a. miniaturized computer keyboard

b. student backpack

c. smartphone

d. beverage cooler for the beach

Use a computer graphics program or craft materials to create a new design for the product that you believe improves on the current design (added features, easier to use, more portable or efficient, etc.). When you and your classmates have finished your designs, display the new products around the classroom. Have a "gallery walk" where small groups walk from product to product and the designer describes the product, its features, and its benefits. [21.2.2]

3. Working in small groups and with the help of your teacher, identify a small business owner from your community who graduated from your high school. Contact the person and arrange an interview. If possible, obtain a video camera and videotape the interview. If it is not possible to meet the business owner in person, it may be appropriate with the permission of your teacher to complete the interview using the telephone, a videoconference, or email. Make sure to take careful notes during the interview.

Ask the business owner the following questions:

1. Why did you decide to start your own business?

2. What did you do to prepare for business ownership?

3. What steps did you take to start your business?

4. What is your target market?

5. Who are your main competitors?

6. What are the characteristics of your marketing mix: product, price, distribution, and promotion?

7. What do you believe are the most important factors in being a successful small business owner?

When your interview is completed, summarize the information your team obtained and prepare an oral report on the entrepreneur to present to your class. [21.1.1, 21.1.2, 21.1.3, 21.1.4, 21.2.2]

Let's Start a Band! Follow-Up Discussion

Work in small teams to discuss the question posed at the end of the opening vignette. What form of legal ownership would you advise for the band?

Build Your Marketing Plan

Build your Portfolio

In this chapter you learned about business organization and the relationship of business planning and marketing planning. You will now apply this learning to the development of your marketing plan. To access the chapter-specific tools that you will need to complete this activity, please navigate to Chapter 21 ➔ Build Your Marketing Plan in MindTap. Alternatively, you can access these tools online at NGLSync. Please visit www.nglsync .cengage.com, and search for the companion website that accompanies this book by entering the ISBN, author, or title. Once you locate this companion website, navigate to Build Your Marketing Plan ➔ Chapter 21.

Start Up Business Plan Event

DECA PREP

Build your Portfolio

The Start Up Business Plan Event provides an opportunity for participants to develop and present a proposal to form a business. The event allows participants to develop and demonstrate mastery of essential skills as they apply to analyzing a business opportunity and developing a marketing/promotion plan and a financial plan.

The body of the written entry must be limited to 10 pages, not including the title page and the table of contents. Participants will have 15 minutes to present and defend their business prospectus to the judge and answer questions about their business plan.

The written plan will have these sections:

Executive Summary One-page description of the business model

Problem Description of the top problems the product/service is solving

Customer Segments Description of target customers

Unique Value Proposition Description of the message that states the unique value proposition

Solutions Description of the top features of the product/service that solve the problem

Channels Descriptions of the pathways to customers

Revenue Streams Description of the revenue model and life-time values; explanation of the revenue and gross margin

Cost Structure Explanation of the customer acquisition costs, distribution costs, human resources costs, and other additional costs

Key Metrics Explanation of the key activities that must be measured

Competitive Advantage Explanation of why the product/service cannot be easily copied or bought

Conclusion Specific request for financing; summary of key points supporting the financial request

Bibliography List of references

You will prepare a proposal to form a business. Your presentation must convince the judge to invest in your idea. The business plan should convince financial institutions and/or venture capitalists to invest money in your idea.

Performance Indicators Evaluated

- Assess opportunities for venture creation. (Entrepreneurship)
- Determine feasibility of venture ideas. (Entrepreneurship)
- Identify company's unique selling proposition. (Product/Service Management)
- Develop business plan. (Strategic Management)
- Describe processes used to acquire adequate financial resources for venture creation/start-up. (Entrepreneurship)

Go to the DECA website for more detailed information. **www.deca.com**

Think Critically

1. Why would financial institutions and venture capitalists want to see financial projections for a proposed business?

2. Why should you analyze the competition when proposing a new business?

CHAPTER 22

TAKE CONTROL WITH MANAGEMENT

See how effective advertising leads to successful marketing strategies.
Click on Chapter 22, Visual Focus, in your MindTap.

Let's Start a Band!

> "Most artists ... spend their entire lives learning how to play music and write songs, and they don't really know how the music business works."
>
> – Moby, Singer–Songwriter

You told me early on that if we started a band, at some point we would need a marketing plan. As you know, we didn't think much of the idea and never got around to doing it. We all thought if we played well enough people would show up, we'd make some money, and everything would be fine.

Well, you were right. Without a plan, things do tend to get out of hand. So I took your advice and told the other members of the band that it's time to write up a marketing plan. I said that we shouldn't have to rethink and redo everything each time we put out a new song or go on the road. I said that now that we have some experience, we can take what we've learned, organize it, and commit it to paper. Then we can evaluate what we're doing and figure out what can be done better as well as what we're wasting our time on.

While all the members said they thought it was a good idea and something we need to do, they said I would have to show them how to do it. So, if you're willing to help me, let's make an outline for a marketing plan that I can take to the other members. Then we can pool our ideas to fill it out.

22.1 THE FUNCTIONS OF MANAGEMENT

Learning Objectives

22.1.1 Explain the role of management in effective marketing.

22.1.2 Describe the five functions of management.

Key Terms

managing
marketing
  management
planning
long-range planning
short-term planning
organizing
staffing
leading
controlling

marketing matters

The people who work in a business complete thousands of activities to achieve certain goals. In order for the goals to be reached, those activities and the people who perform them must be coordinated. Each business activity must occur at the proper time and place, using procedures that accomplish the tasks in the correct way. Resources needed to complete the tasks must be available as well. Making sure that business activities are well planned and occur as planned is ultimately the responsibility of management.

essential question

Why is the work of managers essential to the success of a business or organization?

22.1.1 Coordinate People and Resources

What makes a company successful? A quality product? Satisfied customers? Well-trained and motivated employees? Efficient operations? Profit? Each of these is important, but successful organizations have another key factor—effective management.

Key to Success

Managing is getting the work of an organization done through its people and resources. It is one of the most important functions of a business.

Effective managers are able to organize the resources and work of a company in ways that result in success. Companies with effective managers usually have good products, employees, and operations. Effective managers anticipate and resolve problems, and this results in satisfied customers who continue to purchase from the company.

Marketing Management

Planning and implementing a marketing strategy involve many resources, people, and activities. Customer and market information needs to be gathered and studied. Products and services need to be planned, priced, distributed, and promoted. Each marketing mix element must be coordinated with the others. Products must be distributed in the time and the way that salespeople and advertisers expect, so promises to customers can be kept. Product development costs must match the amounts budgeted to uphold pricing decisions.

Marketing management is the process of coordinating resources to plan and implement an efficient marketing strategy. (Recall that a *marketing strategy* is the way marketing activities are planned and coordinated to achieve an organization's goals.)

Marketing managers are responsible for the success of the organization's marketing efforts. Those marketing efforts are all of the activities involved in planning and implementing a marketing strategy. They manage the people and resources needed to identify markets and plan marketing mixes. Marketing managers also coordinate the work of the various companies involved as products move through a channel of distribution. The channel may include a manufacturer, transportation company, finance company, wholesaler, retailer, advertising agency, and others.

According to the marketing concept, effective marketing results in satisfying exchanges. Marketing managers are successful when customers in the target markets are satisfied and the company is profitable.

CHECKPOINT
What is the role of marketing managers in making sure that a company's marketing efforts are successful?

22.1.2 ▶ Management Functions and Activities

A good way to understand the work of managers is by examining the five functions of management—planning, organizing, controlling, staffing, and leading.

Planning

Planning involves analyzing information, setting goals, and determining how to achieve them. The president of a company is responsible for determining the direction of the business and making sure that plans are in place to move forward. Supervisors determine what their work groups need to accomplish each day and assign duties to each person they supervise. Though the two managers work at very different levels in the organization with different responsibilities, both have planning as a part of their jobs.

Managers complete both long-range and short-term planning.

LONG-RANGE PLANNING In **long-range planning** (also known as *strategic planning*), managers analyze information that can affect the business over a long period of time. Long-range plans are typically developed to cover a year or more and may include goals and direction for as much as five to ten years. Long-range planning includes setting broad goals and direction. Examples of long-range plans in a business are the strategic plan and business plan. The marketing plan often is considered a long-range plan because it sets direction and goals for all marketing functions and personnel. It must be coordinated with the company's overall strategic plan and business plan.

Long-range planning relies on information from a variety of sources. The information available to managers cannot accurately predict the future. Managers need to use the information to help them anticipate what might occur over the time that the plan will be in place. They rely on their experience, a variety of data, and the help of planning experts and tools to make decisions.

SHORT-TERM PLANNING **Short-term planning** (often known as *operational planning*) identifies specific objectives and activities for each part of the business for a time period of a year or less. Often managers prepare a plan for a three-month period and then review or extend the plan on a month-to-month basis. In that way, they are always looking three months in advance.

Short-term planning is based on the long-range plan, so all areas of the business work to achieve the same goals. The objectives and activities of each part of the organization as described in short-term plans must be coordinated to avoid conflicts and inefficiency.

MARKETING PLANNING IN A LARGE FIRM Examining how large firms perform marketing planning provides insight into long-range and short-term

Want to know more about what is trending with this topic? Click on Chapter 22.1, Global Marketing, in your MindTap.

Connect to MindTap

planning. The marketing plan serves as the long-range plan for the company's marketing efforts. It identifies the target markets that the business plans to serve and describes the marketing mix that must be developed to meet the needs of each market. It also sets goals that the company will use to evaluate whether the plan is successful.

The managers of each specific area of marketing—such as marketing information, channel management, sales, and customer service—use the information from the marketing plan to guide short-term planning. They must determine the objectives and activities for each of their areas. They will need to communicate with one another and share information about their plans and activities. In this way, each of the specific short-term plans will coordinate with each of the others to meet the long-range goals outlined in the company's marketing plan. **Figure 22-1** explains how four managers within marketing departments of large firms contribute to marketing planning.

Organizing

Organizing resources ensures the work can be accomplished effectively and efficiently. As a management function, **organizing** involves arranging people, activities, and resources in the best way to accomplish the goals of an organization. Many businesses develop organizational charts to illustrate how the company is divided into divisions or departments and to show the relationships among those work units.

There are many ways to organize the work in a business. Managers assign responsibility and authority to others to get work done. They identify the resources employees will need including buildings, equipment, materials, and supplies.

Marketing Managers	Marketing Planning Activities
Marketing information managers	• Determine the information needed to make good decisions about each part of the marketing mix • Ensure the information is available to all other managers when needed for their planning
Channel managers	• Determine what products to move to specific locations at the appropriate times and quantities • Determine how products will be packaged, stored, and transported at the lowest cost with the least damage.
Sales managers	• Provide training and product information to salespeople • Help identify detailed information about customers and prepare the salespeople to use the information • Make sure customers understand the entire marketing mix and how it meets customer needs
Customer service managers	• Ensure that personnel and resources are available to respond to customer needs after a product purchase. • Coordinate delivery, installation, and repair services. • Make sure problems are solved and customers are satisfied with their purchases

FIGURE 22-1 Managers in various areas of marketing coordinate to meet long-range goals outlined in a company's marketing plan.

Managers develop effective working relationships within the work group and with other work groups to make sure the organization operates effectively.

Staffing

Managers prepare job descriptions, recruit and select employees, determine how personnel will be compensated, and provide the necessary training so that employees can complete their work well. These activities make up the management activities known as **staffing**.

Staffing often is considered the most difficult of the management functions. There are a number of activities involved in staffing, and the manager must be able to work well with a variety of people to accomplish those activities. It may be difficult to find people with the skills that match the jobs in a company. Effective training requires time and money. Some companies are not willing to invest in good training programs, making the manager's job more difficult. Managers also are responsible for evaluating the performance of each employee. They can reward those who are doing well, but they may need to dismiss employees who cannot meet the requirements of their jobs.

Leading

Is there a difference between being a manager and being a leader? What are the characteristics of an effective leader? Who do you identify as leaders—in your class, school, community, or country? Today in business, leadership is considered one of the most important qualities of effective management. **Leading** is the ability to communicate the direction of an organization and to influence others to successfully carry out the needed work. Effective leadership includes having commitment and motivation, using effective communication,

Want to know more about marketing in the information age? Click on **Lesson 22.1, Digital Marketing,** *in your MindTap.*

Connect to MindTap

establishing good working relationships, and recognizing and rewarding effective performance.

Controlling

When **controlling**, managers measure performance, compare it with goals and objectives, and make adjustments when necessary. If a company establishes a goal that 95 percent of all customer orders will be delivered within 24 hours, the manager must regularly review information on order processing and delivery to be certain the goal is met. When the manager sees that fewer than 95 percent of the orders are being delivered on time, quick action must be taken. The manager must determine why orders are late and take steps to improve performance so the goal can be achieved.

Specific controlling activities include setting standards, collecting and analyzing information, considering methods of improving performance, changing plans when necessary, solving problems, and resolving conflicts. Managers use several common tools to control operations, including plans, budgets, financial reports, and management information systems.

CHECKPOINT
What are the five functions of management?

22.1 ASSESSMENT

What Have You Learned?

1. When are marketing managers deemed successful? [22.1.1]
2. What does the organizing function of management involve? [22.1.2]

Make Academic Connections

1. **Technology**   List the five functions of management. Then identify one technology product a manager could use in completing each function. Write a short description of the technology and how it supports the specific management function. [22.1.2]

2. **Math**   A marketing vice president estimates her work week is divided among the management functions in this way: planning, 16 hours; organizing, 8 hours; staffing, 4 hours; leading, 20 hours; and controlling, 18 hours. Prepare a pie chart to illustrate the hours and percentage of time devoted to each function. [22.1.2]

Connect to ◇DECA

Build your Portfolio

Develop a three-minute presentation on why each management function contributes to an effective marketing strategy in a business. Prepare visual aids to support your ideas. Give your presentation to your teacher (judge). [22.1.2]

Planning a Career In...
BUSINESS COACHING

How can you learn from the experience of other businesspeople and have them pass their business expertise on to you? One way is to hire a business coach.

Business coaches are experts in many aspects of business. They provide individualized information, advice, support, evaluation, and feedback to people who are trying to improve their job performance and career success. Business coaches differ from mentors in that they work on specific tasks for defined periods of time and are paid for their efforts. Business coaches may be hired by a company to provide support for one or more employees or by individuals looking for professional support. Business coaches work with top executives, beginning managers, employees in key positions in a company, or individuals who want to move up professionally. A coach may be called in to help with difficult issues facing an employee or to help speed a career move.

Job Titles

- Business Coach
- Career Coach
- Life Coach
- Executive Coach

Needed Skills

- A broad knowledge of business derived from a variety of successful business leadership positions
- Expertise in problem solving, performance evaluation, and planning
- Ability to build rapport, listen, provide positive feedback and encouragement, and motivate improved performance

What it's like to work in... Business Coaching

Joshua Mannes is now in the third month of his new business and loves his work as a business coach. Today he has meetings with three clients. The first is a CEO who is having difficulty communicating with her board of directors. Joshua is working with her on ways to keep the board members updated with short written reports and follow-up telephone calls. The second client is a sales manager who has accepted his first international assignment. Joshua is drawing on his eight years as a sales manager in South America to provide advice on working with different cultures. At the end of the day, he will meet for the first time with a young entrepreneur who wants to be sure he has the management skills needed to lead his rapidly growing business effectively. Joshua is especially interested in working with this new client because he wants to see the young person realize his dream.

What About You?

As you increase your knowledge and experience in business, would you like to pass what you know on to others to help them succeed in their careers?

Discover more about the outlook for this career and watch a video about a related career. Click on **Chapter 22, Planning a Career In...** *in your MindTap.*

22.2 MANAGE WITH A MARKETING PLAN

Learning Objectives

22.2.1 Describe how a marketing plan serves as a guide for effective marketing management.

22.2.2 Explain how marketing managers determine marketing effectiveness.

Key Terms

performance standard
marketing effectiveness
self-directed work team

marketing matters

Marketing plans help marketing managers perform each management function effectively. Details in the marketing plan provide direction and support for each of the other management functions—organizing, staffing, leading, and controlling. The act of developing a marketing plan establishes direction for marketing management. A marketing plan also provides a means for evaluating the company's marketing efforts.

essential question

Can an organization meet its goals without satisfying customers' needs? Why or why not?

22.2.1 Management's Use of the Marketing Plan

Successful companies develop and follow written marketing plans. **Figure 22-2** shows the outline of a typical marketing plan. The marketing plan provides information for planning, directions for organizing, support for staffing decisions, and the means to gain control of the marketing process by evaluating effectiveness and changes in the business environment.

Information for Planning

The marketing plan is a long-range plan that sets goals and direction for the company. The first part of the plan, Market Analysis, describes and reviews internal and external information that affects marketing. By studying this part of the plan, managers learn about the competition, the economy, and other factors that can affect the success of their plans. They are made aware of strengths and weaknesses of the business so that weaknesses can be improved, and strengths can be emphasized.

The second section of the marketing plan is the Marketing Strategy. In this section, target markets are identified, and the marketing mix is described. Most important, the goals and outcomes that will be used to measure the success of the marketing plan are described. Every planning activity in the company is directed at implementing that strategy and achieving those goals and objectives. The managers responsible for each marketing function

MARKETING PLAN OUTLINE

I. Market Analysis
- A. Purpose and Mission of the Business
- B. Description of Current Markets and Strategies
- C. Primary Competitors and Their Strengths/Weaknesses
- D. External Environment Analysis
  1. Economy
  2. Laws and Regulations
  3. Costs
  4. Competition
  5. Technology
  6. Social Factors
- E. Internal Analysis
  1. Strengths
  2. Weaknesses
  3. Anticipated Changes

II. Marketing Strategy
- A. Marketing Goals/Expected Outcomes
- B. Target Market Description
  1. Identifying Characteristics
  2. Unique Needs, Attitudes, Behaviors
- C. Marketing Mix Description
  1. Product/Service
  2. Distribution
  3. Pricing
  4. Promotion
- D. Positioning Statement

III. Action Plan
- A. Activity Schedule
  1. Responsibilities
  2. Schedule
  3. Budget
- B. Evaluation Procedures
  1. Evidence of Success
  2. Method of Collecting Evidence

FIGURE 22-2 A marketing plan sets goals and direction for the company.

must determine how their function supports the overall marketing strategy. The goals and objectives they develop for their part of the business must contribute to the goals identified in the marketing plan.

The final section, the Action Plan, identifies activities and responsibilities to guide short-term operations. It identifies the work needed in their part of the business and guides them in planning day-to-day activities, including schedules and budgets. Most companies require all managers to prepare written operational plans and to show how their plans support the marketing plan.

Direction for Organizing

Much of the organizing work in a company is done before a marketing plan is developed. A company decides which marketing functions and activities it will perform and which will be provided by other companies. It develops a structure that organizes marketing personnel and activities into departments. It identifies the responsibilities of managers for the various departments and activities. Those decisions will be reflected every time a marketing plan is written. If a company is successful with its target markets and makes only minor adjustments in the marketing mixes, it will not want to change its basic organizational structure unless it sees ways to improve performance or save money with the change.

Support for Marketing Staff

Effective marketing requires people with the skills necessary to perform the required marketing activities. Again, the marketing plan provides a useful tool for managers to determine staffing needs. The Action Plan is helpful because it describes activities and responsibilities that marketing personnel need to accomplish.

Managers match those activities with the current marketing employees. If the employees do not have the necessary skills to perform the activities, managers will need to develop training programs. If there are not adequate numbers of employees to perform the necessary work, new employees must be hired, or other businesses can be brought into the marketing channel to perform those activities. In some instances, current employees may not be needed for the activities required in a new marketing plan. Managers will have to make difficult decisions about the future for those employees and may need to help them find other jobs in the company or elsewhere.

Using the marketing plan to evaluate staffing needs is an important way for managers to determine where problems are likely to occur. Some businesses have problems because they do not have adequate numbers of employees or the employees do not have the needed skills or motivation to serve customers well. Managers who pay careful attention to staffing needs, training, and employee motivation often have a decided advantage over their competitors.

Many marketing efforts fail because the people responsible for the activities do not perform them well. Poor performance does not always occur because people do not have the skills to do the work. It may be due to a lack of leadership. A marketing manager who develops an effective plan and has the people and resources needed to carry out the plan needs one more ingredient to be successful. That ingredient is leadership.

Employees need to feel like they are part of the business for it to be successful. They want to be involved and understand why the work they do is important. A marketing manager who is a leader involves employees in developing the plan and discusses the plan with employees when it is completed. In that way, the employees see why the plan is important. They understand how it can lead to success for the business and the people who work for it. They recognize their role in the plan, how it relates to other marketing activities, and what will determine if their activities and the overall plan are successful.

Gain Control of Marketing

A marketing plan clearly identifies the markets the business wants to serve, what marketing activities are required, and

Flying Colours Ltd/Photodisc/Getty Images

Why should managers involve employees in the business planning process?

the goals the business expects to achieve. Each of those decisions is used to measure the effectiveness of marketing. Evaluating changes in the business environments and evaluating effectiveness are part of the controlling function of management.

EVALUATE ENVIRONMENTAL CHANGE There is another valuable way that the marketing plan helps managers with the controlling process. The first part of the marketing plan carefully describes the internal and external environment on which the plan is based. A change in any part of that environment could affect the success of the marketing plan. Managers read research reports, magazines, and newspapers. They attend conferences, talk to colleagues, and review other information so they will be up to date and prepared to respond to changes.

The types of environmental factors that often change are the economy, technology, competition, and laws and regulations. For example, during 2008 and early 2009, the U.S. and global economy experienced a severe downturn based on major problems in the financial and housing markets. As consumer and government spending dropped, manufacturers began to adjust their own inventory levels and production capacities so they would not have too much inventory or have to write down the value of outdated products. It took many years for businesses and consumers to regain their confidence and for production and employment to begin to rebuild to previous levels.

EVALUATE EFFECTIVENESS
Marketing managers study how well they are reaching and serving each target

How can managers learn about changes in the external environment that may affect their marketing plans?

market. They determine the market potential, the company's market share, and the share held by each competitor. Most businesses evaluate customer satisfaction with products and services as well as with other parts of the marketing mix. They want to see high satisfaction levels. A business becomes concerned if satisfaction begins to decline or if customers rate competitors higher.

The marketing mix is developed as part of the overall marketing strategy in the marketing plan. Then the activities and resources needed to implement each mix element are identified. Schedules, budgets, and other planning tools are prepared to guide implementation. Finally, performance standards are developed for marketing activities. A **performance** **standard** specifies the minimum level of expected performance for an activity. Marketing managers evaluate each activity as the marketing plan is implemented to see if the performance standards are being met. Whenever managers receive information that shows activities are not being performed as expected, they must take immediate action to correct problems.

CHECKPOINT
Why is a marketing plan key to effective marketing management?

22.2.2 Determine Marketing Effectiveness

Managers may not always agree on what effective marketing is. The definition of marketing presented at the beginning of this book states that effective marketing results in satisfying exchanges. Accordingly, **marketing effectiveness** means that both customers and the business are satisfied. Based on that definition, to determine if marketing is effective, marketing managers need to determine when both the customer and the business are satisfied.

Measure Customer Satisfaction

Customers are satisfied when they select a company's product or service to meet a need, use it, and choose it again when they have the same need. Therefore, an increasing level of sales is usually a good indication of customer satisfaction. However, companies should be careful to gather information on repeat purchases and use. They should be able to identify the level of sales for specific target markets and, if sales are growing, how much is from new customers and how much is from repeat purchases by satisfied customers.

Many companies spend a great deal of time and money studying customer satisfaction. They telephone customers or ask them to complete surveys. They may ask customers to provide feedback on their purchase, shopping experience, and satisfaction.

Many retailers and other businesses have customer service centers in each store to make it easy for customers to return products, make exchanges, or get help with problems. Internet businesses

MATH IN MARKETING

Use the Rule of 72 for Projections

Determining market share is not always as simple as it looks, even when companies have information about the current size and spending habits of a target market segment. This is because market segments are always shifting, and businesses want to target those that are growing or that can be expected to grow if the right strategies are applied. What is really important is not the size of the segment today, but its size in the future. In other words, what will be the anticipated rate of change in the size of the target market? Rate of change is the increase or decrease over a specified time period such as a year expressed as a ratio or percentage.

While the Rule of 72 most often is used to project the number of years required for an investment to double in value, marketing managers can use it to quickly estimate how fast a market share can be doubled, assuming a constant rate of change each year. Here is the formula:

$$Years = 72 \div Rate$$

where Rate is the annual rate of growth and Years is the number of years needed to double a beginning value.

The formula also can tell you how fast a market needs to grow if a business wants it to double in a given number of years. In that case the formula is:

$$Rate = 72 \div Years$$

The Rule of 72 works well for rates of growth up to about 20 percent per year. For rates ranging from 20 percent to 36 percent, substitute 78 for the 72 in each formula.

Do the Math

1. If Samco Inc. wants to double its Midwest sales in five years to justify a new warehouse, how fast must sales grow each year?

2. If Samco's marketing manager estimates that segment sales will grow 12 percent annually indefinitely, how long will it take to double sales? How long will it take to quadruple sales?

try to make customer service easy by providing options for customers to contact the business through telephone, email, or instant messaging. Simple procedures to make product returns or to obtain service and repairs are also important to companies that sell products via the Internet, telephone, or catalog.

Businesses must keep records of customer questions, problems, and complaints as well as positive responses. Customer service employees should complete a report of each contact, the reason for service, and the results so that common problems can be identified and eliminated. Any customer contact, its purpose, and the actions taken should be documented.

Companies should not ignore the satisfaction of other businesses in the channel of distribution. Retailers and wholesalers are customers of manufacturers. If they are not satisfied with the manufacturer's products and services or their working relationships, they may decide to work with a competitor. Manufacturers need to gather information from retail and wholesale customers regarding any problems they have with the company's products so the problems can be resolved. Many businesses now involve other channel members in planning customer service and evaluation procedures. They regularly check with those businesses to make sure they are receiving the support needed to be effective and to provide customer feedback that relates to the cooperating business.

Measure Business Satisfaction

Every business and organization operate for a purpose. For many businesses, the purpose is to make a profit, but this is not always the case. Some people start and operate a business because they enjoy the work. Organizations are developed to contribute to society. The success of schools, churches, city missions, public health centers, and other similar organizations is determined by looking at how the community or society improved as result of their work.

ANALYZE GOALS The success of a business is determined by whether or not it is meeting its goals. If the goal of a business is to increase sales or market share, it will not be successful if sales or market share decline. If a business sets a goal to achieve a profit of 4 percent of all sales or an 11 percent return on the owners' investment, it will be successful when it achieves that goal. If the goal of an organization is to change the attitudes or behaviors of people (stop smoking, stay in school), it will be successful if people in its target market change those attitudes or behaviors.

Most goals of businesses and organizations are quite specific and can be measured. Businesses gather information on sales, costs, market share, and profits to determine their success. Nonprofit organizations gather information on increases in attendance, use of services, changes in behavior, or differences in attitudes and beliefs.

FINANCIAL ANALYSIS When people think of marketing, they often fail to recognize the importance of budgets and financial performance. Marketing managers must understand and use financial information to determine the success of marketing activities. Sales of products in various markets can be compared from one year to the next. Costs associated with specific activities can be analyzed. Profits from one target market can be compared with those from another. The profitability of a specific marketing strategy can be analyzed.

EMPLOYEE SATISFACTION Managers also need to be concerned about the satisfaction of the people who work for the business. There is a great deal of evidence that employees who enjoy their work are more productive. Marketing managers need to determine the level of employee satisfaction. Some companies ask their employees to complete surveys. Others hold regular meetings where employees can discuss problems and make suggestions.

Many companies form self-directed work teams. A **self-directed work team** is a group of employees that works together toward a common purpose or goal without the usual managerial supervision. Although the work team is not a part of management, it is given many of the management responsibilities for planning, organizing, and evaluating its work. Members need to possess (1) technical job skills, (2) interpersonal skills, such as writing, speaking, and negotiating, and (3) administrative skills such as the ability to conduct meetings, to think analytically, and to maintain records.

The teams also have a great deal of responsibility for setting goals. They may determine the ways that work should be completed or how to solve customer problems. They may even be responsible for hiring other members of the team and determining how bonus money or other rewards are distributed. Involving employees in decisions usually increases their satisfaction. A company that uses self-directed work teams will want to evaluate the effectiveness of that strategy and prepare the team members to be able to evaluate the results of their work.

Why do you think people who enjoy their work are more productive than those who don't?

CHECKPOINT

When marketing managers use the marketing concept, how do they measure marketing effectiveness?

22.2 ASSESSMENT

What Have You Learned?

1. What does a performance standard indicate? [22.2.1]
2. How do companies measure customer satisfaction? [22.2.2]

Make Academic Connections

1. **Management**   Identify three activities you complete on a regular basis at home, school, and in your after-school activities or hobbies. For each activity, prepare a specific performance standard that specifies the minimum level of expected performance for the activity in order for it to be completed successfully. For example, "A student can have no more than two unexcused absences in a semester." [22.2.1]

2. **Research**   Use the library and Internet to locate information on factors that contribute to employee satisfaction. Prepare a two-page report of your findings. Make sure to reference the information sources you used to prepare your report. [22.2.2]

Connect to ◇DECA

Build your Portfolio

Your team has been asked to develop a survey that can be given to customers of a local movie theater to determine their level of satisfaction with important aspects of the entertainment experience. Prepare an easy-to-complete survey of no more than 10 items. Present the survey to your teacher (judge) and discuss the importance of each item as a measure of customer satisfaction. [22.2.2]

22.3 THE MARKETING MANAGER ROLE

Learning Objectives

22.3.1 Describe the kinds of activities marketing managers perform in carrying out the planning and organizing functions.

22.3.2 Detail the way in which marketing managers staff, lead, and control their organizations effectively.

Key Terms

policies
procedures

marketing matters

The activities managers perform while carrying out the five management functions vary. The activities depend largely on the specific management position and the type of organization. Senior executives focus on long-range planning and develop strategies. Lower-level managers spend time implementing the decisions senior executives make. Marketing managers work on marketing activities, while other managers concentrate on the business functions for which they are responsible.

essential question

How is the work of a top-level marketing manager similar to and different from the work of a lower-level marketing manager?

22.3.1 ▶ Plan and Organize

In this lesson, we examine and compare the roles of two marketing managers as they relate to the management functions. Oyang Chen is the executive vice president of marketing for an international automobile manufacturer. James Swathmore is a field sales manager for a food products wholesaler. He supervises five salespeople in a large northeastern U.S. state. The partial organization charts in **Figure 22-3** compare Chen's and Swathmore's positions.

FIGURE 22-3 Chen and Swathmore occupy very different positions on their companies' organization charts.

Planning

Ms. Chen spends most of her time planning with four other top executives and the CEO to set the direction for the company. She is involved in long-range strategic planning, which identifies how the company must change over the next five to ten years. Ms. Chen studies consumer purchasing trends throughout the world and how the economies of various countries are developing. She is very concerned about international trade agreements, increases and decreases of quotas, and changes in tariffs among several countries that have a major impact on the international automobile industry. Energy sources and prices, inflation, and the values of world currencies also are concerns for Ms. Chen.

The major responsibility of Ms. Chen's office is to prepare the company's marketing plan. The plan is developed for a five-year period, with specific plans for each of the five years. Each year the plan is revised and extended for another year, so the company is always planning five years in advance. The marketing plan is used by seven regional managers to prepare specific plans for their regions of the global market.

Mr. Swathmore also is involved in planning, but he concentrates on short-term plans. He develops and implements quarterly, monthly, and weekly plans. He is most concerned with the promotional mix element and selling responsibilities. However, he must be very familiar with the product mix element, distribution, and pricing strategies because each of those has a major impact on the work of his salespeople.

Mr. Swathmore spends most of his planning time identifying customers, assigning them to salespeople, developing schedules and budgets for each person, and helping salespeople develop specific sales strategies for major customers.

Organizing

Ms. Chen and Mr. Swathmore have very different organizing responsibilities. The automobile manufacturer is organized into seven worldwide regions. The food wholesaler is organized by customer type and geographically by state. Five common ways that companies organize their marketing operations are shown in **Figure 22-4**.

Ms. Chen's organizing activities focus on developing marketing policies and procedures for the entire company. **Policies** are rules or guidelines a company uses to make consistent decisions. **Procedures** are the steps employees follow for consistent performance of important activities. Policies and procedures will help determine the organizational structure for marketing, the functions that are performed, and the types of companies that will participate in marketing the automobiles.

Mr. Swathmore must follow the policies and procedures his manager established. He is responsible for determining the activities that need to be performed and assigning those duties to the salespeople. He delegates authority and responsibility to each salesperson to complete the necessary selling tasks.

 CHECKPOINT
What are the key distinctions between the types of planning and organizing activities done by a top-level and lower-level marketing executive?

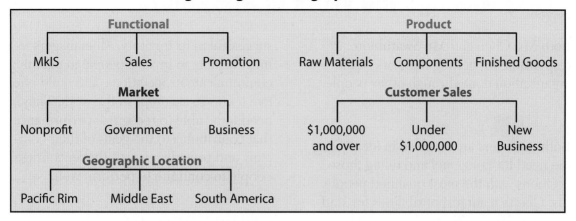

FIGURE 22-4 Marketing activities can be organized in several different ways depending on the type of organization and its markets.

MARKETING COMMUNICATION

Marketing Department Organization

The size of marketing departments can range from one person in a small business to thousands in the nation's largest companies. People who work in marketing can be required to perform a wide variety of tasks or they can be highly specialized. Consider some of the marketing specializations and positions that might be found in a large marketing department. The Chief Marketing Officer would be at the top of the organizational chart. Beneath this top job, any or all of the following departments could be found: Advertising, Branding, Communications, Crisis Management, Customer Loyalty & Relations, Event Planning, Marketing Research, Marketing Strategy, Partnerships, Product Development & Management, Product Pricing, Product Research & Innovation, Programs & Campaigns, Public Relations, Social Responsibility, and Web Production. Because a marketing department can be organized in a variety of ways, it is key to determine the areas of expertise and positions needed to maximize effectiveness and ensure success.

Think Critically

Based on the positions listed above, draw an organizational chart for a marketing department. When you are finished, compare it with examples you find on the Internet.

Both Ms. Chen and Mr. Swathmore are responsible for getting the work of the organization done through other people.

Staffing

Both managers are involved in identifying the need for personnel and filling those positions with the most qualified people. Ms. Chen's main responsibilities for staffing are to work with the company's human resources personnel to develop employment policies and procedures. She makes decisions about the percentage of the marketing budget that will be allocated to employee salaries, benefits, and expenses. She also will hire a few people to be her assistants.

Mr. Swathmore is directly responsible for the salespeople who work in the territory he manages. He may not have total responsibility for hiring each person, but he identifies when an opening exists and describes the requirements for any open position. He helps with recruiting, interviewing, and selecting the person to fill the position. Most sales managers are very active in training new salespeople and helping to improve the selling skills of experienced employees.

Leading

Leading is an important responsibility for each of the managers. Some people would expect that Ms. Chen has more leadership responsibilities because she is the top marketing executive in the company. Yet Mr. Swathmore must be an effective leader if the selling team is to be successful in its territory. All managers must be able to involve people in planning, communicate expectations, and build effective teams to accomplish the work. They need to be able to recognize performance that contributes to the goals of their company and provide rewards that encourage people to continue to perform well.

Controlling

Controlling is another area where both managers have similar responsibilities. Both prepare objectives and plans to guide their work. They develop standards for performance of marketing activities. The major controlling activity is gathering and reviewing information to determine if the objectives, plans, and standards are being met. Ms. Chen is concerned about the entire marketing plan and performance in all of the marketing departments. Mr. Swathmore concentrates on the activities and results of the sales department and salespeople.

Both managers need an effective marketing information system. The marketing information system gathers and analyzes information. It identifies when problems are occurring. Both Mr. Swathmore and Ms. Chen spend a great deal of time studying reports. They must identify the parts of their plans that are working well and the areas in which problems may be developing. Ms. Chen concentrates on products or regions that have high and low performance. Mr. Swathmore is concerned about individual customers and salespeople.

Want to know more about what is trending with this topic? Click on **Lesson 22.3, Marketing Decisions,** *in your MindTap.*

Connect to MindTap

When a problem is identified, the managers work quickly to correct it. They review budgets, schedules, and activities from their plans to determine those not performing as expected. They will revise the plans if it is clear that the original plans will not work.

CHECKPOINT
For which management functions do top-level and lower-level marketing managers tend to have similar responsibilities?

22.3 ASSESSMENT

What Have You Learned?

1. What is the purpose of a company's marketing policies and procedures? [22.3.1]
2. What is the major controlling activity for a manager? [22.3.2]

Make Academic Connections

1. **Career Success** Decide whether you would prefer to hold an executive management position or a specialized position. Prepare a three-paragraph report on the reasons for your choice. [22.3.1, 22.3.2]
2. **Leadership** A student club will operate a school concession stand at the varsity athletic events this fall, and you will manage the project. Using presentation software,

make five slides, one for each of the management functions. For each function, list the activities that will need to be completed. Be prepared to present your slides in class. [22.3.2]

Connect to ◇DECA
Build your Portfolio

Work with another student to prepare two role-play scenarios of a retail store department manager meeting with a salesperson to discuss the importance of customer service. One role-play should demonstrate effective leadership, and the other should demonstrate ineffective leadership. Present both role-plays to your teacher (judge) and be prepared to answer questions. [22.3.2]

Connect to MindTap

*Analyze a case study that focuses on chapter concepts. Click on **Chapter 22, Case Study,** in your MindTap.*

CHAPTER 22 ASSESSMENT

Review Marketing Concepts

1. Every department in an organization has a manager. What do you think the role of the sales manager is in a company? [22.1.1]

2. A manager has several different functions. Which do you think is more important for a manager: the staffing function or the organizing function? [22.1.2]

3. Why is it important for marketing managers to involve their employees in developing a marketing plan? [22.2.1]

4. How have Internet sales businesses, such as eBay and Amazon, changed the way a business measures customer satisfaction? [21.2.2]

5. Explain why it is so difficult for a business to develop a five-year plan. [21.3.1]

6. Why do managers at every level of an organization need an effective marketing information system? [21.3.2]

Marketing Research and Planning

1. Look at the classified ads in your local newspaper or in an online job board. Find at least five ads for management jobs. For each job, list the qualifications needed. Is there one qualification that is common to all of the ads? If so, what is it? [22.1.1]

2. Identify a specific business and the product or service it markets. Write a paragraph explaining how that organization can use each section of a marketing plan as a guide for each of its management functions. Describe the function and the marketing management activities that would be completed to market the product or service. [22.1.1]

3. There are many management tools such as total quality management, six sigma, benchmarking, balanced scorecard, continuous process improvement, and others to help managers improve the effectiveness of their organization. Search the Internet for articles on a management tool of your choice. Write a 400-word paper explaining the tool, how it is used, and whether or not it is considered effective. Cite at least three research sources. Be prepared to present your paper to the class. [22.2.2]

4. Mark Peters is the owner/manager of a wholesale electrical supply house. He has 40 employees and until recently has managed the entire operation himself. Lately his business is growing. He has decided he needs to reorganize the business and have a layer of management that reports to him.

   Eighteen people work in the warehouse. They are responsible for shipping, receiving, and inventory. The supply house has five employees who work the counter, maintain inventory records, and handle some of the more routine paperwork. There are ten truck drivers who deliver and pick up merchandise. Seven people work in the office handling budgets, accounts receivable, and orders.

   Develop an organization chart for the business, adding the new layer of management. Indicate management and employee levels and areas of responsibility. [22.3.1]

5. Managers realize that a good product or service will go unsold unless the employees do the best job possible in dealing with customers. Managers spend a great deal of time motivating and encouraging employees to do their very best. From your personal

experience or using research, identify and describe five ways that managers can support their employees through positive motivation. State which ones in your view are the most effective and why. [22.2.1]

6. A business usually will be successful if satisfactory exchanges are made. Both the company and the customer must be satisfied that they have received the most value for their money. List five specific things that indicate a customer is satisfied and five that indicate business satisfaction. Describe how each of the types of customer satisfaction and business satisfaction can be measured. Be specific. [22.2.2]

Marketing Management and Decision Making

1. A home improvement store sells to both businesses and final consumers. It has recently decided to survey its customers to determine if they are satisfied with the service they are receiving. The results obtained are shown in the table below.

   a. The company surveyed 1,100 final consumers and 550 business consumers. Develop a table that identifies the number of yes and no responses to each of the questions for final consumers and business consumers.

   b. Develop a bar graph comparing the responses of business and final consumers for each of the survey items.

   c. Identify three problems that company managers can address and recommend an action that can be taken to correct the problems.

   d. For each of the actions you identified develop a specific performance standard to measure its effectiveness. [22.2.1, 22.2.2]

2. Form a team as directed by your teacher for this project. Using the Internet, access the website of the U.S. Bureau of Economic Analysis (www.bea.gov). Use the search feature at the top of the page to search for GDP by state. Locate a report of the gross domestic product (GDP) of all states for the most recent year.

   Use a computer to create a spreadsheet. Enter each state name and the state-by-state GDP figures into two columns of the spreadsheet.

   Use a map of the United States to organize the states into 10 contiguous sales regions. Include Alaska and Hawaii in a region with West Coast states. Cut and paste the information in your spreadsheet to organize it into 10 groups representing the sales regions your team developed. Use the spreadsheet functions to calculate the total GDP in dollars for each sales region. Also calculate the percentage GDP (based on total U.S. GDP) for each region. Prepare a report that

	FINAL CONSUMERS		BUSINESS CONSUMERS	
	% YES	% NO	% YES	% NO
Are products usually available?	45	55	75	25
Do you wait more than two minutes to be helped?	15	85	37	63
Is sales staff knowledgeable?	95	5	83	17
Are prices competitive?	50	50	94	6
Is sales staff courteous?	82	18	85	15

identifies the 10 sales regions with their constituent states, showing the GDP in dollars and the percentage GDP for each region. Use the spreadsheet to prepare one or more pie charts for your report that illustrate the sales region information. [22.2.1]

Let's Start a Band! Follow-Up Discussion

Work in small teams to discuss the question posed at the end of the opening vignette. Can you help the band write an outline for its marketing plan?

Build Your Marketing Plan

In this chapter you learned about planning management and evaluation activities and responsibilities. You will now apply this learning to the development of your marketing plan. To access the chapter-specific tools that you will need to complete this activity, please navigate to Chapter 22 → Build Your Marketing Plan in MindTap. Alternatively, you can access these tools online at NGLSync. Please visit www.nglsync.cengage.com, and search for the companion website that accompanies this book by entering the ISBN, author, or title. Once you locate this companion website, navigate to Build Your Marketing Plan → Chapter 22.

Community Awareness Project

DECA PREP

Build your Portfolio

Successful business leaders understand the importance of developing good community relations. Students participating in the Community Awareness Project will demonstrate the skills needed in initiating; planning and organizing; executing, monitoring, and controlling; and closing a project to raise awareness for a community cause.

The Community Awareness Project can be completed by one to three students. The project consists of the written document and an oral presentation by chapter representatives. The body of the written entry is limited to 20 numbered pages, including the appendix (if needed) but excluding the title page and the table of contents. Students have 15 minutes to present their community awareness project and answer questions from the judge about the project.

The body of the written entry consists of the following parts:

Executive Summary is a one-page description of the project.

Initiating provides a historic background of the selected community issue or cause. This section includes the description and purpose of the project, rationale for selecting the project, and description of the benefits of the project.

Planning and Organizing includes an organizational chart, member involvement, and job descriptions. This section includes the schedule, quality management plan, risk management plan and proposed projected budget.

Execution, Monitoring, and Controlling Describe project implementation, unusual or unforseen challenges or successes, and methods of handling them.

Evaluation and Recommendations includes an evaluation of the project and its impact, and recommendations for future projects.

Bibliography is a list of all resources used.

Appendix Inclusion is optional.

Performance Indicators Evaluated

- Explain the importance of company involvement in community activities. (Promotion)
- Propose community issues for company involvement. (Promotion)
- Identify types of public-relations activities (Promotion)
- Utilize project management skills to start, run, and end projects. (Project Management)
- Monitor project and take corrective actions. (Operations)
- Evaluate project success. (Operations)
- Organize and prioritize work. (Operations)

Go to the DECA website for more detailed information. **www.deca.com**

Think Critically

1. Why do businesses have public relations departments?
2. When should publicity be used as part of a community awareness campaign?
3. Why is it important for organizations to establish positive relationships with the local media?

CHAPTER 23

PLAN YOUR FUTURE IN MARKETING

See how effective advertising leads to successful marketing strategies.
Click on Chapter 23, Visual Focus, **in your MindTap.**

Let's Start a Band!

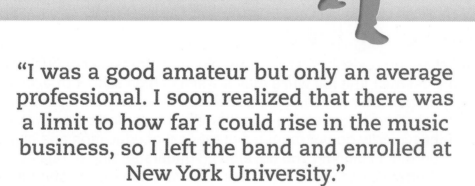

> **"I was a good amateur but only an average professional. I soon realized that there was a limit to how far I could rise in the music business, so I left the band and enrolled at New York University."**
>
> – *Alan Greenspan, Former Chairman of the Federal Reserve*

You've probably already figured this out, but I want to tell you that this is it. Preparing for this next tour has made me realize that I'm not a lifer. So, this is going to be my last tour. I haven't told the rest of the band yet. I'll do that when we get back and help them find my replacement. I know a couple of players who would be a good fit.

I know I'll miss it or at least some of it. I still love performing, but it's the grind of the road that I don't want anymore. What I really like is what you and I always seem to get around to talking about. You know, the business—the marketing—of music. That's what I want to pursue. I really want to learn how to promote and sell music, but I can't do that unless I make a commitment. And I can't commit while still playing in the band. Anyway, can you help me prepare myself for a career in the music business?

MARKETING JOBS AND CAREERS

Learning Objectives

23.1.1 Describe the benefits of choosing a marketing career.

23.1.2 Identify the five employment levels for marketing jobs.

23.1.3 Describe the skills needed to progress through the marketing employment levels.

Key Terms

job
career
marketing jobs
career planning

marketing matters

Marketing jobs exist in every community and almost every business. Many people get their first job while they are still in high school or even earlier. That first job often is a marketing job. It may be delivering newspapers, taking tickets at a movie theater, or serving customers in a fast-food restaurant. Although first jobs typically do not require a great deal of education and experience, they are important in helping you develop an understanding of business operations and important career skills. Business success often means starting at or near the bottom of a company and progressing through the various stages at one or more companies until moving into management.

essential question

What is a potential career path that you might take, and what are the skills necessary for you to navigate that path?

23.1.1 ▶ The Benefits of Working in Marketing

Marketing is one of the most important functions of business today. It provides employment for millions of people. Many of the fastest-growing and highest-paying jobs in our economy are marketing jobs. Whether you are still in high school, have a two- or four-year college degree, or have a graduate degree such as an MBA or PhD, there are employment opportunities in marketing that match your interests and skills.

Marketing Jobs and Careers

You have choices of many different jobs and careers. A **job** is any full- or part-time work in a specific position of employment. Most people hold many jobs during their working lives. On the other hand, a **career** is a chosen area of work, usually made up of a progression of jobs that provides personal and professional satisfaction. Although you may have more than one career in your lifetime, you should base your career choice on your interests, abilities, and preparation. Marketing is an important part of almost every business and many jobs. You will find an understanding of marketing useful to you as you choose and prepare for your career.

For people who have **marketing jobs**, the completion of marketing activities is the most important or only job responsibility. The people who are employed in marketing are responsible for research and product planning, advertising and selling, distribution of products from manufacturers to consumers, customer service, assistance with financing and credit procedures, and many other activities. Because of people who effectively perform their marketing jobs, customers are able to obtain the products and services they need at a fair price, and businesses are able to sell their products and services at a profit.

Marketing jobs are found in all types of businesses. The primary purpose of some businesses, such as advertising agencies and retail stores, is to complete marketing activities. These businesses are responsible for one or more of the marketing mix elements or marketing functions. Most of the jobs in those businesses are marketing jobs.

Businesses and organizations that have a non-marketing activity as their primary purpose, such as manufacturers, service providers, and government agencies, also employ people to complete marketing activities. People who are not directly employed in marketing jobs also need to understand marketing and use marketing skills as a part of their work.

Marketing is a part of every industry. Therefore, you can combine your interest in a given industry with your marketing background for a choice of jobs. Important marketing jobs can be

What is the difference between a job and a career?

© Lisa F. Young/Shutterstock.com

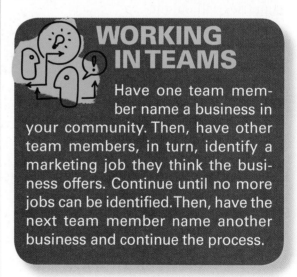

WORKING IN TEAMS

Have one team member name a business in your community. Then, have other team members, in turn, identify a marketing job they think the business offers. Continue until no more jobs can be identified. Then, have the next team member name another business and continue the process.

found in the military and in the entertainment, healthcare, agriculture, and construction industries. Marketers are an essential part of the newest industries, including e-commerce and biotechnology. If you want to work in science, research, publishing, or education, you can find numerous opportunities to combine those interests with your marketing skills.

Some marketing jobs are in business-to-business marketing. Many businesses provide products and services to other businesses rather than to consumers. Steel and plastic producers develop materials used by the auto industry, appliance manufacturers, construction firms, and many other types of businesses. Transportation companies move the products of one company to other companies to be used in their businesses or resold to consumers.

Marketing also occurs globally to meet the needs of people in every country and to support international trade. Many of the products you use daily are produced in other countries. Those products would not be available to you and U.S. companies would not be able to sell their products in other countries without the daily work of millions of people in marketing. International marketing is providing more and more career opportunities.

Specific Benefits of Working in Marketing

Marketing offers many diverse jobs and career choices that fit a variety of individual needs, interests, and lifestyles. Although you may ultimately choose to work in a career area other than marketing, you should still be aware of the many benefits of working in marketing as you make job and career choices.

MANY CHOICES Marketing jobs exist in every industry and within most companies. Marketing jobs are found at the lowest and highest levels of a company and are available for people with varied amounts of education and experience. No matter what your interests, you can find job opportunities in marketing to match them.

*Want to know more about what is trending with this topic? Click on **Lesson 23.1, Global Marketing,** in your MindTap.*

Connect to MindTap

INTERESTING WORK Marketing jobs are not boring. Marketers work with customers and people from other businesses as well as with people in their own company. Most marketing jobs involve creativity and decision making. Marketers are involved in planning, communicating, evaluating, and problem solving. As companies develop new products and services or identify new market opportunities, marketers will be involved from the beginning.

FINANCIAL REWARDS Entry-level marketing jobs sometimes pay the minimum wage. Yet employees who prove to their employer that they understand business operations and have a customer-service attitude are promoted quickly to higher-paying jobs with more responsibility. Marketing jobs are among the highest-paid positions in most companies. Because effective marketing results in higher profits for a company, effective marketers often are compensated with commissions and bonuses to increase the salaries they earn. They also may be entitled to profit-sharing benefits, where they receive a percentage of the company's earnings when the company makes a profit.

STABLE EMPLOYMENT As the economy changes, people may find that job opportunities change as well. People worry they will lose their jobs when the economy is poor. Because marketing activities are so important to the success of most businesses, marketing employees often are the last to be dismissed and the first to be rehired. Marketing skills are useful in many types of businesses and industries. If one industry is not doing well economically, marketing jobs are likely available in industries that are experiencing better economic conditions.

© StockLite/Shutterstock.com

How do marketing skills lead to more stable employment?

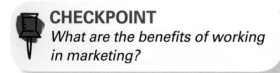

CHECKPOINT
What are the benefits of working in marketing?

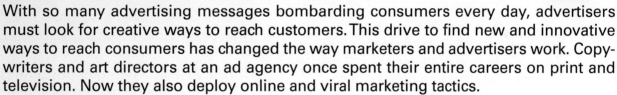

MARKETING COMMUNICATION

Media Redefines Advertising Roles

With so many advertising messages bombarding consumers every day, advertisers must look for creative ways to reach customers. This drive to find new and innovative ways to reach consumers has changed the way marketers and advertisers work. Copywriters and art directors at an ad agency once spent their entire careers on print and television. Now they also deploy online and viral marketing tactics.

Ad agencies such as Crispin Porter + Bogusky, once the advertising agency for Burger King, reach consumers in new and innovative ways. These agencies require their creative department to think outside the box of traditional advertising. In addition to creating print and television ads, they create websites, viral web-based ads, competitions, events, stunts, and even video games. At ad agencies all over the country, traditional roles are becoming less defined, and everyone is being asked to think creatively to help clients.

Think Critically

1. Why is it important for advertisers to be able to think beyond traditional media?
2. If you were in charge of staffing at an advertising agency, what characteristics would you look for in a new hire?

Progress Through Marketing Jobs

Most people will change jobs many times during their lifetime. Entry-level jobs in marketing usually lead to advanced jobs with greater responsibility and higher salaries. A clerk in a store can become a department manager, store manager, and regional manager. Survey specialists working in marketing research can become product and brand managers. A sales associate can progress to salesperson, sales manager, and vice president of sales and marketing. Many chief executive officers (CEOs) of the largest businesses in the United States started their careers in marketing.

Whether you choose marketing or another career, careful career planning is important. **Career planning** is an ongoing process involving self-assessment, career exploration, and decision making leading to a satisfying career decision. You will need to identify the knowledge and skills required for the career you select, the educational preparation needed, and the jobs you will likely hold as you progress through your career. Lack of appropriate preparation often is cited as the reason a person is not considered when a position is filled in an organization.

A number of resources are available to help you plan a career in marketing. Libraries and the Internet provide many career-planning resources and references. Business organizations and many individual businesses provide materials that describe career opportunities and the preparation necessary for each career. People with experience in the careers that interest you often are willing to discuss their work, provide career advice, and even serve as mentors. Career centers and counselors also are valuable planning resources.

Employment Levels in Marketing

Employment opportunities in marketing are available to people with a range of education levels, work experience, and interests. To help with career planning, those opportunities are organized within five levels. The levels of marketing employment are entry, career, specialist, supervisor/manager, and executive/owner (**Figure 23-1**).

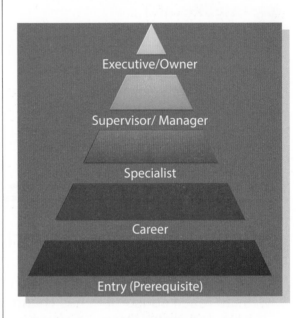

FIGURE 23-1 Marketing opportunities are organized into five levels of employment.

ENTRY LEVEL   People employed in entry-level marketing jobs perform routine activities with limited authority and responsibility. Entry-level jobs require limited education and experience. They often are held by individuals who are still enrolled in high school or who have no education beyond high school. You can often obtain an entry-level marketing job with no previous experience. Entry-level jobs usually pay an hourly wage, often beginning at the minimum wage. Examples are clerk, cashier, and delivery person.

People who hold entry-level positions usually do not view the job as the first step in a career path. They just want part- or full-time employment to earn money. They may move from job to job with no specific plans for the future. Career planning helps people select entry-level jobs that will be interesting, use existing knowledge and skills, and help prepare them for career advancement.

CAREER LEVEL   Career-level positions are more complex than entry-level jobs. People in career-level positions have more control over their work, have a variety of tasks to complete that require specific knowledge and skill to perform well, and usually are involved in problem solving and decision making. As people develop experience and are successful in career-level marketing positions, they may be given limited supervisory responsibilities over a few entry-level employees or may be selected for leadership positions in work teams.

To qualify for career-level jobs, a person will need a year or two of successful experience in the company or a similar business. Instead of or in addition to that experience, a person may need to complete education beyond high school and obtain a two-year or four-year degree.

People in career-level positions usually view the work as more than just a job to earn money. They work in an area of general interest and in a job they think will lead to career advancement. Businesses hire people for career-level positions in marketing who demonstrate understanding of marketing principles and business operations and who have a desire to

develop skills in the area of work that will contribute to the business's success.

SPECIALIST LEVEL   Marketing specialists perform specific work in a business that requires advanced knowledge of a particular area of business operations. They generally will have special training and considerable experience in a particular area of marketing or type of marketing activity. They usually will have a four-year college degree or even a graduate degree or advanced training in their area of work. Examples of marketing specialists include brand and product managers, advertising account executives, lead sales representatives, marketing research specialists, and buyers.

Marketing specialists usually will continue to work in one specific area of marketing and be promoted to advanced positions. They may be hired by other companies because of their specialized marketing expertise.

SUPERVISOR/MANAGER LEVEL
People who have held career-level or specialist positions for some time may want to move into management. They usually will begin as a supervisor or assistant manager with responsibility for a few people in a specific area of the business. Supervisors usually devote only a portion of their work time to management responsibilities. They spend the rest of their time completing the work of their department. If they like managing others and do it well, they likely will be moved to higher levels of management with responsibility for a broader set of management activities.

Supervisors and managers need to understand and usually have some experience working in the area for which they have

Want to know more about marketing in the information age? Click on **Lesson 23.1, Digital Marketing,** in your MindTap.

Connect to
MindTap

management responsibilities. They also must have effective communications, human relations, and leadership skills. People promoted to the position of supervisor or manager usually have several years of experience in the company. However, some people are hired as supervisors or managers with less experience but with specific education or training in management. Companies often have management training programs to help employees learn to be effective managers.

Supervisors and managers are needed in all areas of marketing. Examples include sales manager, inventory manager, customer service manager, marketing information systems manager, and many others.

EXECUTIVE/OWNER LEVEL   The people with the greatest amount of authority and responsibility for marketing are executives and business owners. Executives hold the top marketing positions in a company, such as vice president of marketing or president of international marketing operations. Business owners are responsible for the entire operation of their companies, including marketing.

Marketing executives and business owners need to have a thorough understanding of business principles and procedures, management, and all areas of marketing. They are responsible for all of the major marketing plans and decisions made and the implementation of the plans. They spend most of their time gathering and reviewing information, planning, and evaluating marketing effectiveness to make sure it contributes to the profitability of the business.

Executives will have spent many years in the business, often working in many different marketing jobs. They often have a graduate degree in business. Business owners do not always have as much experience or education. They do have a strong desire to start their own business.

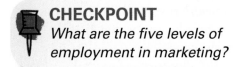

CHECKPOINT
What are the five levels of employment in marketing?

23.1.3 ▶ Skills for Marketing Success

To prepare for a marketing career, you need to understand the skills that will be required for the job you want. Marketing jobs demand two types of knowledge. First, you need foundational skills that are useful in all business careers. Second, you need to develop an understanding of the basic functions of marketing.

Foundational Skills

Marketing is necessary for business success. But marketing skills alone are not enough for a successful business career. Marketing personnel need to develop foundational skills including an understanding of business principles, interpersonal and basic work skills, and academic preparation.

BUSINESS PRINCIPLES   Marketers work closely with people in other parts of the business such as accountants, production personnel, engineers, and information management specialists. Understanding the fundamental principles of business allows people from across the company to communicate and work together effectively. Important business foundations on which marketing is based are economics, finance and accounting, law, technology, business operations, and management. Marketers do not have to be an expert in those areas, but they need to understand basic operations, use business information and reports, and make marketing decisions that support the business's strategy and plans.

INTERPERSONAL AND BASIC WORK SKILLS

Marketers interact with other people. They work with people on their marketing team and with their managers. They communicate with customers to provide information and solve problems, and they are involved regularly with people inside and outside the company. Interpersonal skills including communication, teamwork, human relations, decision making, and problem solving all help to develop and maintain effective work relationships. Additional interpersonal skills include a positive attitude, initiative and responsibility, self-control, creativity, time management, stress management, assertiveness, and flexibility.

Businesses need employees who understand and practice basic work skills. Those skills include promptness, courtesy, motivation, self-discipline, honesty, and ethics. Employees who complete work accurately and on time, use resources wisely, and work to contribute to the success of the business will be recognized and rewarded with opportunities for advancement. Employers also appreciate employees who do more than they are asked, such as finding something else to do upon completing an assigned task. They also want employees who don't create problems with absences or asking for time off at the last minute.

ACADEMIC PREPARATION

Today, most career positions in marketing require education beyond high school. Marketers

© Kinga/Shutterstock.com.

need to have effective writing, speaking, math, and listening skills. Preparation in science, psychology, and technology are helpful in many areas of marketing. Because of the diverse society in which marketers work and the growth of international business, the study of foreign languages and other cultures is also important.

Marketing Functions

Building on business foundational skills, marketers add other skills in one or more of the marketing functions to prepare for a career. Some marketing jobs are specialized and involve one of the nine marketing functions. For example, a person who designs and constructs window displays in a retail mall is performing a specialized promotion activity. In other jobs, the employee must be skilled in several marketing functions. Brand managers for a consumer products manufacturing company need to understand all of the marketing functions. A buyer for a wholesaler or retailer will use skills in finance, pricing, and product management.

Every marketer needs a general understanding of marketing and must be familiar with marketing terms and concepts. In addition, each person will need to develop specialized skills in one or more of the marketing functions to perform their tasks and fulfill their responsibilities (**Figure 23-2**).

CHECKPOINT

What are the two types of fundamental knowledge needed for marketing success?

Marketing Function	Job Tasks/Responsibilities
Market Planning	• Identify and understand the company's markets • Gather and analyze economic, consumer, and competitive information • Recommend marketing strategies
Product and Service Management	• Plan new products and services • Make improvements to existing products • Ensure products are safe, easy-to-use, and perceived as a value
Pricing	• Analyze supply and demand • Set prices that result in a profit for the company • Plan pricing policies • Determine how to communicate price to customers • Determine markdown amounts
Promotion	• Plan promotions that provide customers with necessary information to make a purchase • Plan follow-up to ensure customer satisfaction
Selling	• Represent the company to customers • Build and maintain relationships with customers
Distribution (Logistics)	• Know where customers are located and where they prefer to make their purchases • Plan channels of distribution • Build relationships with other companies involved in the channel • Develop procedures for order processing, inventory management, packaging, shipping, and customer service
Marketing-Information Management	• Provide information to the marketing team, including product information for telemarketers, names of consumers to survey for market researchers, daily sales for product managers
Finance	• Prepare budgets • Identify financial resources to pay for marketing activities • Develop credit plans and policies • Manage leasing process
Risk Management	• Provide security for products, personnel, and customers to reduce the risk associated with marketing decisions and activities • Works with insurance company to identify risks and develop risk-reduction procedures • Purchase insurance to anticipate and manage the cost of possible losses from insurable risks • Identify ways to reduce losses from theft, burglary, shoplifting, and other crimes

FIGURE 23-2 What specific skills will people working in each of these marketing functions need to perform their tasks and fulfill their responsibilities?

© Jacob Lund/Shutterstock.com.

What kind of tasks might you perform if you had a job in market planning?

ASSESSMENT

What Have You Learned?

1. What is the difference between a job and a career? [23.1.1]

2. Explain how marketing jobs can be financially rewarding. [23.1.1]

3. What is career planning? [23.1.2]

4. What foundational skills do marketers need to achieve success in their career? [23.1.3]

Make Academic Connections

1. **Visual Art**   Work with other students to create a bulletin board or other display for your classroom that illustrates the range of marketing jobs in your community. Illustrate jobs that are located in marketing and non-marketing businesses and in business-to-business marketing. [23.1.1]

2. **Writing**   Write a 300-word essay on "The Importance of Career Planning."

The essay should define career planning, explain the career-planning process, the benefits of planning, and what may happen if you do not develop and follow a career plan. [23.1.2]

Connect to ◇DECA

Build your **Portfolio**

Form a marketing research team to study career choices. Survey 25 people and ask them about the primary activity of their employer and get a brief description of their job. Analyze the responses and determine (1) if their employer is a marketing or non-marketing business, (2) if their job is a marketing or non-marketing job, (3) the employment level of their job, and (4) the primary marketing function performed by those with marketing jobs. Prepare charts or graphs and a written summary to report your findings. Present your report to your teacher (judge). [23.1.3]

MARKETING EDUCATION AND CAREER PATHS

Learning Objectives

23.2.1 Describe the importance of marketing education.

23.2.2 Identify non-management and management career paths in marketing.

Key Terms

Marketing Education program
DECA
career area
career path
career plan

marketing matters

Companies need effective managers, but they also need people who are experienced and skilled in particular areas of business operations. Many companies identify the best performers in each area of the business and promote them to management. Businesses also may provide advanced career opportunities for people who do not want to be managers but who are skilled in a particular marketing specialty or function.

essential question

How do you prepare for a marketing career?

23.2.1 ▶ The Benefits of Marketing Education

Preparing for a career in marketing will require both education and experience. It is never too early to start that preparation even if you are unsure if you want a career in marketing. Marketing skills are useful in many jobs. An understanding of marketing principles and the marketing skills you have will make you a valued employee in most businesses and organizations.

You have already begun your preparation for a marketing career with this course and others you have completed in high school. You may have held entry-level marketing jobs giving you some experience and an opportunity to understand many of the ideas you are studying. You must decide if you want to continue your marketing education and what additional

knowledge and skills you need to develop for the career of your choice.

What Is Marketing Education?

You can learn about marketing and develop marketing skills at almost any point in your education. Marketing education begins in middle schools with career exploration programs, job shadowing experiences, and introductory business courses.

At the high school level, many schools offer business and marketing classes as electives designed to develop general knowledge of marketing principles. Specialized marketing courses may be available to allow study of topics ranging from personal selling and advertising to sports marketing or fashion.

Career programs in marketing education provide the most comprehensive preparation opportunities for high school students considering full-time employment in marketing after graduation or for those considering additional education after high school. A **Marketing Education program** incorporates three types of complementary learning experiences—introductory and advanced courses in marketing, business work experiences, and a student organization called DECA. **DECA** is an international association of high school and college students studying marketing, management, and entrepreneurship in business, finance, hospitality, and marketing sales and service.

DECA courses offer understanding of marketing principles in an applied academic environment. Work experience gives students the chance to practice and test their marketing skills in a business, interacting with experienced employees, managers, and customers. Participation in DECA complements coursework and job experiences by providing student-led opportunities to build teamwork and leadership skills, participate in professional development experiences such as conferences and seminars, and enhance and test marketing skills through individual and group competitions.

Beyond High School

Marketing education opportunities expand after high school. Two- and four-year colleges offer marketing degrees as well as

What are the benefits of a marketing education?

Scott T. Baxter/Photodisc/Getty Images

graduate education programs. Today, most marketers complete additional specialized training offered by their employers or by professional associations.

COMMUNITY COLLEGE PROGRAMS Community colleges offer business and marketing courses as a part of an academic curriculum through which students can earn an Associate of Arts degree. The courses and degree will qualify graduates for a number of career-level positions in marketing. In addition, the Associate of Arts degree can become a step toward a bachelor's degree for students who transfer to a four-year college or university.

Community colleges also offer one-year certificate programs that provide very specialized study of a specific set of marketing skills (selling, inventory management, small business management) for immediate employment. Two-year career programs that offer an Associate of Applied Science (AAS) degree are structured in a similar way to the high school Marketing Education programs. They include coursework in English, math, natural science, and social science. Then students can choose to complete a general marketing curriculum or a specialized program such as Hospitality Marketing, Food Marketing, E-Commerce Marketing, Professional Selling, and Fashion Marketing.

Many two-year career programs offered by community colleges include structured part-time or full-time work experiences in marketing jobs and a student organization, Delta Epsilon Chi. Many community colleges now cooperate with high schools to offer college-level courses to students while they are still enrolled in high school. Students who complete those courses successfully can graduate with both a high school diploma and a number of credits toward a two-year degree at the community college.

COLLEGE STUDY   You can earn a bachelor's degree in marketing at most colleges and universities. Those programs incorporate study of advanced marketing skills that prepare graduates for career-level and specialist-level positions in business. Popular marketing courses in colleges today include international marketing, entrepreneurship, e-commerce, sports marketing, and marketing management.

LIFELONG LEARNING   Marketing education is a lifelong experience. Companies spend thousands of dollars each

WORKING IN TEAMS

Have each team member identify a two- or four-year college or university they are interested in attending. Visit the website of each institution and identify the marketing degree programs offered. List them in a two-column table. List those programs that are based on marketing functions in one column and those based on marketing industries in the other.

year to offer training to improve the skills of marketing personnel. Marketers participate in conferences and seminars and read business and marketing magazines to update their knowledge about the best marketing practices. Marketers who want to move into executive management positions usually will complete a graduate program in business such as a Master of Business Administration (MBA). Executive education programs are offered to top marketing managers in companies to improve their understanding of the changing economy, to introduce the latest technology, and to improve decision-making abilities.

CHECKPOINT
What are the three types of learning experiences in a Marketing Education program?

Planning for a career in business or any other field is made up of several components. First you identify a career area. A **career area** is the type of business or the business function in which you plan to work. Examples include marketing, finance, information management, and production. After choosing a career area, you need to consider the career path you want to follow within it. A **career path** is a series of related jobs with increasing knowledge and skill requirements and greater amounts of responsibility.

After choosing the career area and career path, you need to compare your current academic preparation and experience with the jobs in the career path and then prepare a career plan. A **career plan** identifies the progression of jobs in your career path; your plans for education, training, and experience to meet the requirements for those jobs; and a time schedule for accomplishing the plan.

You probably will change your career plan several times during your working life. However, without a plan you likely will not pay attention to important changes and will seldom be prepared to pursue promotions, advancements, and make job changes. People who complete career planning are more likely to have jobs they like and are better prepared to perform them than those who do not have a career plan.

There are so many career opportunities in marketing that it may be difficult to choose a career path. However, because of the many opportunities, it is possible to develop a general career path and then make it more specific in the future as you gain experience and complete further education. One of the decisions that will guide career planning is whether you want to prepare for a management or non-management career.

Moving into Management

Managers are needed for each of the major marketing functions. There will usually be several supervisory positions available in every marketing department. Most companies have one or more executive-level marketing management positions at the top of the company.

Preparing for a management career will require combining the development of marketing skills and management skills. Managers usually have several years of full-time work experience in career-level and specialist-level marketing jobs. They will then become a manager-trainee or supervisor. The career path will lead to an assistant manager position followed by assignments to a series of management jobs with greater and greater responsibilities. To move into senior management positions, you will want to gain experience in several different marketing jobs, learn as much about business operations as possible, take on important projects for the company, continue to improve your management skills, and do more than what is expected of you.

Non-Management Marketing Careers

Businesses recently have reduced the number of management levels and given individual employees and employee teams more responsibility and authority. Management is no longer viewed as the only path to career success. Companies are developing non-management career paths and providing rewards and recognition for non-management employees who offer specific skills to the business.

How can individuals prepare for a management career in marketing?

a career path in one of two ways—either by industry or by marketing function.

INDUSTRY PATHS You might decide to consider the marketing opportunities in an industry that interests you. For example, you might be interested in automobiles, construction, entertainment, or healthcare. After identifying the industry, you should identify the entry- and career-level job opportunities and the advanced marketing jobs to which they lead.

For example, companies recognize that an experienced salesperson who enjoys selling might not be happy or effective as a sales manager. That salesperson should have the opportunity to become a lead account representative rather than a sales manager to advance in his or her career. A creative person who has prepared a number of successful ad campaigns may be more valuable to the company as a senior copywriter than as an advertising manager.

If you choose a non-management career path, you may want to specialize in one area of marketing. You will want to get as much experience as possible in that area to continue to improve your skills. You may be able to move from one company to another to gain experience. You will want to continue your education to ensure that you have expertise in the latest procedures and technology in the area of marketing in which you specialize.

Career Paths in Marketing

You have many choices of career paths in marketing. And, because marketing is a part of almost every business and industry as well as non-business organizations, you have choices of the types of businesses, locations, and working conditions you want for almost any career path. You can select

MARKETING FUNCTION PATHS On the other hand, you might be interested in a specific marketing function such as promotion, distribution, or financing. In that case, career opportunities will exist in a number of specialties. You can study the types of increasingly responsible jobs you will hold in advertising, sales, inventory, transportation, or credit services. Each area will have one or more career paths you can follow.

Examples of career paths related to marketing functions can be found in the areas of advertising, marketing research, and retailing. An advertising career might begin with an internship in an advertising agency. Your career could progress to a job in media traffic where you help to place ads in selected media and monitor the media to ensure the advertisements are run as planned. Advancement in advertising might take you through jobs as an account executive, account supervisor, and finally director of advertising.

A career in marketing research starts as an interviewer or data analyst. The next step may be survey planning and design. You can be promoted to a position as a project director and finally to director of marketing research.

In the retailing career path, most people start as a cashier, stockperson, or salesperson. By demonstrating initiative, a customer service attitude, and effective job skills, you can quickly become an assistant manager for a department. That job progresses to manager, assistant store manager, and store manager. Retail careers can then progress to district and regional management and on to division vice president.

These are only a few examples of common career paths in marketing. Other choices exist within each of the marketing functions we have examined as well as in the other areas of marketing. You need to review the many available career resources and discuss your interests with experienced marketers to identify the various career possibilities open to you.

CHECKPOINT
How do management and non-management career paths differ?

23.2 ASSESSMENT

What Have You Learned?

1. What are the three complementary learning experiences in a Marketing Education program? [23.2.1]

2. What are the benefits of having a career plan? [23.2.2]

Make Academic Connections

1. **Math** Data from the Bureau of Labor Statistics shows the median weekly earnings by educational attainment. Adults working full time who dropped out of high school had weekly earnings of $553. Those who completed high school averaged $730 a week. College graduates earned an average of $862 with an associate's degree, $1,198 with a bachelor's degree, $1,434 with a master's degree, and $1,825 with a doctoral degree. The percentage increase in earnings that results from earning a high school degree is 32 percent ($730 − $553 = $177; $177 ÷ $553 = 0.32).

    a. What is the percentage increase in earnings that results from progressing from an associate's to a bachelor's degree?

    b. What is the percentage increase in earnings that results from progressing from a master's to a doctoral degree? Round answers to the nearest tenth of a percent. [23.2.1]

2. **Decision Making** Prepare a table that compares the advantages and disadvantages of management and non-management career paths. Use the information in the table to develop a three-paragraph statement explaining which career path you would choose at this time and why. [23.2.2]

Connect to ◇DECA

Build your Portfolio

You are interviewing for a job as a salesperson in a new department store. The company wants a person with enough business understanding and leadership experience to begin supervising several part-time salespeople within six months. Your teacher (judge) will ask you to describe why you believe you are qualified for the job. Be prepared to convince the interviewer that you are the best person for both the sales and supervisor positions. [23.2.1]

CAREER PLANNING

Learning Objectives

23.3.1 Describe the steps in preparing a career plan.

23.3.2 Discuss how to successfully apply for a job.

Key Terms

career portfolio
electronic portfolio

marketing matters

How do you prepare for a career in marketing? In addition to the courses you take in high school and college, experience is an important part of your preparation. Some of the experience will be actual work experience in entry- and career-level marketing jobs. But there are many other experiences you can have while in high school that can help you develop skills needed for success in marketing.

essential question

How would you go about preparing for a career in marketing?

23.3.1 ▶ Choices and Decisions

Right now you may think preparing for a career in business is like trying to assemble a jigsaw puzzle. Hundreds of pieces to the puzzle lay before you, but it is almost impossible to envision how they fit together. You know that marketing careers require a combination of education and experience. You must determine what types of education and experience you need as well as where and when to obtain them.

You may know right now that you want a career in marketing and even may have decided on the specific job in which you are most interested. On the other hand, you may have decided on a non-marketing career, but you can see how an understanding of marketing will

benefit you. Or you may be undecided on a career and are just beginning to consider your choices.

Don't be concerned if you have not made a specific career choice yet. People change jobs many times during their lifetime and often move into totally different areas of work than they originally planned. Still, it is important to focus on the impact that education and the employment choices you make will have on your career.

Combine Education and Experience

You are more likely to have a successful business career if you understand the requirements for the entry-level job you want and develop the necessary skills. Career planning becomes a process of determining your interests and abilities, exploring the requirements for the job you want, and planning the education and experience you need to qualify for the job. Employers value both education and experience.

You will need strong academic skills (reading, writing, and mathematics) as well as knowledge of business and marketing. The courses you have completed as well as the remaining courses you will take in high school will prepare you for your career choice. College coursework can add to your academic and career preparation.

Having business experience is always an advantage. Employers value experience because it demonstrates your interest in business, your motivation, interpersonal skills, and the ability to apply what you have learned in your classes. It is relatively easy to find an entry-level job in marketing if you are open-minded about the type of work you will do. Even though a job may not pay as much as you might like, and you will need to juggle your work schedule with school and extracurricular activities, a good work record provides an advantage when you apply for other jobs. You also may gain experience by volunteering to provide marketing services for nonprofit organizations such as the Red Cross or a local hospital.

Students who participate in sports may not have the free time needed to gain work experience in a part-time job or volunteer activities. However, involvement in sports also provides the opportunity to develop skills employers seek, including

*Want to know more about what is trending with this topic? Click on **Lesson 23.3, Marketing Decisions,** in your MindTap.*

Connect to MindTap

communication and teamwork skills as well as the chance to interact with diverse groups of people. Some employers seek out student-athletes because they believe the dedication, determination, focus, and goal orientation needed to succeed in sports are the same qualities that lead to success in business.

If you have successful entry-level experience in high school, you may be able to qualify for more advanced jobs when you seek full-time employment after high school or for jobs you hold while in college. You can add to your work experience by completing internships, working on projects and activities in school organizations, and volunteering in community organizations.

Develop a Career Plan

Planning is an important marketing skill that is necessary to obtain the job you want. By developing a career plan, you not only will increase the chances of obtaining the job you really want, but you also will be practicing an important business skill. Employers will be impressed with the efforts you devote to career planning.

To develop an effective career plan, follow these steps:

1. Complete an assessment of your current knowledge, skills, and interests. Work with teachers, counselors, and others to identify tests and other resources that will improve your self-understanding in order to make the best matches with possible careers.

2. Research to determine the industries and types of marketing jobs available and the work required in the jobs that interest you.

3. Identify the education and experience requirements for the marketing careers that interest you. Interview employees and visit businesses to add to your knowledge. Compare the results with your current education and experience to determine what you need to qualify for jobs in the career area of your choice.

4. Make a list of the knowledge and skills you will need to develop. Meet with experienced people (teachers, counselors, and businesspeople) who are familiar with education and work opportunities to gather advice on the possible choices for additional education and work experience. Share your career plans with them and have them help you make the best matches to achieve your career goals.

5. Prepare a written career plan. The plan may be general at first, but you can make it more specific as you gather more information. The plan should identify the career area of interest to you and possible jobs that make up a career path. You should list the knowledge and skills you will need and the choices of education and experience that you have made to assist you with your career development. You may want to include a timeline that projects how long it will take to complete the experiences listed.

CHECKPOINT
Why do employers value work experience when hiring a new employee?

23.3.2 ▶ Obtain the Job You Want

The importance of career planning will become apparent when you apply for the job you want and are hired because the employer was impressed with your preparation and planning. The information in your career plan will help you complete applications for jobs or for schools.

Prepare a Career Portfolio

A career portfolio is an excellent resource to help you with career planning and job applications. A **career portfolio** is an organized collection of information and materials developed to represent you, your preparation, and your accomplishments.

Select and organize items for your portfolio that you think provide the best evidence of your marketing knowledge and skills. Those items can include tests, reports, and projects completed in classes, summaries of aptitude or interest tests you

have taken, projects and activities you completed in a club or organization, and even work done for a hobby if it demonstrates important business or marketing skills. For example, you may have developed a personal website on your computer that demonstrates technology skills. You may have won an award for a marketing research report you prepared and presented for a state or national DECA competition. Both the report and the award are excellent additions to your portfolio. You also can include materials you created during this class for the Build Your Portfolio activities.

If you have worked for a business or volunteered for a nonprofit organization, you may have work reports or performance reviews that you can incorporate into your career portfolio. If you completed a special project on the job and your employer allows you to have a copy, you should include it.

MATH IN MARKETING

Job Market Outlook

Jobs in the United States are expected to increase on average 7.4 percent between 2016 and 2026. The following table shows the number of employees projected to be hired in five marketing job categories in the growing U.S. job market during this time.

Category	2016	2026
Advertising and promotions managers	31,300	33,000
Marketing managers	218,300	240,400
Sales managers	385,500	414,400
Public relations and fundraising specialists	73,500	81,100
Market research analysts and marketing specialists	595,400	733,700

Do the Math

1. What is the increase in employment in each category? (Hint: The increase in employment for marketing managers is 240,400 − 218,300 = 22,100.)

2. What is the percentage increase in each category? Round your answer to the nearest tenth of a percent. (Hint: The percentage increase for marketing managers is 22,100 ÷ 218,300 = 0.1012368 = 10.1%.)

Source: "Employment by detailed occupation." Bureau of Labor Statistics. January 30, 2018. https://www.bls.gov/emp/tables/emp-by-detailed-occupation.htm

Photos of work you have completed also provide evidence of skills. You should include any awards or recognition you have received in school or on the job.

Make sure your portfolio is well organized so you can easily locate items when needed and others can quickly review your work. You will add to the portfolio as you continue your education and career.

You may prefer to create an electronic portfolio or e-portfolio. An **electronic portfolio** is prepared, maintained, and saved using computer technology. Developing your portfolio electronically not only demonstrates your proficiency with technology but makes it easier to update and share with others. Scan copies of printed materials you want to include and retain the original version of the document.

Apply for the Job You Want

Once you have prepared your career plan and portfolio, you are ready to begin your job search and then apply for the marketing job you want.

IDENTIFY JOBS The first step in a job search is to identify available positions. You can find career opportunities on various Internet sites such as Jobs.com or in the local newspaper. Job listings are usually organized by the type of job or job title.

Most companies maintain a listing of open positions on their websites. There are also websites where companies can list their job openings. Examples are Monster.com and CareerBuilder.com. Many of the websites allow you to search for jobs by job category, specific job title, company name, or geographic location. Many sites allow individuals to develop and post their resumés online. Some will even match the resumés to available jobs and send matching resumés to the businesses with job openings. Other sources of job openings are career centers in schools, job fairs, placement offices, employment agencies, and recommendations from family members and friends.

MAKE A CAREER MATCH   Your career plan will help you identify the companies and select the jobs that most closely match your current interests and abilities and fit your long-term career goal. From the available jobs, select those for which you are qualified and interested.

After you have selected a few jobs, gather information about each company. You will want to know more about the business if you plan to work for it. In addition, by learning about the company, you can show the employer how your skills will benefit the company. By preparing in advance using information about the company, you will be able to clearly communicate the benefits you can provide as an employee.

COMPLETE APPLICATION MATERIALS   If applying for a job in writing, you will want to send a cover letter and resumé. The cover letter makes a first impression, so be sure it is well organized, easy to read, and error free. Address it to a specific person if possible. In the letter, highlight your strengths and emphasize why you want to work for the company.

Your resumé will outline your preparation and experience. The information in your career portfolio will help you complete your resumé and cover letter. Using a computer, you should tailor your resumé and cover letter to each company before you send it. Select the information that most closely matches the job requirements for a given job.

Companies usually will ask you to complete a written application. Have a written copy of all personal information with you when you fill out the application to make sure it is complete and accurate. Print application information carefully to ensure that it is readable and to show that your work is careful and accurate.

COMPLETE A SUCCESSFUL INTERVIEW   If you have not had a lot of experience with job interviews, you may be nervous. Once again, careful and thorough preparation will help give you confidence if you are selected for an interview. You know a great deal about yourself and the job for which you are applying.

Be sure to have a professional appearance in the interview. You want to wear appropriate business apparel compatible with what employees in the business normally wear at work.

Make sure you are on time for the interview. If possible, identify in advance the name of the person who will interview you so that you can ask for that person and use his or her name during the interview.

Unless you are told not to do so, you can bring selected items from your portfolio. You may be given the opportunity to show and describe them during an interview. Refer to examples of your work when answering questions.

Communicate your interest in a marketing career and how the job fits into your career goals. Make sure the employer knows you are interested in working for the company and in pursuing a marketing career.

Demonstrate confidence and professionalism during the interview. Do not be afraid to ask questions about the company and the job. In fact, you should prepare several questions in advance and be prepared to ask them.

When the interview is finished, thank the interviewer for the opportunity. Clarify what will happen after the interview and when you can expect to hear from the company. Send a personal note of thanks to the interviewer as soon as possible.

Use the note to highlight one or two unique qualities you can offer.

THE DECISION   Don't expect that you will be offered every job for which you apply. You are more likely to be hired if you select jobs that are good matches with your interests and qualifications.

You will need to decide whether to accept the job if it is offered to you. The interview gives you the opportunity to gather information to be able to make that decision. If the job is not what you expected or does not fit your career plan, you may choose to decline an offer. The person making the offer probably will be impressed if you clearly communicate why you don't think the job is the best choice for you. If you decide to accept the job, you will do so with the confidence that it is the job that best meets your career plans.

 CHECKPOINT
When is it appropriate to decline a job offer?

23.3 ASSESSMENT

What Have You Learned?

1. In addition to finding a part-time job, what are some other ways you can add to your work experience during high school? [23.3.1]

2. What are the benefits of creating an e-portfolio? [23.3.2]

Make Academic Connections

1. **Research**   Identify one marketing and one non-marketing job that interest you. Use career information from your school's career center or the Internet to identify the important knowledge, skills, education, and experience required for each job. Prepare a table for each job with the headings, "What I Have" and "What I Need." In each column of the table, describe your current qualifications for that job and what you still need to develop. [23.3.1]

2. **Career Planning**   Form a team with three other students. Prepare two role-plays of job interviews. The first role-play should illustrate an ineffective job interview, and the second one should illustrate an effective interview. Present both role-plays to other teams and have them identify what was effective and ineffective. [23.3.2]

Connect to ◇DECA
Build your Portfolio

Use a computer to prepare a professional resumé you could use to apply for a career-level marketing job of your choice. Carefully edit and print your resumé. Present a copy of your resumé to your teacher (judge) and explain why you believe it is an effective resumé for the job you selected. Be prepared to discuss your resumé and answer questions about the information you included. [23.3.2]

 Connect to MindTap

Analyze a case study that focuses on chapter concepts. Click on **Chapter 23, Case Study,** *in your MindTap.*

With the assistance of the Internet and a reliable computer, you can apply for many jobs online. If you have a specific company in mind, go directly to its website. Make sure you find the company's official home page.

Navigate a Company Website

Look for a navigation bar tab on the website that refers to employment. Within the employment section of a website, you may have the option of performing an online job search. Selection criteria might include keyword, location, or department of interest.

Many company websites provide the opportunity to complete and submit online applications for all levels of employment. Entry-level jobs may require only a completed online application form. Applications for higher-level positions may require the completion of a simplified online form and the submission of a resumé, a cover letter, and other written statements as attachments to the application.

Resumés and Cover Letters

Customize resumés and cover letters for specific jobs. Follow the website's directions regarding how to format the resumé for transmission. Use simple formatting as it allows the documents to be scanned more easily.

Submit Your Documents

Before submitting your application documents, read all directions and information carefully. Make sure all information is accurate. Most companies have a policy that inaccurate application information is grounds for dismissal. Also make sure your personal paperwork is in order. If you are chosen for an interview, you will need to produce documentation confirming you are eligible for employment. Personal paperwork may include a driver's license, a

social security card, a birth certificate, or a U.S. passport.

Always use caution when submitting online information. Avoid revealing personal information on a nonsecure website. If you have concerns, call the company before submitting personal information. Also, before you submit the application, carefully review the information to make sure you have completed all sections of the application. Proofread all information to make sure it is accurate and there are no spelling errors. Print a copy of the application for your records.

Personal Networking and Follow-Up

Applying for jobs via the Internet alone is not sufficient. Personal networking is still an effective way to obtain employment. An interested contact inside a corporation who knows about your job search efforts can help "pull" your application through the organization by endorsing your credentials to the decision makers.

Unless you are told otherwise, follow up with a phone call or email to the application decision maker. Be polite when communicating with prospective employers. Time your follow-up contacts to show your interest but do not be annoying.

Develop Your Skill

Identify a job you would like to have. Look for online applications for the job at three different companies. Compare the applications for each of the companies. If possible, print a copy of each application and practice completing it.

Work with a teacher or guidance counselor to review your completed applications. Ask for advice to improve each application.

CHAPTER 23 **ASSESSMENT**

Review Marketing Concepts

1. Marketing jobs can progress from entry level to CEO. Explain why this is important when considering a career in marketing. [23.1.1]

2. Why do you think career planning is considered an ongoing process? [23.1.2]

3. You are hiring salespeople for your business. Which do you find more valuable for candidates: understanding business principles or having good basic work skills and interpersonal skills? [23.1.3]

4. What might prompt you to continue with your marketing education after high school in a community college marketing-related program? [23.2.1]

5. Comparing industry career paths versus marketing function paths, which do you think is the more commonly pursued path? Explain your answer. [23.2.2]

6. Explain why completing an assessment of your current knowledge, skills, and interests is so important in developing a career plan. [23.3.1]

7. Why is it important to send a personal note of thanks to the interviewer as soon as possible after the interview? [23.3.2]

Marketing Research and Planning

1. Marketing jobs are among the fastest-growing opportunities throughout the global economy. Additionally, such opportunities employ the largest number of people in the United States and abroad. The challenge is identifying which jobs are in fact marketing jobs. Use the Internet to locate employment statistics for the United States and your state. Identify jobs you find interesting that you believe to be marketing occupations. List the jobs you would like to pursue and describe why they interest you. Then list how many people such careers employ and how fast the opportunities are growing. Finally, list the skills you need to develop in order to pursue those careers. [23.1.1]

2. Use a library or the Internet to locate information on three 2-year or 4-year colleges that offer degrees in marketing. Study the courses you would have to complete to earn the degree.

   Prepare a table that identifies the college, the title of the marketing degree, the total number of credits needed to earn the degree, and the total number of marketing credits needed to earn the degree. Now determine the combined total number of credits in the academic subjects of communications (English, writing, speech, and literature), mathematics, and science.

   Calculate the percentage of total credits that will be marketing courses, the percentage of credits in the academic subjects, and the percentage of total credits for all other course work. Prepare a pie chart to illustrate your findings. What conclusions can you draw from the table and chart? [23.2.1]

3. Select one of the nine marketing functions that interests you as a possible career area. Using career resources in your school's library, career center, or the Internet, identify three jobs that would make up a career path in the marketing function you selected. One of the jobs should be an entry-level job, one should be a career-level or specialist-level job, and one should be a supervisor/manager-level or executive/owner-level job. Based on your research,

prepare a detailed job description for each job and identify the following:

a. the amount of education you think is necessary to obtain the job

b. the amount and type of work experience you think would be expected of a person hired for the job

c. an approximate wage or salary you think the job would pay [23.1.3]

4. Following the instructions of your teacher, form two teams of students and prepare to debate the following issue:

"Companies should select the most skilled employees in each area to become managers."
versus
"Companies should recognize and reward their most skilled employees but keep them working in the areas where they are the most skilled rather than promoting them to management."

Each team will be assigned one of the two positions for the debate. The team members will work together to develop arguments for their position and against the opposing position. Each team will have five minutes to present the reasons for their positions. Then each team will have five minutes to present reasons against the opposite position or to directly rebut the arguments of the other team.

At the end of the debate, the entire class should discuss the effectiveness of the presentations on each side of the issue. Then other members of the class can present their own views of the debate topic. [23.2.2]

Marketing Management and Decision Making

1. You are the manager of a customer service team for a telephone service provider in your city. Your customer service representatives respond to telephoned and emailed questions from customers who want to add or change their local services or are experiencing problems and are contacting your business for help. The customer service representatives will have specific training so that they know the information about the services provided, and they can access a computer program that will provide suggested answers to customer problems. If the problem cannot be solved, the representative will schedule an appointment with a technician who can go to the customer's home to make a repair.

You will be hiring 15 new customer service representatives. Based on the information provided, write an advertisement for the position. Include an overview of the position and a description of the qualifications you would require of job applicants. What procedures would you follow and what materials would you require of job applicants in order to select the best new employees? [23.1.3]

2. Using an Internet browser and search engine, identify five marketing jobs directly related to e-commerce. For each job, identify the marketing function or functions that are the focus of the work of the employee. Select at least two of the jobs that interest you. Again using the Internet, locate two companies that are currently attempting to hire a person for the type of jobs you identified. For

each company, print the job advertisement that identifies the job title, job description, requirements, and any other information provided. Write a short statement for each position describing how you think the job would be different if it were part of a business not involved in e-commerce. [23.1.3]

3. Begin the development of an e-portfolio using word processing and computer graphics programs as well as a scanning device. Identify the categories of materials that you want to include in your portfolio such as class projects, work products, and others you think are important as evidence of your career preparation. Add items to the portfolio that you already have developed. Prepare a list of the types of items you would like to develop in the future for your portfolio. [23.3.2]

Let's Start a Band! Follow-Up Discussion

Work in small teams to discuss the question posed at the end of the opening vignette. What advice do you have for a musician who wants to work in the business side of music?

Build Your Marketing Plan

Build your Portfolio

You are now ready to determine a format for your marketing plan and assign responsibilities for developing the plan. To access the chapter-specific tools that you will need to complete this activity, please navigate to Chapter 23 ➔ Build Your Marketing Plan in MindTap. Alternatively, you can access these tools online at NGLSync. Please visit www.nglsync.cengage.com, and search for the companion website that accompanies this book by entering the ISBN, author, or title. Once you locate this companion website, navigate to Build Your Marketing Plan ➔ Chapter 23.

Restaurant and Food Service Management Series Event

DECA PREP

Build your Portfolio

The Green Lantern Steak House has been a successful family-owned restaurant for many years. The restaurant is famous for delicious steaks, pasta, chicken, fish, and a large fresh salad and homemade soup bar. Loyal customers come from a 50-mile radius to enjoy the excellent food and service offered at the Green Lantern Steak House.

The Green Lantern Steak House has been in business for 40 years in a community with a population of 5,000 people. Fireworks Grille is a new full-service restaurant that has been the first serious source of competition for Green Lantern since it has been in business. The Green Lantern Steakhouse has lost approximately 30 percent of its business since Fireworks Grille opened.

Fireworks Grille's sandwiches and steaks are more expensive than the Green Lantern's. The restaurant also has live musical entertainment on Friday and Saturday nights.

The manager of the Green Lantern has asked your team to outline marketing and customer-service strategies to recapture customers. You will have 10 minutes to explain your strategies to the manager (judge). During and after your presentation, the manager can ask questions about your proposed marketing and customer-service strategies for sparking new interest in the restaurant.

Performance Indicators Evaluated

- Explain the importance of meeting and exceeding customer expectations. (Customer Relations)
- Demonstrate a customer-service mindset. (Customer Relations)
- Describe factors used by marketers to position products/services. (Product/Service Management)
- Identify factors associated with positive customer experiences. (Customer Relations)
- Identify elements of the promotional mix. (Promotion)

Go to the DECA website for more detailed information. **www.deca.com**

Think Critically

1. What factors should the Green Lantern Steak House emphasize in its advertising campaign?

2. How can daily specials be used to recapture customers?

3. What is the best means of advertising for the target market?

4. How can competition be beneficial for an existing business that has experienced years of success?

Glossary

A

account executive advertising agency employee who is the key liaison between the client and the agency

accounting and finance the business function that plans and manages financial resources and maintains records and information related to a business's finances

account planner advertising agency employee who talks to the target markets, conducts research, and even travels to see how the target market lives, works, and thinks

accounts receivable sales for which the company has not yet been paid

action plan the final section of a marketing plan; it identifies actions needed to accomplish and evaluate the marketing strategy

advertising any form of paid nonpersonal communication that uses mass media to deliver a marketer's message to an audience

advertising agency a company that specializes in creating advertising

advertising campaign a series of related advertisements with a similar look, feel, and theme that centers on a specific product, service, or brand

advertising plan documents that outline the activities to be completed and resources needed to create advertising

ambient advertising any non-traditional medium in the environment of the audience such as stickers on bananas, messages chalked onto side-walks, or hot-air balloons

analysis the process of summarizing, combining, or comparing information so that decisions can be made

approach the first contact with the customer when the sales-person gets the customer's attention and creates interest in the product

art director advertising agency employee responsible for how the ad will look

assets things a business owns

atmospherics elements of the shopping environment that appeal to customers, attract them to a store, and encourage them to buy

attitude a frame of mind developed from a person's values, beliefs, and feelings

attribute-based goods products in which a variety of differences exist and the consumer considers a number of factors to determine the best value

B

balance sheet a description of the type and amount of assets, liabilities, and capital in a business on a specific date

balance of trade the difference between the amount of a country's imports and exports

bartering exchanging products or services with others by agreeing on their values without using money

basic stock list identifies the products a store must have available to meet the most important needs of its customers

benefit the advantage provided to a customer as a result of the feature

benefit segmentation divides consumers into groups depending on specific values or benefits they expect or require from the use of a product or service

bidding several suppliers develop specific prices at which they will meet detailed purchase specifications and other criteria prepared by the buyer

blog a website that contains a consumer's own experiences, observations, and opinions in a journal-like format

boycott an organized effort to influence a company by refusing to purchase its products

brand a name, symbol, or design that identifies a product, service, or company

brand advertising builds an image for a brand or company

brand cannibalization occurs when the promotion results in customers shifting from an established brand to a new brand made by the same producer

brand loyalty a consumer's commitment to repurchasing, using, and even promoting a particular brand over all others

breakeven point the quantity of a product that must be sold for total revenues to match total costs at a specific price

brick-and-click businesses companies that combine traditional business operations with extensive use of the Internet

brick-and-mortar businesses companies that complete most of their business activities by means other than the Internet

broadcast media television and radio; sent via signal from a central transmitter to receivers in a geographic area

budget a detailed projection of financial performance for a specific time period, usually one year or less

bundling the practice of combining several related services for one price

business consumers those who buy goods and services to resell or for use in producing and marketing other goods and services

business cycles periods of expansion and decline in an economy that recur over time

business markets companies and organizations that purchase products for the operation of a business or the completion of a business activity

business plan a written document prepared to guide the development and operation of a new business

business-to-business marketing the exchange of products and services between businesses

buying behavior the decision processes and actions of consumers as they buy services and products

buying motives the reasons that you buy

C

capital expenses long-term investments in land, buildings, or equipment

capitalism *See* **free economy**

career a chosen area of work, usually made up of a progression of jobs, that provides personal and professional satisfaction

career area the type of business or the business function in which you plan to work

career path a series of related jobs with increasing knowledge and skill requirements and greater amounts of responsibility

career plan identifies the progression of jobs in your career path; your plans for education, training, and experience to meet the requirements for those jobs; and a time schedule for accomplishing the plan

career planning an ongoing process involving self-assessment, career exploration, and decision making leading to a satisfying career decision

career portfolio an organized collection of information and materials developed to represent you, your preparation, and your accomplishments

cease-and-desist order legal order to discontinue deceptive advertising

central market a location where people bring products to be conveniently exchanged

channel captain a company that takes responsibility to identify channel members, assign distribution activities, help members agree on performance standards, and facilitate communication among channel members

channel of distribution the organizations and individuals who participate in the movement and exchange of products and services from the producer to the final consumer

channel members businesses used to provide many of the marketing functions during the distribution process

charter a legal document allowing the corporation to operate as if it were a person

click-only businesses companies that complete almost all of their business activities through the Internet

close the step in the sales process when the customer makes a decision to purchase

closed-ended questions questions that offer two or more choices as answers

code of ethics a set of standards or rules that guide ethical business behavior

cold calling a salesperson contacts a large number of people or businesses who are conveniently located without knowing a great deal about each one

collaboration involves people coming together to share information and ideas about solving problems

command economy economic system in which the government answers the three economic questions

communication process the transfer of a message from a sender to a receiver

consumer behavior the study of consumers and how they make decisions

consumer credit credit a retail business extends to the final consumer

consumer decision-making process the process by which consumers collect and analyze information to make choices among alternatives

consumerism the organized actions of groups of consumers seeking to increase their influence on business practices

consumer markets individuals or socially related groups who purchase products for personal consumption

consumer perceptions the images consumers have of competing goods and services in the marketplace

consumer price index (CPI) the change in the cost of a specified set of goods and services over time

consumers individuals who purchase products and services to satisfy needs

controllable risk a risk that can be reduced or even avoided by actions you take

controlling measuring performance, comparing it with goals and objectives, and making adjustments when necessary

copywriter advertising agency employee who writes the words in the ad

corporate advertising brand advertising for a company

corporation a business owned by people who purchase stock in the company

corrective ads ads that correct any false impressions left by the deceptive ads

creative brief *See* **strategic brief**

creative director advertising agency employee who helps guide the creative process and ensures that the creative team's work conveys the right message and is in line with the client's needs

creative strategy how a company positions its brand or product in its advertising

creativity the ability to use imaginative skills to find unique ways to solve problems

crowd-sourcing large-scale virtual collaboration

culture the history, beliefs, customs, and traditions of a group

D

DECA an international association of high school and college students studying marketing, management, and entrepreneurship in business, finance, hospitality, and marketing sales and service

decision a choice among alternatives

decoding the process by which the receiver interprets the transmitted language and symbols to comprehend the message

demand a relationship between the quantity of a product consumers are willing and able to purchase and the price

demand curve a graph that illustrates the relationship between price and the quantity demanded

demographics the descriptive characteristics of a market such as age, gender, race, income, and educational level

demonstration a personalized presentation of the product features in a way that emphasizes the benefits and value to the customer

derived demand a business's demand is derived from, or based on, its customers' demand

direct channel the producer sells the product to the final consumer

direct competition competition in a market with businesses that offer the same type of product or service

direct exporting a company takes complete responsibility for marketing its products in other countries

direct mail any marketing message sent to an audience through the mail

discounts and allowances reductions in a price given to the customer in exchange for performing certain marketing activities or accepting something other than what would normally be expected in the exchange

discretionary income the amount of income left after paying basic living expenses and taxes

discretionary purchases nonessential purchases that satisfy consumers' wants

distribution (place) the locations and methods used to make the product available to customers

distribution center a facility used to accumulate products from several sources and then regroup, repackage, and send them quickly to the locations where they will be used

distribution function determining the best methods and procedures to use so that prospective customers can locate, obtain, and use a business's products and services

E

e-commerce all the activities involved in the exchange of goods, services, and information that relate to buying and selling goods over the Internet

economic market all of the consumers who will purchase a particular product or service

economic resources classified as natural resources, capital, equipment, and labor

economic risk a risk caused by the uncertainty associated with market forces, economic trends, and politics

economic utility the amount of satisfaction a consumer receives from the consumption of a particular product or service

elastic demand market situation in which a price decrease will increase total revenue, and price changes will have an effect on demand

elasticity of demand the relationship between changes in a product's price and the demand for that product

electronic portfolio (e-portfolio) career portfolio prepared, maintained, and saved using computer technology

emergency goods products or services purchased as a result of an urgent need

emotional motives reasons to purchase based on feelings and emotions

employee empowerment an approach to customer service that gives employees the authority to solve many customer problems

encoding sender converts an idea into a message that the receiver can understand

endorsement an advertisement in which a believable person publicly expresses approval of a product or service

entrepreneur someone who takes the risk to start a new business

entrepreneurship the process of planning, creating, and managing a new business

equilibrium the amount of the product demanded is equal to the amount supplied

ethics moral principles or values based on honesty and fairness

executive summary provides an overview of the business concept and the important points in the business plan

experiments carefully designed and controlled situations in which all important factors are the same except the one being studied

exports products and services produced in one country and shipped to and sold in another country

external information provides an understanding of factors outside of the organization

F

feature a description of a product characteristic

feedback the receiver's response to the message

final consumers those who buy a product or service for personal use

financial forecast a prediction of future performance related to revenue and expenses

financial statement a detailed summary of the specific financial performance for a business or a part of a business

fine a monetary penalty imposed on a company that fails to follow advertising regulations

flexible pricing policy allows customers to negotiate price within a price range

FOB (free on board) pricing identifies the location from which the buyer pays the transportation costs and takes title to the products purchased

focus group a small number of people brought together to discuss identified elements of an issue or problem

follow-up making contact with the customer after the sale to ensure satisfaction

foreign direct investment (FDI) owning all or part of an existing business in another country

foreign production a company owns and operates production facilities in another country

franchising a business relationship in which the developer of a business idea sells others the rights to the business idea and the use of the business name

free economy an economic system in which resources are owned by individuals and decisions are made independently with no attempt at government regulation or control; also called **capitalism** and **market economy**

frequency the number of times a member of the target audience is exposed to the advertising message

G

geographic segmentation classifying consumers into markets based on where they live

geo-tagging using mobile devices to add a location to posts on social media platforms

green marketing marketing activities designed to satisfy customer needs without negatively impacting the environment

gross domestic product (GDP) the total value of goods and services produced within a country during the year

gross margin the amount that is available to cover the business's expenses and provide a profit on the sale of the product

gross national product (GNP) the total value of all goods and services produced by a country during the year, including foreign investments

guarantee a general promise or assurance of quality

H

hashtags enable users to track topics on Twitter by classifying or categorizing messages using words or phrases preceded by a hash sign (#)

heterogeneous differences among services resulting from human performance

human risk a risk that arises because of the potential actions of individuals, groups, or organizations

I

image a unique, memorable quality of a brand

imports products or services brought in from another country

impulse goods items purchased on the spur of the moment without advance planning

inbound marketing part of the two-way conversation in social media marketing where potential customers come to the company

income statement a report on the amount and source of revenue and the amount and type of expenses for a specific period of time

indirect channel other businesses between the producer and the consumer perform one or more marketing functions

indirect competition occurs when a business competes with other companies offering products that are not in the same product category but satisfy similar customer needs

indirect exporting the process in which the exporting company is represented by a marketing business that has exporting experience and arranges for the sale of the company's products in other countries

industrial economy economy in which the primary business activity is the manufacturing of products

inelastic demand market situation in which a price decrease will decrease total revenue, and price changes will have little effect on demand

inflation when prices increase faster than the value of goods and services and purchasing power declines

influencers individuals who have established a following and credibility in a specific area that enables them to influence the purchase decisions of others on social media

innovation the introduction of something new that makes a significant change or improvement

input information needed for decision making that goes into the marketing information system

inseparable the service is produced and consumed at the same time

insurable risk a risk faced by a large number of people, is pure rather than speculative, and the amount of the loss can be predicted

intangible incapable of being touched, seen, tasted, heard, or felt

integrated marketing is involved in all important business decisions and considered an essential part of the business

internal information information developed from activities that occur within the organization

international trade the exchange of products and services with people in other countries

Internet advertising advertising delivered through the Internet

interpersonal communication any person-to-person exchange

inventory the assortment of products a business maintains

inventory shrinkage a loss of products due to theft, fraud, negligence, or error

invoice a list of items purchased along with their prices, the total amount due, and a statement of the terms of payment for the order

J

job any full- or part-time work in a specific position of employment

joint venture business relationships in which independent companies cooperate in common business activities

just-in-time (JIT) inventory level is kept low and resupplied by supply chain members as it is needed

L

labor intensiveness the amount of human effort required to deliver a service

law of demand when the price of a product is increased, less will be demanded

law of supply when the price of a product is increased, more will be produced

lead a potential customer for a salesperson

leading the ability to communicate the direction of the business and to influence others to successfully carry out the needed work

lead time the amount of time required to place an ad

liabilities the amounts a business owes

liability a legal responsibility for loss or damage

licensed brand a well-known name or symbol established by one company and sold for use by another company to promote its products

lifestyle the way a person lives as reflected by material goods, activities, and relationships

limited-line retailers *See* **specialty retailers**

logistics *See* **physical distribution**

long-range planning managers analyze information that can affect the business over a long period of time; also called **strategic planning**

M

macroeconomics the study of economic behavior in the economy

management involves developing, implementing, and evaluating the plans and activities of a business

managing getting the work of an organization done through its people and resources

markdown a reduction from the original selling price

market a unique group of prospective customers a business wants to serve and their location

market analysis provides information to help develop a marketing strategy that is competitive, meets customer needs, and can be implemented effectively

market economy *See* **free economy**

marketing the creation and maintenance of satisfying exchange relationships

marketing concept using the needs of customers as the primary focus during the planning, production, pricing, distribution, and promotion of a product or service

Marketing Education program incorporates three types of complementary learning experiences—introductory and advanced courses in marketing, business work experiences, and a student organization called DECA

marketing effectiveness both the customers and the business are satisfied with the exchange

marketing information system (MkIS) an organized method of collecting, storing, analyzing, and retrieving information to improve the effectiveness and efficiency of marketing decisions

marketing jobs the completion of marketing activities is the most important or only job responsibility

marketing management the process of coordinating resources to plan and implement an efficient marketing strategy

marketing mix blending of the four marketing elements—product, distribution,

price, and promotion—by the business

marketing plan a clear written description of the marketing strategies of a business and the way the business will operate to accomplish each strategy

marketing research a procedure to identify solutions to a specific marketing problem through the use of scientific problem solving

marketing strategy the way an organization plans and coordinates marketing activities to achieve its goals

market intelligence the process of gaining competitive market information

market opportunities new markets as well as ways to improve a company's offerings in current markets; identified markets with excellent potential based on careful research

market opportunity analysis studying and prioritizing market segments to locate the best potential based on demand and competition

market position the unique image of a product or service in a consumer's mind relative to similar competitive offerings

market potential the total revenue that can be obtained from a market segment

market price the point where supply and demand for a product are equal

market segment a group of similar consumers within a larger market

market segmentation the process of dividing a large group of consumers into subgroups based on specific characteristics and common needs

market share the portion of the total market potential that each company expects in relation to its competitors

markup an amount added to the cost of a product to determine the selling price

mass communication an attempt to reach a wide audience through mass media such as radio, television, magazines, newspapers, and the Internet

mass marketing directs a company's marketing mix to serve a large and heterogeneous group of consumers

media the method by which the message travels; also called **message channel**

media plan a detailed listing of where and when ads will run

media planner advertising agency employee who develops the media plan

merchandise plan identifies the types, assortments, prices, and quantities of products that will be stocked by the business for a specific period of time

merchandising offering products produced or manufactured by others for sale to customers

message what is being communicated

message channel See **media**

microcredit provides low-value loans to people who cannot qualify for traditional bank loans

microeconomics the study of relationships between individual consumers and producers

mission statement identifies the nature of the business or the reasons the business exists

mixed economy an economic system in which some goods and services are provided by the government and some by private enterprise

mixed merchandise retailers businesses that offer products from several categories

model stock list identifies the complete assortment of products a store would like to offer to customers

money system the use of currency as a recognized medium of exchange

monopolistic competition the type of market where many firms compete with products that are somewhat different

monopoly a market in which one supplier offers a unique product

motivation the set of positive or negative factors that direct individual behavior

multinational companies businesses that have operations throughout the world and that conduct planning for worldwide markets

N

natural risk a risk caused by the unpredictability of nature, such as the weather or an earthquake

need anything you require to live

netiquette the informal code of conduct regarding acceptable online behavior

net profit the difference between the selling price and all costs and operating expenses associated with the product

new product a product that is entirely new or changed in an important and noticeable way

noise any distracting information in the transmission, the message channel, or the receiver's environment that may inhibit or distract from the message

non-business organization focuses on something other than providing products and services for a profit

nonprice competition business emphasizes elements of its marketing mix other than price by developing a unique offering that meets an important customer need

non-store retailing selling directly to the consumer at home rather than requiring the consumer to travel to a store

O

observation a way to collect information by recording actions without interacting or communicating with the participant

oligopoly a few businesses offer very similar products or services

online-to-offline retailing (O2O) designed to create awareness by digital interaction with customers that encourages visits to physical stores to make purchases

one-price policy all customers pay the same price

open-ended questions questions that allow respondents to develop their own answers without information about possible choices

operating expenses all costs associated with business operations; the costs of day-to-day marketing activities

operational planning See **short-term planning**

operations the ongoing activities designed to support the primary function of a business and keep it operating efficiently

opportunity the possibility for success

opportunity cost the value of alternative items or activities that are not pursued as the result of an economic choice

organizing arranging people, activities, and resources in the best way to accomplish the goals of an organization

outbound marketing part of the two-way conversation in social media marketing where a company initiates contact with potential customers

outdoor advertising any marketing message designed specifically for ads outside the home, such as those on the sides of buildings, bus shelters or benches, or signage at sporting events

output the result of analysis provided to decision makers

owner's equity the difference between the amount of assets and the amount of liabilities for a company

P

packing list an itemized listing of all of the products included in the shipment

partnership a business that is owned and operated by two or more people who share in the decision making and profitability of the company

partnership agreement a legal document that specifies the responsibilities and financial relationships of the partners

pass-along rate the number of people who read a single copy of a printed magazine or newspaper

patronage motives reasons to purchase based on loyalty

penetration price a very low price designed to increase the quantity sold of a product by emphasizing value

performance standard specifies the minimum level of expected performance for an activity

perishable incapable of being stored for use at a future time

perpetual inventory system determines the amount of a product on hand by maintaining records on purchases and sales

personal identity the characteristics that make a person unique

personality a pattern of emotions and behavior that define an individual

personal selling person-to-person communication with a potential customer in an effort to inform, persuade, or remind the customer to purchase an organization's products or services

physical distribution the process of efficiently and effectively moving products and materials through the distribution channels; also called **logistics**

physical inventory system determines the amount of product on hand by visually inspecting and counting the items

planning involves analyzing information, setting goals, and determining how to achieve them

policies rules or guidelines a company uses to make consistent decisions

population all of the people in the group that the company is interested in studying

positioning statement a specific description of the unique qualities of the marketing mix that make it different from the competition and satisfying to the target market

positioning strategy outlines how a company will present its product or service to the consumer and how it will compete in the marketplace with other businesses offering similar products and services

postindustrial economy economy based on a mix of business and consumer products and services produced and marketed in the global marketplace

preapproach gathering preliminary information and preparing a preliminary sales presentation for a customer

preindustrial economy economy based on agriculture and raw material development through activities such as mining, oil production, and cutting timber

price the amount customers pay and the methods of increasing the value of the product to the customers

price-based goods products that consumers believe are similar but have significant price differences

price competition rivalry among businesses on the basis of price and value

pricing establishing and communicating the value of products and services to customers

price lines distinct categories of prices based on differences in product quality and features

price range the maximum and minimum prices that can be charged for a product

primary data information collected for the first time to solve the problem being studied

print advertising any paid message in a magazine or newspaper

private enterprise an economic system based on independent decisions by businesses and consumers with only a limited government role

procedures the steps employees follow for consistent performance of important activities

producer advertising agency employee who facilitates everything that happens after the client agrees to develop an ad or campaign

producers businesses that use their resources to develop products and services

product anything offered to a market by the business to satisfy needs, including physical products, services, and ideas; anything tangible a business offers to a market to satisfy customer needs

product advertising relays the benefits of a specific product or service and uses rational arguments to explain why a customer should buy it

product assortment the complete set of all products a business offers to its market

product cost includes the cost of parts and raw materials (or the price paid to a supplier for finished products), labor, transportation, insurance, and an amount for damaged, lost, or stolen products

production the business function that creates or obtains products or services for sale

productivity the average output by workers for a specific period of time

product liability insurance provides protection from consumer claims arising from the use of the company's products

product life cycle identifies the stages a product goes through from the time it enters the market until it is no longer sold

product line a group of similar products with slight variations in the marketing mix to satisfy different needs in a market

product usage how frequently consumers use products and the quantity of product used

professional liability insurance provides protection against claims of negligent or harmful actions by business professionals

profit motive the use of resources toward the greatest profit for the producer

promotion the methods used and information communicated to encourage customers to purchase and to increase their satisfaction; any form of communication used to inform, persuade, or remind consumers about a company's products or services or even itself

promotional mix the combination of advertising, public relations, personal selling, and sales promotion that marketers use to reach a target market

promotional plan the blueprint for how the elements of the promotional mix will work together to deliver a consistent message

proprietor a person who has sole ownership of a business

proprietorship *See* **sole proprietorship**

prospect a lead (potential customer) that has been qualified

prototype a model product used to test quality and costs before beginning full-scale production

psychographics people's interests and values

publicity any nonpaid mention of a product, service, company, or cause

public relations (PR) the effort to reach consumers by generating positive publicity

pull strategy producer promotes the product directly to the customer so that the customer will request the product from retailers who will then request the product from the producer

purchase order a form listing the variety, quantity, and prices of products ordered

purchase specifications detailed requirements for the construction or performance of a product

purchasing determining the products and services needed, identifying the best sources to obtain them, and completing the activities necessary to obtain and use them

purchasing power the amount of goods and services that can be purchased with a specific amount of money

pure competition the type of market in which many suppliers offer very similar products

pure risk a risk that presents the chance of loss but no opportunity for gain

push strategy producer promotes the product to wholesalers and retailers who then promote the product to customers

Q

qualifying gathering information to determine which people are most likely to buy

qualitative research research that looks deeper into the why and how of people's opinions

quantitative research collecting data that can be interpreted into meaningful numerical values

quotas limits on the numbers of specific types of products that foreign companies can sell in the country

R

random sampling a procedure in which everyone in the population has an equal chance of being selected in a sample

rational motives reasons to purchase based on facts or logic

reach the total number of people who see an ad

real-time marketing gathers information about consumers' online activities as they are occurring through the use of advanced consumer analytics

receiver the person or persons to whom the message is directed or any person who understands the message that is sent

receiving record a list of the merchandise received in the shipment and its condition

reciprocal trading a form of bartering in which the products or services of one company are used as payment for the products or services of another company

reference group a group of people or an organization that an individual admires, identifies with, and wants to be a part of

relationship marketing focuses on developing loyal customers who continue to purchase from the business for a long period of time

reorder point level of inventory needed to meet the usage needs of the business until the product can be resupplied

request for proposal (RFP) contains a specific description of the type of product or service needed and the criteria that are important to the buyer

retailer the final business organization in an indirect channel of distribution for consumer products

revenue the money received from the sale of products and services

risk the possibility that a loss can occur as the result of a decision or activity

risk management providing security and safety for products, personnel, and customers; reducing the risk associated with marketing decisions and activities

risk-taking a willingness to accept the chance of failure in order to be successful

S

sales promotion any activity or material that offers consumers a direct incentive to buy a product or service

sample a smaller group selected from the population

scarcity the result of unlimited wants and needs combined with limited resources

secondary data information already collected for another purpose that can be used to solve the current problem

self-concept an individual's belief about his or her identity, image, and capabilities

self-confidence a belief in oneself and one's own abilities to be successful

self-directed work team a group of employees that works together toward a common purpose or goal without the usual managerial supervision

self-regulation taking personal responsibility for actions

self-sufficient not relying on others for the things you need to survive

selling direct, personal communication with prospective customers in order to assess needs and satisfy those needs with appropriate products and services

selling price the price charged for a product or service

sender the source of the message being sent

service an activity that is intangible, exchanged directly from producer to consumer, and consumed at the time of production

service quality the degree to which the service meets customers' needs and expectations

service retailers businesses that have services as their primary offering with a limited number of products for sale that complement the services

short-term planning identifies specific objectives and activities for each part of the business for a time period of a year or less; also called **operational planning**

shopping goods major consumer purchases that are typically more expensive than convenience goods

simulations experiments where researchers create situations to be studied

skimming price a very high price designed to emphasize the quality or uniqueness of the product

sociability the inclusion of one or more aspects of social media in marketing a product or service

social media any technology that allows people to have conversations and share content they have created

social network website that links people or organizations into communities based on common interests, goals, or beliefs

social responsibility concern about the consequences of actions on others

sole proprietorship a business owned and managed by one person

specialization of labor concentrating effort on one thing or a few related activities so that they can be done well

specialty goods products that have strong brand loyalty

specialty retailers businesses that offer products from one category of merchandise or closely related items

speculative risk a risk that presents the chance to gain as well as the chance to lose

staffing the activities needed to match individuals with the work to be done

standard of living a measure of the quality of life for a country's citizens

staple goods products that are regular, routine purchases

storage the resources used to maintain information, including equipment and procedures, so that it can be accessed when needed

strategic brief document that defines the target market and conveys the main message of the advertising; also called **creative brief**

strategic planning *See* **long-range planning**

strategy a plan that identifies how a company expects to achieve its goals

subsidy money a government provides to a business to assist in the development and sale of its products

suggestion selling offering additional products and services after an initial sale in order to increase customer satisfaction

superstores very large stores that offer consumers wide choices of products at low prices

suppliers *See* **vendors**

supply a relationship between the quantity of a product that producers are willing and able to provide and the price

supply chain flow of products, resources, and information through all of the organizations involved in producing and marketing a company's products

supply curve a graph that illustrates the relationship between price and the quantity supplied

surety bond provides insurance for the failure of a person to perform his or her duties or for losses resulting from employee theft or dishonesty

survey a planned set of questions to which individuals or groups of people respond

SWOT analysis identifies a business's strengths and weaknesses and the opportunities and threats it faces

T

target market a clearly defined segment of the market to which a business wants to appeal

tariffs taxes a government places on imported products to increase the price for which they are sold

technology the practical application of scientific knowledge

test market a limited quantity of a new product is produced and the marketing mix is implemented in a small part of the market; specific city or geographic area in which a marketing experiment is conducted

total quality management (TQM) specific quality standards for all procedures

trade credit credit offered by one business to another business, often because of the time lag between when a sale is negotiated and when the products are actually delivered

trademark the legal protection provided to the owner for the words or symbols used to identify a product or service

trade shows exhibitions where companies associated with an industry gather to showcase their products

trending a topic or discussion that is currently popular in social media or other Web-based formats

trial close providing the customer with the opportunity to buy during the sales presentation

U

uncontrollable risk a risk that cannot be reduced or avoided by the actions you take

uninsurable risk a risk for which it is not possible to predict if a loss will occur or the amount of the loss

unsought goods products that consumers don't know about or don't think of buying

V

value an individual view of the worth of a product or service

vehicle the specific broadcast or print choices associated with a message channel

vendor analysis an objective rating system that buyers use to compare potential suppliers on purchasing criteria

vendors companies that offer products for sale to other businesses; also called **suppliers**

viral marketing a promotional approach utilizing word-of-mouth marketing that encourages people to pass along marketing messages via the Internet, which allows the information to spread rapidly

W

want a culturally defined way the consumer can fill a need

warehouse a building designed to store large amounts of raw materials or products until they can be used or sold

warranty a specific written statement of the seller's responsibilities related to the guarantee

wholesale member clubs businesses that offer a variety of consumer products to members through a warehouse outlet

wholesalers companies that assist with distribution activities among businesses

word-of-mouth (WOM) passing information among people through oral communication, often in the form of storytelling

word-of-mouth marketing occurs when a consumer is somehow rewarded for passing along information about products and services

Z

zone pricing different product or transportation costs are set for specific areas of the seller's market

Index